Oman

the Bradt Travel Guide

Diana Darke
Tony Walsh

www.bradtguides.com

Bradt Travel Guides Ltd, UK
The Globe Pequot Press Inc, USA

edition
4

W9-BYK-264

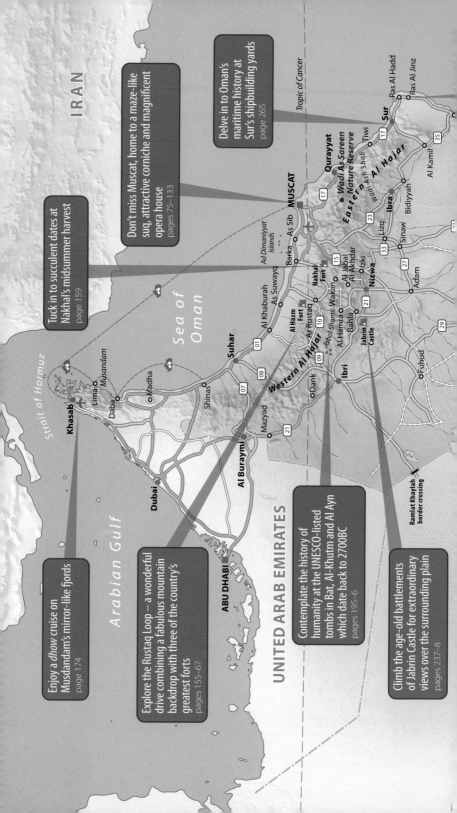

IRAN

Tuck in to succulent dates at Nakhal's midsummer harvest
page 159

Don't miss Muscat, home to a maze-like suq, attractive corniche and magnificent opera house
pages 75–133

Delve in to Oman's maritime history at Sur's shipbuilding yards
page 265

Tropic of Cancer

Ras Al Hadd
Ras Al Jinz

Sur
17

Qurayyat
MUSCAT
17
Wadi As Sareen Nature Reserve
Eastern Al Hajar
Wadi Ash Shab
Tiwi
As Sib
Barka
Al Kamil
35
Ad Dimaniyyat Islands
Nakhal Fort
15
Al Jabal Al Akhdar
Ibra
23
Bidiyyah
Lizq
Izki
Sinaw
33
Nizwa
27
Adam
21
Bahla
Al Hamra
Jabrin Castle
29
Fuhud

Sea of Oman

Al Khaburah
As Suwayq
01
Al Hazm Fort
Ar Rustaq
Jabal Shams Wakan
08
Dank
Ibri
Suhar

Strait of Hormuz
Khasab
Lima
Musandam
Madha
Daba
Shinas
Mazyad
07
21
09

Arabian Gulf

Dubai
Al Buraymi

ABU DHABI

UNITED ARAB EMIRATES

Ramlat Khaylah border crossing

Enjoy a *dhow* cruise on Musandam's mirror-like fjords
page 174

Explore the Rustaq Loop – a wonderful drive combining a fabulous mountain backdrop with three of the country's greatest forts
pages 155–67

Contemplate the history of humanity at the UNESCO-listed tombs in Bat, Al-Khutm and Al Ayn which date back to 2700BC
pages 195–6

Climb the age-old battlements of Jabrin Castle for extraordinary views over the surrounding plain
pages 237–8

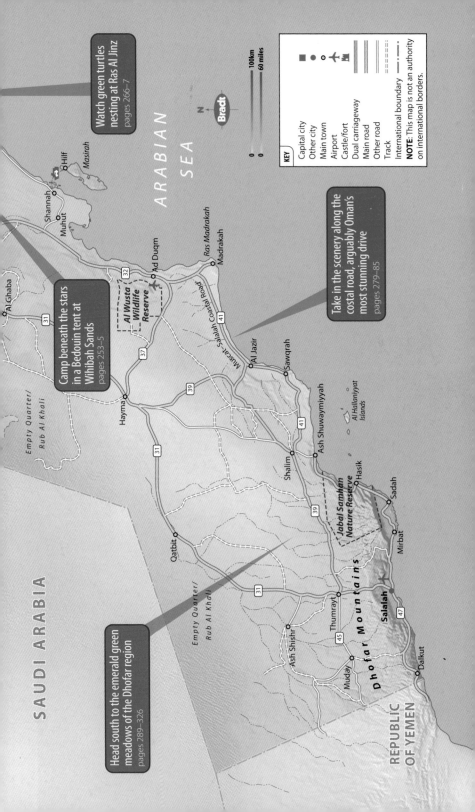

Watch green turtles
nesting at Ras Al Jinz
pages 266–7

Camp beneath the stars
in a Bedouin tent at
Wihibah Sands
pages 253–5

Take in the scenery along the
costal road, arguably Oman's
most stunning drive
pages 279–85

Head south to the emerald green
meadows of the Dhofar region
pages 289–326

KEY

■	Capital city
●	Other city
○	Main town
✈	Airport
⚑	Castle/fort
	Dual carriageway
	Main road
	Other road
┈	Track
─·─	International boundary

NOTE: This map is not an authority
on international borders.

0   100km
0   60 miles

N

Bradt

ARABIAN

SEA

SAUDI ARABIA

REPUBLIC
OF YEMEN

*Empty Quarter/
Rub Al Khali*

*Empty Quarter/
Rub Al Khali*

Al Ghaba

Al Wusta
Wildlife
Reserve

Hilf
Masirah
Shannah
Muhut

Ad Duqm

Ras Madrakah
Madrakah

Al Jazir
Sawqrah

Hayma

Shalim

Ash Shuwaymiyyah

*Al Hallaniyyat
Islands*

Hasik
Sadah

*Jabal Samhan
Nature Reserve*

Mirbat

Qatbit

Ash Shishr

Muday

Thumrayt

Dhofar Mountains

Salalah

Dalkut

Musqat–Salalah Coastal Road

31

32

37

39

41

41

39

31

31

45

47

Oman
Don't
miss...

Trekking
Oman's terrain, along with its climate, makes it perfect for mountain trekking, such as here at Wadi A'Nakhr, Oman's 'Grand Canyon' (TW) page 234

History
There's plenty to keep those interested in history occupied in Oman – from forts and museums to shipwrecks and UNESCO-listed World Heritage Sites. Pictured here: Jabrin Castle
(TW) pages 237–8

Muscat

Stroll along the corniche, hunt for treasures in the suq, explore 'Old Muscat' or spend a night at the Royal Opera. Pictured here: Al Alam Palace

(TW) pages 75–133

Diving

Warm waters and colourful fish make Mirbat a diver's paradise

(SS) pages 296–7

Culture

From traditional crafts to camel racing, Oman's rich culture is in evidence across the country

(TW) pages 34–8

Oman in colour

top left The National Museum is state-of-the-art in both displays and conservation of artefacts — pictured here, a depiction of what the Majan reed boats looked like 4,000 years ago (TW) pages 111–12

top right Mutrah Suq is the largest suq in the country, a maze of shops selling everything from coffee pots and incense burners to an animated toy camel (TW) pages 104–5

above left Muscat's Grand Mosque is simply awe-inspiring — it's worth a visit just to appreciate the architectural achievement it represents (OMOT) page 128

below left The spectacular Royal Opera House, housing a concert theatre and shopping mall, dominates the Al Qurum skyline (TW) page 94

above & right   Nizwa is a verdant oasis city in Oman's interior with a lively animal suq on Friday mornings (IP/S and TW) pages 217–25

below   Like Suhur, Sur is another Omani town that lays claim to being the fictional Sindbad's birthplace (TW) pages 261–6

above left	Some mountain villages are abandoned while others are still clinging to life thanks to their terrace agriculture (F/A)
above right	The name Al Jabal Al Akhdar translates as 'green mountain' and, at 2,000m, it is an ideal place to chill out away from the heat of Muscat (TW) pages 214–17
below	The area around the village of Bald Sayt has been settled for over 3,000 years (BO/S) pages 160–1

ABOUT THE AUTHORS

Tony Walsh has been writing about Oman since 1999. His chosen topics reflect his interests and have included camel racing on the edge of the desert, diving for abalone in Dhofar and, more recently, Oman's World Heritage Sites. Having purchased Diana Darke's first guide to Oman all the way back in 2006, Tony is delighted to have been able to contribute towards this comprehensive guidebook.

The original author of Bradt's *Oman*, **Diana Darke**, first worked in the country for the Omani government in 1980, and remained acquainted with Oman for over 30 years. With a BA in Arabic (Oxford) and an MA in Islamic Art and Architecture (SOAS, London) her in-depth cultural background knowledge is second to none. She is the author of 16 guidebooks on Turkey and the Middle East including Bradt's *Eastern Turkey* and *Syria* guides.

AUTHOR'S STORY   Tony Walsh

Stepping out of the plane at what was then Seeb Airport in Muscat into the heat of a humid March day in 1986, I had little idea of what I would find in Oman. My work in Muscat meant that I travelled through much of northern Oman and met a whole range of people. At weekends I explored, taking my two-wheel drive saloon through unpaved valleys in the mountains and into the desert. The people I met were warm, hospitable and frequently astounded that a single traveller had made it into their corner of Arabia. After two years working in Saudi Arabia, I returned to Oman, which was my home until 2016. There have been vast changes in the country since I first arrived, as there have been throughout the Arab world. Oman, however, has been fortunate that a caring ruler has enabled a state that hasn't subsumed its human population into an anonymous mass but has built their many positive attributes into the remarkable country that Oman is today.

PUBLISHER'S FOREWORD *Hilary Bradt*

Oman came to my attention when we first published *Zanzibar*, many years ago. I learned about the historic links between the two countries – going back to the 1800s when, bizarrely, Zanzibar was the capital of Oman – and thought that any country in the Middle East that was once governed from East Africa would be a perfect addition to our list. Oman is now firmly established as a holiday destination, and I'm delighted to see the book move into its fourth edition. Thoroughly updated and overhauled by Tony Walsh, this guide continues to unearth the very best attractions and hotels to satisfy visitors who no longer have to rely on the trade winds to reach this exotic country.

Fourth edition published January 2017
First published 2006
Bradt Travel Guides Ltd
IDC House, The Vale, Chalfont St Peter, Bucks SL9 9RZ, England
www.bradtguides.com
Print edition published in the USA by The Globe Pequot Press Inc,
PO Box 480, Guilford, Connecticut 06437-0480

ISBN: 978 1 78477 020 4 (print)
e-ISBN: 978 1 78477 165 2 (e-pub)
e-ISBN: 978 1 78477 265 9 (mobi)

British Library Cataloguing in Publication Data
A catalogue record for this book is available from the British Library

Photographs
Alamy: FRIEDRICHSMEIER (F/A); AWL: Matteo Colombo (MC/AWL), Niels van Gijn (NG/AWL); Dreamstime: Askme9 (A/D), Imrandr (I/D), Typhoonski (T/D); Omani Ministry of Tourism (OMOT); Shutterstock: Andrea Seaemann (AS/S), Byelikova Oksana (BO/S), Ivan Pavlov (IP/S), lightpoet (L/S), Marcin Szymczak (MS/S); SuperStock (SS); Tony Walsh (TW)

Front cover Mutrah harbour (MC/AWL)
Back cover Nakhal Fort (L/S); Wadi Bani Habib (NG/AWL)
Title page Henna painting (OMOT); Wihibah Sands (TW); Date palm tree (TW)

Maps David McCutcheon FBCart.S

Typeset by Dataworks
Production managed by Jellyfish Print Solutions; printed in India
Digital conversion by www.dataworks.co.in

Acknowledgements

Tony Walsh would like to thank all of the individuals who, unbeknownst to them, have helped to create this book. Friends, especially Ibrahim Al Busafi, those in Dhofar who took him through their mountains, many in Al Raka Bidiyyah who explored the Wihibah Sands with him, and neighbours in Al Bustan village who created a sense of community. He is indebted to the former foreign residents and visitors to Oman whose names often opened up connections for him across the country.

His involvement in this edition of the guide is due to Rachel Fielding at Bradt, whose leap of faith made it all possible, Maisie Fitzpatrick, whose editorial skill and management polished the text into a Bradt guide, and his brother, Michael, who enabled him to stay focused on the book over the summer.

DEDICATION

To Oman and its people

FEEDBACK REQUEST AND UPDATES WEBSITE

At Bradt Travel Guides we're aware that guidebooks start to go out of date on the day they're published – and that you, our readers, are out there in the field doing research of your own. You'll find out before us when a fine new family-run hotel opens or a favourite restaurant changes hands and goes downhill. So why not write and tell us about your experiences? Contact us on ☎ 01753 893444 or e info@bradtguides.com. We will forward emails to the author who may post updates on the Bradt website at www.bradtupdates.com/oman. Alternatively you can add a review of the book to www.bradtguides.com or Amazon.

Contents

LIST OF MAPS

HOW TO USE THE MAPS IN THIS GUIDE

KEYS AND SYMBOLS Maps include alphabetical keys covering the locations of those places to stay, eat or drink that are featured in the book. Note that regional maps may not show all hotels and restaurants in the area: other establishments may be located in towns shown on the map.

GRIDS AND GRID REFERENCES Several maps use gridlines to allow easy location of sites. Map grid references are listed in square brackets after the name of the place or sight of interest in the text, with page number followed by grid number, eg: [76 C3].

A NOTE ABOUT SPELLING In Oman, road signs, and many other types of signage, are in Arabic and transliterated into English. Over the course of Oman's rapid development the official transliteration of some names has changed. To complicate matters further, some place names may have an official name and a more common – almost universal – name.

In this guide we have used what we believe is the current official use as used on maps produced by the National Survey Authority, a division of the Ministry of Defence, and the official Oman government map authority.

Introduction

Oman is not a country to visit if you want to be overwhelmed by modern architecture or a cacophonous urban buzz. This is a country of nuances that – when knitted together – create one of those places that you wish you had visited before and will be raring to visit again.

Oman is often described as a 'new' tourist destination, but tour groups have been visiting the country for over 30 years, and cruise ships for 20. Step back further in time and Oman has been trading with the USA since 1790, during the time of George Washington, while the first British ship to visit Oman called into Raysut Salalah in 1613, during the reign of King James I (VI of Scotland). The Omanis themselves have been just as well travelled: trade with China began at least 1,900 years ago and the Omani influence along the east coast of Africa is well known. This is a country of outward-looking people who are eager to meet those from elsewhere and proud to welcome visitors to their country.

Despite this international outlook, Oman's economy was moribund from the mid 19th century when Oman and Zanzibar separated in 1856, through to 1967 when oil exports commenced. This inflow of capital enabled Oman's current ruler to speed up development from his accession in 1970 and most of what you will see in Oman dates from then. Muscat International Airport and the port of Mina Sultan Qaboos are the principal points of entry for many of Oman's visitors and both date from the early 1970s.

Since 1970, the country has enjoyed almost unbroken stability and increasing prosperity. Despite the dramatic recent drop in oil prices, per-capita GDP stands at over US$15,000, compared with the US at over US$55,000 and the UK at US$44,000. If purchasing power parity per person is used, Oman jumps to US$38,000; the USA remains at US$55,000 and the UK drops to US$41,000. This means that Omanis noticeably enjoy an excellent standard of living, comparable to much of western Europe. This inflow of wealth means that it's not only Muscat that has well-maintained roads with street lighting, but that now they extend throughout the county. In the north of Oman, an impressive, fully lit 26km road will take you from the plains up into the mountains at 2,000m (pages 214–16). In the mountains you can relax and gaze out from the edge of a cliff into the abyss below or meander through fields of fragrant pink damask roses. From Muscat, fast ferries can take you and – if needed – your car on a sea journey to the Musandam Peninsula 400km away. Great lake-like 'fjords' await you with their mirror-calm waters, ideal scuba-diving spots and unfrequented beaches.

Direct, non-stop flights into Oman by British Airways (Terminal 5 at Heathrow) and Oman Air (Terminal 3) mean that Muscat is an easy 7-hour flight away from the UK. Getting into the capital of Muscat is just as straightforward, with most hotels only 20 minutes' drive away. The transport infrastructure that takes you from A to Z, with very little effort, makes it tempting not to stop and look at D and G along the way. Between Nizwa and the Wihibah Sands are plenty of fascinating villages to visit, be it the Iron-Age fortification at Lizq or the oasis and mansions of Al Mudayrib. While these settlements lack the bright lights and headline attractions of Muscat, they make for an intriguing experience and offer up lots of unexpected sights.

One of Oman's most outstanding achievements has been in emerging from many years of conflict, poverty and national fragmentation to become the stable and prosperous country that it is today. Travelling down to Salalah illustrates how remarkable the change that Sultan Qaboos has enabled really is. Books by Wilfred Thesiger and Jan Morris, both of whom used Salalah as the springboard for their journeys, describe poverty and anxiety as part of the tapestry of Oman. Today the picture is very different, with opulent mansions radiating away from Salalah's town centre and carefree children enjoying life in their neighbourhoods. Whether you travel alone with this Bradt guide as your companion or with a local guide, you'll discover that what makes Oman truly special is the journey and discovering what you come across along the way.

FOLLOW BRADT

For the latest news, special offers and competitions, subscribe to the Bradt newsletter via the website www.bradtguides.com and follow Bradt on:

f www.facebook.com/BradtTravelGuides
🐦 @BradtGuides
📷 @bradtguides
📌 www.pinterest.com/bradtguides

Part One

GENERAL INFORMATION

OMAN AT A GLANCE

Location Southeastern edge of Arabian Peninsula at 21°N, 57°E
Neighbouring countries United Arab Emirates, Saudi Arabia, Yemen
Size 309,500km²
Population 4.28 million (Oman National Centre for Statistics and Information, 2015)
Life expectancy at birth Male: 74; female: 79 (WHO, 2013)
Capital Muscat Capital Area; population 1,274,159 (Oman National Centre for Statistics and Information, 2015)
Other main towns Salalah, Suhar, As Suwayq, Ibri, Barka, Nizwa, Ar Rustaq, Sur
Ports Mina Sultan Qaboos, Salalah, Ad Duqm, Suhar
Climate Predominantly arid, with regional variations. Summer (April–September) finds northern coastal regions hot and humid with the interior hot and dry (average 40°C) and southern coastal areas humid and warm; winter (October–March) is warm and dry throughout, with high mountains in northern areas becoming cold, sometimes with snow. Rainfall is rare and irregular but can be intense.
Status Monarchy
Sultan and head of state Qaboos bin Said (since 1970)
Ethnic divisions Arab, Baluchi, south Asian (Indian, Pakistani, Sri Lankan, Bangladeshi) and Zanzibari
Languages Arabic (official), English (widely spoken), Mahari, Shahri, Baluchi, Urdu, Swahili, Hindi, Indian dialects. German and French spoken in larger hotels.
Religion Predominantly Muslim: Sunni (50%), Ibadhi (45%), Shi'a (2%); other 3% (mainly Hindu, Christian and Buddhist). Figures related to the population breakdown by religion are not gathered by the Oman government, so these figures are interpretative.
Chief exports Oil, liquid natural gas, organic chemicals, steel, aluminium, fertiliser, textiles and garments
GDP US$81.80 billion GDP at market prices (World Bank, 2014)
Currency Omani rial (OMR/RO)
Exchange rate £1 = RO0.47, US$1 = RO0.38, €1 = RO0.43 (October 2016)
National airlines Oman Air
International telephone code +968
Internet domain .om
Time GMT+4
Electrical voltage 220–240v AC; British three-pin plugs widely used
Flag Three equal horizontal bands of white, red and green with a broad, vertical, red band on the hoist side; the national emblem (a *khanjar* dagger in its sheath, with its belt superimposed on two crossed swords in scabbards) in white is centred at the top of the vertical band.
National emblem The *khanjar* (a silver-sheathed curved dagger)
National holidays Non-religious: National Day (officially 18 November but variable), Renaissance Day (officially 23 July but variable); religious (dates alter each year according to the Islamic Lunar Calendar): Eid Al Fitr (at the end of Ramadhan), Eid Al Adha (during the Hajj), Mawlid Al Nabi (Prophet's birthday), Muharram (Islamic New Year). See also pages 62–3.

1

Background Information

Oman is located on the southeastern edge of the Arabian Peninsula and is bordered by Saudi Arabia (to the west), Yemen (to the southwest), the Arabian Sea (to the east), the Strait of Hormuz (to the north) and the United Arab Emirates (to the northwest). The third-largest country in the peninsula, after Saudi Arabia and Yemen, it covers an area of around 309,500km², and is about 25% larger than the United Kingdom, 15% larger than New Zealand and comparable in size to the US state of New Mexico.

The name 'Oman' may be derived from the town Omana mentioned by Pliny and in the *Periplus of the Erythraean Sea* (Itinerary in the Red Sea), a manuscript that may have been written around 50AD by a Greek sailor listing the region's ports and coastal landmarks. The Arab historian Ibn Al-Qabi wrote: 'Oman means those who occupy an area, as in the adjective *aamen*, or *amoun*, i.e. settled man.' Others ascribe it to the name of one of several Arab personages. Its formal name is the Sultanate of Oman or Saltanat 'Uman, but it is simply known as Oman in everyday speech.

GEOGRAPHY

Oman's coastline extends some 1,700km from the Musandam Peninsula to the Empty Quarter around the Yemeni border; much of it is undeveloped. The northern coastline sits astride the Arabian Gulf (called the Persian Gulf in the Arab World) and the Sea of Oman. The Sea of Oman, which extends from the Strait of Hormuz to the peninsula at Ras Al Jinz, borders about a third of Oman's eastern coastline, while the remaining two-thirds of the coastline is bordered by the Arabian Sea, which is the portion of the Indian Ocean between the Arabian Peninsula to the west and the Indian subcontinent to the east. The Sea of Oman is one of the world's most important strategic waterways, providing a shipping lane for oil from the Gulf States. Tankers pass through the Strait of Hormuz – a narrow waterway linking the Arabian Gulf with the Sea of Oman.

The country's topography is varied, with mountains in the north and south, sand desert and gravel desert in the central plain, areas of oases and coastal plains. The **Al Hajar Mountains** rise out of the Strait of Hormuz at the northernmost tip of the country and continue southward, like a spine, for approximately 600km, to finish at Sur, near the eastern end of the peninsula. In many places these mountains reach well above 2,000m, with some peaks of just over 3,000m. At the southern extremity of the country, the **Dhofar Mountains** rise to around 1,800m with escarpments of some 1,000m in height.

Oman's mountains have deep water-cut valleys, or wadis, some of which are up to 1,000m deep. Given their height, the mountains have their own climate and clouds frequently form, resulting in intense downpours. The mountain slopes which face inland have a drainage basin focused on the vast salt flat (*sabkha*) of Um As Samim in northern Oman. Roughly 82% of the land is made

In the past, Arab geographers divided Oman like the human anatomy. The head is the Musandam Peninsula, called Ru'us Al Jabal (Head of the Mountains), the backbone or spine is the Al Hajar Mountains, while the back (Arabic: Adh Dhahirah) is the stretch from the mountains to Al Buraymi. The interior (Arabic: Ad Dakhiliyah) encompasses the Al Jabal Al Akhdar range (Green Mountain) and the historic towns of Nizwa and Bahla; the stomach or underbelly (Al Batinah) is the fertile coastal plain down to Muscat. The bulge from Muscat south to Sur and its hinterland is the eastern province of Ash Sharqiyyah (sharq, meaning 'east'). 'Jaa'lan, the eastern coastal stretch of this region, extends from south of Sur to the coast north of Masirah Island. The name Jaa'lan جعلان means 'to give a gift' and refers to the pledge given by Malik bin Fahm, the legendary leader of the Arab tribes which came into Oman from Yemen, that whichever son of his conquered the area would receive the region as a gift.

The Al Wusta region (meaning 'central') is the empty midriff of the country covered by the vast dry gravel plain, stretching for 800km between the Al Hajar Mountains in the north and the Dhofar Mountains in the south. This plain (also known as the Nejd) is edged by the perilous Empty Quarter (Rub' Al Khali) – a vast desert of sand that extends into Saudi Arabia. The huge gravel desert of the Jiddat Al Harasis is also in Al Wusta region, Harasis being the name for the local Bedu tribe. The southernmost region is Dhofar, the capital of which is Salalah.

up of sand and gravel desert and valleys, about 15% is mountainous and the remaining 3% is coastal plain.

The northern mountains are principally limestone, ranging in age from the Cretaceous period of around 145.5–65.5 million years ago through to the Eocene epoch of around 55.8 to 33.9 million years ago, and in places much older still. These mountains are thought to have been disfigured by the impact of the ophiolite sequence of rocks. These ophiolite rocks were formed when the continental plates moved apart creating a rift valley. Subsequent movement of the continental plates resulted in the Oman ophiolite being 'obducted' (a process whereby the rock was forced on top of other rock) from 90 million years ago. This is unusual, as ophiolite is a heavy, dense rock. Copper and chrome are mined from the ophiolite rocks, and limestone is also commercially important. The geology in Dhofar to the south is equally varied, with granites found behind Mirbat containing debris which is well over one billion years old. Like the north, however, much of Dhofar's mountains are limestone, albeit of a softer, almost chalky variety dating from the Eocene epoch of around 55.8 to 33.9 million years ago. Most of Oman's oil-bearing rocks lie near the Saudi Arabian border in the northwest, around Fahud, and southeast towards Marmul and the Arabian Sea.

CLIMATE

Oman has a hot desert climate, with precipitation far below the upper limit of desert classification. Within this overall climate, it is possible to distinguish climatic variations: the northern coastal regions, the interior plain, the northern mountains and the southern coastal mountains and coastal plain, as well as the two Omani seasons of winter and summer.

During the **winter** months, which fall between October and March, the northern coastal areas are warm and moderately humid with a daytime temperature of 20–30°C in Muscat. In winter, the interior plain is warm and dry. The northern mountain heights are relatively cool and dry with occasional sharp drops in night-time temperature that may cause frost and, on rare occasions, snow. The southern mountains and coastal plain are warm and moderately humid, with Salalah enjoying a daytime temperature of 18–30°C.

During **summer**, which runs from April to September, the northern coastal regions are very hot with Muscat ranging between 30°C and 48°C during the day. The interior plain is very hot and dry, the northern mountains heights warm and dry, and the southern mountains and coastal plain warm and humid, with temperatures in Salalah between 25°C and 30°C. In the south, the crescent of mountains behind Salalah traps the southwesterly monsoon cloud – locally called the *khareef* – which occurs from June to September. This brings dense mist and precipitation, giving rise to a lush, green landscape. The Dhofar region is at its most beautiful after the cloud has lifted in mid-September, until mid-October. The astounding transformation is created by the monsoon clouds, which create a 'cloud forest' on the sea-facing slopes of Dhofar's mountains. Luxuriant vegetation of grass, flowering plants dominated by *Impatiens balsamina*, and trees spring into leaf from late June and are best seen after the cloud lifts from mid-September; indeed, the period from mid- September to mid-October is the best time to visit the Salalah region. Visitors from other GCC (Gulf Co-operation Council) countries and Omanis from the north take advantage of this Dhofar spectacle during school holidays in July and August and the population of Salalah may double during this period. By November the greenery has vanished in all but the most fortunate valleys and sea cliffs.

Overall, the country receives little rainfall. The rain that does fall is due to the mountain ranges, whose height creates cloud cover and occasional, sudden downpours, causing flash floods. Most major roads are all-weather, with the main carriageway elevated above ground level and culverts and bridges allowing water to drain off into the wadis. Local roads may, however, be impassable during and immediately after such floods. Cyclones are rare, but can occur from May to early June or from late October to early November, when sea temperatures provide the heat needed. Recent occurrences have been in May 2002, June 2007 when 'Gonu', the Arabian Sea's most intense cyclone, tracked just offshore along the northern coast, May 2010, October 2011 and November 2015. Apart from raising the sea temperature and providing the energy for cyclones, climate change has also increased the occurrence of 'coral bleaching', causing corals to die off in the warmer seas.

NATURAL HISTORY *with Andrew Grieve*

NATURE CONSERVATION AND RESERVES Oman can be broadly split into four **ecosystems**: the mountains of northern Oman, including Musandam; the desert plains and plateau of central Oman, lying about 350m above sea level; the Dhofar Mountains in the south; and the cloudforest escarpment woodlands and monsoon belt of Dhofar. These very different environments support and sustain their own unique types of flora and fauna. Professor Reginald Victor of Sultan Qaboos University speaks of the importance of a National Biodiversity Strategy and Action Plan (NBSAP) for the country, which would aim (under the guidance of the World Zoo Organisation) to conserve these ecosystems or habitats. The diverse nature of Oman's climate and terrain provides the perfect habitat for thousands of species of plant, animal, bird and marine life and makes the country an ideal destination for lovers of nature and the outdoors.

Enthusiastically 'green' in its outlook, Oman has possibly the most enlightened policy on conservation in the Middle East, with a government ministry, the Ministry of Environment and Climate Affairs, overseeing the relevant matters. It is party to international agreements on biodiversity, climate change, desertification, endangered species, hazardous wastes, marine dumping, the Law of the Sea, whaling and ozone layer protection. In 1984, it became the first Arab country to create a ministry dedicated to environmental issues, and environmental protection laws have been in place since 1974. In addition to preserving its historical monuments and forts, it is committed to protecting the natural habitats of its unique species of flora and fauna, and has established several designated nature reserves, protected sites and research centres. Responsibility for this comes under the Ministry of Regional Municipalities, Environment and Water Resources, through its Directorate of Nature Conservation. Oman is a member of CITES (the Convention on International Trade in Endangered Species of Wild Fauna and Flora), which forbids commercial trading in specific live or dead animals and animal parts.

Wildlife conservation is actively carried out at the country's nature reserves. However, for endangered species, the two principal centres are the Al Wusta Wildlife Reserve at Jaaluni in the Jiddat Al Harasis (Al Wusta region) and the Oman Mammal Breeding Centre at Bait Al Baraka in As Sib (Muscat region), which is not open to the public. Mammals being bred in captivity in these locations include Arabian oryx, Arabian tahr, Arabian gazelle, Arabian wolf, white-tailed mongoose, striped hyena and Gordon's wild cat.

The most popular of Oman's reserves is indisputably the **Ad Dimaniyyat Islands** (along Al Batinah coast, see page 144), which is a designated bird sanctuary, but is renowned for its marine wildlife too. Nineteen species of dolphin and whale have been recorded in Oman's waters, and the Ad Dimaniyyat Islands are probably one of the best locations from which to spot them. Boat trips for dolphin-, whale- and birdwatching can be easily arranged (there is a no-landing policy throughout the bird-breeding season between May and October), and the area is also a highly ranked world dive site.

The protected turtle-breeding beaches at **Ras Al Jinz** (pages 266–7) are a popular place to visit, with the turtles here a key element in the Omani government's tourism strategy. There are seven sea turtle species in the world, of which five occur in Oman's waters and four breed: the females of green, hawksbill, loggerhead and olive ridley turtle lay eggs on Oman's beaches (so far no nesting by the fifth, the leatherback, has been reported). A visitor and research centre has been established at Ras Al Jinz, where an on-site ranger leads you to the sea's edge in the dark for your night-time and dawn turtle-watching adventure.

Other reserves have been established to protect the natural domain of mammals, including two species of gazelle, striped hyena, Arabian leopard, Arabian tahr, Arabian oryx, Blanford's fox, Nubian ibex and Gordon's wild cat. The Saleel Nature Reserve at Al Kamil and Al Wafi (in the Ash Sharqiyyah region) is home to Arabian gazelle and other animals, in addition to varieties of tree, including samr (*Acacia tortilis*) and ghaf (*Prosopis cineraria*). A nursery has been established here to propagate and preserve Oman's endangered wild flora.

Although its central focus is on the endangered Arabian oryx, the **Al Wusta Wildlife Reserve** (pages 278–9) in the Jiddat Al Harasis (central Oman) is home to Arabian gazelle, red fox, Gordon's wild cat, sand cat, caracal, honey badger and possibly the Nubian ibex, among other mammals.

Jabal Samhan, the mountain range in the Dhofar region, was declared a national nature reserve in 1997. These mountains include the highest point in Dhofar, at 1,800m, and are believed to be home to the Middle East's largest population of the endangered Arabian race of leopard, which is being continuously monitored. Other species found in the Jabal Samhan Nature Reserve include the Nubian ibex, striped hyena, caracal lynx, Gordon's wild cat and Blanford's fox.

The five **Al Hallaniyyat Islands** (pages 316–17) off the Dhofar coast are an important breeding ground for turtles and seabirds, although not yet designated a nature reserve. A turtle-counting and tagging programme has also been set up on Masirah Island, one of the most important loggerhead sea turtle nesting sites in the world, with large numbers of loggerhead sea turtles laying their eggs annually. The importance of Oman for sea turtles is highly significant and the opportunities for turtle viewing excellent.

The area from Ras Al Had down to the southern borders of Oman and for 200 nautical miles out to sea from the coast has been declared a protected marine area by the International Maritime Organization (IMO), with the aim of conserving the sea's resources by regulating tourist and ship activity.

The commissioning of books and studies covering the country's wild flowers, butterflies, birds and other forms of wildlife has made Oman one of the best-documented countries of the Middle East in this field. As visitors it is important that we are aware of Oman's conservation policies and respect the habitats and environs of the country's wildlife. The destruction of living plants or killing of wild animals or birds is prohibited by the Oman government.

FLORA Taken together, the northern mountains (including the Musandam Peninsula) and the Dhofar region are home to much of Oman's 1,200+ species of flora, of which about a hundred are endemic to Oman or regionally to Arabia. Nurseries have been established at the Saleel Nature Reserve (in the Ash Sharqiyyah region), Qayrun Hayriti (in Dhofar), Al Qurum Natural Park (Muscat) and the Botanical Gardens within Sultan Qaboos University (Muscat) and most notably the Oman Botanic Garden, a major facility that will be of worldwide scientific importance when it is completed.

Oman's most famous plant is the **Boswellia sacra**, which produces frankincense resin. Found naturally in Dhofar and parts of East Africa, it is a contorted tree that grows up to 8m tall. One tree can produce up to several kilograms of frankincense in a season, and at the height of the trade 2,000 years ago, over 3,000 tonnes of the resin were exported by camel caravan or by boat to the wealthy civilisations of Egypt, Greece, Rome and India. In recent times, however, the trade in frankincense has declined. Research is currently ongoing into the cancer-curing properties of frankincense, as it is thought to contain an agent that stops the cancer spreading by resetting the DNA code. The ancient Egyptians considered it to be the tears of the god Horus.

Also in Dhofar can be found the baobab **Adansonia digitata**, a species more familiar in the African savannah. The majority of these are found in Wadi Hinna (locally called Wadi Ahzer) on the coastal escarpment between Tawi Atayr and Mirbat.

The first decade of the millennium saw a large coastal afforestation project take place, with approximately 188,000 **mangrove trees** planted in the lagoons (*khawrs*) along Oman's coastline. A permanent mangrove nursery and research centre has also been established at Al Qurum Natural Park.

Rose water, extracted from the **Damask rose** (*Rosa* × *damascena*), is used extensively in Oman in the preparation of *halwa* (see box, page 163), as well as in perfumes, incense (especially at Eid and weddings), *qahwa* (page 67) and in traditional medicines. The rose is grown on the Sayq Plateau of Al Jabal Al Akhdar; it is thought to have been introduced there from Persia. The rose petals are simmered in water for several hours and the resulting condensed rose water is stored for over a month to allow any sediment to settle before the product is bottled and sold.

FAUNA
Mammals Around 76 species of mammal have been recorded in Oman, of which one, the endemic Dhofarian shrew, is critically endangered.

The endangered **Arabian leopard** (*Panthera pardus nimr*), Arabia's largest cat, survives in the remote mountains of southern Oman and there have been unconfirmed reports of sightings in Musandam. Usually solitary, it comes together with other leopards only for breeding. A survey into the animal has been carried out both in Dhofar and in Musandam. Modern techniques of camera-trapping and satellite collars have meant that the ecology of this shy and very secretive animal has been studied for the first time. An important sanctuary for the leopard is Jabal Samhan Nature Reserve. The **rock hyrax** (*Procavia capensis*), found especially in better vegetated areas, and the **Nubian ibex** (*Capra ibex nubiana*), found in rocky escarpments, form the bulk of the leopard's diet. This is an extremely rare mammal and even dedicated researchers very rarely see one, as they live on the steep escarpments of the mountains.

The **caracal lynx** (*Caracal caracal*) is found throughout Oman, where it hunts small animals and ground-dwelling birds. Smaller cats are the **sand cat** (*Felis margarita*), with very few living in extreme isolation, and **Gordon's wild cat** (*Felis silvestris gordoni*), which roams throughout a large territory, usually in rocky areas.

In southern Oman the **honey badger** (*Mellivora capensis*) can be found, as can the **striped hyena** (*Hyaena hyaena sultana*), which has almost certainly disappeared from northern Oman. In scrubby coastal areas it is possible to see the **white-tailed mongoose** (*Ichneumia albicauda*). The **common genet** (*Genetta genetta*) inhabits the wooded mountains of Dhofar.

Throughout the mountains are limited numbers of **Arabian wolf** (*Canis lupus arabs*). The ubiquitous **red fox** (*Vulpes vulpes*) is found thoughout most of Oman, including the sand deserts, where **Ruppell's fox** (*Vulpes ruppellii*) also lives. The smaller **Blanford's fox** (*Vulpes cana*) has a more limited terrain, with a preference for mountainous areas.

In the Wihibah Sands the honey-coloured **Cheesman's gerbil** (*Gerbillus cheesmani*) is common. **Brandt's hedgehog** (*Paraechinus hypomelas*) and the smaller **Ethiopian hedgehog** (*Paraechinus aethiopicus*) are found across much of the country.

Among the bat species seen are the large **Egyptian fruit bat** (*Rousettus aegyptiacus*) and in northern Oman the **Muscat mouse-tailed bat** (*Rhinopoma muscatellum*) can be found roosting in undisturbed buildings, including forts.

The **Arabian oryx** (*Oryx leucoryx*), a type of antelope, was extinct in the wild by the early 1970s due to hunting. In 1975, Sultan Qaboos launched Operation Oryx, a captive breeding programme conducted at the sultan's Omani Mammal Breeding Centre, Bait Al Barakah (at As Sib, near Muscat), with donated animals from London Zoo, the Hadhramaut (Yemen), Jordan, Kuwait, Saudi Arabia and Arizona. The programme drew upon the knowledge of the World Wildlife Fund, the Fauna Preservation Society and the International Union for Conservation of Nature and Natural Resources, who assisted with the project. The oryx were then reared at Jaaluni in the Jiddat Al Harasis in central Oman before being successfully reintroduced into the wild in the early 1980s. UNESCO had proclaimed the Jiddat

Al Harasis a World Natural Heritage Site, but in 2007 withdrew this status as the numbers dwindled and the park size was reduced by 90% (see box, page 278). In the years since the numbers have increased, although it is now in protected 'pens' of several hectares each.

The largest single population of **Arabian gazelle** (*Gazella gazella*) can be found in the Al Wusta Wildlife Reserve (pages 278–9). Small groups of gazelles made up of a male and a few females with any young inhabit mountainous and plain areas. The larger male has thick horns while the female's horns are finer and straighter, and they feed on shrubs and grasses.

The **Reem gazelle** (sand gazelle) (*Gazella subguttorosa* ssp *marica*) is a less common species and can be found on the sandy terrain at the edges of the Empty Quarter. In contrast to the Arabian gazelle, the reem gazelle can give birth to twins, and unlike the territorial Arabian gazelle, covers long distances searching for new pastures.

The **Arabian tahr** (*Arabitragus jayakari*) is a separate monotypic genus, one of the rarest animals in the world and an endangered species. The ideal habitat for the Arabian tahr is at altitude, between 1,000m and 1,800m, and so the Wadi As Sarin Nature Reserve in the Eastern Al Hajar Mountains is its natural home. The Arabian Tahr Project began in 1976 and continues to work for the animal's conservation.

The **Nubian ibex** (*Capra ibex nubiana*), another globally endangered species, is a wild mountain goat that lives in small groups. During the annual mating season, groups of up to 30 animals come together, with the large adult males fighting for the right to breed. The Nubian ibex can be found in the Jabal Samhan Nature Reserve and may be seen on the escarpment near the Al Wusta Wildlife Reserve. It does not occur in northern Oman.

As Oman is a desert country with intense daytime temperatures wild animals have adapted to an almost nocturnal existence. You may, however, see occasional gazelle in hilly areas, hyrax are relatively easy to see around water springs in Dhofar, and fox and rodents can often be seen around dawn and dusk. Other larger mammals are almost all rare and extremely secretive, with the inevitable exception of the camel, which is a domesticated animal.

Reptiles There are around 64 species of reptiles in Oman, of which at least 21 are endemic to Arabia and seven are globally threatened. Oman's snake species include the venomous **Arabian cobra** (*Naja arabica*), **Arabian horned viper** (*Cerastes gasperettii*), **Oman saw-scaled viper** (*Echis omanensis*), **Persian horned viper** (*Pseudocerastes persicus persicus*), **puff adder** (*Bitis arietans*) and **small-scaled burrowing asp** (*Atractaspis microlepidota*).

Other land snake species such as the **Arabian cat snake** (*Telescopus dhara*), **false cobra** (*Malpolon moilensis*) and **Wadi racer** (*Platyceps rhodorachis*) are non-venomous. All sea snakes are venomous; these include the **pelagic sea snake** (*Pelamis platura*).

Lizards thrive throughout Oman. A species commonly seen inside buildings is the **yellow-bellied house gecko** (*Hemidactylus flaviviridis*), an excellent insect hunter; other geckos include the small rock geckos *Pristurus carteri* and *P. rupestris*, which uses its curled tail to signal. The northern mountains are home to **Jayakar's Oman lizard** (*Omanosaura jayakari*), which can reach more than 50cm in length, and its smaller relative, the **blue-tailed Oman lizard** (*Omanosaura cyanura*). **Grey monitors** (*Varanus griseus*) are found in gravel plains or sand desert. These are usually pale brown in colour and can grow to over 100cm long. Other inhabitants of the plains are the endemic **Omani spiny-tailed lizard** (*Uromastyx thomasi*) and **Egyptian spiny-tailed lizard** (*Uromastyx aegyptia*), which can be seen absorbing the sun's heat, making them paler as their body temperature rises. In the coconut plantations of Salalah, **oriental garden lizards** (*Calotes versicolor*) are most obvious just before the summer *khareef*, when the males signal using their throat flap in territorial displays. The coastal facing slopes of the mountains and vegetated plain around Salalah are home to the **Arabian chameleon** (*Chamaeleo arabicus*), which naturally turns green during the *khareef*.

Amphibians   Only two species of amphibian are known to live in Oman: the **Arabian toad** (*Duttaphrynus arabicus*) and the **Dhofar toad** (*Duttaphrynus dhufarensis*), which is an Arabian endemic.

Birds   (*with Andrew Grieve*) A total of 524 bird species have been recorded in Oman according to the Oman Bird Records Committee (OBRC), which publishes an official bird list. Familiar widespread wintering species in Oman include **great cormorant** (*Phalacrocorax carbo*), **western cattle egret** (*Bubulcus ibis*), **Eurasian spoonbill** (*Platalea leucorodia*), **greater flamingo** (*Phoenicopterus roseus*), **northern shoveller** (*Anas clypeata*), **little stint** (*Calidris minuta*), **ruff** (*Philomachus pugnax*), **black-tailed godwit** (*Limosa limosa*), **common kingfisher** (*Alcedo atthis*) and **Siberian stonechat** (*Saxicola maurus*). Other more soughtafter wintering species in different parts of Oman include the **steppe eagle** (*Aquila nipalensis*) and the **eastern imperial eagle** (*Aquila heliaca*), found in the foothills of mountain ranges, most readily near rubbish dumps. The **Indian pond heron** (*Ardeola grayii*), **pallid harrier**

BIRDWATCHING IN OMAN

Oman sits at the crossroads of three continents: Europe, Africa and Asia, and is therefore well placed along bird migratory routes, which makes it an excellent location for seeing transitory species as well as interesting resident and wintering birds. The best times to see the migrating species are from late August to November and from February to May, with December through to February being the best for winter birds and also the coolest time of the year. Most of the indigenous species can be seen in the winter, although some breeding species do not arrive until May, particularly in Dhofar. There are good birding sites in every region of the country (see regional chapters for further details). The coastal *khawrs* (lagoons) offer perfect spots for wintering and migrating waterbirds, including ducks, waders and terns. The Ad Dimaniyyat Islands hold substantial numbers of breeding **bridled and white-cheeked terns**, with small numbers of **common noddies** (*Anous stolidus*), **ospreys** (*Pandion haliaetus*) and **western reef herons** (*Egretta gularis*). The As Sawadi Islands and Al Fahl Island (about 4km off Ras Al Hamra, in the Capital Area) hold breeding **sooty falcons** (*Falco concolor*), with the latter site also having nesting **red-billed tropicbirds** (*Phaethon aethereus*); boat trips around Al Fahl Island can easily be arranged from Muscat (page 136). Al Ansab Lagoons (about 30km west of Muscat) and Al Qurum Natural Park in Muscat itself are good places to see typical Omani breeding species such as **grey francolin**, **red-wattled plover**, **laughing dove** (*Spilopelia senegalensis*), **little green bee-eater** (*Merops orientalis*), **yellow-vented bulbul** (*Pycnonotus xanthopygos*), **Arabian babbler** (*Turdoides squamiceps*), **purple sunbird** and **Indian silverbill**.

Bar Al Hikman and Masirah Island (the latter is accessible by ferry only) hold perhaps a million wintering waterbirds, mainly herons, egrets, waders and gulls. Exciting species such as **crab plover** (*Dromas ardeola*) and **great knot** (*Calidris*

(*Circus macrourus*), **lesser sand plover** (*Charadrius mongolus*) and **pin-tailed snipe** (*Gallinago stenura*) are found on coastal areas near *khawrs* (lagoons).

The **Egyptian nightjar** (*Caprimulgus aegyptius*) is usually seen in the stony central plateau, while the **isabelline shrike** (*Lanius isabellinus*) can be found on the edge of the vast 'pivot fields' in the desert. The **citrine wagtail** (*Motacilla citreola*) is found near water seepages, while the **redtailed wheatear** (*Oenanthe chrysopygia*) frequents open rocky plains. The **eastern pied wheatear** (*Oenanthe picata*) is often seen on mountain slopes up to 1,000m, while the **plain leaf warbler** (*Phylloscopus neglectus*) needs a more vegetated habitat. The **rosecoloured starling** (*Pastor roseus*) is an occasional winter visitor in eastern Oman. Many geographical influences can be detected in Oman's breeding birds, with the influence of India provided by **yellow bittern** (*Ixobrychus sinensis*) and **pheasant-tailed jacana** (*Hydrophasianus chirurgus*) nesting in Dhofar, and **grey francolin** (*Francolinus pondicerianus*), **Indian roller** (*Coracias benghalensis*), **purple sunbird** (*Cinnyris asiaticus*) and **Indian silverbill** (*Lonchura malabarica*) along Al Batinah coast. The mangroves along this coast also support interesting species including **red-wattled plover** (*Vanellus indicus*) and the **white collared kingfisher** (*Halcyon chloris kalbaensis*), an endemic subspecies.

Typical African species that are resident in the Dhofar region include the huge **lappet-faced vulture** (*Torgos tracheliotos*), **Verreaux's eagle** (*Aquila verreauxii*), **spotted thick-knee** (*Burhinus capensis*), **Namaqua dove** (*Oena capensis*), **Bruce's green pigeon** (*Treron waalia*), **African scops owl** (*Otus senegalensis*), **African paradise flycatcher** (*Terpsiphone viridis*), **shining sunbird** (*Cinnyris habessinicus*),

tenuirostris) are present in winter, the latter found south of the Shannah ferry terminal for Masirah Island when the tide is rising. A good area to watch at high tide is Filim, 19km south of the town of Al Hij, where **great white egrets** (*Ardea alba*), **greater flamingos** (*Phoenicopterus roseus*), crab plover, **terek sandpiper** (*Xenus cinereus*), **broad-billed sandpiper** (*Limicola falcinellus*) and **slender-billed gulls** (*Chroicocephalus genei*) can be seen. Other locations offering good birdwatching opportunities include Musandam, where breeding **Lichtenstein's sandgrouse** (*Pterocles lichtensteinii*), **chukar** (*Alectoris chukar*) and **Hume's wheatear** (*Oenanthe albonigra*), and wintering **eastern pied wheatear, red-tailed wheatear** (*Oenanthe chrysopygia*), **Eversmann's redstart** (*Phoenicurus erythronotus*) and **plain leaf warbler** (*Phylloscopus neglectus*) can be seen. The desert oasis and resthouse of Qatbit (pages 277–8) on the desert road between Muscat and Salalah is an excellent place to stay over to see desert species such as **crowned** (*Pterocles coronatus*) and **spotted sandgrouse** (*Pterocles senegallus*) and **greater hoopoe lark** (*Alaemon alaudipes*). A series of *khawrs* along the Dhofar coast each side of Salalah are also excellent sites for a range of waterbirds throughout the year, particularly Khawr Taqa and Khawr Rawri (sometimes spelt Rouri). For Arabian endemics and Dhofar specialities, the wooden ravines inland of the coast are the places to visit in the spring, particularly Ayn Hamran just 22km from Salalah. Birdwatching excursions can easily be arranged through many of the tour operators in Muscat (pages 83–5). They cost around RO30 per person for a half-day tour. Several books have been published by the authors Hanne and Jens Eriksen, who operate birding tours in Muscat through some of the tour operators listed within this book. Readers might like to get hold of a copy of their *Birdwatching Guide to Oman* (page 335) or any of their other publications.

black-crowned tchagra (*Tchagra senegala*), **Rüppell's weaver** (*Ploceus galbula*), **African silverbill** (*Lonchura cantans*) and **African rock bunting** (*Emberiza tahapisi*). Some of the summer visitors to Dhofar are also typically African in distribution, with the striking **diederik cuckoo** (*Chrysococcyx caprius*), brightly coloured **grey-headed kingfisher** (*Halcyon leucocephala*), **Forbes-Watson swift** (*Apus berliozi*) and **singing bush lark** (*Mirafra cantillans*) all breeding during the monsoon period. The remaining breeding species are mainly Arabian endemics, seabirds, desert species or typical European and Mediterranean birds. The Arabian endemics include **Arabian partridge** (*Alectoris melanocephala*), **Arabian wheatear** (*Oenanthe lugentoides*) and **Yemen serin** (*Crithagra menachensis*), which all breed in Dhofar. **Yellow-vented bulbul** (*Pycnonotus goiavier*) (northern and southern Oman) and **Tristram's grackle** (*Onychognathus tristramii*) (Dhofar only) are mainly restricted to the Middle East. The elegant and graceful **sooty falcon** (*Falco concolor*), **osprey** (*Pandion haliaetus*) and **crab plover** (*Dromas ardeola*) all breed on island groups.

Breeding seabirds and herons on these islands feature **striated heron** (*Butorides striata*), western **reef heron** (*Egretta gularis*), **red-billed tropicbird** (*Phaethon aethereus*) (which also breeds on mainland sea cliffs), **masked booby** (*Sula dactylatra*), **Socotra cormorant** (*Phalacrocorax nigrogularis*) (Arabian endemic), **sooty gull** (*Ichthyaetus hemprichii*), **swift tern** (*Thalasseus bergii*), **white-cheeked tern** (*Sterna repressa*), **bridled tern** (*Onychoprion anaethetus*), **common noddy** (*Anous stolidus*) and **Saunder's tern** (*Sternula saundersi*). **Jouanin's petrel** (*Bulweria fallax*) probably breeds and is another endemic to the region.

Desert and mountain species are typified by **golden eagle** (*Aquila chrysaetos*), **pallid scops owl** (*Otus brucei*), **sand partridge** (*Ammoperdix heyi*), **cream-coloured courser** (*Cursorius cursor*), four species of **sandgrouse**, black-crowned **finch-lark** (*Eremopterix nigriceps*), **Dunn's lark** (*Eremalauda dunni*), **desert lark** (*Ammomanes deserti*), **greater hoopoe-lark** (*Alaemon alaudipes*), **long-billed pipit** (*Anthus similis*), **Hume's wheatear** (*Oenanthe albonigra*), **scrub warbler** (*Scotocerca inquieta*), **trumpeter finch** (*Bucanetes githagineus*) and **house bunting** (*Emberiza sahari*).

Palearctic species that breed around the Mediterranean and also in Oman include **little bittern** (*Ixobrychus minutus*), **Egyptian vulture** (*Neophron percnopterus*), **black-winged stilt** (*Himantopus himantopus*), **collared pratincole** (*Glareola pratincola*), **turtle dove** (*Streptopelia turtur*), **blue-cheeked bee-eater** (*Merops persicus*) and **southern grey shrike** (*Lanius meridionalis*). The shy **houbara bustard** (*Chlamydotis undulata*) is a desert bird that by 1996 was near to extinction in other parts of Arabia, where it was largely hunted out by Arab falconers. Now protected by CITES, it is also the subject of a conservation survey in Oman, whose anti-falconry laws add further protection. Jaaluni in the Jiddat Al Harasis in central Oman is a good place to look for this species.

For further information visit www.birdsoman.com.

Butterflies (*with Andrew Grieve*)

There are around 80 classified species of butterfly in Oman, none endemic to either Oman or Arabia, and many can be seen in either Musandam or Dhofar mainly between October and May. Familiar colourful species such as the cream-coloured **lime swallowtail** (*Papilio machaon*) can be seen in the date oases of northern Oman, which together with the much darker **African lime butterfly** (*Papilio demodocus*) in the Dhofar region and the **lime butterfly** (*Papilio demoleus*) in northern Oman creates a trio with a wingspan of around 10cm, relying almost entirely on citrus trees. A large, bright species likely to be seen in all parts is the **plain tiger** (*Danaus chrysippus*), a large orange butterfly with black wing-tips, whose caterpillars feed on near-toxic plants. The consumption of these plants by caterpillars makes them in turn toxic if eaten. The **pomegranate**

playboy (*Virachola livia*) breeds in Al Jabal Al Akhdar, with its caterpillars feeding off pomegranate fruits. The **desert white** (*Pontia glauconome*) is widespread and relies on a range of plants. A widespread pale butterfly is the **caper white** (*Belenois aurota*), with large numbers congregating around shrubs. The aptly named **blue pansy** (*Precis orithya*), which feeds especially on Acanthaceae, is found throughout Oman and is a migratory species. The large **death's-head hawkmoth** (*Acherontia atropos*), whose wings span up to 13cm, feeds on honey from honey bees, while the larger, dramatic green **oleander hawkmoth** (*Daphnis nerii*) has caterpillars that feed on the poisonous oleander found in many mountainous areas.

Marine life

The waters of the Arabian Sea and the Sea of Oman provide diverse marine habitats, which give rise to and accommodate an abundance of sealife. At least 1,170 species of fish and around 85 varieties of hard and soft coral exist in Oman's waters, which firmly places the sultanate on any diver's itinerary. **Spotted eagle ray** (*Aetobatus narinari*), **honeycomb moray eel** (*Gymnothorax favagineus*), **barracuda** (*Sphyraena barracuda*) and **Indian frogfish** (*Antennarius indicus*) are just some of the species of fish that inhabit these waters. Coral varieties such as **lattice table coral** (*Acropora clathrata*), **black coral** (*Antipathes* spp), **wire coral** (*Cirrhipathes spiralis*), **teddy bear** (*Dendronepthya* spp) and **cabbage coral** (*Montipora foliosa*) can all be found in Oman, Al Fahl Island offering the widest variety in one location. For information on diving, see the regional chapters; for books on the subject, see page 335.

Whales, dolphins and sharks

Omani waters are home to 19 species of whale and dolphin. The coastal waters near Muscat from Al Fahl Island to near Al Bustan Palace Hotel are the key location for dolphin sightings in northern Oman. Species found include **common bottlenose dolphin** (*Tursiops truncatus*), **spinner dolphin** (*Stenella longirostris*), **long-beaked common dolphin** (*Delphinus capensis*), **pantropical spotted dolphin** (*Stenella attenuata*), **striped dolphin** (*Stenella coeruleoalba*), **roughtoothed dolphin** (*Steno bredanensis*) and **Risso's dolphin** (*Grampus griseus*). Musandam and coastal waters south of Ras Al Jinz are a home to **Indo-Pacific humpback dolphin** (*Sousa chinensis*). Larger cetaceans include **pygmy blue whale** (*Balaenoptera musculus brevicauda*), **sperm whale** (*Physeter macrocephalus*), **humpback whale** (*Megaptera novaeangliae*), **Cuvier's beaked whale** (*Ziphius cavirostris*), **pygmy killer whale** (*Feresa attenuata*), **orca or killer whale** (*Orcinus orca*), **Bryde's whale** (*Balaenoptera edeni*), **false killer whale** (*Pseudorca crassidens*), **dwarf sperm whale** (*Kogia simus*), **melon-headed whale** (*Peponocephala electra*). Whale sightings are less predictable than the smaller dolphins and are usually in remote locations such as south of Ad Duqm and Ras Janjari east of Mirbat, which is a good land-based whale- and birdwatching viewing point. Oman is a member of the International Whaling Commission and follows the CITES regulations, which prevent all of these species from being traded. The Whale and Dolphin Research Group is a voluntary organisation which works within the Environment Society of Oman (ESO) and shares the same excellent website (*www.eso.org.om*). The various sharks spotted in Omani waters include **zebra shark** (*Stegostoma fasciatum*), **whale sharks** (*Rhincodon typus*) and **black-tip reef sharks** (*Carcharhinus melanopterus*). Overfishing of shark for their fins, which are shipped to the Far East, means that you are unlikely to see them except when scuba diving.

Sea turtles

The other creature to merit its own sanctuary is the sea turtle, particularly the green turtle, which is found on designated beaches south east of Ras Al Had on Oman's southeastern tip. Well-organised turtle watching is possible at the Ras Al Jinz Scientific Centre; tickets are obtained at the centre and advance booking is advisable during holiday seasons. Several thousand green turtles lay eggs over the year, with peak season in midsummer. Hatchlings emerge two months after their eggs have been laid. For further details, see Turtle Beach Resort and Ras Al Jinz Scientific Centre (both page 267). There are five species of turtle (out of the world's seven) that populate the seas of Oman, of which four do so solely for the purpose of laying their eggs: the **olive ridley** (*Lepidochelys olivacea*), the **loggerhead turtle** (*Caretta caretta*), the endangered **green turtle** (*Chelonia mydas*) and the critically endangered **hawksbill turtle** (*Eretmochelys imbricata*), which nests on the Ad Dimaniyyat Islands. The fifth species, the **leatherback turtle** (*Dermochelys coriacea*), occurs as a visitor offshore. Several thousand loggerhead turtles nest on the east coast of Masirah Island.

Sea turtles, like all wild creatures, enjoy official protection in Oman. Green turtles may live for up to 100 years and most only start to breed once they are between the ages of 25 and 50. Each female can lay up to 100 eggs in a clutch and several clutches in a breeding season. She spends hours excavating and then recovering holes in the sand for their protection. She then returns to the sea for around a fortnight before she returns to lay another clutch, in a cycle that is repeated approximately four times during the season. It will be another two to four years before that female will lay more eggs. The sex of the hatchlings is determined by the internal temperature of the nest site, often affected by proximity to the relatively cool sea water. A temperature below 28°C and all the hatchlings will be male; a temperature that is over 31°C and they will all be female, while a mix of sexes occurs between 28 and 31°C. The eggs take around two months to hatch, and the sight of tiny baby turtles emerging from the sand is extraordinary. They struggle through the sand, making their way to the sea, but only a small proportion will make it, as many are eaten *en route* by seagulls and other predators.

HISTORY

Archaeological evidence has provided evidence of man's occupation in Oman for over 70,000 years, with large fields of flint flakes in Dhofar's northern valleys. Northern Oman is believed to be at the heart of the ancient 'Majan' region referred to in Mesopotamian texts of the 3rd millennium BC. Copper mined in the ophiolite mountains was traded into Akkad and the Indus Valley was also an area whose products have been excavated in Oman. Trade in Dhofar's frankincense resin grew and it was traded with Rome, Mesopotamia and later imperial China.

Oman's people have historically been astro-navigators, sailors and merchant traders, occupying, as they did, a prime geographical position on the sea trading route between eastern and western continents. The indigenous natural resources of copper and frankincense (both extremely important commodities in the past) transformed the country's prosperity in ancient times through trade with ancient Egypt, Mesopotamia, Greece, Rome and China, to where these goods were shipped. Evidence of Oman's prosperous seafaring history can be found in ancient texts from these regions.

Persia ruled Oman periodically from the 5th century BC until the Arab invasions of Persia after the death of the Prophet Mohammed. Islam was accepted by Arab tribes in Oman following the Prophet Mohammed's embassies in AD627 and has remained an Islamic country since. There was a short rule by the Portuguese from 1507 until they were expelled from Muscat in 1650 by Sultan bin Saif Al Yarubi. The **Yarubi dynasty** continued to rule, though during the early decades of the 18th century there were periodic Persian invasions, one of which occupied Muscat until the invaders were expelled in 1744 by the founder of the present-day dynasty, Imam

Ahmed bin Said. From 1783 through to 1958, Oman ruled Gwadar in modern Pakistan and periodically Char Bandar in neighbouring Persia. Gombroon (modern Bandar Abbas), the island of Hormuz and a section of the mainland coastline were ruled under a lease agreement with Persia, whereby the Omani ruler paid rent to the Persian ruler and was thereby able to retain the lucrative customs duty. This agreement continued from 1794 through to 1868.

It was in East Africa that the overseas territories of Oman reached their zenith. Arabs have traded with East Africa since at least the 1st century AD. Al Jahiz, a 9th-century African scholar, wrote that an Omani prince organised an unsuccessful military expedition against the 'Zanj' (the people of East Africa) in the 7th century. This may have been Sulayman bin 'Abbad Al-Julanda, together with his brothers, the sons of an Omani ruler who fled from the Caliph 'Abd-al-Malik to East Africa, where they died in AD700. In 1698, Zanzibar was ruled by Oman, as was much of the East African coast from Mogadishu south to the Mozambican border. After the death of Sultan Said bin Sultan, the last ruler of the unified territory of Zanzibar and Oman, in 1856, the territories were separated, with one son (Majid bin Said Al-Busaidi) becoming Sultan of Zanzibar and another (Thuwaini bin Said Al-Said) becoming the Sultan of Oman. The peripheral territories of both Oman and Zanzibar gradually separated from their former overlord. Persia retook the leased lands from Oman and in East Africa, while Germany and Britain acquired Tanganyika and Kenya.

UNESCO WORLD HERITAGE LISTS

Oman has four inscriptions on the **UNESCO World Heritage Site list**. These are: Bahla Fort (1987) in the Ad Dakhiliyah region; the archaeological sites at Bat, along with neighbouring Al Khutm and Al Ayn (1988) in Adh Dhahirah region; the Land of Frankincense (2000) in the Dhofar region, which includes the archaeological sites at Al Balid and Samharam/Khawr Rawri; and the *aflaj* irrigation systems of Oman (2006).

The **UNESCO Intangible Cultural Heritage list** includes:

- Arabic coffee, which is traditionally part of the welcome for guests;
- The *majlis*, the sitting area where men meet for celebrations and discussions;
- *Al-Ayyala*, a dance from northern Oman which involves drum music, dance and chanted poetry to portray a battle scene;
- *Al-Bar'ah*, a performance from the mountains in Dhofar involving ten to 30 men and women as a musical ensemble, with two male dancers holding *khanjars* as they dance in unison;
- *Al-Razfaa*, a celebratory dance from northern Oman in which male performers form two facing lines with dancers filling the space between. Led by the main singer, the two rows create a dual chorus, singing chants;
- *Al Azha*, one of the major expressions of northern Omani cultural and musical identity. It takes the form of a poetry contest punctuated by sword and step movements and poetic exchanges between a singer-poet and a choir;
- *Al-Taghrooda*, traditional Bedouin repetitive chanted poetry composed and recited by men travelling on camelback through desert areas of the United Arab Emirates and the Sultanate of Oman. Bedouins believe that chanting entertains the riders and stimulates animals to walk in time.

1

After the separation of Zanzibar and Oman and the ongoing changes in trade following the opening of the Suez Canal and the advent of modern steam shipping, Oman entered a period of economic and political decline. Political decline was exemplified by the Treaty of Seeb (now As Sib) in 1920, which was at the very least an administrative division of northern Oman between Taimur bin Faisal Al Said based in Muscat and the religious imam Salim bin Rashid Al-Kharusi in Nizwa, and was considered by some to be a political separation. This treaty was followed by civil conflict in northern Oman, focused on the Al Jabal Al Akhdar mountains, an attempt to solidify separation and a second more serious conflict in Dhofar that gradually sucked in regional participants.

The presence of numerous castles and forts in virtually every village is testament to Oman's warring past, serving as protection from both outside invaders and neighbouring tribes.

Historic explorers have passed through Oman and many legends have become associated with these explorers. The legend of Sindbad the Sailor, of *Arabian Nights* fame, is believed to have originated here around the 10th century AD. The Moroccan traveller Ibn Battuta visited in around 1331, while Zheng He the Chinese admiral stopped here on his fourth and sixth voyages in 1413 and 1421. Wilfred Thesiger, the explorer and writer, lived and travelled with the Bedu of southern Arabia in the 1940s. His writings illuminate the traditional way of life in Oman, which he deeply cherished. Oman is home to the famed 'Atlantis of the Sands' (the lost city of Ubar), alluded to in the Quran, the Bible and *Arabian Nights*.

Since 1970 the country has seen a radical upswing in its prosperity and outlook under the leadership of the well-respected Sultan Qaboos, made possible by the country's oil reserves. Oman has been modernised and is now a destination for discerning travellers, with accommodation for all budgets throughout much of the country. Airport expansion and improved air links will enable continued growth in Oman's leisure industry. Modern resorts include international-standard golf courses and marinas. Relatively large shopping malls with cinemas, an increasing range of restaurants away from major hotels and more live entertainment add to the leisure mix for residents and visitors alike. This appeal is supported by a number of property developments where non-nationals can own property.

CHRONOLOGY There is no specific history section in this guide, since historical background is woven into the text as and when relevant. For an overview therefore, the following detailed chronology is provided as a handy reference and summary.

c3000BC	Earliest-known references to Oman, as Majan (also Magan), found at Ur in Sumeria, confirming it as a thriving and wealthy seafaring state, the source of Mesopotamian copper. Settlement and graves established at Bat.
2500–2000BC	Umm Al Nar period of rich trade between Oman and Mesopotamia (the Tigris and Euphrates region of Iraq), mainly in copper. Camels domesticated for transportation.
2500BC	Ras Al Jinz settlement established.
2000BC	Rise of Dilmun (Bahrain) eclipses Oman's trading power.
2000–1300BC	Wadi Suq period; sites include Samad A'Shan, where Oman's main trading partner is Dilmun.
1300–300BC	Iron Age. Frankincense trade using caravan routes through Arabia to the north. Sites established at Ubar, Khawr Rawri, Lizq and Bawshar.

c1000BC	*Falaj* system of irrigation in Oman.
350BC	Samharam established by the rulers of the Hadhramaut in Yemen.
145BC –AD570	The continuing failure of the Marib Dam in Yemen gives rise to the emigration of the Al Azd peoples throughout Arabia and the arrival of some, under their leader Malik bin Fahm (c AD 196–231), in Oman.
AD200–400	Sassanians in power, having moved from Iran across the Gulf. Sassanian governors in Suhar and Ar Rustaq.
400–500	Christianity arrives in Oman with suggestions of an early Nestorian church in Suhar and an Omani bishop.
630	Amr Ibn Al As, Muhammad's envoy, arrives in Oman to convert the country to Islam. Oman is one of the first lands to embrace Islam.
633	Battle of Daba. Caliph Abu Bakr sends an army to defeat apostates as part of the Ridda Wars.
750	Julanda bin Masud elected first *imam* (spiritual leader) of Oman. Oman remains under imam rule until 1154.
8th–10th centuries	Oman gradually separates from the Abbasid Caliphate, which periodically sends military expeditions to gain submission.
9th–10th centuries	Extensive trade with the Far East and India, supplying the wealthy.
	Abbasid court of Baghdad. Sohar enjoys great wealth as the principal city of the Wajihid dynasty. The interior of Oman deteriorates under attacks by Qarmathians and Wajihids. These attacks are finished by the regional dominance of the Persian Buhids from Baghdad until c1073.
1151	Dynasty established by Banu Nabhan. The dynasty rules much of northern Oman's interior between 1154 and 1624.
12th century	Hormuz, an Arab principality on the Persian mainland near modern Bandar Abbas, is established. It becomes the principal controller of shipping through the Strait of Hormuz, which forms the entrance to The Gulf, becoming a watchword for wealth. The town relocates shortly after 1296 to the island which now bears its name. Hormuz becomes renowned for its wealth, as noted in Milton's *Paradise Lost*: 'High on a throne of royal state, which far outshone the wealth of Ormus and of Ind'. The Omani town of Qalhat is the southern satellite town of Hormuz and possibly the origin of the Hormuz ruling dynasty.
1330	Ibn Battuta, North African traveller and geographer, visits Dhofar and northern Oman.
1428	Dynastic rule disrupted by the imams following the installation of the first imam for over 250 years.
1507	The Portuguese under Albuquerque reach Oman. They burn Oman's fishing fleets and pillage the towns of Qalhat, Qurayyat and Muscat, followed by Suhar. Their commercial success is based on supply of spices (pepper, cinnamon, camphor, nutmeg and cloves) to European markets. The coastal area and city and port of Muscat fall under Portuguese control.
1527	Forts of Al Jalali and Al Mirani built by the Portuguese in Muscat harbour.

1

17

1624	The Yarubi dynasty begins with its first imam, Nasir bin Murshid Al Yarubi.
1649–68	The Yarubi dynasty builds up its navy and undertakes expeditions to liberate Omani settlements and occupy Portuguese coastal settlements in India and Africa.
1650	The Portuguese are evicted from Oman after 150 years of coastal domination by Sultan bin Saif, the powerful Yarubi leader.
17th–18th centuries	Under the Yarubi rulers, Oman dominates The Gulf and trade routes to East Africa. By the end of the 18th century, the Omanis control an extensive empire, ruling areas of the East African coast from Mogadishu south to Cape Delgado in Mozambique, including Mombasa and Zanzibar. Ports in The Gulf under Omani control include Bandar Lengeh, Bandar Abbas, Qeshm Island and, on the northern coast of the Sea of Oman, Jask and Gwadar.
1724–39	Civil war during the final years of Yarubi rule as the result of the installation of Muhammad bin Nasir Al-Ghafiri as imam. This solidifies tribal groupings around the Hinawi (traditionally south Arab Yamani/Qahtani) and Ghafiri tribes (traditionally north Arab Adnani/Nizari).
1749	End of the Yarubi dynasty with the death of Bilarab bin Himyar Al Yarubi.
1737	Persian forces invade Oman under General Latif Khan, contributing to the country's chaos until their final expulsion in 1748.
1749	Founding of the Al Bu Said dynasty (Al Said becomes the royal family's name) by Ahmed bin Said, who is elected at Ar Rustaq. (Today's Sultan Qaboos is his direct descendant.)
1789	Muscat becomes Oman's capital under Hamad bin Said Al Said.
1750–1800	Oman is wooed by Britain and France, both seeking political alliance and favour. French influence dwindles, weakened by the Napoleonic Wars. Napoleon lands in Egypt *en route* to India. Muscat would have been on his route, but he never got that far, having been forced to retreat from Egypt. Conservative tribes in the interior elect their own imam, feeling that the sultan in Muscat has grown too liberal.
1798	Treaty of friendship with the British East India Company signed.
1800	Al Buraymi is occupied by Wahhabi invasions from Saudi Arabia that raid Al Batinah coast, so now it seeks alliance and support from Britain.
1804	Sultan bin Ahmed Al Bu Said is killed at Qeshm Island. His son Said bin Sultan comes to power at 18 after killing his cousin Badr bin Saif (who was regarded as regent). His 50-year reign brings Oman the greatest prosperity it has known since Yarubi days. Trade from Oman and Zanzibar to locations as widespread as the east coast of the USA and east Asia is the key to its success. Agriculture grows dramatically in Zanzibar based on black pepper, cloves, cinnamon, copra, and nutmeg, with slave labour. Slavery is also a key element of trade between the east coast of Africa and Arabia and Asia, along with ivory and gold.

PORTUGUESE NAVAL DOMINATION

The golden age of The Gulf under the Hormuz princes ended with the arrival of the Portuguese in the Indian Ocean. The beginning of the end was when Vasco da Gama reached India in 1498, guided by an Omani navigator Ahmed Bin Majid, from Malindi on the coast of Kenya. In the following 30 or so years the Portuguese carried out a series of devastating attacks on key strategic points and secured maritime domination of the Arabian seas. The Portuguese were able to achieve this through great organisational skills, benefiting from strong political and economic direction from their homeland, and inspired by religious crusading zeal. On a more down-to-earth level, they also had new and faster ships and superior arms.

Their aim was to monopolise trade, in particular the long-distance luxury trade of the Indian seas. They took Hormuz in 1507, but though they built some forts and bases in the region, their practice was to leave power in the hands of local governments as much as possible and to rule indirectly. This avoided the manpower demands, expense and trouble of a direct European administration. The Portuguese were repulsed from Hormuz in 1622 by the combined forces of the Persian Safavid Shah Abbas and the English East India Company, leaving Oman and its chief port city Muscat to dominate the Gulf until the British again established European supremacy in the 19th century. Portugal's rule was too loose rather than too harsh, and it was remarkable that such a small country was able to retain control of an area as vast as the Indian Ocean for as long as it did. In the period from the end of the Portuguese domination in the mid 17th century until the 19th century, the English, Dutch and French all sailed the Gulf, but their interests were commercial rather than political. Gradually over the course of the 19th century, the British increasingly allied themselves with the Omanis against the Arab 'pirate' sheikhdoms.

1822, 1839, 1845, 1873	Anti-slavery treaties established with Britain.
1839, 1891	Treaties signed with Britain for friendship, commerce and navigation.
1833	Treaty signed with the USA building on contacts established since the first ship from Boston, *The Rambler*, arrived in Muscat in 1790.
1840	First embassy from Oman to the USA arrives in New York. Sultan Said bin Sultan moves his capital to Zanzibar and visits Oman less and less frequently.
1854	Kuriya Muria (Al Hallaniyyat) Islands ceded to Britain. They are exploited for guano. The exchange gift is a silver snuff box.
1856	Sultan Said dies. One of his sons rules in Muscat, another in Zanzibar. The separation of Muscat and Zanzibar is subsequently formalised in 1861 under Lord Canning when Zanzibar agrees to pay an annual amount to Muscat by way of compensation for Muscat renouncing all claims on Zanzibar.
1860–95	Oman's economy slumps after the separation of Oman and Zanzibar. Wahhabi incursions from Saudi Arabia take advantage of the country's weakened state and the lack of unity within the ruling family.

1890–1905	Renewed rivalries between Britain and France for influence in Oman. These are settled by a combination of a judgement at The Hague in 1905 and the Entente Cordiale of 1904.
1913	Sultan Faisal bin Turki dies. His 27-year-old son Sultan Taimur bin Faisal begins his rule.
1920	The Treaty of Seeb is mediated by the British to avert the possibility of civil war between Sultan Taimur bin Faisal and the imam Salim Al Kharusi, who holds influence over Oman's interior. It covers, among other areas, non-interference by the sultan in the 'internal affairs' of interior Oman and sets customs duty on goods moving between the coast and the interior at 5%. The treaty is upheld until the death of Imam Salim's successor, Imam Muhammad bin Abdullah Al Khalili, in 1954.
1925	Oil exploration licence granted to the D'Arcy Exploration Company.
1932	Sultan Taimur bin Faisal abdicates. He dies in Bombay in 1965.
1932	Sultan Said bin Taimur, who was educated in India at Mayo College (often called the 'Princes College' as it was founded in 1875 for the education of the sons of India's princely families) becomes Oman's ruler, aged 22. Oman has been on the verge of bankruptcy since the Zanzibar split of 1857. Said bin Taimur balances the books, never going into debt, believing this is the best course of action for the country. He would later write: 'From 1933 to this present day there has been no financial deficit in the government's budget.'

THE TRUCIAL COAST

In the early 19th century, Britain's main concern in the Gulf was to secure its imperial communications to India. When some of its ships got caught up in the war that had been ongoing for some years between the Omanis and the Arab sheikhs of the Gulf coast, they viewed it as simple piracy. They had no understanding of the cause of such attacks, no realisation that they were casualties of a local naval and trade war. Instead, they accused the Wahhabis (a highly conservative Islamic group) of initiating attacks on British shipping and talked of the 'predatory habits' of the maritime Arabs. With Omani support the British attacked 'the pirates' three times between 1805 and 1820, and then imposed a maritime peace, which had the effect of forbidding the Arab states of the Gulf to fight one another at sea without British permission.

Over the next few decades a series of other treaties followed, some formal, some informal, for establishing a set of special privileges for those who co-operated with the Western powers and restricted their participation in the slave trade. In this way, insidiously and over a long period, Britain's policy of 'non-interference' in the Gulf States' internal affairs in practice radically altered the tribal status quo, and removed the method by which Gulf principalities and city-states used to dominate each other and vie for position in the Gulf. Britain saw itself as a benevolent policeman in the Gulf, preventing piracy, slave trading and maritime war. It also saw itself as gradually introducing, true to the imperial philosophy of the time, progress and civilisation to the Arab Gulf States. As a result of these truces, the Arab side of the Gulf became known as the 'Trucial coast'.

FINANCIAL ORTHODOXY

Said bin Taimur had a horror of debt and strove never to become dependent on creditors. In his only public statement, made in January 1958, he wrote: 'Doubtless it would have been easy to obtain money in various ways, but this could only have been by a loan with interest at a set percentage rate. This amounts to usury, with which I completely disagree, and the religious prohibition of which is not unknown.' Having seen the mistakes of his predecessors he also decided it was dangerous to delegate – better to do everything oneself to be sure it was done as you wanted. The sultan followed these principles utterly consistently, controlling every issue in his country in minute detail, leading, alas, to a rigid form of centralised administration which became increasingly inappropriate in the 1960s, though it may have been suitable in the 1940s and 1950s. When PDO (Petrol Development Oman) announced in 1964 that it had found oil in commercial quantities and would start exporting in 1967, the sultan could have easily obtained credit, but he never took a penny because of his debt principle. He continued to sit, apart from it all, mistrusting all, unapproachable except by those who had obtained special permission to visit Salalah and had arranged a prior appointment. Those who were fortunate enough to meet him were generally won over by his charm and powers of persuasion.

1937	The oil exploration licence given to the D'Arcy Exploration Company is superseded by one granted to the Iraq Petroleum Company (IPC).
1950s	Said bin Taimur regains control of the interior, backed by the British because they want to prospect for oil and therefore require the sultan's authority to be absolute, within defined borders between Oman and both Saudi Arabia and Abu Dhabi.
1954	A serious search for oil commences following the death of the imam Muhammed bin Abdullah Al Khalili, as Sultan Said bin Taimur seizes the opportunity to reunify Oman, a necessity for oil exploration.
1954–59	A growing conflict between the new imam, Ghalib bin Ali Al Hinai and Sultan Said is initiated by an imamate request for recognition as an independent state by the Arab League. After the success at Al Buraymi, Sultan Said makes a trailblazing journey through the country by Bedford truck. He travels over the New Year 1955/56 from Salalah, occupying the imamate capital of Nizwa *en route* before moving on to Al Buraymi, Suhar and eventually Muscat, and then returning to Salalah. In 1955, Saudi Arabia is ousted from the Al Buraymi oasis by Said, the imam and the British in a rare show of unity. Renewed conflict flares in 1957 with support from Saudi Arabia. In January 1959, with prior support by the RAF and Omani forces, two squadrons of Britain's SAS make an overnight ascent to the mountain plateau and secure the area over the course of the next day.
1962–65	A small group of men from Dhofar, supported by Saudi Arabia, undertake the small-scale sabotage attacks that lead to the Dhofar War. Units of the Oman army are deployed in southern

Oman for the first time in 1965. The communist regime in south Yemen supplants Saudi Arabia as the main support for the rebellion as the group expands its aims, renaming itself the Popular Front for the Liberation of Oman and the Arab Gulf (PFLOAG). Government forces become bogged down through lack of support and PFLOAG becomes the dominant force.

1962–67   **Petrol Development Oman** (PDO) discovers commercially viable oil deposits at Yibal (175km southwest of Nizwa), followed by larger oilfields in adjacent Natih and then Fuhud (1964). Oil exports commence from Al Fahl near Muscat in 1967, transforming Oman's economic prospects.

1970–75   Sultan Qaboos bin Said (aged 30) stages a coup against his father Said bin Taimur with British support. Said bin Taimur goes to London in exile. Sultan Qaboos takes over power and immediately establishes a more dynamic approach to the Dhofar War, leading to success by 1975. The country's name is changed to 'Sultanate of Oman' as opposed to 'Muscat and Oman' and implementation of the blueprints drawn up by Sultan Said bin Taimur are accelerated, including sea ports, civilian airports, health, education and infrastructure.

1976   Sultan Qaboos marries but later divorces. He has no children.

1980   USA and Oman sign a security co-operation agreement.

1981   Oman plays a key role in the establishment of the six-member Gulf Co-operation Council, whose other members are Saudi Arabia, Kuwait, the UAE, Bahrain and Qatar.

1986   Oman's first university, the co-educational Sultan Qaboos University, opens.

1991   Elections are held for the Majlis Ash Shura, an elected consultative body comprising 82 elected members from the *wilayats*. The electoral process has developed so male and female Omani citizens aged 21 and over can now vote for the candidate of their choice, with the person (or in more populated areas two people) with the largest number of votes in each area automatically elected.

1998–2012   Salalah Port opens with world-class container terminal facilities. It is one of the top 50 container ports in the world. The adjacent Free Trade Zone (FTZ) includes major chemical plants. Sohar Port opens in 2002 along with an adjacent FTZ that includes major aluminium and steel smelters. Duqm Port opens in 2012, with facilities including a major dry dock. These ports are a key element in Oman's strategy to diversify the economy away from oil.

1999   Oman's oil reserves are estimated at five billion barrels; gas reserves are estimated at over 20 trillion cubic feet. Tourism is estimated to contribute a mere 1% to gross national product. Oman and the neighbouring United Arab Emirates (UAE) settle their border disputes.

2000   Oman joins the World Trade Organization (WTO).

2001   The Sultan Qaboos Grand Mosque opens in Bawshar.

2004   The Ministry of Tourism is established, tourism being a major component of the government's economic diversification plan to move away from its reliance on oil. The minister of tourism is the country's first female government minister.

2006 Royal decree announces a new property law, which enables foreign freehold ownership of real estate on designated major tourist developments such as Shangri-La, Muscat Hills and The Wave (now called Al Mouj). Residents start to move in during 2009.

2007 Cyclone Gonu, the most powerful cyclone in the region for decades, hits Oman, killing over 50 people and causing over US$4 billion of damage to infrastructure and homes. Oil and gas exports are disrupted and the northern coastline is damaged.

2007 Oman's Oryx Sanctuary is removed from UNESCO's World Heritage Site list after poaching decimates the herd size. The government reduces the park size by 90%, enabling oil exploration.

2009 A free trade agreement is implemented between Oman and the USA. Somali pirates hijack a cargo vessel off the coast of Oman, the first such attack in the area.

2010 Scottish firm Aggreko wins a £50 million power supply contract. Muscat holds the Asian Beach Games.

2011 Outbreak of discontent in the wake of Arab Spring protests across the region. Young Omanis demand an end to corruption, improved work opportunities, higher salaries and media freedom. There are no calls for regime change. Two protestors die in Suhar at the hands of security forces. Sultan

THE MILITARY

The SAF (Sultan's Armed Forces) were formed in 1958 from various loosely organised groups with military assistance and a subsidy from the British government. It initially had a British colonel as its commander, but by the mid 1970s it had grown to include over 13,000 personnel, an expansion forced upon it by the bitterly fought Dhofar War against Marxist-led guerrillas. It used to be top-heavy with British officers on secondment and many of these stayed as contract officers once they left the British army. In recent years, however, strenuous efforts have been made towards Omanisation, with Omanis increasingly taking the place of senior British officers. The subsidy Britain paid to SAF stopped in 1967 when the sultan was thought to have enough money from oil revenues to pay for it himself. In the Gulf Wars, the 2001 US invasion of Afghanistan and the 2003 invasion of Iraq, Oman (Masirah Island) acted as a base and staging post for both Britain and the US. In 2001, Oman hosted the British army in exercise Saif Sareea II (which translates as 'Swift Sword'), in which 12,500 members of the SAF also participated. It was an exercise to practise rapid deployment and test equipment in severe conditions, but it so transpired that the Afghan invasion intervened. Today the SAF consists of the Royal Guard, land forces, the Royal Navy of Oman (RNO) and Royal Air Force of Oman (RAFO). The RNO is thought to be one of the most modern in the region and RAFO is highly respected. It acts more as a para-police force than a military machine, and thus is entirely appropriate for a country like Oman.

2012	Qaboos responds by creating 50,000 new jobs in the public sector, increasing benefits and raising salaries.

2012   Activists are put on trial for criticising the government online. Six are given jail sentences of 12–18 months and fined US$2,500 each. Amnesty International issues a statement of support for the detainees. Most are subsequently released. Qaboos reshuffles his cabinet in response to protests, removing three ministers.

2012   Tourism is estimated to be 3.1% of Oman's GDP; it is a key element in the government's economic diversification strategy.

2013   Peaceful protests are permitted but freedom of expression and assembly remain limited. The cabinet outlines plans to limit the expatriate workforce to 33% of the population. Qaboos promises youth participation in nation-building through entrepreneurship and investment opportunities.

2014   Mina Sultan Qaboos port is largely closed to freight shipping. The resultant focus for the port will be on leisure, especially cruise shipping.

2015   Sultan Qaboos returns to Oman after lengthy medical treatment in Germany. The new terminal at Salalah Airport opens, increasing the airport's capacity and enhancing its services.

GOVERNMENT AND POLITICS

Prior to 1970, Al Said leaders assumed the political title of 'Sultan of Muscat and Oman', which implied the existence of two separate political sectors. Indeed, the coast ('Muscat' represented all coastal areas, while 'Oman' referred to the interior of the country) was more cosmopolitan and accepting of new ideas, largely because of its international trading history, whereas the interior was more insular, tribal and conservative, ruled by an imam with traditional Ibadhist ideologies. Under Sultan Qaboos's leadership (since 1970) the country was reconciled under the title the 'Sultanate of Oman', and has carefully and cautiously established its position within the global scheme, and embraced an international, diplomatic mindset.

Administratively, Oman today is divided into 11 governorates and these are in turn divided into administrative areas, or *wilayats*, each overseen by its own chief governor, or *wali*. Under Sultan Qaboos, as head of state, the government remains essentially autocratic: he acts as the prime minister and can accept or reject any legislation. Political parties are prohibited, the death penalty is still in force, internet usage is monitored and the media exercises considerable self-censorship. However, Sultan Qaboos has recognised that such a situation will not go on indefinitely: 'The time will come when this will have to stop and the voters' decision will be final.'

In 1970, when Qaboos came to power, the sultanate had diplomatic relations with just three countries. Now it has relations with over 140, as well as belonging to a network of over 105 regional and international organisations including the United Nations and the Gulf Co-operation Council (GCC). The Oman government has appointed female Omani ambassadors, notably to Washington. The US government has appointed two female ambassadors to Oman, and other countries with female ambassadors to Oman include Italy. Unusually for the Arabian Gulf States, Oman maintains good relations with Iran.

The Council of Oman (Majlis Oman) is a bicameral system, comprising the Consultative Council (Majlis Al Shura) and the State Council (Majlis Al Dawla). The Consultative Council was inaugurated in 1991 and was originally made up

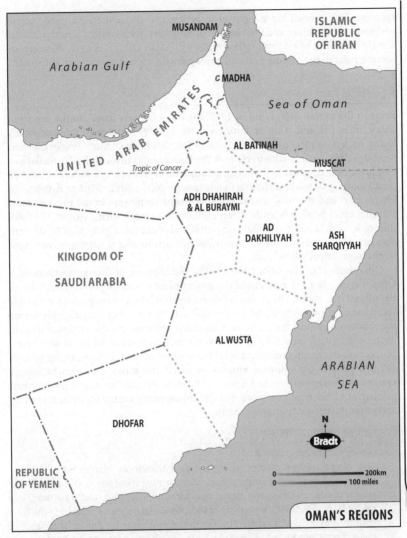

OMAN'S REGIONS

of 59 publicly elected members, representing each of the then 59 *wilayats* of the country. As a result of increases in the population and administrative change, this has now expanded to 85, one member for each *wilayat* and a second member for *wilayats* with a population of 30,000 or more. This council acts as a consultative body only, proposing legislation and expressing views on laws once they are passed. It covers legal matters, the economy, health, education and the environment, but has no say in Oman's foreign, defence or security policies. The committees of which it is composed have free rein to interrogate ministers. Elections are held every three years. The State Council has 84 members who are appointed by the sultan on a three-year renewable term. Members are selected for their high status in society, their experience, reputation and expertise. The State Council acts as the upper chamber, playing a central role in the country's development. It holds four 'ordinary' sessions each year, with the option to hold further 'extraordinary' sessions. This council has the power to review and revise draft laws and submit proposals to the sultan and the Council of Ministers. Each of the councils includes female members, albeit in a marked minority. Sultan Qaboos is by far the longest-serving ruler in the Middle East and among the four longest serving in the world.

ECONOMY

Prior to the exploitation of oil in 1967, the economy was based on the export of dates, limes, fish and skins, and otherwise the country had a subsistence economy based on agriculture and fisheries. As of late 2014, agriculture employs almost 85,000 people, mainly labourers from the Indian subcontinent. By far the largest employer of manpower is the construction industry, which employs over 608,000 on all manner of work, including major new projects such as Muscat Airport, Ad Duqm Port and the road network. Other major employers in the private sector include retail and wholesale (over 189,000), manufacturing (over 176,000), domestic work (almost 161,000) and hotels and restaurants (over 92,000). As with agriculture, the majority of the over 1,700,000 private sector employees are expat workers, principally from Asia.

Omanisation of the labour force – the replacement of foreign workers with Omani staff – is a key element of the government's planning objectives. Like all the other GCC states, Oman has relied on foreign labour to augment a relatively small national population and supply skill sets that had been unavailable before the modernisation of the state. This has been more successful in Oman than in most of the GCC, especially in office work such as finance. In 2014, the Omani proportion of the private sector workforce stood at over 11%, equating to over 197,000 people. Government employees of all categories are overwhelmingly Omani, with over 86% out of a total 178,000 within the principal government ministries. Other major employers of Omani nationals are the uniformed services and other government establishments.

THE WILAYAT SYSTEM

The *wilayat* system (*vilayet* in Turkey) is a traditional Islamic term and system for larger administrative areas with a *wali* (*vali* in Turkey) as the chief administrator. In Oman the sultan appoints them himself, and they then report back to him via the Ministry of the Interior. There are 61 *wilayats* in the country and the *wali* is responsible for all civil matters in his district. This has been the system for many centuries, throughout the sultanate, and before that the imamate, except for times when they evolved into near-independent city-states, defying any attempts at centralisation.

Before 1970 the *wali* might, if he was lucky, have an old Land Rover and even an old wireless link to Muscat. Some places, like Izki, had neither. The *wali* in Sur had a wireless but no Land Rover and was once on tour on his donkey when the wireless operator received an urgent message that he should report to Muscat. The *wali* was fetched and given the message, whereupon he caught a dhow and was in Muscat 12 hours later. There, he was made to wait three days for an audience with the minister of the interior on a matter that was trivial. The *Wali* of Al Buraymi was once likewise summoned and kept waiting for four months until he was allowed to return. Such treatment was not regarded as unusual.

Islamic or shari'a law applies to all members of the community and a *qadi* (Arabic judge) serves alongside the *wali* in every *wilayat* to administer justice according to this law. There is then a chief *qadi's* court in Muscat. In all Arab countries where shari'a law applies it is interpreted more or less strictly in accordance with the outlook prevalent in that country. For Oman this meant an Ibadhi interpretation of Islamic law, which draws from the Quran and the Hadith (traditions) of the Prophet, right up to 1970 when Sultan Qaboos's father, Said bin Taimur, saw no reason to alter matters. Since Qaboos's accession in 1970, however, there has been a modernising shift towards adapting shari'a law to cope with situations of the 20th and 21st centuries while still adhering to Islamic principles. Most Arab countries have had to face this issue of how to modernise Islamic law, and most have adopted a compromise where the legal system is based either on English law or on the French Napoleonic code, depending on their historic associations. Owing to its longstanding links with Britain and Sultan Qaboos's own ties to the British way of life, Oman favours the British legal system. This has enabled the commercial law system to be easily adjusted to accommodate free trade agreements with the USA.

The Omani economy is largely dependent on oil revenues, despite the fact that this dependency has been substantially reduced. Oil production in 2014 was an average of 943,000 barrels a day, according to the Ministry of Oil and Gas (about 10% of that of Saudi Arabia). Gas production was 35.7 billion cubic metres during 2014 (about 23% of that of Qatar). In 1982, oil and gas provided 62% of GDP, but in 2014 they accounted for 47%; the aim is to reduce it to 19% by 2020 by expanding the non-oil sectors, thereby diversifying the economy. Oil and gas accounted for 80% of government revenue in 2014; the aim is to reduce that to less than 70% by 2020.

ECONOMIC DIVERSIFICATION AND VISION 2020 Oman is a relatively small oil-producing state and the remaining years of oil production are said to be limited, though with oil the quantity that is possible to extract is determined by the prevailing world oil price, as with a high price oil that is costly to extract becomes more viable economically. The relatively limited future timescale for oil production, coupled with a drop in oil prices, revealed a vulnerability within the Omani economy and alerted the government to the need to diversify its economic base away from a reliance on oil. The country's focus has now shifted to other areas, such as trade and tourism, manufacturing and building, construction and real estate, directives for which have been outlined in its Vision 2020 economic programme. This 2020 vision was a response to fluctuating oil prices in the mid 1990s and became a key target in Oman's ongoing five-year economic planning periods. Essentially the aim has been to reduce dependence on oil as the engine for the economy, to maximise the economic benefits of Oman's geographical location, utilise the country's climate and scenery to drive tourism and to create added value from Oman's raw materials. It remains to be seen whether these aims will be achieved over the coming years.

TOURISM Tourism in Oman is still underdeveloped and is one of the more prominent areas identified for expansion. Until the 1980s, no-one was allowed into Oman without a No Objection Certificate (NOC), which could only be obtained through an Omani sponsor. If you simply wanted to visit the country out of curiosity, you were not allowed in. Journalists in particular were almost never allowed in and were regarded with great suspicion. This rigorous entry system was devised by the sultan's father, Said bin Taimur, and in his day his own personal permission had to be obtained for entry. The first organised group of tourists – 14 of them – visited the country in 1983, led by the wife of a former ambassador. Today, Oman is far more accessible and accommodating, and ecotourism and adventure tourism are being actively promoted. Oman offers a less glitzy travelling option than neighbouring tourist-dense Dubai, and it is the most successful example in the Middle East of how a country can be gradually modernised without giving up its cultural identity. In 2012, Oman was the only Arab country to feature in *National Geographic*'s 20 Top Tourist Destinations, showing how its politically stable image has made it a direct beneficiary of the tourist fallout from Arab Spring countries like Egypt and Syria. Tourist numbers in 2013 reached 2,121,229, with 177,577 arriving by cruise ship; of the others 371,741 were European (British, German, French and Italian as the major nationalities) and 793,466 from the neighbouring GCC countries.

The Ministry of Tourism and the Ministry of Heritage and Culture have instigated restoration projects to restore old stone buildings and upgrade original mountain tracks, introducing *barasti* (palm frond) shades, toilets and proper signage. There are plans to develop mountain villages and old forts as exclusive retreats to showcase Oman's distinct heritage, culture and natural attractions, drawing upon the expertise of Spain's Paradores Consultancy. Even children can undergo a one-year programme to equip them with the tools to interact with tourists, which includes an English-language course.

The Omani government aims to double tourist revenue and increase it to 5% of GDP by 2020. As around 45% of the population is 19 and under, it is hoped that the tourism sector will absorb many young Omanis entering the job market. Unlike neighbouring Dubai, which encourages visitors from all backgrounds, Oman has repeatedly stressed its desire to encourage upmarket tourism, focusing on cultural and heritage attractions. Backpackers will remain something of a rarity for the foreseeable future. Travel restrictions have now been eased and visitors from 68 countries can get a visa, valid for either ten days (RO5) or one month (RO20) on arrival at Oman's entry points (pages 45–6). There is a joint visa facility with Dubai (not with the other Emirates), from which Oman obviously hopes to attract some of Dubai's 15 million visitors. A similar arrangement is in place with Qatar.

Salalah International Airport is in a new modern terminal in the north of the town. A new terminal for Muscat International Airport is under construction, and media reports in Oman – based on official briefings – have stated that it will be

BRITAIN AND OMAN: THE SPECIAL RELATIONSHIP

Every year around 2,000 Omanis come to Britain to study at schools, universities and training institutes, a higher number than from any other country in the Arab world, and around 7,000 British citizens live and work in Oman, the largest Western expatriate group in the country.

Britain also has a strong defence relationship with Oman, thanks to Sultan Qaboos being a graduate of Sandhurst. Nearly a hundred British military personnel are on loan to the Oman Armed Forces at any one time, the second-largest such group in the world.

complete by the end of 2016. A key development will be the 29 air bridges, rather than the current system whereby a bus ferries passengers from plane to terminal. Apart from Oman Air, key carriers are Air Arabia, British Airways, Emirates, Etihad, flydubai, Gulf Air, Swiss, and Turkish Air, all of which fly from European destinations. Salalah has seen a particularly marked year-on-year increase in air passenger arrivals, and Oman Air, flydubai, Qatar Airways and Air Arabia have all increased their year-round flights.

EMPLOYMENT AND OMANISATION Omanisation is the government policy of replacing foreign workers of all types with appropriate Omani nationals. With over 1.5 million foreign workers, there is vast scope to improve employment opportunities for Omani nationals and reducing remittance outflows. Providing work for the country's growing national population is of increasing concern to the government and with around 45% of the population estimated to be 19 and under, the need for employment is growing. The government's solution is to try to broaden the economic base, so that manufacturing and services businesses will be created and thus begin to absorb the growing workforce. Apart from encouraging Omanis to take on work that since 1970 has been considered as the remit of foreign workers (eg: petrol-pump attendants, waiters, cleaners, tailors and shop assistants), Omanisation has targets of certain percentages of the workforce within a particular field being Omani. Construction has a target of 30%, while banking has a tiered target of 75% management, 95% clerical and 100% non-clerical. Overall, banks achieved 92% Omanisation in 2014.

INFRASTRUCTURE AND DEVELOPMENT Huge improvements to the infrastructure have been made over the past few years, especially in the network of tarmac roads and highways. One notable example is the Muscat Expressway, which has transferred traffic away from the only previous through-route from Muscat along Al Batinah. New dual carriageways have been completed from Muscat to Sur along the coast, Suhar to Al Buraymi, and the mountain route to Sur via Bidbid is being upgraded to provide an all-weather dual carriageway. Beyond Sur the coastal route is tarmac to Salalah and beyond, and the existing Nizwa–Salalah road is in the process of becoming a dual carriageway, slashing journey times. There is a plethora of Al Maha, Oman Oil and Shell petrol stations along all roads, with attended pumps, often small shops and usually toilets.

Within Muscat the arterial routes have been upgraded, in many cases with elevated sections and the more congested roundabouts have been replaced by signalled junctions. Muscat and other major conurbations are still more focused on vehicles than pedestrians, although there is increasing awareness that more pedestrian bridges are needed.

PEOPLE

The Omanis are a conservative people, and a respect for their privacy and religion are courteous gestures from any visitor to their country. They are friendly and giving, and keen to communicate and demonstrate their culture and heritage to those who are interested. They are known for their hospitality and are deeply committed to a sense of family. Omanis are generally keen to assist and welcome outsiders. There is a less rigid attitude towards scheduling than in an Anglo-Saxon environment. In part, this is a result of prioritising the relative importance of a particular activity over its timing. For instance, if a senior person requests your attendance that request is immediately prioritised over a pre-arranged coffee with friends. You are likely to hear 'inshallah' often, which means 'if God wills it, it will happen' – an indication in the absolute faith of Omanis in God's role in all aspects of life.

The core of Oman's most prominent culture is around the northern mountains, with other cultures in the southern mountains, coastline, desert and Musandam Peninsula. The northern mountains are the heartland of the Ibadhi, one of Islam's earliest sects (see box, page 33), whose role in Oman is exemplified by the royal family and previous imams. On the coast along Al Batinah are prominent Shia populations who have traditionally been notable traders. Leading groups among them were the Baharina, originally of Persian ancestry, and the Khojas or Hyderabadis, who are Shi'ites of Indian origin. Their families often had strong trading links up and down the Gulf and Arabian Sea, with cousins and brothers running businesses in Bahrain, Kuwait, Dubai and Qatar and relatives in more distant trading towns such as Zanzibar and Surat in northwest India. There are substantial populations of Omanis of Baluch descent, resulting from Oman's rule along the Iranian and Pakistani Baluch coast. They live principally in Muscat and along Al Batinah coast, but also have communities in disparate areas such as Ibri and the Ash Sharqiyyah. Sunnis, who may form the majority of the population, live throughout the country, especially in Dhofar, the Ash Sharqiyyah and northern areas bordering the UAE.

POPULATION STATISTICS As of September 2015 the total population of Oman is around 4.3 million, of which some 55% are Omanis and 45% are expatriates. The expatriates are mainly from the Indian subcontinent, with others from Arab countries, Europe and the Philippines. Al Batinah coast from Shinas to Muscat is an almost unbroken chain of villages and towns that together are home to over 50% of Oman's population. Muscat is the most densely populated city; its administrative area has a population of some 1.32 million (30% of Oman's total population), and although this does include rural villages, the overwhelming majority live in its urban conurbation. Salalah's administrative area has a population of around 280,000. Other major population areas are Suhar, whose *wilayat* population is around 208,000; Nizwa with a *wilayat* total of around 110,000, including the town plus mountain and other rural settlements; and Sur, which has just 103,000, including areas like Tiwi and Ras Al Jinz as well as the town itself. The least populated region is the central governorate of Al Wusta, with fewer than 45,000 people in an area of just under 80,000km^2.

Family size is relatively large compared with Europe and North America, but the fertility rate has reduced from over eight children per woman in the early 1980s to fewer than three today, according to UNICEF. Life expectancy has also changed dramatically, from 50 in 1970 to 77 currently.

LANGUAGE

Despite the ethnic mix, Arabic remains overwhelmingly the spoken and official language of Oman. Unlike in the United Arab Emirates next door, Oman's larger indigenous population means that the dominance of Arabic is unchallenged. However, the numbers of immigrant Indian, Bangladeshi and Pakistani workers do mean that loan words from Hindi and Urdu are found in Oman's everyday Arabic conversation, especially in Muscat, with its large population from the Indian subcontinent. The Arabic spoken in Oman without these recent colloquial loan words is also one of the purest dialects it can be, and is close to the classical, written Arabic, equating to the erstwhile BBC English, but you will have to be quite determined to use it in the Capital Area. There are regional dialects that are distinctly different, much as Glaswegian differs from

A tribe is a grouping of people who share a common identity, frequently through lineage. Each tribe has its sheikh and major tribes or tribal groupings have a paramount sheikh, a *tamimah*, who is consolidated in this position by the sultan, though not appointed by him. The sheikh acquires his position through the consensus of the tribe, and usually has a lineage from what it considered to be a sheikhly family. He is responsible if the tribe commits an offence, and he receives from the sultan an 'honorarium' which varies depending on the tribe involved.

One interesting issue is the relationship between the sheikh and the nearest *wali* (local governor), which invariably depends on the sheikh's power in relation to the *wali's* influence. The sheikh, like the *wali*, generally approaches the sultan via the Minister of the Interior.

Oman is one of the few remaining places in the Arab world where the tribal system continues to matter and remain strong, though of course its force is inevitably waning. Even so, rivalries between tribes still occasionally flare up, though today they are more likely to be over allegiances to different football teams.

cockney English. Arabic is everywhere on street signs and in advertisements so there is plenty of opportunity to practise your Arabic alphabet (but don't panic; the English translation invariably accompanies it).

Together with Islam, the written Arabic language is one of the unifying factors in the Arab world. It means that newspapers published in Egypt can be distributed and read from Morocco to Oman, Iraq to Somalia. In the spoken language, however, the 22 countries of the Arab League also express their individuality, to the extent that a Moroccan and an Iraqi speaking their local dialect will understand each other only with difficulty. In order to communicate they have to compromise and speak a form of modern classical Arabic which is understood by educated Arabs everywhere, and it is this middle Arabic that you generally speak as a foreigner. The Arabic spoken in the Gulf is the closest to classical Arabic as you might expect, since the Arabian Peninsula has been least influenced by external factors and has never been fully colonised by a foreign power. By contrast, the forms of spoken Arabic furthest away from the pure written classical Arabic are Lebanese and Egyptian, since these countries have been most exposed to foreign influences; ironically, the television and cinema output of these countries ensures that even the remotest settlement will be familiar with the voices of their stars.

RELIGION

The official religion of Oman is Islam, and has been since the 7th century, with most people adhering to the Ibadhi tradition, which is very conservative in approach. Sunni Muslims, the mainstream of orthodox Islam throughout the region, and indeed the world, may now be over half the Omani population. There are a substantial number of Shia Muslims, though their numbers are relatively small and concentrated in Muscat and parts of Al Batinah coast. The Indian and Pakistani expatriates are a mixture of Muslims, Hindus and Christians. Oman is tolerant of other religions, which is borne out by the presence of churches and Hindu temples.

The Islamic religion has five essential pillars of faith. These are the professing of faith, that there is only one god (Shahadah), the making of prayers (Salat), fasting (Sawm), the giving of charity (Zakat) and the pilgrimage to Mecca (Hajj). Salat occurs five times a day just before dawn, noon, mid afternoon, 1.5 hours before sunset and just after sunset. Muslims are alerted to prayer times by the *muezzin*, who chants a call to prayer from the mosque, originally by his naturally amplified voice, but today by loudspeaker.

The Islamic calendar is calculated as starting from the Hijrah, which is the day of departure of the Prophet, as instructed by God, from Mecca to Medina in AD622. The Islamic calendar is a lunar one, so each Islamic year has ten days (or 11 in a leap year), fewer than that of the Christian calendar. It comprises 12 months, one of which is Ramadhan, and has weeks of seven days. The start of a new month in Oman is dependent on the actual sighting of the new moon's crescent by an authorised body, as it is in all Islamic countries, though there have been attempts to either have a scientific dating or to accept that the date should correspond with that in Mecca. Other countries use an astrological calculation regarding the moon's phase. It is likely that the first day of Muharram (the first Islamic month of the year) will be on 20 September 2017, 10 September 2018, and 31 August 2019, depending on the moon being sighted.

RAMADHAN Ramadhan is the holy month, when Muslims abstain from eating, drinking and smoking between sunrise and sunset during the entire month. Non-Muslims are affected because it is considered disrespectful to be seen eating, drinking (in any form) or smoking in public places during daylight hours in Ramadhan. As a result, most restaurants are closed (though large hotels keep a screened-off area for non-Muslims), all bars are closed and hotels are not permitted to serve alcohol publicly. Even after sunset, alcohol is not sold in restaurants or bars throughout Ramadhan, and therefore many are shut down. Consumption of alcohol is

MOSQUE ETIQUETTE

This is something that varies from country to country across the Arab world, but in the Arabian Peninsula non-Muslims are not generally allowed to enter mosques, as the assumption is that they will be unsuitably dressed and only interested in taking pictures of everything. The same applies in Oman, but there are notable exceptions, including the superlative modern **Sultan Qaboos Grand Mosque** in Al Ghubra, Muscat, which opens to non-Muslim visitors from 08.00 to 11.00 daily except Friday. Children under ten are not allowed. Women should be fully covered from head to foot and men should wear long trousers and a conservative shirt; the guards will readily refuse entry otherwise. This is a good opportunity to see mosque architecture and design, with a separate prayer hall for women and a public library (early mosques were always places of learning, often combined with schools/colleges).

Also open for non-Muslims are other **royal mosques**, though the following are most accessible; Sultan Qaboos Mosque in Salalah, Al Khawr Mosque near the palace in Muscat, the old Sultan Qaboos Mosque in Nizwa, the Sultan Taimur Mosque in Al Mabilah North in Muscat and the mosque built by the Saud Bahwan charity, the Muhammad Al Ameen Mosque in Al Khuwair. These mosques are best visited between 08.00 and 11.00 Sunday to Thursday. The dress code is as on page 128.

The Ibadhis, named after Abdullah bin Ibadh Al-Tamimi (d AD708), were the most tolerant subdivision of the puritanical Kharijites, who bitterly opposed Ali, the fourth caliph, and the right of the Quraysh tribe, the most powerful Meccan tribe, to choose the caliph. They wanted the Islamic state to return to how it had been before the power struggle of Ali and Mu'awiya, and believed the best person to be caliph should be chosen irrespective of his relationship to the Prophet's family. This disagreement played itself out in Basra (Iraq) and ended in persecution and exile for the Ibadhis. Some took refuge in Oman and some in Libya, Tunisia and Algeria, where they still survive.

The main doctrinal point on which they differ from Sunnis and Shi'a (the two main Islamic subdivisions), is that they do not feel it is essential that a visible leader must exist at all times. If there is no-one suitable, then they feel it is best to wait until someone suitable appears. From the 8th century onwards imams were elected in Oman as spiritual, political and military leaders, best described as tolerant puritans. The Ibadhis were sometimes known as 'quietists' who believed in achieving things through quiet dignity and reasonableness, not through fanatical confrontations. The mosques reflect this style and tend to be simple and devoid of decoration except round the mihrab niche and the windows. Minarets were not used except on the coast, and in the interior the call to prayer was traditionally made from the roof, reached by an outside flight of steps.

Ibadhism has always been tolerant of Christians and Jews, allowing them to practise their own religions in Oman. Singing is suppressed by Ibadhi Muslims as a frivolity, but many Omanis have a natural sense of rhythm and love of music, which tends to escape when they are happy and contented. The Ibadhi areas are predominantly in the interior around the northern core of the Al Jabal Al Akhdar mountains, which also provided the refuge for Ibadhism and the imamate during periods of outside interference and dominance.

permitted only in the privacy of your home or hotel room. Working hours are shorter, with later starts and earlier finishes. Ramadhan is looked forward to and enjoyed by Omanis, as it is a time for self-restraint, religious reflection, and visiting friends and family after dark, when social activity tends to go on into the small hours. During Ramadhan, government offices and banks are open from 08.00 until noon, Saturday to Thursday. As it follows the lunar calendar, Ramadhan moves forwards each year (falls earlier) by about 10 days.

EDUCATION

In 1970, prior to the current sultan coming to power, there were only three government schools in the whole of Oman: one in Muscat, one in Mutrah and one in Salalah; they were for boys only. Now the situation has turned around and there are over 1,000 government-run schools and over 100 private schools providing equal schooling opportunities for boys and girls. In 1986, the co-educational Sultan Qaboos University, the first university in Oman, was established, and now there are over 20 universities and higher education institutions in the country. State education is free, including at university level, with a living allowance provided to all students within the government further education field. Adult literacy centres are plentiful throughout the country, and Oman now boasts one of the highest literacy rates in the Arab world, at 90% (women's literacy is 90% of that for men according to UNICEF).

CULTURE

OMANI TRADITIONAL DRESS

Men The *dishdasha* is the ankle-length robe worn by Omani men. Usually white in colour for daytime wear and required in white when working in government ministries or in the workplace, official and formal, this also comes in a variety of colours for evening and special occasions. The tassel at the neck is called the *furakha* or *farusha* and it is customary to perfume this.

The *mussar* is Oman's traditional formal turban for males. Though there is a specific material that is only worn by members of the royal family, the *mussar* generally does not indicate rank. It is a square of woven material and in Muscat of a similar quality to a pashmina shawl. Folded to create a triangle, the longest side forms the front with the opposite apex as a 'tail' at the neck. The front is then rolled and the rolled ends are wrapped around the head creating the distinctive turban shape.

A more casual and easy to wear head covering for males is the *kummah*, again the wearing of this does not indicate rank. The design is comparable to caps worn from West Africa through to Zanzibar. The *kummah* is a white cotton cap made from a double layer of cloth with a design created by a double row of running stitch. The design is then quilted with several threads creating a raised line between the double stitched rows. The areas which are not raised are then stitched, traditionally by hand, with what may be thousands of small circular or semi-circular designs using a fine buttonhole stitch in an appropriate colour, often to match a *dishdash*'s decorative thread.

The *kummah* may be worn under a *mussar* to give it a more shaped appearance. The *assa* (stick) is another part of the Omani traditional costume, used to control camels in the past, but these days more of a decorative appendage. Leather sandals are worn on the feet. On formal occasions, a *bisht* (cloak) may be worn that in part covers the *dishdasha*. The edges are embroidered in gold or silver threads.

Women Underneath the *abaya* (a black, or increasingly with other colours, cover-all gown worn in public), Omani women can be found wearing brightly coloured traditional ankle-length dresses and headscarves made from a range of fabrics in a variety of styles, according to region and/or personal taste. The name of each part of the costume varies from region to region. Broadly, the traditional woman's *jallabia* (dress) is usually worn over *sirwall* (trousers) and with a *lihaf* (head shawl). In some regions a *burka* (face mask) is worn. Some women wear Western clothes, but cover up with the *abaya* outside the home. Fabrics are embroidered with lace, sequins, jewels, beads, coins and other materials. Tailors are plentiful throughout the country and so costumes can be speedily made to order according to any personal design. It is traditional for women to have their hands and feet painted with henna at times of celebration. Traditionally, kohl was drawn on the eyes and indigo on the face on special occasions, festivals and weddings. Henna is still used today, pasted on the hands and feet in various patterns and designs which, when dried, leave an orangey-brown decorative stain.

TRADITIONAL SPORTING EVENTS
Bullfighting This takes place on Friday afternoons in the winter months at several places along Al Batinah coast. Unlike Spanish bullfighting, in Oman the sport is bloodless and between two evenly matched bulls. Two Brahmin bulls (who are pampered as pets) push against each other until the first is knocked down or runs away. The event begins at around 16.00 and lasts until sunset. There is no prize

OMANI PROVERBS

In a country where illiteracy was the norm till the 1970s the literary tradition was oral, with storytelling and poetry featuring as the main evening entertainment, though Oman's chief claim to fame was always its proverbs. Proverbs have a very long and important tradition in the Arab world, and the Arabs were the first to gather their own collections as early as the 9th century AD, though they were not translated into English till the 16th and 17th centuries. The origins of some go back long before Islamic times, and provide fascinating insights into the folk wisdom of different cultures. Some are common across the Middle East, but others are specific to a country. For example, the following proverbs on corruption all show a slightly different take, revealing slight differences in national attitudes:

'May God protect the vineyard from its guardian' (Lebanese)

'To destroy the cobweb, destroy the spider' (Maltese)

'It is from the head that the fish first stinks' (Turkish)

'When cat and rat join forces the country is destroyed' (Omani)

money, only honour and prestige for the winner, something that would render it unworkable as an activity in Dubai. In Oman, however, traditions are still valued for their own sake, thereby making this bullfighting a natural spectacle refreshingly devoid of commercialism. No hurt comes to the bulls, as they are matched in age, strength and weight by a panel of judges, and a rope is tied to each bull so that they can be separated if need be. The bulls are often given heroic names from Islamic literature, such as Antar, or even the names of American wrestlers. It is noticeably an all-male event. The fun is in watching the crowd scramble when the bulls get too close and watching the owner try to retrieve his fleeing bull at the end. See page 142 for further details.

Camel breeding and racing Camels are an integral part of the country's culture and history, with references to them in the Quran. Known variously as 'the ship of the desert' or 'the beast of burden', they were also traditionally sources of milk and meat. In Dhofar today, where there are about 60,000 camels according to the United Nations Food and Agricultural Organisation, this is still very much the case: meat and milk are taken from them and they are considered part of the household. Indeed, a female can produce up to 20 litres of milk per day, depending on her reproduction programme. This liquid is low-fat and reportedly good for the human stomach. Elsewhere, select camels have bypassed their traditional use and instead been bred for racing. Much like thoroughbred horses, they have a known bloodline and are fed a healthy diet, groomed and trained, and can become great financial assets to their owners, differing considerably in appearance from their conventional cousins. A good racing camel can still fetch a price of RO300,000 or more.

Camel racing has become a popular and commercial sport in the Arabian Peninsula. In Oman camel-racing events are held at tracks in many areas throughout the country to mark celebratory occasions such as National Day and other public holidays. It is popular in Al Batinah, Adh Dhahirah and Ash Sharqiyyah regions. The Al Felaij track in Barka holds several races each season and is probably the most accessible and best promoted camel-racing venue for people living in Muscat. Racing camels are strictly bred and trained specifically for the sport, and represent big business, competing at both national and international events, and there is even a Directorate-General of Camel Affairs

---

THE *KHANJAR*

The *khanjar* is a curved, sheathed dagger that encapsulates and symbolises the Omani identity. In the past the *khanjar* had a utilitarian purpose, and served as an essential piece of weaponry used to protect against wild animals or the enemy. Today it is valued and respected, and proudly worn as part of a male Omani's traditional dress on special occasions and for official ceremonies. Its image is used on the Omani flag.

The article itself can be broken down into four pieces: blade, handle, sheath and attaching belt, and different skills are required to fashion each piece. The price is largely determined by the material used in its handle. Previously ivory and rhino horn were used, but today sandalwood, ivory-looking plastic or silver are commonplace. It is illegal to import or export ivory and rhino horn, so you will need to opt for the modern versions if taking one out of the country as a souvenir.

Oman has a long silversmithing heritage. The material has been used for centuries and expertly handcrafted into articles of jewellery and ornaments, perhaps the most famous of which is the *khanjar*, a curved dagger worn by men. In the past, both Omani men and Omani women wore decorative silver. They carried keys on fine chains, had silver money holders, tweezers in silver cases, silver toothpicks and ear cleaners on silver chains.

Most of the old silver was unfortunately melted down before traders realised the value of antique silver pieces, so there is remarkably little genuine old silver left. Experienced Omani silver dealers can tell whether a piece is from the Al Batinah, the Ash Sharqiyyah or Dhofar.

Headpieces can be very heavy, weighing 2kg or more, and are worn on special occasions, usually when seated. Dhofari bracelets are adorned with coral beads and spiky silver washers threaded on to elastic. Women's silver necklaces often display Quranic inscriptions, and amulets, anklets and bangles are all intricately engraved. Other articles fashioned from silver include rose-water distillers, incense burners, trays, small engraved silver boxes (used for storing kohl or jewellery) and coffee pots (also made from copper).

within the sultan's administrative ministry. Omani thoroughbreds are well known and sought-after within the region. The training season runs from June to October and the racing season from September to March. Races are generally run 06.00–09.00 on a Wednesday and Thursday morning with free admission; a list of camel-race locations and dates is given on www.omantourism.gov.om.

Equestrian events Oman is famous for its pure-bred Arabian horses and has a centuries-old horse-breeding history. In 1983, the Oman Equestrian Federation was formed, promoting equestrian events. Each winter the federation organises a national show-jumping competition, attracting entries from the Royal Stables at As Sib, the Royal Oman Police, the Royal Guard of Oman and various private stables. It takes place at the Enam Equestrian showground in As Sib, one of the best riding arenas in the world; both Queen Elizabeth and the Duke of Edinburgh were guests at a horse event in 2010. Oman is a member of the World Arabian Horse Organisation (WAHO; *www.waho.org/Reports/Oman*).

ARTS AND CRAFTS
Traditional crafts The craft industry was once an important part of Oman's economy, with artisanal skills handed down from generation to generation. It is artefacts such as pots from Bahla, decorative chests, silver bracelets, *khanjars* and coffee pots that most embody the spirit and identity of Oman; they are tangible samples of its ancient tradition and heritage.

Jewellery Women's necklaces and bracelets, whether in silver or gold, play an important part in marriage ceremonies in Oman – a bride's dowry is expected to contain a certain amount of jewellery. The wealth and status of a family may be judged by the jewellery worn by the women. There is a belief that its wearer will be protected from the evil eye (see box, page 67). Silver is said to be representative of the moon and gold representative of the sun.

1

The use of natural dyes continued in Oman late into the 20th century. The most desirable and expensive was a deep mauve created by *Indigofera tinctoria* or *I. articulate* – indigo. The plant, known locally as *nil*, once grew over large areas as both a wild and cultivated plant. The leaves were cut and soaked in water for two days; the dye in the leaves would sink to the bottom and the surface water would be drained off. The pasty residue was hung out on a thick cloth to dry for two or three days, and then cut into small tablet-like segments. These could be sold locally or, as they had high value, might be traded. The professional dyers used cloth that could be worn by either sex and in particular the face mask (*burka*) worn by Bedouin women. This indigo-dyed fabric, if beaten vigorously, became iridescent creating an almost glittering mask for the woman of the desert or a distinctive shawl still worn today by the Jabali men of Dhofar. Before the advent of the pharmacy, the drying and healing properties of indigo were utilised to cure skin diseases and heal wounds such as the umbilical cord on a new-born baby or on a boy's penis after circumcision. Over the past 20 years or so, the industry has all but disappeared, and the dye is instead largely imported from India.

Pottery   Bahla, in the Ad Dakhiliyah region, is famous for its potters and potteries. Today there are two working factories there, which you can visit to watch the potters at work. Traditionally these pots were used as water containers and dispensers.

Incense burners   These *majmars*, made from clay, are ubiquitous and make the perfect gift or keepsake from Oman. Salalah's frankincense suq (in Dhofar), Mutrah Suq (in the capital) and Nizwa Suq (in the Ad Dakhiliyah) are prime locations for these items. Some are painted in bold colours.

Mandoos   These are Omani chests that have been traditionally used to store valuables. It is said that this stemmed from a Portuguese tradition that Oman inherited when it was invaded in the 16th century. Today, *mandoos* can be bought in a variety of sizes (down to jewellery-box dimensions) and are usually made from either walnut or rosewood. On the surface they are inlaid with brass, gold or silver, in Islamic and geometric designs, and sometimes decorated with precious stones. You will spot them all as decorative furnishing all over Oman, in hotels, official buildings, offices and private homes. They are sometimes referred to as bridal chests.

Omani doors   Intricately carved doors have long been a tradition, and today you will find that their usage has been extended: the carved door – or rather a modern imitation of the traditional Omani door – is now used as a coffee-table top. These can be found for sale in many of the artisan and souvenir shops in Al Qurum, or in the suq at Mutrah, as well as in other artisan workshops scattered throughout the country.

2

Practical Information

WHEN TO VISIT

The **winter season** (October to March) is the peak time to visit Oman as the temperature is broadly on a par with summer in the Mediterranean. The **summer season** (April to September) is the cheaper option, as it is generally deemed too hot for most visitors – inland temperatures can reach 48°C. However, by choosing to visit the cooler mountainous areas, the coast, Dhofar or simply sightseeing in the early morning or late evening, a visit during this time is still possible with some careful planning. Hotel prices differ depending on the season.

During the winter season the **Muscat Festival** is an annual month-long event running from late January until late February (see box, page 125), when replicas of traditional Omani villages are erected at a few specific locations in the city and artisans demonstrate Oman's array of traditional crafts. Funfairs, rides and fireworks all add to the festivities of this time, when Oman promotes its culture and heritage. It is an interesting time to visit as you get a taste of Oman condensed into one area, although, inevitably, early-evening traffic gets extremely busy and congested, especially going towards Al Amrat Park and Al Athaiba Beach.

During the weeks of **Ramadhan** (pages 32–3 and 62), no alcohol is served in restaurants, bars or private clubs, and minibars in hotel rooms tend to be emptied. You are permitted to order alcohol to your room through room service, but this must be consumed within the privacy of your room. No independent restaurants are open in the day at all, and hotel restaurants that are open have their windows draped over and obscured for discretion and in order not to offend local sensibilities. Ramadhan, then, may or may not affect your choice of time to visit the country.

HIGHLIGHTS

MUTRAH SUQ AND CORNICHE Meander through the narrow alleyways of an old Arabian/Indian suq just behind the attractive corniche, still very much in use by local people.

THE RUSTAQ LOOP Take in three of Oman's greatest forts, Al Hazm, Nakhal and Ar Rustaq, against their fabulous mountain backdrop and nearby hot springs.

MUSANDAM Enjoy a boat trip through the mountainous fjords accompanied by leaping dolphins, then picnic on Telegraph Island.

BAHLA FORT Oman's oldest and largest fort, a UNESCO World Heritage Site, with a largely abandoned adjacent mud brick village and the traditional suq close to it.

WADI A'NAKHR (GRAND CANYON RIM) Trek along waymarked paths to the abandoned mountain village of As Sab.

SAYQ PLATEAU Drink in the clear, cool spring air while walking among the blossoms and fragrant roses of the mountain terraces and villages.

SUR Get a feel for the country's maritime links with Zanzibar while strolling in the last working shipbuilding yard for wooden dhows.

RAS AL JINZ Spend the sunrise with baby turtles as they hatch out in their protected reserve and scurry across the sand towards the sea.

DESERT EXPERIENCE Camp out in the remote Wihibah Sands in a Bedouin tent among the silent dunes with camels for companions.

UBAR/ASH SHISR Marvel at the haunting remains of Oman's largest frankincense city, linked with the legendary 'Atlantis of the Sands'.

SUGGESTED ITINERARIES

One week is fine for a holiday here, but if you want to get a fuller taste of what Oman has to offer you will need to travel out of the Capital Area. The average stay is ten days. Three weeks is a great amount of time, which will allow for a full round trip where you will see pretty much everything. Below are itineraries that may be helpful in giving you some idea of how much time to allot to each location. Juggle these around to suit your preferences.

DAY TRIPS FROM MUSCAT
- The Rustaq Loop (pages 155–67) makes a great day out. Take along a picnic and find a spot at the Nakhal Springs. A 4x4 is not necessary.
- Nizwa (pages 217–25) can be visited as a full-day trip from Muscat. Steeped in history, it provides a real sense of the Oman of old. A 4x4 is not necessary.
- Take a wadi trip (either independently or with a tour operator) to Wadi Bani Awf (pages 160–1); it will give you an idea of the amazing mountain scenery of the country. You reach an incredible mountain village oasis (Bald Sayt) at the top, along with the entrance to dramatic Snake Canyon. A 4x4 is necessary here.

OVERNIGHT TRIPS
- Visit Ras Al Had or Ras Al Jinz to see the turtles. Stay overnight there, or in one of the Sur hotels.
- Take a boat trip to the Ad Dimaniyyat Islands and stay in Suhar.
- Visit the slopes of Oman's highest mountain, Jabal Shams, the forts of Bahla and Jabrin, and the archaeological site of Salut, staying at a hotel in Nizwa.

SHORT VISIT If your time in the country is limited, here are some recommendations for sites relatively close to Muscat.

If you have time for only one old town, make it Nizwa. Located in the interior, it is truly evocative of the Oman of old. If you have time for only one wadi trip, make it Wadi Bani Awf, where you can climb in your 4x4 up the mountainside, taking in spectacular gorges and ravines, and finally witness the amazing, thriving village of Bald Sayt, which clings to the side of the mountain. If you can do one short trek along a ravine, go to Wadi Ash Shab (on the coastal road to Sur), and let the boys guide you along and show you the cavernous mountain pool at the end – the peace and the colours of nature here are outstanding. If you can fit in a suq, make it the historical suq at Mutrah, where you can also take in the ambience of the harbour. If you can, visit Al Bustan Palace Hotel, one of the best hotels in the world, with its awe-inspiring atrium. For a unique culinary experience, try Al Angham (page 91) adjacent to the Royal Opera House for excellent Omani food served in a truly opulent setting. If time allows, catch a performance at the Royal Opera House (page 94), one of the world's outstanding opera venues.

ONE WEEK
Day 1 The Grand Mosque; Muscat 'Old Town'; Al Alam Palace; Al Jalali and Al Mirani forts; Bait Al Zubair; Mutrah corniche and suq; dhow cruise; overnight Muscat.

Day 2 Birkat Al Mawz; Nizwa Fort and suq; Bin Ateeq for traditional Omani food; Tanuf ruins; overnight Nizwa.

Day 3 Al Hamra old town; Misfat Al Abriyeen (usually Misfah) mountain village; Wadi Ghul, the 'Grand Canyon'; Bahla town, fort and suq; overnight Nizwa.

Day 4 Ibra Suq and Al Minzifah ruins; Wihibah Sands (with suitable safety precautions); overnight desert camp.

Day 5 Wadi Bani Khalid; Al Kamil Old Castle; Bani Bu Ali; coast from Asilah; evening and dawn turtle watching; Ras Al Jinz.

Day 6 Sur dhow yards; Wadi Ash Shab; Tiwi village; Hawiyat Najm sinkhole; overnight Muscat.

Day 7 Rest and relax in Muscat.

TWO WEEKS With an additional week you can add on a flight to Salalah to enjoy the different atmosphere in the frankincense town. You can reach Salalah by air or road (pages 297–325).

Day 8 Fly to Salalah.

Day 9 Drive over the mountains to Thumrayt and on to Ash Shisr (Ubar), the legendary town discovered by Sir Ranulph Fiennes. Continue to the mega sand dunes after Al Hashman (with suitable safety precautions) and search for geodes. Camp overnight.

Day 10 Return to Salalah, visit Bithnah where black camels may be herded; visit Muday with its enigmatic triliths, ancient rows of stones; overnight Salalah.

Day 11 Visit Mirbat with the Yemeni-style Bin Ali Tomb; Mirbat harbour; Tawi Atayr; Wadi Darbat; Khawr Rawri; Samharam; overnight Salalah.

Day 12 Visit the coconut plantations; Al Balid; Job's Tomb; Mughsayl Beach; Shaat cliffs; return to Salalah; frankincense suq at Haffa; overnight Salalah.

Day 13 Game fishing in the Arabian Sea.

Day 14 Flight home.

TOURIST INFORMATION

The Ministry of Tourism was founded in 2004. The official online tourist service for Oman is www.omantourism.gov.om. There are no tourist information offices in the country, so you have to approach private tour operators for information on tours – see pages 83–5.

TOURIST INFORMATION Oman now has tourist boards and PR companies operating in the following countries:

UK and Ireland	www.fourcommunications.com
Australia and New Zealand	www.tourismoman.com.au
Belgium, Netherlands and Luxembourg	www.visitoman.nl/www.visitoman.be
French-speaking countries	www.omantourisme.com
GCC countries	www.omantourism.me
German-speaking countries	www.omantourism.de
India	www.tourismoman.co.in
Italy	www.aigo.it
Scandinavia	www.omantourism.dk/www.omantourism.se

TOUR OPERATORS

UK

Package holidays from London Heathrow start at around £650 per person for five nights (based on a double room), including flights, airport transfers & bed-&-breakfast accommodation. There are weekly cruise departures from Dubai which call into Khasab & Muscat, giving a brief but comfortable insight into part of Oman. For up-to-date listings of UK-based tour operators who specialise in Oman, consult http://www.travel-lists.co.uk/travel/listings/destinations/asia/middle-east/oman/uk-tour-operators. A handful that have been recommended are:

Cox & Kings ✆020 3797 4936; www.coxandkings.co.uk. Offers group tours as well as private tours to most areas in Oman.
Eastravel ✆01473 214305; www.eastravel.co.uk. Among a variety of other tours, Eastravel can organise a self-drive tour in northern Oman.
Exodus ✆0203 131 6467; www.exodus.co.uk. Activity-based guided group tours including several nights' wilderness camping with the supervision of qualified guides.

Martin Randall ✆020 8742 3355; www.martinrandall.com. An annual small group tour led by an academic. The land-based programme travels from Muscat through the northern mountains & down the east coast to Salalah.
Nature Trek ✆01962 733051; www.naturetrek.co.uk. Escorted birdwatching tour that drives from Dubai via Muscat, Bar Al Hikman to Salalah. The trip should enable sightings of rarities & common birds in a variety of habitats.
Odyssey World ✆01453 883937; www.odysseyexperience.co.uk. For over 25 years the company has organised tours into Oman. Their programme includes small group, private tours with activities that can include a several-day cycling trip around the northern mountains & a golf-oriented stay in Muscat.
Omantravel ✆01295 730950; www.oman-travel.co.uk. Oman specialist offering tailor-made holidays for all budgets, including visits to camel races & wine.
Original Travel ✆020 3773 1976; www.originaltravel.co.uk. Offers a range of tours and activities including the Empty Quarter, scuba diving & Musandam.

Royal Caribbean ☎0844 493 4005; www. royalcaribbean.co.uk. From Dec to Apr a weekly cruise departs from Dubai & includes a day in Khasab & 2 days & an overnight berthed in Muscat.
Safari Drive ☎01488 71140; www.safaridrive. com. Specialises in private, tailor-made 4x4 safaris & offers trips throughout Oman.
Steppes Travel ☎01258 787426; www. steppestravel.co.uk. Specialises in private holidays based on personal specifications, starting from a couple of days. Occasional escorted group tours are organised that may include both Muscat & Salalah.

US

Few tour operators have ever offered regular tour programmes to Oman from the USA, with the exception of Travcoa. Their tours are very upmarket & the cost of US$8,000 per person includes a stay in The Chedi in Muscat.
Travcoa ☎866 591 0070; www.travcoa.com. Luxury holidays either individually or in small groups. They offer programmes to include Oman with other GCC countries or can readily organise a private tailor made itinerary.

OMAN

Major tour operators based in Oman usually have their head offices in Muscat & tours should be booked at least 3 or 4 days in advance. See pages 83–5 for listings.

RED TAPE

VISAS All visitors except GCC nationals require visas. For visitors from 68 countries (including the UK and other EU countries, the USA, Canada, Australia and New Zealand), these can be easily purchased on arrival at Muscat International Airport or at any of the border posts (after filling in a form); a new short-term business/tourist visa is available costing RO5 for up to ten days, which can be extended for a further ten days for a further RO5. A 30-day business/tourist visa costs RO20 and is extendable for a further 30 days for another RO20. Make sure that you pay in Omani cash, because if you pay by credit card or non-Omani currency the rate is higher, around US$20, when it should be closer to US$15. Cruise-ship visitors are entitled to a free visa if their visit is for less than 48 hours. For all nationalities, under 18s are free. Your passport should be valid for at least six months from the date of entry.

Multiple-entry visas can be applied for in advance from your local Omani embassy, allowing visits of up to three weeks, and are valid for three months from date of entry, at a cost of RO50. They are usually only granted to businesspeople and your passport must be valid for at least a year from the date of entry.

For visitors from those 68 countries there is a joint visa facility with Dubai (but not the other Emirates) and Qatar. On arrival into Oman directly from either of these two places with a valid visa, you should receive an Omani visa at no additional charge.

Unusually for the Arab world, having an Israeli stamp in your passport is not currently a problem. Visas to Yemen are obtainable on the border at Sarfayt for all EU nationalities and nationals of the USA, Australia and New Zealand, although it is strongly recommended to obtain them in advance from a Yemeni embassy. They cost US$30 and are valid for one month from entry, three months from issue. In this case your passport must not contain an Israeli stamp. Do check the relevant travel advice (*www.gov.uk/government/world/yemen* or *www.travel.state.gov/content/passports/en/country/yemen.html*). The position regarding Oman entry regulations can change, so it's best to check beforehand either with the Royal Oman Police (e *ropnet@OmanTel. net.om; www.rop.gov.om*) or the Foreign and Commonwealth Office (*www.gov.uk/government/world/oman*) under 'Travel advice'. The US State Department provides an informative page on Oman (*www.travel.state.gov/content/passports/en/country/oman.html*), with 'Safety and security' found in a drop-down section.

CUSTOMS REGULATIONS Firearms, narcotics and pornographic material are banned. Drug smuggling carries the death penalty in Oman, and any prescription drugs should be accompanied by the doctor's prescription; for instance, a prescription is required for codeine. Drug users are subject to lengthy jail sentences accompanied by fines. Magazines, videos and books are sometimes confiscated and examined for subversive or overtly sexual material. Alcohol may be purchased and brought into the country at Muscat and Salalah airports by non-Muslims, and it is available at the Arrivals duty-free shop at Muscat International Airport, situated just before baggage reclaim. The limit is two litres per person, 100ml of perfume and 400 cigarettes. There are spirits and wine at UK supermarket prices. Alcohol is not sold in supermarkets or shops and is only available to residents on a liquor licence, but it is available at licensed hotels, bars and restaurants. Alcohol is forbidden in private vehicles at land border crossings and vehicles are searched quite thoroughly to find it among parties of expatriates travelling over from Dubai for weekends or holidays. If found, it is confiscated and the person carrying it fined. There are no restrictions on camera equipment, computers or music players for personal use.

As for taking goods out of the country, be aware that some handles of the more expensive *khanjars* (see box, page 36) and old ones available in the suqs are made from rhino horn or ivory. It is illegal to take these out of the country and indeed import them to your own. Although these materials are no longer allowed to be used in the making of *khanjars*, the authorities still permit old stocks to be used up. Cheaper varieties of *khanjar* are widely available as souvenirs (pages 63–4).

There is a departure tax of RO10, which all airlines usually include in your flight ticket charge.

EMBASSIES AND CONSULATES

OVERSEAS A comprehensive list of Oman's embassies overseas can be found at www.embassypages.com/oman.

IN MUSCAT Many countries have embassies in Oman, and these are largely concentrated in the Shati Al Qurum diplomatic area of Al Khuwair in Muscat (between the government ministries and the sea). Opening hours generally are 08.00–14.00, with some slight variations. They are closed on Fridays and Saturdays and during Oman's public holidays and their own national holidays.

📧 **Canada** (consulate) 7th Flr, Getco Tower, Way 2728, CBD area; 📞 24 703113; e CanadianConsulate@daud.om

📧 **France** Al Khuwair, Diplomatic Quarter, Jamiyat Al Dowal Al Arabiya St; 📞 24 681800; www.ambafrance-om.org

📧 **Germany** Ruwi, Way 4911, Villa 953, Hillat Al-Jazeera, near Al-Nahda Hospital, Ruwi 📞 24 835000; www.maskat.diplo.de

📧 **Ireland** (consulate) Ruwi, OC Centre, 8th Fl, Suite 807; 📞 24 701282; e ireconmct@gmail.com

📧 **New Zealand** (consulate) Madinat Al-Sultan Qaboos, Villa 2869, Way 2333, Madinat Al Sultan Qaboos St; 📞 24 694692; e nzconsul@omantel.net.om

📧 **South Africa** Hse 1384, Way 3017, Shati Al Qurum; 📞 24 647300; www.dfa.gov.za/foreign/sa_abroad/sao.htm

📧 **United Arab Emirates** Al Khuwair, Diplomatic Quarter, Jamiyat Al Dowal Al Arabia St; 📞 24 400000; e muscat@mofa.gov.ae

📧 **UK** Al Khuwair, Diplomatic Quarter, Jamiyat Al Dowal Al Arabiya St; 📞 24 609000; www.gov.uk/government/world/oman

📧 **USA** Al Khuwair, Diplomatic Quarter, Jamiyat Al Dowal Al Arabiya St; 📞 24 643400; oman.usembassy.gov

📧 **Yemen** Al Khuwair, Diplomatic Quarter, Jamiyat Al Dowal Al Arabiya St; 📞 24 600815; e yemb-muscat@mofa.gov.ye

GETTING THERE AND AWAY

BY AIR Muscat International Airport, located 40km west of the old town of Muscat (about a 40-minute drive), is the country's main international airport and also a hub for domestic flights. Salalah Airport, in the south of the country, is the only other international airport, receiving flights from other GCC countries and charter flights from Europe, as well as domestic flights from Muscat (*for flight information;* ☎ *24 519456/223*).

Flight prices are always subject to change, and it is worth doing a thorough search online using sites such as www.ebookers.com. A standard direct return flight from Heathrow with Oman Air, which flies morning and evening to Muscat, costs around US$900. Oman Air is scheduled to start flights between manchester and Muscat in April 2017, thus enhancing it's hub status for onward flights to Asia. Oman Air also flies from Frankfurt, Milan, Munich, Paris and Zürich to Muscat. Other Oman Air international destinations include Bangkok, Cochin, Colombo, Goa, Jaipur, Kathmandu, Kuala Lumpur, Male, Manila, Singapore and Zanzibar. Other airlines flying into Muscat include British Airways direct non-stop, Turkish Air (via Istanbul), Gulf Air (via Bahrain), Etihad (via Abu Dhabi), Emirates (via Dubai) and Qatar Air (via Doha). Direct flights into Salalah are from Muscat by Oman Air, Doha with Qatar Air, Sharjah with Air Arabia, and from Terminal 2 Dubai with flydubai. Charter flights for package holidays fly to Salalah from Cologne, Milan and Warsaw. If you are looking to cut costs more, find the cheapest flight to Dubai, then catch a bus to Muscat. This also saves you the Oman visa fee, thanks to the joint Dubai visa agreement (page 43). There are no direct flights from the US to Oman.

Airlines

Oman Air Sales office, Ruwi ☎ 24 531111; holidays ☎ 24 765129; www.omanair.com. The national carrier has flights from Muscat to destinations including Abu Dhabi, Al Ain, Bahrain, Bangkok, Beirut, Cairo, Chennai (Madras), Colombo, Dammam, Dar es Salaam, Delhi, Doha, Dubai, Goa, Hyderabad, Jaipur, Jeddah, Kathmandu, Kochi, Kuala Lumpur, Kuwait, London, Male, Manila, Milan, Mumbai (Bombay), Munich, New Delhi, Paris, Singapore, Trivandrum, Zanzibar & Zürich, as well as domestic flights to Salalah, Ad Duqm, Khasab & Suhar.
Air Arabia ☎ 24 700828; www.airarabia.com
Air India ☎ 24 818666; www.airindia.com

British Airways ☎ 24 568777; www.ba.com
Egypt Air ☎ 24 794113; www.egyptair.com
Emirates Air ☎ 24 404400; www.emirates.com
Etihad Airways ☎ 24 823555; www.etihad.com
fly dubai ☎ 24 756091; www.flydubai.com
KLM ☎ 24 657575; www.klm.com
Lufthansa ☎ 24 796692; www.lufthansa.co.uk
Qatar Airways ☎ 24 162700; www.qatarairways.com
Saudi Arabian Airlines ☎ 24 789485; www.saudiairlines.com
Sri Lankan Airlines ☎ 24 796680; www.srilankan.com
Swiss International Airlines ☎ 800 77452; www.swiss.com

BY ROAD Oman borders three countries, but almost all entries by road are through the **United Arab Emirates** whose entire international border is fenced. There are three locations where crossing is possible into the UAE from the main part of Oman (ie: south of Al Fujayrah); these are Al Buraymi, Hatta and Al Fujayrah. The Al Farjah border with **Saudi Arabia** (west of Ibri), crosses directly into Shaybah, Saudi Arabia, and is therefore of use only to non-GCC nationals who have a Saudi entry visa stamped in their passport. Crossing into **Yemen** from Salalah is possible by local bus and car; the suggested border is Sarfayt on the coast. Women travelling solo into Yemen have no additional requirements than men. That said, the tedious and often exasperating bureaucratic requirements by the Yemeni authorities for travel throughout the country make solo travel difficult within Yemen. These requirements include the need to present a travel itinerary, obtain a pass to travel between towns and usually to have an armed escort. See page 43 for visa requirements.

Border crossings with the UAE From the United Arab Emirates there are six entry points: Dubai's Hatta border (Al Wajajah) (if this one is used then the joint visa with Dubai applies); two Al Buraymi borders – one in Al Buraymi town at Hilli and one at Jabal Hafit; and the Khitmat Milahah border at Kalba/Al Fujayrah. The final two entry points are into Musandam in the north at Tibat near Ras Al Khaymah and a rather strange crossing at Daba which, although you cross into Oman from the UAE, has no Omani immigration control. This results in people who are not GCC nationals and who are not resident in the UAE requiring a letter from either of the two hotels in Daba, Oman, confirming that a room reservation is held. The journey from Dubai to Muscat International Airport takes approximately 7 hours and is on a relatively busy dual carriageway for the entire journey.

BY SEA **International** sea voyages have only just started and are currently on a trial basis, running between Khasab and Dubai, Khasab and Qeshm Island within the Strait of Hormuz, and Khasab and Bandar Abbas on the Iranian mainland (Iranian visas required). Contact National Ferries head office (✆ *800 72 000; www.nfc.om*) or their office in Mutrah (✆ *24 713366*) regarding the current situation. **Domestic** services to connect with the international ones at Khasab are well established. Taking the ferry between Khasab in Musandam and Mina Sultan Qaboos means that you will have already undertaken all the immigration procedures before embarking on the ferry. An increasing number of **cruise ships** do call into Mina Sultan Qaboos as part of their itinerary and many also call at the ports of Salalah and Khasab. Several offer a round trip of a week from Dubai that visits Khasab and Muscat during winter months. Cruise ships occasionally use Mina Sultan Qaboos, as a terminus for part of their voyage; the ship's staff will handle the logistics of entry and exit provided that you are included among those nationalities eligible for a visa or have already obtained one.

HEALTH *with Dr Felicity Nicholson*

PREPARATIONS From a health perspective, Oman is a relatively safe country to visit. Vaccinations are usually required only for longer-term visitors or those staying in rural areas. There are pharmacies, clinics and good private medical facilities throughout the country. The heat of the country does mean that it is important to drink plenty of water.

Vaccinations There is no risk of **yellow fever** in Oman. However, the only compulsory vaccine for visitors is the yellow fever vaccine if you have been in an area where yellow fever is endemic, such as sub-Saharan Africa or South America, in the last six days. A valid certificate is then required, which is active ten days after vaccination and lasts for life. Since 11 July 2016, all countries have to accept that any certificate, no matter how long ago the vaccine was given, must be accepted. If the vaccine is contraindicated then ask your doctor or travel clinic (page 49) for an exemption certificate and wherever possible obtain a letter from the Oman embassy in your starting country to accept this.

Generally, however, it would be wise to be up to date with childhood vaccines for tetanus, diphtheria, polio, and measles, mumps and rubella. Hepatitis A would also be recommended. Long-term visitors and expatriate residents are usually advised to have a hepatitis B injection. A course of pre-exposure rabies vaccine (page 48) is also advised for long-term visitors who will be in rural areas. It is best to check with your local clinic several weeks before departure.

Leishmaniasis This cutaneous and visceral disease is spread by sand flies, *Phlebotomus alexandri* and *Sergentomyia* spp, initially causing extremely itchy bumps or a rash, followed by skin lesions and swollen glands. These flies occur in the Ash Sharqiyyah and Adh Dhahirah regions. Prevention methods are as for malaria (see below).

Malaria There is a sporadic risk of both benign and malignant malaria due to importation of cases from other countries. In 2010, local outbreaks were reported

---

LONG-HAUL FLIGHTS, CLOTS AND DVT

Any prolonged immobility, including travel by land or air, can result in deep vein thrombosis (DVT) with the risk of embolus to the lungs. Certain factors can increase the risk and these include:

- History of DVT or pulmonary embolism
- Recent surgery to pelvic region or legs
- Cancer
- Stroke
- Heart disease
- Obesity
- Pregnancy
- Hormone therapy
- Older age
- Inherited tendency to clot (thrombophilia)
- Being over 6ft or under 5ft

A deep-vein thrombosis causes painful swelling and redness of the calf or sometimes the thigh. It is only dangerous if a clot travels to the lungs (pulmonary embolus). Symptoms of a pulmonary embolus (PE) – which commonly start three to ten days after a long fight – include chest pain, shortness of breath, and sometimes coughing up small amounts of blood. Anyone who thinks that they might have a DVT needs to see a doctor immediately.

PREVENTION OF DVT
- Wear loose clothing
- Do anti-DVT exercises and move around when possible
- Drink plenty of fluids during the flight
- Avoid taking sleeping pills and excessive tea, coffee and alcohol
- Consider wearing flight socks or support stockings
  (*www.leghealthwarehouse.com*)

If you think you are at increased risk of a clot, ask your doctor if it is safe to travel.

If someone was seriously ill and in a great deal of pain, the old Arab practice was to apply the *wussum* burn. A girl who had been bitten by a poisonous snake on one leg thus had a series of deep burns inflicted on her other leg that was then brushed with fresh camel dung. The effect was to outweigh the original pain, and sometimes to cause gangrene and death. The old customs ran deep and even in the late 1960s a trained Omani doctor commented: 'Our people will burn and bleed a patient through trying to cure him before they would even think of taking him to the American hospital in Mutrah. That is done only as a final resort when all else has failed.'

Freya Stark in her travels in southern Arabia commented on the same tendency. As a consequence of having two windows in every wall there were often strong draughts in Arab houses. Many caught measles, shivering, then bronchitis and pneumonia, as she herself did. But as she noticed: 'Few came to the chemist. They preferred to run hot irons down their backs.' She also noted that the people of the Hadhramaut had a horror of soap or scent and were convinced that it weakened or even killed you if you were already poorly. After measles no-one would use it for 41 days.

in the northern Ash Sharqiyyah region, and it may also occur in Musandam. *P. falciparum*, *P. vivax* and *Anopheles stephensi* do occur in Oman, although anti-malarial tablets are not currently recommended for the majority of travellers.

Although malaria tablets for prophylaxis are not recommended it is important to protect yourself from mosquito bites, so keep your repellent to hand at all times. There are a variety of diseases that can be transmitted by day-biting *Aedes* mosquitoes, including chikungunya, dengue fever, yellow fever and Zika. You should use a product that contains 50–55% DEET and apply as often as is necessary. Remember to reapply after being in water.

You also need either a permethrin-impregnated bednet or a permethrin spray so that you can 'treat' bednets in hotels. Permethrin treatment makes even very tatty nets protective and prevents mosquitoes biting through the impregnated net when you roll against it; it also deters other biters. Putting on long clothes at dusk means you can reduce the amount of repellent you need to put on your skin, but be aware that malaria mosquitoes hunt at ankle level and will bite through socks, so apply repellent under socks too. Travel clinics usually sell a good range of nets, treatment kits and repellents.

Rabies Rabies may be carried by all mammals (beware the village dogs) and is passed on to humans through a bite, scratch or a lick of an open wound. You must always assume any animal is rabid and seek medical help as soon as possible. In the interim, scrub the wound with soap and bottled/boiled water for 10 minutes, then pour on a strong iodine or alcohol solution. This helps stop the rabies virus entering the body and will guard against wound infections, including tetanus.

If you intend to have contact with animals and/or are likely to be more than 24 hours away from medical help, then pre-exposure vaccination is advised. Ideally, three doses should be taken over a minimum of three weeks. Contrary to popular belief, these vaccinations are relatively painless.

If you are exposed as described, treatment should be given as soon as possible, but it is never too late to seek help as the incubation period for rabies can be very long. Those who have not been immunised will need a full course of injections together with rabies immunoglobulin (RIG), but this product is expensive (around US$800) and may be hard to come by: another reason why pre-exposure vaccination should be encouraged in travellers who are planning to visit more remote areas.

Tell the doctor if you have had pre-exposure vaccine, as this will change the treatment you receive. And remember that, if you do contract rabies, mortality is 100% and death from rabies is probably one of the worst ways to go.

Travel clinics and health information
A full list of current travel clinic websites worldwide is available at www.istm.org. For other journey preparation information, consult www.nathnac.org. Information about various medications may be found on www.netdoctor.co.uk/travel.

Personal first-aid kit
Pharmacies are so plentiful throughout Oman that it is not the end of the world if you don't take your own personal first-aid kit. However, if you prefer to go prepared, then the following may be helpful:

- A few small plasters or dressings
- Suncream
- Painkillers
- Antiseptic cream
- Insect repellent (only needed if camping, and then only in some remote areas)

IN OMAN
Medical facilities
In the late 1960s there were only three hospitals in the country and eight out of ten babies died within ten months of conception. Old and young alike were riddled with trachoma (a contagious disease of the eye). Tuberculosis was common, as were malaria and chronic anaemia. Leprosy was endemic with no enforced segregation. Flies were everywhere, transferring disease from the faeces of villagers to their food with regularity and crawling over the faces of oblivious children.

Today, the situation in Oman is remarkably different. There is an extensive public health service, which is free to Omanis. Foreigners, however, are often expected to pay cash to use these services, and costs can be high. Private medical services are excellent, with many well-equipped clinics and hospitals. Cosmetic surgery is widely available, as is laser eye surgery. Travel insurance is advised as medical treatment can be costly for foreigners. Those with specific medical conditions should wear medical alert tags and carry a list of medications related to their condition. Health expenditure now accounts for 3% of Oman's GDP.

Hospitals
There are a number of hospitals with emergency rooms in the Capital Area. The main government hospitals are Al-Nahda (✆ 24 831255), Khoula (✆ 24 563625) and The Royal Hospital (✆ 24 599000); the main private hospital is Muscat Private Hospital (✆ 24 583600).

Pharmacies
There are several pharmacy groups in Oman. The largest, Muscat Pharmacy, has branches throughout the country, including at Muscat Al Sarooj, Muscat Al Hail, Salalah, Barka, Ar Rustaq, Ibri Suq, Al Buraymi, Nizwa, Ibra and Sur. A few are open 24 hours – you can find their details in any of the English-language newspapers.

Having wheelchair access is not yet obligatory for Oman's tourist facilities, and the further you venture from Muscat, the more challenging life becomes for travellers with mobility problems. However, the tourist industry is growing rapidly and this is having a positive influence on what is available for the disabled traveller. On top of this, Omani culture is one of exceptional hospitality and friendliness, and therefore local people will always offer support and help.

ACCOMMODATION Since most hotels have been built post-1980, access is fairly good. The government has been putting pressure on hotels to provide special facilities and many have responded well (especially in Muscat and Salalah). Most hotels in Muscat will all have at least one room with roll-in showers and grab handles and disabled toilets, and lifts and access ramps make movement within the public areas of the hotel easier. Access to beaches is never easy, but, as always, staff are willing to help. The international chains of hotels of course apply their standards to hotels in Oman, but wherever you book do make it clear if you require disabled facilities within the room.

GETTING AROUND As with tourist accommodation, most public buildings have been built in the past 30 years, meaning they are fairly accessible. In the cities, the situation is constantly improving and several modern shopping malls and pedestrian areas even have disabled toilets and access ramps. The main mosques and museums don't cater especially for wheelchairs, but most are fairly flat with wide doors and level access. If you are intending to visit forts and castles, you can expect to find them as inaccessible as they were designed to be. There is ramped wheelchair access to Bait Zubair Museum, Mutrah Suq and Sultan Qaboos Grand Mosque is especially accommodating, with ramped access even on low steps.

By road There are some taxis with wheelchair access in Oman, but not many, so you may need help when transferring in and out of the vehicle. This will be even more likely if you are planning to venture off the beaten track as 4x4s are higher than normal cars. Drivers/guides are normally happy to assist, but are not trained in this skill, so you must thoroughly explain your needs and always stay in control of the situation.

Distances can be great but thankfully the condition of the roads throughout the country is excellent. However, if you plan to go off-road in any way, for example on a wadi trip or a desert or mountain safari, then it will be bumpy. Anyone prone to skin damage should take extra care. Place your own pressure-relieving cushion on top of (or instead of) the original car seat and, if necessary, pad around knees and elbows.

Oman's red, full-size 'Mwasalat' coaches have limited disabled space. Depending on your ability, you may need assistance to get on and off buses.

By air Aisle chairs are used for international arrivals in Muscat, making entering and exiting the aircraft easier for non-ambulant people, and Muscat International Airport has disabled toilets. The local carrier – Oman Air – is also

Emergencies An ambulance service has been introduced to the Capital Area, using US equipment and US-trained staff. Otherwise, the availability of roadside or ambulance assistance is poor. The Royal Oman Police will assist with transportation in an emergency. In case of an emergency (police/fire/ambulance), call ❜9999.

reported to be of a high standard, though that is not to say that an aisle chair and full facilities are to be expected at every domestic terminal.

ACTIVITIES Local operators have assured me that the dolphin-watching and desert and wadi visits should all be possible. More challenging activities like trekking or *via ferrata* trips (mountain routes traversable by fixed cables, ladders and bridges) would obviously require more planning, but, again, depending on your ability and motivation, they are not out of the question.

HEALTH General healthcare in Oman is excellent. However, as with anywhere, you must understand and be able to explain your own particular medical requirements. Comprehensive insurance is essential, and be sure that the insurance company is aware of any existing medical conditions.

Pharmacies are well stocked, but it is always advisable to take all necessary medication and equipment with you, and to pack this in your hand luggage during flights in case your main luggage gets lost. You should always bring prescriptions with you; codeine, for example, needs evidence of a prescription.

Oman is hot all year round, but every hotel is equipped with air-conditioning units for your comfort. Aerosol water sprays are widely available at chemists, and provide welcome relief as an instant cooling aid, although a cheaper and more environmentally friendly device is a plant-spray bottle filled with water.

SECURITY Oman is a relatively safe travel destination and the crime rate is low. However, it is worthwhile remembering that, as a disabled person, you are more vulnerable. Stay aware of who is around you and where your bags are, especially during car transfers and similar. These activities often draw a crowd, and the confusion creates easy pickings for an opportunist thief.

SPECIALIST OPERATORS There are, as yet, no operators specialising in disability travel to Oman. Having said that, most travel companies will listen to your needs and try to create an itinerary suitable for you. For the independent traveller, it is possible to limit potential surprises by contacting local operators and establishments by email in advance.

FURTHER INFORMATION The most accurate and up-to-date information is available from tour operators. I found the following people most helpful:

Oman Association for the Disabled ✆24 490502; e oadisabl@omantel.net.om. Mainly for nationals but does give some information for visitors.
Peter and Margaret at Omantravel ✆+44 (0)1235 200444; e margaret@omantravel.uk.com; www.omantravel.co.uk
Muscat Diving & Adventure Centre ✆+968 24 485663; e info@holiday-in-oman.com; www. holiday-in-oman.com

Drinking water
The water supply throughout much of Oman is from desalinated seawater, obtained through either flash desalination or reverse osmosis. Outside of the Capital Area, water should be regarded as being potentially contaminated. Bottled water or water that has been boiled is advised

for drinking, brushing teeth and making ice. Several brands of bottled water are from Oman's own mountain sources.

Protection from the sun The summer months (April–September) can be extremely hot. Be careful to keep your skin covered and wear loose-fitting clothes for comfort. Sunglasses and hats will provide welcome relief and are recommended. Do use a sunscreen or at least a high-factor protection cream, ideally 25SPF or above, and reapply after swimming. Try to keep out of the sun between 11.00 and 15.00 when the sun is strongest. Drink plenty of liquids to keep yourself well hydrated.

SAFETY

The crime rate in Oman is low and the streets of the Capital Area are safe even for lone travellers after dark.

WOMEN TRAVELLERS Oman is one of the easiest Arab countries for foreign women to travel in without hassle, if their dress and demeanour are appropriate. There is little risk for women in using taxis, buses or hiring a car. In the Capital Area, despite the fact that the hotel bars and private clubs are a male domain (in Omani culture), you will find that, broadly, Omanis are chatty, relaxed and helpful. For a lone female traveller, Omani men (and for that matter Omani women, who are increasingly to be found independently in public places) can make excellent, respectful and supportive company. The important thing is to wear unprovocative loose-fitting clothing and to conduct yourself with politeness and friendliness, but making sure that a respectful distance is maintained. In general, shaking hands or making physical contact with members of the opposite sex is not polite behaviour and will probably be misinterpreted.

GAY AND LESBIAN TRAVELLERS As in many Muslim countries, homosexuality is illegal in Oman. Partners travelling together should be discreet and especially careful not to make overt physical contact with each other. If caught engaged in homosexual practices, especially with a local Omani, the penalties for non-Omanis range from deportation to imprisonment. It is not a polite or normal topic for discussion in any social situation with Omanis.

TRAVELLING WITH CHILDREN Like all Arabs, Omanis love children and, as a result, hotels and restaurants welcome them warmly, though high chairs are

CHANGING SOCIAL PATTERNS

As Omani society becomes more urbanised and living standards improve, traditional patterns of society are changing. In the cities Omani women now get married later, often not until the age of 28–30, while most men wait until the age of 35. There are fewer arranged marriages and Omani men as a rule take only one wife, unlike many of their counterparts elsewhere in the Gulf. The average number of children per female (fertility rate) has now dropped from six or seven to fewer than three – a direct result of the rise in women's education. Some Omani women will even now marry foreigners, if their families agree and they are able to obtain the permission of Oman's Ministry of the Interior.

a rarity. Children love the desert, the mountains and the beaches, and their greatest danger will be sunburn, so take care to protect them properly. There is a growing number of fast-food outlets, and many restaurants offer child menus or child discounts. Supermarkets and chemists sell nappies, as well as baby food in jars and packets.

WHAT TO TAKE

CLOTHES For comfort, loose cotton clothing is best and a pullover will often be required in the evenings in the winter months (October–March). In the top-class hotels smart casual for dinner is normal, while in the smaller hotels, especially inland, the style is much more informal. For more details, see page 68.

FOOTWEAR If you are going on a more intrepid tour, you will find that a lot of the trails have rocky and uneven surfaces, so ensure that your footwear can cope. Open-toed sandals offer little protection against impact or bites and stings and minimal support on the loose, pebbly terrain.

OTHER USEFUL ITEMS There are pharmacies and food stores throughout the country and so medicines, plasters, batteries, etc, will all be readily available. In most larger towns there are substantial supermarkets that have excellent stocks of virtually everything you can get at home. For female travellers, sanitary towels as well as tampons are available in major supermarkets, although the non-applicator variety of tampon is most usual.

Electricity/plugs Unusually for a Middle Eastern country, Oman has British-style square three-pin sockets at 240v, thanks to its close historic ties with Britain. The majority of electrical items are sold with two-pin plugs; three-pin adaptors to take two-/three- pin plugs are sold in most supermarkets and hotels will generally have one available if needed.

Camping equipment Camping equipment is available in major supermarkets, especially Carrefour and the Sultan Centre in Al Qurum. Lulu have a smaller variety. In addition there are local shops in every village selling pots, pans, and odd bits and pieces that are cheap enough and will equip you for your trip.

MONEY AND BUDGETING

CURRENCY The currency is the Omani rial (RO), usually referred to as the rial. One rial is made up of 1,000 baisas (bzs). Since 1986 the Omani rial has been pegged to the US dollar at RO1 = US$2.60 and the exchange rate has remained stable since then. That said, at the time of writing there is considerable pressure on the exchange rate owing to lower oil prices, so you should actively review the actual rates for any change.

The rates of exchange in October 2016 were as follows: £1 = RO0.47, US$1 = RO0.38, €1 = RO0.43.

CASH It is best to change money in Oman as the rates are better than can be obtained overseas. Money changers are licensed and most offer similar exchange rates, especially when changing dollars. Money changers can be found in most retail shopping areas and are easy to locate with clear signs above the office.

Oman is not a cheap destination for the visitor, but it is possible to tour the country on a budget if you are prepared to forgo some comforts and luxuries. These pointers may help.

- Fly to Dubai (often cheaper than Muscat) and get a bus to Muscat (*7hrs, RO11 return*). This way the Omani visa fee is waived at the border (pages 43 and 60).
- You can eat very cheaply at unlicensed Indian and Omani restaurants and coffee shops. A meal for two with drinks is likely to be under RO5.
- Buy fresh breads of all varieties, hot chicken, delicatessen foods, pre-prepared salads, fruit and cold drinks from any of the supermarkets for great beach or mountain picnics. A litre bottle of water costs around 250bzs, and canned drinks cost around the same. A whole chicken straight off the rotisserie costs only RO1.20.
- Camping will reduce your costs considerably, but do not attempt it in the hot months from April to October; November to March are the best months. Of course, this is only possible outside towns. In rural areas camp well away from villages. Beach camping is possible south of Muscat (pages 115–16).
- Car-hire companies operate within residential areas such as close to Al Hamriyyah roundabout, and these are cheaper than those in the airport, but maintenance is not as good, cash payment is required and CDW insurance is often unavailable. If a 4x4 is not necessary, go for a saloon, which is significantly cheaper. Petrol is cheap (180bzs per litre) and there are monthly

The large numbers of foreign workers needing to send money home to their families creates tremendous demand and on pay day the queues may stretch outside the office. The airport exchange kiosks have a slightly less favourable exchange rate. ATMs are plentiful throughout the country, with an integrated national system where several hundred rials may be withdrawn in cash on any one day. Your own card issuer may wish to be advised if you intend to use your card abroad.

TRAVELLERS' CHEQUES These are almost impossible to exchange and will entail considerable delay and identification requests. The best location to exchange these will be the foreign department of a bank's head office.

CREDIT CARDS Credit cards are widely accepted in hotels, larger restaurants, shopping complexes, some petrol stations and major businesses throughout Oman. It is recommended that you advise your credit-card provider that you intend to use the card in Oman, so as to ensure that you will gain full approval and encounter no hiccups. In smaller hotels, shops, suqs and restaurants it is likely that you will need cash, especially in the interior (those areas away from the Capital Area). Cash is used in the traditional suqs, as it also allows for easy bargaining, which is to be expected in this setting.

TIPPING In hotels a 17% charge is added to the bill (9% government tax, 8% service charge), so tipping over and above this is a matter of personal choice. Larger 'international' restaurants add the 9% and no service charge, so one will certainly be appreciated. Any other tipping, for example for hotel porterage,

announcements that set the price throughout the country. Taxi fares can mount very quickly within the Capital Area, making it cheaper to hire a car, especially if the cost is shared between several people.

- A cheaper option for getting around is to use the shared taxis or minibuses operating in the capital (page 80) and coaches for inter-city travel (page 60).
- Cheapest of all is to hitchhike, though bear in mind that tourists, especially those from the West, are an extreme exception, and solo women should definitely not consider it. The correct gesture to indicate that you want a lift is to hold out your right arm straight and waggle your hand downwards. The Western custom of sticking out a thumb is not used.
- If you're lucky enough to have Omani friends or acquaintances, or know expats with Omani residence, then it is likely that at some point you will be invited along to one of the many private clubs in the cities. Here you will save a fortune on food and drink, which are expensive in hotels.

It is possible to stay in Oman for RO40 (around £72) per day, staying in a budget hotel, renting a saloon car and eating in local coffee shops and budget restaurants. This figure can be reduced further if you forgo the hire car, or intend to camp in the country (although if you're camping, you will need the car and equipment). In this case, you can get by here on a rock-bottom budget of RO25 (around £50) per day. This figure would be sufficient for one or two people sharing a room.

airport assistance, room service or taxi service, is also appreciated and expected in five-star properties. Around 10% is the norm.

GETTING AROUND

BY AIR Within Oman there are domestic flights to Khasab in Musandam (*twice daily; approx. RO25 one-way; 1hr*), Salalah in Dhofar (*up to 6 flights a day; approx RO32 one way; 1.5hrs*). Oman Air also flies to Ad Duqm (*Sun, Mon, Wed & Thu; approx RO25 one-way; 80mins; bookings only through www.duqmair.com*).

BY SEA A ferry service runs between Muscat and Musandam, and three other ports have local services within the Musandam area. There are several crossings each day between Shannah and Masirah Island. Information is available at www.nfc.om, which includes schedules and prices. Advance booking is suggested for all services, and note that identification is required and vehicle documents should be produced.

BY ROAD The **road network** in Oman is excellent, so a saloon car is largely all you need to get about (noting that any use is for tarmac only). Major roads have street lighting, as do many minor roads even away from towns. The crash barriers and road surfaces are well maintained and road signs are in Arabic and English, though occasionally the location of a sign might be improved. The Muscat Expressway, which has three lanes in each direction, goes all the way to Barka from Muscat and is being further extended towards Suhar, is particularly good, though it has limited petrol stations. The three-lane highway past Muscat International Airport continues northwest through Barka to Suhar and links to the UAE from there. This road runs through towns and villages whereas the Muscat Expressway is set well away from existing settlements. There is a good dual carriageway inland to Nizwa and beyond to Ibri and Al Buraymi. The coastal road between Muscat and Sur is a dual carriageway and the inland Bidbid–Sur road is rapidly being upgraded to three-lane highway. Beyond Sur the coastal road to Salalah is single-lane until it reaches Salalah. The Nizwa–Salalah highway is single track for much of its route, except for the initial and final sections, which are dual carriageways. Directions are clearly signposted in phonetic English, so getting around is easy.

There are, however, a few off-road trips where a **4x4** is necessary, and these vehicles can easily be hired, although you should always check the small print to make sure you are covered when driving off-tarmac. Do not assume that driving a 4x4 is the same as driving a saloon car. If you do, you will almost inevitably have problems with the gear ratios, axle lock and more. Ask the car-hire company to clearly show you how to operate the vehicle. Alternatively, if you arrange these trips through a tour operator, rather than going independently, the vehicle and driver/guide will be provided and included in the price with no insurance worries. The Wihibah Sands, the Empty Quarter and the wadi trips each require a 4x4, as does the ascent to Al Jabal Al Akhdar. As such, it may be an idea to hire a saloon which you can use either to Birkat Al Mawz or Al Mintarib, then organise a 4x4 with driver to provide the local service needed.

In terms of **regulations**, driving is on the right-hand side of the road, so all vehicles are left-hand drive. Muscat rush hour is from 07.00 to 09.00 and from 16.00 to 18.00, but with the dramatic increase in vehicles within Oman the traffic is rarely free-flowing. Be sure to carry your passport or identity card with you, along with your driving licence and hire-car agreement and insurance, in case you are asked to produce them at any time. In the event of an accident, however minor, the police must be called and the vehicles involved not moved until they have arrived. You might wish to photograph the situation for ease of reference. The Royal Oman Police (ROP) have a 'zero tolerance' policy for motoring offences. When driving any vehicle you should ensure that the insurance will cover your needs. For example, if you drive into the UAE you will need to ensure that you have international coverage and that you have a collision damage waiver. Vehicles in Oman are insured based on the maximum number of occupants detailed on the car registration document. If you intend to drive off tarmac roads, try to find 4x4 vehicle insurance that will include recovery.

Driving under the influence of alcohol or any psychotropic substances renders your insurance void in the event of an accident and carries heavy fines, jail and may include a ban. Two-wheel drive cars are not covered for damage incurred whilst being driven off-road, so think carefully before you venture off the tarmac. The lowest jail terms for offences will be ten days while the maximum sentence is three years and fines range from OMR100 but could reach OMR3,000. Wearing a front seatbelt is mandatory and there is a fine for non-compliance. It is against the law to drive with a mobile phone or any electrical equipment in one's hand. You can even be fined for driving a car that is too dirty!

Be aware that there may be camels, goats or donkeys crossing the road at any time. Oncoming cars may flash their headlights at you to warn you to slow down for a possible hazard up ahead.

The **speed limit** on the highways is 120km/h (75mph) and cars are fitted with an insistent beeper or dashboard light that is triggered automatically if you exceed this speed limit. The speed limit in urban areas on minor roads is no more than 60km/h.

In the Capital Area, especially around Mutrah and Al Qurum, an increasing number of **parking spaces** require pay-and-display tickets. Make sure you always have some coins on you for the meters: half an hour costs 50bzs at the time of writing, although an increase is expected. Parking is free on Fridays and at non-working hours during the day – the signs give details.

Shell, Al Maha and Oman Oil fuel stations abound throughout the country. Fuel is cheap – in the Muscat area it costs approximately 180bzs per litre and is officially updated monthly, as the government regulate the price based on the current oil price. Most fuel stations are attended service and have toilets (albeit in various states of cleanliness), and generally have a small convenience store with often other useful services such as a small restaurant and vehicle cleaning and oil change on the forecourt.

Vehicle assistance The AAA (Arabian Automobile Alliance) (\ *24 697800*), provides 24-hour roadside assistance.

Car hire There is no difficulty in getting a hire car in Oman. Plenty of car-hire firms have desks in the arrivals area of Muscat International Airport, and car-hire desks/offices can also be found in the upper-range hotels, if you prefer to wait until you are rested before arranging things. The budget and mid-range hotels will also arrange a car for you on request. Most companies will drop a car off at your hotel.

Some car-rental companies re-use paper, resulting in an ID theft risk. The Omani car-registration documents can, for example, be photocopied on to the back of a photocopy of other people's passports or driving licences. This practice is also commonplace in Dubai, even with big companies, so always double-check and get them to change it if necessary.

As in most places, you will be asked for a copy of your passport, your driving licence (either from your country of origin or an International Driving Permit) and a credit card or cash for a returnable deposit. Always check for the spare tyre and jack and make sure that you have either a copy of the car's valid registration document or a copy of the hire agreement. Drivers have to be 21 or over. Rates for small cars with major car-hire companies are around RO17 per day or RO80–100 for a week, including insurance. A 4x4 jumps up to approximately RO40 per day. The costs usually include 200km mileage, collision damage waiver, theft waiver, third-party insurance and local taxes. Personal accident insurance is optional, and costs around RO2 per day, and mileage above 200km is charged at approximately 80bzs per kilometre. Smaller, less expensive car-hire offices do not accept credit cards and their cars are considerably less well maintained, but they are also significantly cheaper, from around RO10 per day; in this case, caveat emptor. Check child-seat availability in advance with all car-hire companies as you may have to bring your own. Always keep documentation with you in case of an accident or a police stop.

Petrol is cheap – at 180bzs per litre; RO5 buys 27 litres. Busier petrol stations are open 24 hours and an attendant fills the tank for you; if you are driving and your tank drops below half full, fill it up at the next opportunity as distances can be long and petrol stations do occasionally run out of fuel.

If you intend to cross any of the **border posts** into the UAE (even if simply in transit to Musandam or Al Buraymi) it is necessary to obtain permission from your car-hire company and to confirm that the vehicle is insured in both countries. You may have to obtain original vehicle documentation to ensure that you are permitted to cross the border. It is not possible to rent a car in one country and leave it in another. In your own car it is possible to cross any of the borders as long as your insurance covers you to do so. Insurance offices are available at major border crossings to provide cover. For more details about crossing borders, see pages 43 and 45–6.

Practical Information GETTING AROUND

2

If a road or any track is covered in water, especially flowing water, hazards under the water are not visible. This makes driving through a flowing wadi potentially dangerous. If the flow is strong and a vehicle halts in the water, the force of the water flow, together with any debris it carries, may lift the vehicle away. It is advisable to wait until the flooding halts and certainly watch what happens if other vehicles try to cross; do not tailgate them through – if they stop, so will you. Cross where the water is at its widest, as this tends to be where it is shallowest and with the weakest current. If the water is likely to be above any part of the vehicle's body and there is a flow of water you should not attempt to drive through. Keep your speed down if the water is fairly shallow so that you do not splash your electrics.

If your engine does get drowned, do not attempt to start it as water may have entered the tops of the pistons via the exhaust or air filter, which could result in a bent crankshaft or, in the worst case scenario, a piston breaking through the side of the engine. Tow the vehicle out of the water, remove and dry the spark plugs, dry the ignition system, then turn on the ignition, which will pump the water out of the combustion chamber. Once the water is out, you can reassemble the spark plugs and leads (taking care to get them in the right order!), then try the ignition or push start if your battery is low.

Note that if you are returning your hire car to the airport, you need to go back to the Arrivals desk (even though you are departing), as there are no car-rental desks in Departures. So remember to park the vehicle closer to this end of the airport entrance. Please note that the new terminal for Muscat International Airport is scheduled to open in 2017 and the details provided here will change when it does – go to www.bradtupdates.com/oman for the latest information.

Car-hire companies The majority of the car-rental companies listed here are in Muscat. Where they have branches in Salalah, this has been indicated. If you require something special, a chauffeur-driven limousine service is available and can be arranged through most of the larger hotels or major car-hire services.

AST Car Rental Head Office Muscat Al Khuwair: 24 571311; Salalah: 23 298085; e info@astoman.com; www.astoman.com

Avis Rent-a-Car Muscat International Airport: 24 510342; Al Bustan Palace Hotel: 24 769392; Muscat InterContinental Hotel: 24 601224; Salalah Airport: 24 601224; e avisoman@OmanTel.net.om; www.avisoman.com

Budget Rent-a-Car Muscat Airport: 24 510816; Head Office, Al Khuwair: 24 683999; Salalah Crowne Plaza: 23 235160; Salalah Airport: 23 290097; Suhar: 26 840392; Sur Plaza Hotel: 25 443777; e budgetom@OmanTel.net.om; www.budgetoman.com

Europcar Muscat Airport: 24 121165; Salalah Airport: 23 367186; e reservation@europcaroman.net; www.europcaroman.com

Global Car Rental Shati Al Qurum: 24 697140; Salalah: m 95 033731; Suhar: 26 840193; e global@alhashargroup.com; www.globalcarrental-oman.com

Hertz Al Wutayya: 24 566208; Muscat Airport: 24 521187; Salalah: 23 217338; Suhar: 26 943089; e nttoman@OmanTel.net.om; www.nttomanhertz.com

Mark Rent-a-Car Hatat Hse, Muscat: 24 562444; Muscat Airport: 24 510033; www.marktoursoman.com

Sixt Head Office, Al Qurum: 24 594922; Al Khuwair: 24 600793; Salalah: 23 290908; www.sixt.com/car-rental/oman

Thrifty Car Rental Al Khuwair: ☏ 24 489248; Muscat Airport: ☏ 24 521189; Salalah Airport: m 99 323619; Salalah City Centre: ☏ 23 211493; Suhar: ☏ 26 845565; e haditha@OmanTel.net.om; www.thrifty.com

Value Plus Rent a Car Muscat Head Office, Al Wutayya: ☏ 22 307000; Muscat Ghala: ☏ 24 597264; Muscat Airport: ☏ 24 510292; Suhar: ☏ 26 846470; Salalah Airport: ☏ 23 211058; e valueplus@otegroup.com; www.valueoman.com

By taxi Taxis are frequent and reliable and are the easiest means of transport in urban areas of Oman. Their orange and white colouring makes them particularly conspicuous. The turquoise and white versions are the airport taxis and the only taxis permitted to pick passengers up from the terminal, although dropping people off is open to all.

It is a good idea to clearly agree the fare beforehand and not accept the driver's 'you decide' suggestion, as taxis are unmetered, and there have been many stories of foreigners paying two or three times the going rate. The usual rate from Muscat Airport to Al Qurum is RO8, and this price is now fixed by the central airport taxi kiosk (page 79), whose licensed taxis are turquoise and white. All taxi drivers are Omani nationals, as this has been designated a protected profession (page 29). They can be hailed on any street, and, on quieter roads, if the driver sees you walking he may sound his horn to see if you need a taxi. The system is that you can share one of these taxis with other people if your destinations happen to tally, which is obviously cheaper, but in practice with foreigners the taxi drivers just tend to charge more and keep the taxi private to you. Tipping is not necessary, unless you particularly want to. The local etiquette is for women to sit in the back if the taxi is private.

Plans are afoot to introduce a metered taxi service in Muscat, operated by Mwasalat, but the general public and the government want metered taxis while the majority of drivers do not, so metering may never be generally introduced.

By minibus Sometimes called baisa buses, these are orange and white 13-seater van-type vehicles. They operate fixed routes and can be flagged down along the highway. Tell the driver your destination and he will tell you if he is going there. Be sure to confirm the fare before getting in. There is limited space for luggage. This is certainly the cheapest way of getting around and is used largely by the Asian workforce. A trip within Muscat will cost from 300bzs to around RO1.

BY BUS For longer journeys you might like to consider taking a bus. The long-distance ones have air conditioning and stop at regular intervals for refreshments. Bollywood and kung fu movies are the staple on-board entertainment, which will either help you to sleep or keep you awake, depending on your inclination. From Muscat it is possible to get a bus from Ruwi bus station (just off Al Jaame Street along from the Sheraton Hotel) adjacent to the old Sultan Qaboos Mosque in Ruwi (not the Sultan Qaboos Grand Mosque). They go to Salalah (in the south), Nizwa (in the Ad Dakhiliyah), Suhar (on Al Batinah coast), Al Buraymi (in the Adh Dhahirah), Ibra and Sur (in the Ash Sharqiyyah), and Dubai and Abu Dhabi (in the United Arab Emirates). Buses make several stops along the way at allocated pick-up/drop-off points. It is recommended that you make your booking a few days in advance, although it is possible to join any of the coach services on the spot if space allows, and simply pay your fare to the driver. The air-conditioned buses take around 40–45 people. No food is provided on the coaches so you might like to take some snacks and drinks along with you. Children under 12 travel for half price. Journeys that take you into Dubai, Abu Dhabi and Al Buraymi cross border posts where the coaches stop for the necessary visa procedures. For more on visas to the UAE, see page 172.

Mwasalat (previously the Oman National Transport Company) (*head office:* 24 701294; *Ruwi office:* 24 708522; *Salalah office:* 23 292773; e *ontc01@omantel. net.om; www.mwasalat.om*) is state-owned and the only company to offer the full range of destinations: Salalah, Dubai, Al Buraymi, Abu Dhabi, Sur and Suhar. There is a detailed timetable on its website. Its services include **Ruwi to Salalah** (*12hrs*) on the Salalah Express. Make your booking a few days in advance, or join any of the coach services on the spot if space allows, and simply pay your fare to the driver. You can pick up the bus at Ruwi, Burj Al Sahwa car park and Nizwa on the Salalah Road near Firq. Rest stops are made at Nizwa, Hayma and Thumrayt, with variable other stops. It is best to check on the website for up-to-date timings. Some people find the overnight bus to Salalah is preferable to relieve the boredom of the largely featureless landscape *en route*. If you are on a tight budget it also saves one night's accommodation. Other routes are Muscat to Salalah (route 100), Muscat to Al Buraymi (route 41), Muscat to Ibri (route 54), Muscat to Sur (route 55, stopping at Ibra and Al Mintarib), Muscat to Bani bu Ali (route 36, stopping at Qurayyat and Sur), Muscat to Dubai (route 201) and Salalah to Dubai (route 102, stopping at Nizwa and Al Buraymi).

The **Gulf Transport Company** (24 790823; *Salalah office:* 23 293303) operates daily coach services from Muscat to Salalah and from Salalah to Dubai. **Salalah Line Transport** (*Muscat office:* 24 709709; *Salalah office:* 23 293323; e *sltsalalah@yahoo.com*) offers coach services to and from Salalah only. It runs three daily services from Ruwi bus station in Muscat and three from Salalah.

MAPS Maps of Oman are available through Apex Press and Publishing. These can be bought online (*www.amazon.co.uk*) before departure more cheaply than in the country itself. The Ministry of Tourism also produces a decent free road map of the whole country, marking all the new highways, with the bonus of good city maps of Muscat, Mutrah, Suhar, Sur, Nizwa and Salalah on its reverse; pick one up just after immigration at Muscat International Airport. There are no detailed Ordnance Survey-type maps of Oman.

ACCOMMODATION

Muscat is home to some excellent **four- and five-star hotels** such as Al Bustan Palace, the Grand Hyatt, the Radisson Blu, the Chedi, and the Shangri-La Barr Al Jissah Resort (which comprises three hotels designed to appeal to different types of client). There are many **mid- and budget-range hotels** too, which offer good, clean

ACCOMMODATION PRICE CODES

Accommodation listings are laid out in decreasing price order, under the following categories: luxury, upmarket, mid range, budget and shoestring. The following key (also on the inside front cover) gives an indication of full prices. Prices are based on a double room (including tax) per night. In practice, discounts are often available and should be asked for.

$$$$$	RO150+
$$$$	RO110–150
$$$	RO70–110
$$	RO35–70
$	RO20–35

accommodation, so it is a misconception that the country can be visited only by the more affluent traveller. **Hotel apartments** are a cheaper way of staying in one place for longer periods, and a growing number of these can be found in Muscat. As tourism increases, the facilities and services available are likely to improve and become more competitive. In the off-season summer months many hotels advertise attractive discounts, while in the high seasons of autumn and spring, especially at festival times, there is a lot of pressure on availability of rooms. **Resthouses** offer good value for money and can be found along the main highways throughout the country. **Wild camping** is permitted anywhere well away from habitation or on undeveloped beaches. A range of accommodation listings is given in each chapter.

EATING AND DRINKING

Travelling around the country you will find plenty of local café-type restaurants. Although these are very basic, they offer a good, cheap way to eat when you are on the road. Chicken, mutton and fish are frequently on the menu. Vegetarians are also well catered for as large numbers of Indian expatriates are also vegetarian for religious reasons, so many Indian restaurants offer a range of vegetarian dishes, with fried vegetables and dhal available in most local restaurants. A big range of vegetarian *mezze* or starters based around tomatoes, onions and aubergines are on offer in all Arabic restaurants.

Each of the resthouses on the main highways has a restaurant, and although these are basic and unlicensed, the curries tend to be very good. Snacks can be bought at the food stores found beside most petrol stations, and within the shops of the petrol stations themselves. Supermarkets sell a good range of food and soft drinks suitable for picnics, and the Omanis themselves have a strong picnicking tradition, with the favourite weekend pastime involving the whole extended family bundling into the car, taking large quantities of food out into the countryside and sitting on mats with the children running around while the men wrestle with the barbecue and the women prepare the other food.

Higher-end restaurants can be found in hotels in major towns such as Nizwa. The star rating of the hotel is indicative of the price range of the restaurant. The capital has many excellent mid- to high-end restaurants both in and out of hotels.

Typical Omani cuisine is quite simple, with rice eaten as the main accompaniment to beef, mutton, chicken or fish. Spices are used to flavour the meat and fish, not hot and spicy ones but rather subtler and more aromatic

RESTAURANT PRICE CODES

Restaurant listings are laid out in decreasing price order, under the following categories: luxury, upmarket, mid range, budget and shoestring. The following key (also on the inside front cover) gives an indication of prices. Prices are based on the cost of two main meals (including tax).

$$$$$	RO25+
$$$$	RO16–25
$$$	RO11–16
$$	RO4–11
$	RO2.50–4

seasonings like cardamom, cinnamon, cumin, ginger, turmeric and saffron. Salads are simply lettuce, cucumber and tomato, with a slice of lime for dressing. A few local dishes to look out for are *maqbous*, a saffron-coloured rice dish cooked over spicy meat; *harees*, a wheat-based dish with chicken, tomato, onion and seasoning; *rabees*, boiled baby shark fried with liver (a Dhofari speciality); *shuwa*, marinated meat (goat, mutton, calf or camel) cooked for 24 hours in an earth oven with date juices and spices, wrapped in banana leaves and served on a giant communal tray called a *fadhl*; and *mashuai*, a whole spit-roasted kingfish with lemon rice. The main meal is eaten at midday, while the evening meal is lighter. If cutlery is not provided, only the right hand is used for eating.

Favourite **local drinks** are *laban*, heavy salty buttermilk and yoghurt flavoured with cardamom and ground pistachios. Fresh juices are also popular, made from fruits like mango, banana, pineapple and pomegranate, and are very cheap by Western standards. The sweet, sticky *halwa* is a popular dessert similar in concept to Turkish delight, and is made by men, with the recipe handed down from generation to generation. After the meal bitter cardamom coffee is traditionally served from brass long-spouted coffee pots into tiny china cup-like bowls.

The Omani government's attitude to **alcohol** is much more relaxed than in other parts of the Arabian Peninsula. It is widely available at hotels and some higher-end restaurants (both within and outside hotels) throughout the country. There are no standalone bars on the streets and the cheap local restaurants in every town or village throughout the country are unlicensed. Non-Muslim expatriates resident in Oman are permitted to apply for a liquor licence based on a percentage of their salary. This entitles them to buy alcohol from the discreet 'retail' shops distributed about the capital, and to drink in their homes. During Ramadhan, however, no alcohol is served, even in hotels. If you want to have some alcohol discreetly while visiting, your best bet is to buy some from the duty-free shop in the arrivals area at Muscat Airport (page 79) and to drink it in your hotel room.

PUBLIC HOLIDAYS

RELIGIOUS HOLIDAYS AND CELEBRATIONS Every year the religious holidays move forward by approximately 11 days in accordance with the lunar calendar. For local festivals, see the relevant chapters.

Prophet's Birthday (Mawlid Al Nabi)	11 December 2016*, 30 November 2017*, 19 November 2018*, 10 November 2019*
Ramadhan	27 May 2017*, 16 May 2018*, 6 May 2019*; Ramadhan lasts for 29 or 30 days
Eid Al Fitr (end of Ramadhan)	27 June 2017*, 16 June 2018*, 6 June 2019* for 3+ days
Eid Al Adha	2 September 2017*, 22 August 2018*, 12 August 2019* for 3+ days
Islamic New Year	22 September 2017*, 11 September 2018*, 31 August 2019*

*Islamic dating should be based on the actual observance of the crescent new moon at the start of a month from within a country. There is considerable debate about using a scientific method instead and there is also a concurrent debate regarding an announcement from Mecca to set the schedule. Oman generally sights the crescent moon a day after Saudi Arabia.

NON-RELIGIOUS HOLIDAYS

Renaissance Day   23 July (the date Sultan Qaboos became ruler) every year
National Day   18 November (also the birthday of Sultan Qaboos) every year

The actual 'day off' for a holiday may be given to provide an extended weekend.

SHOPPING

The main shopping complexes are in the Al Mawalih, Al Ghubra and Al Qurum areas of Muscat. In Nizwa the main shopping complexes are to be found in the Firq area, in Suhar on the main Al Batinah highway road 1 between the Yanqul Road and Wadi Hibi Road, and in Salalah near the junction of Route 49 and Atin Road. These are in the form of modern, air-conditioned malls and plazas, and sell perfumes, gold, souvenirs, furniture made in India or Egypt (to Omani style), household goods, stereos, computers, mobile phones, sports equipment, clothing and photographic equipment. Familiar brands include Body Shop, Boots, Carrefour, H&M, Mango, Marks & Spencer and Next, and for fast food Burger King, KFC, McDonald's and Pizza Hut. Of course, it's far better to discover new places to shop, and you will find Oman's acclaimed Amouage perfumes and from other countries Raymond's men's fabrics and suits, Al Faisal for perfumes and watches, and Leather and Later for exactly that. Most of these malls contain the chains Home Centre, Baby Shop, Giodano for jeans and the excellent Lulu supermarkets.

A traditional shopping trip is a must, and the suq (or traditional market) at Mutrah is *the* place to go for this Arabian experience, selling souvenirs, crafts, jewellery, perfumes and oils, wooden chests, fabrics and *dishdashas* (the usually white gown worn by Omani men), not to mention frankincense (pages 310–11). Suqs have been part of Omani culture for centuries, and many towns and villages in the country have one. It is a traditional market that doubles up as a meeting place. Those selling fruits and vegetables are well worth a visit, as they display a fantastic array of bright colours.

SOUVENIRS Omani silver *khanjars* (see box, page 36), traditional Omani silver jewellery, coffee pots and small silver boxes all make excellent souvenirs. A real antique *khanjar* will cost anything up to RO600, but souvenir imitations are available from RO40. Old Bedouin silver jewellery is also becoming increasingly scarce and pricey. Silver Maria Theresa dollars, which used to be the country's unit of currency, can still be bought fairly cheaply at around RO5. Omani rose water, perfumes, frankincense and myrrh are cheaper, smaller, yet still distinctive souvenirs. Frankincense, or *bakhoor* (a mixture of fragrances; see box on pages 310–11), and a frankincense burner make the perfect gift – Oman being famed for its frankincense production and trade throughout history. Slightly more intriguing, and certainly a topic of conversation when you get back home, would be the *hookah* pipe, also known as the *shisha* or *nargileh*, or simply as the water-pipe. Larger items are Omani and Indian chests, and Omani coffee tables (which use the concept of the traditional Omani door as the table top), which can be shipped or air freighted to you in your home country. *Mandoos* (Omani chests) come in all sizes, so the smallest (which is jewellery-box size) may be a more practical purchase in terms of transporting it home. See also pages 97–8 for artisan/furniture shops.

The *dishdasha* makes a souvenir gift to be worn, and is great to wear about the house after a shower or as a dressing gown. Omani dates make a consumable small gift for friends and family, and you can always combine this with a packet of Omani coffee (mixed with cardamom), which will undoubtedly evoke memories of your Oman experience. Visit the suqs at Mutrah, Nizwa and Salalah for your souvenirs.

ACTIVITIES

The terrain of Oman, along with its climate, makes it perfect for the adventure tourist with a love of the outdoors. Since mountain and desert dominate the country's geography, mountain trekking, rock climbing, caving and wadi driving are all widely available. The treks, climbs and caves are graded in terms of difficulty. There are now many bolted climbing routes in the mountains, and for the real enthusiasts there are even *via ferrata* wire-lines in places such as the upper reaches of Snake Gorge. The Ministry of Tourism (*www.omantourism. gov.om*) has developed a set of walking tours and a booklet describing these routes. There are spectacular gorges and old mountain villages to see, and camping is very popular.

The beaches are also public, so you can walk a full 20km along the sand from Al Qurum to As Sib, for example. If you prefer water-based activities, then scuba diving, sailing, snorkelling, canoeing, dolphin and whale watching, dhow cruising and game fishing are all available. See pages 136, 173 and 296 for details of specialist local tour operators offering these activities. Nature and wildlife lovers can birdwatch, turtle watch, camp or picnic in the mountains or quiet coastal bays.

If local history or architecture are of interest, there are museums, mosques, forts and castles to explore (and these proliferate throughout the country). Culture lovers also have the Royal Opera House Muscat (*www.rohmuscat.org.om*) to satisfy their need for high-level opera, ballet or theatrical performances, often from internationally renowned touring companies (page 94).

For those keen on physical fitness, there is a good selection of gyms and health clubs within the hotels, with swimming pools and tennis and squash courts attached. The beaches or beach roads are perfect for jogging. Visiting the suqs provides a fascinating glimpse into traditional Oman, while air-conditioned, modern shopping complexes give it its familiar Westernised feel. If you want to do nothing, there are some excellent, luxury hotels, some with private beaches, where you can simply relax.

ENTRY FEES AND PERMITS Oman's focus on the promotion of its tourism industry means that its forts and other historical buildings of significance are on rolling schedules to undergo restoration programmes. As a result, one or other of the forts is always likely to be closed for restoration, because their mud-brick constructions require regular maintenance, especially after heavy rains.

It costs between 500bzs and RO1 to visit most forts (payable at the door); others have no-one at the door and you can wander around freely at no charge,

Announcements are made in the local paper of the names of people who are being given their automatic 600m^2 of land by the state. Men have been entitled to this gift from the sultan since 1970, but in 2010 the law was amended to allow women to benefit as well. Unmarried women are prioritised, as are divorced women. Everyone is entitled to this land in the province where they were born, hence the massive land housing boom around Muscat in areas like Bawshar. The plot size is generous, enough to build a spacious detached villa with a large garden. The usual pattern is to start by building a high wall around the perimeter for privacy, then to continue as and when funds permit.

and some may be closed during opening times, so do interpret the opening times shown in this guide generously.

For turtle-watching sites you can get a ticket at the entrance of the Ras Al Jinz site itself (page 267) if visiting numbers permit (pre-booking is suggested through Ras Al Jinz Hotel). To dive the Ad Dimaniyyat Islands (page 144), the permit is easily obtained for you by any dive centre arranging the dive trip, at a rough cost of RO30 for two dives. The bureaucracy involved in obtaining permission to visit places of interest has been relaxed as part of the country's initiative to facilitate tourism.

PHOTOGRAPHY

The scenery of the country is superb for photography. The only places where it is not permitted are government and military buildings. Photographing Omani women can be offensive to them – it is safest to ask permission (and permission should generally be asked of men as well). '*Mumkin sura, minfadluk?*' is Arabic for 'May I take your picture, please?' If it's a woman, it is likely that you will be refused. By contrast, Omani men are usually happy to be photographed.

MEDIA AND COMMUNICATIONS

NEWSPAPERS The English-language newspapers in Oman are the new-entry *Muscat Daily* (*www.muscatdaily.com*), which now boasts the largest circulation in the sultanate, with 33,000 copies distributed daily from Saturday to Wednesday; the *Times of Oman* (*www.timesofoman.com*); the *Oman Observer* (*www.omanobserver.om*); the *Oman Tribune* (*omantribune.com*); and *The Week*, a free weekly tabloid (*www.theweek.co.om*). *Muscat Daily* is owned by Apex Publishing and caused a stir by covering the 2011 Suhar protests extensively. Foreign newspapers can be bought in the larger hotels, supermarkets and in some bookshops, but they are not cheap.

MAGAZINES The *Oman Economic Review* (*oeronline.com*) and *Business Today* (*www.businesstoday.co.om*) are monthly business magazines, while *Faces Oman* (*www.facesoman.com*) and *Y* magazine (*www.y-oman.com*) are weekly free general-interest magazines. Gulf editions of glossy and not-so-glossy magazines from Dubai also cover Oman, among them *Ahlan!* (gossip), *Arabian Business*, *Cosmopolitan Middle East*, *Emirates Home Magazine*, *Esquire Middle East*, *Harper's Bazaar Middle East*, *Masala!* (Bollywood), *Men's Health*, *OK! Middle East* and *Time Out Muscat*.

TELEVISION AND RADIO There is one terrestrial television broadcaster in Oman, namely the state-owned Oman TV, which is operated by the Ministry of Information. It broadcasts two channels, one in Arabic and the other in English.

Radio stations include the English-language Merge 104.8 FM and HiFM 95.9 FM, both of which focus on pop music and local interest, while the government-owned Oman Radio 90.4 FM plays an eclectic mix of pop and classical music and local interest pieces. The BBC World Service is also available on 103.2 FM. All frequencies given here are for Muscat.

TELEPHONE The **country code for Oman** if dialling from abroad is 968 followed by the local number. International calls made from Oman are cheapest from 21.00 until 07.00. Local calls are around 25bzs for 3 minutes.

Public telephones are rapidly becoming unusable as they are not maintained owing to lack of use, and the cards to use them are not widely available.

Land line numbers are six digits and are prefixed with a two-digit area code (eg: 24 for Muscat, 23 for Dhofar, 26 for Musandam and Al Batinah coast, and 25 for the interior and Ash Sharqiyyah).

Mobile phones

Your first option is to check with your mobile-phone provider in your country of residence as to whether they have a roaming agreement with one of the networks in Oman. An alternative is to purchase a SIM card from OmanTel, Ooredoo and Frendi, available at airport counters (and in the phone company's retail outlets which can be found throughout the country, most readily in the major malls). OmanTel has good network coverage throughout the country. Ooredoo has good 4G coverage, especially in major towns, as does Frendi, a mobile virtual network operator that uses the services of either OmanTel or Ooredoo.

Internet packages for mobile phones are available but need to be 'programmed' into your mobile (it's an easy process – if you buy a SIM card at the airport, ask the counter staff to assist you).

Scratch cards and computer-generated slips are used to top up your balance and these are readily available at petrol stations, supermarkets and in some small shops, in various amounts. They last an age. Hayyak top-up cards are used for OmanTel phones (*www.omantel.om*), with Oredoo (*www.ooredoo.om*) and Frendi (*www.friendimobile.om*) mobiles requiring cards of the same name as the brand.

Mobile numbers are prefixed with a 9 and have the same country code as fixed lines.

Useful telephone numbers

AAA (car breakdown services) ☎24 605555
OmanTel call centre ☎1234
Ooredoo ☎1500 (from an Ooredoo number; m 95 011500 (from any other number)
Emergency services ☎9999
Royal Oman Police Muscat: ☎24 560099; Salalah: ☎23 290099

Flight information Send an SMS with your flight number from an Oman-registered mobile number to ☎90016. For Oman Air flights use ☎90910 (Ooredoo customers only). Alternatively, check online at www.omanairports.co.om.

INTERNET Oman has two fixed-line internet service providers, OmanTel and Ooredoo. Both also offer **USB modems**, which operate a 4G connection dependent on signal strength and can be connected to a computer. SIM cards are purchased with the USB modem and recharged by scratch card.

Wi-Fi is available in many coffee shops, restaurants and hotels (very few charge) and also available in some public areas such as airports and Muscat's public parks; a sign-on is required.

There are a few **internet cafés**, notably on Mutrah's corniche, just east of the suq entrance. The old and the new sit side by side like respectful neighbours. Aside from the financial savings to be made by visiting an internet café on the street, it is also a good way of immersing yourself in local culture.

In Oman the internet is monitored and any site considered offensive to the country's religious, moral, cultural or political mores will be blocked.

POST OFFICES Post offices are open 07.30–14.00 Sunday–Thursday. They aren't always easy to find, but their blue and white envelope logo is distinctive. See page 98 for a list of post offices in Muscat.

This is the cheapest way of sending postcards or parcels home, with a postcard to any country outside the GCC region costing only 300bzs. More expensive but more convenient is to ask your hotel to do it for you. Some souvenir shops, bookshops and newsagents also sell stamps.

CULTURAL ETIQUETTE

On greeting, people of the same sex shake hands. For friends and family the handshake is often accompanied by kissing, which is a gentle touch to both cheeks, and is sometimes repeated for close friends. Kissing between men in this way is common. Some people from desert areas will lightly touch noses. Omanis themselves do not shake hands with the opposite sex, especially if they have never met before. If you are female it is for you to offer or refuse to shake an Omani man's hand; a polite refusal is suggested.

If you are invited to an Omani's home, it is customary to remove your shoes at the door before entering the house. *Qahwa* (a strong, bitter coffee flavoured with cardamom) and dates are offered, and it is considered impolite to refuse, even if you are not hungry or thirsty. Once the first cup of coffee (served in a tiny bowl-like container) is consumed, it is then fine to refuse further top-ups. To indicate that you have finished, the cup is gently shaken (or tilted) from side to side. Usually, even

THE EVIL EYE

The concept of the evil eye is common throughout the Arab and Islamic world, even though the origin of the evil eye is Roman, not Islamic. Early Roman mosaics such as those found in Antakya (ancient Antioch) in modern Turkey have graphic depictions of a huge human eye being attacked by a range of weapons and surrounded by devils, illustrating the concept behind it, namely that to openly admire something that belongs to someone else will cast an evil spell on it and bring harm. To protect from this, there are set prayers from the Quran that people can say and expressions such as 'Mashallah' (literally 'what God wills'). The commonest form of protection, however, is the glassy blue eye that can be bought everywhere and is to be seen hanging in people's cars, homes and elsewhere, often on keyrings, bracelets and pendants. Newborn babies are always given such pendants by their families and close friends to protect them from the envious glances of admirers.

in less traditional domestic settings, food is served to be eaten while sitting on the floor. It is quite normal for gatherings to be single-sex groups. The right hand is used for eating from a communal plate, and the same hand is used for holding drinking glasses, though if the right hand is covered with rice the left hand holds the glass and the right hand is placed symbolically at the base of the glass. There is not much talk at Omani mealtimes. This is normal, as the focus is on eating, so do not feel that you have to make small talk to fill the silences. The custom is to leave almost immediately after eating. Often the food is served late, especially if there is a surprise visit, so talking and socialising take place beforehand.

DRESS CODE Considering Oman is a Muslim country, the dress code is relatively relaxed. While Omanis may not comment on it, your style of dress is noted and interaction based on that. As a gesture of respect it is advisable for men to wear loose clothes that cover the shoulders and long trousers that are therefore not too revealing. Shorts, T-shirts and sleeveless tops are fine for the beach, but to be avoided in the shopping complexes and suqs, or for touring the villages and sites of the interior (where the dress code is more conservative). Women will find lightweight and loose-fitting opaque cotton long-sleeved blouses, ankle-length trousers and long 'maxi' style skirts are perfect all year round. Lightweight jackets, jumpers or shawls may be needed for your comfort in winter. Swimwear, preferably one-piece, not bikinis, is fine for private hotel beaches and pools. If Omani women do enter the sea they may do so fully clothed, even including their black *abaya*. During the holy month of Ramadhan it is respectful to observe the dress code strictly.

BUSINESS ETIQUETTE In business, it is advisable to wait for the Omani party to initiate the greeting. As in social etiquette, people of the same sex will shake hands and a female will be the person to decide to offer her hand to shake a man's hand. A customary greeting is *salaam alaykum*, meaning 'peace be with you'. This is followed by *kaif halek*, meaning 'How are you?' When offered coffee, it is considered impolite to refuse. It is acceptable, however, to refuse refills.

The left hand is considered unclean, so always eat with your right hand. Showing the bottom of your shoe or foot is offensive. Using a 'thumbs up' gesture might in the past have been considered rude, but times have changed and Facebook has made it a universally known symbol of approval. When offered

---

ARABIC LANGUAGE SCHOOLS

Oman is capitalising on the flight of foreigners wanting to learn Arabic from the previous favourites of Egypt, Syria and Tunisia. The turbulence of the Arab Spring barely touched Oman and it continues to be seen as a rare model of stability in the Arab world. The **Sultan Qaboos College for Teaching Arabic Language to Non-Native Speakers** (◊ 25 212044; www.sqca.edu.om) in Manah (just outside Nizwa) is the ideal way to learn Arabic to the highest standard. The courses include theoretical and practical language tuition and accommodation is provided close to the classrooms. Also offering tuition is the **Noor Majan Training Institute** (*www.noormajan-institute.com*) in the more remote town of Ibri, 2 hours' drive inland from Muscat. Accommodation is with host families, with small classes of up to six students and four-week courses of 4 hours' teaching per day at beginner, intermediate, advanced I and advanced II levels.

BUYING PROPERTY AS A FOREIGNER

In 2005, the Omani government introduced new laws permitting foreigners to buy property, but only within integrated tourism complexes like Al Mouj close to As Sib, Muscat Hills Golf and Country Club, As Sifah, Barr Al Jissah south of Muscat, and the Salalah Beach Resort. This was followed in 2007 by residency rights, extendable to immediate family members, once the title deed has passed to the buyer's name. By opening up the country to foreign investors and simultaneously expanding its tourism infrastructure, the thinking is such projects will play a big role in offsetting the country's future reliance on oil revenues. Property ownership in these complexes is 75% foreign, mainly comprising Indian nationals. Prices are reasonable and very stable, with a one-bed flat costing around US$275,000 and a five-bed villa with pool US$3,900,000. Foreign owners are also permitted to have 'buy to let' arrangements. The property can be sold any time after its construction is complete, and residency then passes to the new owner. If you die owning Omani property the laws of your native country apply to inheritance, so make sure that you have a valid will. If no heirs present themselves within a year the Ministry of Tourism will manage the property for up to 15 years, then take ownership itself. There may be an extension of the locations in which foreigners may buy property.

Useful websites include www.expatarrivals.com and www.engelvoelkers.com.

a gift, it is impolite to refuse. On visiting an Omani's home take a gift of chocolates, nuts or dates, not flowers. Do not come empty-handed. Most mosques in Oman are not open to non-Muslims, but if your host invites you to view a particular one and presses the invitation, you are then able to enter after removing footwear. Women should wear a large headscarf. Do not discuss the subject of women, even if to enquire about an Omani man's wife or family. Avoid admiring an item to excess, as your host may feel obliged to give it to you.

Expect communication to be slow. Do not feel obliged to speak in periods of silence. Meetings can often be interrupted by phone calls and visits from your host's friends and family. Bear in mind that the Omani doing all the talking is often not the decision-maker. The decision-maker may be the silent observer, most especially if a more senior person.

Business dress code For foreign businesswomen, high necklines are a must and sleeves at least to the elbows are expected. Skirts should cover the knees well and preferably be ankle-length. An alternative is loose ankle-length trousers. As with the general social dress code (page 68), clothes should not be figure-hugging; aim for a baggy, loose-fitting look. For foreign businessmen, a lounge suit with traditional shirt and tie are ideal for business meetings. Men should avoid wearing visible jewellery.

TRAVELLING POSITIVELY

When travelling through Oman there are many small things you can do to give something back to the place that you have had the privilege of exploring. Every action, no matter how small, counts. Consider that in a village or even the terraced fields of Al Jabal Al Akhdar, you are enjoying the result of hundreds of years of work, so do try to make a contribution to the local economy.

The structure of Arabic names is quite different from what we are used to in the West. Everyone has a name given at birth, often taken from the Quran, such as Mohammad, Ali or Fatima, and also taken from a government-approved list. The government is able to veto names it deems unsuitable. This first name is then followed by *bin,* meaning 'son of' in the case of a boy, or *bint,* meaning 'daughter of' for a girl, followed by the name of their father, such as Mohammad bin Ahmad or Fatima bint, Ahmad, where a brother and sister's father is called Ahmad. The final part of the name is the family or tribal name, which is very important and helps distinguish between the thousands of Mohammads and Fatimas. So a full name might be Mohammad bin Ahmad Al-Harthy, showing that this Mohammad bin Ahmad is from the Harthy tribe. Again, unlike in the West, when a woman marries she does not change her name to her husband's, but simply stays the same, as her tribe has not changed – the total opposite of what we might expect. Arabs find it very odd, given the supposed equality of women in our society, that Western women often take their husband's name on marriage.

Respect the locals and their right to privacy. Bear in mind that it is their home territory, so when driving in a 4x4 in remote areas, do not zoom straight through the middle of a village, but explore on foot (noting any signs prohibiting entry). It is also essential to show respect by being dressed conservatively, with women especially being well covered up with loose clothing at least to the knee and at least three-quarter-length sleeves – no cleavage, tight-fitting tops or bare shoulders. The less flesh on display the better. Women should not swim in pools within a village environment, and at all times wear conservative one-piece costumes. Naked swimming in wadi pools is a no-no and if done you may spend several nights in prison before deportation. Ask permission before taking any photographs, and be aware that Omani women and girls will often refuse. Omani men and boys will often enthusiastically oblige. If you have a digital camera, showing Omani children their picture on the screen invariably delights them. Be aware that most adults do have smartphones with cameras and that high-end DSLR cameras and their expensive zoom lenses are also surprisingly common, so you are not demonstrating a novelty and the subject that you are surreptitiously taking a photo of may be very much aware of what you are doing.

Look after your immediate environment. Limit your water usage. Do not leave water running. Take a shower if you can, rather than use the bath. Turn lights off in hotel rooms when they are not absolutely necessary. Re-use towels (hang them back on the rail, so they will not be considered laundry). Limit your use of air conditioning, if possible. Always dispose of your own rubbish after camping or picnicking.

Purchase any locally made artefacts. Buy a pot from the Aladawi pottery factory in Bahla, or a rug from the locals selling their weavings in Jabal Shams and Al Jabal Al Akhdar. Don't forget the essential purchase of frankincense and a burner – you will have become part of an ancient trading history in this commodity. Every small amount you give helps to sustain the heritage and keep alive longstanding Omani traditions.

Eat at local restaurants and coffee shops – your valued rials will help in keeping these small businesses running. Buy some fruit at a suq or roadside stall. Stay at any of the static camps in the country, for example those in the Wihibah Sands; these make trips out to Bedouin camps where you will share lunch in a traditional home. Simply by demonstrating their way of life to you, the Bedu are able to benefit financially, so by using the camps, you are making a contribution to their living.

Respect the rules when visiting nature reserves and sanctuaries. Take care not to disturb the wildlife in any way. This is their habitat. Adhere to the list of dos and don'ts when it comes to viewing the nesting turtles (see box, page 266). Don't touch the coral when scuba diving or snorkelling – it causes damage.

Make that little bit of extra effort to find out more about the local charities shown at the end of this chapter. There are also collection boxes in some supermarkets, especially at the checkouts in Lulu. You might be able to help. Perhaps you can volunteer your time, knowledge or assistance in bringing awareness to their cause in some way when back in your country of residence. There may be a new project underway at the time of your visit. Do give them a call.

CHARITIES AND ORGANISATIONS

A'Noor Association for the Blind ✆ 24 483118; e anoorab@omantel.net.om; e bshahbal@hotmail. com (email address of the vice-president, who speaks good English); www.alnoor4blind.org.om
Association for Early Intervention for Children with Special Needs ✆ 24 496960; e earlyint@omantel.net.om; www.aei.org.om. Looks after children from birth to 6 years of age. Hassan Moosa (m 99 324882) is responsible for marketing & fundraising.
Association for the Disabled ✆ 24 490502; e oadisabl@omantel.net.om. Provide support & equipment to disabled people 16 years & older.
Association for the Welfare of Handicapped Children ✆ 24 596502; e awhoc@omantel.net. om. Looks after children from 6 to 15 years of age.
Dar Al Atta ✆ 24 692996; e info@daralatta. org; www.daralatta.org. A charity that since 2002 has given assistance to underprivileged families throughout Oman.
Geological Society of Oman e gso.network@ gmail.com; www.gso-oman.org. This organisation

facilitates knowledge-sharing among the country's geology experts, advancing science & increasing awareness in the lay community of the importance & relevance of its work.
Oman Cancer Association ✆ 24 498716; e ocancer@omantel.net.om; www.oca.om. This well-established charity aims to create awareness, support patients & their families & fundraise.
Omani Charitable Organisation Al Khuwair St 33, Bldg no 173, Muscat; ✆ 24 297992; e oconet@ omantel.net.om; www.oco.org.om. Assists needy families, orphans, senior citizens & the disabled.
Royal Geographical Society www.rgs.org. Promotes geographical research & advances geography, nationally & internationally. The Queen is its patron. In Oman it ran the Wahiba Sands Project (page 255).
United Nations Children's Fund (UNICEF) – Oman www.unicef.org. International aid agency assisting & advising Oman on all aspects of child development, malnutrition reduction, education & protection.

Practical Information TRAVELLING POSITIVELY

2

Part Two

THE GUIDE

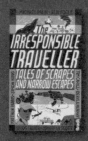

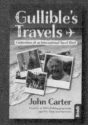

3

Muscat مسقط

Muscat, which is on the northeast coast of Oman, lies on a trade route that is both internationally and regionally important, and has been for centuries. The Sea of Oman, which Muscat faces, in the past was a route to Mesopotamia, Persia and northwest India, while today it is a conduit for oil flowing out of the Arabian Gulf and manufactured products coming in. Regionally it straddles one of the few natural routes from the Sea of Oman through the Al Hajar Mountains to the areas beyond.

Muscat is like a *matryoshka* doll, with smaller versions of itself inside. There are four areas called Muscat, and depending on the context the place being described might be the little tiny Muscat in the centre or the larger one that envelops the others.

Muscat is one of Oman's 11 governorates and to cover its **administrative area** would mean driving 187km from end to end, from near An Naseem Park in Muscat Governorate's northwest to near Fins in the southeast, north of Sur. This area includes empty mountain plateaux of almost 1,500m in height and Muscat's commercial heartland. Within this area is the built-up city that is also referred to as Muscat, a largely linear city set between the striking mountains to the south and the Sea of Oman to the north; its coastal plain is never more than 12km wide. This version of Muscat includes the areas of As Sib, Al Athaiba, Al Khuwair, Madinat Al Sultan Qaboos, Ruwi, Al Amrat, Mutrah and Muscat (one of the smaller versions), a drive from one end to the other of around 73km. In this book the area between As Sib and Muscat is referred to for the most part as the **Capital Area**. Then there is what is increasingly referred to as **'Old Muscat'**, the area between the Muscat Gate Museum and the residential area south of Al Alam Palace. Finally, and being more precise than is really needed there is the **area enclosed by Muscat's city walls**, which includes Al Alam Palace, the two Portuguese forts and the historic harbour. These make up the original, historical Muscat. All these other areas outside the walls have different names which are useful to know if you need to ask the taxi driver to take you to the mosque in Al Ghubra South rather than the mosque in Old Muscat. When mentioning Muscat in this guide, the built-up city known as the Capital Area is meant, while 'Old Muscat' is used to specify the area between the Muscat Gate Museum and the residential area called Takia south of Al Alam Palace, though occasionally the 'governorate of Muscat' is specified where needed.

Muscat's Capital Area has a grand yet intimate setting. A range of mountains tower over the city, rising to a height of 500m. These mountains have a number of valleys that have been cut into the mountainsides and where settlements have been built, while the separation of each one by the hills has enabled those more interlinked communities such as Al Hamriyyah, Al Wadi Al Kabir and indeed Old Muscat itself to develop separate identities.

There are two distinct rock formations in Muscat's Capital Area, the higher being sedimentary limestone and the lower igneous ophiolite rock. The limestone ranges between the Permian period limestone of approximately 299 to 251 million years

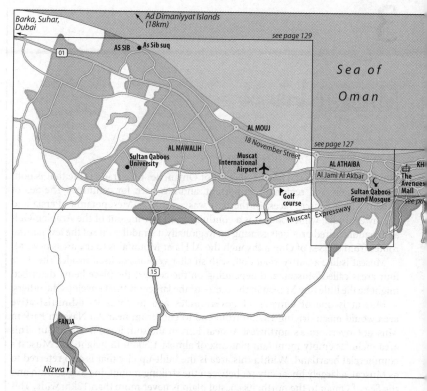

see page 129

see page 127

ago and the Eocene epoch of around 55.8 to 33.9 million years ago. Ranged around Mutrah and Old Muscat are the chocolate-brown ophiolite formations of igneous rock that were obducted onto the Arabian plate from about 90 million years ago (see page 4 for further information).

Muscat dominates all aspects of Oman's economy. The engine of Oman's wealth – oil – is delivered into Muscat by underground pipeline from the deserts all over the country and transferred to oil tankers just off the coast at Mina Al Fahl port. Other industry is located in the Ghala industrial area and Ar Rusayl Industrial Estate southwest of the airport. Service businesses are scattered throughout the city, with banking head offices moving away from the Mutrah Business District towards the airport. Muscat International Airport and the sea port of Mina Sultan Qaboos are key players in the arrival of people into Oman. Retailing and wholesaling are still dominated by Muscat nationally, although less so than a few years ago, with major shopping malls found in Al Qurum, Al Ghubra South and Al Mawalih. Private education and healthcare are becoming increasingly important to the economy and act alongside the excellent government-provided services. Government ministries are scattered from Old Muscat to Al Khuwair, where most of the ministries are found, though a few have relocated to just south of the airport. The cultural scene is dominated by the Royal Opera House and National Museum, with other much smaller cultural centres and art galleries in several areas of the Capital Area. The popularity of football is supported within the Capital Area by several major stadiums and football clubs from Oman's football league.

With 1,281,232 people, **Muscat Governorate** has 32% of Oman's population. The most populous areas are Bawshar (which includes the residential areas of Al Qurum,

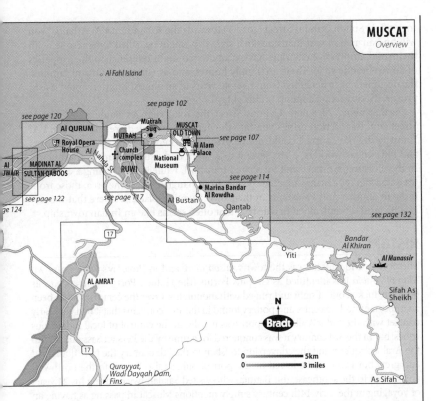

MUSCAT
Overview

Al Fahl Island

see page 120

see page 102

Mutrah
Suq

AL QURUM

MUSCAT
OLD TOWN

Royal Opera
House

MUTRAH

see page 107

Al Alam
Palace

AL
JWAIR

MADINAT AL
SULTAN QABOOS

Al Nahda St.

Church
complex

National
Museum

RUWI

see page 122

see page 117

see page 114

Marina Bandar
Al Rowdha

ge 124

Al Bustan

see page 132

Qantab

Bandar
Al Khiran

Yiti

Al Munassir

AL AMRAT

Sifah As
Sheikh

N

Bradt

0 ———— 5km
0 ———— 3 miles

Qurayyat,
Wadi Dayqah Dam,
Fins

As Sifah

Al Khuwair and Al Athaiba) with 395,725 people and As Sib with 362,102, followed by Mutrah, Muscat, Al Amrat and Qurayyat. Overall, the Muscat population is 62% non-Omanis, most of whom are from the Indian subcontinent, and 38% Omani nationals.

Muscat, as with the rest of Oman, has a built environment that is very much human in scale. Though buildings may hope to impress they never overwhelm you in the way that Dubai has done with the canyon of the Sheikh Zayed Road. The overall impression of Muscat has to be one of restraint, expressed in a style that is increasingly recognisable as Omani. As with much in Oman, this is a top-down influence: the buildings associated with Sultan Qaboos, such as the guest palace, National Museum and Royal Opera House, have had an influence on other government buildings. Oman does not have an iconic world-renowned building simply because, as yet, Oman does not attract the numbers of visitors who would spread its fame. However, two are world class in all respects and deserve to be more widely known. The understated exterior and immensely impressive interior of the Sultan Qaboos Grand Mosque (page 128) should be more generally appreciated. The quality of craftsmanship is remarkable and sense of purpose clearly defined. A more recent arrival is the Royal Opera House (page 94). It shares with the Sultan Qaboos Mosque a quality of material that is superb and enjoys an auditorium whose seats, with few exceptions, have an intimate connection to the stage that should provide an evening of pleasure whatever the performance. If you can, book a seat for any performance during your visit to Muscat.

Driving away from the airport's terminal, the overwhelming impression is of a spacious, well-planned and affluent city. New and remarkably clean vehicles glide along the broad highway, whose street lights are capped by gilded crowns. Taking a

Muscat

3

turn off Al Sultan Qaboos Street (road 1) towards the sea and into Al Athaiba, you will find an area of vast mansions in a style that might be called Omanesque, with their solid, impressive exteriors having an ever so slight reference to the fripperies of an Arabesque style. These are family homes, and as with most Omani families, the occupiers have benefited from over 40 years of an almost uninterrupted rise in prosperity. Supercars abound in this glitzy boomtown.

Further along Al Sultan Qaboos Street the road changes name to Al Nahda Street, and this section brings you into the densely populated area of Ruwi and Al Hamriyyah. The contrast could not be greater, for here live the foreign labourers and blue-collar workers, often several to a room and usually sharing apartments. In the morning, workers wait for shared transport, while in the evening a chat over tea and a cigarette brings together people from Bangladesh in one area, those from India in another and Pakistanis in their own favoured place. It's here that the city is at its most vibrant, albeit in a district that often seems like an Indian township.

HISTORY

The port in Old Muscat was the town's *raison d'etre* and in Ptolemy's 1st-century-AD *Map of Arabia* it is identified as Cryptus Portus (the Hidden Port), a reference to its position, tucked out of sight and ringed with mountains. Over the centuries it has been an important trading centre and pottery found in the area confirms that it had very early contact with the Indus Valley. The port was usually in the control of local indigenous tribes, but in the 3rd century it was conquered for a time by the Persian Sassanids. With the Arab conquests and the conversion to Islam in the 7th century the port flourished and grew but was overshadowed by the port of Suhar (also Sohar) to the northwest and Qalhat to the southeast. Ibn Battuta, who visited Salalah twice during his 24 years of voyaging in the early 14th century simply mentions Muscat in passing as having an abundance of fish. However, by the end of the 15th century the town had become a key port of call in the Arabian Sea trade, with its first Russian visitor, Afanasy Nikitin, in 1472 and the Arab merchant Ahmed Bin Majid calling it 'a port unequalled in the world' in 1500. However, it was the visit by another foreigner, Afonso de Albuquerque, who despite destroying the town also sparked Muscat's rise to power.

In 1507, the Portuguese, led by Afonso de Albuquerque, arrived in Muscat and, upon encountering resistance, proceeded to slaughter the men, women and children of the town. They then went on to occupy it, holding it for over a century. After the conquest of the town, de Albuquerque wrote:

> Muscat is a very large and populous town, flanked on both sides with high mountains, and the front is close to the water's edge; behind, towards the interior, there is a plain as large as the square of Lisbon all covered with salt pans. There are orchards, gardens and palm groves with wells for watering them by means of swipes and other engines. The harbour is small, shaped like a horseshoe, and sheltered from every wind.

Through the 16th century Portugal ruled Muscat and most of Oman's major coastal ports. The Ottoman Turks, who since 1509 had been sending military expeditions against Portuguese holdings around the Arabian Sea, briefly captured Muscat in 1552 and in 1580 looted the town. By the mid 17th century Portugal's strength was insufficient to retain most of their fortified settlements around this vast ocean and in 1650 their time in Oman drew to a close. The imam who ruled the north of Oman sent an army of fighters who eventually forced the Portuguese to leave. In the 18th century, the Persians made a few attempts to take Muscat, adding to regional insecurity, but the Al Bu Said dynasty's founder saved the situation and restored Muscat to local control. By assuming power in 1744 he gave rise to the current dynasty, which has ruled Oman ever since.

GETTING THERE AND AWAY

BY AIR Most international airlines serving Oman fly into Muscat International Airport on the western edge of the Capital Area, close to the coast and a 30- to 40-minute drive from the centre. See also page 45.

There is a currency exchange desk immediately in front of you as you enter the airport building from the plane, and you need to pay for your tourist visa here. Visas cost RO20 for a month or RO5 for ten days and may be paid for in foreign currency or by credit card. If you pay in foreign currency, you will be given your change in rials.

Once through passport control/immigration, there is a small duty-free shop on the left, which also sells alcohol. You are permitted to take two litres into the country (and if you are staying at one of the upper-range hotels, you might like to consider doing so, if you want to save a small fortune on the cost of the same in the minibar in your room). A little further on past this shop are the luggage carousels. Once you have taken your luggage through the security check, you reach the Arrivals area where there are some cafés, cashpoints (which accept a multitude of cards), plenty of car-rental desks and also phone company desks selling SIM cards onto which you can load paid internet access.

When leaving Muscat by air, the departures area has two business-class lounges on the ground floor. If you don't have access to these, take the escalators up to the first floor, where there is a licensed bar, some cafés, a bookshop, music shop, souvenir shop and a small duty-free shopping area.

Airport transfers You can catch a **minibus** (*600bzs pp into central Muscat, paid directly to the driver at the end of the journey*), or take a normal saloon/sedan orange and white **taxi** from the main road (*RO5 for a typical journey to Mutrah*). Both of these options will drop you at any place along the road on their route. The alternative and best choice for a private hire from the airport is to take one of the turquoise and white taxis immediately outside Arrivals into the city centre (📞 *24 341297;* e *taxi@omanairports.com; RO15 to the Shangri-La or RO24 to the Sifawy Hotel*). To hire one of these turquoise and white taxis approach the kiosk to the right after you exit the terminal and tell the man in the office your destination. You pay the fixed fare to him and receive a chit in exchange, which is then presented to the taxi driver. This payment is only for these turquoise and white taxis and though the fare is higher, the convenience on arrival is probably worth the extra cost.

Burj Al Sahwa roundabout, a few minutes' drive west of the airport, is the main taxi hub for locations to the north, northwest of Muscat and some eastern areas, while the main car park is used by taxis to Nizwa, Ibri and also Ibra. Taxis congregate for Al Batinah areas on the eastern side of the roundabout. Prices for a fully 'engaged' taxi (page 80) are RO15 to Barka and RO40 to Ar Rustaq and Suhar; bear in mind that all of the fares given here can be negotiated down. Fares will be less if the taxi is 'shared' or in a minibus, in which case you would pay RO5 to Suhar at the very most. If you are sharing, be prepared to take one taxi part of the way and have to take a different taxi farther on. Do not take any taxi without clearly having an agreed price from the driver or having paid for a fare at the airport kiosk.

Mwasalat red **buses** are available from the footbridge, with the fare less than RO1 to any destination in Muscat. **Long-distance coaches** stop either near the

Be prepared for several different spellings of the same place names on road signs, in books and so on. Maps and spellings in Oman are often very different from those in French-speaking North Africa: as an example, a mountain in Oman is officially *jabal* (often *jebel* in books), whereas in North Africa it may be given as *djebel*. This is because of varying interpretations of the transliteration and pronunciation of Arabic. In general, if they would sound similar and are in the same general location, two different spellings in Roman script may well refer to the same place.

Landmarks are often used to provide reference points; these may be a monumental sculpture on a roundabout, proximity to a shopping mall or major building such as the Royal Opera House. Within built-up areas, the minor streets (ways) are numbered in blue with white lettering rather than named. The numbered streets are broadly grouped, for example Way 4803 and Way 4806 share a common junction. However, 4870 and 4806, which also have a common junction, have no other street 4871/2 and so on in the vicinity, so some searching may be needed to find the correct way once you have arrived in the rough location.

Buildings are numbered in blue with white lettering, and within a building the municipality also allocates a number in blue with white lettering that may be different from the one allocated by a landlord.

entrance to Departures or at the main car park near Burj Al Sahwa roundabout, just to the west of the airport; to get to Burj Al Sahwa take a taxi from the airport. Fares for these coaches are less than RO7 to any destination in Oman.

As Muscat has a limited public transport system, there are innumerable orange and white **saloon taxis and minibuses** that can be flagged down on the road. Neither saloon taxis nor minibuses show their ultimate destination or route and neither has any indication that it is available for hire. There are two fare types: **engaged**, which is usually only undertaken by the saloon taxi, and **shared**, which both saloon taxis and minibuses offer. Engaged is to hire the taxi privately so that you are the only passenger(s), and the driver will take you to any destination. A shared taxi will stop to pick you up and drop you at any roadside location on his route. You need to ask where he is going and if your destination is somewhere along the route, get the price. Of course, this does mean that you need to know his destination and route in relation to where you wish to go. Whether you choose engaged or shared, confirm the price before getting in and be prepared for a surprising lack of knowledge of the Capital Area – although all taxi or minibus drivers are Omani, most are from rural areas often hundreds of kilometres away. To tell the driver to stop simply ask him to stop about 100m before the location, or in a minibus tap the window so that he can hear.

OVERLAND See pages 45–6 for travelling to Oman overland. A handful of operators in the capital offer longer-distance buses that go to Dubai and Salalah. From Muscat's Capital Area it is possible to get a bus trip to Sur and Salalah; the Salalah bus makes stops at strategic points in the interior such as Nizwa. Buses also travel to Dubai and Abu Dhabi in the UAE, making stops at Suhar (in Al Batinah region) and Al Buraymi (in the Adh Dhahirah) along their respective routes. For all bus information, see pages 59–60.

BY SEA Currently the only scheduled service that offers a sea route into Muscat is by ferry from Khasab in Musandam (pages 46 and 55). One option is a Dubai arrival and onward sea journey into Muscat with a stopover in Khasab.

ORIENTATION

Muscat's Capital Area is linear, stretching from Old Muscat in the east towards Barka in the west. The arterial roads run parallel to the mountains and sea for much of their route, making general navigation easy. Signage is easy to read in Arabic and English, and traffic lights function well, with a flashing green indicating that they are about to turn orange and then red. Car drivers, though sometimes adventurous and often tailgating, usually maintain reasonable road discipline and can be surprisingly courteous. If you are intending to hire a car, some familiarisation with the names of the suburbs and their geographical relationship prior to your drive will be time well spent. The city is low density but reliance on vehicles creates congestion during much of the working day. Two major parallel routes run through the town from Al Qurum going west: the Muscat Expressway, which takes through-traffic as it runs below the mountains, and Al Sultan Qaboos Street (road 1), which flows through the built-up areas, including Al Qurum, Al Khuwair, Al Athaiba, the airport and beyond to As Sib and Al Batinah coast. There are two secondary parallel roads: Al Jami Al Akbar serves the Ghala Industrial Estate through to the Muscat Hills development, while 18 November Street links the coastal areas of Al Athaiba (Al Azaybah and Al Udhaiba on some official maps) and Al Mouj (previously The Wave).

GETTING AROUND

BY TAXI Taxis are certainly the easiest option for getting around in the Capital Area, especially if you are unfamiliar with the lie of the land. They are a distinctive orange and white. They are not metered, so once the driver has told you what he wants to be paid, you will have to bargain. Make sure that he doesn't simply make the broad suggestion 'You decide', which can lead to disagreement when payment is made. Ensure that you tell the driver if you want an 'engaged' taxi, in which case you are the sole occupant. All taxi drivers are Omani in line with the Omanisation principle (pages 26 and 29). Their English is generally reasonable as far as their work is needed in the Capital Area, less so in the interior (ie: those areas of Oman outside the governorate of Muscat).

Taxi fares (the private engaged service as opposed to the shared non-engaged service) between suburbs should cost about RO4, although taxi drivers may try to charge you RO7–10 if they think they can. Thankfully, from the airport the system is different (page 79).

For all other journeys, fares should be agreed before getting in. The official taxi fare from Muscat Airport to Mutrah corniche is RO10 and it takes about 40 minutes to cover the 40km. A transfer to any of the central hotels, such as the Radisson Blu, Grand Hyatt or InterContinental (about 20km away) will take roughly 15–20 minutes and will cost RO8. The journey to Al Bustan Palace will take some 45 minutes and cost RO12, while the Shangri-La Barr Al Jissah Resort will take up to an hour and cost RO15.

BY MINIBUS Local white minibuses seating about 12 to 14 people pass the airport regularly 24 hours a day, though from midnight you may have some time to wait. To go to As Sib and beyond, walk to the main road and flag one down. To go towards Old Muscat, cross by the footbridge and flag one down if one is not waiting. There is little room for luggage and if you have a large case a taxi with a boot is the best option. The maximum fare into Ruwi by minibus (normally the farthest these will go) is around 600bzs. For travelling around on main routes within the Capital Area these minibuses are the cheapest option, and short journeys cost about 300–400bzs.

In Ruwi, the minibuses and taxis cluster around the flyover beside the Oman Commercial Centre (usually called the OK Centre as it was named the Oman and Khuwait Centre when it was built) and in Mutrah both gather near the 'fish roundabout'. To go to areas to the north of the Capital Area, see the references to Burj Al Sahwa on page 139. To travel to Qurayyat (*RO1 minibus; engaged taxi RO7*) and on to Sur the minibuses and taxis congregate on the edge of the Shell petrol station at Wadi Adai. To travel to Sur you will probably have to go to Qurayyat and transfer to a different vehicle, where you will need to take a taxi, not a minibus.

BY HIRE CAR There is no difficulty in renting a car at Muscat International Airport, although you may decide to rent from your hotel rather than have the stress of negotiating the unfamiliar road network after a long flight, especially if you arrive at night. Plenty of well-known car-hire firms operate both here and from local hotels. There are also some cheaper local firms throughout the city, especially west of Al Hamriyyah roundabout, where there are a dozen offices with varying standards of saloon cars for hire. Don't worry if you haven't pre-booked; you will find something (for details and car-hire firms, see pages 58–9).

BY BUS Muscat has a limited urban bus system with fares comparable to the minibus. These buses are red and fares start at 500bzs. There are routes from Ruwi bus station to Al Mawalih, Wadi Adai and Al Wadi Al Kabir.

ON FOOT The Capital Area is increasingly designed for vehicle use. The city is so stretched out that in the hot summer months walking is often impractical. Footpaths do not exist in many areas or may finish in a random location. Main roads have limited crossing places. There are a few exceptions: the Mutrah Suq area through to Old Muscat is excellent, for instance.

There are also short trekking paths such as the way-marked trail from Riyam Park near the Incense Burner monument into the mountains and round to Mutrah harbour (see box, page 101). Otherwise, save your walks for the endless stretches of beach at Shati Al Qurum, most of which are public (page 121).

TOURIST INFORMATION, TOURS AND TOUR OPERATORS

See pages 42–6 for tourist information.

ORGANISED TOURS Many tour companies operate within the Capital Area (listed on pages 83–5), most offering similar tours. The Ministry of Tourism regulates them. If you don't want to make the arrangements yourself, explain your requirements to your hotel and they will arrange things for you; they usually work closely with one or two tour operators. Guests can be picked up from any of the city hotels or from a private address, and this is included in the price.

Tour options Half-day **city tours** include the Sultan Qaboos Grand Mosque at Athaiba, the exterior of Al Alam Palace in Old Muscat, the exterior of the Portuguese forts of Al Mirani and Al Jalali, Mutrah Suq and Bait Al Zubair Museum. Other programmes in Muscat include **sunset dhow cruises** (a dhow being a traditional wooden boat, part of Oman's seafaring history) along the coastal bays of Muscat, **dolphin-watching tours, snorkelling and diving tours** and **fishing safaris**.

Off-road **4x4 safari tours** are largely to destinations beyond the Capital Area and include full day trips up into the mountains, the wadis and the desert. A 4x4 is essential, and it is advisable to go through a tour operator who will provide the vehicle and an invaluable driver/guide. For safety and comfort, these 4x4 trips offered by tour operators are generally based on a maximum of four passengers in one vehicle with a driver/guide, and cost upwards of RO150 per vehicle. Some tour companies allow you to join a tour in a convoy if you have your own rented 4x4, and this will work out cheaper, but of course you miss the information provided by the guide *en route*, and you also take responsibility for the driving, which requires skill and experience. It is better to leave the driving to the guides, and more or less essential to do so for trips into the Wihibah Sands (Ash Sharqiyyah) and the Empty Quarter (Dhofar). Wadis may be more manageable for the inexperienced, but only if conditions are dry. Some of the roads up into the *jabals* (mountains) can be narrow and precipitous. In this case, it is still recommended that at least two vehicles go in convoy. If in doubt, arrange your trip through a tour operator rather than driving independently.

The 4x4 tours can work out expensive if you are a lone traveller, as the price is comparable irrespective of whether you are one or four passengers. In such a situation, and if you would like to bring the cost down substantially, enquiries at any of the tour operators will establish whether it is possible for you to join other passengers for your chosen trip. However, you may prefer the privacy of your own car and driver/guide, regardless of cost.

TOUR OPERATORS Below is a comprehensive list of tour operators. These are all based in Muscat but arrange tours throughout the whole of the country. Some have desks within the upper- to mid-range hotels and this is generally the most convenient way to arrange a trip.

Abdullah Al Shuhi Photography Tours
m 99 346900; e abshuhi@gmail.com; www.
omanphotoholidays.com. For the last 20 years,
a leading photographer for the *Oman Observer*
newspaper, Abdullah Al Shuhi has also been
leading tours in Oman. Though based in Muscat, he
specialises in photography tours in Oman's interior.
Book several weeks in advance.

Al Nimer Tourism m 99 550535;
e alnimertourism@gmail.com; www.
alnimertourism.com. Located in the Ramada Hotel
at Al Qurum Beach (page 89), offering all the stock
tours as well as parasailing, sea tours, water rides for
families & children on the Matrix, Viper or Jumbo Dog
(inflatables, towed by a speedboat), & camping trips.

Alwan ☎ 24 594002; e info@alwantour.com;
www.alwantour.com. Based in Al Ghubra, the
company offers group bus tours from Muscat
to Nizwa, Wihibah Sands & Wadi Ash Shab for
RO35pp including lunch. This is a good option if
you are a single traveller. Private tours to other
destinations are available.

Arabesque Travel e tours@arabesque.travel;
www.arabesque.travel. Offers a full range of tours
including trips starting from Dubai. Self-drive 4x4
& private tours from
1 to 4 days, as well as tailor-made private tours.

Arabica Orient Tours ☎ 24 490500; e sanjay@
arabicaorient.com; www.arabicaorient.com.
With an office near The Chedi, the company
offers a range of private day trips & longer
excursions throughout Oman. They also offer
MICE (Meetings, Incentives, Conferences,
Exhibitions) services for businesses.

Bahwan Travel Agencies ☎ 24 704455, 706798;
e subrat.mishra@bahwantravels.com; www.
bahwantravels.com. Bahwan has over 20 offices
throughout the country though most are outbound
focused. Locations in the Central Business District:
MQ Shopping Centre: ☎ 24 601192; Ruwi:
☎ 24 706134; Sabco Centre: ☎ 24 564678; Golden
Tulip Hotel: ☎ 24 510720; Al Khuwair: ☎ 24 603898;
Salalah: ☎ 23 294665, 290908. Established 25 years,
offering a full range of tours & safaris.

Desert Discovery Tours; ↘24 493232; m 92 009427; www.desertdiscovery.com. This company's facilities include Al Areesh Desert Camp in Wihibah Sands, Al Naseem Turtle Beach Camp at Ras Al Jinz (close to the turtle reserve), Al Qabil Resthouse (approx halfway between Muscat & Sur, & a good stop-off point), as well as mobile camping units. It offers guided tours from 1 person to a large group, including cultural, historical & adventure tours.

Eihab Travels ↘24 683900; e oman@ eihabtravels.com; www.eihabtravels.com. Also operates Budget car rental and UPS courier. Their tours include most of the country & they have a conference & business operation.

Elite ↘24 499797; e info@elitetourism.com; www.elitetourism.com. With offices in Muscat & Salalah, Elite can provide extensive services throughout Oman. They also have an office in Dubai, which makes them a good option if you wish to fly into Dubai & travel into Oman by road. The company offers programmes including fixed tours lasting several days &, for golfers, programmes that take in all 3 of Muscat's public golf courses.

Global Tours ↘24 484156, 695959, 695994; e globtour@omantel.net.om; www. globaltoursoman.com. For wadi & dune bashing, camping & caving, & a range of other tours.

Golden Oryx Tours ↘24 489853; e info@ goldenoryx.com; www.goldenoryx.com. Based in Ruwi, this is one of the longest established tour operators in Oman. As well as the more common tours offered by other tour companies, Golden Oryx Tours offer cooking classes in Muscat as well as a longer tour combining Oman with Zanzibar – a good combination considering their history.

Hud Hud Travels m 96 779099; e jo@ hudhudtravels.com; www.hudhudtravels.com. Hud Hud offer the closest version in Oman of an East African-style safari camp set-up. They can offer luxury camping for a group of friends or family in remote areas of Oman.

Mark Tours ↘24 562444, 565567, 560975, 561466; e marktour@omantel.net.om or admin@marktoursoman.com; www. marktoursoman.com. Main office is in Hatat Hse at Wadi Adai roundabout, & there's also a desk at Muscat Airport & in the Radisson Blu Hotel (page 88), plus a franchise in Salalah. They will send you a list of tours on request.

Mezoon Travel ↘24 796680; e info@ mezoontravel.com; www.mezoontravel.com. Located in Al Burj St, Ruwi. Established more than 25 years with branches in Salalah (↘23 297846) & Al Fahl Island (↘24 568220), although all tours are arranged through the Muscat office. Offers an impressive, well-structured range of tours, trips & safaris through mountain, wadi & desert, including rock climbing & trekking, & can organise overnight camping tours, which are priced on any tailor-made route intended. Will send you a detailed list on request.

Muscat Diving & Adventure Centre ↘24 485663; e info@holiday-in-oman.com; www.holiday-in-oman.com. This company offers excellent adventure tours, from trekking to caving, with knowledgeable, qualified guides & equipment. Rock climbing, trekking, surfing, kayaking, game fishing & diving.

National Travel & Tourism ↘24 660300; e tours@nttoman.com; www.nttomantours.com. NTT tours is part of the largest group in Oman who also operate Hertz & have been operating tours for over 20 years. Located at Wutayya, Al Qurum (↘24 564783), Salalah (↘23 295016) & Al Buraymi (↘25 650716). They do offer tours for individuals but probably are better for a large group requiring substantial numbers of vehicles.

Oman Geo Tours ↘24 536629, 600914. Located in Al Qurum. Specialises in geological & scientific tours, but offers other tours as well.

OmanHoliday.co.uk www.omanholiday. co.uk. Based in Al Hamriyyah in Muscat, have been operating for more than 20 years & will arrange bespoke trips for everyone from single visitors to large groups & business visitors.

Passion-Trek ↘22 005560; e info@sultanat-d-oman.com; www.passiontrek.com. Focused on the French market, Passion Trek offer a range of trekking tours in Oman that are unavailable from other operators. You will need to be reasonably fit & able to keep up with a group, though of course you can have a private tour organised by them.

Tour Oman ↘24 760800; e touroman@ travelcity-oman.com; www.touroman.om. Tour Oman is part of a larger group that has been in business for some 20 years. However, the last few years has seen the company expand dramatically with over 30 offices around Oman. From Muscat they

Oman's brief version of its own Arab Spring lasted just four months from January until May 2011, with most of the demonstrations taking place in Muscat, Salalah and Suhar. The protests focused on perceived corruption within the government, lack of work opportunity and salary levels. Several government ministers were replaced, increased minimum wages for Omani workers were introduced and the creation of thousands of new jobs was announced. Since then court cases have been held to try those accused of corruption. Omanis now have improved standards of living and increased wage differentials compared with Asian expatriates.

The Arab Spring has also changed the dynamic of tourism in Oman to some extent. Before 2011, foreign visitors from Europe – mainly the UK, Germany, Italy, France, Benelux, Austria and Switzerland were a key contingent among inbound tourists. Post 2011, Arabs from Gulf countries were no longer able to spend their holidays in Syria, Lebanon and Egypt, so many came to Oman instead. Now there is a more even balance between Europeans and visitors from other Gulf countries. Summer occupancy in hotels used to be only 20%, when it was considered too hot for Europeans, but now occupancy in summer is closer to 45%, thanks to the increase in GCC visitors well accustomed to the heat.

organise day excursions & longer tours, including spa-oriented stays.

United Tours ✎24 787448; e utours@omantel. net.om or utours@unitedoman.com. Located in the CBD; also in Salalah (✎23 297948). Large, established firm with numerous 4x4 vehicles & a fleet of buses offering the full range of tours, including comprehensive 8–12-day tours of Oman, camping, safari & culture.

Zahara Tours ✎24 400844; e inbound@ zaharatours.com; www.zaharatours.com. Located in Madinat Al Sultan Qaboos. Also at the InterContinental Hotel (✎24 699862), Grand Hyatt Hotel (✎24 696596), Salalah (✎23 202581, 202582). Large, established firm, with Avis car hire, travel & diving insurance, & the full range of day trips, city tours, camel & 4x4 safaris, scuba diving & adventure trips.

WHERE TO STAY

Muscat and its Capital Area have a greater choice of hotels than anywhere else in the country. As you might expect from the Oman government's stated focus on top-end tourism, four- and five-star hotels enjoy prime beachfront locations. There is a good selection of in-town hotels in the medium price range and a reasonable choice of lower-cost hotels and furnished apartments. The listings on pages 86–91 attempt to give a fair selection of places to consider. The cheap hotels along the Mutrah corniche are very convenient, although at the time of writing three are closed for rebuilding, which will increase demand for the two remaining. If you want easy access to a beach at reasonable prices, head for somewhere like the Al Qurum Beach Hotel (page 89).

From the airport it is never too far to a good hotel, irrespective of where you are staying in the city. The closest is the Golden Tulip, which is virtually opposite the airport; the farthest are Al Bustan Palace and Shangri-La's Barr Al Jissah, which are both about a 40-minute drive away on good roads, and Sifawy, a 90-minute drive. A more central choice from which to explore the city would be The Chedi (about 15 minutes from the airport), the Grand Hyatt or the Intercontinental Hotel (both roughly 20 minutes from the airport). The Radisson Blu, Ibis and Park Inn offer a good central base in town (again about 15–20 minutes from the airport).

Some hotels in the city provide a complimentary transit from the airport. If you are travelling independently, it may be a good idea to confirm with your chosen hotel whether this service is included.

If you prefer a self-catering arrangement, perhaps for a stay of a longer duration, hotel apartments are widely available around the Capital Area. Again, these vary in quality, but all are basically clean and comfortable. You will often get a discount for a longer stay.

Note that all room rates are subject to a 9% government tax and an 8% service charge, making a total of 17%, so always ensure that you know the total cost when making a booking. In the same way, check whether breakfast is included.

HOTELS
Luxury and upmarket

🏠 **Al Bustan Palace Hotel** [map, page 114] (250 rooms) 📞24 799666; e albustan@ritzcarlton. com; www.ritzcarlton.com/en/properties/albustan. About a 45min drive from the airport just off the Al Bustan roundabout to the east of Old Muscat. Set on its own private beach within 200 acres of lush parkland, complete with helicopter landing pad & stark, mountainous backdrop, the famous Al Bustan has a magnificent foyer & upmarket souvenir shops. Its bay location means that the sea is clear & calm. The hotel in the past was regularly voted top in the Middle East, though now the glitzy hotels in the UAE have that distinction. Over half of its rooms overlook the sea. Sports & leisure facilities are extensive. Offers gourmet dining, including a traditional Omani dinner in the gardens on Wed, a beach bar & restaurant & an award-winning buffet restaurant. A new spa building has been added to the facilities. The hotel's location is a little less exclusive since the Omani government decided to build a massive parliament complex just inland, housing the Majlis Oman, Majlis A'Shura & Majlis A'Dawla, along with VIP areas, an information centre, library & other offices. **$$$$$**

🏠 **The Chedi** [map, page 127] (161 rooms) 18 November St, Al Ghubra North; 📞24 524400, 524401; www.ghmhotels.com. This is one of the most stylish of Muscat's luxury collection of 5-star hotels & only about a 15min drive from the airport (7km). It is well signposted. It is a single- & 2-storey hotel & spa, with 1 deluxe room & private villas, 2 swimming pools, tennis courts, treatment rooms & a boutique (which is also an art gallery). There are sports facilities, 3 bars & 2 poolside *cabanas*. One of the bars is sunken & has a beautiful outlook past the glass-like stillness of the infinity pool & directly on to the postcard-like blue ocean.

The intention is an uncluttered Zen experience of peace & tranquillity, with beauty & bathing rituals on offer, & body elixirs, in the form of massages, scrubs & wraps, for which there is a menu in your room. The award-winning restaurant (called 'The Restaurant') is regarded as one of the best in the city (📞24 524343; **$$$$$**). There is a choice of Arabic, Asian, Indian & Mediterranean cuisine cooked in the 4 open-display kitchens. In addition, there is an extensive cellar, which houses over 300 imported wines on full display in the floor-to-ceiling glass library in the bar (called 'The Bar'). Alternatively, there is The Chedi Pool Side Cabana for evening dining, which serves a Mediterranean menu & has a resident pianist (Sat & Sun). There are 3 semi-private dining rooms, all with sea views, called The Datai, The Setai & The Legian. Suites are impressive, with high ceilings & minimalist designs. Outside, a maze of paved pathways leads to the pools & private beach. **$$$$$**

🏠 **Grand Hyatt Muscat** [120 A3] (280 rooms) As Saruj St, Al Qurum; 📞24 641234; e hyattmct@omantel.net.om; www.muscat.grand. hyatt.com. About 20km from Muscat International Airport, the Grand Hyatt is next to the embassy area. This 5-star hotel is set in 10 acres of gardens, in a good central location on Al Qurum Beach.

It has an opulent stylish design in traditional Arabian architecture, the preference of its owner, a Yemeni prince. There are 4 restaurants & 2 bars. There is a superb Italian restaurant (The Tuscany), decorated as a Tuscan villa, complete with iron gate & courtyard; the Mokha Café is down the stairs, & serves buffet b/fasts & Middle Eastern lunches & dinners. There is also a poolside Asian restaurant & bar (The Marjan). The John Barry Bar, with its sea theme, was named after the wreck of the SS *John Barry*, which sank off the coast of Oman in 1944. There are all the usual 5-star facilities & services in the hotel, & watersports are available at the **Hyatt Boat House** (📞 *24 485663*) situated on the public beach. **$$$$$**

🏠 **Hormuz Grand Hotel** [map, page 129] (231 rooms) Just over 1km south of Muscat Airport on Al Matar St; 📞 24 340500; e receptions@hormuzgrandhotel.com; www. hormuzgrandhotel.com. The Hormuz Grand's style is grand & it's very good for access to the airport & Muscat Hills & Al Mouj. **$$$$$**

🏠 **Shangri-La Barr Al Jissah Resort & Spa** [map, page 114] (680 rooms) Located to the east of Qantab & accessed by the Qantab Rd; 📞 24 776666; e slmu@shangri-la.com; www.shangri-la. com/muscat. This is a resort of 3 top international-class hotels, set in 124 acres of landscaped gardens with a remarkable mountainous backdrop. This is the farthest hotel in the city from the airport & takes up to an hour, depending on the traffic, on roads of excellent condition. This resort is sheer relaxation & escape, just as that offered by Al Bustan a few bays earlier (page 86). The 3 hotels are geared towards different target markets: Al Husn ('The Castle') is a 5-star luxury hotel, while Al Bandar ('The Town') is aimed at the business guest. Al Waha ('The Oasis') is aimed at families, providing a kids' club called Little Turtles, 2 kids' pools & an internet café. The Chi Spa, adjacent to the gym, has treatment rooms in 12 private villas & offers traditional Himalayan & Chinese treatments. There is a 'turtle cove' area where turtles come to nest, & a ranger informs & educates guests on how to respect the species & their natural environment. Guests of Al Bandar & Al Waha can use each other's facilities, & a lazy river can be swum or followed, adjoining the two. There is a central bar amid the pools & surrounding flower gardens. There are over 15 food & drink outlets in total. There is a dive school & watersports facilities, with a lifeguard present. Al Husn remains exclusive, & with a huge chandelier from the Czech Republic, wall light shades from Morocco & carpets from Iran, the décor is opulent. When combined with 3 crystal-ceiling ballrooms with retracting walls (which allow it to convert into 1 impressive 700-seater), this place is seriously luxurious. Transfers from Muscat International Airport can be arranged for a hefty RO35. **$$$$$**

🏠 **City Seasons Muscat** [map, page 124] (175 rooms) Al Khuwair; 📞 24 394800; e info@ cityseasonsmuscat.com; www.cityseasonsmuscat. com. The rooftop pool here, though not that big, has one of the best views in Muscat overlooking the ministry area & sea. There are several restaurants (without alcohol). The price is competitive, though the overall experience is perhaps not as good as you'd expect from such a large hotel. **$$$$**

🏠 **Crowne Plaza Hotel** [120 E1] (207 rooms) Overlooking Al Qurum Beach & easily accessed off Al Shati St; e mcthc@interconti.com; www.cpmuscat. com. The Crowne Plaza has a superb location perched on a cliff in Al Qurum Heights. This is one of Muscat's oldest-established hotels & used to be the Gulf Forum Hotel. There is a Lebanese restaurant (Shiraz), an international buffet restaurant (Tropicana), Arabic food (Palm Café), casual dining (The Edge) & an English pub (Duke's Bar). It is recommended that you reserve a table in advance for any of these restaurants. There are good sports & recreational facilities, while dive trips can be organised. **$$$$**

🏠 **Golden Tulip Seeb** [map, page 129] (177 rooms), 📞 24 510300; e admin@goldentulipseeb. com; www.goldentulipseeb.com. This is the closest hotel to Muscat International Airport, & accessed from the flyover at the original airport terminal on Al Sultan Qaboos St. Guests can use the facilities of the Oman Aviation Beach Club & the Oman Automobile Club (which has go-karting & an 18-hole brown (sand) golf course, located a few minutes from the hotel) & offers free transfer to these on request. There is an international restaurant (Le Jardin), with themed buffet nights, & a nightclub. Seafood night is well worth seeking out, with an awesome buffet & endless wine included in the set price of RO15, open to non-residents as well. PADI dive course packages are also available. **$$$$**

🏠 **Grand Millennium Muscat** [map, page 127] (332 rooms) Al Sultan Qaboos St; 📞 22 342222; e reservations.gmm@millenniumhotels. com; www.millenniumhotels.com. A modern hotel next to 2 of Muscat's best shopping malls, if that's important to you. It is also very convenient for government ministries & the Muscat Expressway if you want to get out of town quickly. **$$$$**

🏠 **InterContinental** [120 B1] (261 rooms) 📞 24 680000, 600500; e muscat@icmuscathotel. com or muscat@interconti.com; www. intercontinental.com. On Al Qurum Beach, about a 20min drive from the airport (21km), close to Al Qurum Natural Park & the museums. Set within 35 acres of private well-maintained gardens, its brown-cement structure doesn't make it the most attractive building from the exterior. The hotel is a little dated, but the staff are friendly & efficient, & it has good leisure & sports facilities, though you should ask about any impact by the construction immediately next to InterContinental of the 290-room 5-star 'W Hotel'. There is an American-style steakhouse (OK Corral), a Mexican restaurant (Señor Pico's), international snacks round the pool (Pool Deck) & Far Eastern food (Coconut Grove). The bar (Al Ghazal Pub) serves food & is popular with expats. It has a live band playing most evenings, & offers quiz nights, sport on the large-screen TV & a pool/snooker area. There is a good cocktail bar & restaurant, **Trader Vic's** (24 698028; $$$), situated just outside the front of the hotel & on the left (as you face it), serving Caribbean & Pacific food. $$$$

Park Inn [map, page 124] (175 rooms) Al Khuwair; 24 507888; e reservations.muscat@ rezidorparkinn.com; www.parkinn.com/hotel-muscat. Well located with good road connections to the airport & major attractions, this is one of Muscat's newer hotels. The rooftop pool & bar are worth a visit; however, the maintenance is not in keeping with the relatively high price demands & the rooms & main restaurant lack character. $$$$

Radisson Blu Hotel [map, page 124] (156 rooms) Al Khuleiah St, Al Khuwair; 24 487777; www.radissonblu.com/hotel-muscat. This hotel is about a 15–20min drive from the airport (signposted from the highway, & situated just off 23 July St). It has an excellent standard of modern décor & there is a great steak restaurant here (Al Tajin Grill), set opposite a romantic, dimly lit piano bar (The Coral), for pre- or post-dinner drinks. There is a nightclub (The Cellar – accessed around the back of the hotel & down the stairs), an all-day indoor & outdoor dining restaurant (Olivio's Coffee Shop), which is also a Wi-Fi zone, serving buffet & à la carte meals, & the Fontana Heath Club. The garden has a bar by the pool, open late afternoon & evenings. The business centre provides free internet & computer services to all guests. The beach club for the Radisson is located next to the Grand Hyatt & transport is provided. The staff give an excellent smiling welcome, & a swift, efficient check-in & delivery of bags to your room.

Reception offers a full explanation of what the cost of an overnight stay includes without being prompted. A courtesy bus will take you to the airport & also does trips to Mutrah Suq at 16.00 with pick-up at 19.00 on request. $$$$

Sheraton Oman Hotel [map, page 117] (230 rooms) Bait Al Falaj St, Ruwi; e oman@ sheraton.com; www.sheratonoman.com. Located at the top of Ruwi, Muscat's Financial District, the Sheraton Oman provides good access to most areas in the Capital Area. Completely refurbished in 2016, the hotel is a landmark of the city & is minutes away from the Mutrah corniche & Muscat Old Town. Each deluxe room offers uninterrupted views of the Al Hajar Mountains. The hotel's several dining experiences include the Argentinian steak house Asado, or high tea in the Tea Library. The hotel also features a recreation area with 2 gyms, a spa, a tennis court, & indoor & outdoor pool. $$$$

Mid range

Al Falaj Hotel [map, page 117] (143 rooms) Off Al Burj St, Central Business District, Ruwi; 24 702311; e sales@omanhotels.com or reservationruwi@omanhotels.com; www. omanhotels.com/alfalaj. One of Muscat's oldest hotels & rated 4 star. Private beach facilities are available on request. On the 8th floor there is a Japanese restaurant (Tokyo Taro) & a pub (Le Pub) with live band & bar-food menu, & each has scenic views over the city. Al Falaj also has a Lebanese restaurant, an Indian restaurant & a coffee shop. The sports facilities include glass-sided squash courts. $$$

Beach Hotel Muscat [120 B2] (20 rooms, 20 suites) Close to the beach & the InterContinental Hotel; 24 696601; e reservations@ beachhotelmuscat.com; www.beachhotelmuscat. com. This lovely small hotel is under friendly new Omani management & has a quaint design with rooms surrounding a small swimming pool. Its international restaurant is unlicensed. $$$

Bowshar International Hotel [map, page 127] (38 rooms) On the sea side of the highway, off the Al Ghubra roundabout, signposted; 24 491105; e bwshrhtl@omantel.net.com; www. bowsharhotel.com. 15mins from the airport, this hotel is rated 3 star by the Ministry of Tourism. Al Mas Brasserie is its licensed restaurant. Accepts credit cards. $$$

⌂ **Dream Resort** [map, page 129] (30 rooms) Near the beach, As Sib; www.rameehotels.com/dream-resort.html. This well-established hotel is certainly the best choice if you are planning on staying in As Sib. Rooms surround the 2 pools – request one on the ground floor if you want your accommodation to lead straight out to the pool. There is the Café Lounge, an international restaurant & the Black Out nightclub. It also has a large screen for sporting events. **$$$**

⌂ **Haffa House Hotel** [map, page 117] (120 rooms) \24 707207; e reservations@haffahouse.com; www.shanfarihotels.com. This hotel is situated on Ruwi St close to the CBD & is part of the Shanfari group of hotels. It has a swimming pool & an unlicenced restaurant. **$$$**

⌂ **Holiday Inn Al Sib Muscat** [map, page 129] (186 rooms) 8km from Muscat Airport off As Sib St in Al Mawalih; \22 080555; e HolidayInnMuscatAlSeeb@ihg.com; www.ihg.com/holidayinn. The ease with which you can travel from here to other regions in Oman make the Holiday Inn a good choice for a short stay. The rooms are relatively small. There is 1 on-site restaurant, & there are lots of others within a few moments' taxi drive. **$$$**

Hotel Al Madinah Holiday [map, page 127] (107 rooms) Ghala; \24 529700; e hmh33@omantel.net.om; www.holidayhotelsoman.com. This Oman hotel is well established (it was a Holiday Inn) & has a coffee shop & licensed bars with live entertainment, as well as a health club with exercise machines. **$$$**

⌂ **Majan Continental Hotel** [map, page 127] (159 rooms) \24 592900; e info@majanhotel.com or sales@majanhotel.com; www.majanhotel.com. The hotel has a 24hr licensed coffee shop (Khaboura Café) & 5 bars with live bands performing daily. It can arrange diving packages to the Ad Dimaniyyat Islands, car hire & tours. Accepts credit cards. **$$$**

⌂ **Muscat Holiday Hotel** [map, page 124] (129 rooms) Just off Al Sultan Qaboos St, Al Khuwair; \24 399100; e info@holiday.co.om; www.holidayhotelsoman.com. The former Holiday Inn, now run by a local Omani company, is very well located for access to the key government ministries & other areas in the central Capital Area (pages 119–25). Churchill Pub, Layalina Bar & the Al Maha Coffee Shop Restaurant are old favourites in Muscat. The hotel is showing its age but the refurbished rooms do make this very good value for money. **$$$**

⌂ **Ramada Al Qurum Beach** [map, page 122] (92 rooms) Close to the beach, Al Qurum; \24 603555; e ramadaom@omantel.net.om; www.ramadamuscat.com. This hotel has a good location very close to the beach & the InterContinental Hotel, about 10–15mins from the airport. Rated 4-star deluxe by the Ministry of Tourism, it is an Arabic-style construction & the room décor is of a good standard. Inside the hotel is Nauras Al Shati Restaurant & the Petit Café. **$$$**

⌂ **Ruwi Hotel** [map, page 117] (116 rooms) Al Nahda St (Ruwi roundabout); \24 704244; e sales@omanhotels.com; www.omanhotels.com/ruwi. This is one of a chain of 5 hotels, the others being Al Falaj (page 88), Sur Plaza (Sur), Al Wadi (Suhar) & Desert Nights in the Wihibah Sands. It is set close to the Central Business District & has a 3-star Ministry of Tourism rating. It has 2 licensed restaurants: the Coffee Shop offers all-day dining & Al Fakhr Restaurant has live entertainment from an Arabic band. There is also the Club Bar & the Mehfil Bar, each with live entertainment. **$$$**

⌂ **Sifawy Boutique Hotel** [map, page 132] (67 rooms) \24 749111; e info@sifawyhotel.com; www.sifawyhotel.com. Located just outside As Sifah, about a 50km drive from Al Qurum, this is a small property set around a marina with an ideal location for those who want to relax. The rooms have a fresh, modern design with balconies overlooking the Sea of Oman. **$$$**

Budget and shoestring

⌂ **Al Bahjah Hotel** [map, page 129] (52 rooms) On the one-way system into town, As Sib; \24 424400; www.rameehotels.com. About 15km from the airport. The hotel's rooms have full facilities, including swimming pool. On-site restaurants & bars include Al Saadah Café, Keranadu Restaurant, Al Massarrat Sports Bar, Al Rafahia Arabic Restaurant & Al Marrah Indian Restaurant. If you are not staying here, it still makes a good stop for a cup of tea (*400bzs*) or something to eat while visiting As Sib. Accepts credit cards. **$$**

⌂ **Al Qurum Beach Hotel** [120 E1] (64 rooms) Al Qurum Heights; \24 5640705; e qbhotel@omantel.net.om. Located a short walk from the beach & Al Shati St, this hotel provides good cheap accommodation & is in a great location with plentiful parking. Up the road to the entrance, it is almost African in feel due to all

3

the greenery around. It also has 2- or 3-bedroom apartments, an international restaurant (Maymoon) & a nightclub in the Ramee Hotel next door, which can be a bit noisy into the early hours. Still, there's a real holiday feel about the place. The hotel will store your excess baggage if you are taking short trips up or down the country. Members of staff are friendly, professional & accommodating. You are a short walk away from the fantastic stretch of beach that runs from the Crowne Plaza Hotel all the way up past the Grand Hyatt & InterContinental hotels. Fantastic value for money. Accepts credit cards. **$$**

⌂ **Hotel Golden Oasis** [map, page 117] (62 rooms) Al Wadi Al Kabir St, on the road to Al Bustan; \24 811655, 814062; e hotgoldn@ omantel.net.om; www.hotelgoasis.com. This hotel is rated 2 star & is located on the road to Al Bustan. To get here, exit the highway at Al Wadi Al Kabir roundabout (about 25mins from the airport) & follow Al Wadi Al Kabir St. The hotel has a licensed bar & 3 licensed restaurants with live entertainment: Mer-Maid Bar, Captain's Café, Ubar Restaurant & Cleopatra Restaurant. It makes a good base for divers using the Oman Dive Centre, a 5min drive away. The hotel provides a shuttle service & can organise courses & dive trips. Accepts credit cards. **$$**

⌂ **Ibis Muscat** [map, page 124] (171 rooms) Dohat Al Adab St, Al Khuwair; \24 489890; www.ibis.com. Functional & neutral but comfortable & clean hotel with all-day restaurant & 24hr bar with snacks. **$$**

⌂ **Marina Hotel** [map, page 107] (20 rooms) Mutrah corniche; \24 713100, 714343, 711711; no direct website, but can be reserved through www.booking.com. The 3-star Marina is arguably the best of the hotels along Mutrah corniche & has a good restaurant, Dolphins Bar & Shark Night Club, all licensed. Even if you don't stay here, do take a trip up to the terrace floor 'P', where the restaurant & bar are located, for a fantastic view over the port, the corniche & the minarets of the mosques. Accepts credit cards. **$$**

⌂ **Midan Hotel Suites** [map, page 127] (35 suites) Just off 18 November St in Al Ghubra North; \24 499787; e rooms@midanoman.com; www.midanoman.com. Midan Hotel Suites offers 35 suites ranging from studios through to a 3-bedroom penthouse. All suites are Wi-Fi enabled, have a well-equipped kitchen, a separate living room

& are all furnished in a contemporary style. The Thai restaurant offers a nice location for dinner. **$$**

⌂ **Ramee Guestline Hotel** [120 E1] (90 rooms) Close to Al Qurum Beach; \24 564443; e salesoman@rameehotels. com; www.rameehotels.com. This hotel has traditional Omani-style architecture & is in a good location. It has an international licensed restaurant (Yamamah). Sea View Grill Restaurant at rooftop. Accepts credit cards. **$$**

⌂ **Sun City Hotel** [map, page 117] (35 rooms) Al Jaame St, Ruwi; \24 789801. A bright, modern hotel with big windows & spacious rooms right next to the Ruwi main bus station, making it convenient if you have a bus to catch. Friendly staff. **$$**

⌂ **Naseem Hotel** [map, page 107] (29 rooms) Mutrah corniche; \24 712418; e naseemhotel@gmail.com. Extremely well located for taxis & Mutrah Suq. The rooms are simple but clean. There is no restaurant but it does provide room service with food from nearby eateries. Ask for a sea-facing room; there are only a few. **$**

HOTEL APARTMENTS

⌂ **Millennium Executive Apartments Muscat** [map, page 127] (115 rooms) Off Al Sultan Qaboos St; \22 323477; e reservations. meam@millenniumhotels.com; www. millenniumhotels.com. These serviced 1-, 2- & 3-bedroom apartments are centrally located in one of Muscat's better shopping mall complexes, including the Muscat Grand Mall & next to The Avenues. Car parking is a slight hassle & there are plenty of other furnished apartments in town, but these offer probably the best mix of all, at a price. **$$$$**

⌂ **ASAS Oman Hotel Apartments** [120 E2] (35 apts) Nr Al Qurum Natural Park; \24 568515; e asasoman@omantel.net.om. This complex comprises fully furnished en-suite apartments, all with AC, equipped kitchens, washing machines, satellite TV, 24hr reception, daily housekeeping service, phone, business centre, temperature-controlled swimming pool & car park. There is disabled access & pets are allowed. There is also an unlicensed restaurant. Accepts credit cards. **$$$**

⌂ **Al Khuwair Hotel Apartments** [map, page 124] (9 apts) Off Al Hadiqa St; \24 478171. This is one of 4 properties owned by the Safeer Hotels & Tourism Company. Large but run-down rooms. **$$**

⌂ **Safeer Plaza Hotel Appartments** [map, page 122] (44 suites) Al Kuliya St; 📞 24 471000; www.safeermallhotel-muscat.com. Big rooms, good value & service. 15mins from the airport. International restaurant. Car rental, packed lunches & tour desk in reception. **$$**

✗ WHERE TO EAT AND DRINK

Dispersed around the city are plenty of restaurants offering cuisines from around the globe. In addition to the ubiquitous Arabic and Indian cuisine, American, African, Chinese, French, Greek, Italian, Japanese, Mexican, Middle Eastern, Mongolian and Thai can all be found.

Most of the upmarket restaurants are situated within the five-star hotels, but other excellent places, like D'Arcy's Kitchen in the Jawharat A'Shati shopping complex and Madinat Al Sultan Qaboos (page 93), the Mumtaz Mahal (Indian) (page 92) or the Golden Oryx (Chinese/Thai) (page 92), for example, are independent. While hotel restaurants are usually licensed to serve alcohol, not all of the independents are, so if needed be sure to check this before making your choice.

There are many **pub-like bars** inside the hotels and generally these all serve bar food. Again, the star rating of the hotel usually reflects the price bracket. **Churchill's** in the Muscat Holiday Hotel (page 89), **Duke's Bar** in the Crowne Plaza (page 87), **Al Ghazal** in the InterContinental (pages 87–8), **Club Safari** in the Grand Hyatt (pages 86) and **Feeney's** next to Grand Hyatt are some of the bars popular with expats and locals alike. The **Up Town** restaurant is like an English pub and located on Rex Road, Ruwi (📞 24 706020; map, page 117).

The restaurants below are the ones outside of hotels and are in price-range order.

INDEPENDENT RESTAURANTS
Upmarket
✗ **Al Angham** [120 B2] Entered from the ground floor of the Royal Opera House, Al Qurum; 📞 22 077777; www.alanghamoman.com; ⊕ noon–15.00 & 19.00–23.00 Sat–Thu, closed Fri. Without doubt, this is the place to go to impress your companions. The décor & place settings are luxurious, in keeping with the overall style of the Royal Opera House. The timings only allow for a meal after a performance at the opera. The menu is Omani cuisine, including lobster, camel & frankincense ice cream. The service is excellent though the food has a very hard time making it worth the cost. Booking is essential & no alcohol is served. **$$$$**

✗ **The Indus** [120 B2] Entered from the ground floor of the Royal Opera House, Al Qurum; 📞 22 022888; e theindus@kr.om; www.theindus.om; ⊕ noon–15.30 &18.30–23.30. With its bright, restrained décor, The Indus is an inviting location for meals. The food is northern Indian-style & well spiced, though the chef will prepare it to suit each person. The highlight of any meal here has to be the outdoor terrace, which overlooks the Royal Opera House; occasionally alcohol may not be served on the terrace. **$$$$**

Mid range
✗ **Bait Al Luban** [map, page 107] Mutrah corniche; 📞 24 711842; www.baitalluban.com; ⊕ noon–23.00 daily. The food here is Omani in style, but for what it is, the menu is somewhat overpriced; however, the ambience is good & the overall experience excellent. If you eat here & the weather is not hot, ask for a balcony table – ideal for 2 people. **$$$**

✗ **Bellapais Restaurant** [map, page 129] Rusayl commercial complex, As Sib; 📞 24 521100; ⊕ noon–15.00 & 18.00–23.00 Sat–Thu, 18.00–23.00 Fri. This pleasant licensed restaurant serves Greek cuisine & offers take-aways & home delivery. Your steak is cooked at your table for you. **$$$**

✗ **Blue Marlin** [map, page 114] Marina Bandar Al Rowdha; 📞 24 737288, 737291; www.marinaoman.net; ⊕ 09.30–23.00 Sun–Thu, 08.30–23.00 Fri, 08.00–23.00 Sat. This international seafood restaurant is licensed, &

you don't have to be a member to access it. Very popular alfresco b/fast buffets by the pool. $$$

✗ **Chez Sushi** [120 G2] Sayh Al Malih St, Al Qurum; www.chezsushioman.com; ⊕ noon–23.45 daily. There are 2 outlets, one in Al Mouj & a second in Al Qurum near the Natural Garden. A fresh take on Japanese sushi – choose your ingredients & they are combined for you. $$$

✗ **The Golden Oryx** [map, page 117] Al Burj St, Ruwi; ✆24 702266, 706128; ⊕ noon–15.00 & 19.30–midnight Sat–Thu, closed Fri. This licensed restaurant has an extensive menu including Cantonese, Szechuan, Beijing, Mongolian & Thai. It is also good for vegetarians. Dimly lit, it has a peaceful atmosphere with instrumental versions of familiar songs playing softly in the background. The food is good & the waiters are consistently efficient & friendly. The Thai Pavilion at the back provides a nice private spot for dining. $$$

✗ **Kurkum** [map, page 107] Just under the fort on Mutrah corniche; ✆24 714114; www.kurkumoman.com; ⊕ noon–15.00 & 18.00–23.00 daily. This is a quirky, stylish restaurant serving Indian cuisine. The food can be spicy, so ask for it to be cooked to suit you. The fish dishes are worth trying. The cost is on the high side, however, the Montblanc pen to sign the bill & extraordinary tray of perfumes at the end of the meal may make you think it was worthwhile. $$$

✗ **Mumtaz Mahal** [120 E3] Off Sultan Qaboos St; ✆24 605907, 607103; ⊕ noon–14.30 & 19.00–23.30 Sat–Thu, 13.00–15.00 & 19.00–midnight Fri. Partly because of its hilltop location, which provides an elevated view over Al Qurum Natural Park & the city, & partly because of its good food, its ambience, its faultless waiter service, its dim lighting, & its very reasonable prices, this award-winning Indian restaurant is one of the best in Muscat. There is a good wine list, but if you are keeping an eye on costs, the carafe of house wine is cheap & easy to drink. From around 21.00, Indian musicians play softly on the low-level stage which fronts a calming waterfall feature. $$$

✗ **Murchi Curry House** [120 E1] In the Ramee Guestline Hotel (page 90). Offers excellent curry, is licensed, has good service & a pleasant atmosphere with live Indian music. $$$

✗ **O Sole Mio** [map, page 124] Radisson Blu Hotel (page 88); ✆24 487777; ⊕ noon–15.00 & 18.00–23.30 daily. This is an excellent Italian restaurant with an extensive wine list. $$$

✗ **Passage to India** [map, page 117] Behind the Hatat Hse compound, near Wadi Adai roundabout; ✆24 568480, 563452; ⊕ noon–15.00 & 19.00–23.30 Sat–Thu, evenings only Fri. Both the food & service are excellent here & there is an open kitchen where you can watch your meal being prepared. $$$

✗ **Pavo Real** [map, page 122] Al Madina Plaza, Madinat Al Sultan Qaboos; ✆24 602603; ⊕ noon–15.00 & 18.00–midnight Sat–Thu, evenings only Fri. A fun, licensed Mexican restaurant with live music. Friendly waiters serve up great food. Do go here for a good fun night out & try the cocktails! $$$

✗ **Sama Terrazza** [map, page 124] Park Inn; ⊕ noon–15.00 & 18.00–01.00 daily (14.00–01.00 Fri). The pool bar at the Park Inn is normally busy each night as its location is excellent & views across the town superb. However, service is patchy & a need to comply with bureaucracy for opening hours & formal customer dress combine to reduce its appeal. $$$

✗ **Ubhar** [120 B2] In the Bareeq Al Shati Mall, Al Qurum; ✆24 699826; www.ubharoman.com; ⊕ 12.30–15.30 & 18.30–23.00 daily. Ubhar was the first Omani restaurant that raised itself from the traditional sit-on-the-floor style. The almost psychedelic pink plastic chairs may distract from food, which is excellent. Try the kingfish *makhboos* with a *halwa* dessert. Don't forget to make a booking, as the restaurant is relatively small & popular. $$$

Budget and shoestring

✗ **Al Makan** [120 C2] Al Shati St, Al Qurum; ✆24 545311; www.almakancafe.com; ⊕ 11.00–02.00 Sun–Thu, 13.00–02.00 Fri. A local restaurant chain of Middle Eastern restaurants with the almost inevitable water pipes. The food & service are patchy but generally acceptable, & the location is outstanding, with views over the sea & mangroves. $$

✗ **Bar B Q Tonight** [map, page 122] Shati Al Qurum; 🄼 97 673304; www.bbqtonight.ae; ⊕ noon–16.00 Sat–Thu, 13.00–16.00 & 19.00–23.30 Fri. Just around the corner from the Ramada Hotel in Shati Al Qurum. Focused on meat, this is part of a Pakistani franchise that is spreading in the Gulf. A mix of buffet & menu choices offers marinated meats & rice-based meals that are tasty & well priced. $$

✗ **The Candle Café** [120 A3] On the beachfront just east of the Hyatt, Al Qurum; 🄼 96 002233; ⊕ 07.00–16.00 daily. This place has a terrace right by the sea & offers simple food like mixed grill & sandwiches. It is unlicensed but has very good juices. The atmosphere is relaxing, making it a perfect place to smoke *shisha* or watch big football matches with local people. In summer they rig up fans to keep you cool. $$

✗ **Copper Chimney** [map, page 117] Fair Trade Hse, CBD; ✆ 24 706420, 780207; ⊕ noon–15.00 & 19.00–midnight Sat–Thu, 13.00–15.00 & 19.00–midnight Fri. A decent licensed restaurant serving good Indian food. $$

✗ **The Crafty Kitchen** [map, page 122] Madinat Al Sultan Qaboos shopping area; ✆ 24 696660; www.thecraftykitchen.com; ⊕ 07.00–20.00 daily. This cross between an old-fashioned English tea shop (think Bettys in Harrogate) & a modern cookery school is a very popular place to eat. The tea selection is excellent & the savoury choice is a great match for its cakes. For what it offers prices are fair, but be prepared to wait for a table at weekends. $$

✗ **D'Arcy's Kitchen** [120 A1] Jawharat A'Shati Complex near the InterContinental Hotel; ⊕ 08.30–23.00 daily. This cheerful place, with its comfortable bamboo chairs set out on the pavement, serves everything from b/fasts & light snacks to full meals. There's a new branch at Madinat Al Sultan Qaboos [map, page 122]. $$

✗ **Golden Dragon** [map, page 122] Behind the shopping complex in Madinat Al Sultan Qaboos; ✆ 24 697374; ⊕ noon–15.00 & 19.00–23.30 Sat–Thu, 13.00–15.00 & 19.00–23.30 Fri. A licensed Chinese & Thai restaurant offering a nice ambience & décor. Also does take-aways. $$

✗ **Grill House Co** [map, page 122] Suq El Mal; ⊕ 09.00–21.00 daily. Serves excellent buffets during Ramadhan. Very clean. Highly recommended. $$

✗ **Japengo Café** [120 G2] Al Shati St, Al Qurum; m 92 892868; ⊕ 11.00–23.30 daily. Far Eastern cuisine with a good selection of sushi set in a bight airy restaurant. The location adds to the meal as you overlook the entire sweep of the beach at Al Qurum & the mangroves. $$

✗ **Kamat** [map, page 117] Off Al Burj St, Ruwi; ✆ 24 479243, 793355, 783300; ⊕ 10.00–13.00 & 17.30–23.00 daily. An award-winning Indian restaurant. $$

✗ **Kargeen Café** [map, page 122] Madinat Al Sultan Qaboos shopping centre; ✆ 24 692269; www.kargeencaffe.com; ⊕ 09.30–15.00 & 17.00–01.00 daily. This unlicensed café is segregated into separate outdoor eating areas, some alfresco, some tented, screened (to enable AC units to function), benched & cushioned, some for traditional eating at floor level, some for families, & some for smoking

shisha. Overall, it imparts a real sense of being in traditional Arabia. An attractive labyrinth & a true oasis, where the bread & food on the international menu is cooked outdoors in full view. $$

✗ **Khana Khazana** [map, page 117] New CBD area; ✆ 24 813466; ⊕ 12.15–15.15 & 19.00–23.30 daily. Indian, Chinese & Tandoori restaurant. $$

✗ **Khyber** [map, page 117] CBD, next to the National Bank of Oman; ✆ 24 781901; ⊕ noon–15.00 & 19.00–midnight. Licensed restaurant serving Indian cuisine. $$

✗ **More Café** The Walk, Al Mouj [map, page 129] & Sayh Al Malih St [120 F2]; ✆ 24 547446; www.oman.morecafe.co; ⊕ 08.00–23.00. With 2 locations in Muscat, More Café is a small chain of casual & stylish all-day restaurants where you can choose from just soup & coffee to a 3-course meal. $$

✗ **Nuovo La Terrazza** [map, page 117] Behind the Hatat Hse compound, near the Wadi Adai roundabout; ✆ 24 571126; ⊕ 19.30–midnight daily. A good Italian located behind Hatat Hse, close to the Passage to India (page 92). $$

✗ **Richoux** [120 B2] On the ground floor of the Opera Galleria; ✆ 22 005165; ⊕ 10.00–23.00. This is a franchise of a London café & offers a take on an English meal. The service is a little hit-or-miss but overall it makes for a nice, easy place to eat. $$

✗ **Shang Thai** Branches in Al Mouj [map, page 129], Muscat Grand Mall & The Avenues Mall [map, page 127]; ✆ 24 554774; www.shang-thai.com; ⊕ 11.30–23.00 daily. This local restaurant offers a consistently good experience, with Thai chefs ensuring authenticity. If you like the food, you could ask to join one of their cookery classes. $$

✗ **Shuwa Express** [120 B2] Bariq Al Shati Mall, Al Qurum; m 98 072498; ⊕ 11.00–23.00 daily. *Shuwa* is Oman's signature meat dish, marinated & slow cooked; Shuwa Express is a fast-food take on the taste of Oman. You choose the way the meat is served. $$

✗ **Al Deyar Restaurant & Café** [map, page 122] Opposite Al Shati Plaza, Al Qurum; ✆ 24 696247; ⊕ Sat–Thu. This local budget restaurant occupies a good location close to the sea. $

✗ **Automatic Restaurant** Al Qurum [120 B2] (✆ 24 561500), Al Khuwair, behind the Radisson Blu [map, page 124] (✆ 24 487200) & Al Athaiba [map, page 127] (✆ 24 424343); ⊕ noon–midnight Sat–Thu, 13.00–midnight Fri. Award-winning Lebanese food chain restaurant serving good Arabian, Mediterranean & Lebanese food, all at good prices. $

THE ROYAL OPERA HOUSE MUSCAT دار الأوبرا السُلطانية

The sultan first ordered this magnificent addition to Oman's cultural life in 2001. Building work started in 2007 and the Royal Opera House (*Al-Kharjiyah St, Al Qurum;* ✆ *24 403332/3/4; www.rohmuscat.org.om*) opened in late 2011 with a performance of *Turandot* and Placido Domingo singing the lead role. The design borrows from contemporary Islamic and Italianate styles, and several government buildings now look like this. Inside it houses a concert theatre, auditorium, small upmarket shopping mall and restaurants. Artists from around the world perform in the state-of-the-art space, equipped with the latest multimedia technology. Performances for the coming season are first announced by August. The season runs from September to May and tickets can be bought online at www.rohmuscat.org.om with prices ranging from RO5 to RO80. If you can't make a performance, take a short tour at 08.00 from the box office (RO2).

✘ **Bin Ateeq** [map, page 124] Next to Shell petrol station on the Khuwair slip road; ✆ 24 603225; ⏱ all day, 7 days a week. Traditional Omani food at very reasonable prices, served in the traditional Omani way at floor level. $

✘ **Camelia** [map, page 117] Bait Al Falaj St, Ruwi; m 92 450927; ⏱ 07.30–02.00 daily. In the CBD area, on the other side of the street from the Sheraton Hotel (page 88). This may be one of the longest-established restaurants in Muscat. The Turkish-style food is good value & tasty, & given how busy they are & the excellent price, the patchy service is an easily overlooked issue. Try the fresh juice selection. $

✘ **China Town** [map, page 114] Capital Commercial Centre (CCC); ✆ 24 567974; ⏱ 11.00–15.00 & 18.00–midnight Sat–Thu, 13.00–15.00 & 18.00–midnight Fri. Serves good Chinese food. $

✘ **Golden Spoon** [map, page 124] Located on the Al Khuwair slip road, between the ice-skating rink & the Shell petrol station; ✆ 24 482263, 478215; ⏱ 11.30–15.30 & 18.00–midnight Sat–Thu, 13.00–15.30 & 18.00–midnight Fri. Serves good Chinese & Indian food. Also at As Sib Suq (✆ 24 424204). $

✘ **Intaqiah** [map, page 107] Mutrah St, within 100m of the back of Mutrah Suq; ⏱ all day daily.

This place is best after dark when its garden is attractively illuminated. It serves set meals freshly made every day, free of the constraints of a menu, accompanied by a selection of salads & *mezze*. $

✘ **Jean's Grill** [120 F4] Upstairs in the Sultan Centre, Al Qurum; ✆ 24 567666; ⏱ 07.00–23.30 daily. Restaurant/café serving good buffet b/fasts. $

✘ **Woodlands Restaurant** [map, page 117] Europcar Bldg, CBD, Ruwi; ✆ 24 700192; ⏱ noon–15.00 & 18.30–23.30. Licensed restaurant serving Indian cuisine. $

✘ **Pizza Muscat** [120 F4] Al Harthy Complex in Al Qurum. Serves pizza made with halal meat, salads & lasagne. $

COFFEE SHOPS

Both **Costa Coffee** & **Starbucks** have a major presence in Muscat now, with outlets at Madinat Al Sultan Qaboos (MQ), Jawharat A'Shati, Muscat City Centre food court, Muscat Airport, Lulu in Al Ghubra, Oasis by the Sea (Shati Al Qurum), Al Asfoor Plaza in Al Qurum & the beach road running from Shati Al Qurum up to the Crowne Plaza Hotel.

ENTERTAINMENT AND NIGHTLIFE

BARS AND PRIVATE CLUBS There are no independent bars as such in Muscat; instead you will find 'pubs' and bars inside hotels and private clubs. You can access a private club only as a guest of a member. If you are lucky enough to have Omani or expat acquaintances, then you can get food and drink in these clubs for a fraction of the amount you pay in the hotels. A couple of these are the **Muscat Rugby Club** (*Bawshar;* ✆ *24 604890*) and the **Civil Aviation Club** (*Al Athaiba Beach;* ✆ *24 498882;* e *info@caaclub.org*).

CINEMAS Films are shown in the capital in English, Arabic, Hindi, Tamil and Malayalam. The cinemas listed below all show films in English.

Al Shati Plaza [map, page 122] Shati Al Qurum; ✆24 607360, 692656; ⏱ 13.30–midnight
Ruwi Cinema [map, page 117] Ruwi; ✆24 780380; ⏱ 09.00–13.00 & 17.00–23.00

Star Cinema [map, page 117] Central Business District, Ruwi; ✆24 791641; ⏱ 14.30–00.30
Markaz Al Bahja Cinema [map, page 129] Al Khawd; ✆24 540855; ⏱ 13.30–02.00

NIGHTCLUBS Nightclubs, such as they are in Muscat, are found within the better hotels. They need to tread a very difficult line, as the more conservative elements in Oman are putting considerable pressure on the government to close them. Periodically some form of restriction is made, which is gradually relaxed until the next time. The result is that the weekend rush to Dubai sucks the commercial foundation from all but the larger hotels. Nonetheless, younger Omanis and expats do enjoy nights out at clubs in Muscat, especially the Copacabana in the Hyatt (page 86). The music in all is international and occasionally DJs add their style to a venue.

☆ **Al Hamra** Al Bustan Palace Hotel (page 86); ✆24 799666
☆ **Sur Nightclub** InterContinental Hotel (pages 87–8); ✆24 600500

☆ **Copacabana** Grand Hyatt Hotel (page 86); ✆24 641234

SHOPPING

Evening shopping is a popular pastime with Omani families. The city's malls often contain good restaurants and some independent shops. Muscat also has a plethora of art galleries and shops that make for an interesting browse. There is also an atmospheric suq worth visiting in As Sib (pages 128–30).

SHOPPING MALLS There are several modern, air-conditioned shopping complexes close to Al Sultan Qaboos Street from Al Qurum towards As Sib. Each of these complexes or malls has its own selection of cafés, food courts and play areas and amusements for children. Most have a mix of fashion shops, upmarket brand-name products (such as watches and sunglasses), computer shops, sportswear outlets, CDs and DVDs, photographic retailers, electronics, perfumes, florists, opticians, interior design shops, artisanal handmade furniture and gifts, internet cafés, cards and bookshops, footwear and beauty products (for more details, see below).

Among the biggest and most modern malls are the Qurum City Centre near the Al Qurum interchange, The Avenues and Muscat Grand Mall in Al Ghubra and Muscat City Centre, out past Muscat International Airport. There are small, modern suqs in the Sabco Centre and Capital Commercial Centre, if you haven't the time to visit the real thing in Mutrah. In Ruwi there is Ruwi Suq Street, which is often referred to as Ruwi High Street, and its side roads.

Al Qurum

Al Qurum is home to the older shopping malls; to access these you will need to keep straight on the dual carriageway & come off at the main Al Qurum roundabout (the next one along from the Al Khuwair roundabout). Taking the left turn at the roundabout (last exit) & the subsequent first

right will lead you into the main group. They are all generally open 09.00–13.00 & 16.00–22.00, with some variations.

Sabco Commercial Centre [120 F3] ✆24 563943, 562761, 566701; www.sabcogroup.com; ⏱ 09.00–13.00 & 16.00–22.00 Sat–Thu, 16.30–

22.00 Fri. This is the longest-established complex (opened in 1985) & contains the Amouage perfume retail outlet, jewellery & fashion outlets, a pet shop, a beauty salon & a small-scale, modern, AC suq, which has 27 small individual units selling silver jewellery & handicrafts, incense burners, *dishdashas*, *kummahs*, *mussars*, pottery, *khanjars*, leather goods, *bakhour* (traditional scented wood), frankincense & other artefacts. If you haven't got the time to visit the real thing at Mutrah, this miniature suq is a good place for buying gifts to take back home.

Al Araimi Complex [120 F3] Opposite Sabco, on 3 floors with mainly fashion clothing. The basement has the Canon camera shop & a number of other electrical showrooms.

Qurum City Centre [120 F3] On the Muscat Expressway, near the terminus with Al Nahda St; ✆ 24 470700. This is part of the ubiquitous City Centre chain of shopping malls that revolutionised retailing in the Gulf in 1995. Mostly franchises from the West including Carrefour, M&S & McDonald's.

Sultan Centre [120 F4] Al Nahda St; m 94 265385. An excellent supermarket with a restaurant upstairs serving good buffet meals. For access keep straight on the highway towards Ruwi & once you have passed the Al Qurum flyover get over to the right for the entrance. There are ATMs & an Oman Oil petrol station.

Al Qurum Beach

The Al Qurum Beach area has a number of small shopping malls that house locally developed shops, rather than the franchised shops often found in the larger malls.

Al Shati St [120 D2] This is a place to enjoy the sea views. The road runs between the mangroves & Al Qurum Beach. The restaurants have open-air & indoor seating, from east to west; Japengo Café offers East-meets-West fusion cuisine, Tche Café has Lebanese-style food, while the Al Makan Café has *shisha* water pipes.

Bareeq Al Shati [120 B2] ✆ 24 699949. On Al-Kharjiyah St next to the Royal Opera House, this is a nondescript mall that has some of the more interesting restaurants in Muscat: the excellent **Steak Company** (✆ *94 116600*; *$$*); **Ubhar** (✆ *24 699826*; *$$$*) with fusion-style Omani food; **Automatic** (✆ *24 605735*; *$$*), a Lebanese restaurant (one of a chain); **B+F Roadside Diner** (✆ *24 698836*; *$$*); and the Japanese **Wasabi Sushi** (✆ *24 699490*; *$$*).

Opera Galleria [120 B2] Royal Opera House Muscat, Hay Al Saruj; ✆ 24 403300; e info@rohmuscat.org.om; www.rohmuscat.org.om. On Al-Kharjiyah St & part of the same building complex as the Royal Opera House, this is intended as an upmarket shopping mall & has a number of premium outlets for perfumes & jewellery. The main draw are the restaurants, including Richoux, The Indus & Al Angham (page 91).

Jawharat A'Shati [120 A1] Hay Al Saruj; ✆ 24 692113; e jasco@omantel.net.om. The turning for this mall is from the traffic lights adjacent to the Royal Opera House – go north along Way 2817, following the route to the InterContinental Hotel. There is parking to the front & rear, but in the evening it can get busy. Inside the complex there is a Starbucks coffee shop, D'Arcy's Kitchen (page 93), the Omani Heritage Gallery shop (page 98) & Muscat Pharmacy perfumes. This area is popular with Omani families in the evening, as access to the beach is good. You might like to pop into the Sheraton Beach Hotel (the beach club of the Sheraton in Ruwi) & have a drink in the Route 66 bar (⊙ *noon–15.00 & 18.00–midnight*). This area is within easy walking distance of both the InterContinental & Beach hotels.

Oasis by the Sea [120 A1] Hay Al Saruj, opposite Jawharat A'Shati mall. This small complex has numerous small casual dining restaurants & a Costa coffee shop. Seating for several of these places directly overlooks the beach & makes for a fabulous place to watch the sunset. Within the complex is Bateel, a date shop, & its neighbour selling Havana cigars.

Al Khuwair *Map, page 124*

Centre Point Near Safeer Plaza Hotel; ✆ 24 698988. Sells sportswear, clothes, makeup, toys & Western-style furniture & homeware.

Zakher Mall ✆ 24 489884; e info@zakhermall.com; www.zakhermall.com. In an area far less busy than both Al Qurum & Ruwi. There is a CD/DVD shop inside here, an internet café, clothes shops, sporting & diving equipment, a card shop, a Body Shop, a café area, a large furniture store & a good Iranian restaurant (unlicensed).

Al Athaiba *Map, page 127*

The Avenues Mall Al Ghubra junction of Al Sultan Qaboos St; ✆ 22 005400; e infoavenuesmall@gmail.com; www.

omanavenuesmall.om. With a large Lulu supermarket & a range of stores that are largely unique in the region, this mall is worth visiting. The 2nd floor has a food court & children's play area, with department stores on the 1st & ground floors. There is excellent car parking space both at street level & underground, so accessing this from the car park adjacent to Lulu is very easy.

Muscat Grand Mall Al Ghubra junction; ☎ 22 000022; e mgm@muscatgrandmall.com; www.muscatgrandmall.com. Like The Avenues, this is a mall where you will find stores unique to the Gulf. There is also a Vox Cinema & Carrefour supermarket. Parking is limited & in the basement.

As Sib *Map, page 129*

Markaz Al Bahja Al Mawalih roundabout; ☎ 24 540200; www.albahja.com. This mall is just west of the airport. On 3 floors, it includes mostly local shops & a few cafés. There is limited outside parking.

Muscat City Centre ☎ 24 558888; www.muscatcitycentre.com. This is one of a Gulf-wide chain of malls. Inside is a Carrefour supermarket, M&S, H&M, Monsoon, Body Shop, among others. Costa Coffee, fast-food outlets, Starbucks & other coffee shops, Vox Cinema & a children's amusement arcade. There is ample parking in the adjacent multi-storey car park.

SUPERMARKETS The supermarkets dotted about everywhere have a fantastic selection of fresh fruit and vegetables, fresh breads and hot ready-to-go foods.

The **Lulu** chain has some excellent hypermarkets here, one near the Bait Al Falaj flyover/roundabout and another by the Al Ghubra flyover/roundabout (on the mountain side of the highway). Grab a hot rotisserie chicken, Arabic bread and hummus, *taboule* salad, fruits and cold drinks, and head to any close destination (there is plenty of spare beach available).

Al Fair is a chain of supermarkets worth a browse around, especially if you fancy taking a picnic to the beach or into the mountains. Simply driving the short distance from Al Fair at A'Saruj to Al Shati Street (the beach road leading up to the Crowne Plaza), parking the car and eating on the beach is great fun. Al Fairs are dotted about throughout the city, including a branch in the Madinat Al Sultan Qaboos shopping area.

BAKERIES Branches of the **Muscat Bakery** are dotted around the capital and the country and are worth a peek. Try those on the Al Khuwair slip road in Al Ghubra, or Ruwi. There are also excellent bakeries in Lulu supermarkets (see above).

TAILORS Tailors' outlets are ubiquitous. Virtually every parade of back-street shops in the city has its collection; try Ruwi, Al Khuwair or Al Ghubra. You can take in an article of clothing and they will copy it for you very cheaply in a material of your choice, in no time at all; or, alternatively, select a design from their range of catalogues.

ART AND ARTEFACT GALLERIES AND SHOPS

Al Madina Gallery Rd 2, Villa 1691, Madinat Al Sultan Qaboos; ☎ 24 691380; www.almadinaartgallery.com; ⊕ 09.00–18.00 daily. Sells prints, watercolours & oils.

Gallery Sarah Al Sayidiyyah St, Old Muscat; ☎ 22 084747; www.gallerysarah.com; ⊕ 09.30–18.30. Sells original paintings by Omani artists, prints & gifts.

Khazir [120 B2] ☎ 24 562370; www.khazirworld.com; ⊕ 10.00–22.00 daily. Located in the Opera Galleria, Al Qurum, Al Araimi Complex, the Grand Hyatt, Al Bustan Palace, Shangri-La & other locations. The largest group for quality oriental-style furnishings & gifts.

Marina [120 F3] Al Araimi Complex, Al Qurum; ☎ 24 562221; www.marinagulf.com; ⊕ 10.00–22.00 daily. Also in Muscat City Centre (☎ 24 537055) & in Jawharat A'Shati (page 96). Stocks rustic wooden furniture & other unique furnishings. Arranges international shipping.

Murtada AK Trading Al Noor market, Mutrah Suq; ☎ 24 711632, 793248; ⊕ 10.00–21.00

daily. Selling original paintings by Omani artists, gifts, handicrafts & jewellery.

Omani Heritage Gallery [120 A1] Jawharat A'Shati Commercial Complex, Al Qurum; 24 696974; 10.00–20.00 Sun–Thu. Selling Omani handicrafts made by Omani Artisans, this is a not-for-profit organisation. Very good for gifts & souvenirs, from jewellery to T-shirts with turtle motifs.

Raj Relics Al Ghubra; 24 490620; by appointment. Behind Bahar soap factory (near The Chedi Hotel), selling & restoring antique & reproduction furniture, Indian & Omani chests, antique doors, dining & coffee tables & artefacts.

Sabco Suq [120 F3] Sabco Commercial Centre, Al Qurum; 24 660100; 10.00–22.00 daily. Several small independent shops selling handicrafts & artefacts; haggling expected.

Stal Gallery Al Inshirah St; 24 600396; e info@stalgallery.com; www.stalgallery.com; 10.00–18.00 Sun–Thu. Modern gallery with exhibitions of Omani & local artists.

OTHER PRACTICALITIES

HOSPITALS Government hospitals will require payment to treat non-Omanis and are generally extremely busy, although they do offer a very good standard of healthcare.

⊞ **Al Nahda Hospital** 24 837800. The oldest government hospital in Oman. Essentially a non-emergency service that is available elsewhere.

⊞ **Khoula Hospital** 24 563625, 560455. This is the principal government emergency hospital in Muscat. It's located just off the Al Qurum Heights Rd on Maydan Al Fath St.

⊞ **Muscat Private Hospital** 24 583600, emergencies 24 583790; www. muscatprivatehospital.com. Accessed on Bawshar St south from junction 6 on the Muscat Expressway. The largest private hospital in Muscat. Offers a wide range of services.

⊞ **Qurayyat Hospital** 24 645003. A small government hospital south of Qurayyat town, accessed off the roundabout on Al Husn Rd.

⊞ **Royal Hospital** South of Sultan Qaboos Grand Mosque on Al Ghubra St; 24 599000, 599977; www.moh.gov.om/en/web/royal-hospital. This is the main referral hospital in northern Oman & has associated speciality centres adjacent to it.

POST AND COURIER SERVICES
Post offices
This is by far the cheapest way of sending anything home, costing just baisas rather than rials. Post offices are generally open 08.00–14.00 Sun–Thu, with some exceptions.

✉ **Central Post Office** On Al Matar St, accessed from the flyover at the original airport terminal on Al Sultan Qaboos St; 24 510343; 07.30–14.30 Sun–Thu. Possibly the quickest postal method, as this is the central sorting office.

✉ **Mutrah** Opposite Way 805 southwest of Mutrah Fort

✉ **Mina Al-Fahl** Sayh Al Malih St; 24 565465

✉ **Jawharat A'Shati** On the upper floor of the Jawharat A'Shati Bldg, Al Qurum; 24 692181

✉ **Ruwi** South of Bait Al Falaj St on Markzi Mutrah Al Tijari St; 24 700922. This post office houses the philatelic department in the main service room. First-day covers & full sheets are available.

Courier services
DHL South of the airport on St 62, accessed from the flyover at the original airport terminal on Al Sultan Qaboos St; 800 77008; 07.00–21.00 daily

FedEx Sinaw Hse, opposite Al Nahda Hospital; 24 833311; e fedexmct@omantel.net.om; 08.00–19.00 daily. FedEx is represented in Oman by a service contractor. For further information, call **Oman Postal Express** (24 833311).

UPS Hala FM Bldg, Dohat Al Adab St, accessed from junction 4 on the Muscat Expressway; 24 683943; e kvijayan@ups.com; 08.00–19.00 daily. UPS is represented in Oman by a service contractor; the office is shared with Eihab Travels.

INTERNET Internet cafés are a rapidly dying business in Oman as smartphones and USB modems become prevalent. The most accessible for visitors is on the corniche in Mutrah, just east of the suq entrance. It is signed 'OmanTel Internet', but in fact this is a private company (**m** *99 562708; ⊕ 09.30–13.30 & 17.30–22.00 daily*). This office also sells Garmin navigation systems. These internet cafés in general charge far less than the business centres of the hotels.

SPORTS AND ACTIVITIES

There is a variety of things to see and do in the Capital Area, including scuba diving, dolphin-, whale- and birdwatching, dhow cruising, fishing, watersports, sailing, mountain trekking, beach walking and jogging or a gym (for further information, see pages 99–101). There are museums, mosques and forts to visit; cinemas, ten-pin bowling alleys, ice skating and opera, or you can go horseriding, play golf or play tennis. Throughout the Capital Area there are modern shopping complexes and the older suqs in Mutrah and As Sib. If you wish to see the city, hop on a Big Bus Tour, book your own private tour with one of the many tour operators (pages 83–5), or hire a car and travel independently (pages 58–9). For the less active, there are endless beaches and bays within the capital that are crying out for you to relax, perhaps with a picnic. Or if you don't want to move far from your hotel, there is the beach or pool of your hotel. Public beaches tend not to have any facilities or lifeguards, just long stretches of flat sand, so be sure to take your own sun protection as there will be no shade. If you want to use the beaches of the big hotels, which are equipped with beach shades and showers, you can do so, but at a price, usually around RO10 for a sunlounger for the day.

BIRDWATCHING Birdwatching sites in the capital include Al Qurum Natural Park (page 121), Haya sewage treatment plant, the gardens of the InterContinental (pages 87–8) and Grand Hyatt (page 86) hotels, and any of the beaches.

In Al Qurum Natural Park species such as the purple sunbird, Indian silverbill, laughing dove, Indian roller, little green bee-eater, yellow-vented bulbul, graceful prinia, grey francolin, the common mynah and the house crow are likely to be spotted. On the beaches species such as western reef heron, swift tern and sooty gull will undoubtedly be seen. For further detailed information, the publications by Hanne and Jens Eriksen are highly recommended (page 335). Speak to any tour operator in the capital if you would like to join a set birding excursion.

DIVING
Dive sites The *Al Munassir* wreck was offered by the Royal Navy of Oman for an artificial reef project and was sunk on 22 April 2003. It is a short boat trip from Marina Bandar Al Rowdha to its location at Bandar Al Khiran.

Al Fahl Island, 4km offshore, is also an excellent dive option and is almost the same distance away, albeit in the opposite direction. Diving here involves finning through an L-shaped tunnel through the island. There are many corals to be seen and the area attracts numerous sharks. Other popular dive sites include Cemetery Bay, Cat Island just off the coast from Marina Bandar Al Rowdha, and the Kalboo (also Kalbuh) area east of Mutrah harbour. East of Al Bustan Palace Hotel (page 86) there are the three bay areas of Bandar Al Jissa, Bandar Al Khiran and Sifah As Sheikh. Any dive centre will provide you with further information.

HEALTH CLUBS Health and fitness clubs and gyms can be found throughout the city. Many hotels have fitness facilities and, as expected, the standards vary according to the star rating of the venue. If you are resident in the country you can arrange annual membership at most of the clubs. If you are a guest usage is included in your room rate. Non-guests might be able to use these for the day, for a charge of approximately RO8 per person – check with the specific venue.

BOWLING **City Bowling** (✆ 24 541277) is located opposite the Muscat Holiday Hotel in Al Khuwair (page 89), and there is also one in Al Hail in the Markaz Al Bahja. Bowling is also available at **Al Masa Mall** [120 B3] (*As Saruj St;* ✆ 24 693919) and **Fun Zone** [120 E2] (*Al Qurum, next to the Natural Park;* 24 662951).

GOLF Three green courses operate in Muscat, all with easy access.

Ghala Valley Golf Club Ghala; m 98 831558; www.ghalagolf.com. Centrally located just off the Muscat Expressway; run by the members.
Almouj Golf, Al Mouj (The Wave) As Sib; ✆ 22 005991; e info@almoujgolf.com; www. almoujgolf.com. Seafront golf north of the airport.

Muscat Hills Golf & Country Club Muscat Hills, south of the airport; ✆ 24 514080; e booking@muscatgolf.com; www. muscathillsgolf.com. Spacious course set within a private residential complex.

HORSERIDING The Royal Stables at As Sib (✆ 24 420444) are considered one of the top riding arenas for watching equestrian events, although the best breeders and trainers are located in the Al Kamil and Al Wafi regions in the Ash Sharqiyyah. The Royal Stables offers horseriding lessons and trails. Riding groups are kept small in the interests of safety, and are accompanied by an experienced guide.

Other riding schools are based within easy reach of Muscat, at Al Qurum Natural Park and by the sea:

Al Qurum Equestrian School [120 E2] Al Qurum Natural Park; m 99 832199. Signposted once inside the park. For an hour's ride it is RO10, but if there is a group of you, this reduces to RO8 pp, with a max of 6 people in the group.
Al Sawahil Horse Riding m 95 177557; e ahmad-565@hotmail.com; ⊕ 16.00–19.00 daily. Located at the seaside, behind the park, at Al Bahja, Al Hail. RO8 per hour for lessons; beach RO14 per hour for a ride along the beach. Beginners welcome.

Shah Mohammed Al Khalili Al Qurum Natural Park [120 E2]; m 99 386978. Shah Mohammed will meet you & your group at the main gate of the park. Beginners are welcome & can take a ride through the park & along the beach for RO10. For the more experienced, the ride can be tailored. An experienced guide accompanies all rides. Lessons are also available at RO12, but if you have a group of 4 people (which is the max for a group ride), this reduces to RO8.

ICE SKATING Sessions at the **Fun Zone** [120 E2] (*Al Qurum, next to the Natural Park;* ✆ 24 662951; ⊕ 09.00–midnight Sat–Fri) cost RO3.50 including skates.

MOTORSPORTS The **Oman Automobile Association** in As Sib (✆ 24 510239, 510630, 522177; *www.omanauto.org*) offers a range of go-karts, motorbikes, motocross/dirt bikes and rallies.

SPORTS CLUBS For those planning a longer stay in Oman, or, more specifically, in Muscat, there are also several sports clubs:

Team sports
Basketball Oman Basketball Association ✆ 24 793802
Cricket Oman Cricket Association ✆ 24 703142;

British Cricket Club ✆ 24 673910; Oman Cricket Club ✆ 24 791270
Football Muscat United Football Club ✆ 24 542920

From the parking area beside the Riyam Park (pages 105–6) you will notice a brown trekking signpost which is the start of the waymarked walk C38. In the winter months or in the late evening or early morning in the hotter months, this walk up a steep rocky path will give you a proper feel for the setting of Mutrah and Old Muscat. It follows part of the ancient overland route that linked Mutrah and Old Muscat before the arrival of roads and vehicles. The total distance one-way is less than 2.5km and it takes 90 minutes to 2 hours, ending behind Mutrah. From the highest points (200m above sea level) you will gain an excellent view over the coast. At one point the path also descends towards an ancient abandoned settlement with its old water cistern and *falaj* irrigation system. The path then diverges into two, with both sections descending back to sea level. You will need to scramble over fallen rocks and navigate seasonal water pools along a wadi bed before reaching a water dam, on either route, into Mutrah, where you descend carefully at the side of the dam and walk down a street towards the fort in Mutrah. The total route is less than 2km and as the rock is crystalline it breaks very easily into small pieces, so do be careful on any slopes. A walking stick is recommended, as is travelling in a small group to discourage the yapping 'wadi dogs' and offer mutual support on the scramble down past the dam.

Hockey RAH Hockey Club Muscateers ↘ 24 675355
Netball PDO ↘ 24 675334; Red Devils Costains ↘ 24 595011
Rugby Muscat Rugby Club e chailmanamuscatrugby.net; Women's Rugby Team ↘ 24 544806; Dhofar Nomads Rugby Club m 99 291548
Softball Muscat Softball League ↘ 24 680453; m 99 336015, 235291
Volleyball Oman Volleyball Association ↘ 24 705567

Cycling and running
Cycling Muscat Cycling Club m 99 324594
Running Muscat Hash House Harriers ↘ 24 316127; Jebel Hash House Harriers ↘ 24 494226; Oman Athletic Association ↘ 24 797233; Muscat Road Runners ↘ 24 692903

Watersports
Sailing and boating Beach Catamaran Owners Club ↘ 24 604307; Capital Area Yacht Club CAYC ↘ 24 737712; Castaways Sailing Club ↘ 24 494751; Civil Aviation Yacht & Beach Club ↘ 24 519424; Marina Bandar Al Rowdha ↘ 24 737288

Racquet games
Squash Muscat Squash League ↘ 24 677414
Tennis Oman Tennis Association ↘ 24 751402; Muscat Tennis League ↘ 24 675210
Tennis coaching Alex Tvaliashvili (m *92 235809*; e *info@alextennisschool.com*; *www.alextennisschool.com*), a former coach of some of Oman's budding professional players, offers private & group lessons at various locations in Muscat.

Miscellaneous
Bridge Muscat Ladies ↘ 24 590167; Muscat Open ↘ 24 797597
Darts Oman Darts Club ↘ 24 618426
Game fishing Muscat Game Fishing Club m 99 322779

WHAT TO SEE AND DO

The Capital Area is easy to navigate, with the mountains providing a sense of direction, as they are visible in almost every location. In a linear form, the city stretches from the west, beyond the airport, towards Old Muscat, and is linked by four roads that

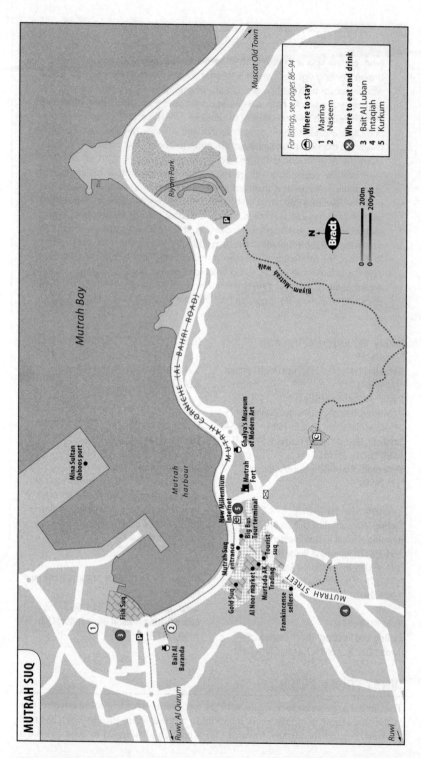

MUTRAH SUQ

For listings, see pages 86–94

Where to stay
1 Marina
2 Naseem

Where to eat and drink
3 Bait Al Luban
4 Intaqiah
5 Kurkum

Mina Sultan Qaboos port

Mutrah Bay

Riyam Park

Muscat Old Town

Riyam–Mutrah walk

Mutrah harbour

MUTRAH CORNICHE (AL BAHRI ROAD)

Ghalya's Museum of Modern Art

Mutrah Fort

New Millennium Internet

Mutrah Suq entrance

Big Bus Tour terminal

Tourist suq

Gold Suq

Al Noor market

Murtada AK Trading

Frankincense sellers

MUTRAH STREET

Bait Al Baranda

Ruwi, Al Qurum

Ruwi

0   200m
0   200yds

N

Brädt

102

A WALK ALONG MUTRAH'S CORNICHE

The walk along Mutrah's corniche is one of the most rewarding in Oman, with whitewashed houses overlooked by mountains and forts; in turn, the buildings gaze at the comings and goings of small and large boats. From the fish suq at the western end, where there is most car parking, the walk will take you east towards Old Muscat along a level paved route, though do look out for drainage holes in the paving stones. The route is under 5km, so allow at least an hour. Highlights will include the two large cream-coloured yachts in the harbour, which are the sultan's personal boats, *Al Said* and *Fulk Al Salamah*. The first of the whitewashed houses is Bait Al Oud, which marks the edge of Sur Al Lawatia, a residential area whose residents actively discourage visitors. This occupies the original Portuguese settlement site that dated from around the turn of the 17th century. The settlement's defences originally had four round corner towers, of which two remain and a third is now a circular coffee shop. Further east, after the fort (not open to the public), is the small, eclectic Ghalya's Museum of Modern Art (page 105) and the start of the original road to Muscat that was constructed in the 1920s and offers an alternative route between the two towns if you take the old road up the hill which overlooks Old Muscat. The corniche continues past the gigantic 'Incense Burner' monument. Passing the community at Kalboo, with its ornamental park (⊕ *17.00–23.00 daily*) and small beach, the Muscat Gate Museum (page 109) can be visited or walked under. Keeping to the left-hand side of the road will eventually take you directly onto Al Alam Palace (page 108), while the right-hand side sweeps around past Bait Al Zubair Museum (pages 109–10) and on towards the National Museum (pages 111–12).

run through much of this area. The key road (known as Road 1 or Highway 1) can take you from the UAE border into As Sib, where its name is As Sib Street. The road then becomes Al Sultan Qaboos Street at the airport and continues past the Sultan Qaboos Grand Mosque and continues as Al Nahda Street, then Ruwi Street, and finally Al Mina Street as it terminates at Mutrah. The road which then continues and goes east past Mina Sultan Qaboos, through Old Muscat and onto Al Wadi Al Kabir becomes the Al Qurum Heights Road, which then merges into Al Sultan Qaboos Street in Al Qurum, so that you could have a 'circular' road tour if wished.

In order to break up the area into shorter, more readily followed sections we have used the administrative divisions used by Muscat Municipality and started the descriptions at the hub of Muscat's tourist area, Mutrah.

MUTRAH مطرح Spreading south from its crescent bay towards the chocolate brown escarpments of the impressive ophiolite hills, Mutrah is the engaging port town that historically served Old Muscat.

Mutrah's success as a commercial hub came despite the nearby harbour of Old Muscat being more sheltered and having a better anchorage, as Mutrah was accessible to camel caravans from Oman's interior. The southern gate behind the suq (if approached from the sea) was the area where the camels, perhaps bearing dates destined for India, would be unloaded and reloaded with manufactured goods bound for the towns of northern Oman. This camel trade continued until the 1960s.

The sweep of whitewashed merchants' houses, which form part of Sur Al Lawatia, the forbidden enclave (page 105), overlook the bay and were previously set directly on the beach; now houses and shore are separated by a modern road, shown as Al Bahri Road on maps but always referred to as 'the corniche'. Until recently there were five well-located, relatively inexpensive hotels overlooking the harbour. At the time of writing, three were closed for refurbishment, leaving a lucky two to take all the guests: the Marina Hotel and the Naseem Hotel (page 90). If you wish to be one, book well in advance as they are small. A few good restaurants augment the numerous coffee shops between the fort and fish market where you can eat Indian or Pakistani food.

Behind the corniche is a maze of streets that run into Mutrah Suq, which is easily the largest suq in Oman. Overlooking the eastern edge of the town and the sea is the old fort, built on an unscalable, dour crag. Though impressive if viewed from the sea approaches, the fort is simply two towers joined by a narrow curtain wall. As in Old Muscat, there were originally two forts guarding Mutrah; the other fort (Arbaq) was demolished when Mina Sultan Qaboos port, which occupies the entire bay opposite the town, was developed as Muscat's harbour in the early 1970s. The western edge of the bay is a mixture of customs and port services, with an active fish suq receiving daily catches including tuna, *hamour* (grouper) and *shari* (emperor) from the local fishermen in the morning.

Mina Sultan Qaboos (*mina* is Arabic for port) has had most of its commercial shipping diverted to the northern port at Suhar and is to be turned into a leisure facility, servicing the increasing numbers of cruise ships that visit in the winter. Plans include building luxury hotels set within landscaped grounds within the port area.

Transport is by taxi, easiest found to the west of the main suq entrance or at the 'Fish Roundabout' at the western end of the corniche, where minibuses also wait for passengers to go into Ruwi. Some of the luxury hotels, including Al Bustan Palace (page 86) and the Shangri-La (page 87), both of which are several kilometres east of Mutrah, offer a complimentary limited shuttle service to Mutrah for their guests.

Mutrah Suq سوق مطرح (🕐 08.00–13.00 & 17.00–21.00 Sat–Thu, 17.00–21.00 Fri) Mutrah Suq (or Suq Al Dhalam – Market of Darkness) is the largest suq in Oman. In reality it is two suqs: the eastern area under the fort is the wholesale market, while the western area is for retail. The main passageway from the corniche entrance through to the town entrance is also a wadi (water course) that floods during heavy rains. During the winter, when the port is visited by cruise ships, the suq can seem like Alexanderplatz, Corso Buenos Aires or Oxford Street depending on the ship that is in port. Since completion of the modernisation project for the corniche for the 35th National Day (in 2005), the suq has been adorned with a green glass domed entrance opposite pedestrian traffic lights; the dome and traffic lights are ideal to orient yourself by.

Suq Al Dhalam takes its name from the darkness provided by the shading over the winding alleys, which are more extensive and complex than anywhere else in the country. As in the 1960s, you can still buy a Taiwanese tricycle, a Mexican gold sovereign, an old bedstead or a Penguin paperback. The original basis of the economy in trading here was selling dates and limes in exchange for cloth, rice and coffee. Today the main passage is increasingly given over to souvenirs; you can buy frankincense sold by men from the mountains of Dhofar, or just beyond the southern town entrance by ladies from Salalah. If you have a yearning for an 'I love Oman' T-shirt or belly dancer costume, this is the place to find them. You will also find coffee pots, incense burners, rose-water sprinklers, henna, Arabic coffee, oregano, dried limes, dried chilli peppers, perfumes, the ubiquitous pashminas, *dishdashas*, antiques, gold, silver, chests, rugs, handicrafts and even the essential animated toy camel. *Khanjars*, the Omani man's ceremonial dagger (see box, page 36), are popular but expensive souvenirs. The aromas from the spices, the incense and the perfume shops evoke an exotic sense of Arabia. Friendly haggling is expected in all of the suqs. Try one of the fantastic milkshakes or fruit juices in the coffee shops just outside the suq on the corniche.

Just after the corniche entrance and before the corner shop of Ghalib Bakheet Salem bait Kalshat Al Mahari is a small alley that leads past shops selling accessories. Follow the alley and eventually you will reach the gold suq, whose shops give the impression that the vaults of Fort Knox have been emptied into Mutrah.

At the T-junction in the gold suq the left turn will take you past more gold shops and onto the main passage. The right turn will take you behind **Sur Al Lawatia**, the private residential area of one of Oman's Shia Muslim communities (uninvited visitors are not permitted within this clearly gated area). The seafront of Sur Al Lawatia includes the splendid blue tiled mosque and whitewashed merchants' houses. Continue in the same direction after Sur Al Lawatia, beyond the conical watchtower and through the maze of small alleys and you will emerge at Bait Al Baranda.

Bait Al Baranda بيت البرندة (*Al Bahri Rd, Mutrah corniche;* ☎ *24 714262;* ⏰ *09.00–13.00 & 16.00–18.00 Sun–Thu, 09.00–13.00 Fri; adult RO1*) This small museum takes its name from the early 20th-century house's veranda, which is now enclosed. The museum's purpose is to offer a broad overview of Muscat's geography, history and culture. Several hands-on displays and periodical art exhibitions add interest. Highlights include interactive explanations of Muscat's geology and a small costume gallery. Though less comprehensive than Bait Al Zubair Museum (page 109) and the National Museum in Old Muscat (pages 111–12), Bait Al Baranda is invariably a less crowded experience and perhaps equally rewarding as a result.

Fish Suq سوق السمك Diagonally across the 'fish roundabout' from Bait Al Baranda is the fish suq. At the time of writing, the current entrance was opposite the Marina Hotel while the yet-to-be-completed new building is adjacent to the fish roundabout. Watch the daily catch being sold here, especially between 06.00 and 10.00. The variety on offer is extraordinary – various tuna caught in the open seas, grouper caught close to the shores and reef fish including parrotfish, sergeant fish and, of course, sardines.

From the fish suq, a walk along the corniche will give great views of the old merchants' houses, the yachts of the sultan and beyond them the ophiolite cliffs that surround the town.

Ghalya's Museum of Modern Art متحف غالية للفنون الحديثة (*Al Bahri Rd;* ☎ *24 711640;* e *info@ghalyasmuseum.com; www.ghalyasmuseum.com;* ⏰ *09.30–18.00 Sat–Thu; RO1/500bzs adult/child*) To the east immediately below Mutrah Fort, this is more a museum than an art gallery. It has small exhibition rooms that include furnishings, ornaments and clothing arranged to give an impression of how a wealthy Omani's home looked in the mid 20th century. A small art gallery has paintings available for sale and there is a gift shop at the exit.

Riyam Park حديقة ريام (⏰ *15.00–midnight Sat–Thu, 08.00–midnight Fri; admission free*) This well-maintained park is clearly landmarked by the large model incense burner that sits atop a cliff. It's a grassy, peaceful spot to wander around in the cooler early evening, or on your walk up the original road between Mutrah and Old Muscat. There is a children's playground, and snacks and drinks can be bought at a kiosk here.

Kalboo Park منتزة كلبوه (⏱ 15.00–23.00 Sat–Thu, 08.00–midnight Fri; admission free) This smaller park also overlooks the sea towards Mutrah, but is located on the seaward edge. The small beach has colourful reef fish on the park side of the sea. Take a left into the small village of Kalboo. Snacks and drinks can be bought here at a couple of kiosks so you can relax and enjoy the sunset over the harbour.

MUSCAT OLD TOWN مسقط القديمة The original old town of Muscat, although only small in area, held a strategic position at the entrance to The Gulf, and so was chosen for its excellent harbour and natural defences. Prior to 1929, Muscat was so ringed by steep jagged rocks that it was accessible only by sea or by footpaths over the hills behind, each of which was closely guarded by watchtowers.

The first land approach by vehicle was made possible in 1929 by the hacking out of a one-lane track through the mountains (from behind the modern Muscat Gate Museum to Riyam) by the British Royal Engineers. The name 'Muscat' means 'place of falling', thought to refer to the falling of the anchor chain (a reference to the harbour). In the late 1830s one European said of Muscat:

> With all its barrenness and unpromising appearance, such is the advantage of position enjoyed by Muscat, commanding, as it does, the entrance to the Persian Gulf, that its harbours are filled with vessels from all ports of the East, and the busy din of commerce constantly enlivens its streets. In few parts of the world can the necessaries, nay even the luxuries, of life, be obtained in greater profusion.

To get there today, take the Al Qurum Heights Road (which is the exit on the right of the Al Sultan Qaboos Street just before the Al Qurum roundabout, where the highway splits) and then follow signs to Muscat; or continue into Ruwi and again follow signage to Muscat. You could take the road through either Mutrah or Al Wadi Al Kabir, both of which arrive into Old Muscat from different sides of the town.

With such an isolated location, it is surprising that Muscat was favoured as the capital city. Mutrah, just a few bays further west, had direct access to the hinterland and was just as good a harbour as Muscat, yet was considered to be more suitable as a commercial area rather than a political capital. Muscat also had very little fresh water within its walls, and the ring of bare hills served as a bowl that magnified the extreme heat and humidity trapped within them, preventing any cooling sea breezes from fanning the walled town.

The town walls that stand today are mostly a reconstruction of the original one built during the time of the Portuguese, and the only original section climbs the cliffs to the east. There were only three gates: the **Al Bab Al Saghir (small gate)** was for pedestrians and donkeys, the **Al Bab Al Kabir (big gate)** was the main gate for smallish vehicles and the **Bab Mathaib (or Matha'eeb)** (this name means location of the waterfall, presumably where water flooded down the cliff during a storm) was the third, used by large vehicles that were only permitted to drive between Mutrah and Muscat, and even then only with a special dispensation, which was granted infrequently. Different tribes had responsibility for different gates: the Hawasina provided ten guards each for the Al Bab Al Saghir and Bab Mathaib, while the Beni Umr guarded the Al Bab Al Kabir gate.

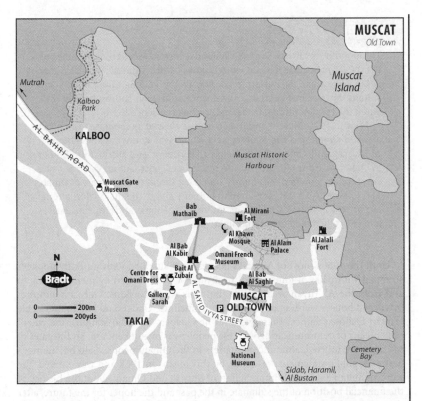

Curfews were imposed on the residents of Muscat: the Al Bab Al Kabir main gate was shut three hours after sunset and could only be opened after that with special written permission from the *wali* (governor). Anyone walking within the walls at this time had to carry a *butti* (a lantern). To ensure that everyone remembered all these regulations, a drum was beaten from the top of Al Mirani Fort for 20 minutes beforehand, followed by three explosions, 3 hours after sunset. In Mutrah, there was one explosion instead of three. Long after the wall either side of the gate in Mutrah was demolished, the doors of the gate were still ceremonially closed each night because no-one gave the order to stop doing so.

The Al Bu Said dynasty, of which Sultan Qaboos is the current representative, made Muscat its seat of power during the rule of Sultan Hamad bin Said Al Said, who died in 1792. Oman's increase in wealth, which flowed in principally from East Africa, resulted in substantial houses being built from around 1820 to 1840. Although appearing huge from the outside, an open courtyard in the house's centre and frequently an interior balcony that also acted as a corridor for access into the rooms around this courtyard resulted in surprisingly small living spaces for the residents. Usually just the first floor was habitable with some five rooms. The ground floor tended to be lost to a spacious reception hall, a small guardroom by the entrance and lots of tiny windowless storerooms. Even the inner walls were massively thick, up to 1m, which helped keep the rooms cool in summer. Their design was a mix of Arab, Persian, Indian and African styles. On the flat roof there was generally a raised wooden platform, high enough to give a view over the rampart wall, offering a peaceful spot on summer evenings to catch the breeze.

Throughout its history, Oman's capital has moved locations and, although the dates are unclear, it has at various times been assigned to Qalhat, Suhar, Bahla, Nizwa and Ar Rustaq, according to the various ruling imams and sultans. Muscat has been its capital since sometime shortly before 1792, when the third Al Bu Said leader established residence there.

Prior to 1970, Muscat and the coast was classed as separate from other areas in Oman and the country as a whole was known as the Sultanate of Muscat and Oman, Oman being the interior and distinctly different in character from Muscat and the rest of the coast. Sultan Qaboos – the current ruler – unified the country, naming it simply the Sultanate of Oman, and today Muscat is its dominating hub: the site of the main international airport, the embassies, ministries, international banks and large businesses and critically the oil export terminal.

Until the 1960s most of Muscat's houses were supplied with water by donkeys strapped with pairs of four-gallon tin drums or even carried by men trudging to and from the Al Tuyan area outside the walls with goatskins. Only a handful of privileged houses were supplied by private pipelines. Under Said bin Taimur's rule (Sultan Qaboos's father) there were no newspapers or radio stations; the ruler's only means of communicating with his people was by noticeboard. So the gates of Muscat were utilised, announcing matters to the Omani people. Said bin Taimur's first ever public statement was made by this means in 1968 and was entitled 'the word of Sultan Said bin Taimur, Sultan of Muscat and Oman, about the history of the financial position of the sultanate in the past and the hopes for the future, after the export of oil'. Said bin Taimur also had total control over all imports to the country. For example, no car could be imported without his express permission, and there were no tractors in the sultanate because he refused to give permission for them to be imported. If he forgot or failed to reply to a request, new businesses that had already invested in buildings were left waiting over six months in limbo, unable to send reminders to the sultan himself as he was in Salalah.

Most of the original buildings of Old Muscat have been demolished. These include the majority of the old mansion houses (the Omani French Museum is a notable survivor – see pages 110–11). The original British embassy, which was immediately below Al Jalali Fort and the building behind it that housed the US embassy for a short period, have also gone. However, the setting of the town still retains its charm, while the forts and watchtowers provide a lasting link to Muscat's history.

Al Alam Palace قصر العلم The sultan's Al Alam Palace (The Flag Palace) was built in the early 1970s at its seafront location here in the old town. The current complex replaced a number of buildings that occupied the harbour front. The blue-and-gold columns provide a sense of glamour, making the building every bit the ideal for an exotic Arabian town. Towards Al Jalali Fort at the eastern edge of the harbour is the more restrained guest palace complex which stretches from the harbour back towards the cliffs. The front of the palace has an English-style garden and the ceremonial entrance is flanked by cannons and raised flower beds. To the rear is a large grass lawn which has been used for receptions on occasions such as Armed Forces Day.

Al Jalali (قلعة الجلالي) and Al Mirani (قلعة الميراني) forts The Portuguese began to build these forts in 1527, though their current versions date from 1587 and 1588 respectively. They were originally known as São João and Fort Capitão. Neither is open to the general public.

Al Jalali Fort, to the east, has a substantial gun platform with eight British ships' cannons dating from the early 19th century. The complex of rooms above the stairs from the harbour includes a small mosque and a museum with a 'son et lumière' presentation of firearms and Omani metalwork. Until shortly after 1970, Al Jalali was Oman's main jail; it is still in use as a garrison for Omani troops. The western fort Al Mirani's principal function today is as a barracks accessed by an elevator concealed in the most prominent tower.

Besides these forts, little apart from the watchtowers on the hills overlooking the main forts remain of the Portuguese occupation of Muscat. Some remnants of the governor's residence and barracks survived as late as 1895, while the cathedral ruins finally succumbed to redevelopment during the first half of the 20th century.

Old Muscat has a number of **museums and galleries**, all within walking distance if you're careful to avoid the traffic. If combined with a walk to view Al Alam Palace, the places detailed below will make for a good day out at a leisurely pace. They are listed in the order that you would encounter them if approaching from Mutrah.

Muscat Gate Museum متحف بوابة مسقط (*Al Bahri Rd;* ✆ *24 739005;* m *99 328754;* ☺ *09.30–12.30 & 16.30–19.00 Sat–Thu; adult 500bzs*) This museum is operated by Royal Court Affairs and is on Al Bahri Road (the continuation of Mutrah corniche towards Old Muscat, literally 'the sea road'). It is located above the gate that spans the road. There is a small car park close to the museum – to reach it, continue through the gate and take the right turn, which takes you to the parking spaces at the base of a flight of steps leading to the museum. This museum covers the history of Oman, with a particular focus on the country's ancient wells, *aflaj,* forts and harbours.

Bait Al Zubair متحف بيت الزبير (*Al Sayidiyyah St;* ✆ *24 736688;* e *museum@ baitalzubairmuseum.com; http://www.baitalzubairmuseum.com;* ☺ *09.30–18.00 Sat–Thu; RO2*) This museum is signposted off the Mutrah–Muscat road about 450m after passing under Muscat Gate Museum and is located just outside the walls on Al Sayidiyyah Street. If coming from Al Bustan, pass through the roundabout opposite Al Alam Palace and the National Museum, continue straight for 600m until the road divides and following the left branch, after an additional 80m, enter the free car park on the right-hand side of the road. This is a purpose-built private museum, located on the site of the house of the owner's family. Opened in 1998 as an Omani heritage museum and cultural centre, it is designed to give an insight into Omani lifestyles and traditions, with early photos and traditional furnishings. Inside the various buildings there is a small lecture theatre, gift shop and coffee shop, as well as a reference library and a *majlis* (meeting room) with an exhibition of old maps, seafaring information and models of traditional dhows. The museum on the ground floor displays *khanjars*, men's dress, swords and weapons, women's dresses, jewellery, chests and household items, all well labelled and explained. There is a second floor with coins and stamps. A separate building, Bait Dalaleel, is an original old house with traditional furniture and a small coffee shop. The third building, Bait Al Oud, holds exhibitions on the ground floor, while the two floors above have household furniture, maps and other historical documents. Outside there are

It was from the harbour of Old Muscat on 23 November 1980 that Tim Severin's ship, *The Sohar*, set sail as part of Oman's tenth National Day celebrations. It was the start of a 6,000-mile journey to China and began amid cannon fire, music and tears from every Omani who had been involved in building the remarkable ship. It took 165 days to construct and was completed ahead of schedule.

The project had been three years in the planning, and Severin lived in the country for 12 months during the preparations and the building of the boat in Sur. He was given a mansion, rented for him by the Ministry of National Heritage and Culture, in Sur in 1980. The house had been built 200 years previously by wealthy Sur merchants, had a large courtyard and was made of coral. He lived in the upper rooms where the original owners would have lived, and even in the height of summer the 3ft-thick walls and wooden shutters kept the rooms cool. When he first arrived, the place was filthy, with goats browsing in the rooms and a cow penned in the yard; it took nearly two weeks for it to be cleaned up by a veritable army of 20 workers. The house was set on slightly raised ground on the foreshore, close enough to walk to the spot where the boat would be built, but too far away to sneak back to during the day.

The boat was built in traditional fashion using timbers held together with coconut rope and antifouling made from lime and mutton fat. Severin went to the coast of Malabar in India (1,300 miles away) to get timber for the ship. All timber for Omani ships had originally come from there, since Oman had always lacked trees large enough to provide first-class boat timber. Severin and his men made excursions into the forest to hand-pick the timber, called *aini*, which did not need to be seasoned for boatbuilding.

entertaining miniature reconstructions of traditional stone and *barasti* houses, with a *falaj* and running water, and even a working model of a pottery kiln.

Bait Al Zubair is also home to the **Centre for Omani Dress** (\22 084700; e COD@ baitalzubair.com; www.centreforomanidress.com), run by an organisation dedicated to preserving and disseminating information about Oman's traditional dress.

Gallery Sarah جاليري ساره (Al *Sayidiyyah* St; \22 084747; e info@gallerysarah. com; www.gallerysarah.com; ⊕ 09.30–18.00 Sat–Thu) Part of the Bait Al Zubair Museum, Gallery Sarah has a separate entrance 120m around the corner on the left-hand side of Bait Al Zubair. This bright, airy art gallery was established in memory of the British curator and artist Sarah White, who helped the Zubair family to establish their museum. This gallery specialises in exhibitions of artists, usually with an Arabic focus, and has limited-edition prints available for sale.

Omani French Museum (Bait Fransa) المتحف العُماني الفرنسي (*Qasr Al Alam* St; \24 736613; ⊕ 09.00–13.00 Sat–Thu; 500/200bzs adult/child 6–12) This museum is on the right-hand side after going through the main gate in the town walls Al Bab Al Kabir (the gate has three tall flagpoles whose flags flutter during daylight hours). Parking is not easy in Old Muscat, but there is a small car park here and several others within walking distance.

Bait Fransa (or French House) was the original 19th-century French consulate and is now an attractive, well-laid-out museum chronicling Omani–French historical links from the 18th century onwards. The lease of the house was only

Severin's boat was named *The Sohar* (the legendary Sindbad's birthplace) on the express wish of the sultan, who sponsored the entire project as a tribute to Oman's seafaring heritage.

The journey to China took a total of seven months. The first stretch from Muscat to Calcutta took one month. There was a crew of 28, eight of them Omani traditional sailors, all volunteers. All but one of these married young Muslim girls when they docked in Calcutta – a custom for sailors in the Arabian Sea as old as the hills. They never had any intention of returning to her, but, as is usual in Omani marriages, the husband paid a handsome dowry to the girl's family, which her family eagerly accepted. There was no stigma attached, even some pride in fact, and after three years the girls were free to marry again if the husband did not return. Indeed, Sindbad himself added to the legend by acquiring a wife at every port. On the recreated journey, boxes of nuts, dried fruit, hundreds of eggs wrapped in sawdust, sacks of onions, dried peas, rice and spices were stowed aboard, along with tinned foods, sauces, Omani dates and fresh fruit. The bilges stank of rotten eggs, giving off hydrogen sulphide gas. The navigation manual that Tim Severin took on board was written by a master of 15th-century navigation, Ahmed Bin Majid, from Julfar on the northern coast of the Oman peninsula and one of the most skilled seafarers of his time. It was difficult to follow, not least because it was written in verse. Nevertheless, on the strength of this manual and after some practice, Severin managed to navigate from the Pole Star using nothing more than a piece of string with a knot and cardboard. Severin's book *The Sindbad Voyage* was published in 1983 (page 335). The dhow now sits on the Al Bustan roundabout opposite the State Council of Oman and near the Al Bustan Palace Hotel.

returned to the Omani government in 1945, despite the fact the last French consul to live there left in 1920. There is a wealth of interest in the exhibits that range from old maps of Muscat and period furniture to copies of Napoleon's correspondence to Oman's ruler in anticipation of Napoleon's military action against British India. Yet for all that, it is the house that is perhaps of greatest interest, as it is the oldest house in Muscat open to visitors.

National Museum المتحف الوطني (*Al Sayidiyyah St;* ✆ *22 081563; www. mhc.gov.om;* ⊕ *09.30–18.00 Sat–Thu; RO1/5/free Omani adults/foreign adults/ children & students*) To reach the National Museum from the corniche, drive to 'old' Muscat and pass under the Muscat Gate Museum and continue for another 1.1km, passing Bait Al Zubair and following the road initially right, then left and then right again along an avenue with date palms, and you will find the museum on your right. From Al Bustan continue into Old Muscat and the National Museum will be on your left as you approach the roundabout opposite Al Alam Palace. Parking is adjacent to the museum.

This museum is purpose-built and state-of-the-art both in its displays and the conservation of its artefacts. Signage is in Arabic and English with Arabic Braille. A guide is usually available to explain the well-marked exhibits. The museum is intended to illustrate Oman's history and heritage, including stone tools dating back to around 500000BC, metalwork from the Bronze Age onwards, traditional Omani costumes in an enormous glass case, the original mihrab from one of Oman's historic mosques and a very impressive doorway from a merchant's house in eastern Oman. Take a morning to enjoy this building, designed by the British museum architect Jasper Jacob.

THE COAST SOUTHEAST OF MUSCAT الساحل الجنوب الشرقي من مسقط From the roundabout opposite Al Alam Palace the coastal route continues southeast.

Sidab سداب If you continue south out beyond Muscat Old Town you come to the small village of Sidab with its fishing community and coastguard operations. The coastal mountains overlook Cemetery Bay, home to two cemeteries with whitewashed graves, one of which contains the grave of Bishop Valpy French, the Anglican Bishop of Lahore, who died in Muscat in 1891 during missionary work. The bays can be accessed by chartered boat most easily from Marina Bandar Al Rowdha (see below).

Haramil حرامل From the roundabout opposite Al Alam Palace a drive of 4.2km takes you to the left turn into Haramil village, with its houses facing directly onto the shingle beach. Fibreglass fishing boats are hauled up onto the beach when not in use and there is a small fibreglass boat repair facility. Shortly after the turn to Haramil is the left turn into the **Capital Area Yacht Club** (✆ 24 737712; ⏰06.00–23.00 Sat–Wed, 06.00–midnight Thu & Fri). This small private members' club has a sheltered sandy beach and a simple European-style restaurant ($$).

Marina Bandar Al Rowdha مارينا بندر الروضة From the turn to Haramil a short drive south of 800m takes you to the access for Muscat's original marina (*www. marinaoman.net*). Those interested in boating, diving, taking a dhow trip or simply having a meal in a beautiful, peaceful location must visit this marina. Located 3.5km south of Old Muscat, it is open to the public and not a private members' club. It has numerous wet and dry berths, a marine control tower, a swimming pool, a licensed restaurant (*The Blue Marlin;* ✆24 740038; $$) and bar, and offers all the sea-based tours. There are numerous independent organisations operating from here (page 136). A traditional dhow is used for sunset trips and scenic coastal tours. The full array of tours includes diving, game fishing, snorkelling, camping, sailing, scuba, whale- and dolphin-watching, dhow cruising and jet skiing, or you can ask to be taken to your own secluded beach and arrange to be collected. You might simply like to visit this place for a meal by the pool or within the air-conditioned restaurant, with full marina views.

Opposite the entrance to the marina is a small **public park** (⏰ 15.00–23.00 Sat–Thu, 08.00–midnight Fri; admission free). The setting is beautiful, as it is surrounded by a horseshoe of mountains and opposite the marina and the Sea of Oman.

Al Bustan البستان Carrying on south from the marina turn and continuing along the road for a kilometre brings you to the junction for Al Bustan village, the place where the inhabitants of the original Al Bustan village were relocated and provided with new housing when their homes were demolished to make way for the domed Al Bustan Palace Hotel (page 86). The village sits on the northern end of Al Bustan Beach, while Al Bustan Palace Hotel has the private beach to the north. At the roundabout leading up towards Al Bustan Palace Hotel sits the *Sohar* dhow, which was used by Tim Severin in his 'Sindbad' journey (see box, page 110).

Set at the base of the mountains is the **Majlis Oman (Oman Council)** building for the bicameral parliamentary body. The two bodies are the Majlis Al Dawla (State Council), a body appointed by Sultan Qaboos from suitably qualified people and the Majlis Al Shura (Consultative Council), an elected body whose members are chosen by the *wilayats*, with one member for a *wilayat* with a population of fewer than 30,000 people and two members for a *wilayat* with more than 30,000 people. Candidates for this elected body must be an Omani national by birth aged 30 and more, educated with a pass from the secondary school final examinations, without a criminal record and not a member of the armed forces or judiciary. Together these two bodies form the Oman Council.

Other buildings close to this roundabout are the National Audit Office to the south, the civil defence complex just north of the Majlis Oman, and the office of the Governor of Muscat opposite the civil defence complex.

Qantab قنتب Qantab, signed from the Al Bustan–Al Wadi Al Kabir road, is a 14km drive from Old Muscat or 21km from Al Qurum. From the Al Bustan–Al Wadi Al Kabir road take the signed route to the Shangri-La Barr Al Jissah, and on the roundabout take the second exit to the left. Qantab is 2.4km beyond this roundabout.

This rapidly growing village was originally a small fishing settlement with a small date garden. It is dominated by a giant limestone crag to the south.

EARLY FOREIGN POLICY

Qaboos's father, Sultan Said bin Taimur, had no links with other countries except Britain and India, the only two countries to have consulates in Muscat immediately before 1970. He considered membership of bodies like the United Nations completely unnecessary, especially as the UN's first involvement with Oman was to condemn Britain for aggression when it responded to his request for help in the 1957 imamate revolution, stating that Oman's right to self-determination was being prevented by the United Kingdom. Said bin Taimur's relations with many of his Arab neighbours and brethren were also hostile, not least because several of them had an imamate representative in their capitals of Baghdad, Damascus, Cairo, Riyadh and Kuwait, and in the case of Saudi Arabia also due to its historical claims to both Omani and UAE territory. The imamates, whose opposition to his father's rule had resulted in the Treaty of Seeb in 1920 and caused the nation to be known as the Sultanate of Muscat and Oman, naturally continued to oppose Sultan Said bin Taimur as the ruler from 1932. Their aim, at the least, was to seek independence for the tribal-led interior of Oman (considered Oman 'proper' as formalised by the treaty).

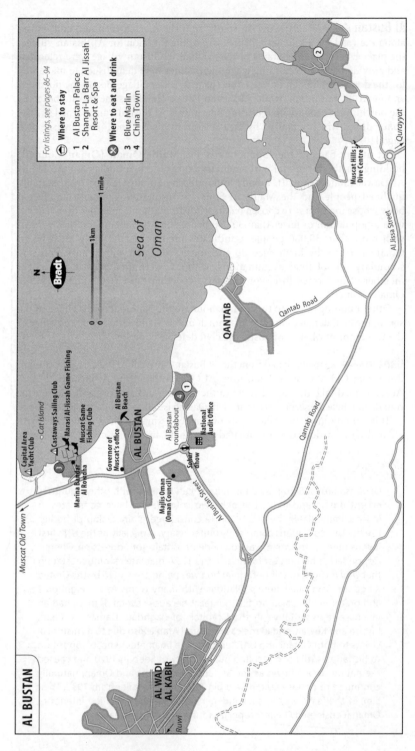

For listings, see pages 86–94

Where to stay
1 Al Bustan Palace
2 Shangri-La Barr Al Jissah
   Resort & Spa

Where to eat and drink
3 Blue Marlin
4 China Town

Sea of
Oman

Capital Area Yacht Club
Cat Island
Castaways Sailing Club
Marasi Al-Jissah Game Fishing
Muscat Game Fishing Club
Marina Bandar Al Rowdha
Governor of Muscat's office
Al Bustan Beach
AL BUSTAN
Muscat Old Town
Al Bustan roundabout
Sohar dhow
National Audit Office
Majlis Oman (Oman Council)

QANTAB
Qantab Road

Muscat Hills Dive Centre
Qurayyat
Al Jissa Street

AL WADI AL KABIR
Ruwi

Qantab Road
Al Bustan Street

The beach has small fibreglass fishing boats that are available for hire at a few rials for leisure trips (albeit without any insurance or safety equipment). To the beach's south is a small ship-construction area where the *Jewel of Muscat* was built. It was constructed to recreate an Arabian Sea dhow that sank off Belitung Island, Indonesia, with a full cargo from the Tang dynasty in China, in around AD830. The *Jewel of Muscat* was constructed using the traditional coconut fibre-stitched hull which was used on Arab dhows until as recently as the middle of the 20th century. In 2010, the *Jewel of Muscat* sailed from Muscat to Singapore, where it and all the artefacts found on the sunk ship are displayed.

Bandar Al Jissa بندر جصة Bandar Al Jissa is a secluded series of bays south of Qantab, with hotel and residential developments by Saraya Bandar Al Jissa in the northern bay area and the Shangri-La Barr Al Jissah Resort and Spa in the southern bay (page 87). Reached by boat from Qantab or any dive centre, there are five dive sites in this area (also spelled Bandar Jussa and Jissah), and its shallow depths are particularly suitable for beginners and night dives. Turtles, spiny lobsters and cuttlefish have all been spotted here.

YITI يتي With a lovely mountain backdrop and a soft sandy beach, Yiti, which lies 25km south of Muscat, is a good place to take a picnic, and close enough if you want to escape the hubbub of the city for an afternoon, though there is no public transport, which may restrict those without cars.

The tarmac road to Yiti branches off from the Al Bustan–Al Wadi Al Kabir road – take the signed route, Qantab Road, to the Shangri-La Barr Al Jissah. On the second roundabout along this road as you're travelling towards the Shangri-La and the Muscat Hills Dive Centre, take the first right. At the first roundabout continue straight and at the second roundabout take the second exit to the left. From this roundabout continue across the wadi and follow the road directly through the small village of Yiti until you reach the sea inlet (the land here is destined to be a marina-based resort). The road then swings right past some more housing and trees and then over a rough sandy track (best accessed by 4x4) and onto the area to the rear of the beach. From the Shangri-La and the Muscat Hills Dive Centre it's a total of 12km.

FRENCH TROUBLES

Although no French consul arrived to live in Muscat until 1894, there had been attempts to send one since a decree in 1795 (issued in Paris) announced the establishment of a Muscat consulate. Mr Beauchamp, the first appointee, spent four years in Egypt *en route* to the post and was then diverted to Constantinople by Napoleon in 1799, where he was arrested and imprisoned. The next attempt was in 1802 when Talleyrand and Napoleon appointed Cavaignac as consul. On arrival in Muscat in 1803 Cavaignac found the imam out of town (he was further up the coast fighting Wahhabi incursions) and was told he could neither disembark his baggage nor occupy the house that had been made available until the imam returned and gave his express permission. When the imam did eventually return, he did not give permission and Cavaignac was obliged to leave. He described Oman with bitterness: 'This country and its people are simply wretched. The sultan is nothing but a Bedouin pawn'.

Bandar Al Khiran بندر الخيران Beyond Yiti the secluded bays of Bandar Al Khiran (or Bandar Khayran) make excellent camping, picnicking, diving and snorkelling spots. There are several dive sites in this area, including *Al Munassir*, a 3,000-tonne ship sunk for wreck diving just to the east of the sea entrance into Bandar Al Khiran. Most of the bays are best accessed by boat (hire from either Marina Bandar Al Rowdha or enquire after the fishermen's boat at Qantab – pages 113–14), though a few rough tracks over or around the rugged hills are suitable for a 4x4 lead into some bays, several of which are fringed with the black mangrove *Avicenia marina*.

AS SIFAH السيفة Continuing on the road past Bandar Al Khiran, which is cut through ever-higher mountains, is As Sifah, a small fishing village set on a soft white-sand beach which extends for 10km, with the tarmac road close to it for part of its length. It is a 52km drive from Al Qurum in the Capital Area, or if you wish to visit the Sifawy Boutique Hotel (page 89), you could use the taxi boat service from Marina Bandar Al Rowdha (\ *24 749111*), which takes less than an hour. The beaches are mostly sand and the mountains behind rise to 1,000m, creating a very picturesque and peaceful location.

RUWI روي These days Ruwi is a busy business district and suburb. It is also the country's transport hub, with the main bus station for destinations all over Oman. The business district is sometimes referred to as the Central Business District (CBD) or the Mutrah Business District (MBD).

Up until the 1960s Ruwi was a small village serving as the market garden for Muscat and Mutrah. It had a large fish shop with an open-roofed kitchen beside the road, and donkeys would bring panniers full of fish from Mutrah Suq to be cooked here. Ruwi was also the location of the customs checkpoint at Wadi Adai, comprising only a mud hut with a red flag, where taxes were levied on

THE INDIAN MERCHANT COMMUNITY

Throughout the Gulf, general trading is dominated by merchants from the Indian subcontinent. In Oman this is nothing new: the chronicles relating the exploits of Afonso de Albuquerque mention the presence of Indians in several towns along the Omani coast. Indeed, the expulsion of the Portuguese was reputedly caused by an Indian merchant called Naretum. A resident of Muscat, he had a daughter who was wanted as a wife by the Portuguese governor. Rather than refuse Naretum agreed, but advised the governor that his food and water were bad and that they should be replaced, and that the gunpowder was damp and needed to be substituted. On the night when all of these supplies had been taken out of the forts in Muscat, the Omani forces besieged the town, and the Portuguese capitulated a short time afterwards.

The flags of a Hindu temple have fluttered for over 150 years above the Al Tuyam district of Old Muscat. Originally the Indians were largely from Sind, but during the latter part of the 19th century a gradual change resulted in people from Gujarat becoming prominent merchants. Today people from Kerala have gained prominence along with the Gujarati merchants. Some Indian families who have been in Oman for generations have Omani nationality, while others chose Indian nationality upon Indian independence but still retain their business operations in Oman.

goods moving between Muscat and Oman. Complex rates of tax were levied – for example 5% for dates and 15% for tobacco, everything having its own rate.

The Ruwi area is built up on either side of the Al Wadi Al Kabir Valley, which eventually exits into the sea at Darsait. The town's two main through-roads are Al Nahda Street to the west and Bait Al Falaj Street to the east. Coming from the airport end of the highway, it is useful to remember that Al Qurum Heights Road (which is the exit on the right, just before Al Qurum, and where the motorway splits into two) leads up and over to the Sheraton. Alternatively, keeping straight on the motorway leads you to Ruwi Suq Street (pages 118–19). There are various budget hotels in the Central Business District off Al Fursan Street and Al Baladiyah Street.

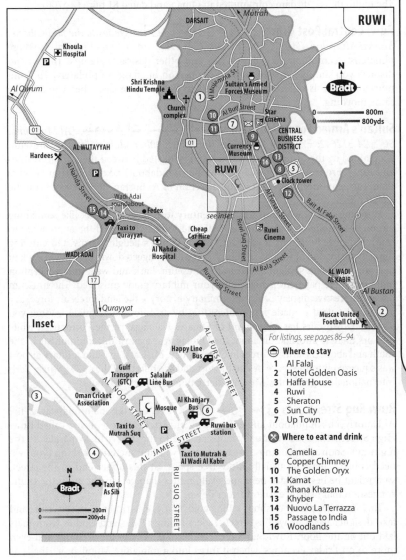

For listings, see pages 86–94

🏨 **Where to stay**
1 Al Falaj
2 Hotel Golden Oasis
3 Haffa House
4 Ruwi
5 Sheraton
6 Sun City
7 Up Town

🍴 **Where to eat and drink**
8 Camelia
9 Copper Chimney
10 The Golden Oryx
11 Kamat
12 Khana Khazana
13 Khyber
14 Nuovo La Terrazza
15 Passage to India
16 Woodlands

The **church complex** is located west of Ruwi Street on Al Farahidi Street, comprising a number of different places of worship. The **Bible Society Centre** (✆ 24 799474; e bsginfo@gmail.com) within the same area is a central contact point for the churches. Behind the church complex is the **Shri Krishna Hindu Temple**, which is also on Al Farahidi Street (✆ 24 798546).

Currency Museum البنك المركزي العُماني (Inside the Central Bank of Oman,
Markzi Mutrah Al Tijari St; ✆ 24 796102; ⊕ 08.30–12.30 Sun–Thu; 500/200/100bzs adult/child/child under 6) This museum showcases a collection of coins and notes. This is a small museum with such a focused area of specialisation that it is probably only of real interest to a numismatic and currency collector, as it sells mint coins. The highlight is a dirham coin minted in Oman and dated 81 hijra (AD700).

Ruwi Central Post Office البريد المركزي في روي (Opposite the HSBC bank,
Markzi Mutrah Al Tijari St; ✆ 24 700922; ⊕ 07.30–14.30 Sun–Thu) This is where philatelists can obtain first-day covers and other desirable stamps. There is no display; you simply sit at the desk of the person in charge of philately. The coin museum and this office are less than 400m apart so can easily be visited in the same morning.

Sultan's Armed Forces Museum متحف قوات السلطان المسلحة (Al Mujamma
St; ✆ 24 312642; ⊕ 08.00–13.00 Sat–Thu; RO1/500bzs adult/child) This museum is operated by the Ministry of Defence and is located between the port at Mutrah and Ruwi. From Al Qurum (Saih Al Malih roundabout) take Al Qurum Heights Road east, continuing straight in the direction of Al Bustan, and the exit is on the left after 6.2km.

It is housed in a whitewashed 19th-century fort, making it look like something out of *Beau Geste*. It was rebuilt in 1845 and initially defended the approaches to Mutrah, before becoming a garrison fort for Oman's fledgling army. On entering the general area, all of which is military, you will be flagged down and should explain that you are going straight ahead to the museum. Park and walk into a reception building where payment is made and your military guide mustered. The museum has an impressive display of Oman's military history – the land force, air force, avy and Royal Guard – made more interesting by an informative guide leading you around. Downstairs has an account of Oman's wars against the Portuguese, while upstairs there is information about the Dhofar War against the communists in the south and about the armed forces in Oman today. Muscat's civil and military airport was squeezed into the space beside the fort and the hills until the 1970s, when 'Seeb International Airport' (now Muscat International Airport) was built.

Ruwi Suq Street شارع سوق روي To get here, exit the main highway at the
Al Hamriyyah roundabout and enter Ruwi Suq Street (almost always called Ruwi High Street). The road eventually loops around to the left (virtually parallel to the highway). Soon after joining this section you will find metered parking (you will need coins). There are usually more free spaces at this upper end of the street, so it might be best to park here and walk, rather than get caught up in the traffic congestion that usually ensues further down.

This street has plenty of shops selling gold, fabric, electrical goods, souvenirs and fake designer wear, as well as street traders selling DVDs and clothes from mats laid out on the floor. Ruwi Suq Street can become busy in the evenings and even more so on Friday evenings, when it turns into a miniature Mumbai or Dhaka as workers from outlying areas congregate to meet friends and while away the evening in conversation.

AL QURUM القرم Originally just a little fishing village of *barasti* huts on the southern end of Al Batinah, Al Qurum (also Qurum and Qurm) is now part of the modern sprawl of the Capital Area and where several of the beach hotels are situated along the wide sandy shore. The marshy estuary is the mouth of the Wadi Adai, which commences in Al Amrat and still floods into the sea after heavy rains. Al Qurum translates as 'mangrove' and the estuary of Wadi Adai is still thick with mangrove trees, now a nature reserve and a natural extension to Al Qurum Natural Park (page 121). It is a good birdwatching spot, more peaceful than most places within the Capital Area. The landscape is enhanced by the rocky headland at the far eastern end of the beach, now built up with apartment blocks and home to the Crowne Plaza (page 87), which benefits from the breezes and elevated views.

Located at the point where the highway has split to approach Mutrah and Ruwi, Al Qurum is still a prime residential and shopping area even as the town has spread west to envelop the airport.

Children's Science Museum متحف الطفل للعلوم [120 D3] (*A'Saruj/Shati Al Qurum;* ⧽ *24 605368;* ⊕ *09.30–13.30 Sat–Thu; 500/100bzs adult/child under 12*) From the traffic lights to the east of the Royal Opera House take Al Shati Street towards the beach and 200m after the traffic lights take the right exit into Way 2601, which then runs due east towards the prominent Beach One Plaza office block and the hill that is home to the Mumtaz Mahal Indian Restaurant. The twin domes of the Children's Science Museum are on the right-hand side, with parking. Operated by the Ministry of Heritage and Culture, this small museum focuses on interactive scientific experiments to promote interest through exploration. There are displays to explain the nervous connection of body parts to the brain and the relative allocation of the brain's resources, together with hands-on microscopes and a skeleton. The museum is worth a visit if you have young children. Unfortunately, it hasn't been updated since it opened some 20 years ago, so don't expect any cutting-edge ideas.

Children's Library مكتبة الأطفال [120 D3] (*A'Saruj/Shati Al Qurum;* ⧽ *24 605368;* ⊕ *09.30–13.30 Sat–Thu*) Immediately next to the Children's Museum, this is a purpose-built library that does as it says, and makes for a good combined visit of the museum and Al Qurum Natural Park (page 121), the entrance of which is adjacent to both.

Oil and Gas Exhibition Centre معرض النفط والغاز [120 G2] (*Sayh Al Malih St;* ⧽ *24 677834;* ⊕ *07.00–noon & 13.00–15.45 Sun–Thu, 08.00–13.00 Sat; admission free*) The exhibition centre can be found on the right-hand side just before Gate 2 of the Petroleum Development Oman (PDO). It was donated to the people of Oman by PDO back in 1995 and guides you through the discovery and excavation of oil in the country. It is interesting for both adults and children, with interactive models and computer information all in English and Arabic.

Planetarium القبة الفلكية [120 G2] (⧽ *24 675542;* e *planetarium@pdo.co.om; www.pdo.co.om/Pages/Planetarium.aspx;* ⊕ *shows at 10.00, 11.30 & 16.00 Sat only; admission free*) The planetarium was built in 2000 and adjoins the Oil and Gas Exhibition Centre (see above). It is best to book in advance for the shows,

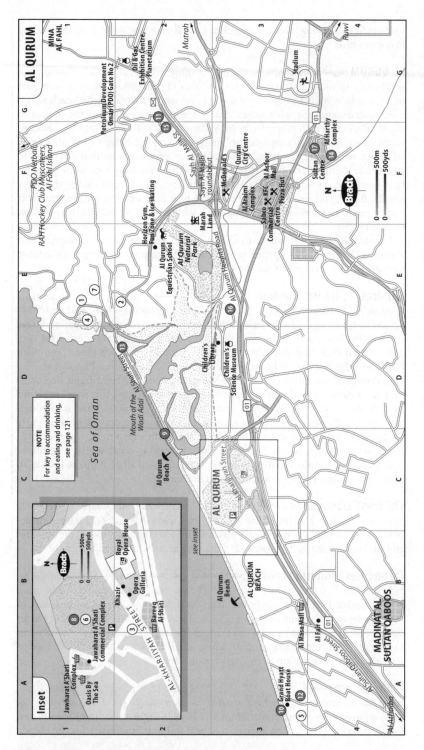

Inset

Jawharat A'Shati
Complex

Oasis By
The Sea

Jawharat A'Shati
Commercial Complex

Bradt

N

0   500m
0   500yds

Khazir

Opera
Galleria

Royal
Opera House

AL-KHARJIYAH STREET

Bareeq
Al-Shati

AL QURUM

NOTE
For key to accommodation
and eating and drinking,
see page 121

Sea of Oman

Al Qurum
Beach

Mouth of the
Wadi Adai

A'Shati Street

PDO Netball/
RAF Hockey Club Muscateers,
Al Fahl Island

Petroleum Development
Oman (PDO) Gate No 2

Oil & Gas
Exhibition Centre,
Planetarium

AL QURUM

MINA
AL FAHL

Mutrah

Horizon Gym,
Fun Zone & Ice-skating

Al Qurum
Equestrian School

Al Qurum
Natural
Park

Marah
Land

Sayh Al Maleh
roundabout

Sayh Al Maleh Street

McDonald's

Qurum
City Centre

Al Araimi
Complex

KFC

Sabco
Commercial
Centre

Al Asfoor
Mall

Pizza Hut

Al Qurum Heights Road

Children's
Library

Science Museum

Children's
Museum

Al Qurum
Beach

AL QURUM
BEACH

Al Qurum Street

see inset

Al Sultan Qaboos Street

Al Masa Mall

Al Fatr

Grand Hyatt

Boat House

MADINAT AL
SULTAN QABOOS

Al Sultan Qaboos Street

Al Athaiba

Bradt

N

0   500m
0   500yds

Ruwi

Stadium

Sultan
Centre

Al Harthy
Complex

120

which illustrate the sky above Muscat through displays on the inside of the domed ceiling. There is comfortable cinema seating. It's ideal for a visit after children have enjoyed the Oil and Gas displays.

Al Qurum Natural Park حديقة القرم الطبيعية [120 E2]

(🕐 *17.00–23.00 Sun–Thu, 10.00–midnight Fri & Sat; admission free*) The park is accessed from two sides: one entrance is just after the Children's Museum (page 119), while there is a second entrance from Al Qurum Street which extends from the Saih Al Malih roundabout towards the Crowne Plaza Hotel. The park has attractive grounds with mature trees and an ornamental lake. It abuts the area of mangroves that exits to the sea by the Crowne Plaza Hotel. The amusement park – Marah Land – boasts rides, games and food outlets.

Al Qurum Beach شاطئ القرم Al

Qurum Beach (Shati Al Qurum in Arabic, plus the official name Hay Al Saruj, which is used on maps) is a prime beach area with two excellent five-star hotels – the Grand Hyatt (page 86) and the InterContinental (pages 87–8) – as well as the four-star Crowne Plaza (page 87). The beach is popular in the afternoon with teams playing beach football, families who stake out their space beyond the match areas, and hotel guests. It is a lovely place to watch the sun go down before going for a meal in one of the restaurants along its length. The housing was built in the late 1980s and early 1990s and conformed to the design requirement of flat roofs, Islamic features on the façade and whitewashed exterior walls. With their size and imposing appearance, they are a popular choice for embassies for those countries that do not wish to build in the main embassy area in Al Khuwair.

Al Fahl Island جزيرة الفحل

Otherwise known as 'Shark Island', this is excellent for diving, offering the largest variety of coral in the capital condensed into one area. There are a couple of wrecks just off the island, offering excellent fish sightings. Black-tip reef sharks, rays and turtles are all to be found here. This island is easily seen from Al Qurum and is directly opposite Mina Al Fahl oil terminal. Boats from Marina Bandar Al Rowdha (page 112) often venture out as far as this to spot dolphin, and scuba-diving operators also leave from there.

MADINAT AL SULTAN QABOOS مدينة السلطان قابوس This area is known locally as MQ, and you may also see it shown as Madinat A'Sultan Qaboos or Medinat Qaboos in different maps and publications. It is a modern, affluent residential area popular with Western expats, and occupies an elevated position on the southern side of Al Sultan Qaboos Street. The central shopping arcade has some good restaurants as well as an Al Fair supermarket, a Muscat Pharmacy, an HSBC cashpoint, Crafty Kitchen café and cooking school, D'Arcy's Kitchen restaurant and various chain fast-food joints and cafés. For memorable places to eat, the Pavo Real (page 92) and Kargeen Café (page 93) all make the district's arcade area worth a visit.

To get there, exit Al Sultan Qaboos Street (road 1) at the Al Khuwair junction and take the signed exit southeast. Continue on Madinat Al Sultan Qaboos Street straight across the traffic lights and take the left turn at the second set of lights. Follow the road straight across the roundabout and the shopping area is on your left after 1.7km from Madinat Al Sultan Qaboos Street.

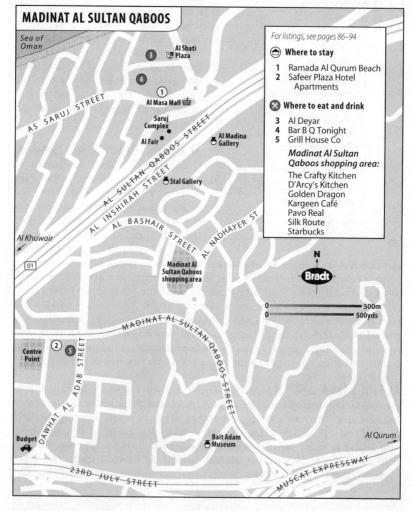

MADINAT AL SULTAN QABOOS

Sea of Oman

AS SARUJ STREET

AL SULTAN QABOOS STREET
AL INSHIRAH STREET
AL BASHAIR STREET
AL NADHAYER ST

Al Khuwair
01

3 Al Shati Plaza
4
1 Al Masa Mall
Saruj Complex
Al Fair
Al Madina Gallery
Stal Gallery

Madinat Al Sultan Qaboos shopping area

MADINAT AL SULTAN QABOOS STREET

Centre Point
2 5
DAWHAT AL ADAB STREET

Budget

Bait Adam Museum

Al Qurum

23RD JULY STREET

MUSCAT EXPRESSWAY

N

Bradt

0 — 500m
0 — 500yds

For listings, see pages 86–94

🛏 **Where to stay**
1 Ramada Al Qurum Beach
2 Safeer Plaza Hotel Apartments

🍴 **Where to eat and drink**
3 Al Deyar
4 Bar B Q Tonight
5 Grill House Co

Madinat Al Sultan Qaboos shopping area:
The Crafty Kitchen
D'Arcy's Kitchen
Golden Dragon
Kargeen Café
Pavo Real
Silk Route
Starbucks

PETROLEUM DEVELOPMENT OMAN

Petroleum Development Oman (PDO) is the country's main oil company. It is owned by the Omani government (60%), Royal Dutch Shell (34%), Total (4%) and Partex (2%). The three latter companies were among the original five partners that first explored for oil in 1937, Total having rejoined after leaving for a number of years. Partex is perhaps the most remarkable, as its founder was the original Mr 5%, Calouste Gulbenkian, who was instrumental in shaping much of the Middle East's oil industry. Oil was discovered in 1963 and first exported from Mina Al Fahl, which has now been swallowed by Muscat's urban spread but was at the time well outside Muscat.

Oman's oil deposits are scattered and small, and the oil heavy and difficult to extract from its rock. This has resulted in oil exploration companies using different forms of technology to extract oil: horizontal drilling to reach more oil, gas injection and steam injection to increase the flow, and fracking to allow the oil to escape more readily. These technologies add to Oman's production costs which are around US$15 per barrel, compared with Saudi Arabia's US$5.

Oil of course is a key generator of wealth for Oman, not only for the government but for its employees. In the early 1970s the PDO directors responded to Omani dissatisfaction with their employment packages compared with expat workers by improving salaries, training and offering mortgages at no interest rate.

The current low oil price and relatively high production costs are adding to the incentive to try and raise production, which now is around one million barrels a day and to diversify the economy from its dependence on oil.

Alternatively, exit the Muscat Expressway at junction 3 and follow the signed route north along Madinat Al Sultan Qaboos Street for 1km. Take the right turn and follow the road straight across the roundabout, and the shopping area will be on your left.

Bait Adam Museum متحف بيت آدم (*Bldg 2881, Way 2 (opposite MQ bridge turning);* ℡ *24 605033;* e *baitadam@omantel.net.om;* ⊕ *by appointment 09.00– 13.00 & 16.00–19.00, visit lasts 2–3hrs in duration; RO5 pp*) Located behind the Arab Open University building, this is more than a museum. This private collector's home displays art, coins, maps, books and treaties as well as other treasures and artefacts from Omani history, dating back to pre-Islamic times. Call in advance to arrange your visit.

To get there, exit Al Sultan Qaboos Street (road 1) at the Al Khuwair junction and take the signed exit southeast. Continue on Madinat Al Sultan Qaboos Street and after 1.6km take the signed route, where you will find Bait Adam on Way 2333. It is the sixth property on the left.

Art galleries Both the Al Madina and Stal galleries are on the same road, easily accessed from the Al Khuwair junction on Al Sultan Qaboos Street. At the Al Khuwair junction traffic lights, take the access road onto Al Sultan Qaboos Street in the direction of Ruwi. Exit right after 300m and enter Al Inshirah Street, continue northeast past the British Council, and the Stal Gallery is first on the right. If you continue along the street, you will find the Al Madina Gallery after another 750m.

3

Al Madina Gallery معرض المدينة الفني (*221 Al Inshirah St;* \ *24 691380;* e *almadga@omantel.net.om*) Near the large mosque on the southern service road of Al Sultan Qaboos Street, this plain, whitewashed villa has been converted into an interesting gallery, with an attached shop offering a framing service and selling local arts and crafts, greetings cards, paintings and photographs taken by the owner.

Stal Gallery صالة ستال للفنون (*145/6 Al Inshirah St;* \ *24 600396;* e *info@ stalgallery.com; www.stalgallery.com*) On the southern service road of Al Sultan Qaboos Street, 450m east of the British Council, this is a gallery specialising in young, up-and-coming artists. Within the building a studio offers space to selected contemporary artists to support their career development.

AL KHUWAIR الخوير Northern Al Khuwair is home to many ministries, which line Al Sultan Qaboos Street. These include the apricot-hued Ministry of Housing, the Ministry of Heritage and Culture and the blue-domed Ministry of Endowments and Religion. Two other ministries, the Ministry of Environment and Climate Affairs, where permits to enter the Ad Dimaniyyat Islands and

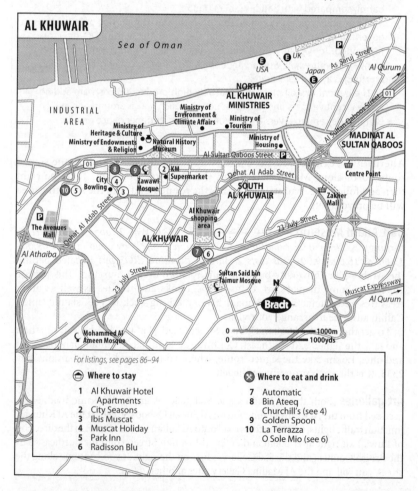

For listings, see pages 86–94

Where to stay

1 Al Khuwair Hotel Apartments
2 City Seasons
3 Ibis Muscat
4 Muscat Holiday
5 Park Inn
6 Radisson Blu

Where to eat and drink

7 Automatic
8 Bin Ateeq
Churchill's (see 4)
9 Golden Spoon
10 La Terrazza
O Sole Mio (see 6)

This is a month-long annual cultural festival held from late January until late February at various parks, beach and shopping-centre locations in the capital, all arranged by Muscat's municipal council. The festival focuses on Omani heritage and culture: traditional villages are constructed, and Omani crafts demonstrated and celebrated. Entertainment includes funfairs, fireworks and raffles. Oman Air offers promotional fare deals, and discounted packages are available at the hotels, which can become full.

other nature reserves can be obtained, and the Ministry of Tourism are on Al Wazarat Street, which is behind and parallel to the other ministries. This area of ministries is clearly signposted as 'Wazarat'. Farther back from the highway and occupying 1.5km of beachfront is the main embassy area. From east to west, you pass the British and US embassies, the Jordanian embassy, in a style that references Petra, and the French embassy with its flying saucer-like dome; this street is the only one in Muscat that may have access restrictions.

Southern Al Khuwair has commercial buildings fronting Al Sultan Qaboos Street. If you are approaching from the airport, access is easiest from the slip road leading off from McDonald's and the Shell petrol station. Commercial establishments include Oman's oldest football club, the appropriately named 'Oman Club' near the Ibis and Hotel Muscat holiday complex, KM supermarket which is alongside City Seasons Hotel, building material and furniture showrooms, the pharaonic-style HSBC bank head office and a private hospital. Further south is Al Khuwair shopping area, with a few small supermarkets plus banks and restaurants. The area is, however, largely residential, with a mix of apartments and houses (which in Oman are usually referred to as 'villas'), extending all the way to its southern boundary along the Muscat Expressway at the base of the mountains. Al Khuwair is also home to the Radisson Blu Hotel, which lies further back from the highway. At the farthest end of Al Khuwair, almost part of MQ, is the large Centre Point department store, packed with furnishings and gifts.

Natural History Museum متحف التاريخ الطبيعي (*Al Wazarat St;* ☏ *24 604957, 614510;* ⏱ *09.30–13.30 Sat–Thu; 500/200/100bzs adult/child/child under 6*) This is a small museum, opened in 1985, within the same complex as the Ministry of Heritage and Culture in the ministries area of north Al Khuwair. The entrance is virtually opposite the large Zawawi Mosque (all the way over the other side of the highway but accessible by a footbridge) and close to the small roundabout. There is limited parking available, so otherwise try the side road.

The displays cover a small area on the ground floor, with examples of the natural environment and wildlife heritage of the country: mammals, reptiles, birdlife, insects and seashells. The Whale Hall next door has an impressive collection of skeletons.

Sultan Said bin Taimour Mosque جامع السلطان سعيد بن تيمور (*Close to the Radisson Blu Hotel, just off 23 July St*) This Ottoman-style mosque is not open to non-Muslims, but its grounds, which are accessible on all sides, are open and include Ottoman-style ablution pavilions.

BAWSHAR بوشر Bawshar (also Bowshar, Boushar), once a remote rural settlement, is now one of Muscat's suburbs. Located at the base of a mountainous spur of the Al Hajar Al Sharqi Mountains, it is signposted from the Al Ghubra flyover/roundabout on Al Sultan Qaboos Street and easily accessed from signed interchange 6 on the Muscat Expressway. As with most residential areas of Muscat, there is no public transport, so you must take a taxi or have your own vehicle.

Under Sultan Qaboos's rule all Omanis, men and women, are entitled to 600m² of land on which they can build themselves a house. If they are from Muscat, that land has to be within Muscat province, so Bawshar has become a favourite spot.

There are two separate areas of Bawshar to explore: one around the signposted Bait Al Maqham, and the other the village of Al Ghala, with the 30°C Ain Ghala hot springs.

Bait Al Maqham بيت المقحم (24 641300, ext 142 (ideally call in advance to ensure the building is open); ⊕ 08.00–14.00 Sun–Thu; 500bzs) Bait Al Maqham was the 19th-century fortified residence of Sayyida (Princess) Thuria bint Mohammed bin Azzan Al Said. This is a restored three-storey mud-brick building with good views over the date plantations and wadi. Given that it currently has no furnishings, it is a long journey to visit if you are able to see one of the major forts elsewhere. The paths through the date plantations are public and are lovely to walk through if you have enough sense of direction to find your way back to your car.

To get there, exit the Muscat Expressway at junction 6 to and take Bawshar Street south for 1.1km before turning turn right into Way 61. Continue south for 2.7km and turn left, continuing for 600m to an area where you can park on rough ground. From here walk south for about 350m with the date plantations on your left and Bait Al Maqham will be to the right.

Ain Ghala عين غلا The hot springs of Ain Ghala lie behind the date plantations of Ghala. Their water, little though it is, irrigates the oasis. The water trickles out of crevices in the mountain. It is used in bathing areas with separate buildings for men and women.

It is possible to drive on a narrow route to the west of the oasis or, if not obstructed by oncoming cars of local residents, along the narrow road between the shops and oasis, but far more enjoyable is to park on the northern edge of the village into which you initially arrive, walk through the area with shops and take the narrow route through the village and oasis to the mountain, veering right to the spring area.

To get there, exit the Muscat Expressway at junction 7 and drive southwest for 1.3km, exit right and take the third exit at the roundabout. Go straight on, and at the second roundabout take the first exit right and continue south for 800m, taking a left turn opposite the Royal Air Force of Oman facility. Continue along this road for 2.7km (do not take a left turn at 1.5km into the village, keep right) before taking a left turn opposite a date plantation. From there it is 750m to the springs; park where you can easily turn around.

AL GHUBRA (الغبرة) AND AL ATHAIBA (الغذيبة) Al Ghubra is largely a residential area, comprising northern Al Ghubra and the beach area close to The Chedi Hotel to the north of Al Sultan Qaboos Street, together with southern Al Ghubra, which is home to the Sultan Qaboos Grand Mosque, Muscat Grand Mall and The Avenues, all to the south of Al Sultan Qaboos Street. There is a variety of small street shops here, selling fruit and vegetables, foodstuffs and building materials, plus a pharmacy, an optician's, a bakery, coffee shops, local restaurants and an internet café.

Al Athaiba is the area of Muscat adjacent to the airport. As with so many locations in Oman, there may be a number of variants of its English spelling as

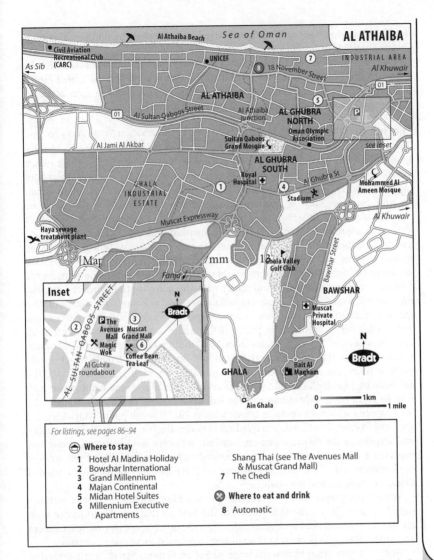

Al Athaiba Beach · Sea of Oman · **AL ATHAIBA**

Civil Aviation Recreational Club (CARC)
As Sib
UNICEF
INDUSTRIAL AREA
Al Khuwair
18 November Street
7
8
AL ATHAIBA
01
5
Al Sultan Qaboos Street
Al Athaiba junction
AL GHUBRA NORTH
Oman Olympic Association
P
see inset
Al Jami Al Akbar
Sultan Qaboos Grand Mosque
AL GHUBRA SOUTH
GHALA INDUSTRIAL ESTATE
Royal Hospital
1
4
Al Ghubra St
Stadium
Mohammed Al Ameen Mosque
Haya sewage treatment plant
Muscat Expressway
Al Khuwair
[Map mm 12
Ghala Valley Golf Club
Bawshar Street
Fanja
BAWSHAR
Muscat Private Hospital

Inset
N
Bradt
AL SULTAN QABOOS STREET
2
P The Avenues Mall
3
Muscat Grand Mall
Magic Wok
6
Coffee Bean Tea Leaf
Al Gubra roundabout

GHALA
Bait Al Maqham
N
Bradt
Ain Ghala

0 — 1km
0 — 1 mile

For listings, see pages 86–94

🛏 **Where to stay**
1 Hotel Al Madina Holiday
2 Bowshar International
3 Grand Millennium
4 Majan Continental
5 Midan Hotel Suites
6 Millennium Executive Apartments

Shang Thai (see The Avenues Mall & Muscat Grand Mall)
7 The Chedi

❌ **Where to eat and drink**
8 Automatic

well as its current official one, including the following: Azaiba, Al Udhaybah, Al Udhaiba, Al Athaibah, Al Azaybah. Al Athaiba is one of the newest residential areas in the city and you will find large, detached and quite grand homes here.

Al Athaiba Beach is excellent for morning or early-evening walks, and local fishermen may sell their latest catch to you. The tides can be strong at times and there have been fatal accidents in the nearby waters, so if you want to swim here, do take advice (talk to any dive-centre representative) and use your common sense. Note that there are no lifeguards on duty at this or at any beach in Oman, unless a hotel has clearly posted notices to that effect. The bays south of Muscat, Al Bustan (page 86) and the Shangri-La hotels (page 87), for instance, offer a far safer and more inviting experience. This same stretch of beach has been enjoyed for many years by recreational clubs for various government organisations. The Civil Aviation Club (*18 November St;* 📞 *24 498882;* e *info@caaclub.org*) does allow guests of members to use the facilities, which are within a smart, sizeable building and a number of smaller private chalets.

To get here, Al Sultan Qaboos Street has two principal junctions that provide access to this area. Al Ghubra junction to the east is ideal for The Chedi Hotel, Muscat Grand Mall and The Avenues, while the exit at Al Athaiba gives access to the Sultan Qaboos Grand Mosque and the beach area.

The Sultan Qaboos Grand Mosque جامع السلطان قابوس الأكبر (⏰ 08.00–11.00 Sat–
Thu; dress requirements: women must be fully covered in loose-fitting opaque clothing & headscarf; the ensemble should only leave face, hands & feet exposed. Men must have long trousers to the ankle & ideally traditional shirts. Clothing should not have slogans, pictures or other symbols, as these may be misinterpreted by the mosque's security. Footwear must be removed to enter prayer halls & bare feet or socks are equally acceptable) This mosque is awe-inspiring and is certainly worth a visit, if simply to appreciate its magnitude, craftsmanship and the architectural design-and-build achievement it represents. Even the non-religious visitor will probably be moved in some way by a tour of its interior. Construction began in 1995 and took six years to complete. Made from marble, sandstone and wood, the four corner minarets measure 45m high, and along with the taller central minaret represent the five pillars of Islam. There are ablution areas, a library, an administrative quarter, stained-glass windows, carved wooden doors and 35 chandeliers. The Persian carpet in the main prayer hall is made of fine wool and cotton in 28 colours, measures 70m by 60m, includes 1,700 million knots and weighs 21 tonnes. It was made in Mashad Khurasan in Iran and occupied 600 female weavers fully for four years. The appearance of the magnificent 50m-high central dome and the 8m-wide by 14m-high central Swarovski crystal chandelier in the main prayer hall, with its 1,122 lights, is breathtaking. The hall has a capacity of around 6,600 and the total capacity within the complex is estimated at 20,000 worshippers, which includes the ladies' prayer room and courtyard set between the two rooms. The tranquillity and serenity of the riwaqs (open-air arcades), archways and courtyards is quite an experience in itself. Each riwaq has decorated niches that hold tiling from areas of the Islamic world. The Grand Mosque in its entirety stands as an assertive symbol of Oman's confidence and spirituality.

Within the prayer rooms of the mosque is a blue fabric strip that is within a roped-off area. This is the only section of the mosque that non-Muslims can walk on and they should not touch material within the mosque's prayer rooms. Camera and video filming is permitted though bags may need to be placed outside.

Access is very straightforward from Al Sultan Qaboos Street in the direction of Ruwi. After the flyover at Al Athaiba, keep in the right-hand lane and exit right after 1km (there is a footbridge at this exit). Turn immediately right and follow the road for 550m from the footbridge, then turn right and again right into the mosque's visitor car park. If required, adjust your clothing and walk into this entrance, which is the only one that non-Muslims can enter. If you are Muslim and appropriately dressed, there is a ramped pedestrian entrance. From the turn-off from the highway at the footbridge, turn immediately right and follow the road for 650m, then turn right and park in the area to your right.

AS SIB السيب As Sib (also Al Sib and Al Seeb) is like Muscat's garden suburb, with
many fine weekend villas of the wealthy set among gardens and palm groves. The **Royal Stables and Equestrian Centre** and the **Royal Guard** of Oman are both here, and just off the dual carriageway is the private road leading to the sultan's As Sib

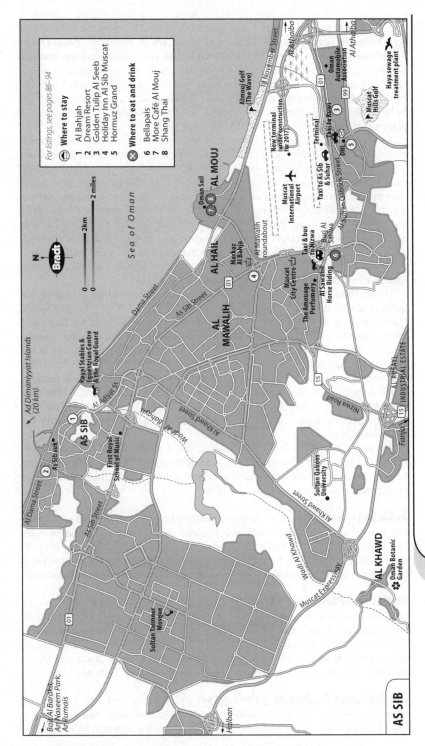

AS SIB

For listings, see pages 86–94

Where to stay
1 Al Bahjah
2 Dream Resort
3 Golden Tulip Al Seeb
4 Holiday Inn Al Sib Muscat
5 Hormuz Grand

Where to eat and drink
6 Bellapais
7 More Café Al Mouj
8 Shang Thai

Sea of Oman

Palace – **Bait Al Baraka** – which is not open to the public. Between the highway and Bait Al Baraka is the First Royal School of Music, which houses the **Royal Oman Symphony Orchestra**, formed in 1985. It may be that you will be in town to hear one of their regular performances (*see local papers for details, or* \26 894021). There is a seemingly endless stretch of beach close by, the potential of which is being harnessed by the development projects of the Al Mouj (The Wave) with a golf course, hotels (to be built), shopping and upmarket housing. A development called 'Journey of Light' is planned on the land to the west of Al Mouj (page 100).

As Sib is a relatively large town, with a one-way system through its shopping area. Well off the beaten tourist track, it is a typical Omani sea town going about its business. The area has an interesting corniche with fishing boats landing their catch on the beach, fishermen's huts along much of the beach's length and finally the interesting fishing harbour and fish suq. Before the harbour is the **As Sib Suq**, which has a wide variety of produce including traditional medicine, frankincense and fabrics of every hue. Wadi Al Bahayis Street, just south of the fishing harbour and roughly parallel to Dama Street, is also where gold shops, clothing and electrical goods are found. The **fishing harbour** is the best place to find small boats that will make the 20km journey across to the Ad Dimaniyyat Islands (permission always required from the Ministry of Environment – see page 144).

To get there, from the Muscat Expressway exit from junction 11, taking the north road signed Sultan Qaboos University onto Al Khawd Street (also Al Khoud). Continue along Al Khawd Street for 11km to the junction with As Sib Street and carry across the traffic lights to follow Al Adiyat Street outlined below. Alternatively, from As Sib Street (which east of the airport is Al Sultan Qaboos Street), exit at the junction for the junction for Al Khawd. Take the north exit into Al Adiyat Street. The road continues for 2.4km before taking a right into street 34 and onto a T-junction which is the corniche, here called Al Dama Street after a total of 3.3km. A right turn will take you in the direction of Al Mouj while a left will continue along the very interesting corniche, past the fishing harbour and fish suq for a total of 5km from the Dama Street junction.

You can also walk from the sandy beach about 5.5km east of the main town, where fishing boats are drawn up, and continue for almost 3km towards the fishing harbour in the main town. Beyond the harbour is the nearly 3km-long landscaped promenade, where there is plenty of seating.

As Sib Suq سوق السيب
As Sib Suq has an extraordinary variety of shops with a wide variety of produce including traditional medicine, frankincense and fabrics of every hue. Gold shops, clothing and electrical goods are found principally along Wadi Al Bahayis Street, while home furnishings are on the adjacent streets. The main suq area is between Wadi Al Bahayis Street, just south of the fisheries harbour, and Dama Street.

An Naseem Park حديقة النسيم
(⊕ *16.00–23.00 daily, women & children only on Tue*) This park, set between As Sib and Barka, has a small lake, waterfall, flower garden, Arabic and Japanese gardens, a maze and a playground, which would all benefit from more care. The park is popular with Omani families and gets crowded at weekends (Fridays and Saturdays). It is about 30km away from the airport on the coast and is signposted from the dual carriageway.

The Amouage Perfumery أمواج للعطور
(\ *24 540757 ext 103, 110 or 111; www.amouage.com; ⊕ 09.00–13.00 & 14.00–16.30 Sun–Thu; free guide for a tour*) Guided tours of the perfumery are offered and an explanation of how the

world-famous frankincense-based Amouage perfume (see box, pages 310–11) is created. There is an opportunity to buy the product. To get there, take Al Sultan Qaboos Street to Burj Al Sahwa roundabout west of the airport. Take the exit west, signed Nizwa road 15. After 650m take the slip road and after a further 800m turn right to the perfumery gates.

AL KHAWD الخوض West of Muscat International Airport is Al Khawd, a modern, rapidly expanding suburb of the Capital Area. The area includes Sultan Qaboos University and old Al Khawd village to its south.

The campus of **Sultan Qaboos University** lies on the flat, open plain. The university took its first (557) students in 1986 and by 1995 had a total of 3,500, one-fifth of whom were female. Now there are more female than male students and a larger number of female graduates than male, with total student numbers exceeding 15,000.

To the west of the university is Al Khawd Street, a direct connection between As Sib Street, the coastal highway which is an extension of Sultan Qaboos Street east of the airport, and the Muscat Expressway. Al Khawd Street leads south into the town of old Al Khawd, the place where the historic Treaty of Al Seeb was signed in 1920. This was a British-mediated truce between the government of Muscat under Sultan Taimur and the tribes of the interior. On a hill to the right, rising above the palm plantations, are the ruins of Al Khawd castle fort, built in 1865, with a Zanzibari carved door and elegant windows showing East African influence. It was lived in continuously by the descendants of the original sheikh until 1979, when the 90-year-old resident finally moved into the modern buildings next door.

The **Oman Botanic Garden** is being constructed here and is open to visitors by agreed appointment only (24 531916; e mail@omanbotanicgarden.com; www. omanbotanicgarden.com).

The adjacent Wadi Al Khawd connects with Fanja (pages 206–7) via a tortuous 4x4 route south through the wadi, which is prone to being washed away by flash floods.

To get to Al Khawd, exit the Muscat Expressway at junction 11. To reach the university take Al Khawd Street north for about 700m, take the first exit right and continue for an additional 3.1km and the left turn is an entrance into Sultan Qaboos University. To reach old Al Khawd exit the Muscat Expressway at junction 11 and take the road south to old Al Khawd for 1.8km; the right turn takes you after 1.1km to the edge of the wadi and on the left is the old castle. For the Botanic Garden drive from the Muscat Expressway south for 2.5km where a left turn will take you after 850m to the offices of the Botanic Gardens. As this is currently being constructed, routes may not be clear. The offices are a few metres south of the greenhouses.

QURAYYAT AND AROUND قريات والمنطقة المحيطة بها Historically one of the main coastal towns of Oman, Qurayyat refused to submit to the invading Portuguese in the early 16th century and had its inhabitants slaughtered as a result. Set at the start of a wide plain, its salty *khawr* (or creek), which centuries ago was a major port and famous harbour, has now silted up and is fringed with mangrove trees. Fishing and agriculture remain important to the local economy and the fish suq is busy in the early morning. It has been known for rows of sharks, including hammerheads, and stingrays to be sold here. The sharks used to be dried in the sun, and then cut into strips of dried flesh, which were used as flavouring for rice. The plain upon which the town is set used to be a breeding ground for the horses for which Qurayyat was famous for exporting.

There are three fortifications here. Opposite the suq is **Qurayyat Castle** (⊙ 08.30–14.30 Sun–Thu; 500bzs), restored and fully furnished to help you imagine

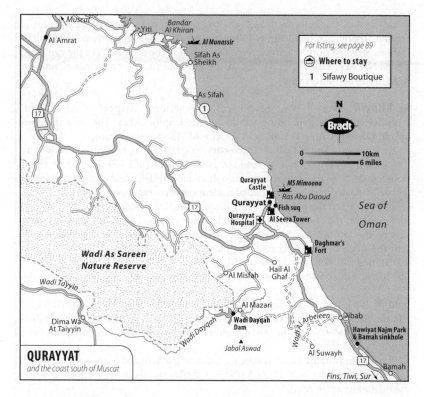

For listing, see page 89

QURAYYAT
and the coast south of Muscat

what life was like for its inhabitants. On the coast is **Al Seera Tower**. The third fort is **Daghmar's Fort**, which overlooks the plain created by the great wadis that exit the mountains around Qurayyat. The last two are not officially open. Inland, the dominant mountain is Jabal Aswad (Black Mountain), which, curiously, is called Jabal Abyad (White Mountain) by the people on the mountain's southern side.

To join the road to Qurayyat, you need to exit the main Al Nahda Street highway at Wadi Adai roundabout. Shared taxis costing RO2 or minibuses costing RO1 can be picked up in the Shell petrol station area near the white mosque for the hour's drive of 99km. Alternatively, if you have your own car, take the Muscat Expressway and exit at interchange 5, taking the signed route – both roads join at Amrat. The dual carriageway to Qurayyat winds through the mountains, passing heavily distorted schist rock formations and always within sight of high mountains on either side. The mountains on the right southern side include the Wadi As Sareen Nature Reserve, created for the protection of the Arabian tahr and not open to the public. After less than an hour's drive from Muscat, you climb to a plateau, from which there is a steep descent for several hundred metres to the plain of Qurayyat (99km from Muscat). Beyond Qurayyat is Sur, a 120km drive along mostly dual carriageway.

Wadi Dayqah Dam سد وادي ضيقة This is Oman's largest permanent freshwater lake, its capacity about 100 million m³. A public park is located on the edge of the lake. The village of Al Mazari below the dam benefits from flood control and an improved supply of water for irrigation. To reach the dam take the signed route to Wadi Dayqah Dam, which is also an exit for Qurayyat on the Muscat–Sur highway. Head towards the signed route to Hail Al Ghaf and take the first exit on the roundabout. After 2.4km turn right at the signed exit to Wadi Dayqah Dam, Al Mazari and Al Misfah, and then after an additional 3km take the left turn. Drive on for 15km to find the signed parking for the dam.

Beyond Al Mazari village is the track for 4x4 vehicles to Al Suwayh. The tarmac track goes through Al Mazari village, which is reached by exiting the dam's road and turning right, continuing for 1.5km and driving down into the wadi, where the road continues before taking a sharp right through date plantations. After the date plantations there is a cream-coloured school building, at which you should take a left turn. Some 650m along the road, take the left turn into the wadi and continue straight, crossing another small wadi, and ascend through the date palms and past a small tower on your right. The route, which here is rough and suitable for 4x4 vehicles, continues for some 22km from the school, without taking any of the left or right turns to terminate at Al Suwayh village. The wadi immediately before Al Suwayh is normally full of water pools formed by low dams that divert the water into the *falaj* system. There are two deep wadis behind the village; the right one has interesting, demanding trekking routes where, if you have undertaken a guided trekking tour from Muscat, your accompanying guide can take you through to more natural ponds. To exit from Al Suwayh, retrace your route for 2.5km and take the right turn into the large wadi. From here, a 12km drive (4x4 only) continues through a deep wadi, occasionally fording water pools, with dramatic scenery all around. The exit is under the Qurayyat–Sur highway at Dibab. After rains this route may be impassable. For places beyond here see the *Ash Sharqiyyah* chapter, pages 239–68.

EXCURSIONS BEYOND MUSCAT

Most of the trips in and around the Capital Area will provide you with a taster of the country. However, a short journey outside of the capital will allow you to see more of Oman's natural wonders, while offering you the chance of a more adventurous trip. You could go 'wadi bashing' (riding in a 4x4 through the dry riverbeds in the mountains) or picnic by peaceful hot springs (pages 158 and 166).

For the seriously adventurous and energetic there is rock climbing, mountain ravine trekking and even caving (page 251). The stock tours include visits to the Wihibah (usually with overnight camping in the desert), the wadis (Wadi Bani Khalid, Wadi Tiwi, Wadi Ash Shab, Wadi Dayqah and Wadi Al Abyadh being the most popular), the jabals (Jabal Shams and Al Jabal Al Akhdar), the turtle reserves at Ras Al Had and Ras Al Jinz, mountain village tours, fort tours, coastal town and village tours and desert town tours.

Most tours to places beyond the Capital Area are ideal if arranged through one of the tour operators in the city (pages 83–5). If you are travelling independently around your chosen region, yet want a sand safari (which requires a 4x4 and a driver/guide), it is safest to pre-arrange this through a tour operator in the Capital Area, who will collect you from your hotel, if you are already in the region.

Al Jabal Al Akhdar makes a great full-day trip (pages 214–17). Nakhal Springs and the Rustaq Loop (pages 155–67) are another excellent day trip from the Capital Area. Wadi Bani Awf and Bald Sayt (pages 160–1) are popular 'wadi bashing' destinations for those staying in the Capital Area and can now be completed as a loop across the mountains to Nizwa, returning via the interior.

LAND-BASED ACTIVITIES
Birdwatching For information on birds and birdwatching, see pages 10–12.

Camping The desert (whether rubbly – that is to say, in the vicinity of mountains – or sandy) and the beaches of Oman are perfect for outdoor adventure. Choose your camping spot and enjoy the vast expanse around you.

The small secluded bays of Bandar Al Khiran (or Khairan) make excellent camping and diving/snorkelling spots; most are accessible by boat only (page 116). As Sifah, too, is excellent for camping (page 116). Camping equipment can be purchased from the Sultan Centre in Al Qurum (taking the escalator up to the first floor), at Carrefour or Lulu.

Caving and rock climbing The more adventurous excursions of caving and rock climbing take you outside the Capital Area. **Jabal Ghul**, **Jabal Misfah** and **Jabal Misht** in the interior regions offer excellent rock-climbing possibilities. Jabal Misht (page 234) has the biggest rock face of all. Specialist tour operators are required and they will advise you of the various levels each site offers. It is necessary to join an organised group session with skilled guides.

The **Al Hoota Cave** (pages 231–2) in the Ad Dakhiliyah region, near Al Hamra, is easily accessible since it has been developed for tourism. *Caves of Oman*, by Dr Samir Hanna and Mohammed Al Baloushi, is published by Sultan Qaboos University and is a recommended read.

Desert safari A 4x4 is a necessity; so too is the driver/guide that comes with it. For a desert safari, or dune bashing as it is otherwise known, you will need to make arrangements through a tour operator because of the potentially dangerous nature of the terrain: a slight loss of concentration or careless bravado will see you axle-deep in sand. With daytime temperatures into the sizzling 50°Cs during summer it's a scenario best avoided. See the listings on pages 83–5.

Mountain trekking Trekking is a fantastic way of seeing and experiencing Oman's mountainscape (see box, page 215). With trekking, a certain level of fitness is necessary and it is always recommended that you join an organised trek, for safety reasons. Trekking trips can be organised through tour operators, who offer a choice of itineraries with different degrees of difficulty.

A global positioning system (GPS) device is a great tool if you like to stay informed of which direction you are walking in, and your position on the globe. You can track your walks, which can be quite thrilling when you take a later trek elsewhere and discover it brings you out very close to where you had travelled previously (perhaps just the other side of the mountain). Some GSMs (mobiles) also work in the mountains and desert. Cell towers are in some surprising places, but of course signals can and do fade even on main routes away from Muscat. Equip yourself with enough food and water for the journey. A useful guide to get hold of is *Adventure Trekking in Oman* (see *Appendix 3*, page 335).

Wadi bashing While the traditional 'wadi-bashing' trips (page 141) are away from Muscat, there are a number of dramatic wadis in this region that are just waiting to be bashed. It's always important to have at least two vehicles and to travel at some distance from each other so that both do not encounter that same problem on a route. Wadi Al Khawd to Fanja is short but full of fun.

Wadi Miah from the Wadi Adai–Qurayyat road at Al Hajar (signed) is less difficult but has plenty of breathtaking scenery. From Yiti (page 115) take a right turn, drive past the health centre and schools, and the road will take you into the

Wadi Al Hulu, where some 30km later you will emerge once again on the Wadi Adai–Qurayyat road, but much closer to Qurayyat.

Wadi Bani Awf (pages 160–1) in Al Batinah region is a 'must-do' wadi, and can be managed easily in a day trip from Muscat. See any of the regional chapters for further details of particular wadis that are worth a visit. Tour operators will arrange a trip for you if you do not wish to explore independently. It is always sensible to go in a convoy of at least two cars for your wadi initiation.

WATER-BASED ACTIVITIES

Diving Oman's waters have much to offer in the way of scuba diving, with 63 registered dive sites. Scuba diving does require a permit and also additional permission for the Ad Dimaniyyat Islands. Both are obtained by the dive centre you use, and all centres will require you to produce BSAC or PADI certificates.

In Muscat the waters offer excellent experiences. Al Fahl Island (page 121), about a 25-minute boat trip northwest of Marina Bandar Al Rowdha, is one of the most popular dive sites in the capital, with two deep-water wrecks. Close to the marina, Cemetery Bay is another good location for diving. Southeast are Bandar Al Jissa and Bandar Al Khiran, with the *Al Munassir* wreck just to its east, offering sheltered and varied dives. Further afield, the island at Ras Abu Daoud and the MS *Mimoona* wreck are both close to Qurayyat and in more open water. The Ad Dimaniyyat Islands (page 144) have several dive locations and are about 1½ hours northwest of Muscat by boat. Night dives, wreck dives and dive courses in the warm waters of Oman are widely available.

Musandam in the north has an excellent range of dives. Most are accessed from Daba (see the *Musandam* chapter for border crossing requirements – page 171) and are between it and Lima.

Southeast of Muscat there is diving from Qalhat (pages 260–1), which also has had archaeological finds, through to wrecks at Ras Al Jinz, famed for its green turtles. However, few operators will undertake these except for large groups of tourists.

In Dhofar there are innumerable dive sites, all only possible from October to May, as rough seas in summer are extremely dangerous. Many are along the coastline east of Mirbat, with the Al Hallaniyyat Islands 60km offshore particularly worthy of note (page 316).

Practicalities Hire of equipment is included in the dive trip or course costs, as are dive permits. The full range of courses, from beginner to advanced diver, are offered, culminating in the award of internationally recognised certificates from PADI (Professional Association of Diving Instructors) or BSAC (British Sub Aqua Club).

The spring months are best for diving, with clear and settled water, but diving is possible all year round, except south of Ras Al Had and especially in Salalah (in the Dhofar region) during the June to September monsoon period.

For night dives in the winter a 5mm-thick wetsuit is recommended; night dives in the summer require a 3mm-thick wetsuit. To arrange a dive, contact or visit any of the dive centres in Muscat (page 136).

Snorkelling Snorkelling away from the beach is tagged onto a scuba-diving trip. Private trips can be organised for four or more passengers. Organising a trip with a dolphin-watching component is also possible.

Dolphin and whale watching Dolphin-watching tours generally last for around 1½ hours and cost about RO20 per person. Sightings are common between Al Fahl Island and Al Bustan Palace. Spinner, common and bottlenose dolphins are usually seen, frequently in their hundreds. Occasional orca whales, false killer whales, sperm whales and Bryde's whales are also seen. Get up early, as the earliest excursion is likely to give the best sightings and calmer seas.

Game fishing It is possible to charter a private boat for a half-day fishing trip (*4–5hrs*) with a boat captain and experienced local fisherman for a cost of RO150, for up to six people (two rods in the water). A full day's fishing costs from around RO220. Spear-gun and arrow fishing are not permitted, and net fishing is permitted for traditional Omani fishermen only. This can be observed along many of the extensive beaches along the sultanate's coastline.

Sailing and boat trips Sailing, boat trips and dhow trips are all available and can be tailored to suit your requirements; speak to any tour operator for full details. Generally, these cost around RO40–50 per person (for a minimum of two people) and last for about 4 hours. You can try your hand at fishing in the traditional Omani way with a handline, or the modern way with rods (all equipment provided). You may even be invited to cook your catch.

Sunset or scenic cruises cost around RO20 per person and can also be arranged through most tour operators. The tour takes you past the two 16th-century Portuguese forts of Old Muscat and the bays of Bandar Al Jissa and Mutrah harbour.

Azzaha Tours m 99 013424; e admin@ azzahatours.com; www.azzahatours.com
Extra Divers m 96 319081; www.extradivers-worldwide.com. Scuba & sea excursions.
Jassa Beach Sea Tourism m 95 599660; e info@ jassabeach.com; www.jassabeach.com. Sea tours.
Lua Lua Diving and Adventure m 96 917330; e info@lualuadiving.com; www.lualuadiving.com. Scuba & sea excursions.
Marasi Al-Jissah m 98 882822; e info@ marassi-charter.com; www.marassi-charter.com. Sea tours & game fishing.
Marina Bandar Al Rowdha \ 24 737288; e bob@marinaoman.net; www.marinaoman.net. Marina & associated services.

Moon Light m 99 317700; e aljoori@omantel. net.om; www.moonlightdive.com. Scuba trips.
Muscat Game Fishing Club m 99 322779; www.mgfa-oman.com. Game fishing.
Nomad Tours m 95 495240; e nomads@ nomadtours.com; www.nomadtours.com. Sea tours.
Ocean Blue m 96 125091; e info@ oceanblueoman.com; www.oceanblueoman. com. Sea excursions.
Omanta m 99 777045; e info@omantascuba. com; www.omantascuba.com. Scuba trips.
Sidab Sea Tour m 99 432782; e contactus@ sidabseatours.com; www.sidabseatours.com. Sea tours.

4

Al Batinah Coast
ساحل الباطنة

Al Batinah (normally just Batinah in English or occasionally Batina) is a coastal region of northern Oman that physically begins at the base of the clifftop Crowne Plaza Hotel at Al Qurum in Muscat. Never more than 35km wide, it continues northwest for some 300km all the way up to the Khitmat Milahah border north of Shinas and, as a geographical entity, though not a political one, beyond that into Al Fujayrah in the United Arab Emirates.

Although its population is spread along the coast and most people think of the region as a coastal flatland, Al Batinah is in fact dominated by the Western Al Hajar Mountains, which have created the outwash plain at the coast. These mountains rise to well over 2,500m, and Oman's highest peak, Jabal Shams, is as much part of Al Batinah as it is of the Ad Dakhiliyah, from which it is accessed (pages 203–38). Deep wadis are cut into these mountains, dissipating into the coastal plain as they gradually descend to the Sea of Oman. Where it meets the sea there is an almost continual strip of settlements. Its beaches are sand, never pebbles, and range from pale cream to a dark grey; again, those looming mountains behind them provide the material that determines their colour. Just offshore are two island archipelagos, which represent the peaks of a crescent of rock that has been separated by erosion away from the mainland.

The highest peaks of the Western Al Hajar Mountains are limestone and stupendously ancient. Wadi Bani Awf, for instance, contains rocks laid down 600 million years ago during the Neoproterozoic era. The dark brown ophiolite that was created under the ocean by continental plates moving apart and then pushed overland by the plates moving towards each other contain chrome and copper that is commercially mined near Suhar.

The region's early **history** was dominated by copper exploitation, and the modern mines west of Suhar still produce the metal today. Copper was exported from Oman to Mesopotamia, and the region imported elements of culture in return: the only known ziggurat (temple) in the Arabian Peninsula lies near the mines. Suhar became an important port after the Abbasid court was established in Baghdad, and its trading routes stretched to China.

The regional **economy** is dominated by Suhar Port, not only due to the trade that it conducts, but also as a result of its major metal-smelting industry and chemical factories. Barka is another important logistics hub that makes use of its location near Muscat. Agriculture has traditionally been an essential part of the local economy, and this is still evident in the almost unbroken line of farms along Al Batinah highway and in major oases such as Ar Rustaq and Nakhal. Suhar is the region's education centre, as home to a major university.

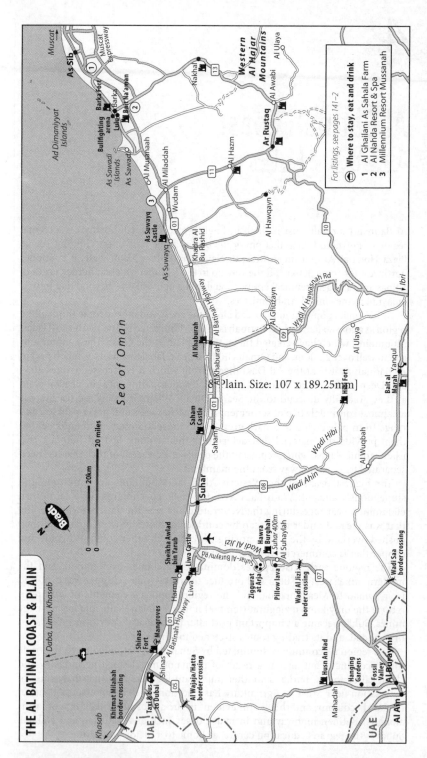

THE AL BATINAH COAST & PLAIN

For listings, see pages 141–2

Where to stay, eat and drink
1 Al Ghailani As Sahala Farm
2 Al Nahda Resort & Spa
3 Millennium Resort Mussanah

Sea of Oman

Western Al Hajar Mountains

Ad Dimaniyyat Islands

Muscat

As Sib

Muscat Expressway

Barka Fort
Barka
Bait Na'aman
Lulu
Bullfighting arena
As Sawadi Islands
As Sawadi
Al Musanaah
Al Miladdah
Wudam
As Suwayq Castle
As Suwayq
Khadra Al Bu Rashid

Nakhal
13

Al Awabi
Ar Rustaq
Al Hazm
11
Al Hawqayn

Al Ulaya
Al Awabi

10

Al Ghuzayn
09
Wadi Al Hawasnah Rd
Ibri

Al Khaburah
Al Khaburah
Al Batinah Highway

Saham Castle
Saham
01

Al Ulaya

High Fort

Bait al Marah
Yanqul

Suhar
Wadi Hibi
Al Wuqbah
08
Wadi Ahin

Sheikha Awlad bin Yarub
Liwa Castle
Liwa
Harmul

Mangroves
Shinas Fort
Shinas
01
Al Batinah Highway

Ziggurat at Arja
Pillow lava
Hawra Burghah
Suhar 400m
Al Suhaylah
Suhar-Al Buraymi Rd
Wadi Al Jizi

Wadi Al Jizi border crossing
07
Wadi Saa border crossing

Khitmat Milahah border crossing

Al Wajaja/Hatta border crossing
05

Taxi & bus to Dubai
UAE

Khasab

Daba, Lima, Khasab

Husn An Nad
Mahadah
Hanging Gardens
Fossil Valley
Al Buraymi
Al Ain
UAE

0   20km
0   20 miles

N

[8 Plain. Size: 107 x 189.25mm]

With 1,057,915 people, this is Oman's second most populous region. The largest administrative areas are Suhar (208,429), As Suwayq (159,052), Saham, Barka, Ar Rustaq, Al Musanaah, Al Khaburah, Shinas, Liwa, Nakhal, Wadi Al Maawil and Al Awabi.

GETTING THERE AND AWAY

BY ROAD Muscat International Airport is situated towards the Al Batinah's southeastern extremity, and the region can be readily reached from there along good roads. The Muscat Expressway has direct access from the airport: take the eastern exit (using the flyover) and turn right onto the signed route for Suhar (also Sohar) and Barka, which leads onto the expressway after 5.5km. Alternatively, and on a far more congested route, use the western exit, which will lead you directly onto road 1 Sultan Qaboos Street, from where you can follow signs to As Sib (also Al Sib, As Seeb, etc), Barka and Suhar.

By taxi Taxis from the kiosk immediately outside the airport Arrivals area cost RO15 to Barka and RO40 to Suhar (pages 146–51). You can also take taxis from Burj Al Sahwa roundabout less than 5km west of the airport on the road that leads from the roundabout towards Suhar.

By bus Buses stop close to the airport Arrivals entrance for various routes, including Al Batinah. Alternatively, you can catch buses from the car park at Burj Al Sahwa west of the airport (*taxi from the airport RO4, about 200bzs for a shared minibus or RO1 for an engaged taxi, or less if you walk 400m south to Sultan Qaboos St & take a taxi from there*). The main Suhar bus stop is at the Shell petrol station on route 1 on Al Batinah highway (As Sib Street continuation after Barka), 3km southeast of Suhar flyover (which is next to Lulu supermarket at the junction with route 8 to Wadi Hibi and Yanqul). Expect to pay RO5 and for the journey to take 3.5 hours.

EXPLORING AL BATINAH استكشاف الباطنة

You may like to explore the whole of the coast up to the Khitmat Milahah border before coming back on yourself and taking the two main roads inland – one being the hinterland of Suhar though to Yanqul (see Adh Dhahirah), the other being the Rustaq Loop. Alternatively, you might like to exit the dual carriageway at the Barka roundabout to do the Rustaq Loop first. Then further up the coast at Suhar's Falaj Al Qabail flyover (after the Suhar flyover at the junction with route 8 to Yanqul) exit the dual carriageway again through Wadi Al Jizi towards Al Buraymi (this route requires passing through Oman immigration facilities, even if you are only travelling within Oman).

OLD-STYLE TRAVEL

Until the 1970s, the easiest way to visit Al Batinah coast was by boat, as the roads between the settlements were poor and intermittent. Eccentric British consuls used to wear bathing suits under their clothes, so that they could disrobe and leap ashore, then reappear in immaculate clothing to meet local dignitaries. In 1930, it took seven days to reach Suhar from Muscat by camel, and the first graded track was not built until that year.

It is quite possible to visit the attractions of the Al Batinah coast as day trips from your base in Muscat. The Rustaq Loop, for example, would make a good day's excursion. Or you might like to visit the Nakhal Springs as a relaxing afternoon trip. It is even possible to dive the Ad Dimaniyyat Islands as a day trip from Muscat; this can be done either as a pre-arranged boat trip from one of the dive centres in the capital. For all of these days out, aside from the diving trip (where food may be provided on the boat), taking along a picnic is highly recommended, as there are no good restaurants hidden amid the date-palm plantations to pander to the needs of the tourist; this is the Omani countryside in its raw and natural state, thankfully. However, as an alternative you might like to pick out a hotel in the region, so that you eliminate the drive from Muscat, which will save you a lot of time gazing at the highway.

WHERE TO STAY

There are several international-standard hotels in the Al Batinah region, including Millennium Resort (page 142), Crowne Plaza (page 149) and Sohar Beach Hotel (pages 148–9), and numerous small hotels and apartment hotels from which to explore, thus eliminating the extra driving time from Muscat. Listings are given under the relevant towns in this chapter.

WHERE TO EAT AND DRINK

Good restaurants can be found within the upper- and mid-range hotels of the region. However, there are many cheap eating places beyond the hotels that are worth a try, largely in the form of Indian-run coffee shops (similar to a British café, serving the local community). They can be found in any row of shops on the street and usually serve chicken, fish and rice dishes.

ACTIVITIES

BULLFIGHTING Bullfighting (pages 35–6) is popular in this region and takes place on Fridays during the year. Barka and Suhar are the main centres but small events are held in many towns, including As Sawadi, As Suwayq and Saham. Ask your hotel whether an event is being held near the town where you are staying. Alternatively, you could arrange for a tour operator to take you from Muscat, taking in other sights as well.

WADI TRIPS These can be arranged either through your hotel in the region, or in advance through any tour operator in Muscat. Wadi Mistal, Wadi Bani Awf and Wadi As Sahtan are the three most popular wadis of the region, all of which are easily explored in day trips from Muscat (pages 158, 160–1 and 162).

USEFUL TELEPHONE NUMBERS

Al Batinah Police HQ ☏ 26 840096
Ar Rustaq Hospital ☏ 26 875055
Suhar Hospital ☏ 26 840299
Suhar Post Office ☏ 26 840003

BARKA برکاء

Barka is the first major coastal town reached after leaving Muscat on route 1, As Sib Street. The town is surrounded by date plantations, with other crops scattered in the fields. Historically, Barka was one of the prosperous cities along this coast, and was important as an area of export to Basra (Iraq), India and East Africa. The town centre is home to a fort, a main suq and a fish suq, and a fishing harbour. The suq area is to the west of the fort and extends to the beach. Vegetables and fresh herbs are sold from mats laid out on the ground or from the back of pick-up trucks surrounding the fish suq. A few interesting old derelict buildings remain near to the suq, while virtually every other shop in the town seems to be for 'Ladies' Tailoring', except, notably, one for the 'Sale of Ice Cubes'.

GETTING THERE AND AWAY Barka is about a 50km drive west from Muscat Airport, and if you do not have your own transport, you can flag down one of the minibuses plying the route. The exit is clearly signposted on the route 1 dual carriageway below the main Barka flyover and, once you have taken the turning, the road continues for 5km north towards the sea, past Lulu, the adjacent Toyota car showroom and countless modem shops.

 WHERE TO STAY AND EAT *Map, page 138.*

🏠 **Al Ghailani As Sahala Farm** (3 reception rooms, 3 bedrooms) East of Barka; m 97 11188, 99 201122; e rashid1122@hotmail.com. A 30min drive west from Muscat International Airport, this family-run farm comes complete with numerous livestock, including goats. The date gardens are extensive & well maintained. As this is a private farm you will not have the antiseptic surroundings that you would in a 5-star hotel. Rooms have en-suite facilities, TV & AC, & there is a large garden & shaded pool. The property is 1.5km southwest off Bait Al Baraka Palace roundabout, along a dirt road. The beach at As Sib is a 20min drive. **$$$$**

🏠 **Al Nahda Resort & Spa** (109 chalets) South of Barka; ✆ 26 883710; e stay@alnahdaresort.com; www.alnahdaresort.com. Located south of Barka, off the Nakhal road 2km south of the Barka

141

exit on the Muscat Expressway. This independent hotel is set in 30 acres of gardens & is marketed as a 'wellness retreat'. The facilities include a gym, fitness studio, spa & volleyball/tennis courts & a bar & live entertainment. This 5-star resort comprises 1- & 2-bedroom villas which need refurbishment to bring them up to date. They are spread throughout the grounds with the farthest some 500m from the main reception. **$$$$**

🏠 **Millennium Resort Mussanah** (308 rooms) On the coast at Al Musanaah, just under 100km west of Muscat International Airport; ☎26 871555; e reservations.mrmo@millenniumhotels.com; www.

millenniumhotels.com. The hotel is well signed & accessed at Al Miladdah (also Muladdah) by taking the north exit at the roundabout at Al Miladdah (the same roundabout that accesses Ar Rustaq). This beachfront hotel overlooks a small marina purpose-built for the Asian Beach Games. Today the fresh, modern interiors offer comfortable accommodation with a choice ranging from standard rooms to apartments. With 3 dining outlets, a coffee shop & bar, the hotel compensates for the lack of good dining in Musanaah. This is an ideal location for exploring the Al Batinah area & offers excellent value compared with similar hotels in Muscat. **$$$**

OTHER PRACTICALITIES

✚ **Barka Polyclinic** ☎26 882055; ⊕ 24hrs. Southwest of the Barka flyover, accessed from the Suhar–Muscat carriageway on route 1, Al Batinah highway, after exiting the road before the flyover; or on the Ar Rustaq–Barka road by exiting left onto the service road & following the road as it curves left to become parallel to Al Batinah highway. Turn left off the service road just after a mosque.

✚ **Capital Pharmacy Barka** ☎26 882490; ⊕ 10.00–21.00. On the service road east of the Barka flyover, 250m west of the Shell petrol station. **Police station** ☎26 882099; ⊕ 24hrs. South of the Barka flyover on route 13 from Nakhal, just over 1km before the flyover junction.
✉ **Post Office** ☎26 882133; ⊕ 07.30–14.30 Sun–Thu. From the suq in Barka take the road west towards the bullfighting arena. The post office is on the left after 1.4km from the junction.

WHAT TO SEE AND DO

Barka Fort حصن بركاء (⊕ 08.30–14.30 Sun–Thu except when the guardian is praying or eating; 500bzs) The town's fort was restored in 1986 and is in fact two forts – the first Yarubi, the second Al Bu Said. This is the reason for the two gates, the original Yarubi one now being on the inside. The inner ground level is raised up to allow good drainage of rainwater or even seawater in heavy storms. There are three gun towers (look out for the bats) and two wells.

In its Yarubi form, Barka Fort was the scene of the historical event that resulted in the ousting of the Persians from Al Batinah coast and the start of the current Al Bu Said dynasty. The story connected with this may have been elaborated over the centuries. Ahmad Al Bu Said, a merchant promoted to *wali* of Suhar, is said to have signed a trick agreement with the Persians in 1748, then invited them to a grand feast in celebration at Barka Fort. After the Persians had feasted themselves witless, the Omanis slaughtered them. Ahmad's position was therefore consolidated and he founded the dynasty the following year in 1749, before setting about the reconstruction of the Omani navy.

Bullfighting arena حلبة مصارعة الثيران This is easiest to access by turning left at the junction in front of the older suq as you arrive from route 1, As Sib Street. After about 3.5km from the suq junction you will find the circular arena where bull butting takes place on your right. This happens on alternate Fridays based on general agreement with the organisers. The trucks with the bulls arrive around 15.00 and the contests start around 16.00. It is far safer to sit on the concrete seating area, as the bulls do have a habit of running through the crowd sitting on the contest floor, scattering men far and wide. It is a man's world here, but all visitors will be welcomed.

Bait Na'aman بيت النعمان (⏰ *08.30–14.30 Sun–Thu; 500bzs; an English-speaking Omani guide is often available*) Signposted off the main dual carriageway 4.3km west of the Barka flyover is the right turn north to Bait Na'aman, which is another 2.3km along a country lane. This unusual castle or fortified country house, restored in 1990 and recently renovated, is easily the most charming of its type in Oman, and made very accessible by the furnishings that bring it to life. The scale, unlike so many of the vast forts, which become rather indigestible after a while, is domestic and homely, and most visitors have no trouble imagining what it would have been like living in such a house a century or two ago. There are also excellent wall plaques explaining the function of each room.

The house was built by Imam Saif bin Sultan (d 1711) in prosperous Yarubi times for his exclusive use as a country retreat (a sort of Chequers or Camp David). In those days, it was three days' journey from Muscat. He planted 30,000 date palms and 6,000 coconut trees around it. The gardens were irrigated by a *falaj* from Nakhal, 35km away to the southeast, which is now dried up. The outside courtyard was where the soldiers would have camped, several hundred of them, to protect the imam, and there was a big raised-up cistern where rainwater was collected. Inside, the high ceilings are attractively decorated and allow for coolness. The accommodation was suitable for a family of eight or nine members. On the ground floor were the toilet, bathroom, date store, kitchen and women's jail, which was needed when Oman's ruler was in residence and had a court case. New carpets have been laid as floor coverings, too big to give an authentic feel – original Omani rugs were and still are very small. Rush matting would have been the usual floor covering.

Halfway up the stairs was the guards' room, to stop people entering the private quarters, and the first floor had living areas only. The towers on the roof floor have cannon holes, though the cannons themselves have been taken off to Barka Fort or to the Ministry, as they were too heavy to get back *in situ* after the restoration. The walls are 1.5m thick, made from traditional Omani *saruj* bricks which were typically soaked for 25 days, not just the one day as is the practice today. As a result, the *saruj* is less strong now than it used to be centuries ago.

PICNIC STOPS ALONG AL BATINAH نزهة تتوقف عند الباطنة

If you travel from Al Buraymi the road towards Suhar passes out of the mountain scenery within 15 minutes, and after that the easiest picnicking spot is not until Suhar, 45 minutes further on. Take the same signpost off towards the coast as for the Sohar Beach Hotel from the Sallan roundabout, and in less than 1km you will see an extensive landscaped park to the left of the road. You can enter it from either end, inland by turning left at the traffic lights, or at the shore end, where you can turn left into a car park. There are toilet blocks and water fountains, shaded pagodas and children's playgrounds with a central lake. You will find it near-deserted, except on Fridays. The Sohar Beach Hotel lies just beyond it.

If you want a wilder spot, another option is to drive further on south of Al Khaburah (1½ hours from the Al Wajaja/Hatta border). Turn off towards the coast at Qasabiyat az Za'ab along dirt tracks through the banana and mango plantations until you reach the tarmac road parallel to the main dual carriageway. Follow this as it winds scenically past date palms until you come to the point where the tarmac crosses a picturesque wadi flowing with a wide river. Leave the car beside the main road and then walk along either side of the riverbank to find a picnic spot among the palm trees. The birdlife here is stunning.

AS SAWADI AND AROUND السوادي

A 17km drive from Barka will take you to the signed right turn to As Sawadi on the beach. There are beautiful stretches of sand at As Sawadi, where there is a beach resort of the same name, and from where you can take boating and other adventure trips out to the Ad Dimaniyyat and As Sawadi Islands.

WHAT TO SEE AND DO
As Sawadi Islands جزر السوادي These islands lie just offshore and boat trips can be arranged after you negotiate with the local fishermen to take you to them; try to get a price per boat of around RO5. One island (Al Mugabra) has a sandy beach where you can picnic under municipal shelters. On another island (Jabal As Sawadi) there is a watchtower whose stairs you can climb. These islands are also good for birdwatching. Snorkellers and novice divers are taken here.

Ad Dimaniyyat Islands Nature Reserve جزر الديمانيات These are a string of small islands situated about 16km off Al Batinah coast (in both the As Sib and Barka *wilayats*). The waters around the islands look remarkable from the air when coming in to land at Muscat Airport.

The islands have been designated a conservation area since 1996, and are rife with bird and marine life. You can explore the waters around the islands by diving, snorkelling or swimming, but the islands themselves are protected and only accessible with specific permission. They are nesting grounds for the endangered hawksbill turtle and the green turtle, and the period from April to September is the birds' breeding season, when ospreys and red-billed tropicbirds, among others, nest here and access is prohibited. The surrounding waters also have protected zones, the purpose of which is to preserve the coral reef. Local dive operators obtain permits from the Ministry of Regional Municipalities and Environment to take guests and tourists to the waters surrounding the islands, and so all the formalities are done for you.

This is one of the best dive sites in Oman, with over 20 set dive locations where coral reef, clownfish, rays, honeycomb moray eels, barracuda, tuna, green turtles, fusiliers, zebra sharks, leopard sharks and whale shark have all been seen. In addition, there are marine and terrestrial snake species and marine mammals such as the bottlenose dolphin, the common dolphin and the humpback whale.

The islands are broken up into western, central and eastern areas, and go by the following names: Al Kharaabah, Al Hayoot, Al Jibaal Al Kibaar Island, Al Joon, Al Jabal as Sagheer, Memlehah, Al Loomiyah, Qismah and Awlad Al Joon. Camping is permitted on Al Jibaal Al Kibaar and Al Joon only, but a specific permit is required and monitoring is maintained by officials on the islands. Permits can be obtained directly from the Ministry of Environment and Climate Affairs (\ *24 404825;* e *nature_oman@meca.gov.om; www.meca.gov.om*), though it is automatically included by reputable tour operators.

AS SUWAYQ TO SUHAR السويق إلى صحار

AS SUWAYQ السويق From Al Batinah highway As Suwayq (also Al Suwaiq) is clearly signposted 51km northwest of Barka, with the town on the right taking the exit from the As Suwayq roundabout north towards the sea (the roundabout is extremely busy and on occasion you may be redirected to an exit farther along Al Batinah highway). It's quite nice to take a detour here, if simply to break the monotony of the dual carriageway. It is a quaint old village with a restored seafront fort and its share of mosques. The beach is deserted during much of the day and makes a great picnic stop. The area is known for its agriculture, with bananas, citrus fruits, mangoes and herbs all grown. Bullfighting also takes place here.

From As Suwayq you can follow the tarmac road close to the coast, which winds through fishing villages, past a crumbling fort and palm plantations for roughly 15 minutes north to Khadra Al Bu Rashid. Between As Suwayq and Al Khaburah further west along the coast there is a cluster of three restored *surs* (walled fort enclosures) standing close to the roadside. They all have either square or round towers at their corners with gun ports. Their doors are always kept locked, but in any event they look impressive from the outside.

What to see and do Located next to the shopping area and overlooking the fishing harbour, with its constant activity, is **As Suwayq Castle** (⊕ *08.30–14.30 Sun–Thu; 500bzs*). It was attacked several times during the 19th century. In 1836, the wife of the governor rallied the defenders and enabled it to withstand an attack when her husband was in Muscat. Today the fort has been restored and overlooks the new fishing harbour. Although it is not large, it is almost two separate units. To enter the fort there is a ramped gloomy passageway of about 15m which opens out into the large *sur*, the walled courtyard that could accommodate large numbers of people from the town. The courtyard adjoins the living accommodation, an almost windowless warren of rooms. By far the most appealing area of As Suwayq Castle is the roof of this residential section, which again can be reached by a second corridor. Here there are a couple of 'summer' rooms that might have caught sea breezes and for today's visitor boast excellent views over town and sea.

AL KHABURAH الخابورة Located 89km northwest of Barka, Al Khaburah itself is unremarkable except as a centre for traditional weaving, the products of which are sold in Muscat's heritage shops. Leather tanning and boatbuilding are other occupations, and sugarcane, dates, wheat and cotton are grown here. Its fort is reached from the Al Khaburah roundabout taking the turn north towards the sea. It overlooks the beach and is in the process of restoration.

What to see and do
Wadi Al Hawasnah وادي الحواسنة At the roundabout in Al Khaburah take the exit west towards the mountains along route 9 southwest towards Ibri. This will take you through the Wadi Al Hawasnah (you will cross the construction work for the new extension of the Muscat Expressway, which will eventually bypass Al Batinah highway). This makes a picturesque wadi day trip through many-hued mountains. Opposite Al Ghuzayn village 22km southwest of Al Khaburah is a small area of pillow lava on the left of the road. This represents the upper section of the ophiolite rock sequence (page 154). The wadi becomes deeper around 51km from Al Khaburah, snaking through the chocolate-coloured ophiolite mountains, with areas of garnet shades interspersed with ochre, and all of it contrasting with the dark green of the occasional date oasis. The road continues towards the village of Miskin, where route 10 to Ar Rustaq can be taken (153km from Al Khaburah via Wadi Al Hawasnah). Route 9 continues through Miskin to Ibri, a drive of 134km from Al Khaburah, taking around 2 hours.

SAHAM صحم Between Al Khaburah and Suhar, Saham lies 169km from Muscat Airport or 107km from the Al Wajaja/Hatta UAE border. Signposted 3km northeast off the roundabout on Al Batinah highway, Saham is an attractive old fishing town with an interesting seafront. Camel and horse racing are popular here, along with bullfighting events, which are held on alternate Fridays to the event held at Suhar (pages 36–7).

Keep straight on over the roundabout with the statues of herons, following signs to As-Suq, until the road leads you to the seafront, where it follows the line of the beach north for 1.3km to reach Saham Castle with its flag flying at the far end. On the way you pass some decayed seafront houses, once the homes of rich merchants. Traces of blue and white paint remain along the decorated arches and windows that look out across the sea from the balustraded verandas. A few old *shasha* (date palm leaf) boats are usually pulled up onto the beach and some are still in use.

Saham Castle (⊕ *08.30–14.30 Sun–Thu; 500bzs*) is at the northern end of the corniche. It is one of Al Batinah's classic *surs*, a fortified walled compound built to protect a town's inhabitants during periods of unrest. It dates from the middle of the 20th century, having been built by Sayyid Shihab bin Faisal Al Said, and is probably the last traditional castle to have been built in the country.

SUHAR صحار

Muscat to Suhar is 195km from Muscat International Airport and 92km (a 2½-hour drive) from the Al Wajaja/Hatta UAE border. Suhar and its hinterland comprise the

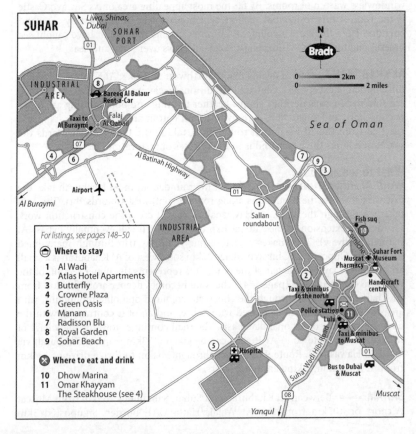

SUHAR

Liwa, Shinas, Dubai
SOHAR PORT

N

Bradt

0 _____ 2km
0 _____ 2 miles

INDUSTRIAL AREA

Bareeq Al Balaur Rent-a-Car

Taxi to Al Buraymi

Falaj Al Qabail

Sea of Oman

Al Batinah Highway

Airport ✈

Al Buraymi

Sallan roundabout

INDUSTRIAL AREA

Fish suq

Suhar Fort Museum

Muscat Pharmacy

Handicraft centre

Taxi & minibus to the north

Police station

Lulu

Taxi & minibus to Muscat

Hospital

Bus to Dubai & Muscat

Muscat

Yanqul

Suhar Wadi Hibi Road

For listings, see pages 148–50

🛏 **Where to stay**

1 Al Wadi
2 Atlas Hotel Apartments
3 Butterfly
4 Crowne Plaza
5 Green Oasis
6 Manam
7 Radisson Blu
8 Royal Garden
9 Sohar Beach

✖ **Where to eat and drink**

10 Dhow Marina
11 Omar Khayyam
    The Steakhouse (see 4)

area that many historians associate with Majan (*ma-jan* means 'ship's frame', with *ma* meaning 'ship' in Sumerian), a hugely important historical region that was a major source of raw materials, in particular copper, for Sumar and Akkad.

In its heyday Suhar was described by the 10th-century Arab geographer Istakhri as 'the most populous and wealthy town in Oman. It is not possible to find on the shore of the Persian Sea nor in all the land of Islam a city richer in fine buildings and foreign wares than Suhar.' His contemporary, the Arab historian Al Muqaddasi, described Suhar as 'the hallway to China, the storehouse of the East'. Traders disembarked from Baghdad into Suhar on their journeys to China, and the legend of Sindbad is said to have originated from here. The city was destroyed in AD972 by the Persian Buyid dynasty and never regained its former glory.

However, for over 1,500 years, until 1749, when the Al Bu Said ruling family moved their headquarters to Muscat, Suhar remained Oman's most prestigious and influential town. The *khawr* (creek) beside the fort, which was once its splendid harbour, is now silted and has almost completely vanished. The only reason for the town's success that remains evident to this day is its location at the end of the Wadi Al Jizi (pages 151–2), one of the few east–west passes across the Oman mountain range, and from where copper was exported to Mesopotamian cities over many centuries.

When the Portuguese arrived in 1507 they found it a thriving town needing 1,000 people to defend the fort alone. An Augustine church was subsequently built there by the Portuguese, who retained it until they were driven out in 1650 by the native Yarubi sultans of Oman.

During the Al Bu Said dynasty Suhar was the stage for just two more moments of high drama: one in 1866 when a sultan was shot by his own son while asleep; and the other in 1952 when the present sultan's father, angered by the Saudi occupation of Al Buraymi, ordered his forces to gather at Suhar for the march up Wadi Al Jizi to Al Buraymi. In the event they never set off, dissuaded from action by the British.

GETTING THERE AND AROUND Suhar's domestic airport is located to the northwest of the town, in a complex of extremely basic buildings. Currently no airline uses this airport.

Mwasalat **buses** run from Muscat (departing from the main Ruwi bus station) to Suhar about four times a day, taking 3 hours and costing RO5, and from Suhar to Muscat twice a day. They drop passengers off at the Shell petrol station south of Lulu and the Wadi Hibi road juction. The **minibuses or taxis** that wait for passengers on all the exit roads at Suhar roundabout can then be used for local travel. Expect to pay about RO40 for a taxi from Muscat, but perhaps less for the journey back from Suhar.

Once you reach Suhar, when driving from the junction on As Sib Street (below the flyover opposite Lulu) take the turn northeast to the town centre. A signed drive of 3.9km will take you through the more modern area into the older settlement beside the fort, which occupies a slightly elevated position opposite the clearly signposted *wali's* office.

Today the sprawl of Suhar is considerable, supported by the rapid growth in Oman's national economy and the port of Sohar, which is in the next administrative area of Liwa. This port is now Oman's principal import- and export- seaport (Salalah is focused on transhipments). In the industrial area adjacent to the port are several aluminium and steel smelters supported by Sohar Power, the largest power generation and water desalination plant in Oman. There are several chemical factories within the same complex and the adjacent Sohar Industrial Estate has a number of smaller, but still important, industrial companies and other industries.

The corniche area is probably the most attractive area in Suhar. This is easily reached from the Al Sallan roundabout 6.3km northwest of the Suhar junction on As Sib Street. Take the northeast exit into Sultan Qaboos Street and continue for 2.5km where on your left will be an attractive park that leads into the sea. Continue along this street past the interesting modern fish suq and take the left immediately after the suq onto Al Bahri Street, the corniche.

Suhar also makes a good base from which to explore Al Batinah Plain (pages 151–3).

WHERE TO STAY *Map, page 146.*

Sohar Beach Hotel (40 rooms) Al Sultan Qaboos St, Sallan; ☎ 26 841111; www.soharbeach. com. The hotel is about a 3hr drive from Muscat Airport – or a 45min drive from the Al Wajaja/Hatta border post. It is roughly halfway between Muscat & Dubai airports & provides a good stopover if you want to split the drive either to or from Dubai. This is a gem of a hotel, on Sallan Beach in Suhar. It sits on the road that loops through Suhar & rejoins the highway, although it is not at all clearly signposted from the Suhar flyover at route 8 to Yanqul. Exit at the Sallan roundabout & travel northeast from the roundabout in the direction of the sea. The hotel is signposted from here, & from this end it is just past the only set of traffic lights on the loop road, & sits within its high walls on the left-hand side. The hotel is like an Omani fort in appearance, with 4 round, crenellated towers. The rooms, suites & chalets are arranged on 2 storeys in a semicircle around a large pool & situated within 11 acres of landscaped gardens. Facilities include the Al Sallan coffee shop & the Al Zafran Arabian nightclub, serving *mezze,* seafood & grills, the Al Jizi lounge for residents & members & the Al Taraif lounge public bar. BBQ evenings every Thu in winter, & private BBQs for 5 or more guests can be arranged. There are lots of activities for kids, including crazy golf, croquet, go-karts, beach buggies, beach volleyball, water scooters, watersports & pleasure boat rides. **$$$$**

🏠 **Al Wadi Hotel** (80 rooms) Al Barka St, Al Batinah highway; ☎ 26 840058, 841995; e gmalwadi@omanhotels.com or reservationsalwadi@omanhotels.com; www. omanhotels.com. To get here, exit the Sallan roundabout towards the mountains & immediately take the service road that will take you north towards the hotel, which lies 1.2km away. The hotel is signposted & has a small pool. Al Sallan is the licensed restaurant, offering continental, Indian & Chinese cuisine (⏲ *06.00–23.00 daily; $$*). There is the Al Waqbah bar (⏲ *noon–15.00 & 18.00–01.00 daily*) & another licensed restaurant, the Oasis (⏲ *19.00–01.00 daily; $$*). Al Majaz is the club bar for residents only (⏲ *19.00–01.00*). This hotel is one of 4 in the group; the others are the Al Falaj Hotel, Ruwi Hotel & Sur Plaza. It does not provide airport transfers. It uses Budget & Hertz for arranging hire cars. **$$$**

🏠 **Butterfly Hotel** (42 rooms) West of the town centre in Sallan next to the Sohar Beach Hotel on Al Sultan Qaboos St; ☎ 26 843501; e info@ butterflyoman.com; www.butterflyoman.com. A modern-style apartment hotel, popular with long-term guests. The restaurant has an African theme, adding a quirky touch to the property. The hotel is a short walk from the (grey) sand beach & public park, & an easy drive from the fish suq & town centre. **$$$**

🏠 **Crowne Plaza Hotel** (126 rooms) On the road to Al Buraymi, not far from the turn west off Al Batinah highway; ☎ 26 850850; e cpsohar@ ihg.com; www.ihg.com/crowneplaza. Located well outside town, this hotel, though modern, is certainly superseded by the Radisson Blu in terms of being up to date, though, it is still very convenient if Al Buraymi is your destination. Ask for rooms at the rear of the hotel, as it is on a main arterial road. B/fast inc. **$$$**

🏠 **Radisson Blu** (179 rooms) Directly on the beach between the port & town centre; ☎ 26 640000; e info.sohar@radissonblu.com; www.radissonblu.com. This modern hotel opened in spring 2016 & overlooks the Sea of Oman. The (grey) sand beach is not public & is occasionally

used to haul in fish in large nets. While the hotel may have some teething problems with its service, the location, good amenities & competitive pricing more than compensate. To get there, exit at the Sallan roundabout north in the direction of the sea. At the junction with traffic lights turn left into An Nuzah St & after 200m look for a track to the right that goes towards the sea. There is no tarmac road, as yet, & you need to carefully negotiate your way towards the hotel, which is in sight all the way. The track is about 1.3km. B/fast inc. **$$$**

🏠 **Atlas Hotel Apartments** (53 rooms) Immediately off Al Batinah highway on the carriageway towards Dubai 1.7km west of the Suhar flyover; ☎ 26 858009, 853010; e royalint@omantel. net.om. Has large double rooms & 1- or 2-bedroom apartments. Opened in 2010 to take advantage of the increase in business caused by the new port, the apartments are furnished with heavy furniture with paisley-type fabrics & a good selection of appliances in the kitchen, but check whether there are plates & cutlery. The location immediately off Al Batinah highway & spacious car parking make it an easy-to-get-to, low-cost option on a drive between Muscat & Dubai; however, the cleanliness is poor & the overall design very basic. **$$**

🏠 **Green Oasis Hotel** (48 rooms) South of Al Batinah highway on Al Muwaylah St, close to the Suhar Royal Hospital & Royal Oman Police; ☎ 26 846442. The Green Oasis has been continually redeveloped over the last 10 years, but unfortunately little attention has been paid to cleanliness. **$$**

🏠 **Royal Garden Hotel** (62 rooms) On Al Batinah highway 1.7km after the flyover at Falaj Al Qabail, the junction for route 7 to Al Buraymi; access to the side of the Al Maha petrol station; ☎ 26 755888; e royalgarden.sohar@ hotmail.com. This hotel is popular with people working in the port. The rooms are spacious & comfortable; the gardens & b/fast outside make this one to consider in Suhar. B/fast inc. **$$**

🏠 **Manam Hotel** (27 rooms) On route 8 from Al Buraymi & just before the junction onto Al Batinah highway at Falaj Al Qabail; ☎ 26 753888; e rameez.shaikh@manamhotel.com; www. manamhotel.com. Comfortable apartment-style hotel that is very convenient for the port & industrial area. B/fast is mediocre, while Wi-Fi is patchy, as is usual in Oman. You can negotiate your room rate to exclude b/fast. **$**

✘ WHERE TO EAT AND DRINK Map, page 146.

✘ **The Steakhouse** Crowne Plaza (page 149); ☎ 26 850850; ⏲ 11.00–15.00 & 19.00–23.00 daily. This is a new addition to the restaurants at the Crowne Plaza. With simple brown-toned décor, you cannot be in any real doubt as to the menu. Unlike Muscat's hotels, where meats are often from Australia, here the steaks are from the US, perhaps delivered from Dubai. The quality & service are excellent. This is very much worth a drive from any location in Suhar & if wine makes a meal for you – unlike most restaurants in Suhar, a reasonable selection is available. $$$

✘ **Dhow Marina** Immediately beside the fish suq at the western end of the corniche; m 96 275963; ⏲ 11.30–16.00 & 18.00–23.30 Sat–Thu, 13.00–16.00 & 18.00–23.30 Fri. You can choose your fresh fish, which is sold by weight, at about RO8 per kilo. $

✘ **Omar Khayyam** Just off the main Al Batinah highway east of Suhar; ☎ 26 844901; ⏲ 11.30–15.00 & 17.00–23.30 Sat–Thu, 13.00–16.00 & 17.00–23.30 Fri. One of the branches of the very well-established Omar Khayyam chain. Pleasantly decorated & very convenient, as it is next to an Oman Oil petrol station. The menu intimidates with the sheer number of choices (over 100). Try the prawns in ginger or ask the waiter to suggest a choice. $

OTHER PRACTICALITIES

Bareeq Al Balaur Rent-a-Car m 91 250570. Next to the Al Maha petrol station to the west of Suhar, not far from the airport & port.

✚ **Muscat Pharmacy** ☎ 26 840211; ⏲ 24hrs. Just behind the corniche, 2km south of the fish harbour.

Police station ☎ 26 840099; ⏲ 24hrs. Just north of the Suhar flyover at road 8 to Yanqul, exit Al Batinah highway & take Suhar St north towards the town centre. The police station is on the right immediately as you exit the highway.

✉ **Post office** ☎ 26 840003; ⏲ 07.30–14.30. Just north of the Suhar flyover at road 8 to Yanqul. Exit Al Batinah highway & take Suhar St north towards the town centre; after 950m take the first exit right into Al Nahda St from the roundabout & drive east for 680m. The post office is on the right.

✚ **Suhar Hospital** ☎ 26 840299; ⏲ 24hrs. On the southbound lane of Al Batinah highway, take a right exit 4km south of the Sallan roundabout & continue on the Al Muwaylah Rd towards the mountains for 5km. This is the principal hospital for the governorate.

WHAT TO SEE AND DO

Suhar Fort Museum متحف قلعة صحار (☎ 26 844758; ⏲ 08.30–14.30 Sun–Thu; 500bzs) To reach Suhar Fort from the Al Sallan roundabout take the route mentioned on page 148 for the corniche. The fort lies at the end of the corniche, as the road veers right. From the Suhar junction on As Sib Street, Al Batinah highway (below the flyover opposite Lulu), take the north exit (Suhar Street) and follow the road straight, crossing two roundabouts. After 2.6km take the right turn into Ash Shizawi Street and continue past the fort-like complex on the left marked 'Ministry of Tourism', then turn left towards the gold-domed mosque and the fort is behind.

At the time of publication the fort was undergoing restoration work and was not open.

Once, Suhar's fort was different from all of Oman's other fortifications by virtue of its whitewashed exterior. Today its fired brick and stonework is exposed and the plaster colour is beige, as with most other forts. Suhar Fort dates from AD795, although it was renovated in the 14th and 15th centuries by the emirs (or princes) of Hormuz. There is said to be a 10km-long escape tunnel, to be used during sieges, that leads from the fort towards the *wilayat* of Al Buraymi. The current buildings are thought to be 200–300 years old. Fully restored in 1985, the fort has a commanding location overlooking the beach, opposite the governor's office. The surrounding gardens have been well landscaped.

Handicraft centre الحرفية الصناعات معرض (⏰ *08.00–noon & 16.00–21.00 Sat–Thu*) Situated 350m southwest of the fort on Ash Shizawi Street – the signage is mainly in Arabic, but it does say 'Ministry of Tourism' in English. This building, built in the traditional style with domes and courtyards, houses a handicraft centre. It looks deserted and may well be if you visit in the afternoon. To avoid disappointment, arrive around 10.00 and you may see some craftspeople at work in their shops. Purchases help those who create the products. The silversmith Hassan Mohammed Al Baloushi sells beautiful handcrafted pieces which are in demand far and wide.

Port of Sohar صحار ميناء Although the port is not accessible to casual visitors, it dominates Suhar (note the use by the port of the older spelling of the town's name). The port was built from 2004 and includes a free trade zone. Its location outside the Strait of Hormuz means that it offers not only reduced shipping times into the Arabian Gulf, if goods are shipped overland via Wadi Al Jizi, but also eliminates a potential increase in 'war risk' insurance charges applied to ships that enter the Arabian Gulf during times of conflict. The free trade zone has attracted heavy industry like Sohar Aluminium, whose partners include Rio Tinto Alcan, and Vale's iron pelletising plant. Both of these industries benefit from low-cost natural gas for power. The port is also the principal inbound container port for Oman, since Mina Sultan Qaboos's container business was relocated to Suhar.

FURTHER AFIELD From near Lulu on route 1 Al Batinah highway is the exit south towards Yanqul on route 8 and Wadi Hibi (also Heebi). The road heads south over the Al Batinah Plain, with Wadi Hibi on your left after 48km. It is another 13km to Hibi with its newly restored small fort in the date oasis (⏰ *08.00–14.00 Sun–Thu; 500bzs*). Continuing on the road will take you to Yanqul and its impressive fort after 61km (page 197).

AL BATINAH PLAIN الباطنة سهل

Al Batinah Plain is fertile from the mineral-rich soil washed down from the mountains into the wadis, namely Wadi Al Jizi, Wadi Hibi and Wadi Ahin, and it is watered by many wells. These have been drilled to excess in recent years, leading to salt-water intrusion into the soil as a result of seawater being drawn inland. However, the land still produces dates and limes together with tomatoes, carrots, onions, aubergines, cauliflowers, peppers, lemons, bananas, mangoes, guavas and even tobacco. Inland, this fertile plain gives way to gravel expanses that reach back to the mountains, broken up only by a few scrubby bushes and trees.

WADI AL JIZI الجزي وادي Few people are aware how much there is to see in the hinterland of Suhar, but with your own transport an enjoyable few days can be spent based at the Sohar Beach Hotel (page 148), exploring Wadi Al Jizi with its ancient copper-mining sites, the medieval stronghold of Hawra Burghah and the ziggurat (temple) at Arja. All are likely to be deserted and all are set in landscapes of wild beauty. There is no public transport. This wadi was one of the two major inland corridors permitting access to the sea from the desert to the west; the other was the Samail Gap that links Muscat with Nizwa and the interior. Suhar grew up here because it was the natural port for the copper dug from the ancient mines along the Wadi Al Jizi – copper that was destined eventually for Mesopotamia.

Getting there and away Wadi Al Jizi is reached by exiting Al Batinah highway below the Falaj Al Qabail flyover some 17km north of the Suhar junction near Lulu. Take route 7 that runs west to Al Buraymi, and the places mentioned below are not far from this route.

Hawra Burghah Fortress قلعة حوراء برغا This worthwhile excursion from Suhar is now easily drivable even in a saloon car since the construction of the wide graded track to the Wadi Al Jizi Dam. The 13th-century fortress is dramatically sited on the summit of a rock outcrop that rises 200–300m, straddling the Wadi Al Jizi.

The medieval fortress was the most important of several forts built by the Nabahina dynasty of hereditary kings in their attempts to resist the invading Hormuz princes. Its strategic location at Hawra Burghah enabled it to dominate the passageway through Wadi Al Jizi to Al Buraymi. Behind Hawra Burghah stands **Suhar peak**, whose white limestone cone rises 400m directly behind the town of Suhar and was used by early navigators as a landmark.

The name 'Hawra' means 'white limestone' in Arabic, while 'Burghah' means 'garden' in Persian. The defensive walls and the elaborate water system of dams, cisterns and plaster-lined *falaj* channels (see box, pages 208–9) make exploring this hilltop site particularly interesting. In its heyday the various terraces and levels may have been lush with crops and vegetation, enabling the inhabitants to hold out against long-term sieges, and testament to the fact that rainfall must always have been high enough to sustain life here.

The ascent of the steep hill takes 10–15 minutes and is best made from the north side, where the track nearly touches the foot of the hill and where there is a breach in the walls through which you can enter. The upper section of the hill is quite a scramble and requires sturdy footwear. Once on top, it takes the best part of an hour to look around the surprisingly extensive city. Try to avoid midday as a time for your visit, as there is no shade on the summit.

Getting there and away Take the Suhar–Al Buraymi road (road 7) inland towards Al Buraymi from the Falaj Al Qabail roundabout for some 16km, and then take the junction at the interchange that allows access to the side route on the south of the road. This initially runs northwest, but you should take the turn south that appears almost immediately. The fortress is reached via a graded track of 4.7km from the main highway.

The ziggurat at Arja الزقورة في العرجاء This archaeological ruin is remarkable not for its scale or size, but for the fact that it exists at all; it is the only one of its kind in the Arabian Peninsula. A ziggurat is a very early kind of temple, built in terraces, similar to a step pyramid. The earliest and most famous ziggurat was at Ur of the Chaldees in southern Mesopotamia. Arja itself was the main centre for copper mining in Oman up until the 12th century. A total of 32 copper-smelting sites have been identified in this area, centred on Wadi Al Jizi. Estimates suggest that in medieval times Arja produced 48,000–60,000 tonnes of copper. Copper was massively exploited here for nearly 4,000 years, the result being the gradual deforestation of the entire mining area to provide fuel for smelting. Omani copper has a high nickel content and the copper deposits here were formed millions of years ago at the bottom of the ocean, in the lavas now exposed in Oman ophiolite rocks.

In his book *Tigris*, Thor Heyerdahl described visiting the site while he stopped briefly in Oman during his 1977 voyage on his replica of a Mesopotamian reed boat. One side of the ziggurat has a clearly recognisable processional ramp leading to the summit, which would have been used by early priests making sacrificial offerings. The exact nature of these practices is a matter of pure speculation, as is much to do with this ziggurat, which appears to be oriented towards a dramatic dark pyramid-shaped peak on the far side of the valley.

Archaeologist Paolo Costa and English orientalist T G Wilkinson conducted an archaeological study in 1978 on Arja and the ancient copper-mining settlements, the results of which were published by the Omani Ministry of National Heritage and Culture.

Getting there and away From the Falaj Al Qabail flyover, take road 7 towards Al Buraymi for 24km from the flyover until you reach the chimney of the industrial area, together with a copper factory and the associated power station. The road passes between these two industrial units, then after 4.5km take the right-hand fork. After a total of 7.7km the ziggurat can be seen to the right, overlooked by a mobile-phone mast.

Pillow lava الحمم الوسائدية East of the village of Al Suhaylah on the old Suhar–Al Buraymi road (which runs almost alongside the new road, route 7) is the 'pillow lava' that overlooks the old road's bridge. This is striking enough to have been featured on the cover of *Geo Times* magazine. It's the upper formation of the ophiolite sequence of rock for which Oman is famed. To get a better view will entail parking your vehicle on the right-hand side of the road, on the Al Buraymi side of the bridge, and walking down a rough track into the wadi. The pillow lava is of no value in itself, but care should be taken not to damage it.

Getting there and away From the Falaj Al Qabail flyover, take road 7 in the direction of Al Buraymi and continue for 26km. Take the slip road to the right and continue for a further 3.5km, where you will see the pillow lava to your left.

Driving to Al Buraymi via Wadi Al Jizi Exit route 1 for Al Batinah at the Falaj Al Qabail flyover and take route 7, the Suhar–Al Buraymi road. There is an emigration/immigration border post after 58km at which, although Al Buraymi is in Oman, you will need to present car registration documents and personal identification, including a valid passport. This tarmac dual carriageway bends and weaves through low-level *jabals* and past old villages with their mosques, forts and watchtowers. (For more information on Al Buraymi, see pages 197–200.)

LIWA لوى

Continuing up the main Al Batinah highway northwest from Suhar, the next town you reach (after 29km) is Liwa. The town's road network is undergoing considerable change due to the Port of Sohar development and an intended new township by the Oman government, costing US$1.5 billion.

WHAT TO SEE AND DO
Liwa Castle حصن لوى (⊕ *08.00–14.30 Sun–Thu; 500bzs*) The elegant castle at Liwa is just 2km east of the Liwa roundabout on the main Al Batinah highway. Its interiors include meeting rooms in the central tower's upper floor with polylobate arches and glistening wooden doors. Five gun towers and the central tower made this a fort with considerable firepower.

Harmul حرمول East of the castle is the small village of Harmul. To the south of the village lies a small *sur*, Sheikha Awlad bin Yarub, which is delightfully unrestored.

Ophiolite is the name for one of the earth's more interesting rock sequences. The structure is typically igneous rock that was formed from oceanic lithosphere (earth's crust and mantle) where the ocean bed was spreading because of the divergence of continental plates, and which therefore became fractured. The fractured nature allows the upward extrusion of magma (hot, viscous rock) into cold seawater. The result of this extrusion is a common sequence that includes the following elements, from the base: the remnants of the mantle; a layering of peridotite, rich in magnesium and with some iron that weathers quickly, creating distinctive holes in the rock; the often clearly defined moho layer, the boundary between the earth's mantle that lies below the earth's crust; layered gabbro, where the granular structure is usually large and easily seen; non-layered gabbro; vertically defined sheeted dykes that intruded into other rock; and finally pillow lava, which represents the intrusion of the molten rock into cold seawater, in much the same way that toothpaste comes out of its tube. The rock is cooled, rapidly forming a pillow shape.

When the continental plates converge they usually ride over the ophiolite as they are a lighter, less dense material. In Oman and some other locations around the world, however, the ophiolite was obducted (overthrust) on top of the continental plate material and in many cases caused dramatic deformation to the rocks. In Oman the dark chocolate-coloured rock found around Muscat, Samail, Nizwa and the lower mountains of Al Batinah are ophiolites. Their natural colour is grey, but exposure to air and water causes oxidation which usually creates this brown colour. This ophiolite rock sequence is the source of minerals which are mined in Oman, notably copper.

To the north of the village is a small lagoon with mangrove trees rich in-birdlife, including the locally rare white-collared kingfisher (*Todiramphus chloris*). As this area is low-lying, care needs to be taken if driving a car off-road, in case the weight of the car makes it sink into the mud.

SHINAS AND REGION شنـاص والمنطقة

This town, the most northerly in Al Batinah region, is 57km northwest of Suhar and has a number of castles and forts, as well as a natural park noted for its forest of mangrove trees (or *qurum*, in Arabic). Bird sightings should include lesser crested tern, great stone plover and, if you are very fortunate, white-collared kingfisher. Fruits and vegetables are grown in the vicinity.

A ferry service runs between Shinas and Khasab (pages 177–9), and an old Portakabin at Shinas Port (☏ 26 748344) provides the office for Oman's National Ferries in the town. Services to Musandam (Khasab, Lima and Daba) can be booked or confirmed here.

WHAT TO SEE AND DO
Shinas Fort حصن شنـاص (⏱ 08.00–14.30 *Sun–Thu*; *500bzs*) Restored in 1997–98 and now open to the public, the fort is signposted 2km off the main highway towards the sea. The fort was built in Shinas's heyday around 1800 when the town was allied with the Persians, and quite separate from the rest of Oman. Shinas fought with the Ras Al Khaymah Qasimi tribe against British shipping

in the Gulf. The British and Omani naval forces retaliated and in 1810 the fort was sacked and forced to surrender. Today Shinas Fort is a very simple classic *sur* of the kind so common along Oman's northern coast. The rectangular walls have a cannon tower on each corner, while inside are a couple of buildings along opposing sides of the vast courtyard. There isn't much to attract visitors; indeed, the scraggly *sidr* trees with nesting house crows are the dominant feature. Make a visit here if you have time to kill while waiting for a ferry at the nearby port.

Shinas mangroves أشجار القرم بشناص (⏰ *08.00–14.30 Sun–Thu; 500bzs*)

Shinas has two areas of mangroves, one on the coast at each side of the town. The northern mangrove is mainly a replanted area that has yet to mature. The southern area is mature and as a result home to a wide variety of fauna. To reach the southern mangrove take the east exit towards the coast at Shinas roundabout. Drive straight at the first roundabout and then after just under 1km at the second roundabout turn right towards the south and continue for 5.7km to a roundabout (near Al Humayra) where you need to take the third exit north and then drive north for 1km and exit right and continue for an additional 1.2km, where you can park. The mangrove is reached across a small footbridge and covers just over 6km^2. Low tides which occur at the early morning are ideal for most sightings as they bring birds to feed. Unfortunately, increased disturbance has affected sightings, but you should look for white-collared kingfisher, Sykes's warbler and Indian pond heron. There are of course innumerable gulls and terns all relying on animals living in the environment, such as crabs including *Thalamita crenata* and snails, especially *Terebralia palustris*.

From Shinas to Khitmat Milahah border post من شناص إلى خطمة ملاحة

From Shinas, the road to the north leads to the Khitmat Milahah border post with Al Fujayrah, which would be the way to travel to reach Musandam, or Sharjah or Ras Al Khaymah emirate. Note the visa requirements to enter the UAE (page 172).

From Shinas to Al Wajaja/Hatta border post من شناص إلى حتا Instead of

continuing straight up the coast road to the Khitmat border and on to Musandam, taking a well-signposted left at the roundabout leads you to the Al Wajaja/Hatta border post and Dubai.

The drive from Muscat to the Al Wajaja (Oman)/Hatta (Dubai UAE) border post, cruising non-stop at the 120km/h speed limit, takes a minimum of 3 hours – roughly 1 hour to As Sawadi Beach, another hour to Suhar and the third to reach the border post – though in practice, with stops for petrol and leg-stretches, most people would allow at least 4 hours. Coming the other way, from the UAE into Oman, the Al Wajaja/Hatta border post is the easiest of all the crossing points. Note the visa requirements for entering the UAE (page 172).

THE RUSTAQ LOOP

The Millennium Resort Mussanah (page 142) makes an excellent base for the inland circuit via Nakhal, Ar Rustaq and Al Hazm, three of Oman's finest forts; add in Al Awabi if you want to have a look at a smaller, simpler fort. Each of the three major forts takes at least an hour to visit, so set aside a day, or ideally two, for the round trip. Alternatively, if time is not an issue, the locations on the loop can easily be visited in a series of outings from Muscat. You can flag down local minibuses anywhere on this route to reach the main towns on the tarmac, but to head into the wadis you need your own transport, preferably 4x4.

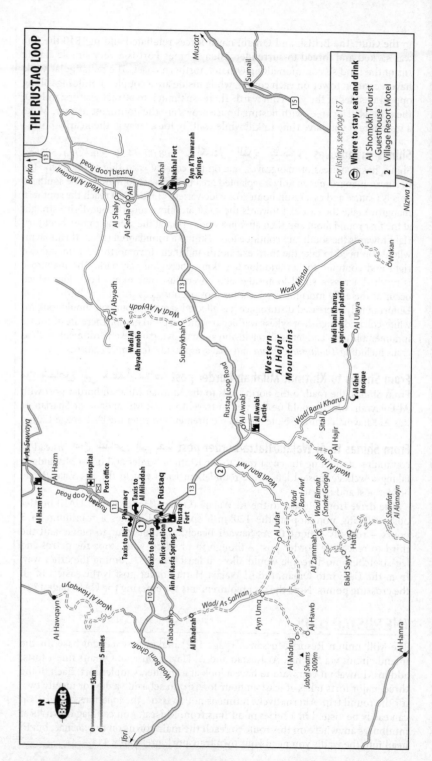

THE RUSTAQ LOOP

Muscat

Sumail

15

13 Barka

Rustaq Loop Road

Wadi Al Ma'awil

Al Shaly

Al Sefala Ot Afi

Nakhal

Nakhal Fort

Ayn A'Thawarah Springs

Nizwa

Al Abyadh

Wadi Al Abyadh moho

Wadi Al Abyadh

Subaykhah

13

Wadi Mistal

Wakan

Western
Al Hajar
Mountains

Wadi bani Kharus
agricultural platform

Al Ulaya

Al Ghel Mosque

Wadi Bani Kharus

Sital

Al Hajir

Rustaq Loop Road

Al Awabi

Al Awabi Castle

As-Suwayq

Al Hazm Fort

Al Hazm

Hospital

Post office

Pharmacy

Taxis to Ibri

Taxis to Al Miladdah

Ar Rustaq

Police station

Ar Rustaq Fort

Taxis to Barka

Ain Al Kasfa Springs

Rustaq Loop Road

11

13

2

Wadi Bani Awf

Al Jufar

Wadi Bani Kharus

Wadi Bimah (Snake Gorge)

Al Zammah

Bald Sayt

Hatt

Sharafat Al Alamayn

Al Hawqayn

Wadi Al Hawqayn

Tabaqah

Al Khadrah

Wadi As Sahtan

Ayn Umq

Al Hawb

Al Madruj

Jabal Shams
3009m

Al Hamra

Ibri

10

Wadi Bani Ghafir

For listings, see page 157

⊙ Where to stay, eat and drink
1 Al Shomokh Tourist
   Guesthouse
2 Village Resort Motel

Bradt

N

0   5km
0   5 miles

The more scenic approach of the two ways into the loop is opposite Barka, taking the inland route marked Nakhal and Ar Rustaq. This brings you to Nakhal after 15 minutes and then on to the 40km stretch to Ar Rustaq, which leads through some spectacular mountain scenery in the approaches to Al Jabal Al Akhdar, with many water-filled wadis and picnic spots. The stretch from Ar Rustaq onwards via Al Hazm to the coast opposite at Al Miladdah is by contrast dull and flat; with no wadis and the mountains ever more distant, there's little to see here.

WHERE TO STAY   *Map, page 156.*

As well as the options listed below, there is also accommodation in Ad Dakhiliyah which might be useful to visitors in this area – see Al Hoota Guesthouse & Shorfet Al-Alamin Hotel (page 228).

Al Shomokh Tourist Resthouse (37 rooms) At the start of the road from Ar Rustaq to Ibri on the left (south) of the road after 600m from the roundabout; \26 877071; e alshomokh234@gmail.com; www.alshomokh.org. This modern hotel sits on a low hill next to Makkah hypermarket & is the only accommodation in Ar Rustaq. The building is on 2 floors enclosing a courtyard with the rooms on the upper floor. Some rooms have balconies with views of the courtyard, while others have views across

to the mountains. The staff have little concept of customer service, which together with the room rate may make the drive to the Millennium Resort (page 142) only 30mins away worthwhile. **$$**

Village Resort Motel (10 rooms) 1km from the beginning of Wadi Bani Awf on the right (west) side of the wadi, between Al Awabi & Ar Rustaq, 31km from Bald Sayt; m 99 214873, 97 588818; e alaufyh2h@hotmail.com. This is quirky, very plain accommodation. The rooms have simple showers & furnishings & may be too basic for some people. However, the setting on the edge of the wadi under a large number of trees may make you decide to stay. B/fast is not available. **$**

AFI AND AL SEFALA افي و الصافية Having turned off the Muscat Expressway onto road 13 towards Nakhal, take the right turn to Afi, which lies 20km south of Barka. Turn in towards the village and follow the road as it curves left. After 2km there is a sharp turn to the right; follow it as it meanders around the date plantations towards the small walled village of Al Sefala, a total of 3.4km from the main road. Parking is on the right just above the track. This is a partially restored village, with a mosque (not open to non-Muslims) that is dated to around 1700. The southern edge of the village is marked out by two of the four original corner towers. If you return the way you came, you could take the left turn after about 300m to the restored fortified house at Al Shaly, which though not open is so close as to make a short exterior view worthwhile.

NAKHAL FORT قلعة نخل (*Nakhal, roughly 77km from Muscat International Airport;* \ 26 781384; ⊕ 08.00–16.00 Sat–Thu, 08.00–11.00 Fri; 500bzs) Built to protect the oasis and trade routes through to the coast, this fort was enlarged several times over the centuries. It is believed to be Sassanid in origin; the water well in the upper bastion is from that era. It was enlarged in the 10th century, and again during the reign of the Yarubi imams in the mid 17th century. It was then reportedly built upon further in 1747 by the Yarubi governor of the fort under Imam Ahmed Al Bu Said. The current gate of the fort dates from 1834, during the reign of Imam Said bin Sultan. Final restoration works were completed in 1990, changing the colour from the well-worn grey to the standard fort beige, at which time rooms were also labelled and furnished with crafts and antiquities.

From a distance it is dwarfed by the mountainous backdrop, but the closer you get, the more impressive it becomes. The fort has a number of bastions and towers, with walls that ingeniously follow the natural contours of the high rocky outcrop on which it sits. Labelled rooms, such as the *majlis*, the judge's room and the jail, aid an understanding of past times. You can then progress upwards and inwards through a second gateway into the private family quarters. This is the most charming area, furnished with cushions and ornaments, and with the guest room boasting a painted ceiling. As in all forts, the layout ensures that the men's living areas, which would also receive guests, catch the prevailing wind through their windows, while the women's quarters get the less comfortable inland side. When you are in Oman you will see Nakhal Fort on the 500 baisa currency notes.

NAKHAL SPRINGS (AYN A'THAWARAH) عين النخل These hot springs are probably the best known of all the springs in Oman and make a popular picnic spot – so popular, in fact, that the plentiful rubbish bins struggle to cope, especially at weekends. The springs are situated about 2.4km through the date plantations of Nakhal. The tarmac road winds on through the date plantations, past houses until it arrives at a parking area which also has a few shops. Park your car and walk on through the picnic area, laid out with basic tables and shades. You can walk further up to the actual source of the springs at the end of the picnic area. There are steps down to the wadi stream, which flows all year round, and little fish swim about in shoals. Children can even splash in the water a bit here when it is high.

These springs are an important water source for the residents of Nakhal, stemming from Wadi Hammam. In spring white lilies grow among the green pastures in the shade of the palms. The waters are said to have medicinal and healing qualities. A notice beside the stream forbids cars from driving across, but local vehicles tend to take no notice and drive over to the houses and village on the other side. The village women still come down to the stream to collect water, balancing the containers on their heads. Together they wash their clothes and dishes in the running water, chatting as they work to ease their chores.

Getting there and away Travel for 26km south of Barka on road 13 to the roundabout signed Nakhal, then take the third exit and drive a further 1.6km. The fort will be on your right and the hot springs are signed from here.

WADI MISTAL وادي مستل With a 4x4 you can take a fork to the left 15km south of Nakhal to explore the natural phenomenon of Wadi Mistal (the Ghubra Bowl), surrounded by the high peaks of Al Jabal Al Akhdar. The initial 25km on the side road is on tarmac, until the black top finishes abruptly and you are on a steep graded road of less than 10km up to Wakan (sometimes Wakkan), a mountain village. The village is at 1,400m and the cooler air allows almond and apricot trees to be grown, along with wheat, garlic and other crops. The setting is beautiful, especially in mid-February when the fruit trees are in blossom. Park in the lower parking area and walk through the village to the fields, beyond which a trekking path ascends through the orchards.

WADI AL ABYADH وادي الأبيض Some 18km beyond the roundabout at Nakhal is a right (north) turn to Subaykhah, which leads into Wadi Al Abyadh (White Wadi). This wadi's name was taken from its blue pools, caused by white calcite covering the pool bottoms that reflect the blue sky, but unfortunately several cyclones have scoured the pools so that it will take time for the calcite to re-form.

Socially and economically, the date is the most important fruit crop in Oman. You can fertilise around a hundred female date palms from a single male date palm (one Omani even called his male palm King Solomon in recognition of its fecundity). Pollination takes place, depending on the variety, during January and February. The dates are harvested from late May through to early August depending on the variety and location. This harvest is an arduous task, as it takes place during mid summer and each tree needs to be climbed to cut down the dates, usually by using a harness (*habl al tuluw*) with back support (*quffah*) made of date palm trunk fibre, which leaves the hands free for picking. A date palm can live for over 80 years and within the date oasis each field may have an individual owner, or perhaps a family owning the plot. Every part of the tree is used: the leaf frond for braiding into baskets, food covers, flooring, sleeping mats and fans; the fibre for ropes and scourers; and the ribs for fish traps, chicken coops and clothes fumigators. Together with timber from local acacia for the beams, homes and other shelters could be easily created from palm leaf midribs, while complete leaf fronds were used in roofing, fencing and the summer housing – *barasti* huts – especially on the beaches or in open desert where the breezes could pass straight through the gaps to give natural air conditioning. Perhaps unsurprisingly, Oman has its own Date Palm Research Centre, based in Ar Rumais near Barka, one of six research centres overseen by the Ministry of Agriculture and Fisheries.

A tarmac road of 1.8km leads from the main road to the wadi's edge. Turn right onto the gravel plain that leads to the narrow wadi. A 4x4 is essential and your speed needs to be steady in a low gear to avoid getting bogged down in the loose gravel. Park your vehicle and walk into the wadi towards the village of Al Abyadh, less than 14km north through the wadi from Subaykhah. Water always flows here and is very plentiful in the winter rainy season. There are pools about 10km into the wadi from the main road and you can walk from that point to reach the village of Al Abyadh. Around 8km after Subaykhah (6km before Al Abyadh), on the east side of the wadi, is a section of 'moho', the boundary between the earth's crust and mantle.

It is also possible to access the wadi from Al Abyadh village, by following signs on the main Al Batinah highway (route 1) about 11km west of Barka, or turning off from route 13 north of Nakhal, with signs from Afi.

AL AWABI العوابي After the Subaykhah turn the road that runs west from Nakhal towards Ar Rustaq now enters some of Oman's most spectacular scenery as it passes through the foothills of Al Jabal Al Akhdar. The foothills are formed of ophiolite, a sequence of rocks that have been obducted overland. The wadi that you cross time and again is the Wadi Bani Kharus, which starts high in the Al Jabal Al Akhdar and extends out here, capturing the flow out of Wadi Mistal, which creates the Wadi Al Abyadh.

Road 13 now sweeps round to Al Awabi, more or less at the centre of the inland loop from the coast. Having virtually passed the town, a tarmac road forks off to the left, taking you towards the old Al Awabi Castle (⏱ *09.00–16.00 Sat–Thu, 08.00–11.00 Fri; 500bzs*) at the head of the gorge leading into the mountains. The fort dates from the early 19th century and is a simple open courtyard with two cannon towers. It has been fully restored to a high standard. A visit inside may take 30 minutes and makes a good stop during any visit to Wadi Bani Kharus.

Al Awabi village has been home to Omani scholars, poets and the literati, and was known as a place of eminent learning.

WADI BANI KHARUS وادي بني خروص

If you have a day to spare, Wadi Bani Kharus has a wealth of places of manmade interest, along with spectacular scenery. The excellent tarmac road through the wadi starts from immediately beside Al Awabi Castle and gives good access to most of the key sights.

The wadi's geology stretches back over 600 million years and is especially noteworthy from Sital through to the upper reaches. At around 10km from Al Awabi Castle, between the turn to Al Hajir and the village of Sital, there is a major 'unconformity' on the left (northern) side of the road. Here the lower rock formation (whose strata is at an angle) is from some 600 million years ago, while sitting directly on this rock is a much younger layer, formed around 270 million years ago.

The village of Sital (also Istal) is the major settlement in the wadi and has places to buy refreshments. Despite the wadi's isolation, it was the birthplace of Imam A'Salt bin Malik Al Kharusi, who ruled much of northern Oman from AD851. The village of Al Hajir, about 19km from Al Awabi, has a small, ancient mosque called Al Ghel, built by Sheikh Assad Al Kindi, a scholar from the village. The mosque is on the far eastern edge of the date plantations. The remotest of the wadi's villages, Al Ulaya (also Al Alya), is only about 28km from Al Awabi Castle along the tarmac road.

Probably the most interesting manmade site in the wadi is a substantial agricultural platform of 3.5 acres on the left-hand side (north) of the road at Murrah about 24km from Al Awabi Castle. The effort that must have been required to assemble the megaliths for the walling speak volumes about the need for a flat surface in a land of mountains. Built in the early 18th century for the Imam Saif bin Sultan Al Yarubi, the crops are watered through a substantial storage tank which is fed by a *falaj* from the mountains to the north.

The subsidiary wadi within Wadi Bani Kharus is the interesting Wadi Al Hajir, signed on the right at around 7km from Al Awabi Castle. The road is mainly tarmac, although the final stretch into the village of Al Hajir, after 5.5km, is graded rough road. Al Hajir has a charming date oasis and an ancient abandoned village behind the date palms. There is a *falaj* that is sourced by the canyon to the south of the village, whose entrance on the right has a number of interesting petroglyphs. Overlooking the canyon's entrance are a number of archaeological ruins.

WADI BANI AWF (وادي بني عوف), BALD SAYT (بلد سيت) AND WADI BIMAH (SNAKE GORGE) (الثعبان وادي)

About 4.6km beyond Al Awabi on route 13 between Nakhal and Ar Rustaq is the signposted start of Wadi Bani Awf, considered by many to be the most scenic and spectacular of any of Oman's mountain drives.

The initial 11km of the route is on a good tarmac road, but it then becomes a progressively more demanding graded track and will require a 4x4 vehicle. The track continues to Bald Sayt village, probably Oman's most picturesque mountain village, with extensive fertile terracing or, if you continue along the track, at Sharafat Al Alamayn, which gives panoramic views over the route along which you have travelled. A 4x4 is essential and the drive is not for the faint-hearted, with steep climbs, extremely narrow tracks and dizzying drops. The scenery is spectacular limestone with towering slabs of mountain soaring above, their strata almost vertical in places. Occasional date oases line the wadi floor and are irrigated by *aflaj* (the plural of *falaj*) running behind the palms.

At 14km from the end of the tarmac the track forks, with one of Oman's most improbable collections of road signs pointing the way in the middle of the mountains. There is a right turn signposted to Wadi As Sahtan, set directly at the foot of Jabal Shams (Oman's highest mountain at 3,009m), and onto Ar Rustaq via the signed route 'Wadi A'Sahtan' (Wadi As Sahtan). However, anyone who has ventured into Wadi Bani Awf will invariably want the left fork, as this leads to Snake Canyon, Bald Sayt and the vast panorama from the 2,000m-high Sharafat Al Alamayn ahead. A good, shaded picnic spot is about 17km from the Nakhal and Ar Rustaq road before Al Zammah, where a deep ravine on the right appears to be blocked by boulders, with a series of pools behind them. You can park opposite in a little side road and walk into the ravine. The village of Al Zammah, 22km from the junction on the Nakhal and Ar Rustaq road, also makes an excellent stop. Park well after the village where the canyon entrance in front of you is the exit from Snake Canyon; you will pass the entrance later on the drive. Climb over the *falaj* – it's only a metre high, but be careful not to damage it – and if you don't mind getting wet it is possible to wade through the water ahead in the canyon. The bottom is often very slimy with algae.

The track makes a sharp turn right and leads onwards and upwards to Bald Sayt and the entrance to Snake Canyon. Bald Sayt (also incorrectly though more commonly Bald Sayt; the latter spelling is for the village just south of Al Hamra) lies a steep 5.1km beyond Al Zammah, requiring a 4x4 for the vertiginous, winding track. Bald Sayt's name is said to be a corruption of 'the town I forgot' (*bilad nasaytuhu*), which it supposedly acquired after a general sacked the villages of the wadi but overlooked this remote one. Park well before the village, as there is limited parking, and enjoy the walk down. The old houses are still lived in, though with satellite dishes on most roofs the village looks like a space listening station. Practise your Arabic greetings here and make sure that you are dressed conservatively. The village area has been settled for over 3,000 years and the agricultural land is fed by the water from 12 water springs on the mountain slopes.

Beyond the turn to Bald Sayt the road continues right to Hatt (also Haat, Hat on various road signs in the wadi) and up to Sharafat Al Alamayn. You will pass the entrance to Snake Canyon (Wadi Bimah) on your left, so called because it twists and turns across pools, rocks and waterfalls. Snake Canyon can be tackled by trekkers and is a 3km walk, bringing you out at Al Zammah. The first 2km of this is very rough going, with jumps into water pools and slippery rocks, making it unsuitable for young children and those who are not fit. People have drowned here in flash floods and it is difficult to monitor the weather when you can see only a tiny piece of sky above you. Speak to a specialised tour operator about this as a separate adventure.

After Snake Canyon continue past a beautiful combination of small date oases and traditional houses and beyond that to the spread-out village of Hatt. Here the road seems to disappear – due to the angle, you can't see the track hidden on the cliff face. Fortunately, as you make the ascent you will find that it reappears in front of you, taking you over a stupendous 900m vertical ascent in less than 11km. If you do this route coming down from Al Hamra, remember to use a low gear to slow you down and avoid overheating brakes which will fail. The summit at Sharafat Al Alamayn gives you a view from right to left of Wadi Bani Kharus, Wadi Bani Awf, Wadi As Sahtan and, overlooking them all, the peak of Jabal Shams at 3,009m. From here the track is tarmac as it continues down to Al Hamra and the occasionally open Al Hoota Cave (pages 228–30 and 231–2).

WADI AS SAHTAN وادي السحتن If you wish to continue your loop around to Ar Rustaq, you should return to the fork marked 'Wadi A'Sahaten' (Wadi As Sahtan, while the wider area is often called the As Sahtan Bowl). Driving west from the signed route you will pass the settlement of Al Jufar after 7.5km. This is one of the many villages in the vast natural As Sahtan Bowl known for their traditional beekeepers. Using date-log hives made from 1m-long hollowed-out palm-tree trunks, the logs are stacked much as you would logs for firewood, but with a small piece of honeycomb inside. The ends are blocked up, leaving only enough space for the bees (*Apis mellifera jemenitica*) to enter. From the time of nesting the bees take two months to produce the honey. Three times a year the beekeeper opens up the ends and smokes out the bees, removing the honeycomb, before starting all over again. It can be a profitable business, with a single honeycomb fetching as much as RO60. A rapport seems to develop between bees and keeper – the beekeepers wear no protective clothing but say that they never get stung. There is a second honey bee in Oman – the dwarf honey bee (*Apis florea*). This species creates a single honeycomb and produces a fine, clear honey that is highly sought-after. Since they have a tendency to relocate if disturbed, it takes skill to manage them as a commercial proposition, but a few beekeepers in the area do keep them as well as the *Apis mellifera jemenitica*.

There are two villages almost immediately below the northern escarpment of Jabal Shams, Al Madruj and Al Hawb, which are used as starting places for ascending **Jabal Shams**. Both villages are accessed from the turn at Ayn Umq (about 40km and an hour's drive from Ar Rustaq), where the schools and health centre cluster. The climb is 2,000m ascent over 3km, and when the top is reached you will be passing very close to a secure military area and your guides may wish to advise the authorities. The descent is best taken by continuing down the southern face to the Grand Canyon (pages 232–4), and you should be prepared to spend an overnight on the route.

Leaving the As Sahtan Bowl towards Ar Rustaq to complete your loop, you enter some 8km of narrow ravine which follows the course of the Wadi As Sahtan. This section, which is tarmac and elevated above the wadi floor, will take you past the oasis of Al Khadrah with its hot-water spring and small ruined castle on the right-hand side.

Once out of the ravine, another 2km along the track brings you to **Tabaqah**, a village with a photogenic fort on a cliff edge, guarding the entrance to the Wadi As Sahtan. From here you access the tarmac road that forks left via Wadi Bani Ghafir to Ibri, or along the tarmac to Ar Rustaq, 9km further on.

AR RUSTAQ الرستاق Ar Rustaq, whose name may come from the Sassanid term for an administrative group of villages, *rustaq*, is about 126km from Muscat International Airport or 55km from Nakhal Fort.

The town served as the Omani capital for some 150 years, first as the Yarubi imams' base from 1624, then in the early part of the Al Bu Said dynasty, from 1744. In the late 18th century Hamad bin Said established Muscat as the capital, and it has retained this status ever since.

Today Ar Rustaq is still a major administrative centre for Al Batinah South Governorate. The town owes its importance to its strategic location at the exit of a wadi on the coastal side of the mountains, so it served as a commercial centre for trade between the *jabal* and the villages of the interior and the coastal Al Batinah towns. The people from the mountains and the foothills of Al Jabal Al Akhdar brought fruits such as grapes, peaches, pomegranates, plums, figs and apricots to sell here, while the coastal people brought fish, lemons and bananas. Pure Omani honey is sought-after and of high quality, and beekeeping is one of the main occupations in Ar Rustaq.

As a result of its political and commercial influence, various industries grew up in Ar Rustaq, notably silversmiths famous for *khanjars*, ornaments, copper work and other traditional crafts. Wooden storage chests and old weaponry can be found at the antique stalls in Ar Rustaq Suq adjacent to the fort (page 165). Date packing has long been carried out here and today there is a date-processing factory close to the cream-domed Sultan Qaboos Mosque on route 11 to Al Musanaah. Omani *halwa* (see box, below) from Ar Rustaq is also famous.

Today the town of Ar Rustaq is a thriving centre of administration and trade, easily the largest of the inland towns on the northern side of the Al Jabal Al Akhdar. The approach is entirely modern, with shops run by Indians lining the dual carriageway as you follow the signposts to Ar Rustaq Fort and the town centre.

Getting there and away By **road** the quickest route to Ar Rustaq from Muscat is along As Sib (Al Seeb) Street to the roundabout at Al Miladdah, 84km east of Muscat International Airport. Here take the third exit (left/south) and continue south past Al Hazm and the Sultan Qaboos Mosque at Ar Rustaq into the town centre. Take a left turn at the traffic lights just after the fruit and vegetable market and continue for 550m, turn right and the fort is ahead of you. **Minibuses** run around the Rustaq Loop and can be picked up on the Nakhal road below the Barka flyover and in the new town centre of Ar Rustaq at the junction to Ibri, near the Sultan Qaboos Mosque. A **shared taxi** to/from Burj Al Sahwa in Muscat or Suhar costs RO5 or less.

Other practicalities

✚ Ar Rustaq Hospital ✆ 26 875055; ⊕ 24hrs. On the main route 11 from Ar Rustaq to Al Miladdah, 6.6km north of the junction to Ibri.
✚ Muscat Pharmacy In the Shell petrol station complex on the junction for route 10 to Ibri; ✆ 26 878631; ⊕ 10.00–21.00 Sun–Thu

Police station 300m north of the fruit & vegetable market in Rustaq town centre; ✆ 26 875099; ⊕ 24hrs
⊠ Post office ✆ 26 875105; ⊕ 07.30–14.30 Sun–Thu. On the main route 11 from Ar Rustaq to Al Miladdah, 6.4km north of the junction to Ibri & next to Ar Rustaq Hospital.

What to see and do

Ar Rustaq Fort قلعة الرستاق (⊕ 08.00–16.00 Sat–Thu, 08.00–11.00 Fri; 500bzs) The fort is said to have been built before the arrival of Islam in Oman, making it one of the country's oldest. It sits at the foot of Al Jabal Al Akhdar and it is easy to miss the left turn at the traffic lights leading directly to the fort, tucked down

> ### HALWA
>
> Ar Rustaq and Nizwa were traditionally the most famous centres of *halwa* making, though in practice it is made in every town in Oman. *Halwa* has a rich brown colour and a consistency like that of heavy Turkish delight. It is the quintessential dessert in Oman. *Halwa* is not made from grapes, as many foreigners may fondly imagine, but from ghee, semolina and sugar mixed for several hours over the fire with a copper spoon, then flavoured with almond and cardamom. There are innumerable variations to the mix, and those with a sweet tooth are bound to find one that is just right. A taste for sugar is widespread in Oman and is associated with the very high rate of diabetes in the country.

Al Batinah Coast   THE RUSTAQ LOOP

4

163

the side of the wadi bed. However, you can just as easily follow the main road as it loops round to the left, giving you views of the fort before you drive through the wadi to reach the main entrance. You can park by the main entrance, beside a telephone box that looks more like a summer gazebo under the shade of a tree, and this will then also serve for visiting the old suq.

A visit to the fort, which is built on three levels, has four towers and is furnished with old items, can take between 1 and 2 hours, depending on your level of interest. It also has a large courtyard area outside the fort itself but inside the curtain wall that you enter upon stepping through the tiny entrance door. Strolling right around the fort will give you glimpses of wonderful butterfly life among the wild plants and the chance to use the old *falaj* system to refresh yourself. The water still flows strongly and is hot. The castle inhabitants used to collect this water in pottery jars and hang it in a shady place to cool, after which it could be drunk.

To the right as you first enter is the large 32-pillared mosque, which used to be the Friday congregational mosque for the town before the large, cream-domed Sultan Qaboos Mosque with its twin minarets was built on the modern outskirts. Known as Bayadha Mosque, it was an institute with a fine reputation, and produced many eminent scholars. To the left as you enter (after shedding your shoes) is a magnificent elaborately sculpted plaster mihrab marking the direction of prayer towards the holy city of Mecca. The mosque is still used on Fridays.

Inside the fort the rooms are not signed and, given that it has had many additions over the centuries, it is somewhat disorienting, to the extent that you may not be certain of seeing all that there is to see. The most splendid rooms, with painted dark red and white ceilings, are the imam's rooms, located on the second storey to catch the prevailing wind. The central beam on the ceiling carries Quranic inscriptions listing some of the 99 attributes of God, such as the King, the Wise and the Holy. Another noteworthy spot is the tiny women's mosque, barely big enough for two to enter, with its minute mihrab to the left. The two more modern towers, the Red Tower and the New Tower, can only be accessed through the *wali*'s offices. On the ground floor of the fort are prison cells, stores and an armoury.

At the southeastern extremity of the complex is the Tower of Winds, the largest of the four towers, with its British iron cannons guarding all directions, set around the huge central pillar. The date of 1821 can still be seen on some, and one has its end blasted off – a poor casting and excess gunpowder sealed its fate. From one of the window seats you will see the domed tomb of Imam Saif bin Sultan on a hill 270m southwest of the fort.

The highest tower of all, to the right (northwest) corner, is the mysterious Burj A'Shayateen (Devil's Tower). You can walk up along the parapet around the courtyard to approach it, giving you superb views over the oasis. The two graves in the tower's courtyard belong to Sayyid Said bin Ibrahim Al Bu Saidi, who died in 1951, and Sayyid Mohammed bin Hilal Al Bu Saidi, who died in 1977.

The earliest castle on this site pre-dates Islam and may have been built around AD600 by the Persian governor who controlled the area at that time. The first Yarubi imam moved his capital here from Bahla and rebuilt Ar Rustaq Fort in 1650. Its greatest heyday was in the 18th century under the Al Bu Saids, when Ahmad bin Said, head of the Al Bu Said dynasty, used it as his capital, from which he co-ordinated the expulsion of the Persians and restored independence to the country. The Red Tower was added in 1744 by the Al Bu Saids, followed by the New Tower in 1906. The fort also featured in the 1950s Jebel War, when it served as temporary home to Talib bin Ali, who led the fight against Sultan Said.

Ar Rustaq Suq سوق الرستاق The old suq has been completely rebuilt, though it is still in the same location by the wadi beside the fort entrance. The best time to visit is before 10.30; bear in mind that Fridays are the busiest days. Unfortunately, in the years that it took to rebuild trade has moved on and is now concentrated in the supermarkets on the road to Ibri near the roundabout. The most interesting and vibrant area of traditional trade is the fruit and vegetable suq just northwest of Ar Rustaq Fort. Here imported fruit is piled high in crates, while local vegetables and fruit are proudly displayed in colourful plastic bowls and buckets.

FORTS

There are innumerable fortifications in Oman – some large, some small, some renovated, and others simply a melting mound of mud. This extensive network of forts, fortified castles and watchtowers sprang up throughout regions to defend against foreign invaders like the Persians or the Portuguese, but more importantly as a power base to defend against and launch attacks against local rival powers.

Forts and fortified castles went beyond defence and also contained law courts, the *wali*'s residence and office and Islamic schools. In mountainous areas small watchtowers on the peaks close to a fort provided lookouts and, if needed, covering fire against attack. Frequently a tower would also act as a guardian for the place where the water of a *falaj* became a surface, as opposed to underground, flow.

The design of forts was intended to delay and disorientate the enemy if they broke through the external defence. Gates would usually have a murder-hole set just above them, from which sticky, boiling date 'honey' *dibs* could be poured onto any unfortunate attacker. Most gates would have a 'wicket' gate set into one or both of the double doors, making any soldier bending down to enter almost literally a sitting target. If they did succeed in entering, they were confronted by narrow passages, usually with right-angle turns enveloped in pitch black. It is often impossible to tell if a room is a new room or an extension of the previous one, and without help it is difficult to find the way out. As the last resort there were also tunnels for an escape route, sometimes linking neighbouring forts, and sometimes so high that soldiers could ride through them on horseback.

After a time, the sheer number of forts in Oman can lead to 'fort fatigue', reminiscent of Freya Stark's 'tomb fatigue' in Lycian Turkey – 'The time came when D B and I looked at each other and said, "Do we really have to go and look at that tomb?"'. The fact that so many exist is a reflection of the need to defend what one possessed against those who wanted it. The fort was the centre of authority, as headquarters of the main sheikh or the *wali*. Any pretender to authority had to control the fort, and anyone who had something to protect, like a water source or fertile ground, would build watchtowers and forts on prominent hilltops to ensure that they stopped a neighbouring tribe from taking it. War was a way of life in order to survive in a country not overly blessed with natural resources. In areas with a more scattered population a *sur* (walled enclosure) was built as a refuge for the villagers.

Since the coming to power of Sultan Qaboos, the major forts of the country have undergone a gradual process of restoration. This is continuing and is being stepped up, in line with the country's relatively recent concentration on and investment in tourism.

Ain Al Kasfa Springs عين الكسفة These hot springs not far from Ar Rustaq Fort are less attractive than the springs at Nakhal, but are nevertheless said to have the same healing and medicinal properties for rheumatism and skin complaints (due to the sulphur content). They have been walled to create segregated bathing areas for men and women. A famous 15th-century doctor Rashid bin Umeirah lived nearby (the remains of his house and clinic can still be seen) and wrote his medicinal expositions on the illnesses of the day and how to cure them in the form of long descriptive poems, which could be memorised more easily. However, these springs are unlikely to be the subject of poetry in modern Oman.

Getting there and away To reach the springs, take the right (north) turn from the traffic lights adjacent to the fruit and vegetable market. Continue north for 600m to the next set of traffic lights and turn left (west). Following the signed road, the springs are reached after 1.4km.

AL HAZM FORT حصن الحزم (*About 20km north of Ar Rustaq Fort on route 11 towards Al Miladdah;* ⊕ *08.00–16.00 Sat–Thu, 08.00–11.00 Fri; 500bzs*) Your first sight of Al Hazm Fort is its battlements peering over the scattered date palms in Al Hazm village, giving no inkling of the architectural complexity within. The date given for its building by the Yarubi imam Sultan bin Saif II is 1708, and it is a superb example of Omani Islamic architecture. Its exterior is plain, even a little disappointing, although once you are close up its scale more than compensates. In Arabic 'Al Hazm' means 'the vanquishing one' and when you have completed your tour you will understand why the fortress was never captured. An Arabic-speaking guardian greets you from his office set in the small courtyard with overhanging greenery. He will take payment and leave you to guide yourself around the fort.

With its coherent, square design, the fort is set around a single open courtyard, making it very easy to explore. The main doors are impressive, with elegant arabesque decoration and the date that they were made, April 1714 (Rabi Al-Akhar, 1126). They open onto the ground-floor corridor that leads past the tomb with the graves of Sultan bin Saif II and his son, Saif bin Sultan II. Near the tomb is a loudspeaker tube, set within the wall, which allowed communication between people on the ground floor and those above. The *falaj* (see box, pages 208–9) gurgles through the building and its water supply, which could so easily be cut, is supplemented by water wells within. The first of the secret tunnels inside the building is accessed from this floor; clearly the architect built in anticipation of hard closely fought attack. The next floor includes the entrances to the two massive gun towers. The northwest one, with its beautifully decorated central column, houses Portuguese/Spanish bronze cannons from the 16th and 17th centuries, including one from the period of Philip II, who ruled both Spain and Portugal from 1581, a few years before the Spanish Armada. The cannons were seized from the Portuguese during the decades after their expulsion from coastal Oman. The southeast tower, which diagonally opposes the northwest tower, houses British iron cannons, including one from 1630, a period when cheaper iron cannons with their superior firepower were being produced by Britain. A secret passageway links the east and west towers. This passageway is the coolest place in the fort, as it is set between the first and ground floors, with massively thick walls, its only connection to the outside world being some small ventilation holes. There are also secret passages leading outside.

The roof gives extraordinary vistas north across the plain towards the coast and south towards Jabal Shams, some 40km away, high above the mountains over Ar Rustaq.

5

Musandam مسندم

The Musandam Peninsula is a paradox. It overlooks one of the world's busiest and most strategic waterways, the Strait of Hormuz, through which a large percentage of the world's crude oil trade passes, yet few have heard its name. Separated from the rest of Oman and closer to the Iranian island of Hormuz than the northern 'mainland' of Oman, it really is different from much of the rest of the country.

Musandam is a great mass of rock literally rising out of the sea. Towering sea cliffs, hundreds of metres tall, create what appears to be an impenetrable wall of rock – and so it has been, until recently. There is little coastal plain and where there is, it is subject to occasional devastating floods that sweep down the valleys, meaning that agriculture is limited. The towns between these vast mountains and the sea could never have grown to become great trading hubs or industrial bases. As such, Bukha, Khasab, Kumzar, Lima and Daba have remained small, while the inland island of Madha, a small exclave of Oman within the UAE, has a political boundary that provides just as much of a barrier as the great mountains do for the other towns.

The higher mountains are limestone and dated mainly between the Permian (which began 299 million years ago) and Cretaceous period (which ended 65.5 million years ago). Around Madha is ophiolite which in Oman generally dates from around 90 million years ago. This ancient limestone forms Musandam's highest peak, Jabal Harim, at around 2,087m high. The whole peninsula is an active subduction zone that experts estimate to sink 6mm per year. This may sound relatively little, but it means that the northern part of the peninsula is dropping at a rate of 60cm every century. This subduction has also created the most memorable tourist sight in Musandam – its rias (sunken valleys), which are similar in appearance to the glacial fjords of Norway.

Musandam has seen various **historical figures** pass along its great mountain mass since time immemorial. Nearchus is believed to have anchored off Musandam, which he called Maceta, in 326BC. The author of the *Periplus of the Erithian Sea* mentions two places in Musandam: the first, Kalon, may be Jabal Harim and the second, Asabon, is the peninsula's northernmost point.

Two great battles took place in Daba in AD632 and 892, defining Oman's relationship with the Umayyid and Abbasid rulers. In 1864, the India-to-Britain telegraph cable was laid, with a station on Jazirat Al-Maqlab, today more usually called Telegraph Island. In the 20th century Musandam was persuaded to remain loyal to the government of Muscat, with gunship diplomacy coming to the fore. It was perhaps the memory of this persuasion, which encouraged the inhabitants to remain part of Oman during the period when Britain pulled out east of Suez and the Arabian Gulf States gradually took on their current political boundaries.

The origins of the **Shihuh people** who live in the region are unclear. They have a distinctive language that is an amalgam of Arabic, Baloushi, English, Persian and Portuguese. Bertram Thomas, who explored Oman in the 1920s and 30s, speculates that they are the southern tribes mentioned in the Book of Job, and that they presumably arrived in Musandam having been pushed north following the arrival of the Azd tribes from Yemen. There are thought to be some 200 Shihuh villages scattered about in the mountains, both on the UAE side and on the Omani side of the border, although few are inhabited today. The numbers are steadily declining; the Al Sayh Plateau, for example, was well inhabited even in the late 1980s, with busy, tended fields, but now migrant workers are often the only permanent residents.

The **mountain villages** represent a pragmatic adaptation to the semi-nomadic way of life. In the summer months, the villages are deserted while the people migrate to the coast to fish or to tend date plantations. The possessions that they leave behind in the villages therefore need to be secured and kept safe until the autumn, giving rise to the invention of the House of the Lock (Bait Al Qufl, in Arabic; see box, page 188). Built of local limestone, whose strata lend themselves to easy splitting into tabular blocks, the foundations and walls go 1.5–2m below ground, giving the structure the strength to withstand the torrential winter rains. The roof of stone and mud is supported by acacia trunks and needs occasional repair. The contemporary Italian archaeologist and art historian Paolo Costa calls this type of structure 'the most extraordinary and unique building in the Arabian Peninsula – the result of local adaptation of the architecture to the semi-nomadic way of life'. These houses are found throughout the mountainous areas of northern Musandam.

Musandam's economy is now dominated by government employment and funds flowing from those Omani citizens working in the UAE. The port and airport in Khasab are important employers, as is the naval base near Goat Island. In 2015, the population of Musandam Governorate was some 48,193 with Khasab and its associated settlements, which include remote Kumzar, having 27,836, followed by Daba, Bukha and Madha.

INACCESSIBLE THROUGHOUT HISTORY

Roads are a recent phenomenon in this peninsula; before 1980 precipitous footpaths were the only links between the mountains and the flat open plains of Al Fujayrah and Ras Al Khaymah. Even donkeys could not be used on such paths, and the Musandam towns of Khasab, Bukha and Lima, with their little harbours, could be reached only by small boats.

Throughout history Musandam has never had any exploitable commodity – no copper, diorite or chlorite in ancient times, and no oil in modern times – so no incentive has existed to defy nature and blast routes through the barren limestone. There is no major coastal plain, and the sheer cliffs plunge straight into the sea in all but the few coves and bays where the towns and fishing villages sit. These are in turn connected by steep paths to a handful of mountaintop plains and terraces where rainfall in winter is plentiful enough to allow for limited agriculture.

Thor Heyerdahl, who in the 1970s sailed down through the Gulf towards the Strait of Hormuz in his replica Sumerian boat *Tigris*, could hardly believe his eyes at his first sight of Musandam:

Above the cloud banks, raised above the earth was land, like another indistinct world of its own. Solid rock was sailing up there ... with rock walls dropping almost perpendicularly into the sea.

Most of Musandam is separated from the rest of Oman by 70km of UAE territory, so the options are either to **fly** or to catch a **ferry** from Muscat to Khasab, or to **drive** in through one of two borders: at Tibat (from the emirates of Ras Al Khaymah and Dubai) or Daba (from Al Batinah coast of Oman, after a stretch through the emirate of Al Fujayrah). The Tibat crossing is the main and more straightforward one. The Daba border can be problematic as there are two possible crossings, of which one is in use at any one time, and the other not. Neither are far from the other, but having to turn around after queueing is frustrating (see below and page 46). At present non-Omanis can cross the border at Daba with a supporting letter from either the Golden Tulip or Six Senses Zighy Bay hotels (page 186). If, however, you wanted to cross over the mountains on rough dirt roads from Daba to Khasab, there is a further checkpoint inland about 50km from Daba at which non-Omanis are currently turned back. There is no doubt that flying in from Muscat or catching the ferry, with your car, are the simplest ways, as there are no visa complications since you never leave Omani territory, although you may be asked to show your passport as a matter of 'procedure'. See above and page 46 for flight and ferry details and the visa position.

The tour section of this chapter follows the route from Dubai, entering Musandam at the Tibat border post, just beyond Sham in northern Ras Al Khaymah, as in practice most visitors come this way. Note that you will have to have valid vehicle insurance for both the UAE and Oman to cross borders.

BY AIR There are currently two flights a day in both directions from Muscat International Airport to Khasab, operated by Oman Air (✆ *24 531111; www. omanair.com*). The Muscat return ticket costs around RO58 and the flight takes 1 hour. There is a 20kg luggage restriction. Seats on the left when flying from Muscat have the better view as you will have the mountains around Muscat and Musandam to look down on rather than the open sea.

In terms of excursions offered by the tour companies in Khasab, one or two nights is probably all you will need to get a flavour of this peninsula. As with Salalah in the south of the country, Oman Air operates package deals (*www.holidays.omanair. com*) with the hotels that include a return economy flight, and you won't have to concern yourself with arranging the short transfer from the taxi-less airport.

The arrival and departure areas of this small airport are modern and clean, with all signs in English and Arabic.

BY CAR Travelling from Al Batinah coast, you exit Oman and enter the UAE at the Khitmat Milalah (or Khatm Al-Mallah) international border, which brings you to Kalba (part of the emirate of Sharjah). You will then drive through various UAE towns and past Madha, an Omani exclave (pages 187–8), and on towards Daba (pages 185–7). This town is divided into three parts, although the divisions aren't clear and the signposts lacking. Critically, two of them – Daba Muhallah of the emirate of Al Fujayrah and Daba Al Hisn of the emirate of Sharjah – are in the UAE, and a fenced border separates these from Daba Bayah, which belongs to Oman. There are two border crossings, neither of which has an Omani border post. Usually only the one to the northeast of Daba Al Hisn on the corniche, just after the harbour, can be used by those who are not nationals of a GCC country or resident in the UAE. To pass through this border (if you are a resident of Oman or a tourist), you should have a letter from either the Six Senses Zighy Bay or the Golden Tulip Dibba (both page 186), confirming you are booked to stay with them. Of course, this requirement can change without notice and you should phone to check with the hotel beforehand.

Beyond Daba the wadi track that runs past the entrance to Six Senses Zighy Bay through Wadi Khab Al Shamsi towards Wadi Bih cannot be traversed the whole way except by GCC nationals due to an Omani military post some 36km north after the water dam at Daba.

These various border restrictions mean that road access for most tourists to Khasab is via a Dubai/Ras Al Khaymah approach, so that you enter Musandam through the Oman border post some 470km from Al Qurum in Muscat. There is only one crossing here and its name is given from the UAE on road signs which use 'Al Dara border' while maps and websites variously use Ras Al Darah or Al Qir.

Travelling through the UAE will also mean that you require a **UAE visa** and, of course, suitable vehicle insurance (page 57). Be sure to check that latest information, especially the new e-visa requirement which currently applies to non-GCC nationals residing in GCC countries; e-visas are obtained through the Ministry of the Interior (*www.gdrfa.ae/GCCIND*). At the time of writing, visiting tourists who are nationals of the 68 countries that are eligible for a tourist visa at Muscat International Airport and not resident in the GCC can also enter the UAE and obtain the tourist entry visa at the border. See page 43 for full visa details and check the Royal Oman Police website (*www.rop.gov.om*) for the current Oman situation, and the UAE website for the latest UAE situation.

BY SEA Ferries operated by the National Ferries Company (\800 72000; *www.nfc.om*) run from Muscat to Khasab and from Shinas, Daba and Lima to Khasab. The Muscat–Khasab service runs one day per week and, unless you are have time to spare, then consider a one-way trip on the ferry and a flight in the other direction. There is a twice-weekly route in each direction to Bahman Port Qeshm in Iran; an Iranian visa is required. Local Iranian boat services run from Qeshm to Bandar Abbas and air services to other Iranian cities. A service to Dubai is planned and this will make an easy route if you arrive into Dubai. Check the website before doing your planning, especially if considering the Dubai or Iranian services. **Catamarans** that can carry passengers and cars are used (not currently available for car transport to Iran), and the journey alongside the mountains of Musandam is spectacular. There are three classes of ticket – economy, first and VIP (not all vessels have VIP) – but the economy section is excellent (page 46).

GETTING AROUND

BY HIRE CAR You can rent a **saloon car** from Khasab Rent-a-Car (m 99 447400), who are most helpful, or Rahal Khasab Rent-a-Car (m 91 323440), for around RO15 per day. However, for proper exploration in Musandam you need a **4x4**, which costs around RO50 per day. If you want a driver the cost for a 4x4 goes up to RO100+ per day and can be arranged through Khasab Travel & Tours (\26 730464; e khastour@ omantel.net.om). Car hire can usually also be arranged through your hotel.

Fuel stations are limited to the two in Khasab and one at Bukha. There is nothing on the rough road between Khasab and Daba if you have a permit to pass the military post. There are several petrol stations in Daba.

BY TAXI Note there are hardly any taxis in Khasab, or in Musandam in general, and those that exist are usually already booked by local people. So it is advisable to organise transport to your accommodation in advance if you're travelling without your own vehicle. In Khasab the airport and port are in the town, as is the port in Daba, so the transfer will be quick, although Six Senses at Zighy

Bay may charge for their transfer from Daba. If you have booked one of Oman Air's packages then the transfer is included and should be arranged as a matter of course. If you haven't, then make suitable transport arrangements in advance.

BY PUBLIC TRANSPORT There are no buses in Musandam and shared taxis only operate erratically. Without your own transport hitchhiking is the only option. Always offer to pay something towards the petrol.

TOUR OPERATORS

The few tour operators that there are in the Musandam region are based in either Khasab or Daba. In Khasab they offer similar dhow cruises, mountain safaris and city tours. The most common attractions are towards Jabal Harim (seen on a mountain safari tour), Telegraph Island (seen on a dhow cruise), dolphin watching, snorkelling, fishing, diving, fjords and birdwatching tours. In Daba you need to consider access in and out of Oman, together with the fact that it's not possible to travel into Oman from a UAE port.

Dolphin Khasab Khasab; 26 730813; e dolphin@omantel.om; www.dolphinkhasabtours. com. Offering an excellent array of tours: inculding the Khasab city tour, a mountain safari to Jabal Harim & dhow cruises. Full-day safaris include lunch while the half-day safaris include refreshments based in the Khasab Hotel.

Extra Divers Musandam Atana Khasab Hotel, Khasab; 26 730501; m 99 877957; e info@musandam-diving.com; www. musandam-diving.com. Part of the Extra Divers group – the staff here are helpful; this is a well-run diving operation.

Khasab Travel & Tours Khasab; 26 730464; e khastour@omantel.net.om; www.khasabtours. com. Operates from Esra Apartments (opposite Khasab Airport).

Musandam Nature Khasab; e pierre@ musandam-nature.com; www.musandam-nature. com. A different kind of organisation that provides excellent trekking & sea-based activities.

Musandam Sea Adventure Tourism Khasab; 26 730069; m 99 346321; e sea_adventure@ msaoman.com; www.msaoman.com. Offers mountain safaris & dhow excursions to the fjords of Musandam.

ACTIVITIES

BIRDWATCHING Many tourists visit Musandam for the purpose of birdwatching alone, although there are no birdwatching tours offered by the tour operators in Khasab. The most common large birds are the Egyptian vulture, Bonelli's eagle and the Barbary and sooty falcon, which can be spotted anywhere by the vigilant as you drive the mountain roads.

CAMPING There are numerous isolated beaches along the Musandam coasts, making beach camping a pleasure. Contact a sea-trip operator to organise transport to and from your choice. Inland the temperatures may make your decision for you; in the winter months try the **Rawdhah Bowl** and the **Sal Ala Forest**. In summer the higher mountains are better, although the terrain is rather rocky for tent pegs. For campfires, never cut trees, even those that appear dead, as rain may magically bring them back to life.

Local fishermen might be a transport option for taking you to remote beaches. Payment after you return to port should ensure that you will be picked up when you wish. Their boats tend to be simpler than those used for organised boat trips, so not as well equipped with such things as shade awnings.

CANOEING The calmness of the fjords offers ideal conditions for canoeing. Musandam Nature (page 173) offers a good variety of trips from Khasab.

DHOW CRUISES/BOAT TRIPS From Khasab harbour the standard boat trips are half-day or full-day dhow cruises that cost around RO20 and RO30 respectively. Children under 12 may have a reduction in price, and if you are a large party it may be worth hiring your own dhow for the day. Half-day cruises include light refreshments, whereas the full-day trips include lunch. The boats are equipped with lifejackets as well as snorkelling equipment, if you haven't got your own. It is best to pre-book with a tour operator on arrival at your hotel to avoid any chance of disappointment. Guests can be collected from their hotels at a small extra charge and taken to the harbour where they join the tour.

There are various degrees in the quality of dhow cruises and it may be that you prefer to go on a larger two-storey dhow for the extra space and elevated views it allows. Ask about the type of boat when booking your cruise.

Trips take you into **Khawr Ash-Sham**, a giant fjord that harbours Telegraph Island and a few other islands, and where the water is calm and sheltered. You will spot the fishing villages of Nadifi, Qanaha, Maglab, Seebi and Sham along the route. You have a good chance of spotting Indo-Pacific humpback dolphins as you enter the fjord, as they like the calm water, but are also attracted by the sound and wake of the engine, swimming with the boat as if it were a giant dolphin. Once the engine is turned off they tend to lose interest. The dhows anchor at Telegraph Island (see box, page 181) and you are given the opportunity to swim and snorkel. If you wish, you can swim up to the island itself and climb the stone steps up to the top.

From October to February visibility is excellent, about 20–30km. From the end of February it drops to about 5km, which detracts somewhat from the overall experience.

DIVING AND SNORKELLING Musandam is an excellent location for diving. As all divers will know, it is necessary to produce original proof of your PADI or BSAC qualification, so remember to pack it.

Those wishing to gain their Open Water qualification can do so here. Extra Divers (page 173) operates from the Atana Khasab with fully certified tutors. So as not to waste time in the region undergoing the theoretical side of diving, you can gain your qualification for this aspect of the course back in your country of residence. You will then be free to concentrate fully on the practical side of diving when in Khasab.

Species include reef and whale sharks, barracuda, sunfish and turtles. Those new to diving are taken to the *khawrs* and bays of the area for their tuition.

Telegraph Island is perhaps the best location for snorkelling in the area, as the coral and marine life is good. If you are not a diver you can opt for snorkelling as part of a dive-boat trip, or as a dhow cruise. The dhow cruise trips make a stop at Telegraph Island to allow for snorkelling and swimming. Trips cost around RO20 for a half day.

DOLPHIN, WHALE AND SHARK WATCHING The hammerhead, nurse, reef and whale shark are found in the temperate waters of the Strait of Hormuz, especially from July to September. Dolphin-watching trips are done as part of a dhow cruise (page 174) and you will almost certainly see Indo Pacific humpback dolphins and, with luck, minke whale.

FISHING Fishing trips, which depart from Khasab harbour, can be arranged through the tour operators or the dive centre.

MOUNTAIN SAFARI If you have flown to Khasab from Muscat and are staying in a hotel there, you will probably have to arrange a mountain safari to see the interior, as you won't have a car to travel independently. The route on page 182 is the one that your driver will take.

BUKHA بخاء

Bukha is west of Khasab and borders the UAE at Ras Al Khaymah. It is potentially large and thriving, but has suffered an exodus to the oil-rich emirates next door, leaving it struggling to retain its remaining population. New capital investment by Oman may help it to revive its potential agricultural resources. In among the new houses are decaying mud-brick ones, some on two storeys with courtyards, which you can see by turning off the main coast road and following a road inland that runs parallel to the coast, and then arcs around to rejoin the main coast road.

GETTING THERE AND AWAY There is no public transport, so you need to have your own transport or hitchhike. Starting from Sham in northern Ras Al Khaymah, take the right fork marked Al Jer at the final roundabout by the mountains. This leads past endless shops selling car spares and hardware to reach the border post on the coast 1km later. Queue at the first counter on the left, marked 'Al Mughaadireen' ('those departing') with your passport and pink form. The second counter is marked 'Al Qaadimeen' ('those coming'), and is where you will queue on your return into Ras Al Khaymah at the end of your Musandam trip. Allow 30 minutes for this UAE section of the border.

The Omani border post is 1km or so further on, and you should again allow 30 minutes for the paperwork, followed by a vehicle search. Go to the first counter marked 'Al Qaadimeen' with your passport and white form. The second counter is marked 'Al Mughaadireen' and is where you will go on your departure with your yellow form. After this, you will be waved on to the vehicle search. Beyond the border is a Shell petrol station just before Burkha in case you forgot to fill up in Ras Al Khaymah. The relatively new tarmac road from now on clings to the coast and had to be blasted in places where the mountain came right down to the waves. It was fully completed in 1998.

Some beaches are equipped with *barasti* sunshades on iron frames (often with their *barasti* roofs missing after high winds), and sometimes have children's playgrounds and water tanks. They tend to be a bit close to the road for comfortable camping. The first town that you come to is Bukha.

WHAT TO SEE AND DO
Bukha Castle حصن بخاء (09.00–14.00 Sun–Thu) The coastal fort of Bukha, 14km from the UAE border along road 2, was built by the Portuguese in the 16th century and renovated in 1990. It sits proudly on the new road, and is open and

accessible only when the watchman is there – usually on working days until 14.00. Its shallow moat, especially visible at the back, used to fill with seawater in the times before the coastline was pushed further away by the construction of the road. A square building of stone blocks faced with mud plaster, its most unusual feature is the pear-shaped tower on the southwest corner which reduced the impact of cannonballs. Inside the castle, the tower has four cannon ports. The earliest areas of the castle are thought to date back to the 16th century, and the recent restoration has retained the remains of rich plasterwork wall decorations and carved doors and shutters. The main gate has the *kuwwa* or *musqat* (literally 'place of falling'), the slit found above a door in many Omani defensive buildings, used for pouring hot date '*dibs*', or honey, onto the enemy or for water to quench any fire that threatened to burn down the door.

Friday Mosque Bukha's historic Friday Mosque stands southwest of the castle, surrounded on all sides by an extensive cemetery of headstones which have the effect of distancing the town buildings. At the back on the inland side a double set of steps leads down into the ablution area. Stairs also lead up onto the roof, so that, as was tradition, the *muezzin* could make the call to prayer from there. Inside, the grand mosque has areas of delicate stucco plasterwork decorating its pillared arches. The motifs are alternate rosettes and arches. The mihrab niche itself is surprisingly plain and free from decoration, as are the *minbar* (pulpit) steps from where the imam would give the Friday sermon. A crude wooden *minbar* was found on these steps, but has now disappeared. The high outer walls of the mosque are pierced with elaborate decorative grilles displaying geometric and plant motifs carved in good-quality strong plaster.

Hill fort Up on the hill behind Bukha stands a fine **hill fort**, a tower ringed with a defence wall. Those with the energy to climb up will be rewarded with an excellent view and a closer look at the unique domed cistern on the summit, complete with a pointed-arch door.

Beyond Bukha On leaving Bukha, the road is a spectacular drive beneath the sea cliffs. Look up to catch sight of any roosting Socotra cormorants on the guano-covered rocks.

QIDA (قدى) AND TAWI (طوي)

Just 4km before Khasab the new road winds round to the fjord-like bay of Qida, with fishing boats lining the beach. Unusually lush and green for Musandam, the oasis of Qida sits in a narrow valley with date palms and many fruit trees. To see some **prehistoric rock art**, take the signposted track to Tawi off the tarmac here, leading in a northeasterly direction into the valley, following a riverbed lined with some interesting old houses. One in particular, raised up on the left side, has attractive plasterwork in semicircular arches above the grilled windows. Follow the track beyond the village until, 2.7km after turning off the Bukha–Khasab road, you come to a second small village, in the centre of which is an enormous cluster of grey boulders to the left of the road, opposite a well between a group of three trees to the right. Look at the boulders and you will see that many are covered in rock art depicting ships, horsemen, ibex and camels. Their date and origins are unknown. Village women, who are used to seeing foreign visitors, may emerge from their houses to sell you their basketry. You can continue up the wadi to explore more mountain villages, some uninhabited.

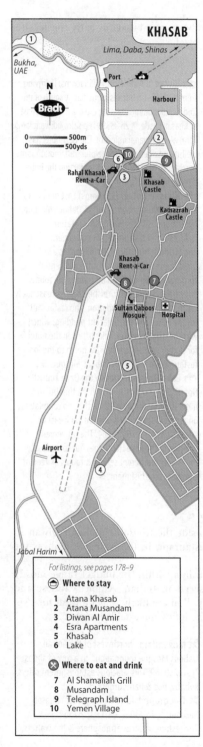

For listings, see pages 178–9

KHASAB

Lima, Daba, Shinas

Bukha, UAE

Port

Harbour

N

Bradt

0 — 500m
0 — 500yds

Rahal Khasab Rent-a-Car

Khasab Castle

Kamazrah Castle

Khasab Rent-a-Car

Sultan Qaboos Mosque

Hospital

Airport

Jabal Harim

For listings, see pages 178–9

⊕ **Where to stay**

1 Atana Khasab
2 Atana Musandam
3 Diwan Al Amir
4 Esra Apartments
5 Khasab
6 Lake

✕ **Where to eat and drink**

7 Al Shamaliah Grill
8 Musandam
9 Telegraph Island
10 Yemen Village

KHASAB خصب

Khasab, 42km from the UAE border, is Musandam's main town (although only a small fishing port) and is the next town that you reach when travelling around the west coast. Khasab and its associated villages are home to 27,836 of Musandam's approximate population of 48,193. This is the northernmost *wilayat* in Oman and overlooks both the Arabian Gulf to the northwest and the Sea of Oman to the east. It acts as the seat of the *wali*, whose influence extends in practice about as far as the limits of the town. Its mainstays are fishing and agriculture, *khasab* being the Arabic for 'fertile'. Khasab has traditionally been a community of fishermen, boat builders, craftsmen and traders. The population swells in summer as people come from Kumzar and the mountain villages to harvest dates and to fish, thereby retaining its old way of life.

The wide bay of Khasab is the mouth of the large wadi that extends inland for several kilometres, and the alluvial silt that has been deposited near the mouth by torrential seasonal flooding has enabled the extensive oases of the date gardens to build up. Khasab town used to have many houses with traditional wind towers, a style introduced from Persia, but few now remain in the age of the air-conditioning system.

Driving inland from the town – past the fort and deeper into Wadi Khasab – you will notice the wide low dam spanning much of the wadi floor. Such dams have been one of the priorities of the Musandam Development Committee, to minimise damage caused by severe flooding. The Royal Geographic Society expedition of 1972 found a few pot shards in the alluvium of the wadi floor, which were dated to the 15th–19th centuries. Anything earlier, if it exists, is likely to be buried deep beneath the silt. Combined with that, the effect of the subduction zone and the post-glacial rise in sea level would have meant that any early coastal sites would now be either underwater or destroyed.

WHERE TO STAY *Map, page 177.*

Atana Khasab (60 rooms) On the main road between Khasab & the UAE, about 5km from the town centre; 26 730777; e stay@ atanahotels.com; www.atanahotels.com. From its elevated location on a low cliff the Atana Khasab overlooks the sea approaches to the town of Khasab. This was the old Golden Tulip, & while the facilities are a bit dated it is still a comfortable hotel &, unlike the Atana Musandam, it has an alcohol licence. B/fast inc. **$$$$**

Atana Musandam (105 rooms) Overlooking the main harbour in Khasab; 26 730888; e stay@atanahotels.com; www. atanahotels.com. Atana Musandam is inspired by a typical Omani village, with a number of low-rise buildings. The majority of them provide private parking – ideal for visitors from the UAE. The location overlooks the sea & mountains but those guests who prefer alcohol with meals might consider its sister hotel down the road, the Atana Khasab. B/fast included. **$$$$**

Esra Apartments (16 apts) East of Khasab airport & 2.3km south of Sultan Qaboos Mosque, this is the last building on the left driving from the Sultan Qaboos Mosque out of town; 26 730562; e booking@khasabtours.com; www.khasabtours. com. The simply furnished self-catering apartments (all with their own kitchen & living room) are supported by a small restaurant that overlooks a small pool. **$$$**

Diwan Al Amir Hotel (55 rooms) If arriving from the UAE this hotel is immediately south of the 2nd roundabout on entering the town & 300m east of Khasab Castle; 26 833991; e sales@diwanalamir. com; www.diwanalamir.com. This new hotel has well-maintained rooms & helpful staff, though some persistence may be needed if contacting the hotel directly by email. B/fast inc. **$$**

Khasab Hotel (35 rooms) East of Khasab airport & 800m south of Sultan Qaboos Mosque, almost opposite the Shell petrol station; 26 730267; e khoman@omantel.net. om. Helpful, friendly reception makes a good impression on arrival, although email communication can be a bit trying. The rooms have been recently refurbished & offer reasonably clean, simple accommodation. The restaurant for the hotel is in the adjacent building, which was the original hotel. Take b/fast in the hotel & for dinner you can easily walk north to the local restaurants near Sultan Qaboos Mosque. **$$**

Lake Hotel (previously the Qada Tourist Hotel) (22 rooms) If arriving from the UAE this hotel is immediately north of the 2nd roundabout on entering the town & a 500m walk east of Khasab Castle; 26 731664. The convenient location of the Lake Hotel does not compensate for its very indifferent service & rooms in need of complete refurbishment. **$**

WHERE TO EAT AND DRINK *Map, page 177.*

There are some fairly basic restaurants inside the Khasab Hotel and Diwan Al Amir Hotel. However, the Al Mawra Restaurant, in the Atana Khasab, is the only licensed one.

Otherwise there are a few local restaurants within the budget range mostly close to Sultan Qaboos Mosque. They serve an Indian, Arabic, Chinese and European menu, and are well worth a try. You are likely to get a meal for two, including soft drinks, for under RO6 at the following establishments:

Al Shamaliah Grill East of the Sultan Qaboos Mosque roundabout, past the banks & money changers & take the first road left; the restaurant is 200m from this junction on the right-hand side of the house with all the trees; 26 730477. This is a popular place; if hooting horns don't bother you, sit outside in the evening & enjoy the grilled fish. **$**

Musandam Northwest of the Sultan Qaboos Mosque roundabout, in a row of shops; 26 730569. This spacious establishment offers kebabs, rice & hamburgers. **$**

Telegraph Island Restaurant Khasab harbour; 26 730577; m 91 367564. The restaurant lacks atmosphere & the waiters can sometimes be overwhelmed by the volume of business, but the food here is good, it's clean & in a very easy-to-find location in Lulu supermarket. If you can sit outside overlooking the fishing boats & mountains, it is perhaps the best dining option outside the Atana Khasab hotel. Try the 'Telegraph Mix Grill', which is large enough to share. $

✕ **Yemen Village Restaurant** Immediately next to the Lake Hotel on the 2nd roundabout in Khasab if driving from the UAE. A simple restaurant that offers Yemeni-style grills & rice. $

WHAT TO SEE AND DO

Khasab Castle خصب حصن (⏰ *09.00–16.00 Sat–Thu, 08.00–11.00 Fri; 500bzs*) An impressive square enclosure with towers at each corner and an old round tower may be an older Omani tower incorporated into the 17th-century Portuguese castle at Khasab. It was the base for the failed attempt by the Portuguese to recapture Hormuz Island. The fort now doubles as a museum with displays of Omani handicrafts, and has been awarded a prize as the best-presented fort in all Oman, as well as the most involved with the local population.

The central tower houses an informative museum with cabinets explaining various aspects of Musandam and its people. The iconic *jirz* (axe) of Musandam, its history and manufacture is explained alongside the crafting of traditional fish traps and the old, almost disappeared, *battil* wooden boats. In the exterior and interior courtyards are original traditional wooden boats whose successors, the fibreglass speedboats, crowd the seawater inlet just to the east of the castle. The corner towers also have excellent displays, including an extraordinarily well-stocked traditional shop and book and documents room.

Kamazrah Castle الكمازرة حصن (⏰ *09.00–14.00 Sun–Thu; 500bzs*) This small fortification may have been built in the mid 19th century by the sheikhs from Kumzar. Although it is of less interest than Khasab Castle, the walk is less than 15 minutes southeast along the road in front of Khasab Castle and it is signed shortly after the end of the seawater inlet. The castle is a single-storey building with rooms opening out onto a central courtyard with a water well and two towers diagonally opposite one another.

Handicrafts Zaree Khasab (🐦 *@zaree_khasab*) is a collective of ladies who offer handicrafts and henna inside the Atana Musandam Hotel. They also set up a tent when cruise ships are in port. This is an excellent initiative and offers visitors a great opportunity to contribute directly to the community.

FROM KHASAB TO WADI BIH   من خصب الى وادي بيح

From Khasab harbour, the road now heads inland past the Khasab Hotel, near the Sultan Qaboos Mosque with its twin minarets. If you have arranged a mountain safari, this is the route your driver will take. The road continues beyond the airport and the water dam into the Wadi Khasab. Some 12km along this road (about 12 minutes' drive from the mosque), you come to a major junction with large signposts. The left takes you to both Khawr A'Najd and Sal Ala, potential camping spots within 30 minutes or so of Khasab. Keeping straight on leads to the steep graded road up past **Jabal Harim**, Musandam's highest peak, down to the checkpoint at Wadi Bih.

The drive over the mountain to the checkpoint takes a good 2 hours with no stops (approximately 61km from the mosque), and with stops on the scenic journey 3–4 hours. For non-Omanis the usual destination is the Rawdhah Bowl, which has no shops or petrol (pages 184–5).

Note: The Wadi Bih checkpoint is only open to Omani passport holders or residents with a special road permit issued by the Royal Oman Police and specifically holders of visit visas are prohibited, so in practice very few non-Omanis use it.

KHAWR A'NAJD خور النجد Taking the southern exit from the roundabout at the Sultan Qaboos Mosque in Khasab's town centre, a drive of 12km along a tarmac road will take you to the major junction for either Khawr A'Najd and Sal Ala to the east of Jabal Harim and beyond to the south (pages 183–5). If you take the left-hand turn and travel an additional 5.8km, then fork off left again and drive up the rough road to reach Khawr A'Najd, the only piece of fjord coastline reachable by road in the whole of Musandam. It passes a military firing range. The track is steep and snakes up to the brow of the hill, from where there is a stunning view out to sea, over the fjord and down to the *khawr* (sea inlet), itself a total of only 6.6km. The total drive, although short, is best for 4x4s only because of the gradient and some bumpy sections. The shoreline is muddy with rocks further out, so most people who want to swim here use boats – either their own or those rented out by fishermen. However, it is the view at the top rather than the shore that makes this a good stop.

SAL ALA سل اعلى Back on the wadi floor from where you turned the track continues straight on to Sal Ala (not to be confused with Salalah, in Dhofar), a dead-end road finishing in a natural silt bowl ringed by mountains on three sides and with a few signs off to several villages on the way. The distance from the turn to Khawr A'Najd to the end of the bowl is 6km. This makes a nice spot to camp and is arguably more peaceful than Khawr A'Najd, which is surrounded by the sound of both cars and boats. The name 'Sal Ala' means 'higher silt flat', reflecting its position at the head of the main valley of the largest drainage system of the Musandam Mountains, flowing into the sea at Khasab.

The silt plain at Sal Ala supports an astonishing open woodland of acacia trees (*simr* and *salam*), as well as *Zizyphus spina-christi* (*sidr*) and *Prosopis cineraria* (*ghaf*). The woodland covers an area of 35ha and the trees reach a height of 9m. After rains during the spring months from January to April, a thick carpet of green grass might grow under the trees, contrasting sharply with the barrenness of the surrounding mountains.

Sheep and goats are in paradise here, and a few donkeys are also to be found. Cows, which one could easily imagine grazing happily here, do not exist in Musandam and are anathema to the Shihuh. Wild animals found in Musandam are wolves, foxes, and possibly the Arabian *tahr* (a sturdy, russet-haired type of mountain goat). Look out for partridge and European bee-eaters.

The spring of **Birkat Al Khalidiya** ('Spring of Eternity') lies southwest beyond the circular playground in the acacia trees, where the track ends. The name is rather ironic as the spring is no longer maintained and has more or less dried up. As the cistern runs low heading into April, hornets are drawn by the remnants of the water. The village over in the left-hand corner of the bowl (the opposite side to Birkat Al Khalidiya) is **Limhas**, the largest settlement in the area. It has a large walled area that used to house a date plantation and fields of crops and fruit trees. The settlement itself has stone Bait Al Qufl houses (see box, page 188), as well as

TELEGRAPH ISLAND جزيرة التلغراف

In the mid 19th century the technological revolution in Europe and the invention of telegraphy via a cable began to change the face of worldwide communications. Britain's empire and its links with colonial India had been transformed too by the introduction of steam ships in 1840 and the British India Steam Navigation Company started a postal service, first to Calcutta and Rangoon, and then to Ceylon and Karachi. Subsequently it extended in 1862 into the Gulf, where the postal service then connected Bombay, Karachi, Muscat and Basra (Iraq). By 1858, a telegraphic land line had been laid between Baghdad and Scutari (Albania), and the proposal was subsequently made to connect this system to India via a land line to Basra, then via a submarine cable down the Gulf. After lengthy diplomatic discussions between Turkey (to which Iraq belonged at that time), Persia and Britain, the land stretch was finally completed in 1854 and the difficult submarine stretch was begun. At the Omani end there were difficulties about the placement of the telegraph terminal on the Musandam tip. This was because the local tribes, specifically the Zahuriyeen, who lived on the Maqlab isthmus – the thin strip of land running between the two major fjord inlets of Elphinstone (Khawr Ash-Sham) and Malcolm (Khawr Habalayn) – disrupted progress for a month while they tried to establish what benefits there might be for them. It appeared that the British too had some doubts about jurisdiction over the area, but after further discussions the sultan reasserted his control over Musandam and the telegraph line was led into Elphinstone inlet and from there on to a small island to be known thereafter as Telegraph Island (although on maps it is officially Maqlab Island). The site was selected as it offered more security than the mainland against potentially hostile local tribes, and the telegraph station was built there in 1854 and maintained until 1869, the year in which the opening of the Suez Canal also brought Britain and India closer.

The terminus functioned for only five years, since no-one wished to live in such an inhospitable place. Its strategic importance was felt by the British to be such, however, that in 1904 they decided to erect flags there, but could not agree what flag should fly – not the Union Jack since it was not British territory, and not the Blue Ensign of the Royal India Marine, for that would mean they might have to defend it. So the flagpoles were all taken down again, except one that was allowed to remain on Telegraph Island with no flag. None of the flagpoles was visible from the open sea anyway, but it is doubtful the decision-makers in London ever realised. Needless to say, this tiny connection with modern technology had no effect on the lives of the Musandam tribes, for whom life went on at subsistence level as before.

The tidal variation of 0.6–0.9m means that it is not always possible to land at Telegraph Island, as the boat would be damaged on the rocks at low tide. Take care when walking about on the island, as the rocks are sharp.

modern houses. It used to take a day for the men of the village to reach Khasab, so they would migrate there for the summer months, but now that it takes only 30 minutes they commute on a daily basis.

JABAL HARIM جبل حارم Jabal Harim is the tallest peak in the region at 2,087m and lies between Khasab and Daba. Returning to the major junction 12km south of the mosque at Khasab, you can now (if you have a minimum of half a day or preferably a full day) continue south on the main mountain road signposted for Daba. Again, if you have arranged a mountain safari, this is where you will head. The road runs very flat along the wadi bed, well compacted and smooth for another few kilometres until signs warn you of the impending mountainous section which requires 4x4 low ratio, especially on the descent. The road, built by the Omani military, is tricky driving, probably more difficult than the drive up to the Al Sayh Plateau or up the Bald Sayt road in the Al Jabal Al Akhdar mountains, both of which are wider routes with better-compacted surfaces. You also require more of a head for heights, as some of the edges on the beginning stretch and just beyond the summit itself are extremely vertiginous.

The first section of the ascent is very steep, but if you can wrench your eyes off the road for a moment, you can spot the Shihuh villages tucked into the mountainsides and perched on the edge of gorges. Old Bedouin houses (now disused) can also be spotted, at rather extraordinary heights. Look out too for the wispy bushes of the wild almond tree (*Amydalus Arabica*, or *Al Mizi*), whose branches are used for the handles of the small axe worn by Shihuh men instead of the traditional *khanjar* of Oman. This axe, called a *jerz*, is unique to Musandam. At each settlement are the white water tanks at the roadside, regularly filled by blue water tankers. If you see the water tanks with no sign of a village, rest assured that there will be a village tucked away somewhere nearby but out of sight of the road. As you get higher it becomes easier to stop and admire the views.

AL SAYH PLATEAU هضبة السيح Towards the upper part of the ascent you will suddenly arrive at the Al Sayh Plateau, a lush miniature plateau about 2km long and 500m wide. In the winter months the plateau is delightfully green, but starts to go brown by mid-April. The settlements, most of which are on the opposite side across grassy meadows, exist to tend the small palm groves and fields of wheat and alfalfa. Donkeys, sheep and goats frolic in the pastureland.

On the opposite side of the plateau is another small settlement with Bait Al Qufl houses (see box, page 188), some of them built into the mountainside like caves. The numbers of villagers are constantly on the decline as men leave for the coastal towns. On the summit of Jabal Harim immediately above, you can spot the grey dome (like a golf ball) that is the radar station set at 2,087m.

A climb of another 10 minutes brings you right up to the summit of the pass, where the Omani Air Force has its austere grey-green buildings. Half a kilometre before the final zigzags to the V-cut in the mountain pass summit is a bumpy track to the right, leading along flat ground for 2km to reach a helicopter landing pad used for delivering supplies to the air-force base. There are a few small walled gardens close by that appear largely disused, and this whole area makes a fine camping spot in the summer months, the altitude providing welcome coolness – though there is virtually no shade and, of course, no water. It's here that most tours will finish, some 24km of rough road from the major junction from Khasab. If you continue on the next stretch of road it's quite likely that you won't see another vehicle.

THE RIDGE This is the dramatic road after the Omani Air Force facilities. Drive to the left of them and then take the right turn (the left one is prohibited, and remember, this is a military area, so don't take photos of the buildings). As you pass through the cutting from the complex to the other side of the mountain range, the most staggering view presents itself and the faint-hearted will quiver at the sight of the road they must follow for the descent. It starts by clinging to the precipitous left side of the mountain, then snakes off to the right over a long thin ridge before the final descent down to the bed of Wadi Bih on the other side, a total of some 45 minutes' driving, though only 18km from the Omani Air Force facilities. The route is definitely at its most spectacular when seen from this direction – the climb back up again gives angles which are less dramatic or vertiginous.

At the very start of the ridge as the road leaves the mountain massif is a small settlement of stone houses to the left of the track (4.8km from the Omani Air Force facilities). If you fork off into this village, following the track through and beyond it for a kilometre or so, you will reach a deserted village which you can explore at leisure, looking at the Bait Al Qufl houses and the walled garden areas. You may also notice the occasional stone plinth, apparently in the middle of nowhere, thought to have been used for the call to prayer. Another unexpected sight is the occasional use of scarecrows in the fields to protect the precious crops. The walled field systems around the tiny village settlement are remarkably complicated, the walls positioned for maximum rainwater run-off collection in harmony with the contours of the ground. Once crops were growing, the tops of the walls were rammed with thorn bushes to prevent goats from jumping in and helping themselves.

WATER PRACTICES IN THE MUSANDAM MOUNTAINS

Today the Khasab municipality runs a system of water tankers that regularly go to each village or to the closest point on a drivable track to replenish large white roadside water tanks for the remaining inhabitants of the mountain villages. This system dates back only to the early 1980s. Before that the Shihuh tribespeople devised other ways of surviving on minimal water.

The *falaj* irrigation channels so common in the rest of Oman are absent in Musandam. The nature of the terrain is such here that there would never be enough water to keep them flowing, so the high mountain villages tried instead to trap as much as possible of the heavy winter rains. To achieve this they built water-deflecting walls (*musaylah*) – following the contours of slopes where they observed the water ran best and most frequently – then caught it in cisterns built of stone and lined with mud. These can still be seen in many mountain villages, where the wall is often mistaken for a defensive structure. One of the best examples is on the raised outcrop directly above the Islamic cemetery at the junction of Wadi Bih with the track into the Rawdhah Bowl.

The other practice was the use of a *khayr* (Arabic for 'good'), a large clay water jar donated by a family for public use. The benevolent donor thereby increased his social standing in the village, and it was his responsibility to keep it full. These jars were generally placed under a tree beside a main track, to facilitate travelling, or sometimes among a group of village houses. A few can still be seen in the remoter villages, and tend to have their tops stuffed with thorn bushes to keep debris out when the village is abandoned for the summer months.

The ridge drive, however, takes you along the ridge of a slope that dips down into Wadi Bih, and after the long ridge the final descent to the wadi floor can be very bumpy, especially after rains have gouged out deep runnels in the steep track. Bulldozers and steamrollers try to repair the damage as soon as they can but occasionally it can take a few days if the rains have been very heavy.

RAWDHAH BOWL تجويف الروضة At the foot of the mountain you come to a crossroads, the left turn of which takes you back along the gravel wadi floor to a minor settlement before reaching a dead end. The right takes you along Wadi Bih to the border checkpoint that is impassable for non-Omanis, but straight over leads you into the Rawdhah Bowl – the best camping spot in the area.

From here into the Rawdhah Bowl is a 5-minute drive along a good track through a narrow defile that suddenly opens up into a large mountain-ringed bowl some 5km long by 2km wide. There are a few settlements in the bowl, and two interesting cemeteries. The area is large enough for you to find houses tucked away, often close to ruined stone homes, deserted in favour of newer buildings.

The wildlife in the bowl is abundant, with owls, hedgehogs, birds of prey, numerous butterflies including tiger moths and blue pansies, and amazing cricket life, as well as the usual sheep and goats. February and March are the best for flowers, and by April the grass is beginning to go brown. The bowl is heavily wooded with acacia, but is nothing like as lush as the forest at Sal Ala (pages 180–3).

Back out at the four-road junction you just left at the foot of the mountain, you should fork left (from the Rawdhah Bowl) on to the Wadi Bih track, even if you do not intend to cross the border, for within just 1km is an extensive cemetery that deserves some attention. The **Islamic cemetery** lies to the right of the road, just around the corner from a large bluff. Its headstones are unusually tall, often over 1m, a few of them with engravings etched onto the rock, like that of the man with a spear and shield. Extremely neat and well arranged, this cemetery is one of the most impressive in the quality of masonry anywhere in Oman. Two slabs marks a male, three slabs a female grave. This is the Sunni, Hanbali style of grave, quite different from the small random stones of the typical Ibadhi graveyard. One unusual structure is circular, reminiscent in style of the foundation of an Umm Al Nar tomb, with pinkish regular blocks.

The only house of the former settlement that is still standing is back at the foot of the bluff on the same side of the road, a remarkable building constructed of colossal stone blocks. This mystery building, undated and unique in the country, is so perfectly crafted that it almost resembles a small rural temple. On the sloping bluff above it is a carefully constructed low double wall for deflecting

GRAZING BY BOAT

Kumzar's houses are so closely packed that there is hardly space to walk between them. There are two small mosques, each with a small graveyard, which were filled centuries ago. Recent burials have therefore been forced to take place under the floors of the houses. Kumzar *baatils* (fishing boats) were unique in the Gulf in having shell-decorated bows and zoomorphic sterns to secure the rigging. The village sheep and goats are taken regularly by boat to pastureland on other coastal bays where grazing is more plentiful. The government has now built a desalination plant at Kumzar, but before that everyone had to rely on a well at the back of the village. Visiting crews used to paint their ships' names on the cliffs behind the harbour, still clearly visible today.

above The sharp ridges of the linear dunes of the Wihibah Sands create mini valleys that lead you towards the distant Arabian Sea (OMOT) pages 253–5

right Some women in the more traditional parts of the Wihibah desert still wear full face masks (TW) page 246

below A typical Bedouin tent where guests are sometimes invited to drink cardamom coffee (TW) page 280

above   Ar Rustaq Fort is said to have been built (from 630AD) before the arrival of Islam in Oman (TW) pages 163–4

left   On a visit to Nakhal Fort, be sure to visit the charming family quarters (T/D) pages 157–8

below   The impressive fortified town of Samharam is believed to have been founded during the 3rd century BC (TW) pages 308–11

above   The tomb of Bin Ali, which is very much in the style of Yemeni tombs, is situated in Mirbat (TW) page 313

right   Al Khandaq Fort at Al Buraymi is surrounded by defensive trenches and has embellishments typical of this area (TW) page 200

below   Sur has long been famous for *dhow* building, and remains the centre of Oman's shipbuilding industry today (TW) page 265

above   Traditional fishing methods are still used along Oman's 1,700km-long shoreline; the journey from net to table is less than 24 hours (TW) page 130

left   Unlike Spanish bullfighting, in Oman the sport is bloodless and between two evenly matched contestants (TW) pages 35–6

below   Rose petals are used extensively in Oman in perfumes and incense – high in Al Jabal Al Akhdar, rose water distilleries run 24 hours a day during April's damask rose harvest (TW) page 216

above   Omani men enjoy playing traditional games like dominoes (AS/S)

below left   Harvesting the sap from *Boswellia sacra* trees to collect frankincense resin (TW) pages 310–11

below right   Bahla is famous for its potters — be sure to visit a working pottery if you're in the area
              (TW and T/D) page 237

top **The virgin white sands of Mughsayl Beach, near Salalah, stretch for several kilometres** (MS/S) pages 317–18

above & below **The landscape of the Musandam Peninsula features towering sea cliffs which form a spectacular backdrop to *dhow* trips into its fjords, with dolphin watching thrown in** (A/D and I/D) pages 174–5

top left	Socially and economically, the date is the most important crop in Oman and its still harvested by hand (TW) page 159
top right	Oman's unique *falaj* irrigation channels ensure water is carefully rationed and distributed into agricultural fields throughout northern Oman (TW) pages 208–9
above	With its rolling grassy meadows following the summer *khareef* (monsoon), Dhofar is different from other areas in Oman (TW) pages 289–92
below	Jabal Misht in the Adh Dhahirah region offers excellent rock climbing possibilities on its sheer southern face of almost 1,000m (TW) page 134

top Dolphin-watching tours are popular in Oman with sightings of spinner, common and bottlenose usually seen, frequently in their hundreds (TW) page 13

above left The *Boswellia sacra* tree produces a sap which becomes frankincense resin when dry (TW) page 7

above right The Al Wusta Wildlife Reserve in central Oman is home to Oman's fabled white oryx (TW) pages 278–9

below Four species of turtle lay their eggs on Oman's beaches – a night-time or dawn turtle-watching trip is a true adventure (TW) pages 13–14

water, a *musaylah*, with a few circular tower-like structures that were probably cisterns for collecting the mountain run-off.

Beyond the Islamic cemetery are a few very collapsed **cairn tombs**, but the better-preserved ones are on the other side of the track over towards the entrance to the Rawdhah Bowl in the wadi plain. These cairn tombs, some 15 in all, are also a mystery here in Musandam, and are as yet undated and unexcavated. One has a long narrow chamber in the centre with roof slabs over the top. It is almost as if the loose stones have been added to cover this above-ground grave structure.

KUMZAR كمزار

Accessible only by boat, Kumzar – a cliffside village – is the northernmost settlement of Oman, crammed into the narrow valley of Wadi Marwan and ringed with bare precipitous mountains. It takes 2 hours one-way to reach it by speedboat from Khasab, and nearly 4 by motorised dhow. Apart from ticking a box to say you have been to Oman's most northerly village, the journey is the real highlight, as the village is not especially welcoming.

The name 'Kumzar' itself is thought to be a contraction of *khawr* (Arabic for lagoon, bay or creek) and *asaba* (the ancient name for the whole peninsula coined by the Roman scholar Pliny in the 1st century AD). Its large shallow bay turns to mudflats at low tide and the type of boat built here, called the *baatil*, was relatively flat-bottomed but big enough for regional trading, taking merchants even as far as India.

DABA دبا

Daba (or Dibba) is located on the southeastern edge of Musandam and has the second-largest population in the governorate after Khasab. The town is divided into three parts, with an impressive chain-link fence between the Oman section and the other two, which belong to the UAE. The southern part is Daba Muhallah and is in the emirate of Al Fujayrah; Daba Al Hisn is part of the emirate of Sharjah; and Daba Bayah is the part belonging to Oman. Excavations have shown that this area was already inhabited in around 1000BC.

GETTING THERE AND AWAY Most people will reach Daba by **road** through the UAE, which does not require a visa, but if you are not resident in the UAE you will need a letter from your hotel in Daba Bayah. If you are one of the few who has managed to secure a permit from the Omani authorities to cross the border via the military checkpoint at Wadi Bih (page 172), it is possible to drive here **from Khasab**, by following the course of Wadi Bih until it reaches the mountain pass, again built by the Omani military and announced by the same warnings of steep gradients. This road is less vertiginous and steep than the earlier section over Jabal Harim, but nevertheless impressive. As you near the top of the slope after the military checkpoint you will notice to the right (west) of the track another narrow track leading upwards. This will take you to a large settlement set about 500m off the road, with extensive terracing. It also has two stone-built towers, one round, one square. The round one – with three levels and rather dilapidated – is thought to have belonged to the wealthiest inhabitant. The square tower is a granary (*yanz*) in which the agricultural produce was stored. There is an opening in the side which was sealed to keep animals out, or to keep it clean when empty. The final section of this route is Wadi Khab Al Shamsi and it continues past the entrance to the Six Senses Hideaway Zighy Bay and into the northern area of Daba, a 6km drive from the Golden Tulip on the coast.

If you arrive by **ferry** then you avoid all the border regulations, though there is not much to see in Daba and you may want to look at timetables to fit in with departure ferries.

WHERE TO STAY *Map, opposite*

Six Senses Hideaway Zighy Bay (82 pool villas) Zighy Bay, Daba Bayah; 26 735555; e reservations-zighy@sixsenses.com; www. sixsenses.com. The hotel is accessed via a signed route to the northwest of Daba Bayah. From the coastal UAE border post it's a 17km drive, initially along the corniche for 2.5km & west for an additional 2km past Sultan Qaboos Mosque. The final section takes you out of town & onto the rough road to the hotel. The ultimate getaway, super-remote, with ultra-clean sandy beaches & lavish service, the Zighy Bay is a Dubai-style resort in Oman for the super-rich. Most customers drive in from Dubai (1.5hrs) via Daba. It has 1.6km of private beach on one side & a mountain backdrop. As well as the pool villas there are 2-bed retreats & a 4-bed reserve. Restaurants are what you might expect, including a hilltop restaurant offering international cuisine & a central restaurant with regional specialities. There is even a choice of arrival methods: a scenic drive down the mountain; a 15min speedboat ride; or as a companion passenger with the Zighy's professional paraglider! *Dbls from RO245.* **$$$$$**

Golden Tulip (54 rooms) Mina Rd, Daba Bayah; 26 730888; www.goldentulipdibba. com. From the coastal UAE border post it's a 5km drive keeping on the main corniche until you reach the hotel, which is the last building to the north of the town & is on the beach. The hotel is a low-rise development. It's classified as 4-star accommodation, somewhat optimistically, but it does offer very good value for money, with plenty of deals at prices well below the rates advertised on websites like www.booking.com. **$$$**

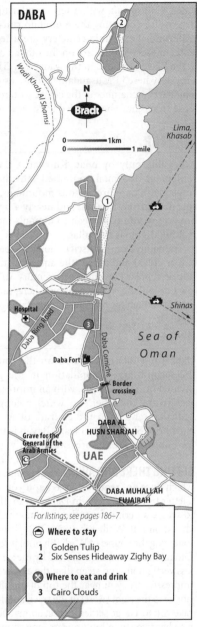

DABA

Wadi Khab Al Shamsi

N

Bradt

0 ——— 1km
0 ——— 1 mile

Lima, Khasab

1

Hospital ✚

Daba Ring Road

3

Daba Corniche

Daba Fort

Border crossing

Sea of Oman

Shinas

DABA AL HUSN SHARJAH

Grave for the General of the Arab Armies

UAE

DABA MUHALLAH FUJAIRAH

For listings, see pages 186–7

⊖ **Where to stay**
1 Golden Tulip
2 Six Senses Hideaway Zighy Bay

✖ **Where to eat and drink**
3 Cairo Clouds

WHERE TO EAT AND DRINK *Map, opposite*

Apart from the hotel restaurants (see above), there is one other option worth a try in Daba.

Cairo Clouds Restaurant South of the harbour on the corniche about 1km north of the coastal UAE

checkpoint; ⊕ 07.00–23.30 daily. This is a busy place that seems to get most of its business from home delivery & take-aways, which may explain the fact that little attempt has been made to improve its appearance. The food is simple, & it's probably the best choice for non-fast food in Daba. $

WHAT TO SEE AND DO
Daba Fort قلعة دبا (*In the middle of the old town, set in a kind of central square, which can be reached from the corniche 800m north of the border crossing & taking a road west for 750m; ⊕ 08.30–14.30 Sat–Thu; 500bzs*) Worth popping in for a few minutes to see the layout, the fort has now been restored and its guardian has even produced a leaflet on it. There are no furnishings but the guardian might offer tea and dates. You can climb up each of the four towers. The fort is probably on the location of the original Portuguese fort, which was part of a larger defensive system.

Grave for the General of the Arab Armies ضريح قائد الجيوش العربية (*Just off the southwestern part of the Daba ring-road, 340m south of the airstrip & opposite a large area of date plantations*) Daba was the site of two major battles during the early centuries of Islam. The first was immediately after the death of the Prophet Mohammed in AD632 during the rule of Abu Bakr, while the second was in 892 during the rule of the Abbasid caliph Al-Mu'tadid bi-llah. Both battles resulted in the defeat of the forces opposing the central Islamic state. The grave ascribed to the General of the Army (there seem to be two graves enclosed) is surrounded by a wall, though which army or general is unclear. Another 200m south of this is an extensive cemetery known as that of the army.

LIMA ليما

Previously Lima was Musandam's most off-the-beaten-track settlement. This isolation has changed since the high-speed ferry started calling into Lima and it will become considerably easier to visit with a new road that will travel over the mountains to the west of Lima and into the Rawdhah Bowl. There is no accommodation here, but camping could be an option in the wadi to the west. The town has an interesting collection of old stone houses rising up the mountain near the small port, while to the north is a small oasis of date palms.

GETTING THERE AND AWAY Lima is reached by ferry on Sundays, Wednesdays, Thursdays and Saturdays, connecting the village with Daba, Khasab and Shinas. See also page 46.

MADHA مدحاء

Madha (or Mudha) is an exclave of Musandam and Oman within the UAE territory and roughly 3km inland from the Sea of Oman near Al Fujayrah in the UAE. At 75km², this makes it slightly larger than San Marino. If you are approaching from the northern main Omani crossing at Khitmat Milahah (Khatm Al-Mallah and variants; page 171) north of Shinas, Madha is about 40km from the Omani border and the road enters next to the Al Maha petrol station. There is no border control at Madha, but valid vehicle insurance for both the UAE and Oman is important in case of an accident. Madha has no hotels, so the closest accommodation is in Al Fujayrah, UAE.

Ruins have been found here dating back to the Iron Age (1500–1000BC). There is rock art and calligraphy to be found at Jabal Al Rukham (the Marble Mountain), and elsewhere in Madha, mostly dating to the 10th and 11th centuries, although some is believed to be pre-Islamic. New Madha is the new administrative part of the town, with schools, health centres and government buildings.

Madha is one of Oman's least-known areas, with peaceful oasis villages, valleys, streams, springs, *aflaj* and date-palm gardens; it is ideal for picnicking. The natural springs are said to have healing properties for skin disorders, as they contain sulphurous water. A local historian who is keen to preserve Oman's heritage, **Mohammed bin Salem Al Mad'hani**, has collected an eclectic and extremely interesting range of materials associated with Madha. These include ancient rock art, coins and photographs. His collection is on display in the centre of the old village, 6.4km from the Al Maha petrol station. The exhibition is basic, and you will need to ask a local person to contact him to unlock the door.

Beyond the old village the road continues through to Nahwa, an enclave within the enclave of Madha; Nahwa is part of Sharjah in the UAE.

6

The Adh Dhahirah and Al Buraymi

الظاهرة و البريمي

Located in Oman's northwest, bordering the UAE and Saudi Arabia, the Adh Dhahirah and Al Buraymi governorates have for long been a route in and out of Oman. Adh Dhahirah Governorate is bordered to the east by the Western Al Hajar Mountains, which include two of Oman's best-known peaks: Jabal Kawr, which rises to 2,716m, and Jabal Misht, whose sheer escarpment ascends to 2,090m. To the southwest are the *sabkha* salt flats of Um As Samim, whose area varies depending on the quantity of water that has arrived from the mountains, but is in excess of 1,000km². Between the Western Al Hajar Mountains and Um As Samim lie the sands of the Rub Al Khali.

Jabals Kawr and Misht are both limestone mountains formed during the Triassic period between 248 million and 206 million years ago. These mountains are two of Oman's largest 'exotics', so called because their material is unrelated to the rock and mountains surrounding them. To their northwest lies an extensive range of ophiolite mountains (page 154), while their southwest edge is fringed by tertiary limestone. The mountain's watercourses, the wadis, flow into the Umm As Samim Depression, where they either sink, creating an aquifer, or evaporate at a potential rate of 3m depth of water per year. Standing water certainly disappears very quickly.

Despite this harsh environment, the region has one of Oman's acclaimed UNESCO World Heritage Sites in the form of Bat, Al-Khutm and Al Ayn, which date back some 5,000 years. The oasis of Al Buraymi has a number of similarly aged sites on its northern outskirts (now in the UAE). There are several impressive historical fortifications, notably in Ibri, As Sulaif, Al Buraymi and Yanqul.

The region's most important economic activity is oil exploration. The oil fields lie to the west in the Rub Al Khali, close to the Saudi Arabian border. Tracks reach out through desolate landscapes to the oil production areas over 100km southwest of Tanam, a settlement 6.5km south of Ibri. Though the government benefits economically from oil production, each 'field' is operated by a company that then shares the profits with the government.

The key commercial areas are in Ibri and Al Buraymi, although the focus is largely on trade and services rather than manufacturing. Both Ibri and Al Buraymi were once important agricultural areas, but a general decline in rainfall has accelerated a degradation of many areas of date oasis.

The combined population of these two governorates was 294,832 in 2015. Ibri is the largest centre, with a population of 148,568, followed by Al Buraymi with 95,874. Other towns include Yanqul, Dank, Mahadah and As Sunaynah, whose tiny population of 595 makes it Oman's smallest *wilayat* (administrative area) by population. Overall, just under 70% of the entire population is Omani national.

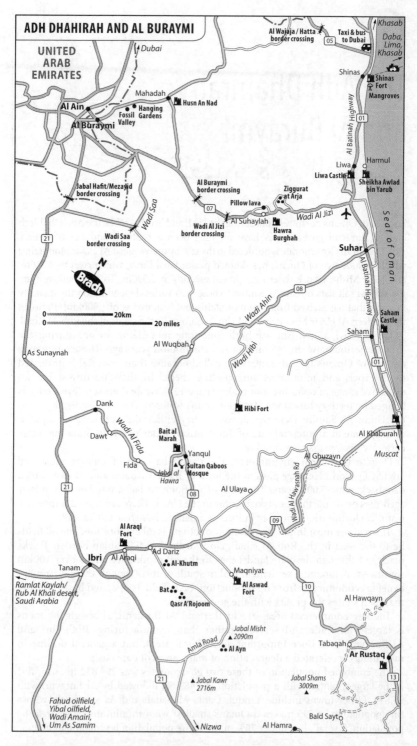

ADH DHAHIRAH AND AL BURAYMI

UNITED ARAB EMIRATES

Dubai

Khasab

Daba, Lima, Khasab

Al Wajaja / Hatta border crossing

Taxi & bus to Dubai

05

Shinas

Shinas Fort
Mangroves

Mahadah

Al Ain

Hanging Gardens

Husn An Nad

Fossil Valley

Al Buraymi

Al Batinah Highway

01

Liwa

Harmul

Liwa Castle

Sheikha Awlad bin Yarub

Jabal Hafit/Mezayid border crossing

Wadi Saa

Al Buraymi border crossing

07

Ziggurat at Arja

Pillow lava

Al Suhaylah

Wadi Al Jizi

Wadi Saa border crossing

Wadi Al Jizi border crossing

Hawra Burghah

Suhar

Al Batinah Highway

N

Bradt

0   20km
0   20 miles

Wadi Ahin

08

Saham Castle

As Sunaynah

Al Wuqbah

Wadi Hibi

Saham

01

Dank

Wadi Al Fida

Hibi Fort

Bait al Marah

Dawt

Al Khaburah

Fida

Yanqul

Jabal al Hawra

Sultan Qaboos Mosque

Al Ghuzayn

Muscat

Al Ulaya

08

Wadi Al Hawasnah Rd

09

Al Araqi Fort

Ibri

Ad Dariz

Al Araqi

Al-Khutm

Maqniyat

10

Tanam

Ramlat Kaylah/ Rub Al Khali desert, Saudi Arabia

Bat

Al Aswad Fort

Al Hawqayn

Qasr A'Rojoom

Jabal Misht ▲2090m

Tabaqah

Ar Rustaq

Amla Road

Al Ayn

13

▲ *Jabal Kawr 2716m*

Jabal Shams 3009m ▲

Fahud oilfield, Yibal oilfield, Wadi Amairi, Um As Samim

21

Bald Sayt

Nizwa

Al Hamra

Sea of Oman

BY CAR From Al Qurum in Muscat the drive is straightforward as you follow the Muscat Expressway west until junction 10B, signed Nizwa. Then continue south on road 15, which along the way becomes road 21, through to Ibri, which you will reach after some 285km. Alternatively, travel to Ar Rustaq on roads 1 and 11 from Muscat, then from the roundabout at Ar Rustaq's Sultan Qaboos Mosque travel west on road 10, which along the way becomes road 9, and you will arrive in Ibri. This route is a little shorter at 266km, but it will take longer, as it is a single carriageway, unlike the Nizwa route, which is a dual carriageway for its entire distance.

Al Buraymi is reached 193km after Ibri. It can also be accessed on routes 1 and 7 from Muscat via Suhar, a journey of 329km. Do remember that for any journey to Al Buraymi you will need to carry your full identity documents, including passport, driving licence and vehicle registration, as – even though it is part of Oman and you do not leave Omani territory – you will pass through border controls.

From the UAE, Al Buraymi is accessed through Al Ain city using the Hilli border point if you are not a GCC national. To access Ibri easily, use the out-of-town Mazayd border near Jabal Hafit, to the south of Al Ain. In addition to the documentation listed above, your vehicle should be insured for both the UAE and Oman. There is an exit charge of UAE 35 dirhams exacted by the UAE and a charge of RO5 for entry into Oman.

The first road and **border crossing between Oman and Saudi Arabia** is expected to open in 2016. Called Ramlat Khaylah on the Omani side and Rub Al Khali (Empty Quarter) on the Saudi side, this is accessed from Ibri via a junction near Tanam 6.7km south of Ibri. From the junction the drive to the Saudi border is 160km through flat gravel plain, with no petrol station. For non-GCC citizens an entry visa for Saudi Arabia should be obtained before travel. Non-GCC citizens travelling from Saudi Arabia should comply with the current exit visa requirements for Saudi Arabia and ensure that they are eligible to obtain an entry visa for Oman at the Omani border (charge as on page 43). From the Omani–Saudi border the road will connect with the road network at Shayba, a drive of almost 300km, and from there an additional 400km to near Al Batha near Qatar. Before making this journey, you should confirm the situation at the border.

BY BUS Bus services run twice a day between Muscat and Al Buraymi via Suhar, taking 1.5 hours and costing around RO4. Check the timetable for this route as at the time of writing the new Mwasalat bus company was intending to upgrade all of its services.

BY TAXI A private taxi will charge around RO45 to drive you from Muscat to Al Buraymi, so it is cheaper to rent a car if you intend to return it to Muscat.

USEFUL TELEPHONE NUMBERS

MEDICAL FACILITIES
✚ **Al Buraymi Hospital** ☏ 25 652319
✚ **Ibri Hospital** ☏ 25 691990

Dank ☏ 25 676099
Ibri ☏ 25 489099
Wadi Jizi ☏ 25 659309

POLICE STATIONS
Al Buraymi ☏ 25 650199
Adh Dhahirah Governorate Police HQ
in Al Buraymi ☏ 25 650099

GETTING AROUND

There is not much public transport for moving around in this region. There are **minibuses** and **taxis** from Nizwa that take 2 hours to Ibri and cost around RO2, and **buses** that run from Muscat to Ibri, taking 5 hours and costing about RO4. To make the most of the region, having your own transport is preferable.

🏠 WHERE TO STAY

There's not much choice in terms of places to stay in this region. There is one mid-range hotel and a few budget hotels in Al Buraymi, a couple of hotels in Ibri, and that's about it.

Your only other option is to camp. One of the best choices for camping is Wadi Fida (off the Yanqul road, pages 196–7), where the tarmac road offers easy access into this stunning gorge scenery.

IBRI عبري

Ibri, located 285km from Muscat, is the main town of Adh Dhahirah. It is thought that the name 'Ibri' may come from the Arabic root 'a-b-r', which means 'crossing' or 'traversing'. It is renowned for its oilfields and its ancient tombs at Bat.

Ibri once had a reputation as a fanatically Ibadhi place with a hostile attitude to Christians, and Wilfred Thesiger avoided the town during his travels for this reason. After the Imamate Revolt was suppressed in 1959 its *wali* (governor) was imprisoned in Jalali Fort, where he died an old man in 1968. Today it has a thriving suq and benefits from its proximity to the oilfield at Fahud. It has its own Arabic-language school for foreigners wanting to learn Arabic (see box, page 68). Nowadays you can safely disregard the description of an early traveller in 1836, who opined that 'to enter Ibri a man must go either armed to the teeth, or as a beggar with a cloth'.

Ibri is also known for its distinctive black-and-red-striped goat-hair rugs, and for its traditional dancing. There used to be about four bands that performed regularly at celebrations such as births, weddings and Eid holidays, but numbers are dwindling now. Dances were performed, as they are today throughout Oman at times of celebration, by men organised in rows and often carrying swords and sticks, who would enact a mock battle to the beat of the drums. In Ibri there was also a dance for women, and even for men and women performing together in rows facing each other. These performances with women are now only held for important events such as a visit by the sultan.

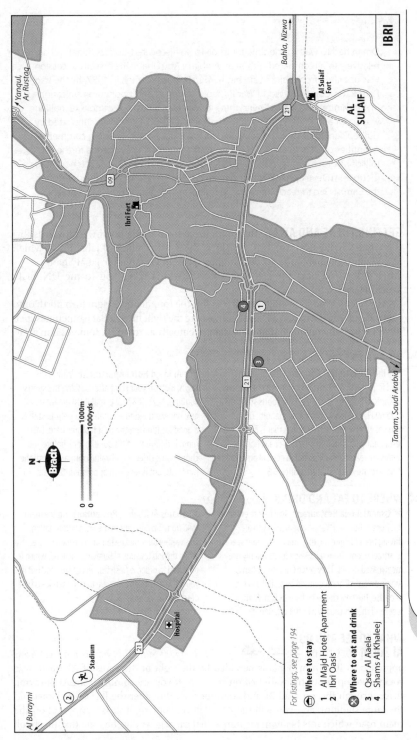

N

Bradt

0 ____ 1000m
0 ____ 1000yds

/ Yanqul, Ar Rustaq

Ibri Fort

60

21

Al Buraymi

Stadium (2)

Hospital

21

21

Tanam, Saudi Arabia ►

Bahla, Nizwa ▲

Al Sulaif Fort

AL
SULAIF

IBRI

(1)
(4)
(3)

For listings, see page 194
Where to stay
① 1 Al Majd Hotel Apartment
2 Ibri Oasis

Where to eat and drink
✕ 3 Qser Al Aaela
4 Shams Al Khaleej

The Adh Dhahirah and Al Buraymi IBRI

6

193

Oman had to wait a long time for its oil to be discovered, and its quantities are relatively small compared with Saudi Arabia or Abu Dhabi. The first oil concession was obtained from Sultan Said bin Taimur, Qaboos's father, in 1937, by the Iraq Petroleum Company. World War II then intervened and poor communications in the hinterland slowed everything down enormously. Around £12 million was spent and, in 1960, most of the partners gave up. Only Shell, supported by Gulbenkian interests, kept trying and in 1964 succeeded in finding commercial quantities of oil in the fields of Fahud, Natih and Yibal. They spent a further £25 million, and actual oil production and export began in 1967 by what is now PDO (Petroleum Develophant Oman). A main pipeline runs from the oilfields through the Samail Gap to reach the tanker terminal at Muscat's oil port, Mina Al Fahl.

GETTING THERE AND AWAY The 96km drive from Bahla northwest towards Ibri is by dual carriageway and initially skirts the southern face of Jabal Kawr, which at 2,716m is probably the second-highest peak in Oman after Jabal Shams. After 44km you pass the right turn north, which takes you to the UNESCO World Heritage Site tombs at Al Ain.

As you enter the sprawling outskirts of Ibri the roundabout's right turn north onto route 9 leads to Al Araqi, Ad Dariz (from where the right turn to Bat (sometimes spelt 'Bath') is found), Yanqul and to Ar Rustaq, eventually as route 10, some 123km away.

 WHERE TO STAY *Map, page 193.*

Ibri Oasis Hotel (29 rooms) On the main road from Ibri to Al Buraymi, over 10km out of town towards Al Buraymi & just after the sports stadium; 25 696172; e iohotel@omantel.net.om. The original hotel in Ibri, with spacious rooms & a restaurant with a limited selection of alcohol. The rooms are reasonably clean but in need of an upgrade & are expensive for what they offer. **$$**

Al Majd Hotel Apartment Within the town, 8km on your right after passing the sports stadium; 25 688272; e majdhtl@omantel.net. om; www.almajdhoteloman.com. Helpful staff & a good location are the best features here. Each room is different, so it's good to look before you choose one. Offers good value compared with the Ibri Oasis, but is less well appointed. **$**

WHERE TO EAT AND DRINK *Map, page 193.*

Qser Al Aaela Restaurant Just before entering Ibri from Al Buraymi. Very convenient if you are driving from Al Buraymi, this small restaurant seems to attract people from far & wide for its mainly rice- & meat-based dishes. They serve Chinese, Indian & Arabic dishes, all homogenised by an Indian chef; of course, the best choice by far is Indian. At the weekend there is usually a buffet offering. **$**

Shams Al Khaleej Restaurant On the main road from Ibri adjacent to the Shell petrol station. This well-established restaurant is a good choice when driving towards Al Buraymi. The food, which is prepared to order, & fresh fruit juices are good but if you are in a rush, do be aware that the service is best described as leisurely. **$**

WHAT TO SEE AND DO
Al Sulaif fort ruins قلعة السليف (⊕ *08.30–14.00 Sun–Thu; admission free*) Your approach to Ibri from Bahla is heralded by the sight of the ruins of Al Sulaif on a rocky outcrop above the wadi bed on your left. If you are coming from Al Buraymi, drive through Ibri on road 21 and continue for 13km after the Ibri Oasis Hotel and the large stadium, and you will see Al Sulaif on your right. It is signposted off the main road which was being made into a dual carriageway at the time that this book

was updated. Once the road work is finished, if you are coming from Bahla you may need to carry on to the first Ibri roundabout 1.5km ahead and do a U-turn back along road 21 and then into Al Sulaif. Park in the car park immediately in front of the fort.

Abandoned in the late 1970s in favour of the new settlement beside it, this fort is a small walled town and is well worth a visit to get a feel for a typical fortified Omani settlement. The town sits on the edge of a cliff that provides a natural defence and has been supplemented by the town wall. The fortification was built by Imam Sultan bin Saif Al Yarubi in the early 18th century. Inside and on the right is one of Oman's more traditional mosques, which has been completely restored. Its pulpit is set within a niche in the main *qibla* wall. There has been some restoration and refurbishment of the settlement in general, which has made it easy to walk around. The extensive views over the surrounding area from the tower to the rear of the walled area make it clear why the location was chosen.

Other forts The three main forts in and around Ibri are Ibri Fort, Al Araqi Fort in Al Araqi and Al Aswad Fort in Maqniyat.

Ibri Fort حصن عبري (08.30–14.30 Sun–Thu; 500bzs) Ibri Fort is in the centre of the town, and over 400 years old. Within its walls is one of the largest mosques to be found within an Omani fortification: it can accommodate about 1,000 worshippers. This mosque – the Friday mosque – has been restored and is still in use today. There is a daily market opposite Ibri's fort which is busy at the weekend, especially with animal sales.

To reach the fort, take road 9 north from the roundabout near Al Sulaif on the Bahla–Ibri road. After 2.7km you reach a roundabout, at which take the third exit, and then take the first right at the next roundabout. Drive along the narrow track under the date palms where the road zigzags for 700m west until you arrive at the rear of the fort, which has ample parking at the front.

Al Araqi Fort حصن العراقي (Al Araqi; 08.30–14.30 Sun–Thu; 500bzs) Al Araqi Fort is a small, well-restored mud-brick fort well hidden under the date palms in the centre of the town. The fort's living areas are set around the interior courtyards, and there is a central tower overlooking the plains beyond the town.

The fort is also accessed from the roundabout near Al Sulaif on the Bahla–Ibri road 9. Drive north on road 9 for 10km to a major roundabout, then take the third exit and follow the road for 1.8km southwest into the centre of Al Araqi.

Al Aswad Fort حصن الأسود (Maqniyat; freely accessible) This fort overlooks the town's main date oasis of the town from a small craggy hill. It is delightfully unrestored, which adds to the picturesque charm of its location, with a flourishing date oasis below.

To reach the fort, take road 9 north from the roundabout near Al Sulaif on the Bahla–Ibri road. Continue in the direction signed Ar Rustaq for 34km to a roundabout and take the first exit to the right (east). From this roundabout the drive is 16km, with the road crossing an open plain before entering the oasis of Maqniyat, where it crosses the wadi and then continues for another 1.3km. The fort is on the hill on the left bank of the wadi and makes a good combination visit with Bat.

BAT (بات), AL-KHUTM (الخطم) AND AL AYN (العين)

The three locations of Bat, Al-Khutm and Al Ayn together make up one of Oman's UNESCO World Heritage Sites. These feature major towers, their purpose unknown, together with tombs that date back to around 2700BC. Though the sites were known locally – indeed, British military personnel re-used some of the fine white limestone found on some tombs as building material – it wasn't until 1972 that a Danish team that had been working in Bahrain received permission to survey in Oman. The three sites are in three different locations, but are usually referred to as Bat, although the most photographed location is the one at Al Ayn.

The site at **Al-Khutm** (also Al-Wahrah), with its single tower, is often overlooked; it is the other two locations, Bat and Al Ayn, that have received the most attention – Bat for the sheer number of different remains and Al Ayn for its dramatic setting.

Bat has a number of megalithic stone towers. These have a well in the centre and several small chambers, yet despite their impressive appearance, their purpose is unclear. Several have been excavated, most notably two towers called Qasr A'Rojoom 1145 and Qasr Al Khafaji 1146. Qasr A'Rojoom (also Kasr Al Rojoom) lies just to the right of the graded track below some restored tombs, most notably a white limestone-faced one that sits on the slope of a low hill. Carbon dating has suggested it is from at least 2570BC, with human use over a period of 1,000 years, until 1610BC. Qasr Al Khafaji lies 383m southeast of Qasr A'Rojoom and is easily accessed by a track off the graded road. The main tomb area is behind a chain-link fence to the north of the track, though access may occasionally be possible if excavators are inside. The tombs within this fenced-off area are from two archaeological periods, the Hafit period starting from 3200BC and the later Umm An Nar period, which finished in around 2000BC.

The other major location is at **Al Ayn**, which has 21 tombs lined in a row on the crest of a low hill of chert, which was used to build the tombs. Dating from the early to middle 3rd millennium BC, these tombs were not a burial place for a single individual but for dozens of people, as archaeologists have found from remains within the tombs. They may have been placed in tombs individually several years or decades after the previous interment. In all cases you may be the only visitors at these sites.

GETTING THERE AND AWAY Since they are a 32km drive apart, seeing all of the sites will take a full day, and though there are several access routes, only one will be detailed here, which uses a well-graded flat road for part of the way. From the Ibri roundabout near Al Sulaif on the Bahla–Ibri road take road 9 north for 17km to a roundabout, then take the first exit right (east) at Ad Dariz (also occasionally Dreez). Almost immediately, take the right turn and then the second left turn next to some shops. From this turn you will find the tower at **Al-Khutm** after 11km, partially exposed to the right of the road on a very low hillock. From here the low hills on the left have many tombs, usually referred to as 'beehive' tombs because of their shape. Continue west and after 14km from the shops at Ad Dariz is a left turn onto a graded track just before a tower for water. Take this track and following a great sweeping bend to the right is the principal archaeological area at **Bat**, the name of the village just to the south. The most easily accessible towers are at about 15km from the shops at Ad Dariz. Continue along the track and after 37km from the shops at Ad Dariz is a T-junction onto the tarmac road from the Bahla–Ibri road 21. A left turn will lead you towards the tombs at **Al Ayn**. Follow the road and after about 5 minutes the tombs should be visible ahead on the crest of a low hill that is dominated by the great escarpment of Jabal Misht. Take the main road left (not into the village), then the right bend, and turn to park your car. At this point you are 44km from Ad Dariz.

WADI FIDA وادي فدى

This attractive wadi is either accessed from the Bahla–Ibri–Al Buraymi road 21 or the Ibri–Yanqul road 8. On road 21 continue towards Al Buraymi for 48km after the first roundabout in Ibri, and take the right turn to Dank. The road passes through the town and continues through Wadi Fida to Yanqul, a journey of 57km. Once you arrive at Dawt, the first village *en route* to Fida from Dank, the gorge narrows again, and there are caves visible in the cliffs. Only when you reach Fida after about 30km from the roundabout does the gorge become really scenic again, with many pools and date gardens offering shade. Yanqul is reached from a turn left at a junction after 48km from the roundabout on road 21.

YANQUL ينقل

Yanqul is surrounded by low but scenically attractive mountains and is an excellent stop if driving between Ibri and Suhar. The town is surrounded by low mountains and its emblem is the pyramidal **Jabal Al Hawra**, just behind the Sultan Qaboos Mosque. Oman's original gold mine, producing 500kg of gold a year, opened near Yanqul in 1994.

Yanqul's principal tourist attraction is the **Bait Al Marah** (⏲ *08.30–14.30 Sun–Thu; 500bzs*). Yanqul's splendid restored fort is a large, sprawling building dating from the mid 17th century. Its courtyard has several complexes of rooms around it and an unusual, almost subterranean-feel mosque that has its entrance in the shade of a large tamarind tree. Beyond the fort is a large *falaj* and a couple of small abandoned mud settlements to the west and north of the fort.

GETTING THERE AND AWAY Yanqul is reached via Wadi Fida or a 54km route from that key first roundabout on the Bahla–Ibri road 21. Take road 9 north towards Ar Rustaq and continue until a roundabout after 24km, then take the third exit left onto road 8 and continue to Yanqul.

The road opposite the hospital runs through to Al Wuqbah (38km) and the pass down to Suhar some 109km away.

✖ WHERE TO EAT AND DRINK In Yanqul's town centre, **Bawadi Fahood** (*on the road between Yanqul & Ibri; $*) stands out from the other restaurants in the area for its helpful service. The food is simple – a mix of fast food and Indian – but they do their best to prepare it your way.

AL BURAYMI البريمي

Al Buraymi and Mahadah are the northernmost *wilayats* of the region. Bordered by the UAE emirate of Abu Dhabi, both are known for their farming and agriculture. In Mahadah corn is the most common crop, along with dates and animal fodder. In Al Buraymi, agriculture is centred on the farming of limes, dates and alfalfa. Al Buraymi has a long history of conflict, with its many forts testimony to this. Its two main forts are Al Khandaq and Al Hillah.

Al Buraymi is significant because of its strategic situation as an oasis on trade routes between Oman, Abu Dhabi, Saudi Arabia and the rest of the Arabian Peninsula. The oasis is in fact a whole group of villages, now mainly belonging to Abu Dhabi, and a handful belonging to Oman. Al Buraymi and Al Ain are tightly juxtaposed, and so, with British assistance, Abu Dhabi and Oman staked out a complex but agreed border, with the Omani part named Al Buraymi and the Abu Dhabi part named Al Ain, after the largest village in each case.

HISTORY In 1800, the Saudi Wahhabis marched into Al Buraymi, planted their governor there and began to dominate the surrounding territory. This first Saudi state attempted to propagate itself into Oman over the next 70 years through a series of raids and invasions from its central Arabian powerbase. Raids were profitable and made in the name of *zakat*, the religious tax of Islam, rather like a church tithe. If the British had not supported the sultan, the Wahhabis might well have conquered Oman. Gradually they were forced to withdraw due to pressure from the rulers of Oman and Abu Dhabi, combined with external powers including Britain and the Ottomans. In 1952, the Saudis renewed their claim to Al Buraymi in an attempt to expand their territory again, following their conquest of Mecca and the west of Arabia by 1934. They were supported by the USA, who were engaged in oil exploration in the adjoining Rub Al Khali area of Saudi Arabia. A legal process was largely unsuccessful in resolving the dispute and in 1955 the Saudis were driven out by the British and the Trucial Oman Scouts. The Saudis later supported the imamate of Ghalib and his brother Talib and the associated Al Jabal Al Akhdar War between 1954 and 1959 in Oman (see box, page 219).

GETTING THERE AND AWAY Those wishing to roam around Oman will undoubtedly be surprised by the internal border controls on entering Al Buraymi from other areas of Oman. They add considerable time and uncertainty to any road journey and all visitors need to ensure that passports and car documents are available.

The two main transport hubs are south of the suq, next to the Al Madheef border for **taxis**; and for **bus** services on the roundabout south of the Sultan Qaboos Mosque.

Entering Al Buraymi There are two options for non-GCC nationals entering Al Buraymi from the UAE. Within the city itself there is a single border crossing through the border fence at **Hilli** well north of the city centre. The border formalities change with little if any notice; at the time of writing, a non-GCC national exiting the UAE pays 35 dirhams at this border and, if travelling beyond Al Buraymi, a RO5 visa charge at the Wadi Al Jizi Omani border 43km away on the road to Suhar. This border at Hilli is congested and not well organised. The border at **Jabal Hafit/Mezayid**, which has both UAE and Omani border posts, is far more sensible to use, especially if you intend to drive on to Ibri (at present, the same charges apply). You can then swing into Al Buraymi from further along the road, although this is a 75km journey. GCC nationals have a third option: the **Al Madheef** border, which is just north of Al Ain city centre and main Al Ain oasis. These three border crossings are also used to exit Al Buraymi into the UAE with the restrictions for entry detailed above.

From the rest of Oman there are two options. From Ibri and the roundabout near Al Sulaif, a journey of 123km will bring you to the roundabout for Wadi Saa. Turn right (west) and after stopping at the **Wadi Saa** border post to show your passport and other documentation, and to get a stamp if you do intend to exit into Al Ain at Hilli, you will eventually join road 7 from Suhar and arrive in Al Buraymi after 72km. Alternatively, if travelling from Suhar on Al Batinah highway, drive from the **Wadi Al Jizi** roundabout using road 7 into Al Buraymi. Again you will cross an Omani 'border' complex in Wadi Al Jizi, about 58km from Al Batinah highway, where you will need your passport and other documents. In the case of both Wadi Saa and Wadi Al Jizi, if you are only holding an Oman visit visa, rather than a residence visa, your visa will be cancelled and a new visa will have to be obtained to return to the rest of Oman. As with all other border formalities, this is subject to change.

Leaving Al Buraymi To travel from Al Buraymi into the rest of Oman, take the dual carriageway east from the roundabout at the Sultan Qaboos Mosque,

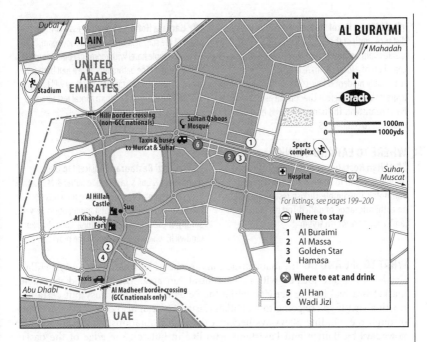

For listings, see pages 199–200

Where to stay

1 Al Buraimi
2 Al Massa
3 Golden Star
4 Hamasa

Where to eat and drink

5 Al Han
6 Wadi Jizi

past the Al Buraimi Hotel and Lulu and under the massive arched entrance gate monument. To reach Wadi Saa and Ibri take the right slip road shortly after passing under this gate, and after the Wadi Saa 'border' post follow the road to the main roundabout, where you turn left to Ibri. Road 7 to Suhar continues along the dual carriageway after the entrance gate monument, swings left and, after undertaking border formalities at the Omani 'border' complex, continues towards Suhar.

 WHERE TO STAY *Map, above.*

There are no upper-range hotels in Al Buraimi. If you are looking for something in this bracket then Al Ain (closely connected with Al Buraimi and to which you are free to travel if you abide by the border regulations) offers the Hilton Al Ain (*www. hilton.co.uk*), the Al Ain Rotana Hotel (*www.rotana.com*), the InterContinental Hotel Al Ain (*www.ichotelsgroup.com*), and the Mercure Grand Jabal Hafit Hotel (*www.mercure.com*), all in the **$$$$$** bracket.

Some hotels in Al Buraimi seem to have abandoned the notion of websites, and in some cases email, so customers rely on online booking websites.

Al Buraimi Hotel (59 rooms) On the main road from Suhar to Al Buraimi town centre; `\`25 642010; e alburaimihotel@hotmail.com. This is a relatively old hotel that is now lacking in glamour & in need of considerable refurbishment to bring it up to the standards just across the border fence in Al Ain. Despite this, the grounds & spacious rooms in the main building do offer a comfortable 1- or 2-night stay if you stay. There is an annex to the rear that has cheaper, lower-standard rooms. At

weekends ask to be in a quiet room as there may be entertainment in the grounds. **$$**

Golden Star Hotel (100 rooms) Just off the main road from Al Buraimi to Suhar, opposite the Al Buraimi Hotel; `\`25 654040. One of the newest hotels in Al Buraimi, this is in relatively good condition. It has a reasonable choice of small restaurants nearby. The staff are helpful & there is a small restaurant that can offer room service. **$$**

🏠 **Al Massa Hotel** (60 rooms) Within walking distance south of the suq & forts; ☎ 25 653007; e sales@almasahotels.com; www.almasahotels.com. Part of a local chain, Al Massa Hotel offers reasonably modern & low-cost rooms & suites. Inspect the room before checking in as cleanliness is not consistent. The Hamasa Hotel is next door if you want to compare. **$**

🏠 **Hamasa Hotel** (28 rooms) Less than 1km south of the suq, next to the Toyota showroom; ☎ 25 651200. Simple hotel with rooms needing complete refurbishment. The bathrooms have a half bath & shower. There is no restaurant, but they will bring food to your room for you from a local restaurant. **$**

✖ **WHERE TO EAT AND DRINK** *Map, page 199.*

✖ **Al Han Restaurant** Just off the main road from Al Buraymi to Suhar & close to the Golden Star Hotel. This Simple Turkish restaurant offers an authentic range of grilled Turkish food. Their lamb chops are worth trying. **$**

✖ **Wadi Jizi Restaurant** Adjacent to the roundabout & bus & taxi stop to Suhar & Muscat. Very convenient if you are waiting for a bus or taxi. The food is nothing outstanding but is served quickly. If you're in a rush, ask for a 'kubz chicken sandwich', which you can eat on the move. **$**

WHAT TO SEE AND DO The main attractions are the Al Khandaq Fort and Al Hillah Castle, which are located within the central suq area. The fruit and vegetable market is a real hub of activity, while the general suq is less busy but certainly worth a visit if you're going to Al Hillah Castle. You can also drive along or stroll through the winding alleyways between the date plantations, which are tended nowadays by Baluch and Pakistanis who live in huts on the edge of the oasis. To the south of Al Khandaq Fort are rolled bundles of date palm leaves, variously used for walling, as they allow a breeze to pass through them, a reasonably solid platform for storing things, or as a covering for laying dates out to dry in the sun.

Al Khandaq Fort حصن الخندق (🕐 *08.30–14.30 Sun–Thu; 500bzs*) This fort is located just over 3km southwest of the Sultan Qaboos Mosque and is in the area of the central suq. Recently restored, it provides a good example of the ancient strategy of using a defensive trench or dry moat to protect and strengthen the stronghold. In its current form, the fort dates from the early 19th century, with its towers giving good views towards the old Al Buraymi oasis and its picturesque, decaying houses.

Al Hillah Castle حصن الحلة (🕐 *08.30–14.30 Sun–Thu; admission free*) This castle is situated not far north from Al Khandaq Fort and overlooks the central suq. It is notable for its plasterwork decorations and motifs. This was previously the residence of the sheikh who governed Al Buraymi on behalf of the sultan in Muscat. Like Al Khandaq Fort, it has been restored.

FROM AL BURAYMI TO MAHADAH من البريمي إلى محضة

Mahadah is located 29km northeast of Al Buraymi; take the road from the roundabout near the Sultan Qaboos Mosque. The road passes **Fossil Valley**, a right turn onto a track about 10km from the Sultan Qaboos Mosque roundabout. The slopes of this horseshoe-shaped escarpment of honey-coloured limestone have small fossils, especially those on the north-facing area.

Beyond Fossil Valley, following the tarmac road to Mahadah, is a continuation of the same range of hills; the **Hanging Gardens**, named after the limited areas of vegetation that are found below the escarpment after another 4km, at the very end of the track. Neither of these are especially worth a specific journey, but make a decent add-on, especially in the morning and if you are interested in fossils. They are usually deserted.

HUSN AN NAD (AL NAD CASTLE) حصن بيت الند *(Mahadah; ☉ 08.30–14.30 Sun–Thu; free admission)* This small fortified residence is in the small town of Mahadah. On the eastern edge of the oasis, it has a circular main tower and domestic rooms set around a small courtyard. To get there follow the road from Al Buraymi northeast and pass through Mahadah town. Immediately after the date oasis on the left there is a road that takes you northwest for 200m to the castle and after the turn there is a substantial water dam on your right.

UPDATES WEBSITE

You can post your comments and recommendations, and read the latest feedback and updates from other readers online at www.bradtupdates.com/oman.

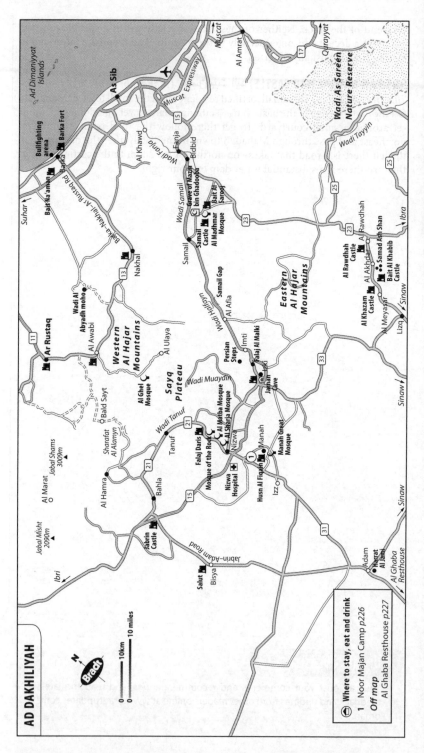

AD DAKHILIYAH

N

Bradt

0 — 10km
0 — 10 miles

Where to stay, eat and drink
1 Noor Majan Camp p226

Off map
Al Ghaba Resthouse p227

Ad Dimaniyyat Islands

Bullfighting arena
Barka Fort
Barka
Bait Na'aman
As Sib

Muscat Expressway
Al Amrat
Qurayyat

Wadi As Sareen Nature Reserve

Baka-Nakhal—Al Rustaq Rd
Al Khawd
Fanja
Bidbid

Wadi Fanja
Wadi Tayyin

Suhar

Nakhal
Wadi Al Abyadh moho
Wadi Samail
Grave of Mazin bin Ghadooba
Bait Ar Saroqi
Samail Castle
Al Madhmar Mosque
Samail

Wadi Halfayn
Samail Gap
Al Afia

Eastern Al Hajar Mountains

Al Rawdhah Castle
Al Akhdar
Samad Ash Shan
Bait Al Khabib Castle

Al Khazam Castle
Al Meyafar
Lizq
Sinaw
Rawdhah
Ibra

Western Al Hajar Mountains
Ar Rustaq
Al Awabi

Al Ulaya

Sayq Plateau

Imti
Falaj Al Malki
Persian Steps
Jabal Akhdar
Cave

Al Ghel Mosque
Bald Sayt
Sharafat Al Alamyn
Wadi Muaydin
Al Matha Mosque
Al Sharja Mosque
Nizwa
Husn Al Fiqayn
Manah Great Mosque

Jabal Shams 3009m
Al Marat
Wadi Tanuf
Tanuf
Falaj Daris
Mosque of the Rock
Nizwa Hospital
Manah
Izz

Jabal Misht 2090m
Al Hamra
Bahla

Jabrin Castle

Jabrin–Adam Road

Ibri
Salut
Bisya

Sinaw

Adam
Harat Al Jami
Al Ghaba Resthouse

202

7

Ad Dakhiliyah الداخلية

The Ad Dakhiliyah translates as 'the Interior' and lies southwest of Muscat. Spread over 31,900km², it incorporates part of the Western Al Hajar Mountains, including Al Jabal Al Akhdar and Jabal Shams. South of the mountains is the vast central plain that extends beyond Adam.

The Western Al Hajar Mountains and the area immediately surrounding them hold the main population centres and places of interest in the Ad Dakhiliyah Governorate. This range climbs abruptly from the wadi and plain, creating an extraordinary wall of rock as you drive around its core. The Western Al Hajar Mountains are over 2,000m and rise to Jabal Shams, at just over 3,000m. Part of the Eastern Al Hajar Mountains also extend into the Ad Dakhiliyah, and although they are lower and less vertiginous, they are also quite dramatic. Steep-sided wadis cut through the mountains and one – Wadi Al Halfayn – reaches the sea near Muhut, stretching a distance of almost 300km. Scattered in close proximity to these wadis are the towns and villages of the region, each having developed around the *aflaj* water systems that literally give life to this region.

The Western Al Hajar Mountains are mainly limestone laid down over several different periods. You will find limestone which ranges in date from the Permian period (299 to 251 million years ago) through to the Cretaceous period (145.5 to 65.5 million years ago) as well as chert from the late Jurassic period (199.6 to 145.5 million years ago). Look carefully, and you are almost certain to spot fossils within the limestone; indeed, several hotels in Al Jabal Al Akhdar are built on rocks littered with fossils of pre-coral structures. There are several caves in the region: Al Hoota Cave near Al Hamra (pages 231–2) has been made into a show cave, while a more recent find, 'Khaslat Al Rowais', is located in the central mountains. The Eastern Al Hajar Mountains in the Ad Dakhiliyah region are ophiolite, the igneous mineral rock formation. The geological movement of these ophiolite rocks colliding with the Western Al Hajar Mountains has caused the dramatic uplifting and tilting of the strata.

This region contains some of Oman's most acclaimed historical sites. They include the historical fortification at Salut dating back to around 1000BC, together with surrounding archaeological finds that are even older. There have been a number of finds at Adam, some of which have been restored, including 4,000-year-old graves. However, the most accessible historical sites are the restored fortifications such as Bahla Fort (pages 236–7), which is probably the oldest original fort, although its current form dates from the 18th century.

Ad Dakhiliyah has played a prime role in many of Oman's cultural and political events for almost 2,000 years. It featured in battles between Arab migrants and Persian generals. The Ibadhi religion developed and became embedded in the region from the 9th century onwards and many of the imams of Oman are from families that have their roots here.

The limited scope for economic development in arid Oman obliged the rulers to look elsewhere for income and gradually this outward-looking, trade-oriented ruling class and other sections of the population resulted in a cultural separation between those who remain in the historical heartlands and those who moved to the coast or overseas.

As the 19th and 20th centuries progressed, the interior and coastal Oman became culturally and economically separated, so much so that the interior was referred to as Oman, and the coast as Muscat. When local people left the coast to go to the interior they would say, 'I'm going to Oman'.

This separation became codified with the Treaty of Seeb (Al Sib) in 1920, which recognised a difference between the interior of Oman and the coastal areas. The interior was administered by an imam and the coast by the sultan. Nonetheless, these differences have gradually become less intense following the reunification of Oman from the 1950s and especially following the accession of Sultan Qaboos.

The region is an important agricultural area, both historically and currently. Apart from dates and fodder crops, the unique climate of the higher *jabals* facilitates the growth of a wide range of fruit trees, plants and shrubs, which are a crucial part of the region's economy. Today there is an increase in industry, focused on Nizwa's industrial area with its food manufacturing and ceramic and plastics factories. Private education is offered at Nizwa University, although there has been some discussion about this becoming a state-run institution. Manah, south of Nizwa, is home to a major private power station. As with much of Oman, there is increasing focus on tourism, giving rise to new hotels.

With a population of 416,858 in 2015, Ad Dakhiliyah Governorate is Oman's third most populous region. The largest towns are Nizwa with 110,256 residents and Bahla with 77,276, followed by Samail, Izki, Bidbid, Al Hamra, Adam and Manah. As with other governorates, there is a substantial proportion of non-Omani within the total population – 22.7% are non-Omanis and 77.3% are Omani nationals.

GETTING THERE AND AWAY

BY CAR The drive from Al Qurum in Muscat is straightforward: simply follow the Muscat Expressway west until junction 10B, signed Nizwa, then continue south on road 15 (a good, tarmacked route with street lighting the entire way). An alternative would be to take the rough 4x4 route through Wadi Bani Awf (pages 160–1). The Nizwa area makes the perfect base for an exploration of the region, and a stay of two or possibly three nights will allow you to experience most of what it has to offer while also providing an interesting and marked contrast to the city of Muscat.

BY TAXI Taxis that will take you to Nizwa are available near Burj Al Sahwa, the clock tower just west of Muscat International Airport. Use your best negotiation skills; getting a shared taxi may cost RO3, while a private one is likely to cost around RO10.

BY BUS Most buses travelling to Salalah in the south go via the interior and drop-offs/pickups can be made at any of the designated bus stops (pages 59–60).

CAR RENTAL

A 4x4 is essential if you want to make the most of this mountainous region and visit Al Jabal Al Akhdar. Your hotel should be able to organise a rental car for you as smaller companies do come and go, or you could arrange it yourself with one of the companies in Birkat Al Mawz.

Buses run to Nizwa during the day from the bus hub around the Sultan Qaboos Mosque in Ruwi, although booking is advised as demand is high. If you wish to get to Nizwa town centre, take a Mwasalat bus from the main bus hub in Ruwi. This can drop you at Firq or some will carry on to the town centre, and from either of these two locations it is easy to find a taxi to take you to your final destination. The journey to Nizwa takes around 2.5 hours and costs around RO3, and the same back again.

TOUR OPERATORS

If you are not intending to travel around the area independently, it is necessary to pre-arrange any tours through operators in Muscat in order to avoid disappointment (pages 83–5). They will either collect you from your hotel in the region (which is likely to be in Nizwa), or transport you from Muscat, whichever suits your needs best.

 ## WHERE TO STAY

Accommodation in this region is mainly concentrated in and around Nizwa, listed on pages 218–21, with other establishments in several mountain locations and Bahla.

CAMPING AND PICNIC SPOTS Away from the towns there are vast open spaces for you to camp in. You can find solitude deep in the wadis, but be careful to keep well above flash flood levels. High in the mountains the winter months are chilly if not freezing, while the summers are cool. Camping is possible all year round.

ACTIVITIES

All major tourist destinations into the *jabals* are signposted from the Nizwa–Bahla road with large brown tourist signposts. You will need a 4x4 to access these. For independent travellers arriving in saloon cars, it is recommended that you pre-book any tours to Al Jabal Al Akhdar, the Al Hoota Cave (check if these caves are open as they do close on a regular basis after flooding by rain and take a very long time to reopen), or any other *jabal* trips with the tour operators based in Muscat, so that you are not disappointed. Caving, rock climbing, trekking and wadi bashing are all possible in this region. For caving and climbing you will need to arrange your trip through a tour operator in Muscat (pages 83–5).

USEFUL TELEPHONE NUMBERS

MEDICAL FACILITIES
- **Adam** ✆ 25 434055
- **Bahla** ✆ 25 419233, 420013
- **Izki** ✆ 25 341755
- **Al Jabal Al Akhdar** ✆ 25 429055
- **Nizwa** ✆ 25 449155
- **Samail** ✆ 25 352236

POLICE STATIONS
Ad Dakhiliyah Police
Headquarters ✆ 25 414899
Nizwa ✆ 25 425222
Bahla ✆ 25 419099
Adam ✆ 25 434099
Samail ✆ 25 350099
Izki ✆ 25 340099
Bid Bid ✆ 25 360099

ROCK CLIMBING AND BOULDERING Numerous climbs and routes have been pioneered in this region. Wadis Kamah, Muaydin, A'Nakhr and Tanuf have tributaries that offer drops of over 50m. Climbs can be organised through specialised tour operators in Muscat (pages 83–5). *Rock Climbing in Oman*, published by Apex, will certainly be of interest to you if climbing is your thing (page 336).

CAVING Al Hoota Cave near Al Hamra is the caving destination of the interior (pages 231–2), and it is now accessible to everyone as a major tourist attraction. For further caving opportunities in other regions of Oman, see pages 251 and 296.

FANJA فنجا

If you're heading out from Muscat on your first exploration of the interior, Fanja will be your first opportunity to explore an old walled town. It is now deserted apart from a few houses at its very edge.

GETTING THERE AND AWAY Fanja is on the Muscat–Nizwa road 15, 27km after Burj Al Sahwa roundabout, or 18km after junction 10B for Nizwa on the Muscat Expressway. The new town of Fanja is signposted off to the right just before the town's Sultan Qaboos Mosque; after taking this exit a right turn a further 3.5km on, just after the bridge, will take you towards the old village area. Park your car shortly after you make the turn. The road is very narrow and the walk is not far. Make your way through the date plantation to a largely abandoned village that looks down on you from its cliff. If you do not have your own transport you will need to be dropped off on the main road by the bus from Ruwi bus station and walk the 2km to the village.

WHAT TO SEE AND DO Look carefully as you get closer to see the old town of Fanja and you will see its two famous **towers** set up high on either side above the old village, built of the same colour as the cliff face and therefore surprisingly easy to miss. Your route is along the tarmac road that carries on upwards. You follow the right exterior walls of the old town until the small entrance gate provides a way in. Once inside you will notice one or two inhabited houses that look quite smartly renovated and boast television aerials, but apart from these the houses beyond are empty. Most interesting, however, is the walk up the sloping escarpment past the old cannon to the fortification towers. The one to the left (south) of the old village is far easier to access than its partner to the north beyond the small wadi. There is a kind of reservoir beside it, originally used by the inhabitants before the days of piped water, and the views out over the date gardens and the majestic sweep of the wadi are very impressive, especially at sunset when the rocks glow a deep ochre. Beyond the gate into the old town are the date gardens, many with splendid entrance doors. This oasis is watered by hot springs that trickle out of the small hill to the west, below the old town.

If you wish to return to Muscat and have a good 4x4 you can also drive down into the wadi bed and then north through water pools and picnic spots along the Wadi Fanja and back towards the coast as far as Al Khawd. Turn into a modern housing area between the bridge and the Sultan Qaboos Mosque, follow several turns, and the winding route will take you down to the only access route to the wadi, just at the base of the ophiolite hill. Al Khawd is the site of a small private castle, the upcoming Botanic Garden and, by tarmac road, the Sultan Qaboos University. Please note that after rains this route through the wadi is not possible.

THE SAMAIL GAP فجوة سمائل

The Samail Gap – the traditional natural pass through the northern *jabals* that separates the Al Hajar Mountains into its western and eastern ranges – is 60km inland from Muscat Airport and the coast, and forms the main access route from Oman's coast to the interior. It starts at Samail and ends at Izki, and following its route is not only the main road from Muscat to Nizwa, but also oil and gas pipelines flowing down to the coast. Flowing in the opposite direction is a water pipeline from the coastal desalination plants into the towns of the interior. The road climbs gradually from the coast to about 600m above sea level.

In geological terms it is also the gap between the limestone range of the Al Jabal Al Akhdar and the lower jagged ophiolite hills that head off into the Ash Sharqiyyah. If you are venturing out of Muscat for the first time, it is the colossal massif of the Al Jabal Al Akhdar, its peaks towering another 1,400m above you on your right, that will draw your eye. The extraordinary tilt of the layers of rock is mesmerising, even for the geological novice, with the occasional cleft snaking off into dark shadowy ravines. Its sharp lines and jagged layers make it immensely photogenic, especially in the early morning and late afternoon. Sometimes around midday, the exceptional heat of the summer months can make it disappear from view altogether behind a haze, a most disconcerting experience when you know it is looming just there behind the shimmering blur.

SAMAIL سمائل Like many Omani towns, Samail is divided into two parts, the lower (*sufelat*) and the upper (*aliyat*). Samail Sufelat is Ghafiri and had the great fort (*husn*) where the *wali* lived until the 1960s, and which also housed a Quran school, judge's office and prison. Samail Aliyat was Hinawi. The two parts of the settlement had many fights against each other. There are around 115 forts or towers defending the area, such was its importance as a trade route. The many small villages of Wadi Samail, with their farms and gardens, are watered by nearly 200 *falaj* channels stretching over 16km. Some of the best dates in Oman come from Samail and are packed in the local date factory 3km east from the castle.

Getting there and away If you follow the signs to Samail from the Muscat–Nizwa road 15, you will **drive** through the new town and out beyond for a few kilometres, where the old town is heralded by two watchtowers on a hill rising above the date gardens.

Without your own transport you will have to get the **bus** from Muscat to drop you on the main road and walk the 2km into the town, or wait on the off-chance of a **taxi** passing by.

Often believed to have been introduced by the Persians in pre-Islamic times, the *falaj* is a water channel that leads from its source to the fields where irrigation is required. Today there is increasing evidence that, at the very least, *aflaj* (the plural of *falaj*) developed independently in Oman. The earliest evidence is reported by the Hajar Project (previously University of Birmingham) team, which dates a *falaj* near Bisya, southwest of Bahla, to around 3000BC.

There are three origins of the water which supplies the *aflaj*. The first of these is an underground water aquifer with horizontal manmade tunnels, which requires innumerable vertical access shafts into it, to take the water from source to supply area. This underground variant is the classic *daudi* (*qanat* in Iran or *khettara* in Morocco) and represents around 23.5% of the 3,000 operational *aflaj* in Oman. Falaj Al Khatmayn in Birkat Al Mawz is a *daudi falaj* and is one of the five *aflaj* registered as a UNESCO World Heritage Site. Secondly, making use of surface or sub-surface flow are *ghaili aflaj*, which represent about 48.5% of Oman's *aflaj*. These will have a manmade dam to pond the water, such as in Wadi Bani Khalid, which then has channels to direct the water into the fields downstream. These *ghaili aflaj*, especially those that have not silted up, are prone to damage by flash floods. Finally, a third form of water supply comes from water springs: these are called *aini*. With about 28% of the total number of *aflaj* in Oman, these are usually found in mountainous areas of which Misfat Al Abriyeen is a good example.

Maintaining the *aflaj* requires much skill and money, and the state of them has therefore tended to be linked to the economic health of the community. During the prosperous Al Yarubi times (17th and 18th centuries) the *aflaj* were, not surprisingly, in excellent repair and many new ones were dug. One ingenious

What to see and do Set on a crag, **Samail Castle** (⊕ *08.00–14.00 Sun–Thu; 500bzs*) is one of two fortifications usually open in Samail. The current castle has been attacked and destroyed several times, notably in the mid 17th century by Imam Nasir bin Murshid Al Yarubi. Most of the accommodation is set below the upper battlements, but the steep climb up to the battlements gives superb views of an extraordinary expanse of date oasis and the original settlement of Sufailat Samail.

The first Omani to embrace Islam, Mazin bin Ghadooba, came from Samail. He was responsible for building one of the world's first mosques, **Al Madhmar Mosque**, in the year 8 Hijri (about AD629) after meeting the Prophet Muhammad in Medina. The mosque can be seen taking the road from the castle, turning left after 250m and then left again at the first turn, a total distance of about 2km. Newly rebuilt, the mosque is not accessible to non-Muslims, but it is possible to visit the **grave of Mazin bin Ghadooba**. This is located 250m northwest of the castle on the opposite bank of the wadi, hidden at the base of the hill behind the palms next to the main road through the area. If visiting it, you should wear conservative clothing (including scarves for women) and remove all footwear.

A second fort can be seen in the Al Khobar district of Samail. From Samail Castle turn right onto the main road that runs through the wadi and continue until a signed left turn after 4.3km. **Bait Al Sarooj** (⊕ *08.00–14.00 Sun–Thu; admission free*), locally called Bait Al Jabri after a family who previously lived in it, is essentially a fortified house. Two watchtowers on the crest of the hill above the fort provided additional defence. Inside, the building has light from two small, deep courtyards and storage rooms on the ground floor, with living accommodation above.

aspect of their construction was the way in which they crossed a wadi bed. They were dug down vertically on one bank to reach below the wadi floor, and then continued horizontally below the wadi bed until the wadi was crossed. A vertical shaft was then dug to a point fractionally lower than the upstream bank, thereby creating a siphon system. This ensured that there was no bridging structure that might be destroyed during a flash flood.

The *falaj* structure tends to be the collective inherited property of the village inhabitants or group of landowners. The water is allocated based on the original share following the construction of a *falaj*, and due to subdivision because of inheritance after death or accumulation after a water rights purchase, the actual ownership of the shares is extraordinarily complicated. Allocation is usually based on a period of time; perhaps a farm will be entitled to water for 30 minutes during a period of a week or ten days. In settlements where the flow of water is little more than a trickle allocation is based on the volume held in a storage cistern. There is usually a certain amount of unallocated water that is auctioned off, with the proceeds helping with the upkeep of the system. An nominated worthy known as the *wakil* is appointed to administer the system, and he is also in charge of repairs, which are usually funded by the sale of the unallocated water and income from land and crops under the ownership of the *falaj* management.

In many village communities the *falaj* is still, but only just, part of the essential way of life, and one of the standard exchanges for a visitor on arrival at a neighbouring village might be 'And how are the *aflaj*?' 'Full, Inshallah.' Times are changing, however, and knowledge and skills are rapidly disappearing as Oman's economy moves away from agriculture and into a system based on industry and services.

IMTI (إمطي) AND AROUND Some 100km from Burj Al Sahwa or 93km from the Nizwa turn on the Muscat Expressway is the turn to the villages of Imti and Izki. From the exit you come to a roundabout, where you should take the first right and continue for a total of 3.2km to reach a parking area opposite a mosque. In front of the mosque, between two buildings, you can join a route that will take you through a linear village that follows a *falaj* channel and is the original settlement at Imti. The houses are built of typical *jabal* drystone walls with arched entrances over the passageways, making an interesting contrast to the mud-brick housing further ahead on the same walk. After about 400m you will see a wall on the left, which runs up the slope for about 170m. Continue on for another 400m and on the hill above the mud-brick houses is what is referred to as the Persian village, although it would be more aptly described as a fortress, given that it has about 4,000m² of stone walling. This is well off the tourist route, though it is difficult to understand why. The stone houses at the start of the walk are still in sufficiently good condition that you can imagine families calling out to you from them, while the contrast between the mountain slope on the left of the *falaj* and the oasis on the right makes it clear just how precious water is for a desert country. It is the fortress, however, that really makes this a treat. The fact that it is standing is remarkable, especially as it is Persian, as has been claimed. Go closer, however, and you will see that the walls are not mud brick, or even bricks secured with a cement, but nothing more than drystone walling and assembled with such skill that the fortress is still standing hundreds of years after being built.

From the parking area opposite the mosque, the wadi to the west leads into the mountains, reaching a dam after less than 2km. The road continues to the left

THE DATE TREE

Date palms are single-sex trees and only a female tree produces fruit; male palms are simply required for pollination. It is not unusual to have a single male palm provide the pollen for 100 female palms. The only way this ratio can be sustained is by hand pollination; a random breeze or insect is of no benefit. In January and February a man has to climb to the crown of a female tree with male flowers and pollinate the female flowers. The dates grow from the size of a small pea to their familiar ripe form. From mid-May the date harvest gets into full swing. The centre of the date trade is to be found at Fanja Suq in northern Oman (pages 206–7), from where dates are traded to Dubai and other Gulf countries. Brought by the truckload from surrounding oases, the dates are bought and sold in a traditional measure called *manns*, roughly 4kg. Between 3 and 3.5 tonnes of dates arrive every day at the suq, from where they are traded by professional date auctioneers, who take a 10% commission. Prices start out high, at about RO5–7 per kilo, then as the season progresses they can drop to as low as 500bzs by peak harvest in mid-June. With up to 150kg of dates produced per tree, the farmer may receive RO100 or more for preferred varieties. The season ends in late summer.

of the dam, where you will see two wadis. The left one will lead you to the base of a further deep wadi after about 2.1km. This is the start of the **Persian Steps** – 1,400 steps cut into the rock of the *jabal* to reach the high plateau at 1,800m. The ascent from where you stand is around 1,300m, reaching the tarmac road between Birkat Al Mawz and the Sayq Plateau. The Persian Steps are reasonably well made, but they're bound to test your joints. The climb up the zigzagging steps takes a minimum of 4 hours and requires a good level of fitness. Locals who live in the mountain villages can do it in under 2 hours in flip-flops, using the technique of gliding effortlessly in one flowing movement from rock to rock. This technique is especially noticeable in their descent, where they appear virtually to run down the mountain with none of the jarring movements so wearing on the knees. As you go higher you will enjoy extraordinary views over the crags and scrubby acacia towards the highway you have driven along and Samail. Overall, the route requires fitness and a full day to do it comfortably one-way. An encouraging guide and more than sufficient water are a must, as you will be trekking in full sun for most of the time. You need to plan what you will do after the ascent, be it have a vehicle collect you, or camp in the cool mountain air.

WADI HALFAYN وادي حلفين About an hour's drive from Muscat will bring you to this spectacular gorge. It makes a fine camping spot, as there are many large *sidr* trees for shade. You will need your own transport to reach it. Take the turn-off to Al Afia some 30km beyond Samail on the Nizwa road, then turn right onto the track 2.8km later, heading towards the nearby gorge. Park by the trees and continue on foot through the large boulders littering the wadi floor. One of them, on the left some 200m from the parking spot, has rock art etched into it.

A disused *falaj*, the **Falaj Sahama**, runs along the right-hand side of the wadi gorge. The easiest option is to climb up to it and walk along it allowing 2 hours to reach where the *falaj* meets the first of many deep pools. The scenery is attractive, with palms and wild flowers. Purple marks on the rocks show the trail on to this wadi's own, less complete version of the Persian Steps (see above).

IZKI إزكي The Samail Gap ends at the inland town of Izki, which lies along the course of the Wadi Halfayn, one of Oman's great wadis. The wadi is normally dry, but after heavy rain a raging torrent runs off into the desert and may block the main road on to Nizwa.

Izki – known as Jarnan in pre-Islamic times, and renamed Izki as a derivative of *zakah* (an Islamic alms tax) – is renowned for its tribal intrigues, and originally had different settlements for its Hinawi (Yemeni from southern Arabia) and Ghafiri (Nizari from the Nejd in Saudi Arabia in the north). Intermarriage between the two was taboo until very recently, and their dialects retain separate characteristics.

Getting there and away To reach Al Yemen, An Nizar and Jarnan Cave (see below), there is a left turn just after the military barracks 2.4km after the roundabout for Imti and Izki. Follow this road to a roundabout after 2.7km and take the first exit right. The road drops into the wadi and passes by some date trees and houses to take you to the main gate of Al Yemen.

After Izki the main Nizwa road bears right to follow the line of the Al Jabal Al Akhdar. On this bend there is a left (south) turn onto a tarmac road to Sinaw, (pages 245–6), and beyond it the road to Masirah Island. If you choose to continue along the main road, it is about 39km by road from Izki to Nizwa's suq.

What to see and do Izki has one of Oman's UNESCO World Heritage-listed *aflaj*, the **Falaj Al Malki**, which has one of its several sources near Imti. Having exited from the Muscat–Nizwa highway at the Imti and Izki exit, drive for 3.1km and you will find the *falaj* on your left. You will see an inverted siphon taking the water below the wadi and into the town. The route of the *falaj* into the gardens is difficult to follow as it disappears underground several times. It is still well maintained and is a superb example of a stone-roofed tunnel, some 6ft (2m) high. In places steps lead down to it where it flows about at 3m below ground level, with a water depth of around 20cm.

The two ancient settlements in the heart of Izki are **Al Yemen** and **An Nizar**. These are separated by **Izki Castle**, which was probably built in 1884. Al Yemen is most easily accessed from the main gateway on its eastern side, overlooking the wadi. This is a well laid-out settlement that was abandoned in the mid 1980s. The old mud mosque is diagonally opposite the gate at the far end of the town.

An Nizar is on the other side of the castle and the modern mosque. The layout is less easy to explore and perhaps more interesting as a result. Immediately below An Nizar is **Jarnan Cave**, which according to legend was once home to a golden bull. The cave itself has the appearance of a manmade tunnel, and unfortunately any trace of the bull has disappeared.

BIRKAT AL MAWZ بركة الموز

From junction 10B for Nizwa on the Muscat Expressway it is 108km to Birkat Al Mawz ('Pool of Bananas'). Birkat Al Mawz (also Birkat Al Mauz/Moz) was a town of the Bani Riyam, whose sheikh, Suleyman bin Himyar, was a rebel leader in the Jabal War.

GETTING THERE AND AWAY If driving, Birkat Al Mawz is signposted off the main Nizwa road at the Imti and Izki exit, and is reached via a right turn some 14km after Izki. From Izki, turn down into Birkat Al Mawz past the date and banana plantations and the old villages.

If you're coming from Nizwa Suq, drive south to Firq, then continue straight across the traffic lights on a signed route to Birkat Al Mawz and Izki. At the third roundabout, which is at Birkat Al Mawz, take the third exit, north, which will take you left into the town. Those coming by **bus** from Muscat or Nizwa will have to ask to be dropped on the main road next to this roundabout and Bank Muscat, from where it's less than 1km on foot to the town's small suq.

WHAT TO SEE AND DO The British RAF was invited by Sultan Said to destroy Suleyman's fine palace at Birkat Al Mawz, which they did. It was restored and opened to the public in 1999, and today the serene two-storey **fortified house (or castle)** is known as **Bayt Ar Rudaydah**. It guards the entrance to Wadi Muaydin, another key route up into the mountains and the point from where the military road up to the Sayq Plateau and Al Jabal Al Akhdar begins. Suleyman, whose base was at Tanuf, had

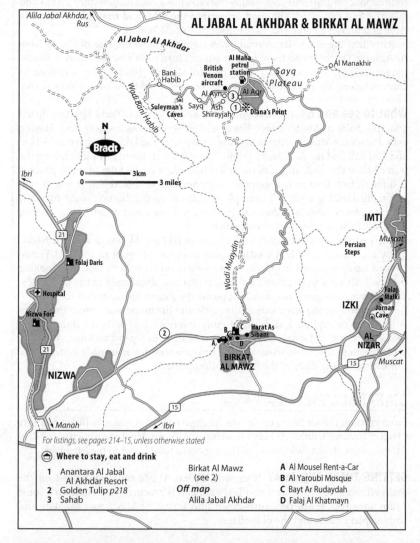

For listings, see pages 214–15, unless otherwise stated

🏠 **Where to stay, eat and drink**

1 Anantara Al Jabal	Birkat Al Mawz	A Al Mousel Rent-a-Car
Al Akhdar Resort	(see 2)	B Al Yaroubi Mosque
2 Golden Tulip *p218*	*Off map*	C Bayt Ar Rudaydah
3 Sahab	Alila Jabal Akhdar	D Falaj Al Khatmayn

a third private palace at Sayq, which has today completely disappeared, bombed again and then utterly demolished to serve as a lesson to the Al Jabal Al Akhdar villagers. A modern white fort was subsequently built for a detachment of the SAF (Sultan's Armed Forces), which has been permanently garrisoned up on the Sayq Plateau ever since.

The castle has an excellent small arms collection inside. At the time of writing the castle seemed to be on the point of opening yet remained permanently closed; if the main door is ajar, speak with the guard and if you are lucky he may let you enter. A visit is very rewarding.

An impressive *daudi falaj* (see box, pages 208–9), **Falaj Al Khatmayn** – built by the imam Sultan bin Saif bin Malik Al Yarubi – runs through the castle from the wadi behind. It is listed as a UNESCO World Heritage Site. You can walk beside it to the northern side of the castle. The small stone-built **Al Yarubi Mosque**, which is dated 1649, gives a rough date for the *falaj*. From the inscription column for the *falaj*, walk towards the shops and turn left; after 450m from the column turn left town a narrow road, and at the bottom turn right into the old mud settlement of **Harat As Sibani** which is reached after a total of 850m from the column. The walk is interesting along the entire route, with more recent housing on either side of the street, children playing and then, as you turn towards Harat As Sibani, a superb vista of an old mud-brick building beneath a watchtower. The *falaj* flows both at the base of the village, near where you enter, and in a separate channel higher up. The **date oasis** beyond is well kept and just under 2km in length, making it another rewarding walk. On your return to the car there is a small coffee shop under the trees to take tea and relax.

WADI MUAYDIN   وادي المعيدن

The road on to Wadi Muaydin (which also leads up to Al Jabal Al Akhdar) runs straight ahead past Bayt Ar Rudaydah, heading for the gorge beyond. About 3.7km past the fortified house the road splits and the right fork brings you, after a further 1.6km, to the police checkpoint which is the start of the military route up to the Sayq Plateau and Al Jabal Al Akhdar (pages 214–17). No permit is required but saloon cars are stopped here and not allowed to continue as there have been some unpleasant accidents on the descent with inexperienced drivers. All drivers must show vehicle registration documents and the driver will be required to show their valid driving licence. You will also be asked your nationality for the Ministry of Tourism records.

Taking the left fork before the military checkpoint will lead you into Wadi Muaydin, a favourite area for walking and camping. In dry weather you can drive a few kilometres into the gorge before stopping in shade and exploring further on foot. The rock strata are noteworthy: near the entrance the massive strata of grey limestone is the Guweyza formation, perhaps 150 million years old, while the left fork of the junction is the Sahtan geological group which is about 199 million years old. Both originate from the Jurassic period which lasted from around 199.6 to 145.5 million years ago. From here is a demanding 6-hour trek up to the plateau and Sayq. In wet weather you may have to stop earlier and wade through running streams. If so, keep a sharp lookout for any signs of rain higher up, which can suddenly rush down the gorge without it ever actually raining where you are.

SAYQ PLATEAU   هضبة سيق

Before the superb tarmac road was finished in 2006, the ascent to the Sayq Plateau was a gruelling 6-hour climb up a near-vertical path. A special kind of *jabal* donkey was used, tough and agile like a goat, as an unburdened, normal donkey would not cope with such an ascent, let alone when loaded. The plateau itself is at 2,000m, with temperatures to match. Even during the day, you will need thick clothing here in the winter months.

Follow the road for 28km from the checkpoint outside Birkat Al Mawz to reach the Al Maha petrol station at Sayq. Your vehicle will consume huge quantities of fuel as it climbs, so make sure that you have at least half a tank full. The road alone is worth the visit: there are several parking areas at higher elevations and on clear days the views are stupendous. There's no need to keep looking over your shoulder, as you will descend on exactly the same road. After nearly 12km of gear-crunching ascent, the road reaches over 2,000m and the general undulating plateau area. The rocks here are limestone, faulted through the collision of the surrounding ophiolite on the plain below.

AL JABAL AL AKHDAR الجبل الأخضر

Al Jabal Al Akhdar, which translates as 'Green Mountain', refers to the mountain range that extends from the Nizwa–Muscat road west until Sharafat Al Alayman, a stretch of about 40km and covering an area of some 2,000km². This is part of the larger Western Al Hajar Mountains, which extend through Jabal Shams to the UAE border. The name 'Al Jabal Al Akhdar' is misleading, as the greenery is confined to the terraces of a handful of villages on the Sayq Plateau, notably between the villages of Al Aqr and Ash Shirayjah. On the south-facing slopes these villages grow almonds, apples, apricots, figs, grapes, lemons, peaches, pomegranates, roses and walnuts and scattered under the trees and bushes barley, garlic and onion thrive.

Everything else is bare rock, predominantly grey karst limestone with little or no vegetation. One convincing explanation of the name Akhdar – green – is that it does not refer to the colour but to the state of 'living', in the sense that it is living limestone rock, not dead ophiolite rock as is found in the foothills around Nizwa and in the Samail Gap.

The *jabal* is home to around 58 separate villages and communities, and about 300 wadis. Water from natural springs flows through *aflaj* (see box, pages 208–9), directing the water to these communities, which also receive regular deliveries of drinking water provided free at its source by the government. The *jabal* has a hospital, some schools, a post office and interconnecting tarmac roads linking the larger villages.

The unique climate of the *jabal* allows for a diverse range of vegetation that cannot grow at lower altitudes in Oman. Fruit trees and shrubs are a major part of the heritage of the *jabal* and all parts of the plants are utilised for culinary, perfumery, medicinal and beauty purposes. Pomegranate and rose are the two most lucrative commodities here, and Sayq, Bani Habib and Al Manakhir are the three main villages involved in growing them. Other Mediterranean fruit trees are being introduced to the region, the climate being ideal; pears are relatively new here. Honey-bee breeding is also carried out in the *jabal's* plateaux.

The best views of the terraces are from **Diana's Point**, named after a legendary visit to the location by Princess Diana, signed as Al Fayyadiyyah. The turn is 300m west of the Al Maha petrol station; continue for 1km, turn right and the car park ahead is next to the viewpoint. A road leads to the small village of Al Aqr from here.

 WHERE TO STAY AND EAT *Map, page 212.*
Al Jabal Al Akhdar has several picnic areas, with toilets, which at the weekend are used by groups of young men for **camping**, who spend much of the night in conversation or playing music.

The Al Jabal Al Akhdar mountains offer superb trekking possibilities and many of the routes are now waymarked. They range from short, easy walks of an hour or two to reach spectacular viewpoints, up to longer, more arduous 14-hour overnight treks to higher peaks. The scenery is stunning on all of these, with mountain gorges, ridges and plateaux. Many of the walks follow old tribal trails and donkey paths that have been used for centuries to reach remote mountain villages. The most spectacular is probably the famous 'Grand Canyon of Oman' walk around the rim of the canyon, a very rewarding experience (pages 232–4). Do remember that at 2,000m above sea level, altitude sickness is a possibility.

The most important things to bring on your trek are comfortable walking boots to cope with the rocky uneven terrain, loose lightweight clothing, sun protection and water supplies. As a rough guide, you should take 1.5 litres for a 3-hour trek, three litres for a 5-hour trek, five litres for an 8-hour trek and ten litres for a 14-hour trek. The weight of this quantity of water for the longer treks will necessitate hiring a donkey to carry it. Do not rely on thirst to guide your water consumption, as this will only give you two-thirds of your daily water requirement. Always carry some sachets of rehydration salts. Energy-rich foods like dried fruit, nuts and cereal bars are good things to keep you going.

🏠 **Anantara Al Jabal Al Akhdar Resort**
(115 rooms) Al Fayyadiyyah Al Jabal Al Akhdar, overlooking Al Ayn; m 99 812410; e aljabalalakhdar@anantara.com; jabal-akhdar. anantara.com. Just opened at the time of writing, the Anantara Al Jabal Al Akhdar Resort overlooks the terraced fields of Al Ayn. This is part of Oman's move towards year-round tourism, and at 2,000m the climate should allow this hotel to draw people up, especially in midsummer. It remains to be seen whether the very high price of this new hotel will be matched by its facilities & service. **$$$$$**

🏠 **Alila Jabal Akhdar** (86 rooms) Near Ar Rus village; www.alilahotels.com. This Asia-based group has created a luxury designer hideaway on the edge of a cliff, boasting spectacular views. It has a good though somewhat overpriced restaurant, spa & kidney-shaped pool with sunbathing terrace,

& the whole complex is built to blend in with the surroundings. The hotel is very isolated with limited activities available away from it. **$$$$**

🏠 **Sahab Hotel** (27 rooms, from studios to family suites) Al Aqr; ☎ 25 429288; e sahab@ sahab-hotel.com; www.sahab-hotel.com. A small, comfortable hotel located at over 2,000m on the Sayq Plateau, beautifully designed to integrate with its natural surroundings but with modern luxuries. The bedrooms have excellent beds with less remarkable showers. The restaurant serves international & local dishes, & there is indoor or outdoor dining with a snack bar overlooking the small swimming pool. The café serving light meals & sandwiches displays 270-year-old marine fossils along one wall, which were found during construction. Organised options for the active include trekking, farming, goat herding, caving & donkey rides. **$$$**

TERRACED FIELDS WALK A short walk or drive 450m northwest to **Al Aqr** village begins from the car park at Diana's Point. From Al Aqr there is a marked walk to the village of **Al Ayn**, and beyond that a slightly more challenging one to **Ash Shirayjah**, offering views of the cascade of rugged mountains disappearing into the distance. Early morning is ideal for this, as the sun will be behind you. The patchwork of small fields and crops are fed by the water channelled along the *falaj* system. In places it is the *falaj* that provides the walking surface, while in others you walk on loose gravel paths or well-worn and slippery bedrock. The three villages that you walk through are still inhabited and in places the paths plunge through a tunnel formed by the upper floors of the houses, which have been built overhead.

The walk is up to 3km and you could spend around 2 hours on it, accompanied for much of the way by the croaking of the toads in the *falaj*. The villages have only one grocery shop in Ash Shirayjah that opens sporadically, so water needs to be carried.

The villages of Al Aqr, Al Ayn and Ash Shirayjah are known for their **damask rose gardens** which flower mainly in April. The paths meander through the fields on top of the terraces that were so laboriously built hundreds of years ago. The best time to see them is early in the morning when the families pluck the flowers. They are then brought to the distillation room, where the petals are plunged into copper jars positioned within receiving holes on the top of a small mud oven. The rising steam from the petals is condensed simply from contact with a copper bowl filled with cold water that is placed over the mouth of the jar. This causes the condensate to drip down into a small receiving bowl. It's a process that is as traditional as these mountains, and the result is a smoky rosewater that is highly prized as a food flavouring. Follow your nose in these villages towards the smoky fragrance and when you have found the source ask if you may have a look ('*mumkin a shoof*'). Individual distilleries operate random hours, so finding one working and open is pot luck.

AL AQR (العقر) TO WADI BANI HABIB (وادي بني حبيب) Having made the walk, if you are with a tour guide they will pick you up at the finish village; otherwise a return to your car is needed. Continuing along the road from Birkat Al Mawz west towards Wadi Bani Habib are the remains of a British Venom aircraft, in a fenced area next to a small wadi on the right of the road 1.8km west of the Al Maha petrol station. The jet was claimed to have been shot down by the rebels on 30 August 1958 in the Jabal War and near it is the grave of the pilot who was buried following the crash. With the agreement of his family, his body has remained there.

You can now drive on to **Bani Habib** village – take a right turn after the military camp and continue until you reach the small parking area some 10km from Al Maha petrol station. There are steep steps down on either side of the toilets which take you into a wadi. The steps on the right pass walnut trees on the way to the rapidly crumbling mud and stone village, which was abandoned several decades ago. Its parlous state is a great shame, because some of the dilapidated mud houses contain colourful wall paintings that are almost unique in traditional domestic architecture in Oman. So far government departments have been unable to agree on how to save villages like these, let alone how to then present them as tourist attractions.

When driving back from Bani Habib, about 3.4km from the parking area look out for **three walled-up cave entrances** in the wadi cliffside facing you at the point where the road does a deep bend and dips into a wadi. You can park on the road opposite the caves and scramble down into the wadi gully and up the other side to the caves, used by Suleyman (see box, page 219) as his final hideout. The story goes that the Bani Riyam, with Suleyman as their sheikh, were the leading Ghafiri tribe, whose territory extended along the base of the mountains and right up into the summit area as well. The *jabal* itself had only once before been conquered by outside forces (in AD972), so Suleyman must have considered himself pretty safe up at Sayq in the third of his palaces. When the British SAS finally made an assault up the mountain in 1959, Suleyman was therefore not prepared for it. Although he had his caves to hide in, the SAS effectively put an end to the Jabal War, and Suleyman chose exile to Dammam, Saudi Arabia, one of the flattest and dullest landscapes in Arabia. The narrow entrance to the caves requires a small adult to get down on all fours with a torch, but once inside, it opens out to be quite spacious. You can even stand up, though no light from outside can penetrate. Spending even a minute in this cave is enough to help you

PATHS TO THE AL JABAL AL AKHDAR

The main footpaths up the *jabal* are via Wadi Muaydin, starting in Birkat Al Mawz (pages 211–13); via Wadi Ghul up Jabal Shams (pages 232–4); the track from Imti near Izki (pages 209–10); from Wadi Halfayn up to Manakhir (page 210); and a couple of tracks from the Ar Rustaq side, the most used of which starts from Wadi As Sahtan (page 162). Most of these ascents have stone steps cut into the rock, thought to have been the work of the Persians when they conquered the *jabal* in the 10th century. The amount of labour involved in such a task is so mind-boggling that one cannot help but wonder whether the summits were green and fertile at that time, to warrant the expenditure of so much effort, or whether slave labour was enlisted.

vividly imagine what it would have been like for Suleyman, waiting for weeks at a time while the furore of the pursuit outside died down.

NIZWA نزوى

The key settlement of the interior, Nizwa is a verdant oasis city, famous for its large, busy suq. It was the capital of Oman in the 6th and 7th centuries. When the traveller Ibn Battuta visited in the early 1300s he described it as a city at the foot of the mountains surrounded by gardens and rivers with beautiful bazaars. He observed the men's habit of bringing their own food to dine together in the mosque courtyard and said of them: 'They are a bold and brave race and the tribes are perpetually at war with each other.' Even when it was not the capital itself, Nizwa was always a centre to be captured by anyone seeking to have power in Oman.

Nizwa is an important crossroads at the base of the Western Al Hajar Mountains, linking Al Buraymi, Muscat and Dhofar, and was once a centre of education and art. The Falaj Daris is the largest single *falaj* in the country. Forty different varieties of date palm grow in Nizwa; fard, khalas and khunaizi are considered the best-quality and most valuable varieties.

Today Nizwa has leapt into the 21st century, with modern malls selling all manner of modernity and car showrooms which, albeit not full of Jaguars, do offer the latest Toyota model – a phenomenon simply undreamt of only a few years ago. The outskirts of the town with their modern mansion-style houses and children playing in the streets speak volumes of the prosperity and security that Oman has enjoyed over the last few decades. As with much of Oman today, however, Nizwa does have a traditional heart. A vast 450ha date oasis envelops the town centre, with Nizwa Fort towering over it.

For an exploration of the region, Nizwa is the recommended base, offering some good hotels. Any of the old villages and places of interest listed on pages 211–38 can easily be reached from here. You will need a stay of two nights or so to fit it all in, but it will certainly provide you with a different feel for the country from the Muscat experience. However short your visit is to the country, a trip to Nizwa and its close surroundings is highly recommended in order to gain a fuller and more rounded impression of Oman.

GETTING THERE AND AWAY

By car Nizwa is about 173km from Al Qurum in Muscat and the drive is straightforward – simply follow the Muscat Expressway west until junction 10B, signed Nizwa, and then continue south on road 15, following the signs to Nizwa; it's a good, tarmacked route with street lighting along the entire way – a pleasure to drive.

ABANDONED VILLAGES

As traditional communities in the interior of Oman change their lifestyles, become increasingly urbanised and move to new housing, they are leaving their ancestral homes and allowing them to fall into disuse. Some are remote mountain settlements like Bani Habib on the Sayq Plateau (page 216), while others are more readily accessible, like the old merchant quarters of Al Minzfah and Al Qanaatir in old Ibra (pages 249–50).

Because a village is composed of many dwellings, with some dwellings having several owners, there will be a wide range of opinions as to what the property or indeed a date garden can be used for. So far these abandoned villages seem destined to become not much more than memories unless a way can be found to enable them to survive in a different guise once again.

These villages, which form an important part of Omani heritage and culture, are currently being surveyed by the Ministry of Heritage and Culture. With over 80 to be included with the survey, this will be a long-term task and the wide range of possible outcomes will hopefully include introducing foreign visitors to these often hidden treasures of Oman's past.

If you're driving, Nizwa is clearly signposted from Muscat Airport roundabout. This is well known as the Muscat–Nizwa Highway. If you are intending to stay at the Golden Tulip Hotel (page 219), remember that you will need to take the exit for Izki, and the hotel is just after Birkat Al Mawz.

At about 3km before Nizwa old town itself is the Falaj Daris Hotel, which sits on the left (pages 219–20). Passing the hotel, you now approach the heart of Nizwa itself, recognisable by the vast round tower of the fort beside the beige dome of the Sultan Qaboos Mosque. Before you reach the old town there is a wide wadi bed, which also serves as the main car park. It's worth remembering that this wadi becomes a raging torrent following rain in the mountains. Unless the weather is looking ominous, park your car here and enjoy the town. **Taxis** from Bahla to Nizwa cost RO3; expect to pay about RO4 from either Adam or Al Hamra.

By bus Mwasalat buses that link all the main cities and towns of Oman start from the Ruwi bus station and run to Nizwa twice daily at 08.00 and 14.30, and from Nizwa (suq) back to Muscat (Ruwi) at 08.40 and 17.50. Check the timetable on their website (*www.mwasalat.om*) for up-to-date timings, as these can change. The trip by bus from Muscat to Nizwa takes 2 hours 20 minutes and costs around RO3. You can catch a bus from Nizwa to Salalah (*10hrs, RO8*) from the major junction at Firq near Lulu where the Salalah highway runs south. Other bus companies such as the Gulf Transport Company (GTC) offer comparable services to Salalah.

GETTING AROUND Once at Nizwa, local minibuses or shared taxis link the smaller towns, with the usual fare being around RO1–2. From the town centre, the minibus fare to hotels such as the Falaj Daris is 200bzs. The bus stop and taxi stand are both in the middle of the wadi in front of the fort/suq area and next to the Sultan Qaboos Mosque in the town centre.

 WHERE TO STAY Map, page 220, unless otherwise stated.

The hotels that serve Nizwa are all on the road from Birkat Al Mawz. In the order that you come upon them from this direction, they are: the Golden Tulip

Hotel, Nizwa Hotel Apartments, Majan Guesthouse, the Falaj Daris Hotel and the Al Diyar Hotel.

🏠 **Golden Tulip Hotel** [map, page 212] (120 rooms) About 4.6km west of Birkat Al Mawz on the old road to Nizwa; ☎ 25 431616; e info@ goldentulipnizwa.com; www.goldentulipnizwa. com. This hotel is the plushest base for exploring the interior. It is about an hour's drive from Muscat International Airport, in its own grounds about 20km before Nizwa town proper. The rooms are in a low-rise modern complex set around a large pool, & with a business centre & 3 bars, 2 of which have live entertainment targeting the local young male population. There is a licensed, pleasant restaurant, a poolside barbecue on most evenings & a lobby café. **$$$$**

🏠 **Al Diyar Hotel** (60 rooms) To the left of the traffic lights 4.2km after the Firq junction if driving to Nizwa; ☎ 25 412402; e al_diyarhotel@hotmail. com; www.aldiyarhotel.com. Located 4km from the town centre, the rooms are a little cheaper than at

the Falaj Daris, but it is unlicensed & so no minibar in your room (although it does have a fridge). There is an unlicensed restaurant attached to it, called Bahjat Al Sham, offering a good, cheap menu. It has a small swimming pool. Hire cars can be arranged from here (with 10 days' advance notice). B/fast inc. **$$$**

🏠 **Falaj Daris Hotel** (55 rooms, 2 suites) To the left of the road to Nizwa 3.1km after the Firq junction; ☎ 25 410500; e fdhnizwa@omantel.net.om; www. falajdarishotel.com. Just the sort of mid-range small hotel Oman needs more of, this single-storey, unpretentious place is situated after the Golden Tulip Hotel as you approach from Muscat & is closer to the centre of the town. Irrespective of the end from which you approach the hotel, the signpost comes up on you at the turn into the entrance; there is no earlier indication. So don't worry if you miss the turning, as you can simply go to the next junction & come back. The hotel is set around 2 attractive courtyards with

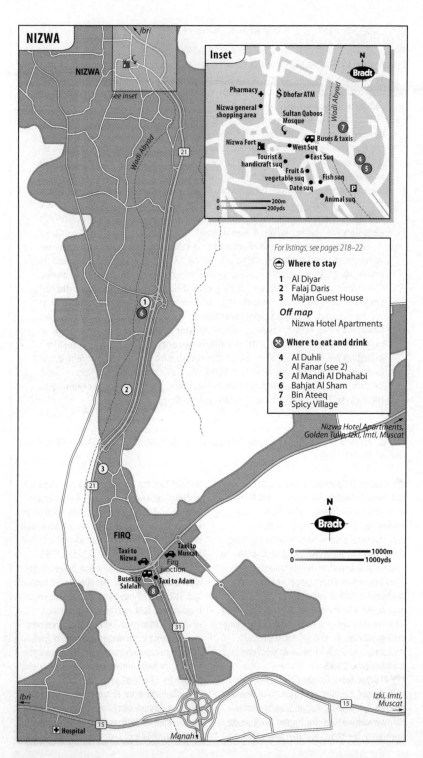

NIZWA

NIZWA

See inset

← *Ibri*

Wadi Abyad

21

Inset

N

Bradt

Pharmacy ✚

$ Dhofar ATM

Nizwa general ●
shopping area

Wadi Abyad

7

Sultan Qaboos
Mosque ☾

Nizwa Fort

🚌 Buses & taxis

● West Suq

Tourist &
handicraft suq

● East Suq

4

5

Fruit &
vegetable suq ●

● Fish suq

Date suq

P

● Animal suq

0 —————— 200m
0 —————— 200yds

For listings, see pages 218–22

⌂ **Where to stay**

1   Al Diyar
2   Falaj Daris
3   Majan Guest House

Off map
    Nizwa Hotel Apartments

✗ **Where to eat and drink**

4   Al Duhli
    Al Fanar (see 2)
5   Al Mandi Al Dhahabi
6   Bahjat Al Sham
7   Bin Ateeq
8   Spicy Village

Nizwa Hotel Apartments,
Golden Tulip, Izki, Imti, Muscat

1

6

2

3

21

FIRQ

Taxi to
Nizwa 🚗

Taxi to
Muscat 🚗

Firq
Junction

Buses to
Salalah

Taxi to Adam

8

N

Bradt

0 —————— 1000m
0 —————— 1000yds

31

← *Ibri*

Izki, Imti,
Muscat →

15

✚ Hospital

15

Manah ↓

pleasant tropical trees & plants, & a small swimming pool in each. It has a licensed restaurant, a bar & a gym. In addition there is an Arabic bar (Sahara Lounge), the entrance for which is outside & to the left as you exit the front doors of the hotel. This has entertainment targeting the local young men. **$$$**

🏠 **Majan Guest House** (21 rooms) 1.6km after the Firq junction on the road into Nizwa; ☎ 25 431910, 431912–3; m 99 453884; www.majangh.com. Roughly 8km before the Falaj Daris Hotel & just after the Firq roundabout on the right-hand side coming from Muscat. Considering this is near to & pretty much half the price of the Falaj Daris it is certainly an alternative option if you simply want to get your head down after your tours. There is no restaurant as yet. **$$**

🏠 **Nizwa Hotel Apartments** (68 rooms) On the Izki–Nizwa road, next to the roundabout that is just west of the sports stadium; ☎ 25 431558; e reservations@nizwahotelapartments.com; www.nizwahotelapartments.com. The best of the apartments & lower-cost hotels in Nizwa. These apartments offer a comfortable stay, especially if you intend to be here for more than

DATES OF NIZWA

Approximately 40 types of date grow in Nizwa, and entire farms now exclusively cultivate the two prized varieties of *khalas* and *khunaizi*. Below is a brief summary of the popular varieties.

FARD Grown in various regions of Oman. It is a mid-season crop, dark brown in colour, with a 65% sugar content. This the date used in many Omani almond-stuffed packed dates.

HILALI OMAN Grown in various regions of Oman. It is a late-season crop, light yellow in colour, with a 60% sugar content.

KHALAS The most valuable date crop. They thrive in this region, as well as in the Ash Sharqiyyah and Adh Dhahirah regions, and in Ar Rustaq. It is 65% sugar and, arguably, the tastiest variety of all. It is bright yellow in colour and oval-shaped. It can be eaten either fresh or half-dry.

KHASAB A late-season crop, which can be dark red or yellowish in colour. Although it grows in all of the date-farming regions of Oman, quality crops stem from the Ar Rustaq, Ibri and Ash Sharqiyyah regions.

KHUNAIZI Cultivated in most areas of the sultanate. They are dark red and can cope with high humidity. They are eaten fresh in season or dry out of season.

MEBSELLI A mid-season crop. This date is cooked, dried, then exported to markets in the Indian subcontinent (in the traditional fashion). It is also eaten fresh or naturally dried. It grows extensively here in the interior, as well as in the Ash Sharqiyyah, Adh Dhahirah and Al Batinah regions.

NAGHAL An early-season crop. It is sensitive to humidity and so thrives best here, in Oman's hot and dry interior. A large percentage of the *naghal* harvest goes to Oman's date-processing factories.

QASHTABAQ This date is reddish-yellow in colour and is oblong in shape. It grows in the interior and the Adh Dhahirah and Al Batinah regions of the country. Sugar content is a significant 68%.

1 night. The staff are helpful & standards good. There is a restaurant that may still be managed by a different company with a less efficient staff & food that is uninspired. **$$**

✗ WHERE TO EAT AND DRINK Map, page 220, unless otherwise stated.

The plushest restaurants of the interior are in the Golden Tulip (page 219) and the Falaj Daris (pages 219–20) hotels, both of which are fully licensed. In general, restaurants in Nizwa close on Fridays until prayer time is finished.

✗ **Birkat Al Mawz** [map, page 212] Golden Tulip Hotel (page 218); ✆ 25 431616; ⏰ 06.30–10.00, noon–15.00 & 19.00–23.00 daily. With an international menu & an excellent buffet, this is the best restaurant in Nizwa. Given that there are 3 bars in the hotel, you can get a surprisingly wide selection of alcohol. **$$$**

✗ **Al Fanar** Falaj Daris Hotel (pages 219–20); ✆ 25 410500; ⏰ 06.30–10.00, 12.30–14.30 & 18.30–23.00 daily. Serves continental, Chinese & Indian dishes. While this restaurant may not be as pleasant as the Birkat Al Mawz, but still a nice choice. **$$**

✗ **Spicy Village** To the south of Firq, in the row of shops close to HSBC; ✆ 25 431694; ⏰ noon–23.00 daily. This place serves Thai, tandoori, Chinese, Arabic, south Indian, north Indian & Punjabi meals. This restaurant is a good choice if there are several people with you, as you can choose to share from a range of ordered dishes. **$$**

✗ **Al Duhli Restaurant** Nizwa town centre, on the eastern side of the car park for the suq & fort; ⏰ 07.00–23.00 daily. Very simple place serving kebabs & *shawarma*. **$**

✗ **Al Mandi Al Dhahabi Restaurant** Nizwa town centre, on the eastern side of the car park for the suq & fort; ⏰ 07.00–23.00 daily. You will come upon this place if you wind your way from Nizwa's suq through the parked cars. The outdoor seating is the best choice, allowing you to watch the world & his goat go by. The food is usually good & is based on a staple rice-&-meat offering. **$**

✗ **Bahjat Al Sham** Next to Al Diyar Hotel, the 1st roundabout after the Falaj Daris Hotel, going towards the town centre; ✆ 25 412409; ⏰ 06.00–23.00 daily. This is an unlicensed restaurant but it has a good-value international & Lebanese menu. The b/fast is not as good as lunch & dinner. **$**

✗ **Bin Ateeq** From Nizwa's main car park, cross over the road & keep to the left of the wadi for about 110m; ✆ 25 410466; ⏰ 09.00–23.00 daily. This offers an eating experience sitting on the floor with cushions in the local style, though within a small windowless private cubicle. The restaurant hasn't changed in about 20 years so you're stepping back in time. The service remains haphazard & the food, which includes dried shark & other authentic Omani dishes, with a nod to Kerala, may not be to everyone's taste. **$**

WHAT TO SEE AND DO Nizwa is at the confluence of two wadis, Wadi Al Abyadh and Wadi Kalbouh. The extensive network of *falaj* channels irrigating its date gardens, which extend for some 8km behind the town, take their under-surface water from these two wadis. While Nizwa's **fort and suq** are undoubtedly prime tourist attractions, this is not a Disney-style experience, and normal cultural etiquette for addressing people and taking photographs should be followed (page 65). If you want to see **old Nizwa**, there is an area south of the fort that has a mix of old mud-brick houses and date gardens. At the entrance to the fort turn left and walk along the tarmac road for about 350m, where there is a left turn that will take you towards the southern end of the car park in front of Nizwa Suq (page 224).

Nizwa Fort قلعة نزوى (⏰ 09.00–16.00 Sat–Thu, 08.00–11.00 Fri; 500bzs) As the chief town of the interior and Oman's capital for many centuries, Nizwa's fortifications are impressive, with the vast circular tower of Nizwa Fort dominating the whole complex. Initially built in the mid 9th century, the castle was enlarged shortly before the addition of the tower. This colossal tower took around 12 years to build under the imam Sultan bin Saif bin Malik Al Yarubi, who captured Muscat from the Portuguese. The tower was completed in 1668 and served to protect the strategic position of Nizwa at the crossroads of the caravan routes. Sultan bin Saif is said to have financed the construction from the spoils of sacking the towns of Jalfar (Ras Al Khaymah) and Diu in India.

Before the massive restoration project (completed in 1990), the *wali* (district governor) lived in the castle and had to move out whenever parts of the roof collapsed following heavy rainstorms. On the roof of the tower itself the army guards lived among scattered iron bedsteads, draped with clothes.

The entire building complex is two separate structures: the massive round tower of the fort and the original and far older castle behind. From the outside, at first glance the round tower appears to be the entire structure, but the other areas that form the original castle are extensive, with prisons, storerooms, kitchens, washing areas, sleeping quarters, a mosque, a Quranic school, *majlis* rooms, a judge's room and living quarters for the *wali*. These rooms are spread over various levels, a veritable maze in which it is easy to lose all sense of direction.

Entering through the main entrance gateway to the left of the round tower, you come to the courtyard, where the sheer extent of the main castle comes as a surprise. The massive round tower is filled in with earth and stones for half of its 30m height and 36m diameter. This solid in-fill created a strong platform for cannon to fire over the tops of the palm trees and made it impossible for rival cannon fire to breach the walls. An additional protective wall with three sets of steps to the top encircles the cannon platform, with excellent vantage points over the town. The round tower is entered via a narrow zigzag flight of steps with seven doors, five having murder holes above, to block off the enemy at each turn. The climb up the tower is rewarded by a panoramic view over Nizwa including the old town and its oasis, with the jagged peak of Jabal Shams in the distance to the west.

As is usual in Oman's forts, signage and information are thin on the ground. On the ground floor within the castle itself is the small **Omani Heritage Gallery** (e *ohgmq@omantel.net.om; www.omaniheritage.com*), a shop selling handicrafts. The prices are higher than those of the suq, but here the objects are from Oman and

CRAFT SOUVENIRS

Items that once featured among every local household's possessions can now be found for sale as souvenirs for visitors. The offerings at Nizwa's suq (page 224) include old silver *khanjars*, silver jewellery, antiques, pottery, metalwork, woodwork, weaving, walking sticks and fans. The flag-shaped fans were used before the days of air conditioning, and each guest was always provided with one. Various baskets and containers were braided from palm fronds, soaked in water for pliability, then dyed and graded in patterns. The basket used for storage is known as a *jrab*, while the basket for the collection of dates is known as a *qufer*. The strange latticework pyramids on sticks are clothes fumigators called *mibkhara*. Clothes were draped over them and placed over incense burners to infuse the clothes with the fragrance and to fumigate them as an added bonus. Pottery coffee pots decorated with red geometric patterns have now been replaced by Thermos flasks, and old cooking pots by aluminium from India. Pottery incense burners are the main souvenirs now, the size compatible with suitcases, their decoration appealing and their purpose exotic.

The old suq at Bahla (page 237), meanwhile, sells silver, spices and herbs. There are two traditional pottery factories if you follow the road through Bahla Suq and around the back of the town. Rugs and other woven products are sold alongside the road to Jabal Shams.

provide pieces made by local craftspeople. It is a not-for-profit organisation that aims to support Omani artisans with a view to preserving their traditional crafts. (There is also another Omani Heritage Gallery outlet in Muscat – see page 98.)

Sultan Qaboos Mosque جامع السلطان قابوس (⊕ *Non-Muslims permitted to enter 08.00–11.00 Sun–Thu*) The mosque, with its cream-coloured dome, was originally founded by Abdulla bin Mohammed Al Ibadhi and lies next to the Nizwa Fort. It was modernised and developed in the 1970s. Views of the mosque and its surrounds are superb from Nizwa Fort.

Nizwa Suq سوق نزوى The renovation programme of the 1990s extended beyond the fort itself into the whole surrounding area, and the modern suq façade conceals renovated areas of pristine cleanliness. Spices, seeds, berries, herbs and all sorts of intriguing produce used in traditional medicinal remedies can be bought here.

Vehicles can drive in through the main gateway in the suq façade and there is some parking within; however, as this is usually full and it takes some time to get in and out, it is best to use the main car park in the wadi. The **central suq** area has been imaginatively recreated, with Omani craft shops selling antiques, silver jewellery, *khanjars*, swords, leather goods, copper, pottery, weaving and wooden artefacts. Artisans go about their craft in a few small workshops behind the main suq area. If you are a poor haggler do check prices in other shops as they may be lower; otherwise ask for a price you consider to be reasonable.

The **animal suq** is usually the highlight of any visit to Nizwa. Live goat and cattle auctions take place on Friday mornings from 07.00–09.00, although they start earlier in summer and on the eve of both Eids in readiness for the feasting that follows. Just around the corner is the **fish suq** (note: there is blood on the floor) where tuna, kingfish and barracuda are the main species for sale. Look for a remarkable variety of local dates to buy in the date suq and a mix of local and imported fruits in the refurbished **fruit and vegetable suq**. In the central suq area is the **tourist and handicraft suq**, which has a mix of imported and local items – this is where your negotiating skills will come in handy. For a chance to see how suqs were before modernisation, head to the **East Suq**; it has an interesting mix of farming tools and spices. Just below the fort is the modern **West Suq** where a good selection of *khanjars* and other silverware can be brought. Beyond Nizwa Fort, outside the central suq area, are local shops selling clothes, perfumes and electronics alongside banks and a good pharmacy if needed.

The Sufi mosques مساجد الصوفيين Spare an extra half hour if you can to make this interesting short diversion to a graveyard on the outskirts of Nizwa, where the Sufi mystics built a series of little mosques on low hills as places where they could worship in seclusion away from the town.

Go out of Nizwa Suq west towards Bahla and after about 2.3km from the Nizwa Suq car park turn left just before a watchtower on a hill beside the traffic lights. The graveyard is to both sides of the road and the section on the right has some important tombs of imams and scholars. Some of the tombs have engraved stones with names and dates going back to the 7th century AD, the first century of Islam. The area is a functioning graveyard and visitors should be dressed conservatively and keep to clear paths.

This road leads on through some of Nizwa's residential areas and its date gardens, giving an unusual contrast to the modern and renovated centre of town, until it leads back to the fort via the road you arrived on from Muscat.

Falaj Daris, Mosque of the Rock and Al Sharja Mosque detour فلج دارس والمنطقة المحيطة به From the car park in front of the suq drive along the road towards Bahla for 7.3km to reach the roundabout for Falaj Daris. Turn right here and then take the right at the T-junction, which leads you immediately to a car park for the public park through which Falaj Daris runs. This is a good picnic spot and men and boys climb down into the waters of this *falaj*, which is one of Oman's largest.

The wadi below the park leads south towards Nizwa town centre. To enter the wadi exit right from the car park and after 400m turn right and follow the road as it curves around and into the wadi on the opposite side from Falaj Daris. The entrance to the wadi is 1.8km from the park. Follow the track south for 2.1km, and to the left of the road you will see the small, square **Mosque of the Rock (Az Al Qadim Sufi mosque)** on the edge of a hill, with a large rock beside it. There is a legend associated with the rock and the mystic who used to pray here alone away from the town: the story goes that the vast rock disappeared and reappeared beside the mosque overnight.

A further 1km along the graded road towards Nizwa town centre are more abandoned mosques, including the charmingly located **Al Matba Mosque** at the top of a flight of stairs on the right. Carry on in the same direction and 1km after that you can see **Al Sharja Mosque** on your left, shielded by the local crops. It has a beautifully carved mihrab dated to 1518 and exterior stairs to the roof from which the call to prayer would be made. You can stay on this track towards Nizwa, forking right to enter the suq car park in the town.

SOUTH OF NIZWA جنوب نزوى

South of Nizwa are the towns of Manah and Adam and settlements associated with them. From the main junction with the traffic lights at Firq take the Salalah road south for 4.9km to the roundabout and take the third exit towards Al Fiqain and Manah.

AL FIQAIN الفيقين From the Al Fiqain roundabout continue east for 7.7km to a right turn, which will lead you to a fortified tower house, **Husn Al Fiqain** (also Al Fayqayn) (⊕ *08.30–14.30 Sun–Thu; 500bzs*). Park near the mosque and castle and cross the *falaj* to the entrance door, which is almost Scottish baronial in its narrow proportions and restored in 1988. The guardian sits below in an adjacent office and lets you take yourself on a tour – hardly surprising given the number of stairs involved. He may offer you coffee afterwards for your exertions. The ruined town of Al Fiqain lies crumbling to the right of the fort, now ringed by modern houses.

The design of Husn Al Fiqain is unique, with massive stone-built walls faced with *sarouj* plaster. Built in the early 17th century, the tall-sided tower to the left as you approach is a wind tower, designed to catch the breeze and funnel it down into the top two floors of living space. This section is approached by the stairs to the left of the entrance door, leading up to the rooftop. Each floor has a perfectly aligned circular hole for the family to shout instructions down to the servants or for raising water or food up on a tray. It is totally separate from the second, slightly larger section, which is approached from the stairs at the back of the entrance hall. The rooms off the hall were for weaponry as well as cooking and storage, and the upper levels were used for the guards and soldiers defending the sheikh's family.

The door through which you now enter the fort was a secret entrance, not discovered until 1991 after an old man in the village told the authorities about it. Before that, the only way of entering was to be hauled up by rope and pulley into the two high windows, still in place in the guard section. All of the restoration work was carried out through these high windows. Note also the two overhanging latrines on the top floor of the guard section.

MANAH مناح Probably Oman's most impressive ruined town, Manah is well worth the short drive (17.5km) south from Nizwa. Restoration work started in 2008 and although work is now largely completed, the site remains closed to visitors at the time of writing, while the government makes decisions about the future use to which it will be put. To reach the site, using the turn to Husn Al Fiqain as the starting point, follow the road east away from the roundabout on the Nizwa–Salalah road. The road swings right and carries on past the Sultan Qaboos Mosque and after carrying straight across a roundabout another right bend will lead you through to the old mud-brick settlement of Al Bilad, a drive of some 3.9km. Outside the settlement is a large cube of a building which is the historic great mosque of Manah. This mosque dates back to 1534 and was renovated in 1991. It cannot be visited by non-Muslims. Just north of the mosque is the old castle and beyond that is the southern entrance to Al Bilad.

At the time of writing the whole walled town has been closed for renovations. However, if either of the main gates allow access, go straight along the main street, where on the right (if entering from the entrance near the mosque and old castle) after about 80m is Masjid Al Ayn, which dates from around 1505, the first of **three 16th-century mosques** on this street. Masjid Al Sharah follows this after an additional 80m and dates from around 1516. Both of these mosques were accessible when Al Bilad was open to the public and have elaborately decorated plaster mihrabs, with Ming china bowls as decorative roundels. The final mosque is Masjid Al Ali, which dates from around 1504. This mosque is part of the main entrance area of Al Bilad and, like the other two mosques, its mihrab was created by Oman's most famous mosque architect, Abdullah Al Hamaimy. It has previously not been open to non-Muslims as it was in continual use.

The north entrance is adjacent to this mosque. The town is mainly built of mud brick and the houses still have many carved doors left; the walls have been stabilised rather than completely rebuilt. Various side streets will take you into different areas, each of which would have primarily been occupied by members of a particular tribe.

The overgrown *falaj* system at Manah is claimed by local folklore to have been dug by Malik bin Fahm, leader of the Yemeni Azdite tribe who settled in Oman after the bursting of the famous Marib Dam in Yemen in the 2nd century AD. This was catastrophic to the Yemeni civilisation and Malik's tribe migrated northeast to Oman, driving out the Persians who were at that time dominant in Nizwa. Coming upon Manah, whose fields must have been bright green with vegetation in the late 19th century, one English traveller wrote: 'Is this Arabia … is this the country we have looked on heretofore as a desert?' Today these words are unfitting, as the *falaj*, thirsty for water in the prolonged drought lies broken and dusty, in a field smothered with dead grass.

 Where to stay *Map, page 202.*
The **Noor Majan Camp** (*13 rooms; 2km from the Manah roundabout on the Nizwa–Salalah road;* m *92 374894;* **$$**) has wooden cabins surrounded by trees, each cabin featuring air conditioning and a private bathroom. This is a rural setting, so expect to share the space with insects and lizards, but it is worth considering if you want something different. The same management as the Majan Guest House in Nizwa (page 221).

IZZ (عز) **AND ADAM** (أدم) Neither part of the Ash Sharqiyyah nor part of the true interior, the towns of Izz and Adam are both situated at the beginning of the road to Salalah. Izz lies some 10km south of the Manah turn-off and Adam about 25km beyond that. Adam is roughly 295km from Muscat and is the main entrance to the interior of the country from Salalah and the south.

Izz was originally a Bedouin nomad settlement surprisingly close to the *jabal*. As such it had little permanent housing but a large date grove; today modern housing has sprung up and the date oasis is still well looked after. Further south, Adam is the last green oasis before the featureless desert that stretches much of the way to Salalah. It has an old walled quarter called **Harrat Al Jami (Mosque Quarter)**, the birthplace of the founder of the Al Bu Said dynasty. The mosque named after him, **Jami Al Bu Said**, has been restored. It has interesting pillars and an ornate mihrab. Inside the walls is an unusual small domed mosque, with two small arched doorways leading in through the mud walls.

Adam's oasis is well kept and worth a stroll through. Its old walled quarter is gradually being restored and sometimes both it and its mosque are not accessible.

Getting there and away To reach Harrat Al Jami in Adam, drive south on the dual carriageway towards Salalah and exit for Adam. Continue for 450m after the Shell petrol station in Adam and turn left. From that left turn continue for 1km and turn left and follow the narrow single-track road for 750m. There is a place to park here for two cars only; an excellent alternative is to park before the narrow track and walk under the cool date canopy for the remaining 750m.

Where to stay and eat on the road to Salalah *Map, page 202.*
Far to the south, the **Al Ghaba Resthouse** (*10 rooms; on the Salalah road at the southernmost point of the Ad Dakhiliyah, 120km south of Adam;* m *99 358639;* **$$**) provides basic accommodation with a simple international restaurant; it accepts credit cards. Owing to its remote location, unless you are driving on towards Salalah the options listed in Nizwa (pages 218–21) or Manah (page 226) are a better bet.

TANUF تنوف

About 19km from Nizwa on road 21 to Bahla is a brown sign marked Wadi Tanuf, along with a sign for Tanuf mineral water. Turn right (north) here and continue to the old ruined mud-brick town.

Today Tanuf is known for the mineral water that is bottled from the springs at the nearby factory. A small **modern settlement** has grown up along the road off the main highway, a sign of how all regions in Oman now have good-quality housing. If you follow the road around immediately behind the ruins this takes you into the wadi. After parking in the shade of a tree before the gorge, you can climb the steps over the *falaj* to explore the ruined old mud-brick town.

This **ghost town** is a stark reminder of the savage Jebel War, fought in the 1950s. Tanuf was singled out for destruction as a reprisal against the Bani Riyam, whose sheikhs were known as Lords of the Green Mountain. From the wadi behind the town there were escape routes up into the mountains, which is how Suleyman bin Himyar, the sheikh at the time, used to slip away up to hideouts in caves high on the Sayq Plateau (pages 213–17). The town was bombed by RAF planes at the request of the sultan (Said bin Taimur) and what remains today is a crumbling collection of houses set on the mountain slope above the wadi. The *falaj* still runs through it, offering a rare opportunity to explore a traditional Omani town without disturbing the inhabitants. The pillared mosque beside the *falaj* has been renovated.

If you cross the *wadi* you can picnic in the playground on the other side, often accompanied by goats who hope you will feed them. Do take care if you cross the *wadi* as, after rains, the flow of water may conceal boulders hidden beneath the surface. If your vehicle hits them the boulders are large enough to stop your vehicle which could be dangerous if the flow of water is sufficiently strong. There are good views of the *falaj* channel built into the sheer mountain wall. After the rains it fills to overflowing and cascades down the wall like a waterfall to join any water flow in the wadi. The track into the gorge is drivable for over 4km, passing to the left of the Wadi Tanuf recharge dam (which was completed in 1989 with the intention of increasing the supply of subterranean water feeding the aquifer for the *aflaj* in Nizwa, especially the Falaj Daris). The wadi at the end, called **Wadi Qashah**, offers a good walk for 10km after the recharge dam to deepwater pools which lie below the villages towards the west of the Sayq Plateau. A whole day can easily be spent in this stunning scenery.

AL HAMRA AND AROUND الحمراءوالمنطقةالمحيطة به

Almost hidden from the wider world within a broad valley, the region around Al Hamra is dominated by the jagged crest of Jabal Shams. The valley can best be seen from The View hotel as it looks over Al Hamra and beyond. The main town of Al Hamra is one of Oman's larger mud-brick towns and, as with all settlements, most of these impressive buildings have been abandoned in favour of splendid new mansions.

Almost a small suburb to Al Hamra is the mountain village of Misfat Al Abriyeen. Its own new mansions overlook Al Hamra, but tucked away on the slopes of the steep wadi is a cascade of old housing. The showpiece of this region is Al Hoota Cave, just east of Al Hamra, making this area an excellent day's outing. See pages 229–30 for directions to Al Hamra.

 WHERE TO STAY *Map, page 229.*

The View (30 rooms) 8km up a track from Al Hamra; 24 400873; m 98 518778; e reservations@ theviewoman.com; www.theviewoman.com. At 1,400m, The View is cool in summer & chilly in winter. Each unit is a self-contained Portakabin with comfortable furnishings & panoramic windows across the entire front of each 'pod', as they are futuristically called. The very front units are the ones to choose, as on a clear day they offer views over Al Hamra to Nizwa, over 30km away. **$$$$**

Misfah Old House (12 rooms) Village centre, Misfat Al Abriyeen; m 92 800120; e bandb.misfah@ gmail.com. A traditionally furnished house with a tiled floor, large windows & rooms with mattresses, blankets & pillows. Shower & shared bathrooms. Omani food provided by local families. Heating, AC. No Wi-Fi. Packed lunches, hiking & horseriding can be arranged. Shuttle service by arrangement. **$$$**

Al Hoota Guesthouse (30 rooms) In the mountains above Wadi Bani Awf on the Al Batinah &

Al Hamra in the Ad Dakhiliyah just before the Sharafat Al Alamayn Pass; m 92 822473; e hootaoman@ hotmail.com. Though high in the mountains, this hotel does not have dramatic views. It is conveniently located adjacent to the tarmac road down to Al Hamra & just around the 1st bend following the steep ascent from Wadi Bani Awf. The rooms are simple in a low 2-floor building, & there are a few chalets. The design is uninspiring while the maintenance & cleanliness work against repeat visits. **$$**

Shorfet Al-Alamin Hotel (30 rooms) In the mountains above Wadi Bani Awf; m 99 449071; e aalabry@gmail.com; www.shorfetalalaminhotel. com. Just over 1,500m from Al Hoota Guesthouse, this simple accommodation at 2,000m is new but like its neighbour hasn't taken advantage of the views, which are literally metres away. The rooms are comfortably furnished small private verandas. The staff are helpful & it does offer a good base for trekking over a wide area. **$$**

AL HAMRA الحمراء One of Oman's most attractive and traditional towns, Al Hamra was founded during the Al Yarubi dynasty (1624–1741) and has Oman's most elegant collection of two- and three-storey mud-brick houses in the old part of town, many dating from the Al Yarubi era. You can reach them as you follow the tarmac road winding and twisting beside the date gardens, which are set down below street level

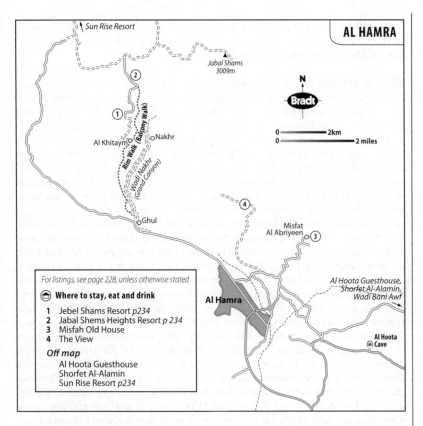

For listings, see page 228, unless otherwise stated

AL HAMRA

Jabal Shams
3009m

Sun Rise Resort

Al Khitaym Nakhr

Rim Walk (Balcony Walk)

Wadi Nakhr
(Grand Canyon)

Ghul

Misfat
Al Abriyeen

Al Hoota Guesthouse,
Shorfet Al-Alamin,
Wadi Bani Awf

Al Hamra

Al Hoota
Cave

🛏 **Where to stay, eat and drink**

1 Jebel Shams Resort *p234*
2 Jabal Shems Heights Resort *p 234*
3 Misfah Old House
4 The View

Off map
Al Hoota Guesthouse
Shorfet Al-Alamin
Sun Rise Resort *p234*

so as to maximise rainwater collection. Unlike so many Omani towns, Al Hamra has no fort and no defensive walls. As a result it was never involved in tribal warfare and the houses are still very well preserved – indeed, some are still inhabited.

Getting there and away If you are **driving**, from the Nizwa–Bahla road 21 turn into the road north to Al Hamra, signposted Al Hamra 17km, at the roundabout near the Oman Oil petrol station. The road heads straight for the foot of the Al Jabal Al Akhdar, where the town lies, about 33km from Nizwa and 8.2km from Bahla. As you drive towards Al Hamra from road 21 note the sections of *falaj*, built of stone and looking like a low wall, running along the side of hills to your right, with the occasional disused building nearby.

As you approach the mountain you can see two roads snaking up the *jabal* to the east, behind Al Hamra. The one on the left leads to Misfat Al Abriyeen, and you can see the new splendid housing looking down at you. The one on the far right is the tarmac road up and over towards Wadi Bani Awf. Continue straight across the roundabout that is signed left to Jabal Shams and carry on over the next roundabout past the various shops and banks until you reach another small roundabout, which is directly in front of a school. Turn left here and follow the road (note the signed turn to Misfat Al Abriyeen) to the right, and continue as the road winds behind housing (you will pass a sign right to The View hotel) until the road descends onto yet another roundabout. Here take the third exit left towards the old housing and then park your car.

Taxis from Nizwa (page 218) to Al Hamra wait near Nizwa Fort and cost about RO4. From Bahla (page 235) they wait near the entrance to the fort and cost RO3 – you could negotiate or take a shared taxi for less.

What to see and do What is unusual about Al Hamra is that a number of old mud houses are still lived in, with air conditioning and television aerials added, especially those on the edge that are easily accessible by vehicle. The least inhabited parts are those up narrow alleys in the centre where no car can penetrate.

The enormous, rapidly collapsing, standalone three-storey mud house with green shutters, close to where you will find various places to park, was the residence of one of the principal sheikhs. This is the start of a varied walk where old mud-brick housing vies for your attention with the beautiful date oasis. The *falaj* and the date oasis are to your right and as you walk through the town you will pass many mud-brick mansions now abandoned in favour of newer housing elsewhere.

The old houses here are fascinating. There are a few houses with the *falaj* actually flowing under the building. From the big standalone mud house continue for about 280m, where on your left is an inviting open area with almost a piazza-like feel. Look for an entrance just on the right of the piazza and walk through it. This takes you into the older section of Al Hamra, dating from the early 18th century; here old men may sit in the shaded alleyways drinking coffee and chatting about old times. From here a walk in the direction that you have been going will take you to the **Bait Al Safa** (House of Purity) (⊕ *09.00–17.00 Sun–Thu; RO3*) after about 140m, where mystical Sufi women once lived together like nuns. The 300-year-old house is now open to the public and is set out like an exhibition, showing life in the old days, usually with demonstrations of food preparation. Opposite it is a small **mosque** built beside the *falaj*, originally for the women's use alone, now air conditioned with its porticoes glassed-in. Women in the Sufi tradition often chose to remain single and celibate, devoting their lives to prayer. Beyond Bait Al Safa the path continues and after about 95m opens out into a public space. On the left is the **Bait Al Jabal** (The Mountain House) (**m** *99 008711*; ⊕ *09.00–17.00 Sun–Thu if open; RO3*), which was set up as a very interesting museum of items associated with Al Hamra by an Omani who cares passionately about his heritage; unfortunately lack of finance means that it is rarely open and lacks informative signage, but if you are lucky and find it open, it is well worth a visit. The entrance is to the left of the large house. The end of the walk is near a *halwa* **maker** on the left, his central freestanding stall piled round with wood for fires which he lights beneath the huge copper bowl.

MISFAT AL ABRIYEEN مسفاة العبريين Misfat Al Abriyeen (also known as Misfah) is the ultimate medieval village, built into a rock face 10km up a winding tarmac road from Al Hamra (pages 228–30). From Al Hamra the drive is a straightforward one of 5.3km up the mountain slope, all tarmac and with street lighting. You will pass a shaded picnic area close to the left bend into the old village, where information boards detail walking tours in the area as well as destinations for day trips by saloon car and 4x4 vehicles. Park well before the village near the small shelter on the left; the villagers built the next section of road with their own hands, so they deserve easy parking next to their village. To walk through Misfat Al Abriyeen, head down the road into the main alleyway, which is straight ahead of you. It's only 300m from the shelter and the walk gives great views over the date plantations which are directly below the village in the wadi. Follow the narrow streets between the tall houses until you pass under a house that has a window with charming water-evaporating clay jars, used to cool drinking water. You will need to take care, as several areas have very slippery walking surfaces. As you walk out you overlook the water cistern of the *falaj* and a veritable Shangri-La with all manner of trees and crops covering the slopes below you. Walk down the steps, exercising caution as they are both steep and slippery, and turn left and out into the main wadi and terraced fields. The truly adventurous can follow the waymarked donkey trail (W9) for a 6-hour trek from here over to Bald Sayt in Wadi Bani Awf (pages 160–1), a distance of 9km, reaching altitudes of 2,000m with a difference of 1,050m. The descent takes 4 hours and will test your knees in a way that you never thought possible. Speak to one of the specialist tour operators in Muscat if you would like to arrange this trek (pages 83–5).

Getting there and away As you approach the mountain towards Al Hamra you can see two roads snaking up the *jabal* to the east behind the town. The one on the left leads to Misfat Al Abriyeen, the other is the route to the old houses in Al Hamra, along which you will pass the signed route up to Misfah.

AL HOOTA CAVE (كهف الحوطة) AND SHARAFAT AL ALAMAYN (شرفة العلمين)

(e *info@alhootacave.com; www.alhootacave.com;* ⊕ *tours 09.00–17.00 Sat–Thu, 09.00–12.00 & 14.00–17.00 Fri; visits by guided tour only – train capacity 48 people; RO6.50/5.50 adult/child 6–12; pre-booking advised*) Al Hoota Cave (also Al Hoti/Hota/Hotta) is one of the largest cave systems in the Middle East, with several lakes providing a home to a variety of different species of fauna. There is a wealth of stalactite and stalagmite formations in the chasms below, and the cave is also home to unusual species of pink-coloured blind fish which sense their way around the lake with feelers, as well as bats and hunter spiders.

The Gulf's only show cave, this used to be accessible only to serious cavers, requiring ropes and climbing gear to descend the 9m into the sinkhole. Now, however, it has been developed for tourism, with a visitors' centre, a Lebanese and international restaurant called Zajal, a ticket counter, a souvenir shop, a geological museum and a railway station with an Austrian-made 36-seater train that makes a 4-minute journey along a tunnel for a distance of 2.7km into the cave. The train often seems to have maintenance problems, so be prepared to walk the 0.7km to the entrance to the cave, then a further 150m along a tunnel to where the guided cave tour begins and where photographic equipment has to be surrendered (photography is prohibited). An illuminated walkway with stairs has been erected to view the cave, which has interesting offshoot chambers. The tour is guided and lasts for less than an hour.

Note: At the time of writing, the cave had been closed more often than it was open. You should contact the cave before visiting to ascertain its current status.

Nearby lies the village of **Sharafat Al Alamayn**, Arabic for 'balcony of the two worlds', and, as its name suggests, this is an excellent vantage point for views from Jabal Shams and along to Wadi Bani Awf and Bald Sayt. The altitude here is 2,000m and the terrain is covered in bushes and juniper trees. Even in May and early June, nights can be surprisingly cool, dropping to 10°C, while the temperature at Nizwa may rise as high as 45°C. Since the improvement in the roads, this route can be followed in a 4x4 over the mountains, visiting Snake Gorge and Bald Sayt on the descent (pages 160–1), to arrive via Wadi Bani Awf at Ar Rustaq and return to Muscat along the coast road. Some tours even offer this route to Bald Sayt as a long day's outing from Muscat.

Getting there and away From the Nizwa–Bahla road 21 turn into the road north to Al Hamra at the roundabout near the Oman Oil petrol station. After 3.7km take the right-hand turn, signposted to Qalaat Al Masalha. Then continue along the road, bearing right at 8.8km, and at 9.5km you will reach a T-junction. For **Sharafat Al Alamayn** the road climbs up from a turn just 90m to your right.

For **Al Hoota Cave** take the right-hand turn at the T-junction and continue for 3.5km to the entrance of the car park on your left.

WADI GHUL AND JABAL SHAMS GRAND CANYON وادي غول وجبل شمس The best

time for an exploration of **Ghul village**, abandoned on its rocky outcrop, is late afternoon to dusk. The colour of the stone is brought to life by the red sunset, and as night approaches the contrast between the eerily empty houses on one side of the valley and the noisily bustling modern village on the hilltop opposite is all the more striking. In Omani Arabic the word *ghul*, which gives this wadi its name, is the wadi racer snake *Platyceps rhodorachis*. In classic Arabic it also means a kind of evil (jinn), usually female, that feeds on dead humans and appears in monstrous shapes, especially to travellers alone at night (and from which we get our word ghoul).

Rug-sellers often set out their wares from the bend that curves left on the road to Jabal Shams; you can also find the track down into Wadi Ghul and the old village here. Entering the wadi, immediately turn left and continue straight; try and get to the left bank of the tributary wadi ahead, Wadi A'Nakhr, if the gravel allows you, about 550m from where you entered the wadi. Leave the vehicle here and look for a little mosque, set at the foot of the slope on which the old stone village is built, just beside the *falaj* system. The path rises up in a zigzag from the mosque until it soon turns into a good walking pathway up through the village, though in places it is heavily overgrown and there are some collapsed stone walls from the adjacent houses.

Clambering about in and among the houses can take anything from 15 minutes to an hour, depending on how exhaustive you wish to be. If you have the time it is well worth gradually making your way to the very top of the rocky outcrop, where the remains of an impressive fortification are to be found. At the entrance is a rock drawing showing a warrior with sword and shield. The views from the summit give a sense of strategic command.

Returning down through the main street, look out for the rock drawings of men on horseback chiselled into the flat grey rock faces. There is a particular concentration of some 12–15 drawings about halfway down the street. Close by is a smooth worn hole in the rock, like a grinding mill in the grey stone, though quite why this is in the middle of the street remains unclear.

Wadi A'Nakhr, where you parked your car, carries on deep into the mountain for about 8km to the eponymous A'Nakhr village. The drive is bumpy and in places the canyon is but a few metres wide – your car will just squeeze through. Here, at the terminus of the track, is where many of the rugs available for sale along the road to Jabal Shams are woven, in a spectacular setting at the base of what is usually referred to as Oman's Grand Canyon. Do be cautious here, as the water catchment area is directed into this narrow canyon, so entry should not be attempted at any real sign of rain. The whole setting is beautiful and if a drive is not possible, why not walk?

At 3,048m above sea level, Jabal Shams ('Mountain of the Sun') is the tallest mountain in Oman. It is a popular tourist destination due to its spectacular gorges, ravines and breathtaking heights. The various peaks are also locally called Al Qannah, Gamhats Shameyli and Jabal Asarah. The rock is limestone, mainly from the Cretaceous period of about 145–66 million years ago. The rock itself is full of fossil shells that show that aeons ago it was the floor of a warm shallow ocean. It rather goes without saying, but good care must be taken with children on account of the precipitous location and the karst limestone with its grykes.

At this height the trees are wild olive and juniper, while on the lower slopes in springtime you will see the delicate pink flowers of the *Moringa peregrina* (*shu* in local Arabic), which for the rest of the year is virtually leafless. Its seeds are crushed to make oil with medicinal properties, said to be beneficial for fevers, skin and stomach problems. Local children will sometimes offer handfuls of *Monotheca buxifolia* (*but*) – delicious and full of vitamin C.

Tiny villages are signposted off the main track and occasionally visible clinging to the hillside with terracing. Children from these villages receive education from a school on the mountain and, as they get older, further away in the wadi and plains below. The local population are keen sellers of their handmade craftwork, with woven rugs at around RO40 and more easily affordable woven keychains at a couple of rials. The striped geometric patterns of the rugs can be very attractive. The predominant colours are red, black, brown, white, and occasionally grey and yellow, made from both vegetable and chemical dyes. The women's job is to spin the wool, but the men do the weaving, something that is perhaps reflected in the more masculine patterns and colours.

Al Khitaym village lies on the edge of the Grand Canyon with fantastic views from its 1,900m height. You can also see Bahla and Al Hamra in the distance from here. The 'Rim Walk', also called the 'Balcony Walk', starts from here. This is a track that runs along the edge of the Grand Canyon, gradually descending from 1,900m to around 1,600m, leading to a small abandoned settlement just under 4km away. This village benefited from constant water dripping down from the wadi immediately above, but the water also caused it to be abandoned in the mid 20th century due to a catastrophic flood. The views are extraordinary along the trek, which is best done either early in the morning when the air is cool, or in the afternoon when the escarpment above provides shade. Bring plenty of water and remember that the gentle slope down will seem a fierce hill on the way back, so set your own pace and allow perhaps double the time to come back as you took to go. In winter, occasional falls of snow dust the upper reaches of the mountain, creating one of the more unexpected sights in Oman.

Getting there and away From the Nizwa–Bahla road 21 turn into the road north to Al Hamra at the roundabout near the Oman Oil petrol station. Carry on north towards Al Hamra and at the roundabout after 12km take the third exit left, which takes you west past the Shell petrol station and a number of shops and restaurants. From this roundabout the road carries on past several villages up to the Grand Canyon, with a tight U-turn at 29km and a critical right turn at 35km that will lead you to the edge of the Grand Canyon and on past a small hotel and campsite to the village of Al Khitaym after 42km. The road was built by Desert Line Projects to enable military vehicles to get to the defence installations on the summit of Jabal Shams. The first 28km is on tarmac before the rough road starts abruptly, and this is where saloon cars lose their insurance coverage if they continue. The tracks around here need careful driving, especially those through Krub. Few vehicles use this section, so your tyres and spare should be in excellent condition.

To add variety to your visit, at that critical turn at 35km to the top of the Grand Canyon you can continue straight (north) and upwards. After about 6.5km along the same track you will arrive at the scattered settlement of **Krub**. You should avoid making turns onto other tracks as they cannot be followed and U-turns will be almost impossible. The open woodland of ancient trees with the soilless mountain slopes makes it seem as if the villagers' goats could not find much to eat, but they seem to thrive here. Follow the track through the village and take the steep ascent to your left, which starts at around 7.3km. After about 10km the road twists through **Al Marat** village, with its houses dotted across the landscape, and shortly afterwards on your right the grand vista of **Wadi Yisab** appears. Plunging down almost from the edge of the road, Yisab's canyon of ochre and slate-grey

GRAND CANYON OF OMAN TREK

This dramatic 3-hour round-trip trek follows the course of an ancient donkey path starting from the Jabal Shams plateau at the village of Al Khateem. The ground underfoot is stony but quite easy going, covering a total distance of only 3.5km, and with a difference of just 100m and a highest altitude of 1,900m. The at-times vertiginous path skirts the western edge of the Wadi A'Nakhr Gorge (popularly known as Oman's Grand Canyon) and leads to the abandoned village of As Sab. It is waymarked as W6 with the yellow, white and red stripes. The village once housed some 15 families who used to grow watermelon, onion, chilli powder, tomato, wheat, pomegranate, lemon and basil. You can still see a flour grinder among the houses. It had its own water supply, still visible above the village in the form of the pool known as Bi'r Dakhiliah (Inner Pool) below a cave. Do not take anything from the houses. There is also some cave housing and a ruined tower.

rock looks as if a vast cheese grater has plunged into the earth, leaving a serrated reminder of its path. As with Oman's Grand Canyon, the rock here is limestone, dating from around 100 million years ago. Here the wadi forms a tributary to Wadi Hawqayn, which reaches the sea, while the Grand Canyon simply feeds into the land south of Bahla and sinks or evaporates. To create a circuit, take the left-hand turn that you reach after about 15km (if you drive straight ahead you will reach Sunrise Resort) and follow the track as it drops down, with **Jabal Misht** eventually appearing over your right shoulder. You reach the road that came from Al Hamra after about 21km and can turn right to follow it down.

 Where to stay and eat   *Map, page 229.*

Jebel Shams Resort (35 rooms) Located just after the cliff edge overlooking the Grand Canyon, see route on pages 233–4; m 99 382639; e reservations@jebelshamsresort. com; www.jebelshamsresort.com. There are various levels of accommodation, though each type has fewer than 10 units, so do check what is available; they usually can help if you want to use your own tent inside the grounds. The chalets & rooms are simply but adequately furnished, complete with en-suite bathroom, veranda, AC & heater. There is a restaurant with terrace & garden that also provides packed lunches to trekkers & BBQ facilities, & hidden away is a swimming pool. Usefully, there is a small shop. Service is very friendly & the location is great, although it lacks a wadi view. **$$$**

Sun Rise Resort (21 rooms, mix of chalets & tents) Talh, Jabal Asarah near Jabal Shams, 40km from Al Hamra – see the route on pages 233–4; m 97 100791; e reservation@sunriseresort-om. com; www.sunriseresort-om.com. Set high in the mountains, with a garden & children's playground. AC & free Wi-Fi. Buffet restaurant serving traditional Omani dishes, offering b/fast, lunch & dinner for up to 50 people. Outdoor pool. Guided walking tours of 3hrs or 6hrs. **$$$**

Jabal Shems Heights Resort (6 chalets & 6 tents) Located just before the cliff edge overlooking the Grand Canyon, see route on pages 233–4; m 92 721999; www.jabalshems.com. A variety of accommodation including an area where you can set up your own tent. Somewhat less organised than the alternatives. **$$**

BAHLA بهلاء

A sense of the previous importance of Bahla can be gleaned from the extraordinarily extensive wall remnants that still surround the town for a distance of some 12km and which you cannot fail to notice as you approach from the direction of Nizwa.

For the best view of Bahla Fort, rising majestically above the oasis palms, drive beyond the town and then double back to approach from the Jabrin side of town, where a large gateway straddles the road. If you have come from Al Buraymi, this will be the first view you get, and it is an impressive one as you approach via the winding road. The walls enclose not only the fort and the town, but also an extensive area of date gardens and irrigated fields. When Bahla was the capital of Oman – a period of four or five centuries (mid 12th to 17th) under the Al Nabhani dynasty – a special group of slaves used to guard the walls. The walls are said to have been designed by a woman named Gaitha 600 years ago, and have 15 gates and 132 watchtowers for sentries at regular intervals.

Approaching from Nizwa, you may like to slow down and take the track towards the **three 'flying' mosques** just 600m after the Shell petrol station on your left. The track leads through a vast cemetery of plain, traditional graves, reflecting Ibadhi beliefs that graves should be as simple as possible. Clearly there was no question of revisiting a grave, as it was impossible to distinguish one from the other. Saint worship was strictly against Ibadhi and Orthodox Islamic beliefs, but in this part of Oman mystical Sufis held sway, with another Sufi fraternity, or more accurately, sorority, dominant in Al Hamra. The three mosques, called Masajid Alabad (Mosques of the Servants), are now in ruins, and have to be walked up to from the track. You should allow 40 minutes to explore all three. They are said to have belonged to religious hermits, and legend has it that the highest one 'flew' here one night from Ar Rustaq.

Back on the road from Nizwa, the turn-off to the right immediately opposite the fort (clearly signposted) leads west into the **old suq area** of town, which lies to your right as you advance slowly along the narrow road. The restored suq has been renovated by keeping the original rather than a wholesale redevelopment, as was done with Nizwa. At the centre of this suq once stood a famous gnarled tree, said to be inhabited by jinn. The villagers were afraid the jinn might fly off with their tree, so they tied the tree down with chains. According to locals, when the tree was cut down, a spontaneous fire arose. A new tree has been planted in its place, surrounded by a low concrete wall. The main market day is Thursday and, as with Nizwa, you should arrive early to see the main action, which includes animal auctions around that new tree.

Bahla Fort (pages 236–7) was built and rebuilt many times throughout its colourful history, sometimes due to rainstorms, and sometimes as a result of enemy attack. One such razing was in 1610, so most of the current fort was rebuilt by the Al Yarubi, the dynasty who were so prolific building fortifications in Nizwa, Jabrin, Ar Rustaq and Al Hazm. Until the 1960s the *wali* used to live in the section immediately overlooking the road.

Bahla has long had a reputation for magic and sorcery, with witches, flying mosques, magic trees and a range of people who continue to claim extra-sensory experiences while in and around the town at night. The town is also famous for its pottery and the ancient craft can be watched at the Aladawi pottery factory (page 237).

GETTING THERE AND AWAY From Nizwa road 21 leads directly to Bahla, and it's 40km between the forts of each town. A **shared taxi** will cost around 600bzs, while a **private taxi** will be around RO6.

WHERE TO STAY

🏠 **Jibreen Hotel** (29 rooms) Situated on the road that leads west out of Bahla towards Ibri at the Jabrin junction, 3km from Jabrin Castle; 📞 25 363340/, 363371; e jibrnhtl@omantel.net.om.

Offers very good value accommodation & a great location, making this a welcome & modern addition to the sparse accommodation found in this area. It also has a restaurant with a varied menu. **$$**

The three mosques on little hills just before Bahla, the Masajid Alabad (Mosques of the Servants), are also known as the Mosques of the Saints (page 235). In Orthodox Islam there are no saints, but to the Sufis, the mystical sect of Islam, saints' tombs are revered and are often held to have miraculous powers such as healing the sick. The origins of Bahla's magical roots are not known, but it may simply be that three mystics or religious hermits settled here and their reputations grew.

The Prophet Muhammad was himself a sincere believer in the existence of good and evil jinn, and the Quran has a *sura* (chapter) entitled Sura Al Jinn. In one of the Traditions of the Prophet it is said that: 'The jinn were created of a smokeless fire.' They were also meant to have a great fear of metal – hence the chains on the Bahla market tree – and someone who felt himself pursued by a jinn would shout 'Hadid, hadid!' ('Iron, iron!'), to protect himself. The existence of jinn in Islam is completely accepted and through the use of magic they have extended into folklore. A man who died by violence, for example, was commonly thought to become a jinn spirit and haunt the place of his death, just like our ghosts.

🏠 **Bahla Hotel Apartments** (32 rooms) Located 2.7km north of Bahla Fort on the right-hand (eastern) side of the road; ☎ 25 421017; e bahlahotel2012@gmail.com. Well located for visits to Bahla & Al Hamra. The rooms are of varied size & include apartment-style accommodation. As the accommodation is relatively new, wear & tear has not set in. The small restaurant in the same building does serve b/fast. **$**

✕ WHERE TO EAT AND DRINK

✕ **Wahat Al Tabiya Restaurant** Town centre, on the main road about 400m south of the fort; ⊕ 06.30–23.00 daily. Consistency in service & food when eating in a local restaurant is no bad thing, as the author has found in over 20 years of eating at this Bahla restaurant. The food can be adjusted to your taste & the smoothie-style fruit juices are definitely worth a try – go for the lime/lemon & ginger if you fancy something thinner. The décor is rather dated & the toilet does still need upgrading but it's a worthwhile stop if you visit any of the nearby locations. **$**

WHAT TO SEE AND DO

Bahla Fort قلعة بهلاء (⊕ 08.00–16.00 Sat–Thu, 08.00–11.00 Fri; 500bzs) Located in the centre of Bahla, the fort sits on a small hill with archaeological remains dating back 5,000 years. It is one of the oldest in Oman, with some evidence of Sassanid remains. With its lofty hall, the main citadel in the southeast of the fort is the oldest area, perhaps dating from the late 13th century and the Al Nabhani dynasty. The upper rooms give excellent views, though the drops below some of the steps which have no side barrier mean care must be taken. The southern and western areas are more modern, dating from the mid 17th century. They were enlarged in the late 18th century, with a new section, Bayt Al Hadith, built in the 19th. The fort is part stone and part mud brick, perhaps reflecting the different periods at which the building took place. It is a UNESCO World Heritage Site, and described as 'a monument of global importance'. The UNESCO restoration project began in 1988 and work finally finished in summer 2012, when the Ministry of Culture and Heritage handed it over to the Ministry of Tourism. The restoration task was enormous and the state of disrepair so advanced that when they began work, the first two years were spent clearing rubble. A dearth of old photos (pre-1960) also meant that they were unsure of what the original looked like in some parts. The oldest-known photo was taken by a British colonel called S B Miles in 1885 and showed two incredibly tall wind towers, probably the tallest towers ever constructed in Oman.

Outside the walls, on a raised terrace in the far southeastern corner, stands the old **Great Mosque of Bahla** (*ask at the fort to find out whether it is open*). As was typical of old Ibadhi mosques, this is an almost featureless building set on a raised platform. The mosque itself has a number of bricks that may date from Sassanid times, while inside is a dated inscription from 1033. The interior has a magnificent plaster mihrab dating from 1511 by the acclaimed craftsman Abdullah Qasim Al Humaymi, who worked in Manah.

Parking for the fort and mosque is just to the west next to the fort.

Bahla town walls The wall that surrounds Bahla still extends for some 12km with bastions and gateways along its length. There are a number of legends associated with the wall: one that it was built by jinn, another by a lady named Gaitha. She lived in Bahla during a period when the Persians took an annual tribute from the town. One year she persuaded them to waive the tribute as there was no money, but assured them that a double payment would be made the following year. On their return the tribute money had been spent building the city wall, which secured the citizens and their property.

Bahla Suq سوق بهلاء The suq is on the other side of road 21 from the fort; it's a short walk of 150m east. The area has undergone sympathetic restoration and remains a charming rural market. There is a good mix of shops and, so far, no souvenir shops. Visit on Thursday, when a vibrant early morning livestock auction is held in the tiny central square.

Aladawi Clay Pots Factory and Shop مصنع ومحل العدوي للفخار (⊕ *08.00–noon Sun–Thu; purchases recommended in lieu of an entrance fee*) To take a look at the pottery factory take the road that runs opposite the car park for Bahla's fort and goes past the suq, carry on for 160m, turn right and then follow the road for an additional 700m, where the signed pottery is on your right. It is not always open, as occasionally the staff are away at an exhibition, but if you catch it at the right time, it's worth the visit. The pots are biscuit-fired and wheel-thrown, although the larger ones are built up from coiled clay. You can purchase those that take your fancy. From the pottery the road continues in the direction you took when coming here; following the right forks will take you to road 21 after 1km; turning right onto it will return you to Bahla Fort, from where the road carries on to Jabrin Castle.

Jabrin Castle قلعة جبرين (⊕ *09.00–16.00 Sat–Thu, 08.00–11.00 Fri; 500bzs*) To reach Jabrin from Bahla follow road 21 west towards Ibri and Al Buraymi. You will pass under the new arched monument. Continue over the roundabouts and after 5.3km take the signed road left to Jabrin. Cross over the Muscat–Nizwa–Ibri highway and straight across the roundabout. After a drive of 5.1km take the third exit at the roundabout and drive into Jabrin Castle's parking area. You can't miss the castle, as it stands by itself in an open plain beside some date gardens.

Jabrin (also Jibreen, Jabreen) is quite unlike all other Omani forts for its elegance and elaborately decorated ceilings, which make it appear more like a palace than a fort. It was built by Bil'arub bin Sultan, an imam of the Al Yarubi dynasty, known for his interest in scholars and poets, initially as a home in 1670, and subsequently used as a sort of retreat by the Yarubi imams or ex-imams. It still retains a calm and peaceful feel. The restoration – which took seven years – was the first to be undertaken by the Ministry of Culture and Heritage, and was completed in 1983. The rooms were then furnished to give as close a flavour as possible of the original atmosphere.

It was not designed to have a defensive role – the two round gun towers at diagonally opposite corners were added later, as was the outer encircling wall. A small village used to nestle at its foot, but this was knocked down after the restoration, and the government built a new settlement some 1km away back towards the main road and clearly visible from the palace roof. The large shady tamarisk tree by the gate is more permanent and has provided shade for over 100 years.

Imam Bil'arub bin Sultan died here in 1692 after a siege by his brother. A later imam, Mohammed bin Nasir, then made Jabrin his headquarters, but after that it remained uninhabited from his death in 1728 until restoration began in the late 1970s. The imam is buried to the left of the main fort door near the *falaj* that runs through its courtyard, said to be his favourite place in the building.

Inside, the three-storey structure is arranged around two separate courtyards, each with different floor levels. The main reception and guest rooms, known as the Sun Room and Moon Room, are the most elegant and elaborately furnished, with charmingly painted ceilings. Some of the ceiling arches and passageways are decorated with Quranic inscriptions and geometric red-and-black patterns. A small room on the second floor was specifically for the imam's favourite horse; it seemed to have been a habit of rulers to stable their horses upstairs.

On the roof was a Quranic school, and Jabrin became an important centre for teaching Islamic law, medicine and astrology. According to an early source, the students were given bananas from the gardens below to keep them alert in their studies.

Near the entrance to Jabrin Castle is a small gift shop and behind it some toilets. If you need accommodation, Jibreen Hotel (page 235) – about 3km from the fort – should meet your needs.

SALUT سلّوت

Salut is an Iron-Age fortification dating from 1300–600BC just north of the village of Bisya. The ruins of the site sit up on a low hill surrounded by a fertile plain, which has a large number of other sites, now covered with silt. The fortification and surrounding area are currently being excavated by the universities of Pisa and Sorbonne. Approaching Salut by rough track provides a good overview of the site to the left, with a fortified entrance complex facing the track. Access into Salut is easiest from the left or eastern side, where a path ascends into the upper area where the remains of what is believed to have been a circular megalithic tower have been found. From the vantage point on top of the hill, you can see an excavated circular megalithic tower 350m to the west and one that is currently being excavated over 500m to the north. On the crest of the hill to the east of Salut are three reconstructed buildings – two beehive tombs, which are thought to date from around 1000BC, and a six-columned structure (excavations revealed the plinth) that may have originally been built during the Iron Age (1300–300BC).

GETTING THERE AND AWAY To reach Salut from Jabrin Castle (pages 237–8), take the second exit from the small roundabout 250m west of the castle, continue for an additional 550m and turn right onto a good tarmac road signed Bisya. Follow the road for 20km from this turn, where, just after a low ochre-coloured hill, a rough track leads off west to the right. The track runs west for 1.3km before the access road leads left into Salut.

By **taxi** from Nizwa (page 218) to Jabrin may cost around RO5; if you ask the driver to wait and take you to Salut, the charge climbs. However, this area does not have a large number of taxis passing, so the wait for a different one may be some time.

8

Ash Sharqiyyah الشرقية

Ash Sharqiyyah is Oman's eastern region, and its name simply means The Eastern (Region). It stretches southeast from Muscat and includes Oman's most easterly point at Ras Al Jinz. This a region of considerable contrast. From Muscat the Eastern Al Hajar Mountains extend south and are flanked by the narrow coastal plain that abuts the Sea of Oman. South of the mountains the small coastal sand desert of the Wihibah Sands extends to the Arabian Sea and covers an area of around 12,000km². A small peninsula, Bar Al Hikman, extends south into the sea, its mud flats covering dozens of square kilometres at low tide. The island of Masirah, which is included in this book's *Al Wusta* chapter to help your driving navigation (pages 285–8), lies off the southern coast of this region.

The high mountains, which peak at around 2,193m, are formed from limestone during the Eocene epoch, making them relatively young – between 55.8 and 33.9 million years old. To their southwest is a substantial area of ophiolite that was obducted overland about 90 million years ago. Both rock formations have steep valleys; notable ones are Wadi Al Arbeieen (also *Arbaeen*), Tiwi, Ash Shab, Bani Khalid and Tayyin. They mostly drain into the sea. The inland sand sea of the Wihibah Sands was mainly formed around 110,000 years ago in the north, while in the south near the coast it is less than 10,000 years old, formed by exposed beach sand being blown inland. Here you will also find sea cliffs of Aeolian sand.

The region's historical legacy includes the prehistoric settlements south of Ras Al Had which date to the 3rd millennium BC, most notably the settlement at Ras Al Jinz, where archaeological finds show trade with Mesopotamia and the Indus Valley civilisation of Harappa. Here also, east of Bani Bu Ali, are rows of triliths that are more often found in Dhofar, and are believed to date from around the 1st century BC–1st century AD. The port of Qalhat was an important medieval trading town as part of the Kingdom of Hormuz, and it was here that Afonso de Albuquerque first made contact with and fought in Oman. As trade with the east coast of Africa increased after the expulsion of the Portuguese from Oman in 1650, the port of Sur became a prominent trading town between Oman, India and Africa. The region has been dominated for many years by the Al Harthy tribe and its sheikhs, who are strongly Ibadhi (see box, page 33). It is believed that the East African cities of Mogadishu and Barawa were founded by Omanis of Al Harthy descent in the 10th century. After the Zanzibar revolution of 1963 many of the Zanzibari who fled East Africa sought asylum in Oman and settled in Ash Sharqiyyah, considering it to be their ancestral homeland. Qabil, the Al Harthy capital of Ash Sharqiyyah, was on the route of the slave trade from the ports at Sur and Al Ashkharah. African goods used to be imported to Oman via the ports of Sur and Al Ashkharah, and dates were exported in exchange. This trade flourished until the introduction of steam ships and the Suez Canal which rapidly made the old coastal trade of sail ships obsolete.

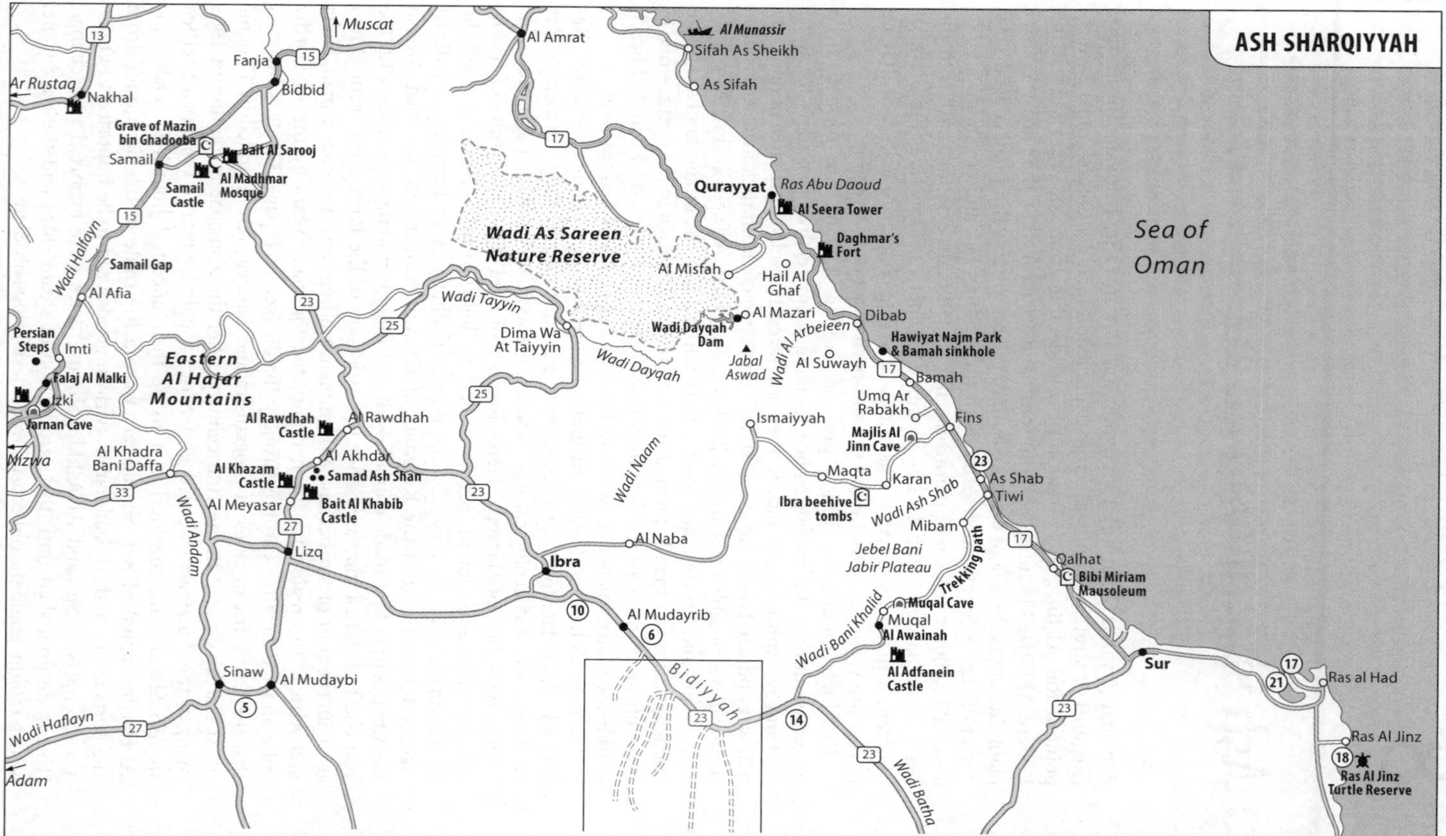

Sea of Oman

Al Munassir
Sifah As Sheikh
As Sifah
Ras Abu Daoud
Al Seera Tower
Daghmar's Fort
Qurayyat
Hail Al Ghaf
Al Mazari
Dibab
Hawiyat Najm Park & Bamah sinkhole
Banah
Al Suwayh
Fins
As Shab
Tiwi
Qalhat
Bibi Miriam Mausoleum
Sur
Ras al Had
Ras Al Jinz
Ras Al Jinz Turtle Reserve

Al Abeleen
Wadi Al
Jabal Aswad
bam
Wadi Dayqah
Al Misfah
Wadi Dayqah

Umq Ar Rabakh
Majlis Al Jinn Cave
Maqta
Karan
Wadi Ash Shab
Mibam
Jebel Bani Jabir Plateau
Trekking path
Muqal Cave
Muqal
Al Awainah
Al Adfanein Castle
Wadi Batha

Ismaiyyah
Ibra beehive tombs
Al Naba
Al Mudayrib
Bidiyyah

Al Amrat
Wadi As Sareen Nature Reserve
Dima Wa At Taiyyin
Wadi Tayyin

Ibra

↑ Muscat
Bidbid
Fanja
Bait Al Sarooj
Al Madhmar Mosque
Grave of Mazin bin Ghadooba
Samail Castle
Samail
Samail Gap
Nakhal
Ar Rustaq
Wadi Halfayn
Al Afia
Falaj Al Malki
Persian Steps
Izki
Imti
Taman Cave
Nizwa

Eastern Al Hajar Mountains
Al Rawdhah
Al Akhdar
Samad Ash Shan
Bait Al Khabib Castle
Al Rawdhah Castle
Al Khazam Castle
Al Meyasar
Liza
Al Khadra Bani Daffa
Wadi Andam
Al Mudaybi
Sinaw
Wadi Haflayn
Adam

Wadi Naam

240

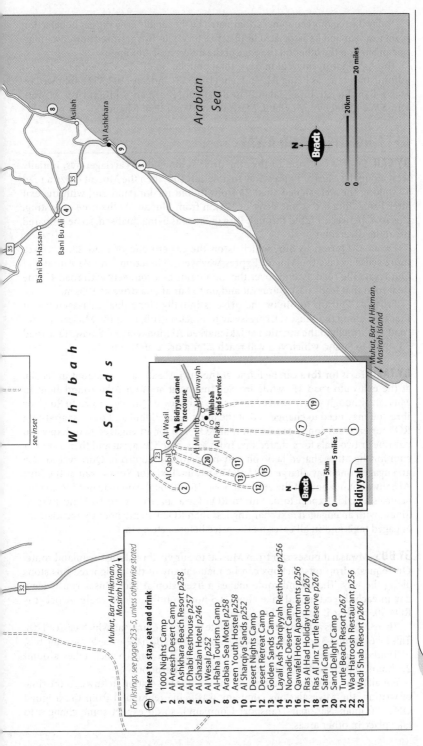

Bani Bu Hassan

Bani Bu Ali

35

35

4

Asilah

8

Al Ashkhara

9

3

N

Arabian
Sea

Bradt

0   20km
0   20 miles

Muhut, Bar Al Hikman,
Masirah Island

32

Muhut, Bar Al Hikman,
Masirah Island

W i h i b a h

S a n d s

see inset

Bidiyyah

23   Al Qabil

Al Wasil

Bidiyyah camel
racecourse

Al Mintirib

Al Huwayah

Al Raka

Wihibah
Sand Services

20

11

13   15

12

2

7

19

1

N

0   5km
0   5 miles

Bradt

Ash Sharqiyah

8

241

Today the region's economy is dominated by the rapidly growing gas liquefaction plant near Sur and its associated fertiliser factory, plus two gas-fired power stations, one in Sur and the other on the edge of the desert near Al Kamil.

The Ash Sharqiyyah region has a total population of 525,575, with the largest administrative areas being Al Mudaybi (105,538) and Sur (102,352), followed by Jaalan Bani Bu Ali, Ibra, Jaalan Bani Bu Hasan, Bidiyyah, Al Kamil Wa Al Wafi, Dima Wa At Taiyyin, Al Qabil, Masirah and Wadi Bani Khalid.

GETTING THERE AND AWAY

BY CAR From Al Qurum to **Ibra** the drive is along dual carriageways, initially west along the Muscat Expressway to junction 10B, then the Muscat–Nizwa road 15, taking the well-signed road 23 from Bidbid for Ibra and Sur, with the exit after Fanja. Ibra is a scenic drive of 171km from Muscat. At the time of writing, this road between Bidbid through Ibra to Sur was being dualised, so be prepared for route diversions.

From Al Qurum to **Sur**, which is on the eastern end of road 23, it makes more sense to take the Muscat Expressway west to junction 5 for Al Amrat and Qurayyat. The road ascends over the mountains and connects with road 17, the dual road that leads past Qurayyat and on to Sur after a drive of 195km.

From Al Qurum to **Sinaw** the drive is initially along dual carriageways, at first west along the Muscat Expressway to junction 10B, then the Muscat–Nizwa road 15 through to the junction at Izki marked Al Mudaybi and Sinaw. Take road 33 south to Sinaw, which you will reach after a drive of 213km.

BY TAXI Taxis for **Ibra** can be found at the Burj Al Sahwa roundabout in As Sib, at the exit onto road 15, while for Sur they wait at Wadi Adai roundabout in Muscat, although you may need to change vehicles at Qurayyat to go to **Sur**. For Ibra you may need to change taxi at the junction at Bidbid and pay a shared-taxi RO2 for each section of the journey, or RO15/20 for an engaged taxi. Expect to pay one or two rials for a shared taxi from Muscat to Qurayyat and then a similar sum for the other shared taxi you may need, to take you from Qurayyat to Sur; an engaged one may charge up to RO20 to Sur. Taxis for **Sinaw** wait at the Burj Al Sahwa roundabout at the exit onto road 15, although you may need to change vehicles at Izki. Expect to pay up to RO3 for a shared taxi to Izki and RO2 to Sinaw, with an engaged taxi charging less than RO20. Remember to negotiate on engaged taxis and in all cases fix the price before getting in.

BY BUS Mwasalat buses run from Muscat to Sur via Ibra along the inland route. On request, drop-offs/pickups can be made at any of the designated bus stops along the way. The inland route makes a fixed stop at Ibra. Buses run twice a day in each direction and take about 4.5 hours on the inland route. A ticket is RO4.50, but less if you travel to Ibra.

There is one bus a day on the coastal route to Sur via Qurayyat, which passes Tiwi. This takes around 3 hours and costs RO4. Both routes do have an early morning bus.

There is one bus a day to Sinaw via Samad Ash Shan, which takes around 2.5 hours and costs RO2. The bus leaves in the afternoon.

For all buses, book at least the day before at the bus station in Ruwi. At the time of writing, the Mwasalat bus company was being rebranded from the original ONTC (Oman National Transport Company), so do expect some changes to take place in other areas.

TOUR OPERATOR

The tour operator **Desert Discovery Tours** (✆ *24 493232;* m *92 009427;* e *tours@omantel.net.om; www.desertdiscovery.com*) is listed on pages 83–5, but is also worth a mention here, as they operate camps and tours in the Ash Sharqiyyah region. They run the **Al Areesh Desert Camp** (page 254) in the Wihibah Sands and also arrange mobile camping units for stays in the Wihibah and elsewhere, including 4x4s, carrying camping gear, cooking staff, food, water, drivers and guides.

🏠 WHERE TO STAY

There are a few guesthouses and budget hotels along the interior route to Sur. On the coastal route, there is one at Tiwi and several in Sur (page 264) and then a few down the coast. If you are after a desert experience, do try one (or more) of the various camps in the region (pages 83–5). You can camp in most places, whether mountain, beach or sandy desert. Basic resthouses are available in Sinaw (page 246) and Bani Bu Ali (page 257). One consideration is that away from Muscat hotel staff tend to be less fluent in English, and finding a good Wi-Fi connection becomes increasingly less likely.

✖ WHERE TO EAT AND DRINK

If you want Western-style meals then you can find them in the main hotels of Sur (page 264). Villages do have their share of basic coffee shop-type places catering to the local community. You might stumble upon a gem, but otherwise keep in mind that these villages, thankfully, weren't designed to cater to the Western tourist. You will find reasonable choices in Tiwi (page 260), Sur (page 264) and Ibra (page 248).

ACTIVITIES

CAMEL RACING Camel-racing events are held at tracks at Bidiyyah and Mudaybi and are announced in the local press. For more information, see pages 36–7.

CAMPING The beaches along the Ash Sharqiyyah coast are ideal for camping. Inland the Wihibah Sands are open to all, which means that you will need to ensure that your chosen site is off any tracks and well away from settlements and bear in mind that for Omanis, proximity when camping is a good thing. If you prefer isolation, do make certain that you are well away from obvious

USEFUL TELEPHONE NUMBERS	
MEDICAL FACILITIES	**POLICE STATIONS**
✚ **Al Ashkharah** ✆ 25 566100	**Sur** ✆ 25 542599
✚ **Bidiyyah** ✆ 25 581167	**Sinaw** ✆ 25 524999
✚ **Ibra** ✆ 25 587100	**Bidiyyah** ✆ 25 583099
✚ **Ras Al Had** m 92 177549	**Ibra** ✆ 25 570099
✚ **Sinaw** ✆ 25 524338	**Al Kamil/Al Wafi** ✆ 25 557420
✚ **Sur** ✆ 25 561100	**Jaalan Bani Bu Hasan** ✆ 25 550420

places. Up in the mountains the ground is literally rock hard, so tent pegs may be futile and a good mattress essential.

CANYONING Canyoning is a special kind of activity that requires some skill and equipment. It usually involves a combination of narrow canyons with sheer rock faces, natural water pools to swim in, caverns and grottos. Most locations in this region are accessed from the coast. There are a couple of specialised tour operators in Muscat who offer canyoning; Muscat Diving and Adventure Centre is the longest established (pages 83–5).

CAVING The cave above Wadi Ash Shab, called Majlis Al Jinn ('Meeting Place of the Spirits') is one of the largest in the world (page 251). It is for advanced cavers only and it is essential to arrange trips through a tour operator in Muscat (pages 83–5).

There is also the Muqal Cave in Wadi Bani Khalid, which you can visit independently. You will need a flashlight and must be prepared to enter the cave crawling on your hands and knees. For more information, see page 255.

DESERT SAFARI Of Ash Sharqiyyah's offerings, a desert safari trip into the Wihibah Sands (otherwise known as 'dune bashing') is one of the best. It provides the 'real' sandy desert experience. It is vital in terms of safety that you have an accompanying guide – someone with demonstrable desert driving experience and logistical knowledge. A minimum of two 4x4s is also recommended, again for safety. It is advisable to arrange a trip into the Wihibah a few days in advance with a tour operator (pages 83–5), as you may be disappointed if you are unable to organise anything while in the vicinity. You can opt for a day trip or an overnighter, which includes a barbecue and sleeping tents or 'barasti' huts. Either trip includes a visit to a genuine Bedouin camp, dune bashing and camel riding if you want it. These trips can be surprisingly expensive, so make sure you investigate the costs fully before committing yourself.

GAME FISHING Sur and Masirah are especially good sites for this, with species such as marlin and tuna living in the waters. Tours can be arranged through operators in Muscat (page 136).

HIKING AND TREKKING Like the rest of Oman, the terrain is great for those with a penchant for trekking and hiking and, as with the rest of the country, you're never far from a mountain, wadi or canyon. Wadi Ash Shab, on the coastal route to Sur, is an easy-to-reach location for this. If you travel to Wadi Ash Shab independently, there are usually young Omanis at the entrance who will guide you through. There are no lifeguards here or in any other public places and these young men may have no skill apart from local knowledge.

TURTLE WATCHING The main turtle-watching site is at Ras Al Jinz, where green turtles come to nest and lay their eggs in the sand on these beaches through the year. The best time to see large numbers is June–November: in January only a few females nest per night, while in July and August the number may be in the hundreds. There is hotel accommodation on the site at Ras Al Jinz (page 267). The beach itself is about 1.2km long, with cliffs at the back and a high sandbank. The nearest village is about 1–2km away, but is not visible from the hotel.

Visitor numbers to the sites are controlled, as these are endangered species. You have to join an escorted tour that goes on to the beaches at around 21.00

The 28km from the coast at Wadi Tiwi to the green inland oasis of Wadi Bani Khalid is the only properly waymarked route in the Eastern Al Hajar Mountains, and probably also the most spectacular, unless you decide on the sheer ascent from west of the highway. However, it is not for the faint-hearted, as it requires either 14 hours with a light pack or 18 hours plus an overnight with camping gear to cover the distance. If you do this without a tour operator you will need to plan ahead and think about how to get back, as there is no public transport at either end. One quite fun idea, if you have two vehicles in your group, is for each party to walk from opposite ends and to meet in the middle and swap keys – make sure you have duplicate keys with someone else in the party just to be sure it all works.

On the Wadi Tiwi side the starting point is the village of Mibam (if you use local support), and you can make an early start by camping on one of the many beaches near Tiwi. On the Wadi Bani Khalid side the walk begins just after the village of Muqal by the pools, where you can camp under the palm trees. The trek follows an ancient donkey trail and is waymarked (E35) using the standard yellow, white and red stripes, and cairns. You must take your own water for the trip and be self-sufficient in food as there is no settlement on the way. The highest altitude reached is 2,100m and the difference is 1,800m, making this one of the more gruelling and challenging treks in Oman. The fabulous landscape, with stunning views over deep canyons and green wadis, will make it a memorable experience. There are no unstaffed overnight huts or similar accommodation here or indeed anywhere in Oman.

and book your place through the hotel (m 96 550606). Places can also be booked through a tour operator or through hotels in Sur, which offer visitation packages.

WINDSURFING Oman offers excellent windsurfing at all levels from beginner to advanced. Lessons are given through Al Bustan Palace, InterContinental Hotel, As Sawadi Beach and the Millennium at Al Musanaah. Once you know the basics you can progress to Asilah on the east coast near Al Ashkharah, 3.5 hours' drive from Muscat. For the real experts, the ultimate windsurfing destination is Masirah Island (pages 285–8).

FROM SINAW TO AL RAWDHAH من سناو إلى الروضة

This route tracks south to Sinaw from Izki through an open landscape scattered with occasional villages. The road is single carriageway and tailgating is common. In front, meanwhile, you need to look out for camels crossing.

SINAW سناو Sinaw is famous for its very vibrant suq and its Thursday goat auction, which also attracts people wishing to sell camels. Yet there is more to Sinaw than this: on the low plateau behind the town are three interesting abandoned walled mud-brick settlements.

Sinaw is a 75km drive south of Izki. From the roundabout at Sinaw on route 33 take the first exit right (route 27 to Muhut) and the suq is about a kilometre south on the edge of another roundabout. The main suq area is to the right of this roundabout, behind large metal green gates.

The **suq** consists of a rectangle of shops with each shop facing into the centre, where there is a roofed, but open pillared area that provides the venue for the goat auction that takes place on Thursdays just after dawn. In the same covered area is the fish selling area, which is buzzing with flies and, probably as a result, shielded by a wall. Some of the shops around the rectangle sell traditional silver jewellery as well as the more modern gold jewellery that has become popular with local women. Unusually, women sell produce in this market alongside the men. The Bedouin women sit on the ground on the suq's eastern side and sell a variety of cosmetics and Oman's traditional *burka*, which is very different in style from its more famous all-enveloping Afghan counterpart. The wearing of this style of face mask is on the wane and they may well be relegated to museums once the older generation passes away. On the other side of the road from the suq are a variety of shops, while over the roundabout is a covered suq selling household goods.

From the southern end of the suq a narrow road rises west up a low hill. On the left as you ascend (preferably by car) is the first of three abandoned mud-brick complexes; the first was principally the old suq. As the hill rises, the next mud-brick area is the Al Burashidi Quarter. The final area is the Al Sawafi Quarter and, as with the Al Burashidi Quarter, it is best entered from the side facing the date oasis. A hoard of coins was found near here in September 1979, their burial dated to the 9th century, including both early Islamic currency and Sassanid coinage.

Where to stay and eat

🏠 **Al Ghazlan Hotel** [map, pages 240–1] (25 rooms) Less than 5km east of the roundabout at Sinaw on the road from Izki; ✆ 25 525261; e alghazlanhotel@gmail.com; www.alghazlanhotel.webs.com. This simple, single-storey hotel is fine for an overnight stay between Muscat & eastern or central Oman.

There is no restaurant, though they can help with getting a meal delivered. **$**

🏠 **Sinaw Hotel Resthouse** (16 rooms) On route 33 just 400m west of Sinaw roundabout; ✆ 25 524560. Basic accommodation that will nevertheless be welcome if you have been camping for a few nights. **$**

Heading onwards to Lizq Returning to road 27, take the right turn at the roundabout (this road was route 33 west of the roundabout, east it becomes route 27) and head northeast to Lizq, which lies 34km away. The route passes a number of settlements with well-tended date oases and scattered hills, including one hill that looks very much like a giant camel sitting down.

LIZQ لزق For those interested in ancient ruins, a hill to the southwest of the modern village of the Lizq has a ruined building complex has been dated to the Iron Age. It must have been an important site, as leading up from the base is an impressive megalith staircase. The hill is not high, at around 60m, but this is the only staircase of its kind to survive in Oman. Good footwear should be worn, as the rocky terrain can be loose and slippery.

Getting there and away From the turn-off road 27 into Lizq drive east towards the village for 2.5km, turn right (south) for 950m, take the left-hand turn (east) and drive ahead towards the hill about 1.9km in front of you (you cross over a very dusty 800m of ground, so close your windows), and you will find the stairs on the left-hand slope of the hill.

Return to road 27 and turn right to continue towards Samad Ash Shan.

SAMAD ASH SHAN سمد الشان Samad Ash Shan is known for its archaeology, including a number of graves on the edge of its wadi seen if you turn left (west) off the road into Al Meyasar (also spelt Maysar) when coming from Lizq after 8.1km. The graves are unmarked in a flat open area on the right after 450m and date from around 300BC.

Continuing away from Lizq, a left turn (west) after 11km will take you to **Bait Al Khabib Castle** (⏰ *08.30–14.30 Sun–Thu; 500bzs*). The castle is set on a small hill overlooking the wadi, with date plantations on either side. Built by Sheikh Said bin Khalfan Al Busaidi in the first half of the 19th century, its rooms open out onto an open courtyard. The two floors are well restored, albeit without visitor information, and are worth a visit. Just 520m northwest is **Al Khazam Castle**, unrestored and crumbling down, on a small hill with an abandoned mud-brick village nearby. You can visit it at no charge with a short walk across the open wadi to the west of Bait Al Khabib Castle and along a narrow vehicle track through the date plantation that runs 130m northwest opposite Bait Al Khabib Castle. Dress conservatively here, as you will be an unexpected outsider.

AL AKHDAR الأخضر Beyond Samad Ash Shan a sign points off left to take you to Al Akhdar, whose brown stone-built tower can be seen from the road. The village, with its picturesque fort in ruins, is rich in history but particularly noted for its **pit-weavers** (all of whom are men). The work is within private homes, so an introduction is needed. If you spend half an hour here and ask a villager they may direct you to where the weavers are at work, sitting in the sunken pits where their wooden hand looms are erected. There is a range of woven items, including wall hangings, bedspreads and shawls. Prices start from RO45, the high price reflecting the labour-intensiveness and skill required to produce beautiful items. You can buy direct here if they have any spare produce. There are several fine old houses around the tower, some of which were lived in until the late 1990s.

AL RAWDHAH الروضة Al Rawdhah is the next and final settlement on road 27. Take the left turn 10km after the access road to Bait Al Khabib Castle and follow the road as it curves left into the wadi, where **Al Rawdhah Castle** (⏰ *08.30–14.30 Sun–Thu, note that the person responsible for the castle will be away around midday prayer; 500bzs*) sits on a hill to the left. The setting is picturesque and the steep climb up to the small castle adds to the flavour of adventure.

Built in the latter part of the 17th century, the castle has two main floors with several small rooms each. A climb up a narrow staircase with a barrel-vaulted ceiling will bring you to the roof, which has views across the wadi and luxuriant green date oasis.

Road 27 ends north after Al Rawdhah. At the junction by the Shell petrol station the left turn is to Muscat and the right to Ibra and Sur.

IBRA, THE WIHIBAH SANDS AND REGION
إبراء و رمال آل وهيبة والمنطقة المحيطة بها

This route follows the inland road from Bidbid via Ibra towards Sur. It is rapidly being dualised and there are plans to straighten the road through the mountains and bypass Ibra and other bottlenecks.

IBRA إبراء Ibra is surrounded by chocolate-brown ophiolite mountains and a major wadi cuts through south behind the town. It is the chief town of the inland Ash Sharqiyyah and used to have close trading links with Zanzibar and East Africa. It is known as the gateway to the eastern region, and is famous for its fine horses and horsemen, situated as it is on the ancient caravan route from the interior to the port at Sur. The houses of wealthy merchants still stand, crumbling among the palm gardens, as evidence of the town's more prosperous days. Ibra is the home of two major tribes: the Al Harthy, who have long been connected with power in the country, with several members holding senior government positions; and the Al Maskery, who also have been connected with East Africa. This has resulted in the town having a spread-out structure based on the original tribal settlement pattern.

The town is the regional capital and although it lacks a substantial industrial base, it is home to university colleges and an army base. There are plans to have a branch line off the planned railway terminate here.

On occasions of celebration such as an Eid, traditional horse events take place at the track on the edge of the shallow wadi east of the roundabout on road 23 in the town centre (just south of the Toyota showroom on the main road).

The town is accessed from the new dual carriageway between Bidbid and Sur. Take the signed exit into the town centre, where a roundabout is situated on the old road 23 (the road number may be transferred to the dual carriageway on future maps).

Where to stay *Map, below.*

The **Ibra Motel** (*25 rooms;* ✆ *25 571777;* e *ibramtl@omantel.net.om;* **$**) is located behind the Oman Oil petrol station just off the main highway. A cheap place,

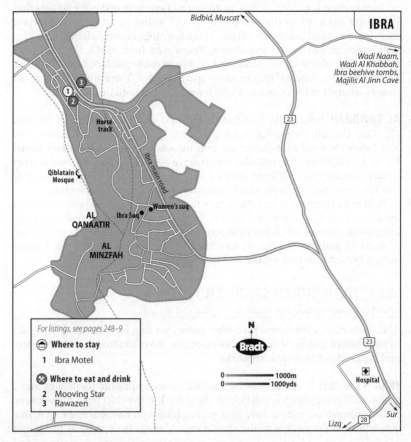

it has the advantage of being central and close to the bus stop. Breakfast can be taken in the restaurant next door for RO2.50. **$**

✖ Where to eat and drink   *Map, opposite.*

There are local coffee shops (all **$**) dotted about on the main road, serving Indian, Chinese and Arabic food.

✖ Mooving Star Traditional Restaurant
Behind the Oman Oil petrol station & next to the Ibra Motel; ⊕ 07.00–23.00 daily. Spelling mistake notwithstanding, this is a worthwhile & convenient stop in Ibra. The food is claimed to be Omani, Indian & Chinese, but the Indian biriyani is a good choice. **$**

✖ Rawazen Restaurant Opposite Oman Oil petrol station, Ibra town centre; ⊕ 10.00–23.00 daily. Walk upstairs & at lunchtime there is usually a buffet. If you have missed the buffet the menu offers a good selection with a great range of soups – the spicy prawn soup comes particularly recommended. **$**

What to see and do

Ibra Suq سوق إبراء The suq, although now housed in modern buildings, is still the heart of the town. It is a lively place, with plenty of traditional outlets including weaponry sellers and rifle repairers. Wednesday mornings are particularly busy, as this is the main market day, with a popular section for women only, offering a range of local items.

From the roundabout in the town centre on road 23 continue east in the direction of Sur for 1.7km and then turn right (south) just after the Shell petrol station. The suq is spread out on either side of the road after 600m, with the women's suq on the left and the main food suq hidden on the right.

The old quarters of Ibra There are two old quarters of Ibra: Al Minzfah and Al Qanaatir. They are on the southern side of the wadi that runs to the south of Ibra. Both settlements were located in an agricultural area which spread south for 2km, but today much of it is dust, as the *falaj* supplying them has dried up completely. At Al Minzfah the old houses reflect not only agricultural wealth but also the trade between Oman and Zanzibar. Today, like the agricultural fields, most of the old houses are returning to dust, though there are sufficient remains to make it a worthwhile visit.

Northwest along the wadi are two small mosques on the left (west) bank opposite one of the few areas of verdant date plantation. The second is called the **Qiblatain** (meaning two *qibla*) as it has two prayer points, one in the original

> ### THE WOMEN'S SUQ سوق النساء
>
> On Wednesday mornings from roughly 07.30 to 11.00 modern Ibra has a suq for women only (the first of its kind in Oman). The suq is in the open air and stallholders set up shop and close as they wish – it's a 'pop-up' market. The women do the selling as well as the buying, mainly of items like perfumes, cosmetics, clothing, lotions, powders and textiles, as well as fruit and vegetables. It was started in 1986 and its popularity is increasing year on year as women enjoy shopping away from the pressures of men's impatience. 'Men do not enjoy shopping like we do,' says Fatima, a regular visitor. 'We like to take our time and chat while buying, but they want to get it over with. This arrangement frees them from the need to do the family household shopping.' Traditionally the household shopping was the man's role, so that his wife was not seen in public. The suq is located south of the Shell petrol station.

8

prayer direction for Muslims, which was to Jerusalem, the other towards Mecca. The change happened during the lifetime of the Prophet Mohammed, indicating that this mosque is one of the few whose origins date back to his lifetime. You should be very conservatively dressed and women should wear a headscarf. The mosque may be locked, as it has increasingly been in recent years.

Getting there and away Take the road past the suq and after about 1.1km from the Shell petrol station take a left turn to drop into the Wadi Al Gharbi. Then continue south along the wadi and after about 2.2km south of the Shell petrol station take the right track out of the wadi and continue to a T-junction. Here you turn right into Al Minzfah to park and walk through; Al Qanaatir is just north of Al Minzfah. To reach Qiblatain mosque, take a track right (northwest) along the wadi from its entrance for about 2km and you will find the mosque on your left.

Further afield High on the Eastern Al Hajar Mountains are two places of interest. Both could be reached from the coast up a precipitous rough track near Fins, but the road from Ibra, though longer, is easier.

Ibra beehive tombs In the mountains of Jabal Bani Jabir at Shir, often called Jaylah, on a high ridge 2,000m above sea level, are over 80 tower tombs dating from the 3rd millennium BC. These are probably the best preserved of all Oman's beehive and tower tombs. Carefully built, many have dressed stone blocks, while others have more simply cut stones that taper in towards the top. Most have a double wall. In 1994, archaeologists opened one to find skeletons, beads and pottery, which enabled dating to take place. The rough track meanders over the plateau and brings you past many good examples.

A 4x4 in excellent condition with a full tank of petrol is needed to reach these tombs, along with the boldness to drive along the steeper sections. Although the tombs are only 81km away from Ibra you may need 2 hours to reach them. After rains it may be several days before the sections around Maqta reopen. From the roundabout in central Ibra take the north exit to Wadi Naam. The road passes under the dual carriageway and continues through open countryside which gradually becomes hillier and is often of startling hues. You pass Al Naba village with its water dam to your left at 18km and carry on towards Ismaiyyah

---

ABANDONED WEALTHY MERCHANTS' HOUSES

After entering through a fine gateway into Al Minzfah (pages 249–50), you will find some of Oman's grandest old merchants' houses, a few of them four storeys high and built of stone faced with mud plaster (*sarouj*) like that used on the old forts. They are in varying states of repair, one or two are locked and inaccessible, while others no longer have doors and can be wandered into freely. A few modern houses have also been built now, their concrete hulks scattered incongruously among these magnificent ruins.

In the 1980s many of these houses still had blue-and-white Chinese plates embedded in the walls and ceilings, but all have now mysteriously disappeared. The Ministry of Tourism has been examining how best to display these unusual examples of Omani residential architecture to the public, and various schemes are under consideration. Sadly, in a few years there may not be much left to display.

(also Isma'iah). Shortly before Ismaiyyah village take a right turn at 54km from Ibra, just before an isolated school, which takes you into the rough road of Wadi Al Khabbah. Follow the main track, veering right as the wadi turns and gradually ascends. Here the road becomes steep and a change into 4x4 drive mode will be useful. To your right is the small settlement of Maqta, whose population has created a number of scattered fields irrigated by water springs. As you reach the initial plateau a left turn at 74km from Ibra takes you higher and carries on until the first tomb after 81km. Other tombs are several kilometres along this track.

Majlis Al Jinn Cave خشلة مقندلي / مجلس الجن The other reason for enthusiasts to come this far is for access to the Majlis Al Jinn Cave ('Sitting room of the Genie'). It is one of the largest known cave chambers in the world at 310m long and 225m wide – about the size of several aircraft hangars. The cave was 'discovered' in 1983 by an American employee of the Ministry of Water Resources, though the villagers living nearby were aware of it.

The cave – correctly known as **Khosilat Maqandeli** – is a vast open cavern. Since it needs a 160m rope descent through a sinkhole to the floor of the cave, it is clearly not going to be undertaken by the average visitor to Ash Sharqiyyah. Experienced climbing guides will need to accompany you and these climbing tours can be arranged through the tour operators in Muscat (pages 83–5), who should also be cleared with Oman's Ministry of Tourism for access to the cave. Camping up on the high plateau here is possible, but chilly and exposed in winter.

From the initial tower tomb on the route from Ibra, the cave entrance is about a 15km drive northwards across the plateau and is located south and high above Umq Ar Rabakh. From the first tombs follow the track for about 3km and then take the left route onwards, where after 8.3km from the first tomb you will pass through a small scattered settlement in a wadi. Follow the left-hand route after the village through the wadi until you reach a junction after about 13km from the tower tomb. Here take the right fork past a few houses until, after just over 15km from the tower tombs, you will see the main cave entrance just under 500m to the left, near a scattering of houses. If you do continue north on this road you will reach the mountain's escarpment and the track down to the Muscat–Sur coastal road 17, some 16km away near Fins. The slope is extremely steep (you will descend 1,360m in around 8km) and using your gears to slow you down will help you avoid complete brake failure. Taking this escarpment in either direction needs experience and a 4x4 vehicle in good condition.

AL MUDAYRIB المضيرب Al Mudayrib is 20km beyond Ibra on the road to Sur. This small town is worth a detour, especially towards the end of the day when the colour of the distant Wihibah Sands reflects a gentle redness.

The attraction here is the fine old buildings in the centre of town built by wealthy merchants who may have been resident in Africa. These were intended for public use as an endowment for the town. They are known as *sablas*, and only ten remain. The public reception areas were used for meetings, wedding celebrations or halls of mourning. Each prominent family would have a *sabla* for use by its extended relations – like a social club for that family. The area to the west of the open area that lies just south of the white mosque has a magnificently carved door, imported from East Africa in the 19th century. The locked door conceals a finely decorated room with painted ceiling beams. Unfortunately it is not possible to enter all of these *sablas*, some of which are fortified and on two storeys.

There are also 20 small **mosques** scattered about the town, and it is worth climbing the hill to the crumbling 18th-century **fort** built on flaky black rock.

8

The old *falaj* channel runs through close to these old buildings and on to the cool and shade of the date oasis. A walk through the oasis is pleasant at any time of the year, and mornings and afternoons will often have agricultural workers busy in the fields.

Al Mudayrib is at its most evocative just before the Eid holidays, when the **suq** comes alive and everyone, man and woman alike, is dressed in their finest clothing and jewellery.

Getting there and away The town lies 1km off the main road 23 between Ibra and Sur, off to the left after 19km if you're coming from Ibra. You can follow the road into the centre 1.4km away, and park on the left under a shady tree in the old town square, encircled by the abandoned stalls of the old suq.

Where to stay and eat *Map, pages 240–1.*

Al Wesal Hotel (was Al Qabil Motel) (16 rooms) On the old main road between Bidbid & Sur just south of Al Mudayrib; `25 581243; e alwesalhotel@gmail.com; www.alwesalhotel. com. The single-storey property is set around an open courtyard & offers comfortable accommodation, though it has a slightly tired feel about it & rooms do vary in décor, so check them to choose the one that is right for you. $

Al Sharqiya Sands Hotel (24 rooms) North of Al Mudayrib on the main road 23;

m 99 205112, 205113; www.sharqiyasands. com. The rooms are of a reasonable standard & have pleasant décor, though they are positioned around a tired garden courtyard area & swimming pool that does not function. It is peaceful & serene here & a major plus factor is that you can buy a cold beer (there aren't many places in Ash Sharqiyyah where you can do that). Rooms are available on a B&B, HB or FB basis. $$

BIDIYYAH بدية Bidiyyah (also Bidiya or Bidiyah) is the name of the *wilayat* that comprises a number of small scattered villages: Al Dhahir, Al Wasil, Al Ghabbi, Al Mintirib, Al Raka, Al Shahik and Al Haweyya. Of these, Al Wasil with its restored fort, Al Mintirib, also with a fort, and Al Raka are most visited by tourists as they give access into the dunes of the Wihibah Sands.

The villages are set on the banks of Wadi Batha, which heads from Al Qabil and Ibra and skirts the Wihibah Sands before reaching the Arabian Sea south of Al Ashkharah. Heavy rains in this area can cause floodwaters from Wadi Batha to cut the base off the sand dunes on the wadi edge, thereby maintaining the edge of the desert in one location.

What to see and do
Al Mintirib (حصن المنترب) *and Al Wasil* (حصن الواصل) *forts* Up until the 1960s the *qadi* (judge) could regularly be seen sitting in the sand in front of **Al Mintirib**

CONTROLLED DEVELOPMENT

Under the previous sultan (before 1970) it was forbidden to replace your house with anything except the materials from which it was already built. So if your *barasti* hut burnt down it had to be replaced by a *barasti* hut unless you could obtain special dispensation, normally only available from the sultan. All controls tended to be negative in those early days and the municipality existed primarily to tell you what you could not do. This prevented an unbridled development boom that has been gripping Dubai for years, but has been criticised for hindering much progress.

Fort (🕐 08.30–14.30 Sun–Thu; 500bzs), holding his *majlis* to decide on legal matters of dispute. This strong, square defensive fort with no towers sits by itself 2km south off the main road. It is set around a courtyard and the rooms are within the tremendous walls. Opposite is a small museum with an interesting collection of artefacts. Nearby, to the left of the fort, your eye will be drawn by a tall tower house which, on closer examination, has painted green crenellations. It is still lived in, with a television aerial attached and a very fine carved entrance gateway.

Al Wasil Fort has recently been restored and is one of several to have been built by the Hajri tribe after they arrived in the area in 1008. The castle inside is a square keep surrounded by a wall that is now open in several areas.

Getting there and away To reach Al Mintirib, from the Shell petrol station on the main road 23 between Ibra and Sur take the right turn (north), and you will reach the fort after 2.6km. To get to Al Wasil, take the market turn right into Al Wasil village 15km after Al Mudayrib, and you will see the fort on your left after 550m.

WIHIBAH SANDS رماة أل وهيبة The sands are about 3 hours' drive from Muscat through either Ibra or Sur. There are several entrances to the northern dunes, but accessing them through Al Raka or Al Wasil (page 252) is the usual method. That said, if you intend to stay in a permanent camp overnight, its location will probably decide what part of the dunes you see. In this northern section they are similar and equally beautiful.

The Wihibah (also Wahiba) is a true sea of sand, measuring 180km from north to south, 80km from east to west, and with dunes 100–150m high. The northern dunes are primarily quartz in origin, with a multi-hued golden sheen from surface oxidisation, while the southern dunes are carbonate sand, pale in colour, and formed by the prevailing south–north wind direction. In the north the wind has created vast linear dunes whose length is in excess of 50km. The ridges of the dunes have created valleys that now contain most routes from the north to the Arabian Sea. In the winter months night-time drops in temperature may cause mist whose dew can sustain both animals and plants. Below the loose dune surface in the south is an older fossil desert made up of Aeolian dunes that become evident along the southern coast. Bedouin camps can be found along trails and tracks in the Wihibah, though today most people are permanently settled in one of the villages of Bidiyyah (page 252).

Al Huwayah is a large oasis on the very edge of the Wihibah with extensive date and banana plantations. The high dunes almost completely encircle the oasis, giving a real sense of the encroaching desert. There is a *falaj* and a narrow one-way road running through the plantation and you can picnic in the shade here, watching the awesome dunes pressing in, or camp just outside the plantation on the very edge of the desert. In the high summer months from June to September the Wihibah Bedouin families come from the sea coast to the oasis and live in the villages harvesting their dates.

Along the eastern edge of the Wihibah near Bani Bu Hassan are extensive woodlands of prosopis (*ghaf*) and acacia (which have been shown to live on dew), with many Bedouin settlements scattered among them.

The easiest and safest option with the Wihibah is to set up an organised trip through an experienced company (pages 83–5). Alternatively, you can contact a desert camp direct (see below).

🏠 **Where to stay** *Map, pages 240–1.*
🏠 **Desert Nights Camp** (24 double units, 2 family tents) **m** 92 818388, 99 744266; can be reserved on www.booking.com. The most luxurious of the desert camps, very stylish & exquisitely

In Islamic architecture the door or gateway to a building is often the most elaborately decorated feature. All the effort is concentrated on the façade side of the door; from the inside it is often quite plain. Oman does not have the right kind of indigenous tree for carving, so the wood was usually imported – perhaps teak from India or sometimes from Zanzibar. Omani carpenters then carved their motifs, often opting for traditional floral patterns of roses, Oman's favourite flower. These days, alas, there are few Omani carpenters left and most wood is carved by Indians imitating local designs. Old Omani doors have become popular with expatriates and tourists who like to turn them into coffee tables. There are two things to look out for if you want to tell the difference between an old door and a new one: colour and texture. Old rosewood or teak (200 years old) is dark with a deep redness to it. Young wood looks more orange. Some dealers stain the doors darker to disguise their age, but this masks the grain of the wood. Newly carved doors also have a sharp feel to their carving and edges, while old doors will have gained the smoother finish that comes from wear and exposure. Today metal doors, often brightly coloured, are increasingly replacing the old carved doors. These metal doors may be locally fabricated or from China, as their often oriental theme suggests.

designed. The accommodation is solid concrete with a roof that looks a bit like a tent. The Two Dunes Restaurant offers AC indoor dining or outdoor under the stars. The Oasis Bar is fully licensed. Excursions can be organised to Wadi Bani Khalid, a local suq or a local Bedouin house, & activities include trekking, sandboarding & camel safaris. **$$$$**

⌂ **Al-Raha Tourism Camp** (77 units arranged in a similar manner to terraced housing, 15 of them more comfortable) 20km off the road; www.alrahaoman.com. Large-scale desert experience, with the central dining tent holding up to 200 people. It offers the full range of desert activities including sandboarding, dune bashing, quad biking, camel riding, archery & shooting. It even boasts its own on-site dune. **$$$**

⌂ **Golden Sands Camp** (20 en-suite chalets & large furnished Bedouin tents) m 99 445092. The Golden Sands office is at Al Wasil. This is where you park to join a vehicle to transport you to the camp. It offers a great place within the Wihibah Desert. The dining & entertainment area is called The Oasis & there is even a small shop for essential items. Quad bikes can be hired, there is a children's adventure playground, & beach volleyball, soccer, archery & golf are all available. Or you can 'star gaze' in a tent away from the camp or take a camel ride. **$$$**

⌂ **1000 Nights Camp** m 99 448158; e info@1000nightscamp.com;

www.1000nightscamp.com. An impressive set-up that even runs to a conference centre, this camp offers 'emir' 'sheikh' & 'Arabic' tents, a small swimming pool, free Wi-Fi, & a proper restaurant & terrace. An extensive range of activities are on offer, from free sandboarding to private dune driving. **$$**

⌂ **Al Areesh Desert Camp** (43 tents) \ 24 493232; m 99 317107; www.desertdiscovery.com. This is the most northerly of the desert camps, signed on the inland Muscat–Sur road, page 242. The accommodation is covered with palm fronds in the traditional Bedu style, & equipped with electric lighting & bedding. The camp has shared shower & toilet facilities. You can experience dune driving (with experienced Bedu drivers), sand skiing, camel rides or a visit to local Bedu homes. There is an evening campfire & entertainment from traditional musicians, dancers & singers. **$$**

⌂ **Desert Retreat Camp** (20 rooms) South of Al Wasil, with the meeting place at the Al Maha petrol station at Al Wasil; m 99 332264; e desertretreat@yahoo.com. This is a medium-sized camp with Bedouin-style tents & European-style beds. The camp does occasionally add bell tents when bookings are high, & the toilets & showers may be shared with guests using other tents. **$$**

⌂ **Nomadic Desert Camp** m 99 336273; e info@nomadicdesertcamp.com; www.

nomadicdesertcamp.com. A more intimate experience of the desert, run by a Bedouin family. There is a handful of *barasti* huts with shared bathrooms; all is clean & simple. *FB inc a camel ride & transport is RO40 pp.* **$$**

Safari Camp m 92 000592; e alwan900@hotmail.com; www.safaridesert. com. Deep in the desert, this spacious camp has private toilet & shower for each room & co-operative staff. **$$**

Sand Delight Camp (6 tents) In the desert close to Al Wasil, but it is essential to contact the camp for directions; m 99 332363; e sanddelight@hotmail.com. This place is ideal if you don't like the idea of staying in one of the larger camps, or if you are in a small group looking to book out the entire campsite. There are only 6 spacious Bedouin-style tents (with 1 toilet/shower for every 2 tents). The owner will usually be the person to meet you & guide you into the camp. **$$**

Other services Wihibah Sand Services (m *99 767494; e saidfromwahiba@gmail. com*) is a family-operated business based in the desert, offering 4x4 transportation to desert camps and excursions into the Wihibah Sands. They can meet clients at the Shell petrol station in Bidiyyah; be sure to book at least a day in advance at weekends.

WADI BANI KHALID وادي بني خالد East of Bidiyyah is the stunningly beautiful Wadi Bani Khalid, one of Oman's most popular wadis. During holiday periods such as Eid it is likely to be full to overflowing with visitors. The wadi reaches high into the mountains above, its tributaries almost meeting those of Wadi Tiwi on the northern side.

In the northern section of Wadi Bani Khalid a turn left at a junction after the descent into the valley will take you after just over 7km to the water pools. Their upper reaches hold **Muqal Cave**, which can be accessed with a 1km walk and scramble through the wadi and its water pools. Although it's not far, you do need to be fit and wear footwear with a good grip. A small fissure allows you to crawl into the cave, and somewhere deep below is the sound of rushing water and bats.

The flow of water through the wadi has been dammed to create a series of water pools which are used to irrigate the date oasis downstream. These clear pools of water have a population of freshwater fish who nibble the toes of adventurous swimmers. If you do swim, remember that this is a public place in

WIHIBAH BIODIVERSITY

The sands were the subject of an expedition by the Royal Geographical Society in 1986, the results of which aroused international scientific interest. The project director wrote:

> No body of sand in the world contains such a full range of study terrains, nor has so much to offer desert scientists urgently trying to piece together the complex jigsaw of arid zone areas. Its isolation and size lend it to field research simply because it can be studied as a complete unit. It can be circumnavigated by Land Rover in three days.

The 35 scientists involved discovered 150 species of plant, 200 species of mammals, birds, reptiles and amphibians, and 16,000 invertebrate specimens.

If you are interested in learning more, there are two titles you might wish to track down. The first is *The Scientific Results of the Royal Geographical Society Oman Wahiba Sands Project 1985–1987*; the second is N Winser's *The Sea of Sands and Mists: Story of the Royal Geographical Society Oman Wahiba Sands Project* (page 71).

a conservative area and dress very modestly. The water pools above the small restaurant towards Muqal Cave are more private. The area below the pools is all lush date plantations that stretch for about 5km downstream.

In the wadi section about 3.7km after the junction is **Al Awainah**, just 100m east of the road through Wadi Bani Khalid. This old settlement has been abandoned for many years, but even today the wealth that the agriculture produced is clear. In the middle of the date plantation is a fortified mansion (now barely recognisable, as it is simply low walling) that once held an elaborately decorated mihrab within a crumbling mosque. The mihrab is now displayed in the National Museum in Muscat (pages 111–12). There are pathways that wander at some length in this area.

At the junction, instead of taking that left turn, carry on ahead past the office of the *wali*. Take a left across the wadi to the north bank and into the village of Al Adfanein. Hidden among the houses and date palms is **Al Adfanein Castle**, which was probably once a fortified home. Its rooms open out onto a small open courtyard. At the time of writing this castle is not open, although it has been restored.

Getting there and away From the Shell petrol station in Bidiyyah, take road 23 east towards Sur. After 14km there is a signed junction to the left with a small coffee shop and toilets. From here there is a very scenic drive up and over the mountains to the junction in Wadi Bani Khalid, some 22km away from road 23.

⌂ Where to stay *Map, pages 240–1.*
The **Layali Ash Sharqiyyah Resthouse** (Oriental Rest House) (*12 rooms;* ❧ *25 584233;* e *onrhoman@gmail.com;* **$**) is a simple place located at the entrance to Wadi Bani Khalid. The meals for in-house guests are simple but quite tasty.

AL KAMIL الكامل This small town on the northeastern edge of the Wihibah Sands is part of the eastern region of Jaalan, administratively linked with Al Wafi to its south. It is an important junction and taxis wait on either side of the main road, by the Oman Oil petrol station.

⌂ Where to stay *Map, pages 240–1.*
The modern and clean **Qawafel Hotel Apartments** (*19 rooms; on the main Sur–Bidbid road, less than 2km west of the junction to Bani Bu Ali;* ❧ *25 558777;* e *qawafelhtl@gmail.com;* **$**) offers a mix of rooms and apartments.

✗ Where to eat and drink *Map, pages 240–1.*
The **Wad Hatroosh Restaurant** (*just to the west of the roundabout in the town on the way to Bani Bu Ali;* **$**) has more room inside that a first glance might suggest, so do look around if it appears to be full. The food is served quickly and they have a good selection of fresh fruit juices.

Old Castle Museum متحف الحصن القديم (m *99 259529;* e *old.castle.museum@ gmail.com; www.old-castle-museum.com;* ⊕ *09.00–17.00 Sat–Thu, Fri by appointment; RO2*) Hidden behind a residential compound just to the south of the post office and east of the large mosque on the roundabout in the town is the Old Castle Museum. As its name suggests this museum is within an old, nicely restored castle. The *falaj* for the town passes through the castle, accessed down some steps. Inside the castle is an eclectic collection of objects associated with Oman, ranging from old Pepsi bottles through to elaborate silver *khanjars* and even a meteorite. It's the very personal collection of the very enthusiastic owner.

The display cases are well laid out and as you have a guided tour the experience is very interesting and not to be missed.

BANI BU HASSAN (بني بو حسن) **AND BANI BU ALI** (بني بو علي) Taking the road from Al Kamil to Al Ashkharah (route 35), you will see the twin towns of Bani Bu Hassan and Bani Bu Ali (7km apart along the main road). They have a certain curiosity value for their forts and splendid fortified houses.

Bani Bu Hassan
Bani Bu Hassan is an area famed for horsemanship. One resident of the town trains 23 horses and has instilled his passion in his 22 children; the youngest son could stand on a galloping horse at the age of nine.

Bani Bu Hassan Castle
(🕐 *08.00–14.00 Sun–Thu; 500bzs*) Although it looks fresh, Bani Bu Hassan Castle is thought to date from the 9th century. There is an extensive wall enclosing the keep, which was constructed in the early 19th century, creating a peaceful monument to this region's past. Climb to the top of the keep to see the nearby date palms.

The castle is reached from the roundabout at the Oman Oil petrol station on the road south from Al Kamil, just after the large mosque with twin minarets. Take the first right and follow that road south for 1.2km, and then right again. Follow the road as it then swings north at a supermarket for 1.2km to find the castle.

Bani Bu Ali
Historically the tribes of Bani Bu Ali town had an uneasy relationship with the government in Muscat. In the first quarter of the 19th century, its people accepted the new Wahhabi creed (pages 197–8), becoming a fundamentalist Muslim sect.

In 1820, men from the town were suspected of 'piracy' by Britain who sent a messenger to ask for compensation. He was killed *en route*. An expeditionary force was then sent by Britain with the support of Oman's ruler, Sayyid Said. Almost 300 members of the force were killed by the local opposing forces. Naturally, Britain felt the need to avenge the defeat. An army that included the 65th Regiment of Foot was sent to Bani Bu Ali in January 1821 under the command of Major General Lionel Smith. In March the tribal forces were defeated, their possessions destroyed and two leading sheikhs were injured, captured and imprisoned for two years; British forces also sustained 'heavy losses'.

The **Al Hamuda Fort** has been rebuilt since its destruction in 1821, although it is now rapidly deteriorating, with sections collapsing on a regular basis. It contains several impressive buildings, including a keep with an iron-plated door and a twin-domed mosque.

Close to the fort is another very unusual small mosque with 52 domes, called **Al Hamuda Mosque**, as the mosque – like the fort – was built by the Al Hamuda sheikhs. It is thought to date from the 11th century and was renovated in 1990. The domes have hidden ventilation for the mosque, making it surprisingly cool inside. With its courtyard and simple arches, its style is almost Umayyad.

Where to stay and eat *Map, pages 240–1.*
The **Al Dhabi Resthouse** (*14 rooms;* 📞 *25 553307;* **$**) can be found next to the Shell petrol station on the road to the coast. It's a simple place with basic accommodation, but it's the only option in town. There's also a small **restaurant** next door (**$**).

Other practicalities The main taxi pickup point of Bani Bu Ali is in the centre of town opposite the hospital.

257

AL ASHKHARAH الاشخـــرة Al Ashkharah is a quiet coastal fishing town where you can see traditional wooden dhows on the beach as a reminder of its prestigious past. Inside the small harbour there are usually several more modern fibreglass ones. In addition, many fishing boats line the beach, these days made of fibreglass. The beaches on either side of the town are soft white sand, although some are rather littered. South of the town, the Muscat–Salalah Coastal Road entices you to explore further. Al Ashkharah was the landing point for merchant ships from India, Yemen and Iran from the 11th century onwards.

🏠 **Where to stay** *Map, pages 240–1.*

🏠 **Areen Youth Hostel** About 4km south of the town on the road to Ad Duqm; ✆25 566266. This is not a youth hostel as known in Europe, but rather a hotel aimed at young families. It makes a clean & modern base for exploring the region, & it also has a good restaurant. Though not directly on the public beach it is less than 400m away. The sea does have undercurrents. Payment is by cash only. **$$**

🏠 **Al Ashkhara Beach Resort** (15 rooms) Just over 15km south of Al Ashkharah on the road leading to Ad Duqm; m 94 082424; e info@ashkhara.com; www.ashkhara.com. On an almost never-ending public sandy beach, this makes a useful stop on a long drive between Muscat & Salalah. The rooms are relatively small & are in need of refurbishment. Meals are fairly basic & you might be tempted to try a meal in Al Ashkharah. **$**

✕ **Where to eat and drink** The **Golden Beach Restaurant** (*on the main route from Sur through Al Ashkharah to Ad Duqm;* **$**) is a busy, simple place in the centre of Al Ashkharah, with seating inside or in a shaded outside area. As is so often the case with local restaurants away from Muscat or Salalah, the meals are based on rice, which here is excellent. Not surprisingly for a seaside town, the fish is worth trying, though do try and persuade them not to overcook it. You may need to share a table, as most of them seat up to ten.

ASILAH أصيلة Also spelt 'Asaylah', this is another quiet coastal fishing village. Close by is the relatively new BBC World Service relay station – the replacement for the closed site on Masirah Island. North of the village is a beach where the kite- and windsurfing is the best on the mainland coast.

🏠 **Where to stay** *Map, pages 240–1.*

The simple, single-storey **Arabian Sea Motel** (*30 rooms; on the coastal road between Sur & Asilah, a few kilometres west of Asilah;* m 97 794244; e arabianseamotel@hotmail.com; www.arabianseamotel.com; **$**) overlooks the public sandy beach on the east coast south of Sur. The hotel has had some recent refurbishment that improves on the homespun feeling of the accommodation. This section of the coast is very popular with windsurfers who may have travelled from Dubai for a weekend. The fish here is fresh and the staff will usually accommodate requests if you have caught your own.

ALONG THE COASTAL ROUTE FROM MUSCAT TO SUR
الساحل من مسقط إلى صور

The most varied route from Muscat to Ash Sharqiyyah is the coastal road to Sur, along a dual carriageway that benefits from street lighting all the way. The journey via this route (195km from Qurum to Sur) offers plenty of diversions. There is fabulous coastal scenery here, with mountains and gorges extending down to the sea, rock pools and good walks into the hills. The stretch of coastline is a series of rocky inlets reaching all the way down to Sur. Whole sections between Muscat and Qurayyat where the road does not follow the coast are reachable by boat only, and some of the villages are still linked only by graded tracks.

GETTING AROUND To join the road to Qurayyat, Sur and the open horizon beyond, you need to exit the main Al Nahda Street at Wadi Adai roundabout in Muscat. Alternatively, take the Muscat Expressway and exit at interchange 5, taking the signed route. Both roads join at Amrat and are then numbered road 17.

You can also get **taxis** from near the Shell petrol station to Qurayyat; shared taxis cost RO2, while minibuses cost RO1, with similar charges from Qurayyat to Sur. Expect to pay around RO20 for an engaged taxi to Sur.

The dual carriageway to Qurayyat winds through mountains and interesting schist foothills. After less than an hour's drive from Muscat you climb to a plateau, from which there is a steep descent for several hundred metres on to the plain of Qurayyat (99km from Muscat). Beyond Qurayyat is Sur, which is roughly a 120km drive mostly along a dual carriageway.

HAWIYAT NAJM PARK AND THE BAMAH SINKHOLE منتزه هوية نجم The beaches around Dibab, which has an exit from the road 112km from Wadi Adai, are particularly good for beachcombing, with unusual shells and birdlife. From the main highway you can also access a sinkhole – take the turning signed Hawiyat Najm Park. Approximately 5km beyond Dibab you come to the park, where there is a picnic site in an area planted with trees. Surrounded by a 1m-high stone wall, the huge natural water sinkhole – 40m across and 20m deep – is known locally as the Bait Al Afreet ('House of the Demon'). Steps lead down to the water, which is clear, turquoise and slightly salty; there are tiny fish visible in the shallower part.

BAMAH (بمة) AND UMQ AR RABAKH (عمق الرباخ) Instead of driving along the main highway (road 17), it is possible to drive along bays and coves rich in birdlife before coming to the village of Bamah (also Bimma). To reach this coastal road, exit at Dibab and follow the road right towards the sea. Bamah is unremarkable in itself, but 2km beyond the village is the right turn that passes under the main highway and continues as a rough graded track that leads inland 16km to the mountain village of Umq Ar Rabakh (usually simply known as Umq). This village is unusual for its old mud and stone houses built into the side of the mountain. The villagers also keep bees whose hives are tucked under cliffs for shelter. The drive is scenically stunning and there is much wildlife in the area, including wolves, foxes and gazelles. You can drive through the impressive wadi on the left (access on the coast over 5km west of Bamah) for up to 8km, depending on flood damage. It has a few old houses in the cliff face.

From Umq there is a difficult 6-hour climb up the 800m cliff face on to the Jabal Bani Jabir Plateau, where the Ibra tombs are located (pages 250–1). The climb is not to be attempted without a guide.

FINS (فنس) TO TIWI (طيوي) From Bimah it is another 10km along that coastal road to Fins, which marks the halfway point to Sur. The stretch of coastline from Fins to Tiwi has both long white-sand beaches and tiny gravel bays with rock pools. The road immediately next to the sea is damaged in several places before Tiwi, and a continuous drive may not be possible. Litter can be a problem, especially on the popular sand beaches like Tiwi (also known as White Beach, 6km beyond Fins). At weekends the beaches can become particularly crowded.

8

WADI ASH SHAB (وادي الشاب) **AND TIWI** (طيوي) These two settlements are both at the mouth of gorges that share their respective settlement's name. If there is one wadi that you must visit during your trip to Oman, it is **Wadi Ash Shab**. It is a place of outstanding natural beauty and peace. The wadi is not drivable, but small boats are available to take you across at RO1 per person return, payable on your return. The youngsters looking after this are on the south side of the wadi just under the bridge roughly where you can park. The 3km walk will take up to 50–60 minutes. In places you will have to clamber down drops of 50cm and negotiate boulders, so some degree of fitness is needed. The walk into the wadi is beautiful, leading through the steep ravine and past pools, waterfalls and lush plantations. On the way are a few abandoned cliff-face dwellings, perhaps just above extreme flood level. The *pièce de résistance* is the mountain pool at the end of the walk, deep in the mouth of the gorge. Here you swim under a vast rock (depending on water levels you may need to dive under for several metres) that opens up into a cavernous mountain pool of turquoise water. There are several villages farther along the wadi that are accessible only on foot.

At **Wadi Tiwi** on the other side of the village the gorge is wider and drivable for 10km or so. The vegetation here, including banana, mango and fig, is very lush and the water flows all year round.

Getting there and away Access to these wadis is via the exit to Wadi Ash Shab signed on road 17. Ash Shab comes first if you are driving from Qurayyat, and is approached by a road that has been cemented because of the steepness of the descent and ascent from/to the cliffs. The road runs down into Wadi Ash Shab and then ascends out of the wadi and on towards Tiwi village, beyond which is Wadi Tiwi.

🏠 **Where to stay** *Map, pages 240–1.*
The **Wadi Shab Resort** (*34 rooms; on the Muscat–Sur dual carriageway just north of Tiwi;* ☏ *24 757667;* e *wadishab@travelcity-oman.com; www.wadishabresort. com;* **$$$**) overlooks a public shingle beach and is well located for a visit to Wadi Ash Shab. The rooms are clean though small considering the relatively high price. Meals are below the standard expected for the price. You will need to book through a Muscat-based tour operator rather than direct with the hotel.

✗ **Where to eat and drink** The menu at **Mubarak bin Juma bin Mubarak Al Araimi Restaurant** (*on the road that winds through Tiwi, next to HSBC;* ⊕ *07.00–22.00 daily;* **$**) has been the same for longer than the author cares to remember: rice with a choice of chicken, beef, fish, dhal or fried vegetables with fresh salad and paratha bread. Everything is freshly prepared and the result is a simple yet very tasty meal. Enjoy watching the activity in the village by sitting outside.

QALHAT قلهات In medieval times Qalhat was one of the key ports in Arabia, but today the ancient town is a ruin and the new settlement hardly more than a village. It is hard to see today why Qalhat was chosen as the site of such an important port, when Sur, just 20km down the coast, seems to have such a superior natural location, with an obvious route to the interior. But until the end of the 15th century, Qalhat had a *falaj* system leading down the wadi from the hills, with many wells to supplement it. There was also enough water for boats to be moored here. Although today the *khawr* (lagoon) is just a stagnant tongue of water by the modern village, centuries ago it was a good anchorage, reaching west into the wadi. For the route to the interior, merchants must have used the donkey path through Wadi Hilm, which ultimately leads to Wadi Bani Khalid.

Qalhat was disastrously affected by major events. First, an earthquake destroyed many of the city's fine buildings at the end of the 15th century. Then in 1507 the Portuguese arrived in Oman and ransacked Qurayyat and Muscat. The following year they attacked Qalhat, killing many of the local population and burning all the ships and buildings. Qalhat was completely devastated and the survivors fled the city.

The town's archaeology is now spread over an area of about 4km², with its prominent mausoleum to the north and the city wall to the south. Most of the major buildings are in the north, lying between the mausoleum and the sea. It is difficult to picture it as the great city that it once was.

The **Bibi Miriam Mausoleum**, named after the woman who built it, has survived earthquakes and invasions since 1311. It was built from limestone and coral and originally covered in stucco with blue Persian tile decoration. It attracted praise from all who wrote about it. In terms of style, it is a familiar cube-shaped building surmounted by a dome, while its interior is decorated with squinches with simple *muqarmas* decoration overlooking the vault below. Bibi Miriam's husband, Baba Ad Din Ayaz, who was the Governor of Qalhat and later Hormuz, predeceased her around 1311 and it is possible that they were both buried below the famous mausoleum on her death, before 1329. The archaeological site is south across the wadi from modern Qalhat. Local people bring small gifts of Omani *halwa* as an offering and occasionally notes are slipped in between the building's stonework. The semicircular arched tunnels are cisterns that were built by the princes of Hormuz in the 13th century.

Getting there and away The new highway bypasses the site, which lies on the seaside a little lower down the hill. To reach it you therefore have to take the Qalhat exit and follow the road down through the village to reach the wadi bed. From here access is on the south side of the wadi. Zealous guardians may not permit entry, so park your car close in order to avoid a wasted walk. If you can walk up the track the mausoleum is on your right and the main town to your left; there will be no charge.

SUR سور

Sur is a quiet coastal town that played a central role in overseas trade with East Africa. It occupies a position on a large lagoon that is still an anchorage today, although at

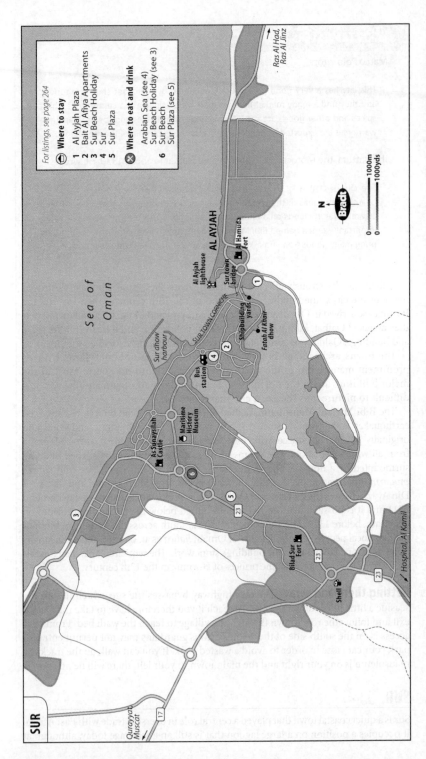

SUR

For listings, see page 264

Where to stay
1 Al Ayjah Plaza
2 Bait Al Afiya Apartments
3 Sur Beach Holiday
4 Sur
5 Sur Plaza

Where to eat and drink
  Arabian Sea (see 4)
  Sur Beach Holiday (see 3)
6 Sur Beach
  Sur Plaza (see 5)

Sea of Oman

AL AYJAH

Ras Al Had,
Ras Al Jinz

Al Ayjah lighthouse
Sur town bridge
Al Hamuda Fort

Sur dhow harbour

SUR TOWN CORNICHE

Shipbuilding yards
Fatah Al Khair dhow

Bus station

Maritime History Museum

As Suwayhah Castle

Bilad Sur Fort

Shell

Hospital, Al Kamil

Qurayyat Muscat

0   1000m
0   1000yds

N

Bradt

low tide areas of it become football pitches. Like Suhar, Sur is another Omani town that lays claim to being the fictional Sindbad's birthplace. It shares its name with the coastal port of Sur in Lebanon, known to Westerners as Tyre, and one attractive theory, based on Herodotus's account that the Phoenicians came from the Gulf area, is that the Phoenicians originally hailed from here, then moved on to Lebanon, reusing the same name as their home town. Archaeological evidence to prove this theory is lacking, but the origins of the Phoenicians are still disputed by experts. To this day Sur's inhabitants have a reputation for being independent-minded, and many of the largest businesses in Oman are owned by people from here.

The coastal town itself never had fresh water, but Bilad Sur, the large village amid the date palms a few kilometres inland, supplied all the necessary water from its wells, and water is still piped in today from the same source.

When Zanzibar and Oman split into two separate sultanates in 1861, Sur had over 100 ocean-going dhows in fleet for trading with the island. Trade declined after the split, hastened by the arrival in the Gulf of the British India Steamer Navigation Company, which also took trade away from Sur. Shipbuilding gradually declined as Sur became a less prosperous port.

The modern town of Sur has a sprawl that extends many kilometres inland and it is difficult to establish when you have reached the centre of town. It is renowned for its horses, hence the model horse statues that flank the road. The passion for pure Arab thoroughbreds survives here in the form of a few trainers who are masters in their field.

If you follow the main tarmac road into the centre of town, this eventually does a big loop around the lagoon, and then crosses the bridge to Ras Al Had and Ras Al Jinz.

GETTING THERE AND AROUND The bus station in Sur is right in the centre of town close to the suq and the Sur Hotel. **Buses** run from here twice a day to Muscat, leaving at 06.00 and 14.30, taking the inland route and costing around RO4.50. **Minibuses** also run early in the morning, costing RO3.50. A shared taxi ride anywhere in Sur should cost around 500bzs.

If you have your own **car**, follow signs for the LNG plant and Qurayyat to get onto the coast road to Muscat. If you follow the Muscat signs you will find yourself on the inland route instead.

A CENTRE OF SHIPBUILDING AND SLAVE TRADING

Sur has long been famous for dhow building and remains the centre for dhow and *sambuk* (fishing boat) building in Oman today. A large dhow (200 tonnes) will take five to six months to build, and only one or two are built in a year. In the 19th century some eight dhows a year were built and launched. The workers today are all Indian.

Many people of Sur had worked abroad in India, East Africa and the rest of the Arabian Gulf, in marked contrast to those from the interior. They particularly focused on the slave trade and arms trafficking. British attempts to eliminate these trades were always met with a certain incomprehension, and Sur was viewed with great disdain by Britain for its chosen activities. Even after the sultan signed anti-slavery treaties with the British, implementing them in Sur was virtually impossible; the established routes inland to Saudi Arabia did not involve Muscat. The first anti-slave trade treaty was signed with the British in 1822, when it was recorded that some 4,000 slaves were imported into Sur. Later, the British began to control shipping more strictly.

WHERE TO STAY *Map, page 262.*

🏠 **Sur Beach Holiday Hotel** (82 rooms) North of the town centre with access from the Qurayyat–Sur highway by turning left to the sea at the 1st roundabout after the large LNG plant; ✆ 25 530300; e surbhtl@omantel.net.om; www.surhotelsoman.com. The hotel is set on a rocky public beach – good for beach combing. The Al Rasag restaurant serves international cuisine with views over the sea. Sur Bar has live music. There is a swimming pool. Accepts credit cards. B/fast inc. **$$$**

🏠 **Sur Plaza Hotel** (102 rooms) On the main road into Sur from Ibra, about 3km after the roundabout with the clock tower; ✆ 25 543777; e reservationsur@omanhotels.com; www.omanhotels.com/surplaza. Part of a chain of hotels that includes Al Falaj Hotel & Ruwi Hotel in Muscat & Al Wadi Hotel in Suhar. It is a large hotel, set inland, with a licensed restaurant & 2 bars, both with live entertainment. The Captain's Bar has easy-listening music played by the resident duo; the Sambuq & Al Shabaka Bar have Arabic/Indian bands. There is a Budget Rent-a-Car desk here. **$$$**

🏠 **Al Ayjah Plaza** (41 rooms) On the other side of the lagoon from the main town, just west of the bridge; ✆ 25 544433; e alayjahplazahotel@gmail.com; www.alayjahplazahotel.com. On the edge of Sur, this hotel is in a good location for visiting Al Ayjah, with the fort & old houses a short walk away. The hotel itself is clean & has an efficient reception. The adjacent restaurant is a good place to enjoy sunset. **$$**

🏠 **Bait Al Afiya Hotel Apartments** (12 rooms) Centrally located in Sur near the Sur Beach Restaurant; the entrance is down a side alley; ✆ 25 544301. This an apartment-style hotel that though not brilliantly clean does offer good value, especially if you want to stay for a few nights; take a meal in one of the outside restaurants. **$**

🏠 **Sur Hotel** (16 rooms) In the centre of Sur with the entrance opposite a good parking area; m 95 566809; e booking@surhotel.net; www.surhotel.net. A good location if you are looking for a simple hotel in town. The hotel dates from the early 1980s but the recent refurbishment has added to its appeal. The rooms are reasonably clean & staff are helpful in making this a worthwhile place for a budget stay. **$**

✗ WHERE TO EAT AND DRINK *Map, page 262.*

Good options for eating out are to be found within either of the two mid-range Sur hotels or at the Arabian Sea Restaurant on the ground floor of the cheaper Sur Hotel, a lively place popular with locals serving good kebabs and even vegetarian bean dishes. There are also plenty of local coffee shops.

✗ **Sur Beach Restaurant** In the centre of Sur on what was the main road through the shopping area; ⏱ 07.00–23.00 daily. This is the best of several similar restaurants in the town centre. The food is on the spicy side, but the cooks can take it down a notch if you ask. **$**

OTHER PRACTICALITIES There are several cash machines in Sur and various money changers in the town centre.

WHAT TO SEE AND DO

Bilad Sur Fort حصن بلاد صور (⏱ 08.30–14.30 Sun–Thu; 500bzs) Set well inland just left of Main Street, Bilad Sur Fort is recognisable by its unusually shaped tower, with a turret on top – just large enough for a person to stand in and gaze out to sea over the date palms. This fort dates from the early 19th century and was constructed from limestone and coral, as coral is both relatively light and insulating.

To get to the fort, drive 750m into Sur on road 23 from the Shell petrol roundabout with the clock tower in the centre. Turn left, take the track ahead of you diagonally to the right and the fort is ahead of you, with its entrance on the other side.

As Sunaysilah Castle حصن السنيسلة (⏱ 08.30–14.30 Sun–Thu; 500bzs) Standing on a mound much closer to the sea and harbour than Bilad Sur Fort, this 350-year-old castle looks far out to sea and provides an excellent first view of Sur. It's a simple design with a square outer wall and round towers. Inside the castle, the entrance hall opens onto a spacious square with only a few rooms, suggesting that the castle was intended for short-term use. The castle is on road 23, about 4.3km east of the Shell petrol station roundabout.

Maritime History Museum المتحف البحري (℡ 24 541466; ⊕ 09.00–16.00 Sat–Thu; contribution recommended) The Maritime History Museum is located in the Al-Oruba (Al Arooba) football club. It is an interesting, very personalised museum about Sur's seafaring tradition and the people involved, comprising three small rooms crammed with exhibits.

From the Shell petrol station roundabout drive east into Sur on road 23, continue across two roundabouts and after 4.6km take a right turn to enter the sports complex immediately to your left. You will need to find the caretaker (haraas) and ask him for a key.

Shipbuilding yards (أحواض بناء السفن) and the *Fatah Al Khair* dhow

(⊕ 08.00–17.00 Sat–Thu) On the edge of Sur's lagoon on the corniche just south of the suspension bridge are the boatyards, which are still in operation but now seemingly under contract to Qatar. The keels and hulls are made from teak imported from India, while the ribs are made from local wood. No plans are ever used: the boats are built by eye, from the outside in, with any and every gap plugged by a specifically cut piece of wood. Though traditional in design and construction, the captain's quarterdeck for these boats, destined for Qatar, is packed full of the latest technology. A small room has souvenirs for sale.

Further southwest on from the boatyards, the road loops around to pass the restored dhow *Fatah Al Khair*, which was built in 1951 in Sur and was the last boat of its kind to be constructed. It was later sold to a Yemeni merchant and then purchased back in 1993. It weighs about 300 tonnes and is over 20m long (a similar size to the ships Vasco da Gama and Afonso de Albuquerque used on their voyages). At low tide the lagoon water disappears and the dhows in the lagoon are beached on an expanse of wet mud.

From the Shell petrol station roundabout drive east for 7km, then at the roundabout take the third exit left and follow the road down the corniche, past the suspension bridge and park on the left. Walk in, avoiding the yapping wadi dogs.

Al Ayjah العيجه There are very few elegant 18th-century merchants' houses in Sur today and you will get a better picture of old prosperous merchant housing in Al Ayjah, a small traditional fishing village. A new suspension bridge takes you across the bay, or else the original road still loops right round from Sur, skirting the edge of the lagoon past small mangrove swamps to reach the district; both routes make the previous ferry trips across the narrow *khawr* unnecessary. The citizens of Al Ayjah, which belongs to the Bani Bu Ali people, used to relish this separation, and in the early 20th century set up their own customs post and flag independent of the customs post in Sur. It then took the sultan two years to get the flag down and back over to the Sur side – he even had to enlist the help of the British Resident in the Gulf.

Late afternoon and early evening are the best times to see Al Ayjah, when the sun sets over the lagoon and casts a reddish-purple tinge over the water. The road winds into the town, passing the **old Al Hamuda Fort** (⊕ 08.30–14.30 Sat–Thu; 500bzs), once the abode of the Hamuda sheikhs from Bani Bu Ali. The fort's entrance is hidden on the eastern side. Inside it is very simple and less interesting than the one in Balid Sur. You can then simply follow the tarmac road southwest through the old houses and turn along the lagoon's edge towards the new lighthouse which overlooks the bay. The road that skirts the lagoon ends there, and the town's youth play football on the sands below.

Take the time to stroll about among the houses, especially those that face directly out to open sea away from the sheltered lagoon. Some of these are imaginatively decorated with maritime memorabilia like old anchors and nets.

Getting there and away Follow the route to the dhow yards on road 23 and cross over the suspension bridge. Take the second exit left at the roundabout, and the same again at the next one, then take the next left and you will be next to the fort.

RAS AL HAD (رأس الحد) AND RAS AL JINZ (رأس الجنز)

Ras Al Had is Arabic for 'headland' or 'land's end'. Scenically unprepossessing, this is the point where the turbulent Arabian Sea meets the calmer Sea of Oman; it is not a dramatic promontory but a flat sandy spit at the end of a monotonous plain, and a lot of litter tends to get washed up here, making the beaches rather unattractive.

An RAF staging post was built here in World War II and the remains of the airstrip are still in evidence. Nearby was a collection of *barasti* huts where simple fishermen lived, with a **fort** (⊕ *08.30–14.30 Sun–Thu; 500bzs*) close to them. This fort still stands and is worth visiting for the views from the towers. Close to the fort archaeologists have found remains from Oman's Bronze Age, and this region in particular was a hub of international trade during that era.

The beaches of Ras Al Had and Ras Al Jinz provide nesting grounds for an estimated 20,000 turtles each year that migrate from as far as the Red Sea and the East African coast. They can be seen virtually all year round, but May through to August is peak nesting time. Other months are considered low nesting season, but the author has been coming here since 1987, often during winter, and has always seen at least one animal, so visit with hope.

Ras Al Jinz (also spelt Junaiz or Junayz) is about 17km southeast of Ras Al Had. The **Turtle Beach Nature Reserve** has been established here, complete with a hotel. It is staffed by guides who escort you to the nesting beach after dusk to watch the large female turtles come ashore and lay their eggs. The evening tour (*RO5pp*) begins about 21.00, and the guide visits the beach to find a suitable turtle and then summons you over. Alternatively, you can go just before dawn (at about 04.00) – also on a

TURTLE-WATCHING RULES

Some visitors demonstrate an extraordinary lack of sensitivity when attending this natural spectacle in their determination to get good photos at any cost. The turtles are easily disturbed and if they feel intruded upon, will simply head back into the sea. To enjoy the process and allow others to enjoy it too, it's important to follow a few guidelines. At Ras Al Jinz you are on a supervised visit.

- Do not make any noise or disturb their peace.
- Do not use flash photography, as the lights unsettle the nesting turtles (at night cameras are prohibited at Ras Al Jinz).
- Do not touch the turtles or their eggs.
- Do not stay overnight on the beach.
- Do not leave any litter.

supervised visit – and watch the eggs hatching and the baby turtles scurrying to the sea before the hungry gulls or crabs have a chance to eat them. Many do not make it. This early morning experience can often be more enjoyable than the evening one, as you can avoid the crowds, probably see the last straggling female return to the beach and when your guide says you may, take some photographs.

A new **research centre** has been built by the Ministry of Tourism and there is a **museum** (*www.rasaljinz-turtlereserve.com*) within the hotel designed to showcase both the turtles and the unique marine ecology of the eastern coast of Ash Sharqiyyah region. The exhibits provide visitors with comprehensive insights into the ecosystems that sustain turtles, charting the complete life-cycle stages of the turtle from hatchling to nesting to migration. In addition, antiquities uncovered during ongoing excavation work in the area are preserved here.

Italian and French archaeological teams have worked at a site behind the turtle beach and the mesa overlooking the beach. A mud brick building divided into several elongated chambers was found, together with some burial sites. Items included bitumen from Mesopotamia, ivory from India, Indus Valley (Harappa) pottery and stamp seals, indicating trading links between Oman, the Indus Valley and Mesopotamia some 4,500 years ago.

GETTING THERE AND AWAY There is no public transport to either Ras Al Had or Ras Al Jinz. By **car**, from the suspension bridge at Sur cross over to the east, at the roundabout take the second exit left and at the next roundabout take the first exit right. After 32km you will arrive at a junction with Ras Al Had, which is signposted to the left, and Ras Al Jinz, signed to the right. Beyond Ras Al Jinz the coastline continues with low cliffs and sandy though debris-ridden beaches to Asilah (page 258), 65km from the junction for Ras Al Had and Ras Al Jinz.

WHERE TO STAY *Map, pages 240–1.*

Ras Al Had Holiday Hotel (60 rooms)
\ 25 569111; e rasalhadd@surhotelsoman.com;
www.surhotelsoman.com. At the junction from Sur,
turn left to Ras Al Had, continue over the roundabout
& follow the road as it swings left; you will arrive at
the hotel, which is on the east side of the lagoon,
after 8.5km. The rooms are good sizes & pleasantly
decorated. There is a licensed restaurant & separate
bar. It is always best to confirm turtle tours in
advance to avoid any disappointment, although you
might be lucky to turn up & arrange something for
the same day. The usual pattern is to leave the hotel
at 20.00 for a short drive & return at least 2 hours
later. A 4x4 is not necessary. Accepts credit cards. B/
fast inc. **$$$**

Turtle Beach Resort (50 beach 'cottages' of
various types) \ 25 540068; reservations
\ 25 543400; e info@tbroman.com; www.tbroman.
com. At the junction from Sur, turn left to Ras Al
Had, then at the roundabout turn left (3rd exit)
& carefully follow the twisty road that skirts the
lagoon. Turtle Beach Resort is almost at the end of
the road; after 7km right turn takes you onto a short

track into the hotel. The simply furnished beach
huts occupy a spot on the private beach, & there is
a dhow-shaped restaurant overlooking the beach
serving an included buffet of international food that
includes chips & ice cream. B/fast is served in a small,
uninteresting restaurant; far nicer if you can tolerate
the occasional fly is to take b/fast at the beachside &
enjoy the view of beach, lagoon & dhows.
The white-sand beach is on the lagoon, making it
a calm area for swimming. The habitat for turtles
about a 20min drive away; you will need to leave for
Ras Al Jinz around 20.20 to see them. **$$**

Ras Al Jinz Turtle Reserve (31 rooms)
m 96 550606; e reservations@rasaljinz-
turtlereserve.com; http://www.rasaljinz-
turtlereserve.com. Behind Ras Al Jinz Beach; the hotel
is 15 rooms within the main building & 16 'eco-tents'
on a low hill overlooking the general area; it takes
about 5mins to walk from these to the main building
for meals & meeting up with the guides for turtle-
watching sessions. All rooms have AC & have private
shower & toilet. If you decide on the eco-tent, ask for
unit 25, which overlooks the sea. **$$$$**

9

Al Wusta الوسطى

The Arabic name Al Wusta means the 'central area' and that accurately describes this chunk of central Oman which is neither north nor south. Al Wusta is bordered to the west by Saudi Arabia, to the south by the governorate of Dhofar, in the east by the Arabian Sea and in the north by Oman's Ash Sharqiyyah, Ad Dakhiliyah and Adh Dhahirah regions.

This is Oman's least-populated province. Its 41,069 people are spread over a vast 79,700km², giving an average of far fewer than one person per square kilometre. Currently Muhut, with 17,208 people within its administrative area, is the most populous zone. However, future plans for Ad Duqm, which has a current population of 8,401, could see it grow considerably, not least due to the expected accommodation for thousands of workers. Hayma, the region's administrative centre, has 9,115 people, while the town of Al Jazir has 6,345.

Masirah Island has been included in this chapter in order to provide a more logical link for the routes given here, even though administratively speaking it is part of the Ash Sharqiyyah region. Its population of 12,881 reflects the draw of the rich fishing waters that both it and Muhut share. Further south again, Ash Shuwaymiyyah and its administrative area of Shalim wa Juzur Al Hallaniyyat have a small population of 4,434.

Most people simply drive through Al Wusta at speed along the long, central, inland road from Muscat to Salalah, longing for a sight of something other than gravel and flat, featureless desert. The region is very much a link between Oman's north and south. The arterial roads are tarmac and are generally in good condition with hard shoulders. From Nizwa to Adam the main road is dual carriageway, as it is from Thumrayt to Salalah, and the central section is rapidly being worked on to achieve a dual carriageway all the way from Muscat down to Salalah. The focus on this substantial upgrade has meant that some small sections of the current road have a cracked surface, though this is periodically repaired. There are petrol stations at regular intervals along the three main arterial roads, which are more than sufficient to assure safety under regular conditions, although it's advisable to refill a petrol tank when it gets below half full. These modern roads mean that it is possible to drive from Muscat to Salalah in a day, but if you choose to take time over the coastal route there are hotels of varying standards scattered down the coast; camping is no longer the only way to enjoy this region.

With such a low population and a previous subsistence economy, there are no forts or buildings of historic significance here. Nature is at its most appealing along the coastline, so it makes sense for travellers to avoid the main Nizwa–Salalah road and take the road less travelled. To do justice to this part of Oman you are probably looking at a week of self-sufficient camping, definitely in the cooler winter months, as there is no shade to be found at all – there is little vegetation to speak of and from April the wind increasingly makes camping difficult near the coast. New hotels offer

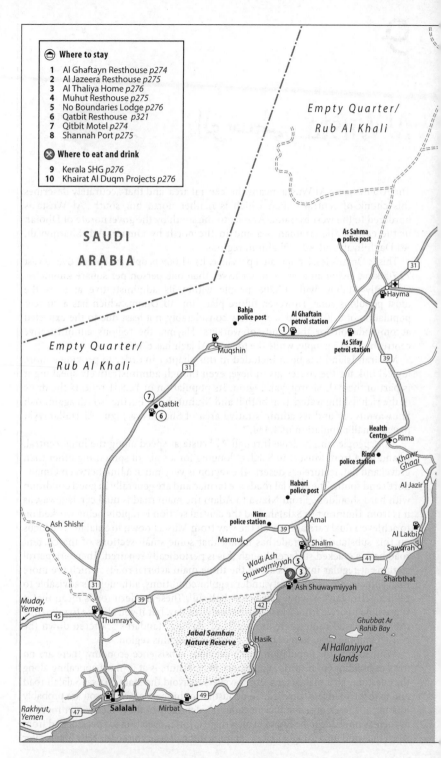

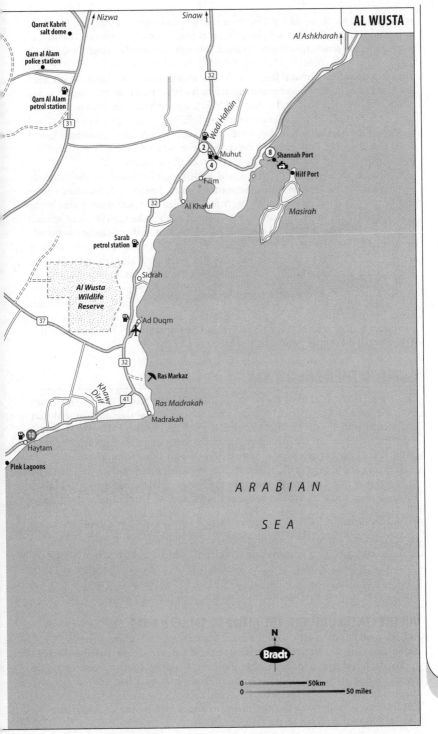

Qarrat Kabrit
salt dome ●

↑ Nizwa

Sinaw ↑

Al Ashkharah ↑

Qarn al Alam
police station
●

Qarn Al Alam
petrol station

🅿

31

32

Wadi Haflain

🅿
2
Muhut
4

○ Filim

8 Shannah Port
⚓
● Hilf Port

32

○ Al Khaluf

Masirah

Sarab
petrol station 🅿

🅿 ○ Sidrah

**Al Wusta
Wildlife
Reserve**

37

🅿 ○ Ad Duqm
✈

32

➤ Ras Markaz

Khawr Dirif

41

○ Ras Madrakah

Madrakah

🅿 10
Haytam

● Pink Lagoons

A R A B I A N

S E A

N

Bradt

0 ────── 50km
0 ────── 50 miles

an alternative for those who prefer more comfort and these are sufficiently spaced out, making it possible to travel along the coast road from hotel to hotel. The arterial roads along the coast are well-paved tarmac, although with only a single lane in each direction on these routes it's also fortunate that the volume of traffic is relatively low. The most dominant physical feature is the low escarpment of the Huqf, which lies a few kilometres inland from the shoreline. Much of the coast is uninterrupted sandy beach, although the headland of Ras Madrakah is dramatic, with stretches of white sand interspersed with black igneous rocks and cliffs. Several shipwrecks have rusted quietly on the beaches where they were washed up. Near Al Jazir (previously Qahal or Al Kahil) are the Pink Lagoons caused by algae, while Ash Shuwaymiyyah has a box canyon quite unlike any other in Oman, with sheer, creamy cliffs.

Birdlife, especially gulls, flamingos and waders, can be found on the extensive beaches and the *khawrs* (creeks). Birds are attracted here for the molluscs, and dolphins and turtles can often be seen offshore. A few Arabian oryx still roam freely in the gravel desert of the Jiddat Al Harasis, reintroduced by the sultan in 1982, having been hunted to extinction in the wild (see box, page 278), and Arabian gazelle can usually be spotted in the same area. Perfectly adapted to the desert, the oryx can go without water for 22 months as long as it has plants to graze on with high water content. The region is also home to caracal lynx and desert hare and possibly Nubian ibex.

The developing port of Ad Duqm is the region's dominant economic focus. It is largely intended to be a service port with dry-dock facilities. The British Royal Navy are thought to be planning to take advantage of this by developing a support facility within it for their Arabian Sea operations. The port may also have a small oil refinery and a fish-processing facility.

GETTING THERE AND AWAY

This region is accessed from the north via three separate routes, two of which start from the main Muscat–Nizwa highway, while the other takes the coast from Muscat and merges with one of the other routes all the way into Salalah in Oman's far south. All of the routes are tarmac all the way. Although mostly single track in each direction, traffic is not heavy so delays are minimal. Here they are listed from west to east.

There are also a number of roads that cross west–east between the routes that start in Nizwa and Izki. One cross route links the Nizwa–Salalah road across to Muhut, while another, route 37, crosses between Hayma and Ad Duqm, and a third, route 39, branches off 23km south of Hayma before looping into Marmul and on to Thumrayt, offering a route via Rima towards the coast at Al Jazir. Route 39 also carries on to Amal and a junction there gives access to Shalim and Ash Shuwaymiyyah.

At Ad Duqm there is a small **domestic airport** which has flights from Muscat on Sundays at 07.45, Mondays at 13.35, Wednesdays at 07.40 and Thursdays at 12.10, returning to Muscat on the same days, departing 30 minutes after arrival. Oman Air provides the service, but booking is done exclusively through www.duqmair.com.

VIA THE CENTRAL DESERT: THE NIZWA TO SALALAH ROAD The desert Nizwa–Salalah road has its junction off the main Muscat–Nizwa highway (routes 15 and 31). This is without doubt the quickest route if you are simply passing through Al Wusta, but it is also indescribably soporific, with the distance between single trees often as great as that between petrol stations, and a flat, endless horizon that neither advances nor retreats. In several sections the road surface is cracked. Resurfacing is underway, but the major overhaul will be the dual carriageway that is being constructed in the middle section.

There are **petrol stations** along the entire road, including at Adam (57km south of the Firq junction at Nizwa), Qarn Al Alam (120km south of Adam), Hayma (198km south of Qarn Al Alam), Al Ghaftain (96km south of Hayma), Muqshin (68km south of Ghaftain), Qatbit (60km south of Muqshin), Thumrayt (195km south of Qatbit), and countless pumps in Salalah (73km south of Thumrayt). Ideally, you should never leave yourself with less petrol than will allow you to drive 300km, in case a petrol station is without fuel and you need to proceed to the next one. Small coffee shops offering food and refreshments can be found either immediately next to these petrol stations or within a very short distance. With little in the way of tourist attractions along this road, the understandable temptation is to drive without stopping. Resist this urge and take a break where practical to at least walk off any doziness.

Companies offering **bus** services along this route include daily services by **Salalah Line Transport** (✆ *24 798470*; e *salalahline@gmail.com*), leaving Muscat at 08.00 and 18.00; the **Gulf Transport Company** (✆ *24 790823*), leaving Muscat at 03.00, 07.00, 10.00, 13.00, 17.00, 18.00, 19.00 and 20.00; and **Mwasalat** (formerly the Oman National Transport Company, page 60), leaving Muscat at 07.00, 10.00 and 18.00. Salalah Line and Mwasalat services arrive in Hayma 6 hours and Salalah 12 hours after leaving Muscat; Gulf Transport Company services reach the Al Ghaftain Resthouse 7 hours and Salalah 12 hours after leaving Muscat. Prices for all of these services from Muscat to Salalah are around RO7 per person one-way.

There is no public transport other than the long-distance bus services on this and the other two routes and there is unlikely to be a taxi unless it is passing through. This does mean that these long-distance buses can unfortunately be used only for passing through the region and little else.

🏠 Where to stay and eat on the Nizwa–Salalah desert route
On the drive along route 31 from Nizwa to Thumrayt there are several simple resthouses, some with basic, unlicensed restaurants. In the order that you meet them on the drive from Muscat, these are: Al Ghabah (in Ad Dakhiliyah, page 227); Hayma and Al Ghaftayn (both in Al Wusta); and Qatbit and Thumrayt (both in Dhofar – page 321). Three of them are in this region and are detailed below, along with Qatbit, which although in Dhofar is so far north within that region as to be only useful on this route. The establishments below are listed from north to south.

The route has only the most basic places to eat, and the restaurants in the hotels are comparable to much of the offering in standalone restaurants. Hayma, with its concentration of simple eating places around the Shell petrol station, makes a sensible place to stop, fill up with petrol and sit down for some food.

USEFUL TELEPHONE NUMBERS

MEDICAL FACILITIES
- ✚ **Hayma Hospital** ✆ 23 436013
- ✚ **Rima Health Centre** m 99 203826

POLICE STATIONS
Al Wusta Police Headquarters
✆ 23 436099
Hayma Police Division ✆ 23 436211

Qarn Al Alam Police Station
✆ 23 385559
As Sahma Police Post ✆ 23 388984
Bahja Police Post ✆ 23 388963
Habari Police Post ✆ 23 388004
Nimr Police Station ✆ 23 382391
Rima Police Station ✆ 23 382272

🏠 **Arabian Oryx Hotel** (50 rooms) South of the Al Maha petrol station just before entering Hayma; 📞 23 436379. This is the newest of the 3 hotels in Hayma, & so far the ravages of time are not showing. Rooms are accessed from a common veranda & there is a shaded central courtyard to sit in. **$**

🏠 **Al Wusta Tourism Motel** (16 rooms) In between the Arabian Oryx Hotel & the petrol station in Hayma; 📞 23 436016. Simple but adequate accommodation with a basic restaurant. If you cannot locate staff ask at the petrol station next door. **$**

🏠 **Himah Motel** (15 rooms) 2km south of the Arabian Oryx Hotel; 📞 23 297103. This is a small hotel offering cheap rooms. No restaurant, & it's desperately in need of complete refurbishment. **$**

🏠 **Al Ghaftayn Resthouse** [map, pages 270–1] (10 rooms) 96km south of Hayma;

m 99 485881. Reasonably clean rooms around a central courtyard. There is also a petrol station within the compound. The restaurant gets busy when the Muscat–Salalah buses run by the Gulf Transport Company arrive, so it's best to try & wait or ask whether your meal can be delivered to your room. **$**

🏠 **Qitbit Motel** [map, pages 270–1] (10 rooms) Qatbit, 223km south of Hayma; 📞 23 212769. Rooms set around a central courtyard similar to but not as well looked after as Al Ghaftayn. There is also a petrol station within the compound. Because the motel is so isolated & there is a water spring with a densely vegetated small oasis a kilometre behind the motel, both the oasis & the numerous trees of the motel's garden attract migrating birds during late summer & early spring. **$**

VIA THE IZKI TO MUHUT ROAD الطريق إزكي إلى محوت The Izki–Muhut road
has its junction off the main Muscat–Nizwa highway. It passes through Sinaw (in the Ash Sharqiyyah) and on towards Muhut (routes 15, 33, 32), where it becomes part of the Muscat–Salalah Coastal Road. The scenery south of Sinaw is generally flat with little of interest, although on a clear day along the central stretch of the road you might have distant views of sand desert to the east.

All of the places of any real interest are on the Muscat–Salalah Coastal Road described on pages 279–85.

There are petrol stations and small restaurants at As Sifay, 126km south of Sinaw.

VIA THE MUSCAT TO SALALAH COASTAL ROAD الساحل من مسقط إلى صلالة The
third route is from Muscat via Sur, Al Ashkharah and Muhut to Hasik (route 17 and on to 32, 41, 42 and 49). This entire route is tarmacked and termed on maps as the Muscat–Salalah Coastal Road, and for much of the route it does precisely that, as it largely follows the line of the east coast.

From Muscat road 17 leads into Sur, where you cross over the suspension bridge in the centre of town, as there is no bypass. The road then continues south to Al Ashkharah, where again the route runs through the town centre. This is a bit of a rabbit warren, with no signage and a very narrow road through the built-up area. However, even if you stray a bit off track in the town, bear in mind that you need to follow the coast south, which is on your left, and adding only a few minutes to your journey. From just outside Al Ashkharah the route is obvious and is initially mostly between the southern dunes of the Wihibah Sands and the Arabian Sea. It then crosses over the *sabkha* peninsula of Bar Al Hikman to Muhut and joins up with the Izki–Salalah road.

The scenery is varied, with isolated mountains in the northern part south of Sur, sand desert in the central area, and south of Muhut a coastal plain where beaches are usually just a short distance away. From Al Lakbi an escarpment adds interest, almost as an appetiser to the splendid wadis and coast from Ash Shuwaymiyyah onwards.

Petrol stations are available along the route, including at Qurayyat (103km southeast of Muscat), Sur (90km south of Qurayyat), Al Ashkharah (130km south of Sur), Muhut (222km south of Al Ashkharah), Sarab (95km south of Muhut), Ad

Duqm (69km south of Sidra), Haytam (149km south of Ad Duqm), Al Lakbi (89km south of Haytam), Shalim (109km west of Al Lakbi), Ash Shuwaymiyyah (38km south of Shalim), Hasik (90km south of Ash Shuwaymiyyah), Mirbat (122km west of Hasik) and several on the way into Salalah. Small coffee shops offering food and refreshments can be found either immediately next to these petrol stations or within a short distance.

A twice-daily **bus service** from Burj Al Sahwa in Muscat to Ad Duqm is provided by **Happy Line** (m *24 798470;* e *info@happylineoman.com*), leaving at 07.00 and 10.30 (*7hrs; RO5; booking essential*). There is an alternate-day bus service by Happy Line from Ad Duqm to Salalah (m *97 473034, 473035*); ask about this when you arrive in Ad Duqm, as it operates on different days each week. Although this bus service does provide access to Ad Duqm, you will need your own hired vehicle once you are there, as taxis are non-existent and, in common with most of Oman, there is no local public transport.

See pages 279–85 for more on the places along the Al Wusta section of this route.

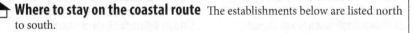 Where to stay on the coastal route
The establishments below are listed north to south.

Shannah Port Hotel [map, pages 270–1] Opposite the Oman Oil petrol station, Shannah; m 91 364014. This is a simple place with basic accommodation, where you might rest overnight if waiting for the ferry. There is a small restaurant next door. **$**

Al Jazeera Resthouse [map, pages 270–1] (18 rooms) On the roundabout of the main road from Sinaw south towards Ad Duqm, next to Al Maha petrol, Al Jubah Muhut; m 99 820882. A simple place, but with adequate rooms & a basic restaurant. **$**

Muhut Resthouse [map, pages 270–1] (16 rooms) Muhut; m 93 232610. Simple accommodation at a reasonable price & situated conveniently to get to Filim if you wish to birdwatch. The restaurant offers reasonable meals throughout the day. **$**

City Hotel Duqm [map, page 282] (118 rooms) Less than 2km southeast of the Shell petrol station in Ad Duqm on the main road or a 25km drive northeast from Ad Duqm's airport; m 25 214900; e rsvn@cityhotelduqm.com; www.cityhotelduqm.com. This modern hotel is very convenient if you simply need a place to sleep in on your drive along this route. **$$$**

Crowne Plaza Duqm [map, page 282] (213 rooms) 11km southeast of the Shell petrol station on Ad Duqm's beachfront area or a 30km drive northeast from Ad Duqm's airport; m 25 214444; e info.cpduqm@ihg.com; www.ihg.com/crowneplaza. All rooms have a sea view &, like other Crowne Plaza hotels, this new hotel offers good facilities with several dining options; overall, it offers excellent value for money. **$$$**

Park Inn Duqm [map, page 282] (73 chalets & apts) Adjacent to the Crowne Plaza, Ad Duqm; m 22 085700; e reservations.duqm@ rezidorparkinn.com; www.parkinn.com/hotel-

---

duqm. This hotel is set further back from the public beach than the Crowne Plaza – it's a 500m walk over the natural rock pavement. Especially good for families who use the chalets with their outdoor sitting area & small kitchen. **$$$**

🏠 **Al Thaliya Home** [map, pages 270–1] (11 rooms) Next to Al Maha petrol station on the edge of Ash Shuwaymiyyah; m 99 499511. Very simple accommodation. No meals, but the small restaurants in the village are a few minutes' drive away. **$**

🏠 **No Boundaries Lodge** [map, pages 270–1] (9 rooms) Located 500m behind Al Maha petrol in a residential area of Ash Shuwaymiyyah; m 95 951810; e noboundariesoman@gmail. com. 3 simple but comfortable lodges that are usually very popular & therefore busy with game fishermen in Oct, Nov, Mar & Apr. **$$**

✖ **Where to eat and drink on the coastal route** There are a number of good restaurants in the hotels in Ad Duqm in addition to the very basic ones that are in the villages on this road. A few of these restaurants are listed here, north to south.

✖ **Coral Reefs Restaurant** [map, page 282] Shell petrol station forecourt, Ad Duqm; ⏰ 07.00–23.00 daily. Simple local food with an emphasis on rice & chicken, served in a busy local restaurant with very simple decoration. **$**

✖ **Suq Restaurant** [map, page 282] Crowne Plaza Hotel (page 275), Ad Duqm; ☎ 25 214444; ⏰ 06.00–22.30 daily. International-style buffet & à la carte offered in a modern restaurant with earth-toned decoration overlooking the hotel's pool. **$$$**

✖ **Ocean Restaurant** [map, page 282] Park Inn Hotel, Ad Duqm; ☎ 22 085700; ⏰ 06.30–10.00, noon–15.00 & 19.00–23.00 daily. International à la carte. The seating area includes a very pleasant shaded veranda overlooking the sea, as well as an indoor dining room in a restrained modern style. **$$$**

✖ **Areesh Restaurant** [map, page 282] City Hotel (page 275), Ad Duqm; ☎ 25 214900; ⏰ 06.00–22.30 daily. Buffet b/fast & à la carte lunch & dinner. This restaurant has a clean, modern appearance with a pleasant outdoor seating area. **$$**

✖ **Khairat Al Duqm Projects Restaurant** [map, pages 270–1] On the east side of the road, Haytam; ⏰ 08.00–22.00 daily. Simple local food cooked to order. Very basic quiet local restaurant with outdoor tables on a small veranda overlooking the road. **$**

✖ **Kerala Restaurant SHG** [map, pages 270–1] In the centre of Ash Shuwaymiyyah, next to a small grocery; m 99 691351; ⏰ 08.00–22.30 daily. Simple local food with a slightly spicy flavour in a small, simple restaurant. **$**

THE NIZWA–THUMRAYT INLAND ROUTE
طريق نزوى - ثمريت

(Route 31; 800km; see pages 272–3) See pages 273–4 for practical information and places to stay and eat along this route.

The 800km tarmac road from Nizwa to Thumrayt can be completed in around 8 hours' solid driving, with a single refuelling stop. Most people find this too strenuous and deadly dull; moreover, regular breaks are essential on this soporific drive, where lack of concentration is the main cause of accidents. An overnight at one of the rather uninspiring series of resthouses along the way will break up the journey or at the very least provide a stop for a meal.

Driving south from Adam in the Ad Dakhiliyah region, the vegetation gradually disappears and the land takes on the appearance and profile of a well-fried pancake. Along the route are signs pointing off to distant locations where some of Oman's oilfields are scattered. If you are expecting a change in scenery your wait will eventually be rewarded with a few outlying sand dunes almost 200km south of Adam. However, these are soon left behind and it's another 136km until the small town of **Hayma** (هيماء) is reached (see page 274 for accommodation listings). The by now familiar scenery continues past Muqshin, which is Dhofar's northernmost settlement and on into Dhofar's second town of Thumrayt, where conical hills finally bring the central plateau to a very welcome end after 740km driving from Adam.

QARRAT KABRIT SALT DOME قارة كبريت With its salt excavations, the Qarrat Kabrit Salt Dome provides a geological link to Oman's past trade and its current oil industry. It is a 45-minute diversion from the main road. At Al Maha petrol station, located 177km south of the Firq junction at Nizwa, take the turn west. Continue for 20km to a track that heads to the north, turn onto it and continue down it for 7km to the small hill. This is not worth making a long journey specifically to see, but it is an interesting short detour just off the highway.

Although it rises less than 50m, the salt dome assumes a dominance over the surrounding flat dusty landscape. The salt, created through evaporation over probably hundreds of thousands of years, was eventually buried several kilometres deep by other sediments. The right conditions underground allowed the downward pressure on the salt to force the salt upwards through weaknesses in the overlain sediments in the form of a giant column. Today salt domes are markers for possible oil deposits.

Quarried over the centuries for rock salt and baked for aeons under the sun, the small hill has a grim appearance. In the past, the salt from here might be shipped by camel and dhow to distant East Africa, where it was bartered for timber, cloves and slaves. Today modern Landcruisers bring it to the local suqs, where it is a cash-only business.

MUQSHIN مقشن This is a small settlement with a petrol station and health clinic 164km south of Hayma. The explorer Wilfred Thesiger described visiting 'Mughshin' in 1945 and 1946, where he mentioned some *ghaf* trees in a protected area called a *hauta*, which meant that no tree could be cut. Today the trees are still there, fed by a small water spring that creates an elongated open woodland 3.6km west of the main road. To reach the trees exit the road into Muqshin and take the third exit left at the roundabout, and almost immediately there is a right turn that takes you along a tarmacked road towards a small, quite unexpected parking area. The pools of water and resulting vegetation attract a wide variety of birds, though in limited numbers; warblers, shrikes and ravens should be seen, with the possibility of sandgrouse.

QATBIT قتبيت At 60km south of Muqshin, Qatbit (also Qatbit) is a small oasis 3km east of the main road. Take the rough track to the right of the Qitbit Motel (page 274) to the extremely dense vegetation on the track's left. Vagrant birds are common

TRIBES OF CENTRAL OMAN

The three major Bedouin tribes of central Oman are the Junaiba, the Wihibah and the Harasis. Since they are all nomads, their tribal areas are never entirely clear-cut. As a rule, however, the Junaiba live along the coast from Sur, with several sub-tribes near the Dhofar border, and they also live on Masirah Island. The Wihibah live in the Wihibah Sands and eastwards to the coast, while the Harasis live in the vast flat expanse of desert known as the Jiddat Al Harasis, northeast of Salalah. The Harasis have always been the truest nomads in Oman, with no date groves to return to, just the inhospitable Jiddat lowland where they move about with their camels, speaking a south Arabian dialect incomprehensible to any other Arab. They are noted for their excellent sense of direction.

THE ORYX LEGEND

The white oryx, a kind of large desert antelope the size of a red deer or reindeer, are iconic in Oman and through the Arabian Peninsula generally, always viewed as part of the local heritage. Their local name *Al maha* is used for innumerable companies, notably by the ubiquitous petrol station chain, and Qatar Air also use it as their logo. They are perfectly adapted to their desert environment, their white coat reflecting the sun's rays and their splayed hooves making it easy to walk in sand. They are very hardy to drought and live solely on the dew that falls every night in the desert here. Legend has it that the oryx is in fact the ancient unicorn, and certainly when seen in profile the horns do often appear as one. The ancient Egyptians were said to bind the horns of young oryx together to make them fuse into one as they grew. Both sexes have horns and the ones of the female are longer and thinner than those of the male.

A law passed in 1982 banned hunting them, and a 40-strong herd was re-introduced at that point, the last animal having been shot in 1972. By the late 1990s the numbers had increased to several hundred. A victim of its own success, the herd was again decimated by intermittent poaching. Oryx were traditionally hunted for their meat and white skins; however, it was a live animal – especially female – that was the prize, to be spirited away elsewhere and used for breeding in private collections. Further attempts to reintroduce the species into the wild in Oman are unlikely, as the same thing might well happen again.

Oryx are extremely hard to spot, as they have a keen sense of smell and tend to disappear over the horizon, leaving their tracks and droppings as the only clues that they were there. Local tribesmen say they can be approached from upwind by lying flat on a camel's back, as oryx have no fear of camels.

here and you will see a wide variety in what is less than a hectare, including scops owl, golden oriole, kestrel, hoopoe, warblers, shrike, ravens and of course what is now probably Oman's most widespread bird, the common mynah.

See page 274 for accommodation in Qatbit.

AL WUSTA WILDLIFE RESERVE محمية المها العربية في الوسطي في جعلوني (*Entrance gates* ⊕ *07.00–noon & 15.00–17.00 daily; RO5*) The Jiddat Al Harasis, Oman's vast central plain, was so isolated and desolate that few people have lived there and even fewer ever visited. In summer the heat is extreme, rising to well over 50°C, while in winter temperatures plunge to a bone-chilling near-zero. It was probably these factors that enabled the Arabian oryx to survive here for so long, as its principal predator, man, was few and far between. By 1972 there were no wild animals to be found and the species was reported as being extinct in the wild. Fortunately, captive Arabian oryx were breeding in several zoos around the world, and these enabled the oryx to be reintroduced to the wild. A decision was made that the location in which they were last seen in the wild would be the best place for that initial reintroduction, and that place was Jaluni in the Jiddat Al Harasis. In 1982, a reintroduction programme began.

The Al Wusta Wildlife Reserve at Jaluni, which was previously called the Arabian Oryx Sanctuary, was such an initial success at breeding the oryx that it was inscribed as a UNESCO World Heritage Site in 1994. At over 27,000km^2 it covered a vast expanse – almost 10% of Oman's land area. The oryx population reached 450. In 2007, following a reduction in the numbers of oryx to 65 due to poaching and the overall size of the sanctuary being reduced to 10% of its original size, UNESCO delisted the site.

Although the Jiddat Al Harasis lacks any hills that might attract rain, it does have a sharp temperature drop before dawn, which allows dew and occasionally fog to form, sustaining life within the area. Inhabitants include Arabian oryx, caracal, Arabian gazelle, sand gazelle, sand cat, houbara bustard, lizards, snakes, spiders, birds and endemic plant species including acacia. The oryx are now kept in pens whose total size is about 3.6km². They hold mostly females; males are left in the pens for a period to mate and then released outside and other males introduced, as a method of trying to maintain genetic diversity. The reserve lies on bird migratory routes between Africa, Europe and central Asia, and provides good opportunities for birdwatching.

If you are in the area this is a worthwhile visit, as you will be able to see the female oryx in their pens and probably a few male oryx roaming around in the general area. A fair number of gazelle can also be seen. That said, it is not an East African-type experience or even similar to a safari park where you can drive or walk among the animals. **Permission to visit the reserve** can only be obtained directly from officials based at the reserve. To arrange this, contact m 99 012132, possibly initially as a text message with a follow-up phone call the next day. The reserve is under the jurisdiction of the Advisor for Conservation of the Environment (e *acedrc@ omantel.net.om*), although at the time of writing they did not handle visit enquiries.

Getting there and away There are two ways of getting to the sanctuary. One is to take the Muscat–Salalah road and, at Hayma, turn left (east) towards Ad Duqm. After 64km on this road take the track north to Jaluni. Alternatively, from the Oman Oil petrol station on the Hayma road south of Ad Duqm, travel west towards Hayma for 99km to the same turn north. Follow this dirt track for some 23km, until you reach a fork in the road, at which point you follow the right fork and drive for another 23km to the camp. There is an entry gate well before the offices and accommodation for the Al Wusta Wildlife Reserve; do not try a cross country-route as there is a perimeter fence to block access. Maps and GPS are needed to tour the reserve, and at least two vehicles should travel together for safety reasons. It is possible to camp at the reserve in a prescribed place, but you will need to be entirely self-sufficient in food and water.

THE MUSCAT–DHOFAR COASTAL ROUTE
طريق مسقط ـ ظفار الساحلي

(*Routes 15, 33, 32, 41 and 42; 1,179km; see pages 274–5*) *See pages 275–6 for practical information and places to stay and eat along this route.*

If you want lots of beach camping in unspoilt landscapes, have your own 4x4 and are completely self-sufficient in supplies, this route may appeal to you.

Although the route is long and lacking in any major tourist sights, it is so full of unexpected interest and stark beauty that it may well be the most pleasurable long-distance drive in Oman. The tarmacked road leads south after leaving the Ash Sharqiyyah region, cutting in between the dunes of the southern Wihibah Sands and the Arabian Sea. At Ras Ruwais the dunes collapse into the sea and, as if running out of material, the splendid hills of sand are almost immediately replaced by the endless *sabkha* at Bar Al Hikman. The beaches here are a magnet for thousands of birds throughout the year and occasional turtles haul themselves up to lay eggs. After Muhut (also Mahout, Mahawt, Mahoot and occasionally Hij, the official name of the town), the main tarmac road turns south, passing the Huqf escarpment on the right and the edge of the white powder sands at Al Khaluf and the sea on the left. Periodically the road ascends a low hill, giving an enticing view of your journey stretching out before you, perhaps with a bend at the end that

In the 1960s the Bedouin of the south had an almost unimaginably harsh lifestyle. They owned nothing save their camels, goats and a few leather bags. The children would sleep squashed among the goats. Their close dependence on nature, where they could perish if a well dried out or a camel died, gave them a deep sense of the will of Allah, and the Quran was their only education. Even though they had so little, the rule of the desert was to share with guests and unexpected visitors, even if this meant their own family going without. No bedu would eat or drink until their companions had all reached the water well; no-one would take more than their share. Petty theft within a tribe was despised as dishonourable, yet it was acceptable, even manly, to raid another tribe's camels and kill the tribespeople in order to steal for your own. This illustrates the overriding loyalty to one's family and tribe above all other considerations; an outsider is often a secondary consideration. In her book *The Southern Gates of Arabia*, Freya Stark observed: 'Crime is practically unknown in the Hadhramaut; such things as robbery and murder, being done according to established rules, come rather under the heading of legitimate warfare.' Blood feuds are also a question of honour; they are not crimes.

The camel – the lifeblood of the Bedouin – does not normally sweat until its body temperature exceeds 104°F, thereby conserving its water for long periods even in excessive heat. As such, the Bedouin were able to rely on camel milk in the desert long after their own water ran out. A Bedouin was said to be able to tell from the footprint of a camel who its owner was, when and where it had drunk last by the amount and frequency of the droppings, and in which wadis it had last eaten, from their texture. If one Bedouin owned she-camels, he would arrange a meeting with a he-camel belonging to another man and borrow its services in exchange for milk or food.

will draw you towards it to see what lies beyond. After Ad Duqm the route heads over a flat plateau, with occasional small settlements, until again an escarpment gradually hems in the road. Eventually the road snakes up the cliff to travel into Shalim, and from there down into Ash Shuwaymiyyah and Jabal Samhan.

MUHUT محوت At 520km from Sur, Muhut is a small town at the southern limits of the Wihibah Sands and on the edge of the Wadi Haflain, which originates in the Al Jabal Al Akhdar mountains almost 300km to the north. It's a new town developed to provide housing and services for the Bedouin tribespeople from the surrounding area. The housing is scattered over a wide area, but unlike so many towns in Oman there is a town centre clustered around the road. See page 275 for accommodation in Muhut.

The road that runs through Muhut leads to **Filim**, a small settlement of fishermen on the edge of the very productive bay surrounding **Muhut Island** with its well-established mangrove swamp to the west. A small fishing boat might be hired from either Filim at high tide or Al Khaluf if you can locate a willing fisherman and want to see both the mangroves and possibly the dolphins that frequent the bay. High tide is also an ideal time for birdwatching at Filim or other areas around the bay, as the water drives waterfowl close to the shore edge; look for flamingo, oystercatcher, crab plover and waders by the thousands. Low tide reveals the mud flats and millions of crustacea. When the tide is at its very lowest it's probably possible to wade all the way out to Muhut Island itself, and you may see the few residents of the island wading out to their boats halfway between the two.

A word of warning: much of the low-lying areas between Shannah and Filim and on towards Khaluf are *sabkha*, a mixture of silt and sand that can be treacherous at high tide or after rain. There may be tracks which lead off a road. To the inexperienced, their crusted surface may look ideal for driving, but below could be a liquid mud. A car driven along them may sink into soft mud and will probably be a write-off, as several intrepid explorers have found to their financial cost.

After Filim a track swings around the bay to the coast at **Al Khaluf** (الخلوف), a small village with traditional houses. A nearby fish plant sells fresh fish and ice. Beyond the village is a track that leads behind a rocky headland and on to one of the most beautiful beaches on the whole coastline. You need to be experienced at sand driving, but at low tide driving on the hard beach sand is possible. As always, drive with an additional experienced guide vehicle. Watch out for the sand above the high water mark, parts of which are *sabkha*, which is much softer and easier to bog in. The beach makes for excellent camping, especially with children, although you will need to ensure that your tyres are deflated and that you can reflate them when driving on tarmac.

AD DUQM الدقم Returning to the main road and continuing south towards Ad Duqm (184km from Muhut), the landscape changes to low hills and cliffs, often in kaleidoscopic colours, and along this stretch, until just before Ad Duqm, you can see some of Oman's oldest rock formations, with black dolomites contrasting against reddish sandstones and shales. A turn east, 133km south of the Al Maha petrol station roundabout near Muhut, takes you to the tarmac road signposted **Sidrah**; follow the road, which after the new white houses becomes a well-graded track at 5.6km and then reaches the coast and more secluded beaches with many birds, especially Socotra cormorants, the only endemic seabirds of the Arabian region, which land and take off in their thousands in February. The small island of **Hamr Nafun**, off the coast between Sidrah and Ad Duqm, is a roost for thousands of these Socotra cormorants.

Your next port of call is Ad Duqm (also Al Duqm, Al Doqum, etc, but mostly just Duqm). Originally not much more than a small village, the town is undergoing massive development covering the port, airport and hotels. A new residential complex for 17,000 workers, mostly from the Indian subcontinent, is planned for 2017. These workers will be involved in the development of an oil refinery, free trade zone, power station, hospital, schools, shops, recreational facilities, dry dock and a shipbuilding yard. The development is planned to open in stages, and will obviously take many years to complete. This is bound to result in a massive population increase, especially when you consider that in 2004 the entire region of Al Wusta had only 22,900 people.

See pages 275–6 for accommodation in Ad Duqm.

Ras Ad Duqm is one of the most splendid bays on the coast and was where the PDO (see box, page 123) first landed in 1954 – an event mentioned in passing in James (now Jan) Morris's book *Sultan in Oman*. The mudflats and *sabkha* of the coast support a large population of indigenous and migratory birds. North of the Shell petrol station after 5.4km is a turn towards the coast. After 2.6km on the

CAR RENTAL

Ad Duqm has a small car-rental service through **Ajnib Al Shamel Trading** (*on the forecourt of the Ad Duqm Shell petrol station;* m *92 910752*).

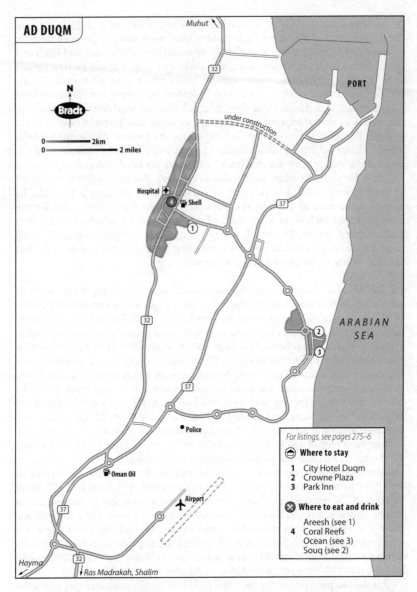

AD DUQM

Muhut

PORT

under construction

N

Bradt

0 ___ 2km
0 ___ 2 miles

Hospital ✚
⬆
🏪 Shell

1

32

37

*ARABIAN
SEA*

2

3

● Police

🅿 Oman Oil

✈ Airport

Hayma

Ras Madrakah, Shalim

For listings, see pages 275–6

🛏 **Where to stay**
1 City Hotel Duqm
2 Crowne Plaza
3 Park Inn

✖ **Where to eat and drink**
Areesh (see 1)
4 Coral Reefs
Ocean (see 3)
Souq (see 2)

right is a collection of *yardangs*, wind- and sand-eroded rock formations which, though they are the key attraction in town, were at the time of writing being put behind a chain-link fence. Unless there is a break in the fence, a distant view of this well-publicised 'rock garden' is all that's possible now

AD DUQM TO RAS MADRAKAH الدقم إلى رأس مدركة   South of Ad Duqm is a land of broad horizons, where a flat iron could hardly have done a better job of smoothing out the bumps and toasting the rest. From the Shell petrol station in Ad Duqm the road goes south out of the town for 12km past the Oman Oil petrol station and shortly after that exits left (southeast) at the roundabout to Al Jazir and Al Lakbi.

In summer the constant wind from the summer *khareef* (meaning 'monsoon')and accompanying sand results in a landscape that, in places, is devoid of any visible vegetation. After 49km the exit to the beautiful beach at **Ras Markaz** brings you, after a further 13km, to a 5km stretch of soft white sand with fishing boats at its northern end, ghost crabs along the central area and sea cliffs at the southern end.

The route to Ras Madrakah is signposted off the main road 56km south of the Shell petrol station at Ad Duqm and the scenery begins to change a few kilometres before you arrive into the relatively large settlement, which is 25km by tarmac road from the main road. **Ras Madrakah** (رأس مدركة) is an almost triangular peninsula of igneous dark rock, forming a very distinctive headland. Its overall area is less than 15km^2 and the contrast between the almost white sand, dark rock and blue sea is surreal; the beach itself is covered with beautiful shells, and dolphin and whale bones.

The village of **Madrakah** itself sits at the foot of these black hills near the beach beside a desalination plant. From the initial roundabout at the entrance to the village turn left (north) and a tarmac road will take you after 6.2km to a small beach. There are rough tracks off this tarmac road, most notably one after 2.1km from the roundabout, which leads 1.8km to a small fishermen's beach. The northern section of this beach has small sandy gullies that lead around the rocks and onto another beach. Rock oysters cover the black rocks and ghost crabs scurry in their hundreds along the sand, looking for dolphin and whale bones to pick clean. The male crabs build sand towers just above the tide line to lure females.

Ras Madrakah has been the location of innumerable shipwrecks; modern ones are usually cleared for scrap metal after a year or so. The old ones have been swept away by several summer cyclones over recent years. To the southwest of the village is a long sandy beach of over 4km which is accessed by a track leading south off the town's entrance roundabout. It makes an excellent camping location away from the housing and overlooking the sea.

RAS MADRAKAH TO ASH SHUWAYMIYYAH رأس مدركة إلى الشويمية The next
section of coast from Ras Madrakah to Ash Shuwaymiyyah (386km from Ad Duqm) has some of the most varied and unscarred scenery in Oman. Having returned to the main road, 45km further south from the Ras Madrakah junction is a small lagoon, **Khawr Dirif**. There is a road sign that reads 'Wadi Dharaf', pointing inland; use it simply as a marker and turn left towards the sea. This is also known as Three Palm Tree Lagoon, although there are more date palms than that. Camels and donkeys come here to drink, and flamingos, spoonbills, herons and ducks are also drawn by the shallow water. It makes another fine camping spot, but make sure you have mosquito protection.

Continuing south, 93km from the Ras Madrakah junction is the small settlement of **Haytam** (Hitam) with its petrol station and cheap refreshment options from cafés or grocery shops. After a further 1km there is a left turn which leads onto a 3km track that ends at the sea, where the fishermen from the village have their boats. From Haytam another 31km will take you to a roundabout that gives an alternative route to Ash Shuwaymiyyah.

For a detour, the right, northern, exit goes north to route 39 and then west to Rima, Amal and Marmul, which are at the heart of Oman's southern oilfields. A turn just after Amal takes you south to Shalim and Ash Shuwaymiyyah. If you want to see 'nodding donkeys', the classic oil pumps, in profusion, then this is your chance. Some 346km beyond the roundabout to Rima is Thumrayt (routes 39 and 31; page 321) on the Nizwa–Salalah road 31. These are vast distances, so be sure that you have sufficient fuel.

Continuing along the Muscat–Salalah Coastal Road, you come to the village of **Al Jazir** with its petrol station and the collection of cheap restaurants on its roundabout, which is about 17km beyond the roundabout to Rima. A short detour here will take you into the largest and most scenic lagoon on this section of coast, **Khawr Ghawi**. This is reached by a detour following the tarmac route east (left turn from the north) of this roundabout for 5.3km and taking a track right for another 2.5km. The vast lagoon is some 7km long and is edged by white sand dunes. In the winter months it can attract thousands of flamingos. High tide will bring the birds towards the shore, where they may be joined by spoonbill, heron, egret, plover, avocet and crab plover. Just over 2km north of the northern open end of Khawr Ghawi are a series of 'Pink Lagoons', which are completely cut off from the sea. With evaporation they have become very saline, encouraging a particular kind of algae which, when it blooms, occasionally gives the water a deep pinkish colour. Local fishermen use the thick red and white salt crusts around the edge to dry their catch. The remoteness of this area makes it an excellent place to camp, provided that you choose an area away from vegetation, which may harbour insects and snakes.

Returning to the main road at Al Jazir, continue south for 47km to the small harbour just after **Al Lakbi** (اللكبي). Turning left off route 41 will bring you to **Sawqrah**, where the road climbs the escarpment and rejoins route 41 (which also climbs the escarpment by a different route), before continuing 105km west to the Shell petrol station at Shalim. After 37km from either Al Lakbi or Sawqrah there is a signed turning left (south) and a graded road can offer a 17km detour down to the sea and the coastal village of **Sharbthat**. West of Sharbthat a 39km track meanders along beaches that provide good camping areas, passing an area of ruined houses at Manji before climbing again to rejoin the road to Shalim.

At **Shalim**, take the left (south) exit at the roundabout towards Ash Shuwaymiyyah, which lies 38km away. After 20km there are turns to the right that will give magnificent views over the creamy cliffs, and down across the coastal plain to the Arabian Sea glittering beyond. Note that parts of this stretch don't have safety barriers in place along the cliff edge, so drive carefully. The road plunges down as a black tarmac streak against the pale rocks to the coast and swings west into the town.

ASH SHUWAYMIYYAH (الشويمية) TO SALALAH (صلالة) The town of Ash
Shuwaymiyyah (386km from Ad Duqm) has petrol, grocery shops, accommodation and some very cheap simple restaurants frequented by Bangladeshi fishermen on what passes for the main street. The town is known as a centre for basket weaving, especially *karmah*, a milking container woven from *Nannorrhops* palm and goat leather and sold by local women.

See page 276 for accommodation in Ash Shuwaymiyyah.

Behind the town **Wadi Ash Shuwaymiyyah** is one of the most attractive wadis in Oman, with creamy white cliffs rising in stepped stages rising to over 300m. The convoluted route that it follows makes it a beautiful location in which to camp; silence and dark skies complete a magical experience. To enter the wadi, drive west along the street in the town which has the grocery shops and restaurants (not the through road beside the beach). The track crosses from one side of the wadi to the other for about 800m before veering right and then continuing along the west bank of the wadi for about 3.6km before again re-entering the wadi bed. At this point the track is reasonably good unless there has been very heavy rain. After 11km from the village, you will see the first of the three travertine waterfalls on the right, formed over the tertiary limestone. If you climb up on the ledge you will find a secret water pool edged with rush. Beyond here the wadi meanders for another 15km, though flash floods may make the track impassable. Children will love exploring the wadi higher up, with more pools and vegetation. Hyena, ibex, gazelle and the small rabbit-like rock hyrax can sometimes be glimpsed along the most remote areas if you are very fortunate; the wadi is on the edge of the Jabal Samhan range – a key habitat for the Arabian leopard – and these are its prey.

To continue to Salalah, exit the wadi on the route you entered and turn right onto the tarmac road. Initially this runs along a 20km sandy beach which offers an alternative place to camp, but if you have camped on beaches on the way down, the wadi makes for a magnificent change. The far end at the base of the escarpment sees the road ascend just after the strange white building on the left, which was a prototype chalet for a hotel that so far has not been completed. The road then disappears high above into a manmade valley cut deep into the limestone, whose manmade cliffs tower overhead. This road is stupendous, as it should be, as the 90km route into Hasik from Ash Shuwaymiyyah village had a budgeted cost of US$288 million.

Driving towards Hasik you can enjoy extraordinary views over a vast fan-shaped valley after driving west around 39km from Ash Shuwaymiyyah, with another view overlooking the distant sea 59km beyond Ash Shuwaymiyyah. Continuing towards Hasik, the road approaches Wadi Sanaq, a major wadi, and therefore the road descends from the plateau height of 650m into the date palm-fringed bed of the wadi, whose *khawr* is dammed at the sea, creating a small lagoon some 68km west of Ash Shuwaymiyyah. Many of the trees along this route are frankincense, and if you look into the valleys on either side of the road you should see more. The last hurrah of the road is the descent onto the coastal strip to **Hasik** – this route description continues on pages 314–16.

MASIRAH ISLAND جزيرة مصيرة

Though administratively part of Ash Sharqiyyah, Masirah Island is approached through Al Wusta. Sitting 20km off the mainland just south of the Wihibah Sands, Masirah is Oman's largest island, about 70km long and 650km² (somewhat larger than the Isle of Wight). It is accessed by boat from Shannah, the small mainland settlement on the eastern edge of the Bar Al Hikman Peninsula. The boats dock at Masirah's only town, **Hilf** (حلف), which is located towards the northern end of the island and extends from the sea up a gradually sloping hill that rises no more than 50m.

Masirah was known to the ancient Greeks, who referred to it as 'Serepsis', the name of a god favoured by Alexander the Great. An RAF base here played a central role in both the Jebel War of the late 1950s and the Dhofar War of the 1960s and 1970s. The BBC World Service had a relay station here – the British Eastern Relay Station (BERS) – which was later relocated onto the mainland at Asilah, close to Al Ashkharah. Today the local economy is dominated by a major airbase at the northern end of the island, fishing and various areas of government employment. A book by Colin Richardson called *Masirah: Tales from a Desert Island* reports the history of the island, enlivening it for the visitor (page 335).

The island remains largely untouched, especially in the south. Camping here is excellent if you come fully equipped. The best beaches are on the open east coast and more southerly area of the west coast, although a strong sea breeze may make the decision for you.

GETTING THERE AND AWAY From Muhut travel east on the Muscat–Salalah Coastal Road for 43km to a right turn southeast, which takes you onto a 13km causeway that leads past the Oman Oil petrol station and the National Ferries office towards the

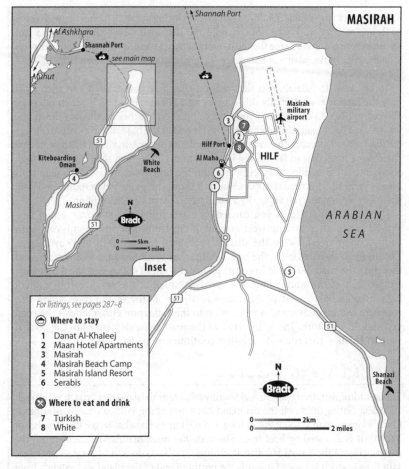

For listings, see pages 287–8

MASIRAH

Inset

Where to stay
1 Danat Al-Khaleej
2 Maan Hotel Apartments
3 Masirah
4 Masirah Beach Camp
5 Masirah Island Resort
6 Serabis

Where to eat and drink
7 Turkish
8 White

jetty for boats to Masirah Island. Access to the island is by three different boat types. Small, speedy **fibreglass fishing boats** which almost skim across the water are the quickest, with the journey taking about 20 minutes depending on the sea conditions for the 16km crossing. Expect to pay a few rials per person after direct negotiation with the owner and to wait until the boat has the number of people the owner wishes to take, which may be seven or eight. These fibreglass fishing boats can be hired from the old jetty close to the Oman Oil petrol station or the new jetty near the ferry access.

The slowest are the old **flat-bottomed ferries** that have character but are a long way from modern shipping standards. The old ferries depart from the modern jetty when they are full and the tide is right. Foot passengers travel for free and vehicles are charged by an official on the boat from RO10; you do not have to book. These old ferries take up to a couple of hours, as they meander around sandbanks at low speed.

The alternative are new **catamaran ferries**, which again depart from the modern jetty and must be booked in advance either in Muscat or at the National Ferry Office at Shannah, which is just before the bridged road onto the jetty (\ 25 216161) or opposite the port entrance in Masirah (\ 25 504884). The ferries take about 1.5 hours as they also need to navigate the sandbanks, and any greater speed would cause the rear end to scrape the sea bed. Although the National Ferry Company does have a website (*www.nfc.om*) it only contains information, which may be out of date, rather than an online booking system. At the time of writing, ferries sailed several times a day from Shannah to Masirah (*09.00, noon, 15.00 & 18.00 Sun; noon & 16.00 Mon; 09.00 & 15.00 Tue; 09.00, noon, 15.00 & 18.00 Wed–Sat*), and back from Masirah (*09.00, noon & 15.00 Sun; 09.00, 15.00 & 18.00 Mon; noon & 18.00 Tue; 09.00, noon, 15.00 & 18.00 Wed–Sat*). Extra services may run on busy days. A one-way charge for a passenger, whether on foot or with a vehicle is RO3 for adults, RO1.50 for children, RO10 for 4x4s and RO8 for a saloon car; you will need to carry vehicle documentation and each passenger's personal ID. Don't skip booking in Muscat, as this ensures that by the time you have driven to the ferry it is not fully booked, and also ensure you have a confirmed return booking from Masirah.

The journey across to Masirah does create a real sense of embarking on an adventure. From the small fishing boats and old ferries you can enjoy the sight of the island's only town, Hilf, gradually appearing over the waters. Unfortunately, on the catamarans you are required to remain in the indoor public seating area for safety on all departures and arrivals, and therefore miss much of the view.

GETTING AROUND MASIRAH There are no taxis in Masirah and no car-hire firms, but your accommodation may be able to organise transfer from the port. The island's petrol stations and other services are in Hilf, so supplies for any activity that you undertake will need to be taken with you. The island can be driven around in a day along a good tarmac road which extends around the whole island, with a couple of tarmac roads that cross from the east coast to the west coast. It's about 130km, with no petrol stations on the route.

For a different view of the island ask your hotel whether they can contact a fisherman and his boat to take you on a trip for a few hours. You may catch fish if you try with a hand line and your hotel will almost certainly be delighted to cook it for you.

 WHERE TO STAY Map, page 286.
Masirah has a better selection of accommodation than only a few years ago. Unfortunately the restaurant choice is still very limited, but places to eat are of a similar standard to local restaurants all over Oman.

⌂ Masirah Island Resort (21 rooms, inc a few chalets) Overlooking the island's east-coast beaches & the Arabian Sea, 10km southeast of Hilf; ✆ 25 504274; e reservations@masiraislandresort. com; www.masiraislandresort.com. Ask for ground-floor rooms & you will have direct access to the grounds with the swimming pool. Set on a beautiful beach on the east side of the island, it offers a pool, tennis courts & a fitness centre, as well as an international buffet restaurant & a bar. You are paying a premium compared with the other hotels, but it might just be worth it. Look in the lobby for the displays of the Masirah Wildlife Museum. **$$$**

⌂ Danat Al-Khaleej Hotel (25 rooms) Less than 2km from the ferry terminal, on the beach on the southern outskirts of Hilf; ✆ 25 504533; e info@ danat-hotel.com; www.danat-hotel.com. With a good sea view & public beachside location, the recently refurbished hotel makes for a good base on the island. The ground-floor rooms at the rear have a small veranda to sit on & enjoy the sunset. A simple multi-cuisine restaurant. **$**

⌂ Maan Hotel Apartments (12 rooms) Centre of Hilf; ✆ 25 504678; e maan.masirah@gmail.com. This is a good option if you are in Masirah for more than a few nights as you can self-cater or just walk over to the 2 best restaurants in Hilf. Be patient & very clear with communication, as the hotel is new & the staff are even newer. **$**

⌂ Masirah Beach Camp 32km south of Al Maha petrol station; ✆ 25 504401; e info@ kiteboarding-oman.com. This is simple beachfront accommodation, but a superb location for nature lovers, as it's on a small sandy peninsula with a few tiny desert islands offshore waiting for their own Robinson Crusoe. The staff are helpful & there's even Wi-Fi, albeit slow, that you can check over the camp's buffet b/fast. **$**

🏠 **Masirah Hotel** (22 rooms) North of the harbour immediately next to the sea & close to the centre of Hilf & the air force base; ☎ 25 504401; e booking@omantel.net.om; www.almajalioman.com/masirah.html. This hotel is next to the island's diesel power station, which chugs away, ensuring the island's houses are supplied with electricity 24hrs a day. The rooms, which have their entrance from a common veranda walkway,

are large, though they never get chilly due to the underpowered AC. The hotel is generally in need of refurbishment. The beach usually has a number of fishing boats. The staff are helpful & the kitchen offers reasonable food. **$**

🏠 **Serabis Hotel** (50 rooms) Overlooking Hilf harbour, less than 2km walk into the centre of Hilf; m 99 446680; e dira2008@omantel.net.om. Newly refurbished, the rooms in this hotel are good, as is the small restaurant with Indian-style food. The views of the petrol station detract slightly from its appeal. **$**

✕ **WHERE TO EAT AND DRINK** *Map, page 286.*

✕ **Turkish Restaurant** 140m north of the roundabout in the central area of Hilf; ◷ 09.00–midnight daily. A good range of Middle Eastern food with great kebabs & fresh fruit juices. The décor is very basic & most of its business is takeaways. **$**

✕ **White Restaurant** 20m west of the roundabout in the central area of Hilf; ◷ 08.00–23.00 daily. A basic restaurant with a reasonable offering of local Indian/Omani-style food with rice-based meals. They also have locally caught fish. Shaded outdoor seating area. **$**

WHAT TO SEE AND DO With its isolated location, Masirah might well be the most relaxing place to visit in Oman, provided that you do not arrive during the rush over Oman's Eid holidays.

Near Shanazi, south of the Masirah Island Resort on the east coast, rock pools will keep any family occupied, and there's added excitement when the dhow fleet is anchored offshore. Further south, all along the east coast, the **beaches** are exceptional. White Beach, 13km southeast of Masirah Island Resort, deserves its name: the sand is dazzling and powder soft, and you may be the only person along its 5km length.

The central area of the island has a limestone mesa of around 200m and ophiolite covering much of the southern end. **Birdwatching** is interesting on the island, with Egyptian vultures, harriers, Socotra cormorants, crab plovers and flamingos, along with gulls and terns. Vagrants are frequently blown in, and if you stay all year on Masirah you might see 300+ species. The sewage treatment plant 2km south of Al Maha petrol station, with trees on either side of the road, is practically the only well-vegetated area in the north of the island, with cormorants roosting in the branches. The bay on the western side 30km south of Al Maha petrol station offers a good variety of waders.

The island is an important **turtle-nesting** location, especially for loggerhead turtles (*Caretta caretta*). The ICUN Red List has recently downgraded their status worldwide to vulnerable, and the northwest Indian Ocean population (which includes those in Masirah Island) is critically endangered. Oman offers excellent supervised turtle-watching opportunities in Ras Al Jinz (pages 266–8), and it is suggested that the turtles of Masirah are not watched in order to avoid disturbing them. Shells here are varied and often beautiful – look for *Acteon eloiseae*, named after Eloise Bosch, the wife of one of Muscat's first Western doctors.

The western side of the island is good for **windsurfing**, and **surfing** is particularly good in the *khareef* (meaning 'monsoon'; June–September). **Kiteboarding Oman** (m 96 323524; e info@kiteboarding-oman.com) provides kitesurfing and windsurfing from its base 32km south of Al Maha petrol station.

10

Dhofar ظفار

Dhofar is Oman's southernmost province, bounded to the west by the great Rub Al Khali Desert on the border with Saudi Arabia, the Mahra Governorate of Yemen to the southwest and the vast Arabian Sea to the south and east. Its northern border is one of those straight lines beloved by administrators, in this case drawn for the oil concession granted to Wendell Phillips in 1952.

With its rolling grassy meadows following the summer *khareef* (monsoon), Dhofar is different from other areas in Oman. For residents and those familiar with Dhofar this blaze of green comes to mind whenever the name is mentioned, but of course with an area of almost 100,000km², there is more to Dhofar than that. Flying into Dhofar by plane from northern Oman's great central plain is the best way of appreciating its **terrain**. Great swathes of the vast orange sand dunes of the Rub Al Khali cover the entire western area, to the east glints the Arabian Sea and as the aircraft descends over the mountains, which rise to almost 2,000m, the distinctive dendritic pattern of the wadis, which fan out onto the central plain, come into view. It is only in the final few moments that the relatively narrow band of grassland and tree-covered escarpment come into view. The airport is on the coastal plain on which the city of Salalah is built. Just off eastern Dhofar is a small archipelago of islands whose geology closely matches that of the Horn of Africa, whose attachment to Arabia failed millions of years ago.

Unlike the rest of Oman, the **temperature** of this narrow band of green mountains and coastal strip rarely exceeds 30°C. From October to February the temperature is warm (26°C), sunny and dry, and therefore attracts European and North American visitors seeking to escape their cold winters. December and January are the coolest months, with temperatures in the region of 18–23°C. From March onwards, and until the monsoon begins in mid-June, the climate is muggy and humid, and there are fewer European and North American visitors, while Arabs from other Gulf countries flock here instead, attracted by the cloud cover, accompanying drizzle and luxuriant greenery. The sea waves can reach a dramatic 8m during the monsoon season and the Arabian Sea is then too dangerous for swimming. The average wave height outside the monsoon season is just 1m, but swimming can still be dangerous because of undertows.

Dhofar's **geology**, though perhaps slightly less dramatic than that of the mountains of the north, is equally interesting and, in the east, includes what may well be Oman's oldest igneous rocks, with material up to 1,300 million years old. They lie in the shadow of the stupendous escarpment at Jabal Samhan. This impressive escarpment of limestone rises to well over 1,000m along all its 70km south-facing edge and to its west increases to around 1,800m. Though blessed with summer monsoon rains, in the past Dhofar had an even damper climate that gave rise to the numerous tufa fossil rock waterfalls. Behind Jabal Samhan is the oil-producing region around Marmul. The rocks here date from between 350 million and 400 million years old and include a conglomerate of

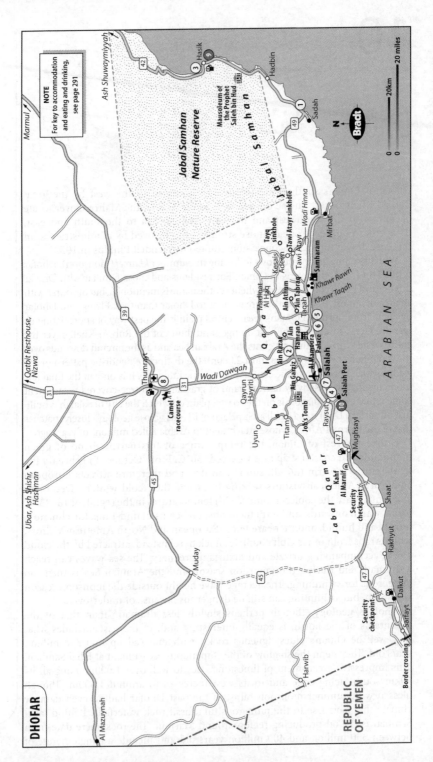

even older rock. To the west around Mughsayl are chalky limestones from the Paleogene period around 65.5 to 23.05 million years ago. To the north of Mughsayl and Jabal Qamar is the Rub Al Khali or The Empty Quarter, which is believed to have been formed during the Pleistocene epoch about 2.6 million to 11,700 years ago.

Dhofar is increasingly thought to have been a major route on man's journey 'out of Africa'. A more hospitable climate would have facilitated movement along the coastline during a period when sea levels were lower. Ample evidence exists of flint tools from at least 70,000 years ago and in places the flakes seem to carpet the ground for many hectares. The UNESCO World Heritage Sites of the Land of Frankincense illustrate the region's place in an increasingly important trade system around the Arabian Sea and Indian Ocean, with Greek and Roman ships appearing to regard the coast as familiar territory. This trade may have been associated with the migration of tribes from Yemen into Dhofar. Certainly the Qara tribal group is believed to have come from the west and still retains a language, Modern South Arabian, that is related to the spoken languages of Dhofar before Arabic arrived.

The region became integrated with northern Oman during the 19th century and for many years the current sultan's father, Sultan Said bin Taimur, resided in Salalah, making it the effective political capital of the country. From the mid 1960s to the mid 1970s, a civil war (pages 293 and 313) tested that unity, but today Dhofar is firmly part of the country.

Although Dhofar is rapidly changing, it still has a unique culture that makes it very different from other parts of Oman. This is exemplified by the claimed descent of many of the Dhofari tribes from Qatan, the historic titular head of the 'original' Arabs who originated in southern Arabia, as opposed to Adnan, from whom the northern Arab tribes, which include the Hashimites, claim descent. Linguistically, the language that many Dhofari speak is Modern South Arabian, a Semitic language group that includes Mahari, whose speakers had been concentrated on the desert side of the Dhofar and Mahra mountains, Shari (*jabali*) spoken by the Qara from the main Dhofar Mountains, and Bathari spoken by those from Ash Shuwaymiyyah. Historically, those who lived away from Salalah were involved in animal husbandry, which, though partially nomadic, did not entail any need to range over vast areas due to the relatively abundant water available around the mountains. The vast herds of camels, cows and flocks of goats today provide a living link with the past of not so long ago.

Dhofar's dominant commercial activity is situated around Salalah Port, a world-class transhipment port. The adjacent free trade zone includes chemical factories, parts assembly for vehicles and companies focused on logistics. Immediately next to the port area are major cement producers and a flourmill. Tourism is also a rapidly growing part of the local economy, making use of the region's year-round appeal to different kinds of visitors. Traditional industries of Dhofar that are still important are agriculture, which is focused on the coastal plain around Salalah, livestock for meat, and fishing.

Dhofar

10

Through a quirk of nature, the mountains of Dhofar and the Salalah Plain are exposed to a monsoon climate, with daily precipitation from mid-June to mid- September blowing in from Africa. Cloud-filled winds brush past the island of Socotra off the southern coast of Yemen, the vacuum created by the vast searing deserts beyond sucking the winds against the Jabal Al Qara mountains. Known as the *khareef* (meaning 'monsoon'), the clouds shed 15 inches of water over those three months, causing the wadi beds to flow and spectacular waterfalls that plunge over sheer cliffs. The area becomes filled with mist and fog. Camels are forced to leave the mountains, which become slippery and dangerous, and are kept in the plains until the rains abate. When they return to the mountains in September, after the rains, the pasture is rich and plentiful. This *khareef* period is the season in which the region is most popular with Omanis from the northern provinces as well as other Arabs of the Gulf, who seek to escape their own hot dry summers, and enjoy the lush green landscape here.

Each year, at this time, there is a six-week-long carnival. Like its Muscat counterpart, it is a showpiece for Omani customs and traditions, and hotels and flights can get booked to capacity. The Baladiya Entertainment Centre is one of the principal centres where festivities take place. It was purpose-built, with a heritage village, two theatres (one open-air) and a fairground. Al Marooj Amphitheatre, which can hold 7,000 people, was opened in 2005 and is located in the east of Salalah, in the Atin Plain. The festivities include folk bands, song and dance, art exhibitions, handicraft demonstrations, information on regional conservation projects and other exhibits displaying and promoting the culture and heritage of the region and country.

Dhofar Governorate's population in 2015 was 382,983, spread over a vast area and with a density of fewer than four per km². Salalah, with 264,652, is by far the largest population centre, followed by Taqah (27,939); other administrative areas include Mirbat, Thumrayt, Al Mazyunah, Sadah, Rakhyut, Shalim Wa Juzur Al Hallaniyyat, Dalkut and Muqshin in Dhofar's north, with only 791 people.

GETTING THERE AND AWAY

BY AIR Oman Air operates several flights a day from Muscat International Airport to Salalah Airport in Dhofar and also flies from Dubai non-stop on most days. Other airlines that fly into Salalah include Qatar Airways from Doha, flydubai from Dubai and Air Arabia from Sharjah. Check their websites (*www.omanair.com*, *www.qatarairways.com*, *www.flydubai.com*, *www.airarabia.com*) for exact timings, which vary seasonally. The flight from Muscat takes 1.5 hours and the price for a return ticket is around RO64. Oman Air usually offers good package deals, so it may be worth enquiring at the time of your visit as to what is available. Travelling independently, a transfer to any hotel in Salalah town will cost roughly RO4 by taxi, although some hotels offer a free transfer. Here, unlike Muscat, there is no kiosk to make a fixed payment, so you need to negotiate. You will find that taxi drivers in Salalah are very hard to get to shift from their price, but do not get into the taxi until you have an agreed price from the driver.

In 1963, the Dhofar Liberation Front consisted mainly of dissatisfied Dhofaris who were nationalists intent on seizing Dhofar back from Oman. They were supported by what was then the People's Democratic Republic of Yemen (PDRY). The Front began as a simple movement of tribesmen who wanted Dhofar for the Dhofaris, but once Russian and Chinese involvement began it turned into a non-Marxist political war, where the ultimate goal for the Russians and Chinese was control of the oil markets through control of the Strait of Hormuz. Dhofaris were trained as Marxist rebels for spells of up to 18 months in Russia or China, and in 1968 the Marxists took over leadership.

By the mid 1970s approximately 2,000 Dhofaris had broken with the movement, and later agreed to support Sultan Qaboos bin Said and fight against the insurgency. They retrained and were incorporated into the Sultan's Armed Forces (SAF). Jeapes and Drury's book *SAS Secret War: Operation Storm in the Middle East* (page 334) tells the story of the SAS involvement in the Dhofar War of the 1970s and the defeat of the communist rebels.

The departure lounge of Salalah Airport is modern, with shops, small coffee shops and a number of car-rental counters downstairs.

Announcements are made in Arabic and English. As the airport is on two levels do allow time to reach the departure lounge.

BY CAR There are three road options into Salalah from Muscat. The quickest is route 31, which runs from Nizwa all the way south to Salalah. The distance from Muscat is approximately 1,000km. This is mostly a single-carriageway tarmac road and runs virtually parallel to the Empty Quarter (or Rub Al Khali) and is a long 11-hour journey (including stops). Travelling by bus is your cheapest option at around RO7 per person one-way, but if you have others in your party who could perhaps share the driving, then a hire car would be a good alternative, although you will need to determine with the car hire company whether this is possible. That said, the drive itself is rather tedious, with long stretches of featureless bleak landscapes, often a flat and gravelly desert.

The Izki–Muhut road, which has its junction off the main Muscat–Nizwa highway, carries on south through Sinaw (in the Ash Sharqiyyah) and on towards Muhut (routes 15, 33, 32), where it becomes part of the Muscat–Salalah Coastal Road.

The Muscat–Salalah Coastal Road, which merges with the Izki–Muhut road, passes through Sur and Muhut to Hasik and on to Salalah (routes 17 and onto 32, 41, 42, 49). This entire route is tarmacked and for much of the way it largely follows the east coast. See the *Al Wusta* chapter for more information.

BY BUS Bus companies which offer transport via the main route (31) include daily services from Muscat by **Salalah Line Transport** (✆ 24 798470; e *salalahline@gmail.com*), leaving Muscat at 08.00 and 18.00, **Gulf Transport Company** (✆ 24 790823), leaving Muscat at 03.00, 07.00, 10.00, 13.00, 17.00, 18.00, 19.00, and 20.00, and **Mwasalat (Oman National Transport Company)**, leaving Muscat at 07.00, 10.00 and 18.00. They all arrive into central Salalah about 12 hours after leaving Muscat. There are several stops *en route*, principally at Nizwa, Hayma and Thumrayt. The journey costs around RO7 per person one-way.

There is no public transport other than these long-distance bus services on this and the other two routes, and there is unlikely to be a taxi unless it is passing through. This does mean that these long-distance buses are simply good for passing through the region, but little else. For buses to **Yemen** from Salalah, the Gulf Transport Company (Salalah office: ☎ 23 293303) runs two buses a week to Al Mukalla in Yemen (🕐 06.00 Mon & Fri; RO11 adult one-way); the return from Al Mukalla is on the following days. All buses are usually on time and tickets can be bought either from the bus company office in advance or from the driver on boarding, though it would be wise to book a day or two in advance.

GETTING AROUND

CAR HIRE If you intend to drive yourself around and explore, you can hire a car from the airport or pre-book one from the Muscat car-rental offices (pages 58–9).

Avis ☎ 24 601224; e kiran@avisoman.com. Available at Salalah Airport.
Budget ☎ 23 235160; e shaweta@budgetoman. com; www.budgetoman.com. Available at Salalah Airport & the Crowne Plaza.
Colors m 91 347405. Next to GTC Transport, available at Salalah Airport.

Dollar ☎ 23 212778; e hiltonsalalah@ dollaroman.com. Available at Salalah Airport.
Etihad ☎ 23 296897; e sony@etihadcarrental. com. Available at Salalah Airport.
Europcar m 99 430608; e salalah@ europecaroman.com. Available at Salalah Airport.

Do note that if you plan to make excursions with tour operators, it is not really necessary to hire a car, as tour companies collect you from your hotel and return you afterwards.

If you plan to go off-road but are thinking about saving money by renting a standard car instead of the pricier 4x4, remember that your insurance will be void if you sustain any damage to a saloon car while driving off-tarmac. Car hire is recommended in Salalah because of the dearth of public transport running to the tourist sites.

TAXIS The airport terminal is on the Salalah bypass and about 23km from central Salalah by road. Few taxis wait at the airport, so your best option is to ask the hotel you are booked into to provide you with an airport transfer or hire a car from your arrival. Taxis are the easiest way of getting from the central Salalah hotels, including the Crowne Plaza and the Hilton. If you are staying outside the city, speak with the hotel front desk regarding a shuttle bus that can transport you from the hotel to the city-centre suqs and budget restaurants, but bear in mind that prices add up, as most taxi drivers charge a minimum of RO3 per engaged journey, especially from the big hotels out of town. Some visitors have reported that they regretted not renting a car as it would even have been cheaper in the long run, especially on the longer journeys; a taxi would easily charge RO15 to Taqah, for example. The taxis and the few shared minibuses all tend to gather in front of the HSBC building on As-Salam Street in central Salalah and run to the various towns in the vicinity, not to the tourist sites. Minibus fares to places like Taqah and Mirbat range between 600bzs and RO1.

BUSES There are no buses or any form of public transport from Salalah Airport or within the town.

TOUR OPERATORS

Tour operators, which can be found inside the Salalah hotels as well as in the streets of Salalah city centre, offer the stock tours of the area, albeit to varying degrees of quality and price. They may vary slightly in the sites they include in each tour. Tours can easily be arranged through your hotel, if you prefer someone else to do the organising. Alternatively, you may prefer to hire a car and travel independently.

Arabian Sand Tours 23 235833; e seavllas@omantel.net.om. A very well-established company. Specialises in off-beat tours, especially in the Empty Quarter.
Bahwan Travel Agencies 23 294665, 290908; e topclass@omantel.net.om; www.bahwantravels.com. This is one of the biggest tour operators in the country, established for 25 years & offering the full range of tours. It's best to arrange Salalah tours through the Muscat office (pages 83–5).

Sumahram Falcon 23 236334; e sumahramfalcon@gmail.com; www.sumahramfalcon.com. Owner-operated company running for some 15 years. Specialises in out-of-Salalah tours & sea-based programmes.
Zahara Tours 23 202581; e inbound@zaharatours.com; www.zaharatours.com. Offers tours principally to standard tourist attractions.

 ## WHERE TO STAY

Apart from a few exceptions, the hotels are mainly to be found in the Salalah area. The Hilton and Crowne Plaza are located on the edge of town, while many of the lower-cost hotels and self-catering apartments are in the city centre. During the monsoon season they can get full, so advance booking will definitely be necessary.

WHERE TO EAT AND DRINK

The plushest restaurants are in the five-star hotels in Salalah, and these are licensed. All other eating places are simple and unlicensed, though there are one or two places offer excellent food in atmospheric surroundings. Outside Salalah, city-centre places to eat are few, so packing a picnic is always a good idea (unless you're visiting the blowholes at Mughsayl, west of Salalah, where there is a simple restaurant).

ACTIVITIES

Places of interest in the Dhofar region are largely based around the southern coastal areas. The stock tours offered by the tour operators (see above) include the 'city tour', 'East Salalah', 'West Salalah' and 'Ubar and the Empty Quarter'. Each set tour lasts for roughly half a day (irrespective of operator), with the option for a full-day tour to Ubar.

Dhofar ACTIVITIES

10

If you want to tour the area, three nights will generally be enough time; however, if you are planning to include a visit to Ubar (which is a little further out), four nights is recommended, and will give you a little time to relax and spend at leisure. There are plenty of deserted picnic spots in spectacular surroundings both east and west of Salalah.

BIRDWATCHING The birds of southern Oman are more African in character than in the north. They include the African silverbill, Verreaux's eagle, Ruppell's weaver, African scops owl, Bruce's green pigeon, Didric cuckoo, grey-headed kingfisher, African rock bunting, singing bush lark, African paradise flycatcher, shining sunbird and Palestine sunbird. Broadly, the three best sites for birdwatching in Dhofar are the Mughsayl Lagoon (west of Salalah; pages 317–18), Darbat (including Khawr Rawri Lagoon; pages 307–11), and Khawr Ad Dahariz (also called East Khawr, about 1km east of Salalah). Add in Ain Razat (page 306) and Ain Hamran (page 306) for more unusual species. It is easy to travel to these sites independently, but if you would like an accompanied tour, speak to a tour operator. For further information on birdlife, see pages 10–12.

BOAT TRIPS Diving centres (see below) can offer full- and half-day boat trips along the southern coast, where it is likely that you will spot dolphins and whales. An afternoon trip means you have the additional pleasure of watching the sunset from the boat. Tours leave from both the marina at Juweira Boutique Hotel and Mirbat harbour (east of Salalah). You will be collected from your hotel. A half-day trip costs from around RO220 for the boat, which takes ten people, and includes refreshments. The cost doubles for a full-day trip, which includes lunch and refreshments.

CANOEING/KAYAKING Canoeing can also be experienced outside of the *khareef* (meaning 'monsoon') season off the Salalah coast. It costs RO24 for a full day and RO18 for half a day, from Saturday through to Thursday. On Fridays there is a special full-day canoeing trip around the lagoon of Khawr Rawri for RO50 including lunch. Guests will be collected from their hotels. All levels are welcome.

CAVING Tayq Cave sinkhole (page 308) is situated in the mountains above Mirbat and is one of the largest sinkholes in the world. Its smaller companion, the sinkhole at Tawi Atayr, has precipitous edges and lives up to its name 'the well of birds' (pages 307–8).

DESERT TOURS AND CAMPING Overnight trips to the desert camp in Ash Shisr (Ubar) (pages 322–3) are offered by local tour operators. A day trip costs around RO150 per car, which includes the driver/guide and lunch, and allows for a maximum of four people in the vehicle.

DIVING Diving is permitted in the waters of the southern coast of Oman at any time outside of the *khareef* season. Avoid the *khareef* if you want to dive, as the waters are far too rough. Operating from Mirbat, **Extradivers** (m 95 410213; www. extradivers.info) offer one of few opportunities worldwide to dive both kelp forests and coral in the same session. Offshore they include a well-established wreck dive.

There are several dive sites off the Dhofar coast. The best are between Mirbat and Hasik (east of Mirbat), along with the Al Hallaniyyat Islands.

The Aquarium, which is located 8km east of Mirbat, is a good, easy shore dive for divers of all levels, and makes a great site for training new divers and snorkellers. Lionfish, stingrays, clownfish, scorpionfish, pufferfish, lobsters, rays and turtles are often spotted. The Eagles Retreat dive site is 10km east of Mirbat. A shore dive is offered from Mirbat to Hadbin towards Hasik (an ancient village whose shores offer some of the best diving in Dhofar), and the Salalah Marriott Resort also has its own dive centre (page 312). Close to the Juzor Al Hallaniyyat there is a British wreck that sank in 1914 on the return leg of its journey to Calcutta, carrying a cargo of tea. The *City of Winchester* lies at 30m depth.

By way of example, a two-night camping trip to the Juzor Al Hallaniyyat, which incorporates ten dives, costs around RO475 per person inclusive of everything (transport from your hotel, gear, food, camping kits), with a minimum of five people required. For one to two dives, including tanks and weights, it costs RO40 per person. Snorkelling costs around RO25 per person.

FISHING Fishing trips can be easily arranged through one of the diving centres (page 296–7). The boat takes a maximum of six people and departs from either Salalah Port (west of Salalah) or Mirbat harbour (east of Salalah). Hiring the boat for half a day costs from RO400, while the full day costs from RO650.

The delicacies of lobster and abalone are plentiful in the waters off Oman, especially in the Dhofar region and around Masirah Island in the Ash Sharqiyyah. Their high commercial value has been steadily exploited, which has led to conservation regulations being established which now restrict the fishing of these species to a few weeks in winter each year.

SALALAH صلالة

Salalah, the capital of the Dhofar region, is located on a crescent-shaped coastal plain at the base of the 1,000m-high Jabal Al Qara Mountains. In summer the mountains are obscured by cloud but in winter there are few areas in the town where their escarpments cannot be seen. The airport occupies the central area south of the mountains and just north of the town. Salalah Port is located just to the town's west, while the east is delineated by the lagoon of Khawr Ad Dahariz.

The beautiful soft white-sand beaches that extend along this entire section of coast are largely public within the town area, though they are not used as sunbathing beaches. The private exception is in front of Al Husn Palace just to the west of Al Haffa Suq (also called Al Husn Suq), and the boundary of this is clear and not to be crossed.

The central area of the town is a commercial one with government ministries, offices, banks and small shops. To the southwest of the airport perimeter fence is an area that is developing into a retail shopping area comprising the large Salalah Gardens Mall, Lulu and several other shopping malls. The modern areas of the town that extend around the older area near Al Husn Palace are laid out on a grid pattern, with the principal through-routes running east–west.

Where northern Oman has its dates, southern Oman has its coconuts. The route from the clock tower (2km north of Salalah city centre) to the Crowne Plaza Hotel winds through lush plantations of coconut, papaya, banana and mango. Along the route there are stalls set up under the coconut canopy selling coconuts with straws, and the prices are well worth stopping for, with fresh, cold coconut milk from the nut at only 300bzs.

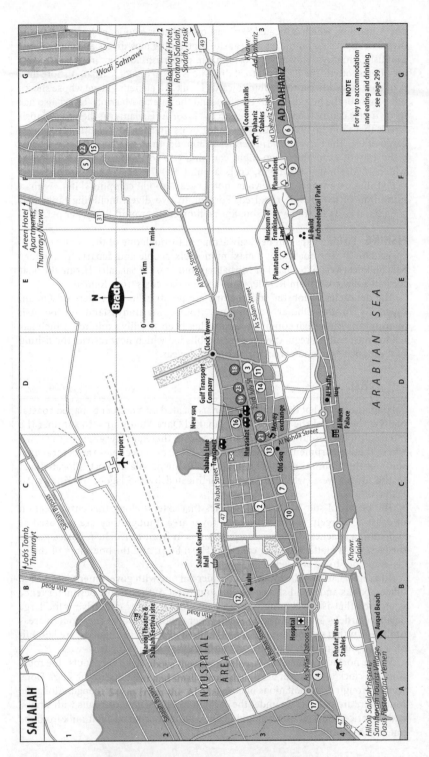

SALALAH

NOTE
For key to accommodation and drinking, see page 299

AD DAHARIZ

ARABIAN SEA

Wadi Sahnawt

Juweira Boutique Hotel,
Rotana Salalah,
Sadah, Hasik

Areen Hotel &
Apartments,
Thumrayt, Nizwa

Job's Tomb,
Thumrayt

Marooj Theatre &
Salalah Festival site

Hiltop Salalah Resort,
Samharam Tourist Village,
Oasis, Restaurant, Yemen

INDUSTRIAL AREA

Salalah Gardens Mall

Airport

Clock Tower

Gulf Transport Company

Salalah Line Transport

New suq

Mwasalat

23rd July St

Money exchange

Old suq

Al Nahda Street

Al Husn Palace

Al Haffa suq

As Salam Street

Al Rubat Street

Plantations

Plantations

Museum of
Frankincense Land

Al-Baleed
Archaeological Park

Coconut stalls

Dahariz Stables

Ad Dahariz Street

Khawr
Ad Dahariz

Khawr Salalah

Auqad Beach

Dhofar Waves Stables

Hospital

Lulu

As Sultan Qaboos St

Al Rubat Street

Atin Road

Salalah Quay Cross

Salalah Quay Cross

Considered Oman's second city with a population of only 264,652, Salalah is the administrative centre of Oman's southern governorate of Dhofar. As with the rest of Oman, there are no high-rise buildings here and the majority of the residents live in two-storey houses. Beyond the town centre the new residential areas are full of opulent mansions that are testimony to Oman's increasingly wealthy middle class.

The name *salalah* means 'shining one' in the *jabali* language. Sometimes known as the 'perfume capital of Arabia' thanks to the local cultivation of frankincense trees, a visit to the Museum of Frankincense Land (page 304) at nearby Al Balid will help you to visualise the importance of this product to the region. Salalah became part of the Sultanate of Oman in the 19th century, becoming its effective capital and the preferred residence of the sultan from 1932 to 1970, following which Sultan Qaboos chose to move both the capital and his main residence to Muscat.

 WHERE TO STAY Note that all the hotels in the budget range provide comfortable, affordable accommodation. Even the cheapest have good, clean rooms, and after your tours and all that fresh air, you can get your head down for a very reasonable price. The prices in summer, which for most hotels is from 1 July to 31 August, are higher. Some prices include taxes, which in Oman is 17%. Confirm whether breakfast is included before you arrive, and it's also worth checking whether a free airport transport service is provided for guests. Hotels at both ends of the scale seem genuinely happy to accommodate you, so if there is anything you need, or would like to change, just ask.

Luxury and upmarket

Al Baleed Resort Salalah by Anantara [298 F3] (20 rooms) Immediately west of the Crowne Plaza & next to Al Balid's lagoon; e albaleedsalalah@ anantara.com; www.salalah.anantara.com. The Anantara Al Baleed Resort on the Arabian Sea in Salalah is a luxury villa resort. With an opening date of autumn 2016, this will offer an upmarket experience previously unavailable in Salalah. The hotel is immediately next to Al Balid, the UNESCO World Heritage Site. The Anantara has a mix of private pool villas & spacious rooms, with 3 dining outlets & Salalah's first *hammam*. The beach is public & further along is the Crowne Plaza Hotel. **$$$$$**

Hilton Salalah Resort [map, page 290] (150 rooms) On the beach 12km from Salalah town centre on the way out to Raysut, not far from the 'fish' roundabout; 23 211234; e salalah@hilton.

com; www.salalah.hilton.com. The Hilton is well placed to catch the business trade from Salalah Port. There is a complimentary airport shuttle service to the hotel. There are 2 restaurants: Al Maha, offering international, Italian & Arabic cuisine, & Palm Grove, an outdoor restaurant situated by the beach, which offers fresh fish in the evening & light snacks during the day. The hotel has an English pub called The Mayfair. There is the Whispers Night Club & an Indian bar called Chequers. Internet access is not cheap in the hotel (*RO4 for 15mins*), but there are internet cafés in the street shops at approx 500bzs for an hour's usage. **$$$$$**

🏠 **Crowne Plaza Resort Salalah** [298 F3] (153 rooms, 7 suites, 19 family villas) About 3km out of town, less than 10mins from the airport; 📞 23 235333; e cpsll@omantel.net.om; www.crowneplaza.com/salalah. From Salalah Airport turn left at the 1st roundabout, right at the 2nd & then left at the 3rd, then follow signs to the hotel. The sandy beach is public but the hotel has put out its own sunshades. There is a large pool, tennis, minigolf & health club with sauna, jacuzzi & gym. There are 3 fully licensed restaurants: Darbat Restaurant on Dolphin Beach, Al Luban Restaurant & Al Khareef (an English/Irish pub). There is also a 3-bar complex located just outside the hotel, a tea lobby lounge (Bird's Lounge), 9-hole green golf course (the 1st green course in Oman) & driving range, squash & children's playground. **$$$$**

🏠 **Juweira Boutique Hotel** [map, page 290] (64 rooms) 18km from city centre, 20km from Salalah Airport; 📞 23 239600; www.juweirahotel.com. An unusual blend of oriental & European design,

with luxury spacious rooms, each with a balcony overlooking the ocean. Private beach, 2 outdoor pools, gym & spa. Al Fanar international restaurant, As Sammak seafood restaurant. Free shuttle. **$$$$**

Mid range

🏠 **Beach Resort Salalah** [298 F3] (60 rooms) Ad Dahariz St, near Crowne Plaza Hotel; 📞 23 236170; e reservation@beachresortsalalah.com; www.beachresortsalalah.com. See ad, page 326. New in 2013, this is a modern hotel with spacious rooms & suites with balconies overlooking the beach, a 24hr reception & complimentary b/fast. **$$$**

🏠 **Hamdan Plaza Hotel** [298 B3] (180 rooms) Al Wadi St, city centre; m 93 201048, 201054; www.hamdanplazahotel.com. Set in the city centre about 5mins' drive from the airport, this 4-star hotel has a host of amenities, including a large outdoor pool with sun terrace, health club, tennis & squash courts, gym, hot-tub & dry sauna, billiards & table tennis. There's also Al Lou-Lou'a Restaurant (Arabic, Indian, Far Eastern & continental food), a coffee lounge, internet café & supermarket. **$$$**

🏠 **Rotana Salalah** [map, page 290] (400 rooms) 17km east of the city centre; 📞 23 275700; e salalah.resort@rotana.com; www.rotana.com/salalahrotanaresort. From the Clock Tower roundabout in central Salalah follow road 47 east & then take road 49 towards Taqah. From Ain Hamran roundabout on the dual carriageway the road leads south towards the sea & the resort's entrance comes after an easy 22km drive. This hotel is just east of Salalah & is a low-rise property spread over more than 20ha that includes

---

OMAN AND ZANZIBAR 1698–1856

Zanzibar, a series of islands off the coast of East Africa once famed as the main centre of the slave market, was absorbed into the Omani empire in the 1690s when the Imam of Oman, Saif bin Sultan, took it from the Portuguese. Over subsequent centuries its importance to Oman grew, until in 1837 the greatest Omani sultan of the 19th century, Said bin Sultan, decided to make it his main place of residence, building fine palaces and gardens there. On his death in 1856 his sons had a dispute over who would inherit the empire, which was eventually resolved with the help of British diplomacy, with the outcome that one son inherited Zanzibar and its East African possessions, while the other son inherited Muscat and Oman. Sultan Qaboos traces his ancestry to the side of the Al Bu Said family which inherited Muscat and Oman. Today, Zanzibar is a semi-autonomous part of Tanzania.

manmade canals. The hotel receives charter flights from eastern Europe, which means it is busy most of the time. The rooms are comfortable with excellent bathrooms, & most have good sea views. Meals are less sumptuous than the 5-star hotels elsewhere in the Gulf. **$$$**

⌂ **Salalah Gardens Hotel** [298 B3] (168 rooms) In the Salalah Garden Mall near the junction of Atin Rd & Al Rubat St (road 49); 📞 23 381000; e reservation.sgr@safirhotels.com; www. safirhotels.com. Unless you're looking for a beach-based hotel this is an excellent choice for a single night or longer stay. The facilities are well managed & modern with ample space with competent & friendly staff. The Salalah Gardens Mall has a good selection of shops & a Carrefour supermarket. If you stay during a weekend or a busy period, do ask for a floor with no families as the corridors are used day & night for games by the children. **$$$**

⌂ **Samharam Tourist Village** [map, page 290] (46 villas, 16 chalets) About 10km from the airport, close to the Hilton; 📞 23 295444, 211420. This 4-star hotel is on the same side as the Hilton. To access it, you need to continue driving past until you meet the next roundabout, where you can turn around & come back. Affiliated with the Shanfari Group, this is a peaceful beachfront resort with chalets that can be let from 1 night to a medium- or long-term stay. Restaurant, coffee shop, large pool & health facilities. **$$$**

Budget and shoestring

⌂ **Al Ghubairah House Hotel Apartments** [298 C3] (21 apts) Al Ghubairah St; www.booking. com. Simple, clean flats with kitchen, satellite TV & balcony, car rental & free parking on offer. **$$**

⌂ **Al Jabal Hotel** [298 A4] (90 rooms) On Sultan Qaboos St in the town centre, close to Sultan Qaboos Hospital; 📞 23 210611, 214020; e jabalhot@omantel. net.om. Has live music & entertainment in the Shahrzad lounge, including Arabian belly dancers. There is a 24hr restaurant. **$$**

⌂ **Arabian Sea Villas** [298 F3] (15 rooms) About 700m west of the Crowne Plaza & directly on the beachfront; 📞 23 235822; e seavllas@ omantel.net.om; www.arabian-sea-villas.com. This accommodation is based on a small complex of villas directly on the sandy beach in Ad Dahariz. The rooms are simply but pleasantly furnished with most, but not all, overlooking the sea. Much of the benefit in staying here is the beach access (as with all beaches

in Salalah, this is not a sunbathing beach) & the remarkable knowledge of the management; make time to talk with them on arrival if possible. **$$**

⌂ **Areen Hotel Apartments** [map, page 290] (48 rooms) Saadah St just east of the main Salalah-Thumrayt highway in north Saadah; 📞 23 234810; e admin@salalah-youthhostel.com; www.salalah-youthhostel.com On the outskirts of Salalah, reasonably priced apartment rooms with kitchenette, fridge & satellite TV. The hotel has an outdoor pool, restaurant but no internet access. There are facilities for the disabled. **$$**

⌂ **Bamsir Tourist Hotel** [298 C3] (35 rooms) On the western section of 23 July St; 📞 23 202556, 202091. The hotel, though modern, has poor housekeeping & indifferent staff. You may be able to get a good price here, after checking the rooms. **$$**

⌂ **Darbat Hotel** [298 C3] (53 rooms) On the western part of 23 July St; 📞 23 295877, 295878; e darbathotel@hotmail.com. This is a well-established property & downstairs has a nice restaurant. **$$**

⌂ **Dhofar Hotel** [298 D3] (86 rooms) South of the Clock Tower; 📞 23 292300, 282300; e dhfhotel@omantel.net.om. A larger hotel, very well established & with easy access to routes out of town. Has a restaurant serving international, Arabic, Indian & Chinese cuisine. Does not accept credit cards. **$$**

⌂ **Muscat International Hotel** [298 C3] (65 rooms) Just west of the junction at the Al Nahda St police station opposite Sultan Qaboos Mosque, 23 July St; 📞 23 297799; e info@al-mashhoor.com; www.almashhoor.net/muscat-international-hotel-plaza-salalah. This modern 7-floor hotel offers good facilities in the heart of Salalah. It is convenient for the government ministries & gives easy access to major roads. **$$**

⌂ **Redan Hotel** [298 D3] (27 rooms) Al Salam St; 📞 23 292266, 288032; e redan@omantel.net. om. Also has 2- & 3-bedroom flats available. **$$**

⌂ **Salalah Hotel** [298 D3] (24 rooms) A'Suq St; 📞 23 295332, 295626. This 2-star hotel is situated close to the central market & opposite the Mwasalat bus station. **$$**

⌂ **Salalah Plaza Hotel** [298 A3] (104 rooms) On the Auqad roundabout on As Sultan Qaboos St; 📞 23 210794; e salalahph@salalahph.com; www. salalahph.com. This modern hotel is in a good location for exploration to the west of Salalah. The rooms need better housekeeping generally but they are an acceptable standard for the price.

The hotel often lets its web address expire &, as with many other hotels in Salalah, simply relies on online booking sites & casual arrivals. **$$**

🏠 **Al Hanaa Hotel** [298 D3] (25 rooms) Eastern part of 23 July St, south of the Clock Tower; ☎ 23 298305, 298306; e msarawas@omantel.net. om. Large, clean rooms. B/fast not offered during Ramadhan. **$**

🏠 **Al Nile Hotel** [298 F1] (80 rooms) In the main shopping area; ☎ 23 225804; e anh@al-mashhoor.com; www.almashhoor. net/al-nile-hotel-salalah. Drive north on road 31 to Thumrayt & turn right 2.2km after the start of road 31. Continue straight over the 1st roundabout and take the 2nd left turn, & after 150m the hotel will be on your left above Al Mashhour supermarket. Well located with a good selection of services in walking distance. The rooms are spacious & quite clean. Does not offer meals but there are restaurants & a supermarket close by. **$**

🏠 **Rotaj Suites** [298 F1] (30 rooms) In the main shopping area in north Salalah; m 97 179663. Driving north on road 31 to Thumrayt, turn right 2.2km after the start of road 31. Continue straight over the 1st roundabout & the hotel is on the left 600m after the roundabout. With a good range of facilities available near these apartments, the accommodation offers very good value, especially in the winter months, if you are prepared to use your negotiation skills. Apartment accommodation is worth considering if you intend to stay in the area for several nights. Cash only. **$**

✖ **WHERE TO EAT AND DRINK** The in-hotel restaurants offer breakfast from 06.30, lunch from 11.30 and dinner from 19.00.

✖ **Al Luban** [298 F3] Crowne Plaza (page 300); ☎ 23 235333. One of the Crowne Plaza's offerings, this restaurant is also a nightclub with live entertainment. **$$$$**

✖ **Al Maha** [map, page 290] Hilton (pages 299–300); ☎ 23 211234. Inside the Hilton Hotel, this restaurant serves international & Arabian cuisine. **$$$$**

✖ **Darbat** [298 F3] Crowne Plaza Hotel (page 300); ☎ 23 235333. Serves b/fast, lunch & dinner, buffet or à la carte, with the option of eating on the terrace overlooking the sea. **$$$$**

✖ **Palm Grove** [map, page 290] On the seafront at the Hilton Hotel (pages 299–300); ☎ 23 211234. 12km southwest of Salalah; international cuisine & fresh fish. **$$$$**

✖ **Al Khareef** [298 F3] Crowne Plaza Hotel (page 300); ☎ 23 235333. Pub-style establishment serving hot & cold bar food & snacks. **$$$**

✖ **Baalbek Restaurant** [298 D3] Eastern part of 23 July St, just east of the Gulf Transport bus office; ☎ 23 298834; ⊕ 10.00–23.00 daily. Very pleasant Arabic restaurant run by Syrians. **$$**

✖ **Bin Ateeq** [298 D3] 23 July St; ☎ 23 292384; e binateeq@omantel.net.om; ⊕ 11.00–23.00 daily. An eating experience sitting on the floor with cushions in the local style, within a small windowless private cubicle. The restaurant hasn't changed in probably 15 years so you certainly are stepping back in time.

The food, which includes dried shark & other authentic Omani-style food, may not be to everyone's taste. **$$**

✖ **Oasis** [map, page 290] Adjacent to Salalah Port on road 47; ☎ 23 219248; e oasisclub@ salalahport.com; ⊕ noon–15.00 & 18.00–23.00 Sun–Thu, noon–23.00 Fri & Sat. Offers good meals for staff of the port & free trade zone, visitors welcome. The location on the cliffs overlooking the sea is excellent. It offers a Western-style menu compared with the Middle Eastern/Indian offerings found in most Salalah restaurants. However, the main attraction here has to be the well-priced alcohol available. **$$**

✖ **Yamal Sea Food** [298 B3] Salalah Gardens Mall near the junction of Atin Rd & Al Rubat St (road 49); ⊕ 11.00–23.00 daily. Has both indoor & outdoor seating options. An excellent choice of food, depending on the availability of fish dishes, & the staff here are very helpful. **$$**

✖ **Al Khabeer Turkish** [298 D3] 23 July St; ⊕ 10.00–23.00 daily. A very well-established & popular Turkish restaurant. The food here is attuned to local tastes rather than totally Turkish. There is a buffet-style counter so that you can eat quickly if you have limited time. **$**

✖ **Chinese Cascade** [298 C3] 23 July St (opposite Sultan Qaboos Mosque); ☎ 23 289844; ⊕ 11.30–23.00 daily. The food here is good & very well priced. Main dishes are around RO1. **$**

Shark fishing is a lucrative business in Dhofar, and the season between October and April brings hundreds of fishermen from as far away as Masirah, Sur and Al Ashkharah for the season. Around 60 different species of shark are known to exist in Oman's waters. The sharks, hunted primarily for their fins and tail, are snapped up by agents principally in the small port at Mirbat. Shark-fin soup is an exotic dish with a strong consumer market, especially in Far Eastern countries. Sharks here are often 5–6ft in length and fetch around RO55–60 each. A single overnight shark fish hunt would probably yield around 12–18 sharks, so it is big business for local fishermen. As sharks have so few young and they reach maturity slowly their numbers are rapidly reducing.

✗ **Mamara Turkish Restaurant** [298 F1] In the main shopping area of Saadah, north Salalah; ⊕ 10.00–00.30 daily. One of the more popular Turkish restaurants in Salalah. The service is efficient & even freshly cooked meals are prepared within a short time. The restaurant also offers an excellent range of fresh fruit juices. The only drawback to sitting outside is

the constant honking of car horns as people wait for take-away orders. $
✗ **Tea Time** [298 D3] 23 July St, about 200m east of the bus area for Gulf Transport Company; ⊕ 07.00–23.00 daily. Serves snacks & a vast range of excellent teas, which are spiced with ingredients including ginger & saffron. The snacks are also good. $

OTHER PRACTICALITIES

✉ **Post office** [298 C3] Located just west of Al Nahdah St (entrance from the service road behind to the west) in central Salalah, opposite Sultan Qaboos Mosque; ☎ 23 292933; ⊕ 07.30–14.30 daily

Currency exchange [298 C3] Along Al Nahda St; ⊕ 08.30–13.00 & 16.00–20.00 Sat–Thu, 08.30–11.00 Fri. The rates at these money changers are better than at the big hotels. There are ATMs throughout the town.

STABLES IN SALALAH Do ensure that your insurance covers you for horseriding, if not, do not ride in either of the stables listed below.

Dahariz Stables [298 F3] From As Sultan Qaboos St the entrance track is 450m west of the Shell petrol station in Dahariz; 📱 96 286622. This small private stable is operated by a couple of very enthusiastic Omani men. The horses include Arab steeds, so the owners do not agree to allow inexperienced people to ride them. The coconut plantations which surround the stables offer an interesting ride as part of the route to the beach.
Dhofar Waves Stables [298 A4] South of Sultan Qaboos St/Auqad roundabout in the coconut

plantations; 📱 92 657978. From Auqad roundabout take As Sultan Qaboos St towards the Jabal Hotel, then at the hotel turn right to the coconut plantations, then turn left & then 1st right & follow the road as it swings right. The stables entrance is opposite the rear of the school building. This is a small stable run by a couple of non-Omani women. They have a paddock & reasonable access to the beach beyond for more experienced riders. The stables also cares for rescued horses.

WHAT TO SEE AND DO
Salalah's suqs Salalah's oldest suq is **Al Haffa** [298 D4] (⊕ 08.00–11.00 & 16.00–19.00 Sat–Thu), named after the Al Haffa district of town. It is close to Al Husn, the sultan's palace, and is therefore often called Al Husn Suq. Lying between As Sultan Qaboos Street and the corniche, it is a sprawling maze of little alleys where some of Salalah's few remaining old houses can still be seen, now

lived in by Pakistanis and Bangladeshis; the Omanis have moved out to more modern suburbs. Here you can bargain for **frankincense** of several qualities – the most expensive white variety, followed by the mixed white and brown, and then brown, the least expensive. Perfumed oils, *bokhur* (see box, pages 310–11) and incense burners are also for sale here.

There are a few shops in the suq selling **old silver jewellery** such as Omani *khanjars*, women's anklets, bracelets and headdresses, though these are diminishing year by year.

From the suq it is a short stroll to the corniche, its coconut palms leaning at amazing angles in line with the prevailing wind. The area immediately along the corniche, which was a mixture of residential and retail shops before being demolished in 2015, will be a new mixed-use development intended to enhance the locality.

The other town suqs are more modern – the **new suq** [298 D3] selling fish (mornings only), fruit and vegetables near the Mwasalat bus station, and the **old suq** [298 C3] packed with tiny shops selling the gold trinkets that are favoured today. The gold in Salalah is very yellow, but is 24 carat. The traditional old silver Dhofari jewellery is increasingly rare, most of it having been melted down to make new items before the value of the old pieces was fully appreciated.

Al Balid Archaeological Park منتزة البليد الأثري [298 E3] (⊕ *08.00–20.00 Sat– Thu; RO2 per car, tour buses RO50 & RO100, depending on size*) Now designated as part of the Dhofar UNESCO World Heritage Site, Al Balid is the site of ancient Salalah, known as Zafar, from which the province of Dhofar gets its name. Descriptions by early visitors like Ibn Battuta (the Arab geographer) and Marco Polo referred to this ancient Salalah as 'a great and noble and fine city'. Today it is an extensive site on the Khawr Salalah (Salalah Creek), a short walk west of the Crowne Plaza. It is 2km long and 600m wide.

A five-year project led by a German team from Aachen University began an archaeological dig here in 1996, discovering that many of the blocks of this ancient Salalah were pilfered to build the modern city, adding to the puzzle.

The extant ruins are from the 10th to 15th centuries, when the city was settled as a port for exporting frankincense and Arab horses, although archaeological finds date the origins of this ancient city to the early Islamic period, and even earlier. The city began to decline in the 16th century as the Portuguese took over the export trade to India.

The remains of the ruler's citadel are still visible today, as are the ruins of the Great Mosque, the Quran school, the cemetery and a large enclosing wall with towers. The impressive sea wall is now faced not by the sea but rather by small modern restaurants set on an elevated bridged walkway. Within Al Balid is one of Oman's better museums, the **Museum of the Frankincense Land** (*opening hours as Al Balid*), which includes two main halls (one historical, the other maritime). The historical and archaeological exhibits from Samharam and Al Balid and other areas in the region include rock art, pre-Islamic pottery, coins dating back to the 11th century, manuscripts and photographs, plus a section on frankincense.

There is a gift shop, restaurant and snack bar, though the opening hours of these depend on the shopkeeper's arrival. There is also a botanical garden behind the buildings with indigenous plant species, which can be visited as part of the Salalah 'city tour'.

TOURS IN AND AROUND SALALAH
Salalah city tour The half-day Salalah city tour is likely to include Al Balid archaeological site, the frankincense suq, the gold suq and the Arabian fish market

(there's a handicraft market near here too). If you prefer to be independent, take a taxi to the gold or frankincense suq, where you can stroll about at leisure. Distances are a little far for walking if you are based at one of the beach hotels. On the coast at the edge of town is the Al Balid Archaeological Park (page 304), easy walking distance from the Crowne Plaza, but a taxi ride from the Hilton.

West Salalah tour The west Salalah tour offered by the operators is likely to include Job's Tomb (also known as Nabi Ayoub; pages 324–5), frankincense trees and the Mughsayl blowholes (pages 317–18), and will take roughly half a day. Beyond Mughsayl is the fabulous road to Yemen which will take a full day or more if you wish to camp or stay in the simple accommodation available. Few companies if any offer this region. There are only a few sites of historical importance on the western side of Salalah, but the natural sites and landscape make up for it. The total circuit is approximately 240km.

As you head out west from Al Husn Palace along As Sultan Qaboos Street you pass the bird sanctuary to your left among the marshes of Khawr Salalah. It is not possible to visit the sanctuary, which is private to the grounds of the palace.

If you still have a couple of hours of daylight left (it gets dark at 18.00 all year around) on returning from your trip west of Salalah, you can continue straight on up to Job's Tomb. By reaching this tomb in time for sunset, you can enjoy a tea on the terrace of the adjacent restaurant overlooking the Salalah Plain and Arabian Sea from on high.

Ubar tour North of Salalah, the tour offered by all the operators is the 'Ubar and the Empty Quarter' tour. It lasts a full day. You will be taken to the archaeological site and small museum (pages 322–3), after which you will be taken for a drive over the dunes of the Empty Quarter.

An early start is usually made, and a 4x4 is not strictly necessary to reach Ubar as the road from the Thumrayt–Nizwa road is tarmac. However, to reach the sand dunes beyond it is graded road all the way, and the road tests the suspension of 4x4 vehicles. Most organised trips to Ubar include a short spell in the desert beyond, to give the visitor a taste of the Empty Quarter and to experience the sensation, however briefly, of being surrounded by silence and sand. You may find that camels lurk at a particular point beyond Ubar, the young owner ever hopeful that a party of tourists will want to experience a ride.

EAST OF SALALAH باتجاه الشرق من صلالة

Salalah has a natural eastern boundary at Wadi Sahalnawt, which creates the Khawr Ad Dahariz lagoon that is so excellent for birdwatching. The landmark Burj An Nahda (which in English is referred to as the Clock Tower) that lies opposite the new municipality building makes a natural distance marker. From here the coastal plain stretches 71km east to the town of Mirbat, while the small coastal settlement of Hasik lies 190km from the Clock Tower. The main route, road 49, is well tarmacked and in good condition, and beyond Mirbat it is single track in each direction. Fortunately there are petrol stations along the route, most of which have toilets and a small shop. Initially the Arabian Sea coastline here is soft white-sand beach, before developing into low coastal cliffs beyond Taqah until another stretch of soft sand beach with an attractive series of coastal dunes that almost run into Mirbat. Beyond Mirbat the coastline is principally rugged bays cut into the granite coastal plain that stretches with little interruption into Hasik.

Overlooking the coastal plain and sea are the Jabal Al Qara mountains and, farther east, Jabal Samhan, both of which gradually diminish in height as they extend north to the plains of central Oman. There are several access roads up into the Jabal Al Qara mountains, most of which are tarmacked, although poorly signposted. The principal roads are into Madinat Al Haq and Tawi Atayr, both of which lie on the undulating plateau at around 600m above the Arabian Sea. From the *khareef* (monsoon) until early October the plateau is open grassland, albeit with a very rocky surface, dotted with acacia, *Anogeissus dhofarica* and *Euphorbia smithii*, which are perhaps the three most common trees on the southern slopes.

AIN RAZAT (عين رزات) AND OTHER WATER SPRINGS Ain Razat (Razat water spring) is a constantly flowing series of springs within a valley at the base of the mountains. The water irrigates the gardens of the principal residence of the sultan in Dhofar, Al Mamoura Palace. Ain Razat is some 23km east of the Clock Tower and is well signposted after taking the third exit to the north at Al Mamoura roundabout on the dual carriageway road 49. Passing the 2ha ornamental garden, which is very popular at weekends, a car park lies on the edge of the spring area.

Although many local residents swim with abandon in the water, do note the sign warning of the disease bilharzia (schistosomiasis), which is spread by parasitic worms carried by freshwater snails; you should regard all springs and pools in Dhofar as their potential habitats. A dry, partially paved walk across the stream will take you up to a cave that gives views of the valley beyond.

Farther east along road 49 are several other major water springs; Ain Hamran is set in a generally scrubbier setting, but it is often good for birdwatching, while Ain Tabraq and Ain Athum are set at the end of attractive valleys, both of which are accessed from the same left (north) turn from the main road.

TAQAH طاقة Taqah (also Taqa) is the first town you come to, after 30 minutes (30km), on the easy dual carriageway (road 49) that runs east of Salalah. It was once a prosperous port. Its location between sea cliffs which offered shelter from rough seas, while a substantial area of cultivated land allowed self-sufficiency in food. Take the right turn on the roundabout on the edge of Taqah and you will pass **Khawr Taqah**, which has been developed from a natural lagoon into an ornamental one, the reed beds providing habitat for a variety of birds.

Less than 500m after the roundabout as you approach the town centre is a right turn down to the beach area, where fishermen are joined by seabirds which congregate by the hundred.

If you choose not to take the turn down towards the beach, carry on into the town centre for 2.5km, where a left turn takes you into the small 19th-century **Taqah Castle** (⊕ *09.00–16.00 Sat–Thu, 08.00–11.00 Fri; 500/200bzs adult/child*), which is often signed as Hosn Taqah. *Hosn* (Husn/Hisn) is the Arabic used in Oman for castle. This is well maintained with interesting furnishings in the rooms, which are set around an open courtyard. This fort was built in the 19th century by Sheikh Ali Al Mashani but became a government building during the early years of the 20th century. The rooms within the fort are accessed from an open courtyard: those on the ground were used for storage and retainers, and those on the first floor were accommodation for the family of the sheikh.

On the hill above this castle is a mid 20th-century **fort** which is not open, though the views from it over the town are worth the ascent. South of Taqah Castle is the whitewashed **Sheikh Al Afif Mosque** where a small cemetery near the entrance has the grave of Sultan Qaboos's mother and several of her family members.

Where to stay Within Taqah there are two major apartment buildings run by **Adam Homes** (*35 rooms; 1 building at each end of the main street, Taqah;* m *94 268564;* e *ravip@hfpoman.com; www.taqah.hfpoman.com;* **$$**), and they both usually have apartments available for one or more nights. The apartments are of good standard, with the one to the east of Taqah Castle exceptional for its reasonable price. No services are provided, although the staff in the supermarket on the ground floor of each building are helpful. They take cash only.

WADI DARBAT وادي دربات Rejoining road 49 from Taqah you will access a roundabout, at which you should take the second exit to head north towards the mountains that will lead you into Madinat Al Haq. The first exit right continues along road 49 towards Mirbat. Some 3.9km east of this roundabout is the signed left turn to Tawi Atayr (Tawi Atair). This well-tarmacked road continues in a loop and returns to road 49 towards Mirbat (for the direct signed way to Mirbat, see pages 311–14). If you take the left turn you will find yourself climbing towards Tawi Atayr. After 2.7km from road 49 you will pass a small coffee shop that overlooks what the Victorian explorer Theodore Bent described as 'one of the most stupendous natural phenomena we have ever seen' when he travelled here in 1890. He was referring to the **'tufa dam'**, a precipitate of lime mineral spanning 1.3km that has blocked the exit from Wadi Darbat and which, occasionally, has a waterfall that cascades over the edge to crash into the base some 100m below. Beyond this coffee shop, the tarmac road into Wadi Darbat meanders between the wooded escarpments of a 'seasonal cloudforest' caused by the clouds brought in by the *khareef*. After 6km there is a small car park with a coffee shop and toilets, although sitting under the vast tamarind tree 200m before the car park is far more enjoyable.

On its right-hand side, the road runs beside seasonal lakes whose water volume gradually decreases after the *khareef* (monsoon), but they almost never completely dry up. This water enables large herds of camels, cows and goats to graze their way through the valley throughout the year.

TAWI ATAYR طوي أعتير Exiting from Wadi Darbat by the route you entered, you should turn left towards Tawi Atayr (Tawi Ateer, Tawi Atair and variants), which is a drive of 15km from this junction. The tarmac road carries on up to the plateau, around 600m above the sea. Almost devoid of trees except on the slopes into the valleys, this is a seasonal grassland that sustains the cattle that wander freely. The village of Tawi Atayr has a number of small coffee shops and a single restaurant. Just before the village is a left turn signed Kesais Adeen and Atayr sinkhole. Shortly after taking this left turn the road forks and you should take the right fork, after which it's a 500m drive to a right turn onto a short track that leads to the parking area for Tawi Atayr. There is a simple coffee shop here, with public toilets available during and just after the *khareef*. The paved path will lead you to a viewing platform overlooking the sinkhole.

The **sinkhole** was a vertical series of caves within the karst limestone, the oldest at the top and the youngest at the bottom. Over time the roofs of the caves collapsed, starting at the lowest level until, eventually, the final upper cave roof collapsed, revealing the vast chamber, which is now 211m deep and up to 150m across. Standing on the viewing platform, the calls of the numerous birds make it easy to understand how it received its name epithet of 'the well of birds'.

Leaving the car park, turn right and then left after 3.6km. This will take you to the other major sinkhole in the area, **Tayq Cave sinkhole (كهف طيق)** (also Tayq/Taiq/Teiq cave). After an additional 8.3km you will find the parking area for this attraction on the right. This massive chamber is approximately 300 million m³ and can be accessed by a path that descends from its southern edge. The base of the sinkhole has a water drainage exit on its western side. Geologists from Sultan Qaboos University have speculated that the flow is connected with Tawi Atayr, and from there to a known cave on the edge of the sea.

Return along the 8.3km route that you took to the second sinkhole and then turn left, which will lead you to the **escarpment edge of Jabal Samhan**, 1,200m above the town of Mirbat to the south.

Returning to the village of Tawi Atayr and using the left turn into the village as a reference point, a drive of 9km on this good tarmac road will bring you to the start of the descent from the plateau onto the coast. After an additional 2km there is a sharp right turn onto a rough track that takes you 300m to **Wadi Hinna** (locally called Wadi Ahzeer), an area that is home to a baobab forest (غابة شجرة الماشوة). These flower in May and the pendulous seed pods ripen by December. After a series of bends the tarmac road straightens out. You are now in an area referred to as an anti-gravity or magnetic road, which some people believe enables cars to roll uphill without engine power. Unfortunately for the seekers of unlimited energy, it's an optical illusion, but fun if you can get a performance. Carry on down to road 49, where a left turn takes you to Mirbat after 12km; the right returns you to the roundabout at Taqah after 25km.

KHAWR RAWRI (خور روري) AND SAMHARAM (سمهرم) If you have decided to press on towards Mirbat instead of making the detour to the mountains, about 5km after leaving Taqah you will see a right-hand turn to the UNESCO World Heritage Site of Khawr Rawri (Khor Rori/Ruri), which also includes the fortified town of Samharam (also Sumhuram on road signs) and a small museum. The topography of Khawr Rawri is reason enough to visit this site, quite apart from its historical remains. Overlooked by the Jabal Qara and the impressive tufa dam in Wadi Darbat (page 307), and with the Arabian Sea to the south, Khawr Rawri is the largest lagoon in southern Oman, with a surface area of almost 60ha. The mouth is blocked by a substantial sandbar that bridges the gap between the two mesa-like promontories. Set within this imposing setting is the fortified town of Samharam. In winter it becomes the workplace of the excavation team from the University of Pisa, whose work may add a wealth of future information.

Continue along the entrance road. The natural paving will force you to drive sedately until you reach the entrance gate, where you will need to park and pay an entrance fee at the kiosk on the right. The charge is not based on the number of people, but is based on the size of vehicle (⊕ *08.00–20.00 Sat–Thu; RO2 per car, tour buses RO50 & RO100 depending on size*). After 600m take the right-hand turn and park your car. Opposite the turn is a small cave tomb, one of several found in the area. The metal gates, set within a low wall, are usually open; if they're not, simply open them and walk in.

The town, which is included under UNESCO's 'Land of Frankincense', has been extensively excavated by the University of Pisa in conjunction with Oman's Ministry of Heritage and Culture since 1996. Earlier excavations were made by Wendell Phillips in 1952 and intermittently by others after that date.

The Victorian explorers the Bents, who were so enthusiastic about Wadi Darbat, mentioned these ruins and felt that they were the port town of 'Abyssapolis', which featured in the geography by Claudius Ptolemy the Greek, who lived in Alexandria around AD150. The Bents also concluded Abyssapolis was another name for the harbour 'Moscha' mentioned in the *Periplus of the Erythraean Sea*, a text describing ports and coastal landmarks around the Erythraean Sea, part of today's Indian Ocean, which is believed to have been authored by a Greek living in Egypt around AD50. In this *periplus* the author described a harbour, Moscha, and its unnamed port where frankincense gum was received and traded to places including Rome, Persia and India.

Samharam is currently believed by the University of Pisa to have been founded during the 3rd century BC by a kingdom, Hadhramaut, from what is today's southern Yemen. The town's name is also that of a king of the Hadhramaut. Principally a trading town, Samharam's main commodity was frankincense, the sap from the *Boswellia sacra* tree. Trade through the town was greatly enhanced by the arrival of Roman trading fleets into the region following the Roman conquest of Egypt in 30BC. Frankincense became a substance of ostentatious consumption within Rome, all to the ultimate benefit of Samharam. The decline of the town seems to have happened during the 5th century AD, when it became abandoned, possibly as a result of the sandbar developing and restricting access to the creek and creating today's lagoon. Trade may also have reduced substantially following the AD380 edict by the Roman emperor Theodosius the Great that Christianity was the sole state religion and the subsequent prohibition by him of offerings to gods, which included burning incense.

There are two possible means to enter the town. One is from the path that gently rises and loops around the exterior of the walls, with a couple of entrance places (or exits if you choose). However, by far the most convenient entrance is through the massive gateway that protrudes by some 20m from the north-facing wall.

The substantial entrance gateway with its zigzag passageway is formed by substantial honey-coloured megaliths. The same stone is used throughout the town, although usually on a smaller scale. From the time of the town's foundation this gateway was enlarged several times: as you walk through, look for the two inscriptions in the ancient south Arabian script behind perspex. The initial inscription on the left explains that a servant of the Hadhramaut king Yalut living in Shabwa (a town in Yemen) directed the construction at the behest of the military commander of the frankincense region. Also on the left, before entering the town itself, is a small postern gate.

Once inside the gateway, you will see an entrance on the right into what is currently described as a 'monumental building' due to its size, although its purpose is unclear. Previously the American excavation team classified it as a palace, later investigators called it a temple. This building has a water well and excellent draining channels.

In the far northwest corner of the town is a temple complex, thought to have been dedicated to worship of the moon god Sin. The large troughs here may

FRANKINCENSE

In ancient geography, the southern area of Arabia was named Arabia Felix (meaning 'happy' or 'fertile'). Compared with the dry interior and the barren mountainous north of the region, it was richly fertile, and home to the frankincense tree. Its valuable gum allowed the region to flourish, giving rise to the name 'felix', meaning 'happy' or 'flourishing'.

Frankincense was used in religious rites and for medicinal purposes in most civilisations throughout the ancient world. Used in temples and at funerals, and as tribute to be paid by the Arabs to Darius the Persian king, it was a much sought-after substance. In the famous words of the 'Song of Solomon': 'I will get me to the mountain of myrrh, and to the hill of frankincense.'

Ancient Greek and Roman writers such as Herodotus, Ptolemy, Pliny, Strabo and Diodorus relate that frankincense from Dhofar was taken by sea to all parts of the world. It has been suggested that frankincense was the first commodity to lead to the whole idea of international trade routes. A Roman army under Aelius Gallus went into Yemen in 24BC to try to acquire trade domination but, as recounted by several authors including Strabo, the expedition failed with substantial loss of life and prestige. In the 1st century AD the countries of southeast Arabia were believed by their contemporaries to be the richest people in the world as a result of the frankincense of Dhofar. At the height of the trade in the 2nd century AD roughly 3,000 tonnes was being shipped from southern Arabia to Rome, Greece, Egypt, India and the Mediterranean world. Khawr Rawri was a key entrepôt.

Two thousand years later, frankincense is still at the centre of Dhofar's heritage. *Boswellia* trees grow in southern Oman, in Wadi Hadhramaut in Yemen and in Somalia, but *Boswellia sacra* from Oman is usually considered to be the best. The best of the best comes from Sadah, Hadbin and the valleys of Jabal Samhan. The Arabs divide the sap into four types, of which Hojari, from dry valleys, produces the highest quality. The medium-quality frankincense comes from the slopes and hill summits, while the inferior type is collected near the coast.

Between March and August small incisions are cut into the *Boswellia* tree bark to allow the milky sap to seep out, taking three to five days to dry into

---

have been used in cultic ceremonies. To the southeast are rooms that were used to store frankincense. These would have had a single access point from within the town and a single exit through the town's exterior walls to the waiting ships. The other areas in the town are mainly residential and commercial, and metalwork seems to have been carried out in several of these.

Included within Samharam are several other areas of interest. To the northwest of the car park at the end of a 300m path are the remains of a small temple which was built and then destroyed by flooding shortly after Samharam's foundation. There is a small **museum** 400m to the east of the car park. Inside are a few items excavated from the site and information about the region. This museum is worth a visit if only for the clean toilets to the rear of the building. South of the museum is an **historic dhow**, *The Wolf*, which was a sailing *sambuk* built in Taqah in 1953; the full-size replica next to the original is a few years old.

Birdwatching is possible from many areas around the **lagoon**, as it abuts a variety of habitats that mean that it is visited by various species. The area close to the dhow, especially the two small tributaries to the east, are visited by ibis, crake, and snipe. The more central area will often have a number of flamingo

semi-opaque lumps. In ancient times, according to Pliny the historian, only a small number of privileged families were permitted to carry out the harvesting and tending of the trees. He explained:

> These persons are called sacred, and are not allowed, while pruning the trees or gathering the harvest, to receive any pollution, either by intercourse with women or contact with the dead; by these religious observances it is that the price of the commodity is so enhanced.

Frankincense burns well on account of its natural oil content and is used throughout Oman today largely in this capacity, burnt on specially manufactured charcoal roundels to fragrance a room as a gesture of hospitality and in fumigators to scent clothing. Travelling around Oman, you will soon become accustomed to the aroma of frankincense in suqs, in the shopping malls, in hotel lobbies and on the clothes of Omanis. It is also a component of a fragrance called Amouage (*www.amouage.com*), one of the most valuable perfumes in the world (pages 130–1). The burning of frankincense is an essential part of wedding and Eid festivities and birth celebrations. An exotic incense, which is a mix of aromatic materials including frankincense, is *bakhoor* (or *bukhour, bokhur*). The ingredients vary and can include *oudh* (scented wood from India and the Far East), rose water, sandalwood, attar, myrrh, other perfume oils, aromatic resins and extracts. These are blended in their varying quantities, cooked, then ground down into a powder for burning on coals.

Salalah's frankincense suq is an ideal location to buy the product and a variety of perfume. The traditional hand-painted pottery frankincense burner (*mejmarr*) has had a revival after being used as packaging for Amouage's new perfume Salalah. Dhofari women make the pottery and then hand-paint it, thereby helping to supplement their family incomes. Frankincense and a frankincense burner make the ideal souvenir of your travels here.

and grey heron, while the sandbar should provide sightings of gulls and tern, and a clamber up to the eastern promontory may reward you with masked booby, red-billed tropicbird and Socotra cormorant. This promontory also has an archaeological site from the period after Samharam was largely abandoned.

Returning to road 49 and turning right, the town of Mirbat is a 32km drive to the west. Along the drive at 20km from the Khawr Rawri turn is the descent from the baobab trees and Tawi Atayr (pages 307–8). An additional 3km after this Tawi Atayr road is a left turn that ascends the mountain slope via a tarmacked 4km drive to an area of tamarind trees, a beautiful picnic spot with extensive views over Mirbat. Continuing towards Mirbat and shortly after the area of beautiful white coastal dunes, the road sweeps around to the right. Just after the shallow wadi is a sign pointing right to the Mausoleum of Bin Ali (page 313).

MIRBAT مرباط Mirbat (also Marbat, Murbat, etc) is most the easterly town on the coastal plain that includes Salalah. Dominated by the escarpment of Jabal Samhan, which ranges between 1,200m and 1,800m above the Arabian Sea, the town is rarely affected by the *khareef* of the summer, apart from the rough seas.

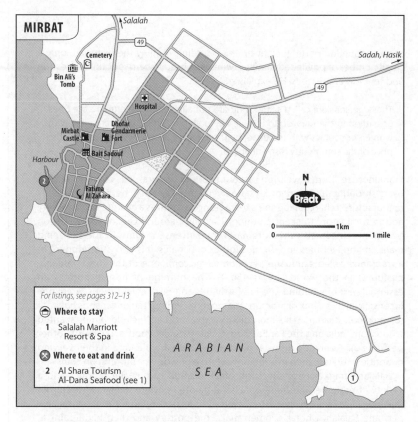

For listings, see pages 312–13

⌂ **Where to stay**

1 Salalah Marriott
Resort & Spa

✖ **Where to eat and drink**

2 Al Shara Tourism
Al-Dana Seafood (see 1)

Historically the town was periodically a capital of its region before the rule of the Al Said dynasty from 1897. In 1169, the historian Al Idrisi wrote that Mirbat was a centre of boatbuilding using the method of stitching the planks together using coconut fibre (coir). It was during this period that Mirbat became associated with the trade in horses to India for use by Indian armies. Later Aboul Feda (d 1331) recounted the export trade of frankincense from Mirbat. During the 19th century the port became a centre for the import of dates from northern Oman and the Gulf. The town today is primarily a local commercial and government hub, the port being a key fisheries centre.

⌂ Where to stay *Map, above.*

⌂ **Salalah Marriott Resort & Spa** Mirbat Cove; ☎ 23 268245; www.marriottsalalahresort. com. The 1st Marriott hotel in Oman has chosen Mirbat Cove, a few kilometres east of Mirbat as its location, well away from any competition & in an excellent spot for diving, watersports & dolphin-watching. The white sandy beach & black rocky sections contribute to the highly scenic spot. There are several dining options, from the plush Al-Dana Seafood restaurant to poolside snacks, an Arabic café & even an English pub. Very much a place for getting away from it all. Diving centre & full health spa, huge freeform pool (the largest in Oman) & tennis courts. Good promotional rates. **$$$**

✖ Where to eat and drink *Map, above.*

If you want to stop off quickly for some food, take the first right after Mirbat Castle, then second right where there is a sign for Shaba Restaurant. This is actually the **Al Shara**

Tourism Restaurant (🕐 *10.20–22.30 daily;* $) and, although basic in appearance, it offers an extensive international menu for a very low price, with friendly staff and views out to sea. If you want to linger, there are of course the restaurants of the Salalah Marriott (page 312), as well as the top-class **Al-Dana Seafood** restaurant (📞 *23 275500;* 🕐 *noon–15.00 & 19.00–23.00, reservation required;* $$$$), plus an all-day restaurant (🕐 *06.30–23.00 daily;* $$$), serving international fare daily.

What to see and do

Bin Ali's Tomb ضريح بن علي The tomb is just under 1km from route 40 and both it and the adjacent cemetery with its associated buildings are in regular daily use. Mohammed bin Ali is a descendant of the Prophet Mohammed through his grandson Hussain. An ancestor of Mohammed bin Ali, Ahmad bin Isa al-Muhajir arrived in the Hadhramaut from Basra in Iraq and Mohammed bin Ali in his turn travelled to Mirbat from Tarim in Yemen, where he became a religious scholar and died in 1161. The whitewashed, twin-domed mausoleum is typical of the sort of structure designed for important personages from the Hadhramaut. Courtesy to people contemplating within the tomb precludes visiting whilst they are inside, and visitors should be extremely conservatively dressed, which means removal of footwear and large headscarves to be worn by women. Surrounding the tomb is an extensive cemetery in which the headstones are inscribed, unlike in northern Oman. As elsewhere, those with three upright stones are for women and those with two are for men.

Mirbat Castle حصن مرباط After leaving the tomb of Bin Ali, take a right turn onto the road into Mirbat's town centre, and after 1.9km you will see a road to the right signed Mirbat Castle. The tarmac road continues out onto the seafront. To the left is Mirbat Castle (🕐 *08.30–14.30 Sun–Fri; 500bzs*), with cannons on a platform

---

THE BATTLE OF MIRBAT

During the lengthy Dhofar War this was the conflict that has gained the greatest renown and was a critical success, enabling the government forces to gradually defeat the rebels. On 19 July 1972, during the height of the *khareef*, around 250 rebels gathered under the cover of night. They made an attack, starting just before dawn, against a small lookout on the hill above the tomb of Bin Ali, which resulted in the position being overrun. The attacking forces then moved towards the town of Mirbat where nine members of Britain's Special Air Services (SAS) had been sleeping in their house, 410m southwest of the Gendarmerie Fort that still lies on a low hill opposite the modern road junction to Mirbat Castle.

The attacking forces were initially held off at the Gendarmerie Fort by SAS Sergeant Talaiasi Labalaba who had run across the open ground to man a World War II artillery gun just outside the defensive wall. He was fatally wounded but three other soldiers had also reached the artillery gun and, with Omani forces from the Dhofar Gendarmerie in their fort, continued to hold off the attack. Other defending forces restricted the movement of the rebels towards the town and by mid-morning support had arrived from Salalah: a helicopter supported by military jets. The rebel attack was repulsed with severe loss of life on their side and three deaths among the government soldiers, including Sergeant Labalaba.

overlooking the sea. The castle probably dates from the period of Mohammed Akil up until 1830 and was the residence of the governor (*wali*) of Mirbat. The castle consists of two floors: the ground floor was used by guards and as a store for their supplies and ammunition. The upstairs section was used for cannons and as accommodation for the governor and his family.

Returning towards the road into Mirbat's town centre there is a small fort about 400m away opposite the junction. It is this fort that gained fame in the Battle of Mirbat in 1972.

The town and the port   A right turn onto the road into town from Mirbat Castle will take you after 450m past an older area of housing. Several of these buildings have collapsed, including **Bait Sadouf**, which is to the right of the modern arch, and according to some local people is between 300 and 500 years old; in the future Bait Sadouf may be restored. To the left of the arch the house with a small protruding *mashrabiya* and embossed wall decoration was the home of Sheikh Abdullah Hassan Al Amari during the 1950s. Continue along the road and past the small shops and restaurants until you reach a junction with the brown **Fatima Al Zahara Mosque** on the right. Here the right turn will bring you to a roundabout; the second right on the roundabout takes you straight into the small port.

The port is a fishing harbour where dhows return after several days at sea with their catches of shark, tuna and trevally. Smaller fibreglass boats set out for a few hours at a time and may catch sardine, grouper and tuna. The waters at Mirbat, and to the east of Mirbat at Hasik, offer excellent scuba diving (page 296) and are the best places for spotting dolphins. Sports fishing tours begin here at the harbour, from the marina in Juweira (page 300) or the jetty at the Marriott (page 312).

EAST OF MIRBAT مرباط الشرق   About 140m south of the junction for Bin Ali is the continuation of road 49 east to Sadah, Hadbin and distant Hasik, which is a drive on tarmac road of 121km. Although Mirbat is comfortably within a day's sightseeing from Salalah, if you wish to visit the area to its east then it is worth considering staying in Mirbat.

Beyond Mirbat the scenery is quite different from the region around Salalah. Jabal Samhan to the north is an impressive escarpment of limestone that rises to well over 1,000m along all its 70km south-facing edge, and is over 1,500m for much of this. The scree (talus) deposited at the base of the cliff leads down to one of Oman's oldest rock formations, a vast area of exposed basement rock that extends from Mirbat to beyond Hadbin in the east. These igneous rocks are some 800 million years old and some contain material up to 1.3 billion years old. For much of the drive the rock is granite with spectacular parallel dyke intrusions of contrasting colour cut through the overlying rock; often these intrusions are many kilometres in length. Probably less than 50 million years ago, this basement rock was just below the surface of the sea, whose wave action resulted in the relatively uniform maximum height, so that it is a form of wave-cut platform. Beyond Hadbin the limestone escarpment reaches the sea and it continues this proximity through to Sawqrah (page 284). The occasional wadi cuts through the granite to reach the sea, giving the coastline an indented appearance of small coves and a mix of pebble or sand beach.

The region's largest settlements are Sadah and Hasik and the wadis have a number of very small villages. Offshore are the Al Hallaniyyat Islands which are outcrops of similar rock to the mainland. Only one of them, Al Hallaniyyat, has a small village on its western tip. The islands are difficult to reach during the *khareef* and a few other months when seasonal winds are at their strongest.

SADAH, HADBIN AND HASIK سدح, حدبين وحاسك From Mirbat continue along road 49 towards the east, where the landscape becomes more incised with valleys and dykes, especially after 30km from Mirbat. **Sadah** is signed to the right after reaching a junction 59km from the Mirbat turn (127km from the Clock Tower in Salalah). With its small but well-protected harbour, Sadah (Sadh, Sudah, etc) was a port for the trade in frankincense, as there are trees growing in the hills to the north of the town. It was once a key area for abalone during the season when diving for the mollusc is permitted, but this trade has now decidedly moved to Hadbin.

At the time of writing, Sadah's small castle, which dates from the early 20th century, was being rebuilt. (Previously it was open 08.00–14.00 Sunday–Thursday.)

Leaving Sadah and continuing east along road 49, you will find that you're mostly always within sight of the sea, including the beach at Haat, where the coconut palms overlook a small very basic restaurant and simple accommodation. The village of **Hadbin**, with its shops and simple restaurants, is reached after 28km from Sadah. Here the small natural harbour, just beyond the village, is a hive of activity during the few weeks when diving for abalone is permitted. The smooth, pillow-shaped rocks close to this harbour are granodiorite, the same form of granite as that used in the creation of the Rosetta Stone.

From Hadbin the road lies at the base of the cliffs, within a few metres of the Arabian Sea, and once again most of the beaches are soft sand.

A left turn into a wadi 15km beyond Hadbin is the short road to the **mausoleum of the Prophet Saleh bin Hud**. In the Quran the Prophet Saleh was a god-fearing member of the idolatrous tribe of Thamud, who were granted a camel for milk by God as a test to see whether they would kill her for meat. They did kill the animal and failed to repent, whereupon God destroyed them, sparing only Saleh and his followers.

The road continues between the sea cliffs and beaches into **Hasik**. This town has a large number of new houses to the right of road 49, while beyond these, closer to the sea, lies the older section where most of the few restaurants and grocery shops are located. If you are driving into Ash Shuwaymiyyah, the Al Maha petrol station is the last place to fill up with fuel for 90km.

Beyond Hasik there are a few seasonal waterfalls at the base of the cliffs before the road, now route 42, ascends to the remarkable tarmac route into Ash Shuwaymiyyah. Although this area is officially part of Dhofar, in this book it has been included within the *Al Wusta* chapter for ease of route navigation (pages 284–5).

 Where to stay *Map, page 290.*

Al Safeena Resthouse (11 rooms) On route 49 at the T-junction for Sadah, turn east towards Hadbin; the resthouse is after 3.5km from the T-junction, directly on the beach; m 99 143217, 294660. This is simple accommodation – private rooms with shower & toilet. Most rooms have a small patio overlooking a beautiful sandy beach & small bay. You might want to rent the room simply to enjoy a day at the beach. There is an extremely basic restaurant; Sadah, with a better choice of

places to eat & some small groceries, is only a few moments' drive away. Cash only. **$**

Hasik Beach Resthouse (7 rooms) At the Hasik Al Maha petrol station turn north towards the sea, continue to the end of the road & turn left for 600m, & the accommodation is on your left facing the sea (sign is in Arabic only); m 92 585896. This is basic accommodation of reasonably clean individual rooms with private shower & toilet. There is a new 'satellite' unit of this accommodation under construction in the same place. The location is ideal to make the journey by road between Ad Duqm & Salalah or if you wish to get a boat out to the Al Hallaniyyat Islands (Juzor Al Hallaniyyat). Do try to contact the accommodation before you arrive & be patient in dealing with language issues if the person in charge speaks faltering English. Cash only. **$**

Where to eat and drink *Map, page 290.*

✗ Adhwa Hasik Restaurant In the old centre of Hasik, reached by turning off the main Mirbat road 49 into the village & going through the convoluted route into the centre; m 99 479660; ⊕ 07.00–22.30 daily. There are a couple of small restaurants in the centre of old Hasik, similar in quality, but this one is slightly better & does have cutlery. Its sign is in Arabic only, but the phone number is on the sign. The food is rice-based & the owner (who is also the cook) will prepare fish & chicken freshly for you. **$**

✗ Sadah Towers Restaurant At the T-junction in Sadah turn right away from the harbour, which is to the left, & the restaurant is on your right after 200m; ⊕ 07.30–23.30 daily. The restaurants in Sadah are simple & unused to Western tourists, & this one is no exception. As a result, the sign is in Arabic only, but ask around & people will show you the location. It offers Indian-style rice & meat; sit outside for an interesting view of life on the main street. **$**

AL HALLANIYYAT ISLANDS جزر الحلانيات These five islands lie 200km east of Salalah, just off the coast of Shalim and Ash Shuwaymiyyah. They used to be called the Kuria Maria Islands, but now are known as the Juzor Al Hallaniyyat, and the intention is to make them a protected zone and reserve. They are a haven for birds including Socotra cormorants and masked boobys; turtles breed here and in the waters Oman's humpbacked whales seem to use them as a terminus for their movements along Oman's coast (the other terminus is towards Masirah Island).

The islands have had numerous shipwrecks. On 6 August 1914, the British merchant cargo ship *City of Winchester* was steaming through the Gulf of Aden from Calcutta with a cargo of tea. The German cruiser SMS *Königsberg* commanded the *Winchester* to stop and she was then boarded. Both ships transferred to the Al Hallaniyyat Islands, where the *Winchester*'s coal and ship's stores were transferred to the *Königsberg*. On 12 August, the *City of Winchester* was scuttled, making it the first British ship to be lost as a result of World War I. Today the ship lies in 30m of water about 1.5km offshore from Ghubbat Ar Rahib bay to the northeast of the Al Hallaniyyat Islands. Also in Ghubbat Ar Rahib bay is an earlier wreck, that of the *Esmeralda*, one of the caravels that sailed in Vasco da Gama's 1502 fleet of 20 ships from Portugal to India. After Vasco da Gama returned to Portugal with the main fleet, five ships remained in the Arabian Sea under the command of Vice-Admiral Vicente Sodré, including the *Esmeralda*. In April 1503, a fierce storm arrived and sank the *Esmeralda* while at anchor in Ghubbat Ar Rahib bay, and most of the crew were lost. The wreck's remains are just offshore and various artefacts are displayed in the National Museum (pages 111–12).

Perhaps the most extraordinary episode in the islands' history was when they were ceded by Sultan Said to Britain on 14 July 1854. There was subterfuge all around, for Britain had said that they wanted to establish a coaling station there. In fact, a Captain Ord wished to extract guano, which was then a key fertiliser and was apparently available in vast quantities on the islands. After Sultan Said, as the apparent ruler of the islands, made a gift of them to Lord Clarendon the British foreign secretary, Lord Clarendon sent him a silver snuff box in appreciation of the island gift after much consideration. Unfortunately, Sultan Said's claim to rule the islands was not uncontested and in 1856 tribes from the mainland forced Ord to evacuate his guano-mining team. Ord returned in greater force in 1857, only to see the venture fail in 1861. The islands were ceded back to Oman in 1967 after Britain withdrew from south Yemen.

Burial in the Islamic world is a quick affair, usually within 24 hours of death, and in a fairly simple grave, often with no coffin, but with the corpse just wrapped in a white shroud. The Prophet Muhammad said that if the deceased were a good man, the sooner he is buried the sooner he will reach heaven; and if a bad man, he should also be speedily buried so that his unhappy lot might not fall upon the others in the house. The actual funeral service is not recited at the grave, this being thought too polluted a place for such a sacred ceremony, so it is usually held in a mosque or in an open space near the house of the deceased, either by the family imam or the *qadi* (judge). The corpse is buried so that the body lies on its right side facing Mecca. As Mecca is due west from Muscat, the body in that part of Oman is aligned north–south and at an appropriate orientation elsewhere in the country or world. As the corpse is lowered all present speak the sentence: 'We commit thee to earth in the name of God and in the religion of the Prophet.' Cremation of the dead is strictly forbidden under Islam, for a dead body was considered as fully conscious of pain as a living body, and Muhammad said: 'It is not fit for anyone to punish with fire but God.'

Today the main island, Al Hallaniyyat, has a small village on its western tip. The islands are a popular scuba-diving location.

WEST OF SALALAH غرب صلالة

Salalah has spread rapidly along the coastal plain west towards the cliffs on the edge of Salalah Port. Beyond the port the mountains curve towards the sea until, just west of Mughsayl's popular beach, they create some of Oman's most iconic scenery. From Mughsayl the landscape rises to a rugged plateau of over 1,000m and extends west beyond the border with Yemen and north into the edge of the Empty Quarter desert. The isolation of this region has meant that it has a very low population density, with most communities close to the coast.

SALALAH PORT ميناء صلالة Located west of Salalah at Raysut on the western section of route 47 (also called Al Rubat Street and then As Sultan Qaboos Street), this modern container port is a key transhipment port between western Europe and Asia, and in terms of volume it is among the 50 largest ports in the world. The area surrounding the port is the Salalah Free Trade Zone, which combined with Salalah Airport are key facilities in Oman's diversification away from reliance on oil income. The port is a mixed-use operation and cruise ships use the berths. Grain and cement bulk carriers are a key element of the shipping tonnage.

Road 47 enters a roundabout near the port 17km west of the Clock Tower. Take the first right and continue for a total of 42km to reach Mughsayl Beach.

MUGHSAYL المغسيل Mughsayl Beach is a magnificent 4km stretch of white sand with high cliffs at either end. The first area, that you can drive onto, has substantial shaded shelters built of breeze blocks, though the quantity of rubbish littering the area is depressing, especially in view of the numerous green government notices in Arabic exhorting citizens to look after the environment and avoid pollution. Picnic shades stretch the length of the beach, at the far end of which is the attractively green and large lagoon Khawr Mughsayl. Grazing camels often join the many birds here, which include flamingos, pelicans and heron. Just after the lagoon is an Al Maha petrol station – you should fill up with petrol here, as the petrol stations at the harbour in Rakhyut and village of Sarfayt, which is 109km from Mughsayl, are remote and may run out of petrol.

Just beyond the lagoon is the sign to **Kahf Al Marnif (Al Marnif Cave)**, complete with the **Al Marnif Restaurant ($)**. The food at this restaurant is very basic but it does offer a place to sit and enjoy the sea views or use the toilet facilities. From the car park there is a short walk up the paved slope to reach the **Mughsayl blowholes**, which are past the imposing rocky outcrop and rock overhang which is the cave. The blowholes are at their most impressive during the monsoon season when the sea is at its most forceful, and water can shoot up to 30m high through one of several holes in the limestone rock. At other times of the year the blowholes are still active at high tide, but at low tide you will mainly just hear the sea slopping about under the rocks, with the occasional soft roar and gentle spray forcing its way up through the metal grids that have been put over the holes to prevent accidents. Even a gentle spray can completely soak you, so be careful what you wear, as watches, leather or cameras could be damaged. It is fun to watch people posing for photos beside the blowholes, tentatively awaiting the arrival of the forceful spray of seawater so that it can be captured on camera, before they hurriedly dart away to avoid getting soaked.

JABAL QAMAR جبل القمر After Mughsayl's Al Maha petrol station the road westwards begins its impressive 22km climb up to the plateau of the Jabal Qamar, 'the Mountains of the Moon'. After about 4.6km the hillsides are covered in frankincense trees and you will see them further on towards the higher plateau. The road's hairpin bends cut through cream-coloured limestone and wind their way down and then up in an impressive ascent from sea level to 1,000m. This section of the route is known as 'the furious road'. Some 14km after Mughsayl a left turn will take you down the rough track to the sea at **Fizayah** (also Al Fazayih), a bumpy road of 6km. Here the beaches are soft sand and there are scattered growths of desert rose of the *Adenium obesum* variety along the final section of track. The countryside here is not as empty as it seems at first. You could find a spot, sit down for lunch quite alone, and then be startled by a Jabali herdsman striding past as if from nowhere.

The landscape of the plateau is very different again, with extensive rolling plains covered in grass (browning by late October), trees and the occasional settlement of cow herders. There is a checkpoint at which you will need your identification, driver's licence and vehicle registration, if you are hiring the car ensure all the documents are correct. There is a second checkpoint 76km after Mughsayl requiring the same documents to be presented. Occasionally people who are not resident in the villages beyond may be turned back if the security forces decide, but this is unusual.

SHAAT شعت The tarmac road on the plateau travels along the divide between the area affected by the *khareef* cloud (monsoon) cover to the south and the northern side, which is almost vegetation-free dry mountain and valley. During August this divide is almost as stark as that between the cultivated and non-cultivated Nile Valley. The left turn to Shaat 31km after Mughsayl will take you by tarmac road to the stupendous sea cliffs that tower 1,000m above the waves below. The greenery on the cliffs lingers throughout much of the year and small picnic shelters are available to rest in.

A right turn at 54km from the Al Maha petrol station in Mughsayl will take you onto the 84km-long, bleak and mountainous rough road 45 to Muday, 81km by road west of Thumrayt. This track has additional security checkpoints and there is no petrol station until Thumrayt.

RAKHYUT رخيوت The tarmac road up on the plateau and the ascent itself have little traffic, with whole stretches where you do not pass another vehicle. Rakhyut, a small fishing settlement and old sea port, is a 61km drive from Mughsayl. The descent by tarmac road from the plateau above the settlement to the sea takes you through almost 23km of undulating hillsides which, following the *khareef*, are covered in grassland and green woodland. Immediately after the *khareef*, this is one of the most attractive drives in Oman, with panoramic views on the way down over pastureland and sea. There is a small coffee shop in the group of more modern houses on the left as you enter Rakhyut and a second one just outside the small hotel.

Where to stay The **Rakhyut Tourist Motel** (*12 rooms; on the eastern edge of Rakhyut between the mountains & sea;* m *92 630784;* $) is the only accommodation in Rakhyut. The rooms are very basic and not especially clean, but they do have their own shower and toilet. Staying here after the magnificent drive may be something of a let-down. They take cash only.

Where to eat and drink On entering Rakhyut, there are a number of single-storey houses at the base of the mountain on the left. The **Rakhyut Restaurant** (⏱ 08.00–22.00 daily; $) is on the street where these houses are. This very small restaurant offers a selection of basic meals including 'Lebanese' pitta bread sandwiches. This is the local venue for the children to eat, so you will soon be the centre of attention. Ask for a take-away (the local term is *parcel*) if you want to eat on the beach.

DALKUT ظلكوت This is the final settlement of any size before the Yemeni border and after a 104km drive from Mughsayl the town rewards you with its superb setting, wooded cliffs that overlook a splendid beach and the Arabian Sea. The beach is soft sand, stretching almost 2km from the small harbour in the east to the sea cliffs at the west, while the escarpment is 600m high, through which pale grey crags protrude and eagles search. Within the harbour is a petrol pump, while outside the harbour's perimeter the road leads to a gigantic baobab tree.

Where to stay and eat

🏠 **Dalkut Hotel** (14 rooms) On the main street in Dalkut, about 500m west of the harbour; m 99 245215, 98 206986. Newly opened with the best accommodation in the area, though there is little competition. This is the tallest building in town & cannot be missed. The rooms have basic furnishings & if you ask for a sea view you do have uninterrupted views, although a mountain view is also spectacular. Cash only. $

🏠 **Dalkut private accommodation** (2 rooms) On the main street in Dalkut, about 900m west of the harbour on the north side of the road;

m 92 733920, 95 401594. Part of a private Omani house, this accommodation comprises 2 rooms with individual access from the outside. The rooms have a private shower, though as is normal in some Omani homes, you may sleep on a mattress on the floor. The family have limited English, but somebody will usually be found who can help. Always phone before arrival to try to make a reservation. Cash only. $

✗ **Ahla Restaurant** Centre of Dalkut, close to the main mosque; ⏱ 06.30–23.30 daily. Serves a simple selection of freshly cooked chicken or lamb with rice. $

NORTH OF SALALAH شمال صلالة

North of Salalah the coastal plain stops abruptly with the steep mountain slope of Jabal Qara. The coastal plain, which is naturally vegetation-free, is then replaced not only by slopes but also by what is termed as a 'seasonal cloudforest', formed as a result of the *khareef* clouds descending almost to the level of the plain.

Dissecting the slope are valleys, usually running approximately from the north down to the south. Scattered through the Qara mountains are small settlements whose families traditionally herded cattle and camels. Now, as with the rest of Oman, employment within the government and in commercial organisations provides the greatest income.

The plateau is karst limestone and open grassland from midsummer until October, with free-ranging animals throughout the length of the mountain chain. Undulating at over 700m above sea level, there is a distinct divide between the south-facing slopes that receive the clouds coming in from the sea and the barren hills that drop away sharply to the north. On the eastern side of the Qara mountains these foothills lead north into the Jiddat Al Harasis plain of central Oman, while those to the west meet the Rub Al Khali sand dunes.

Travelling northwards up and out of Salalah there are several tarmacked mountain roads going north from the Salalah dual carriageway bypass. They all eventually meet with the Salalah–Thumrayt–Nizwa highway, which is the only tarmac route north from the mountains. To simplify the routing only two routes are described, namely the Salalah–Thumrayt highway and the Atin Road (also Itin), the latter of which includes Job's Tomb and the link to the Salalah–Thumrayt highway.

GOING NORTH ON THE SALALAH–THUMRAYT HIGHWAY الطريق صلالة ثمريت From the Clock Tower the Salalah–Thumrayt road is 4.6km to the east. Take the exit signed Thumrayt. The 72km drive from here to Thumrayt along road 31 is on a dual carriageway, which for the first 12km traverses the plain behind Salalah. The ascent is initially steep and although there is usually not much traffic, the extremely slow and overladen trucks do take some getting used to – more so if you return on the same route going down, when both you and they need to use low gears to slow down your respective vehicles and avoid overheating brakes. The route has been cut through the wooded mountain slope and it gradually enters the plateau grassland area, which is less steep. There are side roads into these areas, although road signs here are few and far between, and mostly in Arabic only. The area affected by the *khareef* finishes in the general area of the shops and restaurants at **Qayrun Hayriti**, relatively close to a checkpoint after 34km from the start of the Salalah–Thumrayt road. Here, at a checkpoint, you may be required to show vehicle documentation, your identification and driving licence.

Almost immediately after Qayrun Hayriti the roads descends, cutting through cream-coloured limestone on its way towards the barren foothills. To the left of the road and accessed via a turning at 41km from the turn onto the Salalah–Thumrayt road is **Wadi Dawkah**, one of the places inscribed as part of the UNESCO Land of Frankincense World Heritage Site. Here a small information centre (⊕ *08.00–14.00 Sun–Thu, but opening times dependent on staff presence*) overlooks the rows of frankincense trees. The wadi on which the trees are located has cut through the soft limestone, and flint and chert chippings can be found on the tops of many of the inselbergs along this and similar wadis. According to the archaeologist Dr Jeffrey Rose, these chippings are from what must have been vast areas of stone tool production, evidence of man's early arrival into Arabia between 60,000 and 100,000 years ago.

🏠 **Where to stay** Camping is the only option if you are venturing into the Rub Al Khali, where you will be rewarded by superlative scenery, dark skies and deafening silence.

🏠 **Qatbit Resthouse** [map, page 270]
(10 rooms) m 99 085686. North of Thumrayt,
continuing on the main Muscat–Salalah road, this
is the next hotel stop you will reach. This is another
basic resthouse with an international restaurant,
situated 275km from Salalah, & provides a welcome
stop if you need it. Accepts credit cards. **$$**

🏠 **Thumrayt Resthouse** [map, page 290]
📞 23 279371. The Thumrayt Hotel & restaurant
stands over to the right (east) when entering
Thumrayt on the main Salalah–Thumrayt road.
It is a simple set-up despite its lavish marble
entrance. The restaurant is not licensed & serves
Indian or international cuisine. It is a welcome stop
if you are visiting the Empty Quarter & Ubar. **$$**

✗ **Where to eat and drink** There are a few coffee shops, restaurants and fruit-juice stalls in Thumrayt, close to the petrol station. If you haven't brought a picnic, you might like to eat here or inside the Thumrayt Resthouse. The Qatbit Resthouse also has a restaurant.

Thumrayt ثمريت Thumrayt links Dhofar to the rest of Oman and throughout history has therefore acted as an important junction on the ancient caravan routes. The town has a **camel racecourse**, and races are held here periodically, with a camel beauty and milk production competition held in conjunction with the races. The racetrack is on the other side of the dual carriageway from the Shell petrol station; you will need to make the U-turn on the roundabout next to this petrol station.

From Thumrayt the dual carriageway road 31 continues north for a monotonous 795km to Nizwa. For route information, see the *Al Wusta* chapter (pages 272–7). The western exit from the roundabout at Thumrayt is the desert route to Yemen via road 45. After 6.6km the north exit leads to a second roundabout, where the first exit is road 39 via Marmul to Ash Shuwaymiyyah or Al Lakbi.

To explore more of the region north of Salalah, continue along road 31 and after 16km from the roundabout near the Shell petrol station is the left turn onto road 43 to Ash Shisr (also called Ubar). This road is not tarmacked, but continue to 41km north of the Shell petrol station where you'll see a tarmacked road on the left. Take this route to reach Ash Shisr after 52km.

THE JABALI

As their name implies, the Jabali are a mountain people of southern Oman (*jabal* is Arabic for mountain) who have lived, until recently, largely on the milk and meat of cattle, goats and camels. Historically they were dependent on these livestock for their survival and livelihood.

The Omani Jabali language (also called Shahiri) is a different language from Arabic, and (along with the Mahari language) originates from the ancient languages of southern Arabia. Their traditional clothing is an indigo-dyed piece of material, wrapped up and slung over the shoulder and around the waist, forming a skirt, and the older Jabalis can occasionally be seen today dressed in this way. The younger ones have tended towards both the diet and attire of the people of Salalah. Generally, the Jabali have been able to take advantage of the improved situation of their surrounds, in terms of education, medical care, employment and access to a wider range of food since Sultan Qaboos took control.

The Jabali formerly lived in traditional round-stone windowless houses, which had earth and grass roofs, built slightly sunken into the ground; relatively few of these remain today. Instead they occupy modern houses in either the mountains or a town, or perhaps both.

Ash Shisr (site of Ubar, Atlantis of the Sands) الشصر أوبار Ash Shisr (often just Shisr) is on the edge of the Empty Quarter and the confluence of Wadi Ghadun and Wadi Malhit (referred to by Wilfred Thesiger in *Arabian Sands* as Umm Al Hait). The water from the Qara mountains flowing underground has created a number of springs such as at Hashman. One such spring previously was at Ash Shisr too, but the constant pumping of underground water for the pivot fields has dropped the water table to the spring at the base of the collapsed cave over which the town's fort was constructed. This was the source of water that enabled the settlement, but it has since dried up.

Today, Ash Shisr is within an area of pivot fields where water is pumped up and used to irrigate grass fields. The hay from these is then trucked into Salalah to feed the livestock there.

The modern quest that resulted in Ash Shisr becoming one and the same as Ubar (called Wabar by the Oman government) evolved gradually. Bertram Thomas, the first European to cross the Rub Al Khali, was guided in 1930 by Bedouin from the tribes that have now have settled in Mitan and Hashman further into the Empty Quarter. As they travelled in the Empty Quarter the guides pointed out to him, 'Look, Sahib, there is the road to Ubar. It was a great city, our fathers have told us that existed of old; a city rich in treasure, with date gardens and a fort of red silver.' Wilfred Thesiger explored the area in the late 1940s with guides from the same families as those who had helped Thomas. He wrote, 'We watered at Ash Shisr, where the ruins of a crude stone fort on a rocky mound mark the position of the famous well, the only permanent water on the central steppes.' Wendell Phillips, who came to Dhofar in 1952, tells of meeting a Bedouin and, 'When I asked him if he knew the location of Ubar he shouted into my ear, "Only the devil knows." Ranulph Fiennes recollects a conversation he had with an army colleague Nasran, who said, '"Some say the finest city in all Arabia was Ubar, built like Paradise with pillars fashioned from gold." "Will you take me there, Nasran?" I asked. "Inshallah" was his reply.' This set Fiennes off on his quest to discover the lost city, eventually being joined by filmmaker Nicholas Clapp, who had come to Oman in 1980 to film the release of the oryx back into the wild.

At the start, in mid-July 1990, when the expedition to try to discover Ubar was about to begin, Fiennes wryly remarked:

> My polar expeditions normally start in dark, freezing shacks with a handful of comrades who know each other well and understand the minutiae of the straightforward aim to get to the Pole. The Ubar reconnaissance expedition began in Muscat's plush Al Bustan Palace Hotel and involved a group who were mostly strangers to each other, none of whom knew how best to set about searching for their goal, and each of whom had a different motive for being there.

The discovery of **Ubar** (موقع تاريخي أوبار) was announced with much fanfare in *The New York Times* of 5 February 1992 and it was included in the Land of Frankincense Sites in 2000.

From the small roundabout in Ash Shisr towards the end of the tarmac road take the second exit to continue straight ahead. Ahead are a number of houses; to the left a complex whose offices administer the area and to the right is parking outside Ubar. To the left of the entrance to the site is a small shop where soft drinks and snacks are available; do support this business. From here you can walk into the site, which is not large, at less than 1.5ha, while the fort is just over 2,000m².

The feature that dominates the site is the **sinkhole**, into which a substantial part of the fortress collapsed. Behind the ancient fortification is a more **modern**

whitewashed fort, built in 1955 using stone from the older fort. Its purpose was the same as the original fort: to defend its key resource, water, and to control customs revenue along a poorly demarcated frontier.

The **ancient fort** is a distorted oblong shape with its walls fortified by seven towers, some of which would have served as living quarters. The citadel was located in the northwest corner. Set within its wall, the principal gate faced west, the direction for which most camel caravans would have departed. The renovated wall of the fort and a small building within those walls are all that remain of the building.

Evidence points to the site having been used since the Stone Age (around 5000BC) and the style of the fortifications suggests that it was constructed during the late Iron Age (from 325BC). Juris Zarins, the archaeologist involved with the excavations, believes that it was built on an earlier settlement. Though the site continued to be used in the Early and Middle Islamic periods it had lost its importance by the 3rd century AD.

Objects found at Ash Shisr have been eclectic: Neolithic spear points and arrowheads (8th–7th millennia BC); glass bracelet fragments (9th–16th centuries AD), Abbasid coins (8th–10th centuries AD); and, most intriguingly, part of a chess set (8th–10th centuries AD).

Hashman and beyond حشمان و المنطقة A 4x4 is required to continue beyond Ash Shisr into the Empty Quarter, and travelling with at least one other vehicle is important. Return to the small roundabout in Ash Shisr and take the first right, which takes you west and then north. The tarmac road disappears after less than 3.5km next to a useful tyre-repair shed, where tyre pressure can be adjusted, and from here the road is mostly a well-defined track with a very bumpy surface for 72km until the turn to the small village of **Hashman** (previously called Fasad). The village has a small grocery shop with little in the way of products to buy. To the east of the village is a small sulphur spring which has resulted in a thick oasis of date palms. The water that often floods over the sand attracts sandgrouse in the early morning.

Beyond Hashman the track is subsumed by sand and overlooked by the mega-dunes of the **Empty Quarter**. The Empty Quarter or Rub Al Khali is believed to have been formed as recently as the early Pleistocene epoch, which dates from 2.6 million to 11,700 years ago. During this period increases in glaciation substantially reduced sea level, exposing calcium carbonate sand that was previously the sea bed. Winds could then transport this pale, off-white sand inland. However, in the eastern and southeastern areas of the Rub Al Khali the principal source of sand was outwash from the major wadis of the mountains in Dhofar and northern Oman. Hard quartz forms the majority of the grains and oxidisation on the surface has given them a distinctive orange colour. The variable winds have created star dunes interspersed with large flat areas between individual dunes which are often covered in a pale grey deposit of gypsum and marl. In several areas geodes are scattered on the desert floor. These were washed down from the Qara mountains aeons ago.

As you are near the borders of Saudi Arabia and Yemen you must make yourself aware of any security notices and respond calmly to instructions by Omani military patrols if you meet them.

Returning to Salalah from Hashman on the rough track heading east towards Ash Shisr there is a right turn to the south some 42km past Hashman. Continue on this road past the right turn to the small settlement of Bithnah and, eventually, having travelled 105km from Hashman, you will reach a tarmac junction. Turn left (east) towards Thumrayt. After some 53km, you will arrive at the roundabout for the small settlement at **Muday**. Crossing the roundabout towards Thumrayt and continuing for a further 500m or so there are **triliths** (see box, page 325) on the right-hand side of the road. A little further along and also on the right, there are others.

To reach Thumrayt from Muday, continue 81km past the roundabout. Taking this route to Thumrayt from Hashman via Muday is almost 240km with no petrol station *en route*.

GOING NORTH ON THE ATIN ROAD باتجاه الشمال على طريق أتين From the Clock Tower roundabout travel west for 5.7km along road 47, also called Ar Rubat Street, and take the right turn. The road carries on north across the plain and continues over a roundabout until a second roundabout is reached after an additional 7.5km from the turn-off road 47. Here there are numerous small establishments selling cooked food and also small groceries. The first right turn will take you to **Ain Garziz**, a spring that usually has water following the *khareef* (monsoon). There are areas of tufa around the spring. From this second roundabout carry on north and ascend the mountain road. Passing the television studio on the left that broadcasts live chat shows during the *khareef* and small restaurant next to it, the road climbs past scattered small farms whose cattle and camels frequently block the road. The turn to the mausoleum of the Prophet Job is on the left after 14km from the roundabout with all those small shops. Here are some small shops and from here it's a short 1.5km drive to the mosque, which stands next to the tomb.

Job's Tomb ضريح النبي أيوب The mausoleum known as Job's Tomb is set on the upper edge of a wadi overlooking the town of Salalah. As with many of the sea-facing slopes, this is in a well-wooded location.

The Islamic story of Job, who is revered as an Islamic prophet, is similar in concept to his Book in the Bible. Job (Ayoub in Arabic), who is mentioned in the Quran as a descendant of Noah, was described by angels as being a God-fearing person who prayed daily and praised God for giving him wealth and a large family. However, Satan claimed that Job only worshiped God because of his blessings; without these he would no longer pray. God allowed Satan to destroy Job's wealth and give him misfortune, but Job continued to worship God. Job's servants were killed and thieves took his cattle, and his house collapsed, killing members of his family, and Job did not feel angry at this loss and thanked God. Later he suffered from a skin disease and all the people deserted him, with the exception of his faithful wife, Rahima, though eventually she too longed for his death. Job prayed to God and was told to strike the earth with his foot. When he did this, a spring of water started to flow. He washed in the water and was cured of his skin disease. God returned him to wealth and prosperity.

Set within a walled compound with abundant shrubs and a few trees, some of which are nesting sites for Rüppell's weavers, there is a small cemetery and mosque, with the tomb of Job set at the far end of the area. Before entering the tomb, on the left there is an open-air mosque. It is claimed that the walls have two mihrabs, one facing northwest to Mecca and the other said to be facing Jerusalem (it is not), which was the original prayer direction before it was changed to Mecca in the Prophet Mohammed's lifetime.

All visitors should remove footwear and women should cover their heads with a scarf before approaching the mausoleum. Just in front of the tomb's entrance you can make out what appears to be a very large human footprint fossilised in stone. Inside, the tomb is covered in cloth and there is often incense burning, although it is officially prohibited. The walls are undecorated, though there is an interesting tree of the prophets, which apart from Job also shows Jesus (Issa bin Miriam in Arabic) and the Prophet Mohammed.

South of the walled compound is a whitewashed building. This is a small coffee shop that is mainly focused on offering *shisha* pipes (water pipes) with flavoured tobacco, although it does also serve tea. The main attraction, however, is the view. On the same section of road as the coffee shop there is a left turn after 350m which takes you down via a small car park and a zigzag walk to a small spring in the cliff face.

TRILITHS, DHOFAR'S STANDING STONES

Triliths are one of Oman's more obscure and enigmatic archaeological structures. Thesiger described them on his journeys through Oman as standing:

> In groups of three to 15, each one consisting of three stone slabs approximately 2ft high, standing on end and leaning against each other with their base forming a triangle; a few were capped with a fourth and usually round stone. They were in a line a yard apart, each group surrounded by an oval bed of small stones. On one side of each group, parallel with it and about 3yds away, was a line of fireplaces consisting of piles of small stones.

Triliths have been dated to between 400bc and ad300 and are found along the southern and eastern areas of Arabia, from the island of Socotra to just north of the Wihibah Sands. The triple stone component has provided these rows with the name 'triliths' (Thesiger called them 'trilithons'). Usually they are found on the bank of a *wadi* and are parallel to its course. The piles of stones Thesiger mentioned are shallow circular pits filled with large pebbles from the *wadi* bed. These pits have been compared by Ali Ahmed Al Shahri, an authority on Dhofar's history and culture, with the current practice in Dhofar of making a circular cooking pit of hot stones for grilling meat. The overall purpose of triliths is unclear, they are not burial places as they are placed on bed-rock; they are, however, so widespread and built to a common design that their purpose must have been clear to anybody during the period they were built.

OMAN ONLINE

For additional online content, articles, photos and more on Oman, why not visit www.bradtguides.com/oman.

The triliths and the pools of Uyun عيون و المنطقة بها Returning to the junction off the main road, turning left in the direction of Titam and continuing along a tarmac road for 9.3km brings you to a right turn to Uyun (also Ayun, Ayoun, Aiyun) and Hijayf. Turn into this road. The scenery changes almost immediately from grass and open woodland to an increasingly arid landscape where the small valleys either side of the road are peppered with frankincense trees. The road snakes through the hills and comes to a left turn after an additional 17km (26km total). Turning onto that tarmac road, there is another left turn onto a rough track which is better suited to 4x4 vehicles for extra ground clearance. A little way along this rough track there are a several rows of stone structures; these are **Oman's triliths** (see box, page 325). From the junction with the tarmac road, the rough track continues for 3.6km on the slope of a low hill, beyond which lie the reed-filled water **pools of Uyun** (Ayoun). The Wadi Uyun continues through the hills and eventually joins Wadi Ghadun near Ash Shisr. The side valley has a number of frankincense trees along its base. It was here that Thesiger's companion Bin Kabina almost died and was the subject of an exorcism, and also where Bin Ghabaisha was first introduced to Thesiger. Return to the main tarmac road and turn left onto the road to Hijayf, which takes you from the turning to Qayrun Hayriti onto the main Thumrayt–Salalah road after 22km..

Appendix 1

LANGUAGE

The official language in Oman is Arabic, although there are several other languages spoken in various regions and within specific populations. In major towns and often elsewhere many Omanis may also be fluent in English, Hindi and Urdu, which reflect historical and cultural ties. Apart from Arabic, the other languages that can be called indigenous in Oman are Shahi and Kumzari in Musandam; Baluchi on Al Batinah coast through to Muscat; Lawati also on Al Batinah coast through to Muscat; Swahili, which is spoken throughout northern Oman by families who have had recent associations with East Africa; Harasusi spoken by a limited number of nomads in central Oman; Mahri, which is spoken almost exclusively by the Mahri tribe in southern Oman; Shahri (also known as Jabali) in the southern mountains and on the Al Hallaniyyat Islands; and Bathari around Ash Shuwaymiyyah.

Arabic is a Semitic language with a **root system** that is based on an idea or concept represented by a simple verb, usually consisting of three consonants. Other Semitic languages such as Hebrew, Amharic in Ethiopia and Maltese also use this system. In Arabic, variations of meaning around the root idea are expressed by creating different letter patterns around the basic root, usually by including vowels within the root and often by adding a prefix or suffix. Hence, in this simplest and most appropiate of examples, from the root K T B (*kataba* when vowelled), which means 'he wrote', comes *maktab* meaning 'office', *maktaba* meaning 'library' and *kitaab* meaning 'book'. Prefixes and suffixes can add gender, though with a remarkable 12 possible personal pronouns everyday spoken Omani Arabic may simplify this by using the masculine gender only. The vowels are fully conjugated, so *katabnaa* is 'we wrote' and *yatabuuna* is 'they are writing'. For those learning Arabic or even simply wishing to know the meaning of a word there used to be a stumbling block as a traditional Arabic dictionary lists words following their root. As can be seen above these root words will often start with a different letter from the word that is being looked for, so if you cannot identify the root you cannot look up the word. Modern technology has of course simplified this, and any search will show the meaning.

Arabic **lettering** is arguably the easiest thing about the language, with only 29 characters and only one case (no upper or lower cases). The fundamental style is cursive and there are strict rules to determine which characters join on to which according to their position within the word, much as English written letters do, though Arabic does have explicit rigidity. The process of learning the characters and their shapes is therefore purely a memory exercise that can be done easily in a few days and thereafter just requires practice. As for the right-to-left flow of text, it just takes a little time to adjust, rather like driving on the right instead of the left of the road.

Having mastered the script, the task begins in earnest. In most printed media the diacritics are not included and in Arabic these include three that emphasise the vowel sounds; a, e, u. In this case, how do you know which vowels to put where? The answer is that you will know after you have studied the intricacies of Arabic grammar and word structure, which might only take a few months' study. For this reason beginners' texts and children's schoolbooks are fully annotated with vowel signs added in the form of dashes and dots above and below the line. Getting students to read an unvowelled text aloud is always an excellent way of assessing their level, as it instantly reveals the depth of their understanding of Arabic grammar.

Pronunciation is another area that is not as daunting as it may seem. Of the 29 consonants, 18 have direct phonetic equivalents in English, such as b, d, t, l, s. The rest have no direct equivalent and range from emphatic versions of d, s and t, usually transliterated as D, S and T, to a small handful of sounds that are genuinely difficult for Westerners to pronounce. The guttural stop or *'ayn'* as it is called in Arabic, usually represented in transliteration as a reversed comma, is probably the one that gives most trouble, sounding like a vibrating constriction of the larynx. In any case within Oman there are considerable local variations in pronunciation and with so many foreigners also adding their own pronunciation, variants such as Arabic in Queen's English may well be easily understood, while an obscure Egyptian dialect may be unintelligible.

Because Arabic as a written language is directly associated with the delivery and inscription of the Quran, change in its current form of writing may not be possible. The Arabic script has undergone change in the past, as can be observed simply by comparing early Qurans which do not have diacritics to those currently used with their elaborate diacritics. Written Arabic in its current form became established by the end of the 8th century through the contributions of Al-Khalil bin Ahmad Al-Farahidi, who died by 791. He was born in Oman and developed the current Arabic diacritic system that became used in the Quran.

Arabic is, by the very nature of its structure, an extremely rich language, capable of expressing fine shades of meaning, and this is reflected in the wealth of Arabic literature, especially poetry. The average English tabloid reader is said to have a working vocabulary of 3,000 words, while the Arab equivalent is said to have about 10,000. Scholars believe that because Arabic evolved in the deserts of Arabia where life was nomadic and the daily struggle to stay alive extremely tough, the people developed a rich vocabulary to describe every conceivable nuance of material life, natural phenomena and individual activity of their lives, almost as if to counterbalance the uniformity of their environment. So there are more than a hundred words to describe a camel, for example, depending on its gender, age and qualities.

There are also many **interesting features** of the language which hint at the nature and attitudes of the Arab mind, notably the existence of only two tenses: perfect and imperfect. There is no future tense. In the Arabic concept of time there is only one distinction that matters: has something been finished or is it still going on? Another curiosity is that the plural of inanimate objects is treated grammatically as feminine singular.

GREETINGS On first meeting the polite greeting is: *As-salaam 'alaykum*, meaning literally 'May peace be upon you.' The standard reply is: *Wa 'alaykum as-salaam*, meaning 'And on you be peace', though it is also possible to simply reply *As-salaam 'alaykum*, which of course helps to reduce the number of phrases you need to remember.

There are three common phrases you will hear incessantly. *In sha Allah*, meaning 'If God wills it', is used all the time because nothing is certain to happen unless God wills it. So if you say to an Arab 'See you tomorrow', he will reply 'In sha Allah', meaning, 'Yes, if God permits it and nothing happens in the meantime to prevent it.' It can also be a polite way of avoiding commitment, conveying 'Let us hope so …'. The second phrase is *Al Hamdou lillah*, meaning 'Thanks be to God'. This is used for any event either good or bad, for thanking God for his actions and is a natural part of Islam. The third phrase is *TafaDDal*, meaning 'You are welcome', 'Please go ahead' or 'Come in' or 'After you'. It is always said by your host when you arrive and on entering the house or room and before eating. Literally it means 'Please be so good as to …'.

Other greetings

Hello, welcome   *marHaba, ahlan*

Goodbye   *ma'a as-salaama* (literally, 'with the peace' and again the phrase *As-salaam 'alaykum* can be used if needed)

THE ARABIC ALPHABET

Final	Medial	Initial	Alone	Transliteration	Pronunciation
ل			ا	aa	as in 'after'
ب	ب	ب	ب	b	as in 'but'
ت	ت	ت	ت	t	as in 'tin'
ث	ث	ث	ث	th	as in 'think'
ج	ج	ج	ج	j	as in 'jam'
ح	ح	ح	ح	H	emphatic, breathy 'h'
خ	خ	خ	خ	kh	as in the Scottish 'loch'
د			د	d	as in 'den'
ذ			ذ	dh	as in 'that'
ر			ر	r	as in 'red'
ز			ز	z	as in 'zero'
س	س	س	س	s	as in 'sit', hard 's'
ش	ش	ش	ش	sh	as in 'shut'
ص	ص	ص	ص	S	emphatic, strong 's'
ض	ض	ض	ض	D	emphatic, strong 'd'
ط	ط	ط	ط	T	emphatic, strong 't'
ظ	ظ	ظ	ظ	Z	emphatic, strong 'z'
ع	ع	ع	ع	'	gutteral stop, hardest sound for non-Arabs to make, called 'ayn.
غ	غ	غ	غ	gh	like a gargling sound
ف	ف	ف	ف	f	as in 'fire'
ق	ق	ق	ق	q	like a guttural 'k'
ك	ك	ك	ك	k	as in 'king'
ل	ل	ل	ل	l	as in 'lady'
م	م	م	م	m	as in 'mat'
ن	ن	ن	ن	n	as in 'not'
ه	ه	ه	ه	h	as in 'hat'
و			و	w	as in 'will', or 'oo' as in 'food'
ي	ي	ي	ي	y	as in 'yet', or 'ee' as in 'clean'

USEFUL OMANI ARABIC WORDS AND PHRASES

Yes	aiwa, na'am	Is it possible? May I?	mumkin?
No	laa	My name is …	ana ismee …
Please	min faDlak	What is your name?	min ismak?
Thank you	shukran		ana maa afham
Thank you very much	shukran jazeelan	Where are you from?	min wayn inta?
You're welcome	afwan	There is…	fii …
Sorry, excuse me	'afwan, muta'assif	There is not…	maa fii …
Hurry up, let's go	yallah	What?	waish??
More, again, also	kamaan		

Getting around

airport	maTaar	left	yasaar
bus	baas	right	yameen
car	sayyaara	near, close by	qareeb
suitcase, bag	shanTa	straight on	'alaa aT-Toul
taxi	taksee	where?	wayn?
ticket	tadhkira	Where is the	Wayn Al matHaf
petrol	benzeen	museum, please?	min faDlak?
diesel	maazout	How far is it to …?	Kam kiiloometre
far	ba'eed		ila…?

Hotels and restaurants

hotel	*funduq, ootel*	a medium glass	*koop mutawasit*
room	*ghurfa*	a large glass	*koop kabir*
soap	*Saaboun*	glass	*koop (or finjaan)*
toilet, bathroom	*Hammam, ghurfat mai*	I don't eat meat	*ana ma akul laHm*
towel	*futa*	I want the meat	*areed allahum*
the bill	*Al faaToura, Al Hisaab*	cooked rare	*almatbukh nadir*
restaurant	*maT'am*	I want the meat	*areed allahum*
breakfast	*fuTour*	cooked medium	*almatbukh*
lunch	*ghadaa*		*almutawasita*
dinner	*'ashaa*	red wine	*nabidh ahmar*
half litre	*nusf liter*	white wine	*nabidh abyadh*
one litre	*wahid liter*		
a small glass	*koop saghir*		

Food and drink

10g	*ashrat gharam*	meat	*laHm*
100g	*miayat gharam*	sugar	*sukkar*
half kilo	*nusf kilo*	vegetables	*khuDar*
1kg	*wahid kilo*	yoghurt	*laban*
bread	*khubz*	beer	*beera*
butter	*zibdeh*	coffee	*qahwa*
cheese	*jibneh*	mineral water	*mai ma'daniya*
eggs	*bayD*	red	*aHmar*
fish	*samak*	white	*abyaD*
fruit	*fawaakeh*	tea	*shay*
honey	*'asl*	wine	*nabeedh*
jam	*murabbeh*		

Shopping

cheap	*rakhees*	How much	*bikaam?*
expensive	*ghaalee*	(does it cost?)	
money	*fuluus*	I would like a Durex	*areed wasayil mane*
a lot, much, very	*katheer*	contraceptive	*alhamal durex*
no problem	*mafee mushkila*	Where can I find	*wayn yumkinuni*
never mind	*ma'a laysh*	sanitary towels?	*ashoof ealaa alfawta*
shop	*mahl*		*alshiyat annisayiya*
market	*suk*		

Health

chemist	*Saydaliyeh*	neck	*alanq*
dentist	*Tabeeb asnaan*	This man/woman –	*hadha/almar'at –*
doctor	*doktoor, Tabeeb*	is badly injured	*bijuruh balghat*
diarrhoea	*ishaal*	please do not move	*alrijul min fadlik*
ill, sick	*mareeD*	them	*la naqalho*
ankle	*alkahil*	Please phone for	*yourja alhatif lilhusul*
arm	*dhraa*	an ambulance	*ealaa sayarat asraf*
back	*alkhalf*	My ankle is broken	*huwa kasr kahili*
chest	*sadar*	My leg is broken	*huwa kasr saqi*
foot	*qadam*	My arm is broken	*huwa kasr dhiraei*
hand	*yad*	My tooth is broken	*huwa kasr al'asnan*
head	*rais*		
leg	*rajla*		

Numbers

1	*waaHad*	١
2	*ithnayn*	٢
3	*thalaatha*	٣
4	*arba'a*	٤
5	*khamsa*	٥
6	*sitta*	٦
7	*sab'a*	٧
8	*thamaaniya*	٨
9	*tis'a*	٩
10	*'ashara*	١٠
20	*'ishreen*	٢٠
30	*thalaatheen*	٣٠
40	*arba'een*	٤٠
50	*khamseen*	٥٠
60	*sitteen*	٦٠
70	*sab'een*	٧٠
80	*thamaaneen*	٨٠
90	*tis'een*	٩٠
100	*mi'a*	١٠٠
150	*mi'a wa khamseen*	١٥٠
200	*mi'atayn*	٢٠٠
500	*khams–mi'a*	٥٠٠
1,000	*alf*	١٠٠٠
2,000	*alfayn*	٢٠٠٠

Other vocabulary

bank	*bank*
museum	*matHaf*
post office	*maktab bareed*
good	*zain, Tayyib*
bad	*maa zain*
hot	*Haar*
cold	*baarid*
What time will the bus leave?	*waqt ma sekun taghadir alhaafila?*
Where is the ticket counter	*wayn huwa shibak altathkara?*
I would like to speak with the manager	*areed atakallam maa almudir*
Can I speak with somebody who speaks good English?	*areed atakallam maa shakhs yatahadith alinjlayazi jidan?*
I have an appointment	*andee mawaad*
I do have a reservation	*andee tahfaz*
My room is not clean	*ghurfati mush nudhafa*

Days and time

Monday	*Yawm Al Ithnayn*	Saturday	*Yawm as-Sabt*
Tuesday	*Yawm ath-Thalaatha*	Sunday	*Yawm Al AHad*
Wednesday	*Yawm Al Arba'a*	today	*Al yawm*
Thursday	*Yawm Al Khamees*	tomorrow	*bukra*
Friday	*Yawm Al Jum'a*		

ARABIC SIGNS

Open	مفتوح	*maftouH*
Closed	مغلق	*muglaq*
Forbidden	ممنوع	*mamnou*
Police	شرطة	*shurTa*
Men's toilet	دورة مياة رجال	*dorat mai rijaal*
Ladies' toilet	دورة مياة السيدات	*dorat mai sayyidaat*
Hospital	مستشفى	*mustashfaa*

Appendix 2

GLOSSARY

ablution	ritual washing before prayer laid down by the Quran
abu	father
ain	spring
bab	gate
bahr	sea
bait	house
bandar	anchorage
bani	tribal prefix meaning 'son of ...' in Arabic
barasti	made from the branches of palm trees
Bedouin	desert nomads (see box, page 280)
bin	son
bint	daughter
bustan	garden
dhow	traditional Arab wooden sailing boat
Eid	religious holiday
falaj	irrigation channel running from a water source to water crops or date gardens (plural *aflaj*)
Ghafiri	a tribal confederation in Oman
Hadith	collection of anecdotes from the Prophet Muhammad's lifetime
halwa	Omani sticky brown sweet often served to guests with coffee, eaten with the fingers of right hand
Hinawi	a tribal confederation in Oman
Ibadhi	one of Islam's earliest sects, followed in Oman, very traditional and orthodox (see box, page 33)
Imam	spiritual and secular leader who is chosen by consensus among the sheikhs (see box, page 206)
jabal	mountain
jerz	simple axe with wooden handle carried only by men in Musandam, instead of the khanjar dagger
jinn	spirit which can be good or evil like our 'genie'
juzor/jazirah	islands/island
kabir	big
khanjar	Omani silver dagger worn on the belt, with a distinctive curved blade
khareef	monsoon season in Dhofar from mid June to mid September which brings mountain enveloping clouds; the festival held in Salalah during August
khawr	creek or inlet from the sea
madina(t)	town
majlis	literally 'place of sitting', the room where guests are received; a meeting of an important person with others

mihrab	prayer niche in a mosque indicating the direction of Mecca for prayer
mina	port
minbar	pulpit in a mosque from where the imam addresses the congregation
oryx	an antelope which in Arabia has two straight long horns, well adapted to desert life (see box, page 288)
PDO	Petroleum Development Oman, the main oil company in Oman
qadi	Islamic judge
qahwa	Arabic coffee
Ramadhan	Muslim month of fasting (pages 32–3)
ramlat	sandy area
ras	headland
resthouse	simple hotel
sabla	communal hall used for activities like weddings and funerals, belonging to a community
saghir	small
sambuk	small fishing boat
sarouj	mud plaster
shatti	shore/beach
Sheikh	tribal leader or respected senior person; there is a different connotation in the UAE where only members of the ruling families have the title, which is then equated with prince.
Shari'a	Islamic law, according to the Quran and the Hadith
Shi'a	offshoot of Islam from the Orthodox Sunni Muslims, following a hereditary principle of succession after Muhammad rather than an elected or consensus method; mainly found today in Iran
Sultan	head of state and government in Oman
Sunni	Orthodox Islam, following the principle-of-consensus selection of the next caliph or imam
suq	Arab market
sur	fortified walled enclosure
sura	chapter of the Quran
umm	mother
wadi	natural watercourse often associated with a deep valley or canyon
Wahhabi	an ultra-conservative branch of Sunni Islam aspiring to return to what it sees as the fundamentals of Islam (particularly dominant in Saudi Arabia)
Wali	local governor of a wilayat
wilayat	district/area

Appendix 2   GLOSSARY

A2

Appendix 3

FURTHER INFORMATION
BOOKS
History

Aguis, D A *In the Wake of the Dhow: The Arabian Gulf and Oman* Ithaca Press, 2002. Documents the history of the Arabian dhow.

Allen, C H, Rigsbee, W L, and Rigsbee II, W L *Oman Under Qaboos: From Coup to Constitution 1970–1996* Frank Cass Publishers, 2002. Examines the political, economic and social development of Oman since Qaboos.

Clements, F A *Oman: The Reborn Land* Longman ELT, 1980. An appreciation of Oman's past glories and traditions.

Dinteman, W *Forts of Oman* Motivate Publishing, 1993. An overview of Oman's forts.

Eickelman, C *Women and Community in Oman* New York University Press, 1989. Christine Eickelman lived in Al Hamra on the western edge of Al Jabal Al Akhdar in 1979 and writes of her explorations into the culture of Omani women through the life she shared with them. She sheds light on their concepts of family, privacy, propriety, status and sociability.

Frifelt, K *The Island of Umm-an-Nar: Third Millennium Settlement* Aarhus University Press, 1995. Presents the results and the material found at the settlement of Umm-an-Nar. The Umm An Nar culture was the most conspicuous culture in the Oman peninsula in the Bronze Age.

Gwynne-James, D *Letters from Oman: A Snapshot of Feudal Times as Oil Signals Change* Gwynne-James, 2001.

Hawley, Sir D *Oman and its Renaissance* Stacey International, 2005. An immense work on the history, geography and culture of Oman, and a beautiful book to boot.

Jeapes, T *SAS Secret War: Operation Storm in the Middle East* Flamingo, 1996. The ten-year Dhofar War lasted until 1976, taking place under conditions of secrecy. This is a first-hand account of the SAS's secret campaign in Oman.

Joyce, M *The Sultanate of Oman: A Twentieth Century History* Greenwood Press, 2005.

Laing, Stuart and Alston, Robert *Unshook till the End of Time* Gilgamesh, 2012. A detailed history of relations between Britain and Oman from 1650 till the end of the Dhofar War in 1975, by two former British ambassadors to Oman.

Peyton, W D *Old Oman* Stacey International, 1983. A fascinating and valuable album of photographs of a bygone age, with accompanying description, taken from c1900 up to 1970.

Philby, Harry St J *The Queen of Sheba* Quartet Books, 1981. Harry St John Philby was a great Arabian traveller, scholar and writer. He examines the mixture of fable, history, magic and mystery surrounding the visit of the Queen of Sheba to King Solomon, from its origins in the Old Testament and the Quran.

Phillips, W *Qataban and Sheba* Harcourt, Brace and Company, 1955. Wendell Phillips is an explorer, adventurer and archaeologist who has explored the ancient treasures of the exotic civilisations of southern Arabia. In this book he unveils the history of Sheba territory in Oman.

Raban, J *Arabia through the Looking Glass* Harvill Press, 1979. An entertaining journey to explore the complex relationship between the Arabs and the West.

Al-Rawas, I *Oman in Early Islamic History* Ithaca Press, 2000. An in-depth study of the history of Oman from the advent of Islam until the fall of the second Ibadi imamate in AD893.

Richardson, C *Masirah: Tales from a Desert Island* Pentland Press, 2001. A well-researched book which recounts a wealth of first–hand stories of RAF history by those who have known Masirah since the 1930s. Illustrated with photographs.

Salil Ibn Razik *History of the Imams & Seyyids of Oman* Kessinger Publishing Company, 2004.

Severin, T *The Sindbad Voyage* Putnam Publishing Group, 1983. The reconstruction of an ancient trade route mentioned in the legend of Sindbad; an experiment to see if a sewn wooden boat could reach China using only primitive navigational instruments.

Ward, P *Travels in Oman* Oleander Press, 1986. On the track of early explorers, an edited collection.

Wikan, U *Behind the Veil in Arabia: Women in Oman* University of Chicago Press, 1982. Unni Wikan explores the segregation of women, the wearing of the *burka* mask, nuptial rituals and place of women in Omani society.

Natural history

A good selection of natural history books is available in the UK from the NHBS Environment Bookstore (*2–3 Wills Rd, Totnes, Devon TQ9 5XN;* `01803 865913; www.nhbs.com`).

Baldwin, R *Whales and Dolphins of Arabia* R Baldwin, Bowlish, Somerset, 2003.

Batty, P D *Bluewater Fishing in Oman* Muscat Game Fishing Association, Oman 2002.

Bosch, D and Bosch, E *Sea Shells of Oman* Longman, 1982.

Eriksen, H and Eriksen, J *Birdwatching Guide to Oman* Al Roya Publishing, Muscat, Oman 1999.

Eriksen, H and Eriksen, J *Common Birds in Oman* Al Roya Publishing, Muscat, Oman 2005.

Hanna, S and Al-Belushi, M *Caves of Oman* Sultan Qaboos University, 1996.

Larson, T B and Larson, K *Butterflies of Oman* Bartholomew, 1980.

Macgregor, M *Wilderness Oman* Ptarmigan, 2002.

Mandaville Jr, J *Wild Flowers of Northern Oman* Bartholomew, 1978.

Miller, A G and Morris, M *Plants of Dhofar, the Southern Region of Oman: Traditional Economic & Medicinal Uses* Office of the Adviser for Conservation of the Environment, Diwan of Royal Court, Sultanate of Oman, 1988.

Randall, J E *Coastal Fishes of Oman* University of Hawaii Press, 1996.

Salm, R and Salm, S *Sea Turtles in the Sultanate of Oman* Historical Association of Oman, 2001.

Winser, N *The Sea of Sands and Mists: Story of the Royal Geographical Society Oman Wahiba Sands Project* Ebury Press, 1989.

Various *The Scientific Results of the Royal Geographical Society's Oman Wahiba Sands Project* RGS-IBG Field Research Programmes, 1985–87.

Woodward, T *Beachcombers' Guide to Oman* Motivate Publishing, 1996.

Al Zubair M, *Landscapes of Dhofar* Bait Al Zubair, Oman 2003.

Adventure tourism

Dale, A and Hadwind, J *Adventure Trekking in Oman* Cordee, 2001.

Explorer *Oman Off-Road* Explorer Publishing, 2013. Twenty-six routes complete with GPS co-ordinates and maps.

Klein, H and Brickson, R *Off-Road in Oman* Motivate Publishing, 1996.

Mackenzie, A *Oman Trekking Guide* Explorer Publishing, 2005.

Mcdonald, R A *Rock Climbing in Oman* Verulam Publishing, 1994.

Salm, R and Baldwin, R *Snorkelling and Diving in Oman* Motivate Publishing, 1992.

Culture and tradition

Al-Azri, Khalid *Social and Gender Inequality in Oman: The Power of Religious and Political Tradition* Routledge, 2012. Rigorous investigation into the post-1970 barriers to reform in Oman and wider Islamic society, chiefly in the areas where Islamic law still places restrictions on women in marriage, divorce and inheritance.

Kendrick, I *The Bands and Orchestras of Oman* Diwan of the Royal Court, Oman 1995.

Newcombe, O *The Heritage of Oman: A Celebration in Photographs* Garnet Publishing, 1996.

Richardson, N and Dorr, M *The Craft Heritage of Oman* Motivate Publishing, 2004.

Vine, P *The Heritage of Oman* Immel Publishing, 1995.

Biography and autobiography

Beasant, J and Ling, C *Sultan in Arabia: A Private Life* Mainstream Publishing, 2004. A biography providing insight into the character of Qaboos bin Said.

Burrowes, J *Sultan: The Remarkable Story of a Man and a Nation* Mainstream Publishing, 2005. Biography of Sultan Qaboos.

Monroe, E *Philby of Arabia* Ithaca Press, 1998 edition. Explores the life of Harry St John Philby – one of the great Arabian desert travellers.

Taylor, A *God's Fugitive: The Life of C M Doughty* HarperCollins, 1999. Charles Montagu Doughty, an explorer, scholar, scientist, travel writer and poet, was the foremost Arabian explorer, who started a tradition of British exploration and discovery in that region. He spent two years wandering with the Bedu through oases and deserts, and returned to England to write one of the greatest and most original travel books: *Arabia Deserta*. Andrew Taylor brings Doughty to life in this biography.

Thesiger, W *My Life and Travels* Flamingo, 2003. A chronicle, spanning the 20th century, of Wilfred Thesiger's life and travel writing.

Travel writing

Allfree, Philip *Warlords of Oman* Robert Hale, 2008. Reprint of an original classic from 1967. The author (recently deceased) describes many fascinating and colourful episodes from an Oman now long disappeared, based on his unique first-hand experiences.

Barnett, D *Dust and Fury: A Novel Set in Oman* Woodfield Publishing, 2003.

Clapp, N *The Road to Ubar* First Mariner Books, 1999. Nicholas Clapp, a noted documentary film-maker, arranged two expeditions to Oman with a team of archaeologists and NASA space scientists to search for Ubar, the city that had become known as the Atlantis of the Sands. This book is part travel journal, part archaeological history.

Doughty, C M *Arabia Deserta* Peter Smith Publishing, 1960. A classic account of two years spent with Arabian nomads in the late 19th century.

Fiennes, R *Atlantis of the Sands* Bloomsbury, 1992. Ranulph Fiennes – a leader of major travel expeditions around the globe – relates his search for the legendary Ubar in Oman.

Holden, W M *Dhow of the Monsoon: From Zanzibar to Oman in the Wake of Sindbad* PublishAmerica, 2005. William Holden follows Sindbad's journey by dhow relying on the monsoon winds.

Morris, J *Sultan in Oman* Sickle Moon Books, 2003. A fascinating read from one of the world's great travel writers, who experienced Muscat prior to its development.

Owen, T *Beyond the Empty Quarter* Serendipity, 2003. Tim Owen's light-hearted memoir of his experiences in 1960s Oman.

Rollins, J *Sandstorm* HarperCollins, 2004. James Rollins's fiction based around the lost city of Ubar, in the desert of Oman.

Stark, F *The Southern Gates of Arabia* John Murray, 1936. Freya Stark – a travelling Englishwoman – relates her journey to explore the Frankincense Road, catching the spirit of people and place in this travel classic.

Thesiger, W *Arabian Sands* Penguin Classics, 1959.

Thesiger, W *Desert, Marsh and Mountain* Flamingo, 1995. Thesiger's writings are an absolute must for those interested in the accounts of previous explorers and travellers to Oman. Beautifully written. Thesiger recreates his five-year journey with the Bedu at the time before oil and the West transformed them.

Thomas, B *Arabia Felix* Jonathan Cape, 1933. Bertram Thomas writes about his ground-breaking crossing of the Rub Al Khali in 1931. This was the first such journey, predating the now better-known follow up by Wilfred Thesiger in 1947.

Walsh, T *Oman's World Heritage Sites* Al Roya Press & Publishing, 2013. A comprehensive overview of all Oman's World Heritage Sites in a fully illustrated coffee-table hardback format.

Health

Wilson-Howarth, Dr Jane, and Ellis, Dr Matthew *Your Child Abroad: A Travel Health Guide* Bradt Travel Guides, 2014 (eguide only).

Wilson-Howarth, Dr Jane *Bugs, Bites & Bowels* Cadogan, 2006.

WEBSITES

www.almaha.com.om One of four petrol station chains in Oman; the current petrol price is detailed along with their network.

www.almouj.com Major commercial and residential development in Muscat.

www.apexmedia.co.om Includes *Muscat Daily*, *The Week*, *Business Today* and other publications.

www.baitalzubair.com Privately operated museum in Muscat.

www.bankdhofar.com One of several banks in Oman – the website does have a listing of their bank and ATM network.

www.birdsoman.com Information about birds in Oman.

www.booking.com A site for online hotel booking.

www.businessdirectoryoman.com Business directory for Oman.

www.businesstoday.co.om Monthly business magazine.

www.customs.gov.om The Royal Oman Police customs site.

www.destinationoman.com All about Oman and getting there.

www.diveworldwide.com/oman A list of diving holiday options in Oman.

www.du.edu.om Dhofar University.

www.embassyworld.com Details of Omani embassies abroad and foreign missions in Oman.

www.eso.org.om Environment Society of Oman, a semi-governmental environment organisation.

www.gso-oman.org Geological Society of Oman.

www.mofa.gov.om Ministry of Foreign Affairs with details of Oman's embassies and foreign governments' embassies in Oman.

www.mwasalat.om Mwasalat, the government land transport company; the site includes some bus information.

www.nfc.com National Ferries, the government-owned ferry company.

www.nizwa.net A useful site for information about Oman generally but especially the city of Nizwa and its heritage.

www.oapgrc.gov.om The Oman Animal and Plant Genetic Resources Centre gives an overview of organisations focused on Oman's flora and fauna.

www.octm-folk.gov.om Omani Centre for traditional music lovers.

www.oman.om The Oman government portal.

www.omanair.com The Oman Air, the national carrier, with timetable information for flights to Khasab and Salalah.

www.omanairports.co.om Muscat and Salalah airports with near real-time flight information.

www.omanauto.org Oman Automobile Association.

www.omanhotels.com Local chain of hotels in Oman.

www.omaninfo.com Classifieds, news and tourism features.

www.omantel.net.om A mobile and fixed-line telephone and internet company.

www.omantourism.gov.om The Ministry of Tourism's website.

www.omanuaeexchange.com Foreign currency exchange company with numerous offices throughout the country.

www.ooredoo.om A mobile-telephone and internet company.

www.part.gov.om The Oman Public Authority for Radio and Television.

www.pdo.co.om Petroleum Development of Oman.

www.rohmuscat.org.om Royal Opera House Oman.

www.rop.gov.om Royal Oman Police – for visa information and traffic fines.

www.squ.edu.om Sultan Qaboos University.

www.stalgallery.com Art gallery focused on Oman's modern art scene.

www.talabat.com Online meal delivery service from over 100 restaurants in Oman.

www.timesofoman.com Daily English-language newspaper.

www.tripadvisor.com Useful for checking out hotel reviews.

Index

Page numbers in **bold** indicate main entries and those in *italic* indicate maps.

INDEX OF ADVERTISERS

NOTES